The Seventh Million

Tom Segev

The Seventh Million

Translated by Haim Watzman

The Israelis and the Holocaust

Hill and Wang

A division of Farrar, Straus and Giroux / New York

LIBRARY OF CONGRESS CATALOGING-IN-PUBLICATION DATA
Segev, Tom.
[Ha-milyon ha-shevii.   English]
The seventh million : the Israelis and the Holocaust / Tom Segev ;
translated by Haim Watzman.
p.   cm.
Translation of: Ha-milyon ha-shevii.
Includes index.
1. Holocaust, Jewish (1939–1945)—Influence.   2. Holocaust, Jewish
(1939–1945)—Public opinion.   3. Jews—Israel—Attitudes.   4. Public
opinion—Israel.   5. Holocaust survivors—Israel.   6. Israel—
Politics and government.   I. Title.
D804.3.S44513   1993   940.53'18—dc20   92-7372   CIP

Contents

Acknowledgments

This book, like my two earlier ones, has been written at the invitation of Domino Books of Jerusalem. It took much longer to write than planned. My first thanks go, then, to Deborah Harris, publisher, agent, and friend, for her patience and encouragement.

The book is based mainly on thousands of documents, many of which have not yet been published. This is the opportunity to say a kind word about Israel's historical archives. Wherever I turned, I received generous help and good advice. My thanks to the staffs of these archives: the Central Zionist Archives, the National Archives, the Haganah Archives, the Labor Party Archives, the Ben-Gurion Archives, the Lavon Institute Archives, the Moreshet Archives, the Hashomer Hatsair Archives, the Jabotinsky Archives, the Weizmann Archives, the Institute for Oral Documentation of the Hebrew University, the Yad Vashem Archives, the Tel Aviv Municipal Archives, the Aviezer Yellin Archives of Jewish Education in Israel and the Diaspora, the Beth Hatefutsoth and the Kibbutz Hameuhad Archives. I also wish to express my thanks to the Israeli photographic department of the Government Press Office, and the National Archives in Washington.

Two of the book's chapters are based in part on fascinating and extremely important material not made available to all researchers. Reuven Feurstein, Yaakov Rand, and Ada Oz of the Hadassah–WIZO Canada Research Institute, founded by Aliyat Hanoar, allowed me to inspect the personal files of Youth Aliya students, as well as the findings of their research. I am grateful to the late Avner Rom of the United Restitution Organization Ltd. (URO), who generously allowed me to examine the personal files of people who demanded compensation from Germany. Permission to examine the Aliyat Hanoar and URO files was conditioned on anonymity, to prevent invasion of privacy, which is why the files have been quoted without mentioning names.

Naturally, I owe thanks to many researchers and writers. Their names appear in the notes, and some in the body of the text. Some were kind enough to allow me to use their material before it was published, which I appreciate especially. I benefited from the invigorating atmosphere in the reading rooms of the National and University Library in Jerusalem. My thanks also to the staff of the excellent library at Yad Vashem.

During the research for this book I spoke with people involved in a number of the events described here. I also made use of interviews I had conducted earlier, in my journalistic work. I am grateful, therefore, to Uri Avneri, Yitzhak Arad, Hannah Arendt, Gabriel Bach, David Ben-Gurion, Hanzi Brand, Haim Guri, Yehiel De-Nur (Ka-Tzetnik), William Hall, Isser Harel, Haim Cohen, Eliezer Lidovsky, Rolf Pauls, Yossi Peled, Ehud Praver, Victor Frankl, Shimon Peres, Gerhard Riegner, Dov Shilansky, and Eli Tabin.

I owe a great debt of thanks to those Holocaust survivors, among them several members of Kibbutz Lohamei Hagetaot, who shared some of the terrors of their memories with me. I learned much also from the students I accompanied on their trip to the sites of the extermination camps in Poland.

Five friends read the early drafts of the manuscript: Amos Elon, Dr. Yehiam Weitz, Avraham Kushnir, Dr. Eli Shaltiel, and Avi Katzman. Haim Watzman, who translated the book into English, also offered me valuable advice. Sara Bershtel, executive editor at Hill and Wang, invested much wisdom and effort in the manuscript in order to make it comprehensible to the American reader. She was helped especially by David Frederickson, as well as Roslyn Schloss, Sally Singer, Angela Quilala, and Elisheva Urbas. My thanks to all of them.

Translator's Acknowledgments

I would like to thank my father, Sanford Watzman, for spending part of a vacation editing my work, and Kibbutz Tirat Zvi for giving me the time needed to complete the translation during the year I spent there with my family. Most of all, I owe thanks to my wife, Ilana, and my children, Mizmor, Asor, and Niot, for their support and patience.

HW

The Seventh Million

Prologue | Ka-Tzetnik's Trip

Early in 1987, I telephoned the writer Yehiel De-Nur to ask what he thought about the John Demjanjuk trial, which was then in progress in Jerusalem. Demjanjuk, a Ukrainian extradited to Israel from the United States, stood accused of murdering 870,000 people, the vast majority of them Jews, at the Treblinka extermination camp. De-Nur had been among the prosecution witnesses at the trial of Adolf Eichmann, twenty-six years earlier, and now the writer's hushed, choked voice immediately took me back to his testimony about what he had endured at Auschwitz. It was impossible to mistake that voice—the voice of the man from the other planet—or to forget the few sentences he had managed to pronounce in court:

I was there for about two years. Time there was different from what it is here on earth. Every split second ran on a different cycle of time. And the inhabitants of that planet had no names. They had neither parents nor children. They did not dress as we dress here. They were not born there nor did anyone give birth. Even their breathing was regulated by the laws of another nature. They did not live, nor did they die, in accordance with the laws of this world. Their names were numbers. . . . They left me, they kept leaving me, left, . . . for close to two years they left me and always left me behind. . . . I see them, they are watching me, I see them. . . .[1]

He spoke in a hollow voice, with the intensity of a prophet, oblivious to his physical surroundings, "as if reading a page from his book," wrote Haim Guri, who covered the trial. Something in his voice and the tone of what he said charged the atmosphere with almost unbearable tension. The prosecutor and the judge tried to bring him back to the business at hand. De-Nur collapsed in a faint, slumping, almost theatrically, to the floor. All Israel held its breath. It was the most dramatic moment of the trial, one of the most dramatic moments in the country's history. It has since been broadcast frequently on radio and television.

At the time of the trial, De-Nur was forty-five years old. Born Yehiel Feiner, he had grown up on his grandfather's farm in Poland, had studied at the Chochmei Lublin Yeshiva, had been a musician, a writer, a poet. "He was a young boy, a yeshiva student, when he first came to the editorial office," recalled an editor of one of the Yiddish newspapers published in Poland before the war. "He held out a stack of his manuscripts. For some reason, the young man with his long sidelocks and dreaming eyes caught my attention. That evening I looked through one of his stories and a poem of his. I was enchanted by his ability, his talent. His writing first appeared in my newspaper."

After Auschwitz, De-Nur made every effort to consign his early work to oblivion, going so far as to personally remove it from libraries. He also discarded his original name. Auschwitz, having robbed him of his family, had also robbed him of his identity, leaving only the prisoner. He began writing about the Holocaust soon after he was liberated, while recuperating in a British army camp near Naples. His end was near, he felt; he might not finish. But he had sworn an oath to the dead, to be their voice, to chronicle their story. Some forty years later, in the 1980s, he recalled: "I sat down to write, and for two and a half weeks I hardly got up. I handed the manuscript over to a soldier to send on to Palestine. The soldier read the title, *Salamandra*, on the first page; he bent down and whispered: 'You forgot to write the name of the author.' I cried out, 'The name of the author? They who went to the crematories wrote this book! Write *their* name: Ka-Tzetnik.'"

The name comes from the German acronym KZ (Ka Tzet) for *Konzentrationslager*—concentration camp. The inmates were referred to as Ka-Tzetniks, by number; De-Nur had been Ka-Tzetnik 135633, and this was how he signed his works. He also changed his real name, as so many Israelis did theirs, and took the name De-Nur, "From the Fire."

Salamandra was one of the first Holocaust books to be published in

Israel. Later, Ka-Tzetnik also published *House of Dolls, Piepel,* and *Phoenix over the Galilee.* Together they constitute *A Chronicle of a Jewish Family in the Twentieth Century*—a single autobiographical novel. Here, and in his other books, he wrote about the daily routine at Auschwitz, describing sadistic acts in horrifying detail, including the sexual abuse of young girls and boys.

I dialed his number with great trepidation. I was a boy when I first read *Piepel.* I have never since read anything about the Holocaust that so disturbed me. Rereading it, I found no small measure of kitsch and pornography, but I belong to a generation of Israelis whose image of the Holocaust was formed by what they read as teenagers in Ka-Tzetnik's books. Only a few of us knew who Ka-Tzetnik was. At the Eichmann trial, De-Nur was asked for the first time to admit that he was Ka-Tzetnik. That was the reason he fainted, he told me. In the twenty-six years that had elapsed since then, he had done everything he could to wipe out the connection between Ka-Tzetnik and De-Nur. His books had been translated into many languages, but he had forbidden his publishers to print his picture. Readers had written to him from all over the world, but he had rejected all requests for interviews and never spoke in public.

Still, fame was not to be eluded. Every two years a literary prize named for Ka-Tzetnik is awarded by the president of Israel. The prize was created by a man whose drug-addicted son reformed after reading Ka-Tzetnik's books and eventually gave up drugs altogether; the grateful father established a prize for works about the Holocaust. But Ka-Tzetnik does not take part in the award ceremonies. Once he almost did but at the last moment changed his mind and went home. He couldn't bring himself to appear in public, and he feared that his presence at the presidential mansion would be misinterpreted as publicity-seeking. "On my way to get a taxi to Jerusalem," he wrote to the president, "I stopped and returned home with a heavy heart, afraid that they would talk about Ka-Tzetnik and see me: how could I meet the eyes of those who left me in Auschwitz, whose gaze never deserts me?"

By the time I called him, he was seventy years old. He told me what he had told other reporters who called him around the same time, that he was not following the Demjanjuk case and that he didn't have the strength to relive the Eichmann trial. A few months later, I learned that De-Nur had written a new book, about the radical therapy he had undergone in the Netherlands, and I called him again to ask for an interview. De-Nur hesitated. Over the following weeks we developed a telephone acquaintance, in the course of some rather long and strange conversations. Sometimes he was the one who called—once or twice late at night. He spoke from within the storm in his soul, long monologues, parts of which I did not completely understand and parts of which terrified me —memories of Auschwitz atrocities blended with mystical, apocalyptical visions. Sometimes he would call and remain silent. One night he suddenly informed me that he had decided to show me the manuscript of his new book.

The next day, I went to his apartment in Tel Aviv, and we met again a week later. These meetings were not interviews. "I am unable to answer questions," he said, and the manuscript he showed me explained: "This is a trauma that has its source in the Gestapo torture chamber, in Katowicz." He had been tortured, during an interrogation about a cache of weapons discovered in the ghetto. He also told me how he had been summoned to the office of the city's Gestapo commandant, Alfred Dreyer. One of his acquaintances had managed to get him a Honduran passport. It had been sent to him through official channels, through the Swiss embassy in Berlin and the Gestapo headquarters in Katowicz. Dreyer was not quite sure what to do with this man, a ghetto Jew who had suddenly become a foreign national. While he deliberated, a superior officer entered the room. He looked at the papers and, without a word, tore them to shreds. At that moment, as the bits of paper fluttered slowly into the wastebasket, De-Nur said, he felt he had lost his passport to life. Later, he told me, he learned that this superior officer was Adolf Eichmann. When he faced the man in the Jerusalem courtroom he attempted to look him in the eye—but collapsed before he managed to catch his attention.

I tried not to ask questions. I listened. At times his memories were so painful that tears streamed down his face; I feared he would faint again. At other times he was a gracious host. He would smile, but an instant later, he would be back in Auschwitz, lost in an agonizing silence. Then, just as suddenly, he was back with me in his living room in Tel Aviv, joking: quick flights from planet to planet. It was grotesque. He warned me that his identity should not be revealed, lest he be scorched, like photographic film exposed to sunlight. Then, all at once, he agreed, for the first time, to sit for a photographer.

The manuscript he gave me was astounding: it contained a humanistic message and a stern warning. It was a kaleidoscope of visions that he had had ten years before, when he had been treated by Jan Bastiaans, the medical director of the Center for War Injuries in Leiden, Holland. Bastiaans specialized in caring for patients suffering from what he called "concentration-camp (or KZ) syndrome," a posttraumatic phenomenon known in one form or another since the First World War but that appeared in a severe form among the survivors of Nazi concentration camps. For them, the professor explained to me, adjustment to normal life could take as long as thirty or forty years, if it happened at all, and it always required great physical and emotional effort. Bastiaans found that those survivors who appeared well-adjusted actually relied heavily on emotional defense mechanisms. Thus many became extremely introverted—"as if they were in an internal concentration camp." The fences of this camp defended them; they were afraid to open its gates, and so endured their tortures ceaselessly and alone. Relatives, friends, and even doctors generally tended to think that these survivors had recovered from their experiences and that their "normal" daily life was just as it seemed—a fiction convenient for everyone, sometimes even for the survivor himself.

It was some time before the medical world learned to recognize that the survivors of the camps were in fact living on emotional reserves that were often too meager to last them their entire lives. Years after the Holocaust, their strength would give out, they would suddenly fall ill, mentally or physically—or they would commit suicide. Bastiaans's therapy was meant to prevent this ultimate exhaustion.

In the early 1960s, Bastiaans began treating patients with LSD. In a lecture he gave in Jerusalem, he confessed that he had only gradually discovered the correct way to use the drug. It could be given only to relatively strong people, he said, because otherwise the treatment would destroy them. Unlike other drugs, which make patients drowsy and fog their senses, LSD sharpens awareness, brings back the terrors of the past and forces patients to reexperience their tortures. In a drug-induced trance, the patients speak, and their words are recorded on tape, sometimes on video. Afterwards they analyze the recordings. Usually, five or six trances are necessary before patients can learn to live with all the traumas they have endured. The therapy is controversial—medically, morally, politically, and legally; Bastiaans received a special permit to pursue his method only after several Dutch Holocaust survivors sent a petition to their queen.

When told of Bastiaans's therapy, De-Nur at first refused to go to Leiden. His wife tried to persuade him. "How completely I understood her enthusiasm," he wrote. "All the pain that empathy had caused her, the agony she had kept inside for so many years now turned to euphoria at the prospect of my salvation. I held her in my arms, not knowing how to explain that Professor Bastiaans couldn't possibly help me. Professor Bastiaans had never been in Auschwitz. And even those who had been there did not know Auschwitz. Not even someone who was there two long years, as I was." But his wife continued to plead with him.

They had met in 1947, in the wake of *Salamandra*. Nina Asherman, the daughter of a prominent doctor, was a teenager when she first read the book. It made a powerful impression on her, and she decided to search out the pseudonymous author. He had recently come to Tel Aviv; he was living in a dark basement but spent most of his days, and many of his nights, on a bench on Rothschild Avenue. She found him somehow and fell in love with him. She felt a sense of mission that was exceptional in the country at that time: members of her generation tended then to avoid Holocaust survivors, even to turn up their noses at them.

Nina-Elia ("Nike") De-Nur, a poet, had been through difficult years with her husband. "I will never forget the way she suffered silently through my nightmares, hiding her own feelings," he wrote. "My strangled cries would wake me, feverish and dripping. Nike, at my side, dried my terrible sweat with a towel, her eyes brimming with unspoken fear and compassion." She wrote: "And still you did not agree to tell me your name." Their children also suffered; their daughter Daniela told me: "Once a year, on Holocaust Memorial Day, they show on television the film of his fainting at the Eichmann trial. I became the daughter of the fainter. And the children in my own daughter's class say to her, 'Your grandfather fainted,' as if it happened yesterday."

In the end, he agreed to go. In his manuscript, he described the five treatments he received in Leiden. He lay naked, covered with a sheet. Bastiaans sat next to him, offering comfort, then injected him with LSD. De-Nur went into a trance, during which he spoke in English, sometimes in Hebrew. In his visions, he saw a comrade from his barracks being beaten to death on his naked buttocks. He saw another friend who lived only because in his misery he served as jester to the SS men. Lived, that is, until they spread his face with jelly and called the starved prisoners out to lick it off. A thousand prisoners charged the man and in seconds they turned into a single mass of hands and legs and mouths, biting and licking one another. The Germans howled with laughter. On the ground sprawled a bloody corpse, eaten away, as if mice had gnawed at it. He saw an SS man murder a boy who had been the victim of his sexual perversions. The soldier grilled the boy's body on a spit and gulped down the meat piece by piece. De-Nur saw his sister Daniela among the camp prostitutes, and he saw his mother, standing naked in line to the crematorium with all the others, and he saw them going up in smoke. He saw himself at Dr. Mengele's "selection," as the Nazi doctor moved his finger just slightly to indicate who would live and who would die: time after time he was chosen to live. He had psychedelic visions that reminded him of Dali paintings. He saw angels and demons. He saw God, in green, pink, and yellow. He also saw an atomic mushroom cloud, "the king of the world." He was tortured by his nightmares and visions, and he was tortured with the enigma of his identity: who was Ka-Tzetnik and who was De-Nur?

His past continued to pursue him, even after the drug wore off. Two days before his second session, he went to the beach, feeling like a condemned man facing his execution. The tourist season was at its height. Most of the tourists had come from West Germany. "I noticed a group of happy young German tourists, their chests and arms bizarrely tattooed," he wrote.

Amused and fascinated, they stared at the plain, unadorned number they discovered on my forearm. To them, the plain blue number was a novelty, and they seemed transfixed, trying to figure out what it meant. Finally, one of them approached me.

The blood pounded in my veins. This was the very first time that I had exposed the number on my arm. For the thirty years since it was burned into my flesh I had been very careful to keep strangers from seeing it. I had not had a short-sleeved shirt in my closet for thirty years. I had never learned to live with these six digits branded in my flesh and soul. To this day I do not know the number by heart—I have to look at my arm. In fact, because of this trauma, my mind cannot retain numbers.

Only on that beach at Noordwijk, did I finally expose the number to the sun. Perhaps I could do it there because no one knew me. It wasn't Israel, where every schoolchild knows the meaning of a plain blue number on someone's arm, knows where that person has been. I know I didn't conceal the number out of shame or guilt. Not at all. Then why? Only Satan of Auschwitz knows. And there in Noordwijk, where my mind was preparing to be free from the curse on my life, there was a German, of all people, standing over me, staring at the number on my arm and mumbling something. I didn't hear him, didn't notice my surroundings. Any minute something horrible would happen, I knew. A crazed beast was awakening inside me, ready to plunge its fangs into the throat of this creature standing over me. I jumped to my feet, shouting curses, and ran.

I can still see the smiling face of that young German who found the tattoo on my arm so plain and thus unique. I wonder whether coming generations will see my period in German history as a plain, unique tattoo.

In one of his later trances, he found himself in an SS uniform. On his head was a hat with the skull insignia, and then he knew "the most terrible of all the horrors"—that, as a human being, he had a share in the guilt. That, apparently, was the main truth he learned in Leiden: the SS man who sent him to the furnace could have been De-Nur, but De-Nur could also have been the SS man. So he addressed God: "O Lord, merciful and compassionate Lord, am I the one, the one who created Auschwitz?"

One day he knew that his work with Bastiaans was over. He had bridged the gap between Ka-Tzetnik and De-Nur: the treatment in Leiden had given him the awareness that Ka-Tzetnik was De-Nur and De-Nur was Ka-Tzetnik, the same person. Auschwitz was not on another planet but in this world; it was the work of man. He left the "other planet" behind in Leiden. Auschwitz the hellish, the dark, was a nightmare belonging to his past. He was able to sleep: memories no longer tortured him at night. Yet the tormented visions continued during the day. It was no longer the past that tortured him but the future: his fear of a nuclear holocaust. "Wherever there is humankind, there is Auschwitz," he wrote. "Because it was not Satan that made Auschwitz but you and I, just as Satan did not create the [nuclear] mushroom, but rather you and I. Man!" Like King Saul at Endor, he wrote, he had gone to Bastiaans to demand an explanation for the Auschwitz of the night. Where might he go now, to demand an explanation for the Auschwitz of the day?

It was ten years before he could write the Leiden story, and he wrote it in two and a half weeks, as he had *Salamandra*, his first book of testimony. When he showed me the manuscript, he was still undecided. Perhaps he would file it away, he told me, because who, after all, had appointed him to be a prophet in this world? Perhaps it would be best to burn it. He had burned *House of Dolls* twice before publishing it. In the end, he decided to publish *Shivitti*. When the book came out, Ka-

Tzetnik did something that would have been unimaginable before—he agreed to a long interview on television.

¶

Like Ka-Tzetnik's story, the history of Israel's painful confrontation with the Holocaust is a story of uncertain identity. The Israelis' vision of the Holocaust has shaped their idea of themselves, just as their changing sense of self has altered their view of the Holocaust and their understanding of its meaning. Like Ka-Tzetnik's emblematic story, this story contains within it a great human drama of repression and recognition, of agonizing engagement with the lessons of the past.

The Seventh Million tells that larger story. Beginning with the Zionist response to the rise of the Nazis and the arrival of the first German refugees, it documents the less than compassionate response of the Jewish community in Palestine to the destruction of the European Jews—and that community's first pained and uncomprehending encounters with the survivors.

After the war, a great silence surrounded the destruction of the Jews. Then came moral and political conflicts, including the painful debate over relations with Germany, which slowly brought the Israelis to recognize the deeper meaning of the Holocaust. The trial of Adolf Eichmann served as therapy for the nation, starting a process of identification with the tragedy of the victims and survivors, a process that continues to this day.

The most fateful decisions in Israeli history, other than the founding of the state itself—the mass immigration of the 1950s, the Six-Day War, and Israel's nuclear project—were all conceived in the shadow of the Holocaust. Over the years, there were those who distorted the heritage of the Holocaust, making it a bizarre cult of memory, death, and kitsch. Others too have used it, toyed with it, traded on it, popularized it, and politicized it. As the Holocaust recedes in time—and into the realm of history—its lessons have moved to the center of a fierce struggle over the politics, ideology, and morals of the present.

The Seventh Million concerns the ways in which the bitter events of the past continue to shape the life of a nation. Just as the Holocaust imposed a posthumous collective identity on its six million victims, so too it formed the collective identity of this new country—not just for the survivors who came after the war but for all Israelis, then and now. This is why I have called them the seventh million.

PART I

HITLER:
The Yekkes Are Coming

1 | "The Streets Are Paved with Money"

On Prophets Street in downtown Jerusalem there was, in the 1930s, a small and romantic-looking stone house shaded by pine trees. It was the German consulate, which had been opened at the end of the previous century. On one of the first spring days of 1933, shortly after the Nazis took power, an employee climbed up to the roof and raised a red flag bearing a black swastika on a circle of white. Zionist activists, members of the right-wing Betar youth movement, managed on occasion to steal the offending flag. But each time, the Germans raised another in its place, and the swastika flew, there in the heart of Jerusalem, for six of the twelve years of the Third Reich's existence, until the consulate was closed at the outbreak of the Second World War.[1]

Palestine was then ruled by the British. As long as diplomatic relations continued between Nazi Germany and Britain, the German consulates (there was a second one in Jaffa) were allowed to operate in Palestine. Like other foreign legations in Jerusalem, the German consulate did not restrict itself to routine consular affairs but effectively served as a Nazi embassy. It furthered German interests and was in regular and close contact with both Arab and Jewish political bodies.

The League of Nations mandate under which Britain ruled provided for "a Jewish agency" to advise and cooperate with the mandatory authorities on matters related to the establishment of a National Jewish Home. It named in this role the Zionist Organization (later the World Zionist Organization), an international federation of Zionist groups founded by

Theodor Herzl at the turn of the century and later led by Chaim Weiz-mann. In the 1930s, the Jewish Agency operated virtually as the govern-ment of the Jewish state-in-the-making.

Campaigning for influence in the agency and in other organizations were a variety of political parties. Mapai (Labor)—a coalition of the two largest socialist-labor Zionist parties forged by David Ben-Gurion—dom-inated almost everywhere, especially after he became the chairman of the Jewish Agency executive in 1935. Zeev Jabotinsky's Union of Zionist Revisionists was the principal opposition party. The Revisionists' oppo-sition was so firm, in fact, that they seceded from the Zionist Organization and each of the other governing bodies at least once during the tumultuous years between their founding in 1925 and the establishment of the state in 1948. They too pressed for Jewish national rights in Palestine, but they opposed the official law-abiding Zionist policy toward the British as lacking purpose and firmness, rejected the prevailing socialist ethos, and held that private investment was the fastest way to bring large numbers of Jews to Palestine to populate the "maximalist" state—which, the Re-visionists insisted, should eventually occupy both sides of the Jordan River. Betar, whose members surreptitiously tore down the offensive Nazi flag in Jerusalem, was the Revisionist youth movement.

Such demonstrations aside, though, Nazi Germany's ties with Palestine proceeded normally through the prewar years. There were mail, tele-phone, and financial links; many German Jews who had been forced out of their jobs continued to receive their monthly social-security pensions in Palestine. Palestine exported to Germany and Germany to Palestine. People traveled back and forth by sea and occasionally by air. Some came from Germany to scout out conditions in Palestine before deciding to settle there. Others arrived as businessmen, and still others as vacationers and tourists. German government officials also visited, including Wil-helm Frick, Hitler's minister of the interior, who passed through Jeru-salem on his honeymoon.

¶

Readers of the lively Hebrew press in Palestine received a broad range of information on the rise of the Nazis, based primarily on reports from the international wire services, but sometimes on the work of their own special correspondents. In the months preceding the political revolution in Ger-many, stories from Berlin made headlines in all Zionist papers almost every day. The reports of the events that led to Hitler's seizure of power were not accurate in every detail, but the general picture they gave was reasonably correct.

On January 31, 1933, the day after Hitler became chancellor, the independent liberal daily *Haaretz* decried this "hugely negative historical event."[2] Ten days later, it ran a headline that read, "BLACK DAYS IN GERMANY."[3] The paper followed the ongoing "anti-Semitic horror," but during those first weeks it, like the British press, generally aimed at reassuring its readers: "One must suppose that Hitlerism will now renounce terrorist methods: government brings responsibility."[4] The right-wing *Doar Hayom* agreed: "There can be no doubt that Hitler the chancellor will be different from the Hitler of the public rallies."[5] But from the start, *Davar*—the left-wing daily published by the Histadrut (Labor Federation)—was more pessimistic: "It was a bitter and ill-fated day when the New Vandal came to power," the newspaper wrote the day after the change of government in Germany. It described Hitler as a man of hate and demagoguery, who would "tear the Jews out by their roots."[6]

Although the press saw Nazism as a new chapter in the long history of anti-Semitism that stretched from the Middle Ages through the Tsarist regime in Russia, it found the current incarnation difficult to understand. Several weeks after Hitler became chancellor, one writer likened Nazi Germany to the primitive world of Kipling's *Jungle Book*; another writer called Nazism an "obvious example of mass psychosis," suggesting that only psychiatry could explain it.[7]

Already visible at this early stage were the outlines of the debate that would come to preoccupy Israel: What was the proper attitude to take toward the German people? The positions ranged across the political spectrum: *Hapoel Hatsair*, the weekly newspaper of the left-of-center Labor party (Mapai), declared, "Our war against this despicable and mad enemy is a war against a particular regime . . . but it is not a war against the German people."[8] Those on the right tended not to make this distinction: Seventeen million people—the number who voted for Hitler—are more than a minor party, wrote Revisionist leader Jabotinsky, condemning the whole German nation.[9] Then there was the middle way: The fact that the majority of Germans supported Hitler, *Haaretz* thought, attested to the fact that stupid, rude, and narrow-minded national chauvinism was rooted in the German people more deeply than in any other nation; nonetheless, "all the Hitlers in the world cannot eliminate the names of Kant, Goethe, and Schiller from German history." In this connection, the newspaper coined the expressions "the other Germany" and "the different Germany," highly charged terms that would later see much use in Israeli politics.[10]

More than anything else, though, the rise of the Nazis was seen as confirming the historical prognosis of Zionist ideology. *Hapoel Hatsair* described the Nazi persecution of the Jews as "punishment" for their having tried to integrate into German society instead of leaving for Palestine while it was still possible to do so. Now they would have to run in panic, "like mice in flight," the paper said.[11] The Revisionist paper *Hazit Haam* used even stronger language: "The Jews of Germany are being persecuted now not despite their efforts to be part of their country but because of those efforts."[12] The Holocaust would later be the primary argument for the establishment of the State of Israel and for its wars of survival.

The leaders of the *yishuv*—the Jewish community in Palestine—and the heads of the political parties followed the German crisis closely; they seemed to have grasped its meaning quite soon. "Hitler's anti-Jewish plans form an organic part of his ideology and he is likely to try to carry them out," Jabotinsky declared at the beginning of 1933, and two years later he wrote, "The Third Reich's policy toward the Jews calls for a war of extermination. It is being conducted in a way that exceeds the bounds of humanity."[13] In 1934, David Ben-Gurion stated after reading Hitler's *Mein Kampf*, "Hitler's policy puts the entire Jewish people in danger."[14]

Everyone wondered how the persecution of the Jews in Germany would affect life in Palestine. The papers predicted "loss and ruin beyond repair" and described "the dance of death" that was going on in Berlin. Nonetheless, they expected that "the hour of trouble and anguish" would open unprecedented historical opportunities—specifically, increased immigration to Palestine.[15] Ben-Gurion hoped the Nazis' victory would become "a fertile force" for Zionism.[16] Writer and Mapai activist Moshe Beilinson went to Germany and reported back to Berl Katznelson, editor of *Davar* and one of the leaders of Mapai, "The streets are paved with more money than we have ever dreamed of in the history of our Zionist enterprise. Here is an opportunity to build and flourish like none we have ever had or ever will have."[17]

¶

A few months after Hitler rose to power, a senior Zionist official made a trip to Berlin to take advantage of that opportunity, to negotiate with the Nazis for the emigration of German Jews and the transfer of their property to Palestine. Arthur Ruppin, economist and jurist, had been born in Prussia but had lived in Palestine for twenty-five years. A founder of Tel Aviv, he was, at fifty-seven, a central figure in the Zionist movement. By the time he returned to Berlin that summer of 1933, thousands of German Jews had already been expelled from their jobs—civil servants, teachers, professors, doctors, lawyers, judges. Thugs from the SA, the Nazi party's storm troopers, patrolled the entrances to Jewish stores to deter customers from entering; from time to time they would attack Jews in the street or light bonfires to burn books by Jewish authors. The first concentration camps were already in operation, one of them not far from Berlin.

Although Germany lived under a reign of terror, Ruppin could see little visible evidence of the Nazi revolution. "Had I not known from the newspapers and from personal conversations how much the economic and political situation of the Jews had worsened as a result of government decrees, I would not have sensed it at all on the streets, at least not in Berlin," he wrote in his diary. [18] Jewish business establishments were open, he noted. On the Kurfürstendamm, the elegant boulevard in the center of town, the cafés still welcomed Jewish customers and served them as if nothing had happened.

Georg Landauer, a member of the Jewish Agency and formerly a leader of the Zionist movement in Germany, suggested to Ruppin that he travel to Jena, the famous university town that had once been home to Schiller, Hegel, and other great German scholars. There, Landauer said, he could meet Hans F. K. Günther, one of the leading Nazi race theorists. Ruppin would be interested; he had himself conducted some research into the origins of the "Jewish race," looking in particular for a connection between the physical appearance and the mental characteristics of the Jews. During a two-hour meeting, Günther explained to Ruppin that Aryan racial doctrine had not originated with him. The Jews were not inferior to the Aryans, he reassured Ruppin, they were simply different. This meant that a "fair solution" had to be found for the Jewish problem. The professor was extremely friendly, Ruppin recorded with satisfaction. [19]

Ruppin also felt well received at the Nazi foreign and finance ministries, he wrote. On the afternoon of August 7, 1933, he attended a meeting in the finance ministry. The parties agreed that every Jew who emigrated to Palestine would be allowed to take £1,000 sterling (about $4,000) in foreign currency and to ship to Palestine merchandise worth 20,000 German marks (about $5,000), or even more, with the finances to be handled by Jewish and German trust companies.[20] The sum of £1,000 was necessary to receive British permission to settle in Palestine as a "capitalist," as this category of immigrant was called. It was a sizable sum; a family of four could then live in bourgeois comfort on less than £300 a year.[21]

The *haavara* ("transfer") agreement—the Hebrew term was used in the Nazi documents as well—was based on the complementary interests of the German government and the Zionist movement: the Nazis wanted the Jews out of Germany; the Zionists wanted them to come to Palestine.[22] But there was no such mutuality of interests between the Zionists and German Jewry. Most German Jews would have preferred to stay in their country. The tension between the interests of the yishuv (and, in time, the State of Israel) and those of world Jewry was to become a central motif in the story of the Israelis' attitude to the Holocaust.

¶

It is not possible to establish who was the first to propose negotiating with the Third Reich about arrangements for emigration and transfer of property. The proposal, however, had a good Zionist pedigree; Theodor Herzl had suggested similar ideas in his book *The Jewish State*.[23] It would seem that something like the haavara agreement came more or less simultaneously to a number of people.

Sam Cohen, for instance, was a millionaire from Lodz, Poland, who had settled in Berlin and dealt in real estate, most successfully. He was part owner of a small bank and a coal mine and had his own chateau. A seasoned businessman, this adventurer and philanthropist had purchased land in Palestine and ran a company called Hanotea ("the Planter") that rented land to new settlers. When the Nazis seized power, he hit on the idea that transferring the capital of German Jews to Palestine, in the form of goods, would advance Zionist interests (by increasing both immigration and capital in Palestine) and those of Hanotea as well (through sales and commissions). His connections in Berlin had helped him obtain the first permits allowing Jews to take out of Germany the sum of money necessary to settle in Palestine as "capitalists"; presumably Hanotea would manage the transfer of their property as well. It seemed like a good deal for all concerned. Another man with a related idea was Haim Arlosoroff, the head of the political department of the Jewish Agency. Apparently he did not know about Cohen's arrangement when he came to Berlin in June 1933 to try to obtain something similar;

Arlosoroff himself liked to keep the details of his contacts secret. Yet another was a lawyer named Felix Rosenblüth, formerly one of the leaders of German Zionism; he had floated such ideas in conversations with other Zionist notables who had emigrated from Germany—one of whom was Arthur Ruppin.

The various uncoordinated negotiations with the Germans lasted for several months in early 1933. At one stage the controller of foreign currency in the German finance ministry, Hans Hartenstein, was surprised to discover that the Jews sitting across the table from him did not represent a unified interest but rather were competing with one another, threatening the entire arrangement. The leaders of the Jewish Agency wanted to prevent private entrepreneur Cohen from getting a monopoly on the deal, partly because his Hanotea was identified with the Revisionist right in Palestine. Instead they brought in Yachin, a firm affiliated with the Histadrut, whose Berlin representative was Levi Shkolnik, later to be Prime Minister Levi Eshkol. *

Intervention by the German consul in Jerusalem, Heinrich Wolff (soon to be relieved of his post because he had a Jewish wife), was necessary to prevent the collapse of the negotiations. He found himself in a bind —Cohen had apparently bribed him, and the Jewish Agency blackmailed him.[25] In the end the Jewish Agency and Ruppin gained control of the negotiations, but Cohen, the Histadrut, Mapai, and the Jewish National Fund (the Zionist Organization's arm for land purchase and development) all received their shares—some of the profits were used to purchase land for Jewish settlement.

The details of the agreement were adjusted from time to time and new arrangements were added over the years, but in the main the haavara operated through trust companies set up in Germany and in Palestine. Before leaving Germany, the Jewish emigrants deposited their capital with the German trust company, which used the money to pay German suppliers for merchandise meant for export to Palestine. The customers in Palestine who ordered merchandise from Germany transferred their payments to a local trust company, which returned the money to the Jews who had in the meantime arrived from Germany. The system was

---

.* Other future prime ministers were also involved in various stages of the haavara affair. David Ben-Gurion and Moshe Shertok (later Sharett) fought for the haavara agreement at the Zionist Congresses and in the Jewish Agency executive. Golda Meyerson (later Meir) defended it in New York. Menahem Begin was with Zeev Jabotinsky when Jabotinsky fought the agreement.[24]

complex; it required financial expertise and legal acumen, as well as infinite paperwork and patience. All those involved in the agreement benefited. The Nazis got rid of Jews, increased their exports, even though they did not receive foreign currency, and broke the boycott against them that had been initiated by several, mostly American, Jewish organizations. The Zionist movement gained new settlers who, had they not been allowed to transfer their capital, might not have come to Palestine. And the emigrants escaped Germany with more of their property than they might otherwise have done; only slowly did it become clear that they owed their very lives to the agreement, as well.

The haavara system continued to function in one form or another until the middle of World War II. Some 20,000 people were assisted by it, and about $30 million was transferred from Germany to Palestine. Not an earthshaking sum even then, but it gave a certain impetus to the country's economy and to the Zionist enterprise. [26] The immigrants themselves were forced to wait a long time for their money, sometimes as much as two or three years. They lost up to 35 percent of their capital, but according to calculations by proponents of the haavara, they would have lost more had they tried to transfer their capital in any other legal way. [27]

Nonetheless, the haavara was dealing with the devil, and it aroused fierce disputes and conflicts that lasted as long as the agreement itself: a left-wing national leadership versus a right-wing opposition that did not have to prove its rhetoric in policy; pragmatic activism versus emotional populism; the need to rescue Jews and build Jewish settlement versus the desire to preserve the national honor; Zionist interests in the Land of Israel versus worldwide Jewish solidarity. Nothing provoked sharper divisions among Jews at that time than the haavara agreement, David Ben-Gurion commented. [28] The debate was further inflamed by battles for prestige and ideological supremacy, intrigues and accusations, threats, deception, obstruction, blackmail, extortion, and a murder that would haunt Israeli politics for another fifty years.

§

At that time Zionist politics in Palestine were deeply influenced by the ideological currents in Europe, both left and right. Almost everything written in the left-wing press about the rise of the Nazis reflected a sense of social-democratic solidarity and the fear created by the destruction of Weimar democracy. Thus the Mapai weekly *Hapoel Hatsair*, not confining its attention to the danger the Jews were facing, described Nazism as a "black reaction meant to draw Germany back to the darkest ideas of the Middle Ages."[29]

The Revisionist right, by contrast, had long been sympathetic to Benito Mussolini's Fascism and now and then even to Adolf Hitler's Nazism—except, of course, his anti-Semitism. Betar, Jabotinsky's youth movement, fostered classic Fascist ideas and forms. In 1928, Abba Ahimeir, a well-known Revisionist journalist, had a regular column, "From the Notebook of a Fascist," in the newspaper *Doar Hayom*. In anticipation of Jabotinsky's arrival in Palestine, he wrote an article titled "On the Arrival of Our *Duce*."[30]

Four years later, in early 1932, Ahimeir was among those brought to trial for disrupting a public lecture at the Hebrew University. The incident and the resulting trial are worthy of note only because of a declaration by defense attorney Zvi Eliahu Cohen in response to a speech by the prosecutor comparing the disruption of the lecture with Nazi disturbances in Germany: "The comment on the Nazis," Cohen said, "went too far. Were it not for Hitler's anti-Semitism, we would not oppose his ideology. Hitler saved Germany." This was not an unconsidered outburst; the Revisionist paper *Hazit Haam* praised Cohen's "brilliant speech."[31]

When it came to the struggle between the Nazis and their Communist opponents, the right-wing press in Palestine had a clear preference. Ahimeir heralded the Führer's appointment with an article that placed Hitler among other "shining names": Mustafa Kemal Atatürk, Jozef Pilsudski, Eamon De Valera, and Benito Mussolini.[32] "Hitler has still not caused us as much evil as Stalin has," asserted *Hazit Haam* a few weeks after the change in the German government; there was a difference between the attitude of the Zionist left toward the Nazis and that of the Revisionists: "Social democrats of all stripes believe that Hitler's movement is an empty shell," the newspaper explained, but "we believe that there is both a shell and a kernel. The anti-Semitic shell is to be discarded, but not the anti-Marxist kernel." The Revisionists, the newspaper wrote, would fight the Nazis only to the extent that they were anti-Semites.[33]

Jabotinsky, however, was less sympathetic than some of his followers: He chastised the editors of *Hazit Haam*: the articles on Hitler were "a knife in the back," "a disgrace," and "verbal prostitution"; such articles, he insisted, must no longer be published. Within a few weeks, his followers, too, learned to forsake the distinction between shell and kernel.[34]

¶

The haavara agreement was a central issue in the elections in the summer of 1933 for representatives to the Eighteenth Zionist Congress. The Revisionists rejected any contact with Nazi Germany. It was inconsistent with the honor of the Jewish people, they said; Jabotinsky declared it "ignoble, disgraceful, and contemptible."[35] The Revisionist press now castigated the Zionist Organization and the Jewish Agency as "Hitler's allies," people "who have trampled roughshod on Jewish honor, on Jewish conscience, and on Jewish ethics, . . . dark characters who have come to trade on the troubles of the Jews and the land of Israel, . . . low types who have accepted the role of Hitler's agents in Palestine and in the entire Near East, . . . traitors, . . . deceivers who lust after Hitler's government."*[36]

The Zionist establishment found it hard to counter the emotional Revisionist opposition to contact with Germany. As would happen more than once thereafter, the Mapai leadership advocated a more temperate approach than most of its voters wanted; for this reason it tried, as it would also do in future controversies, to conceal the details of its contacts, including those concerning the haavara agreement. These details were acknowledged only after they were leaked to the press. And then the leaders offered purely practical justifications; what they proposed was not

---

* In the tense battle between left and right, party leaders often compared their opponents to the Nazis; Adolf Hitler's name thus penetrated public consciousness not only as a danger but also as an all-purpose political insult.

David Ben-Gurion was in Berlin for a conference at the time of elections for the fifth Reichstag on September 14, 1930, when the Nazis became the second-largest faction in the Weimar parliament. He wrote the next day that "the deafening victory of the 'German Revisionists' was greater than anyone had feared." After reading the Nazi party newspaper, Ben-Gurion wrote, it seemed to him that he was reading the words of Zeev Jabotinsky in *Doar Hayom*: "the same things, the same style, and the same spirit."[37]

Zionist leader Chaim Weizmann, later the first president of Israel, spoke out that same year against "Hitler-style" political hysteria and stated that Revisionism resembled "Hitlerism in its worst form."[38] In 1932, the editor-in-chief of the Mapai weekly depicted the Revisionists as "children playing with a Jewish swastika."[39] Later that year, Jabotinsky returned the compliment in an anti-Mapai article entitled "The Red Swastika."[40] Two months after Hitler came to power, Ben-Gurion, speaking at a rally in Tel Aviv, called Zeev (born Vladimir) Jabotinsky "Vladimir Hitler."[41]

So they would speak throughout the period of Nazi power and for years to come. Long after the grisly details of the Holocaust became known, Ben-Gurion compared Menahem Begin to Hitler.[42] Berl Katznelson, by contrast, sharply condemned comparisons between the Revisionists and the Nazis.[43]

clothed in glory or crowned with national honor; they spoke only of realistic goals, of what was possible, what could be done. The pragmatists pointedly reminded the Revisionists of the agreement that Jabotinsky had negotiated with the anti-Communist government of Simon Petlura to create a Jewish gendarmerie, even though Petlura's followers had massacred Ukrainian Jews. They quoted Jabotinsky's declaration that for the Land of Israel he was willing to make a pact with Satan himself.[44] Ben-Gurion proposed to his party that it publish a special pamphlet containing the details of the agreement between the Revisionist Hanotea and the German authorities, in order to denounce the hypocrisy of the opponents of the haavara policy.[45]

As the election campaign for the Eighteenth Zionist Congress intensified, the Revisionist newspaper *Hazit Haam* published an article in which it charged that the Hebrew nation's honor, rights, security, and position in the world "had been sold to Hitler for a whore's wages," unconditionally and without anything in return. The Jewish people, the newspaper threatened, "will know how to respond to this odious act."[46] Among the villains condemned for having a hand in the agreement was Haim Arlosoroff.

That same day, June 16, 1933, Arlosoroff had lunch with Sir Arthur Wauchope, the British high commissioner for Palestine; two days earlier, Arlosoroff had returned from conducting haavara business in Germany. That evening he went for a walk on the Tel Aviv beach with his wife, Sima. Two men loitering there approached them. While one shone a flashlight in Arlosoroff's face, the other pulled out a pistol and shot him. Arlosoroff was rushed to the Hadassah Hospital, where he died on the operating table soon after midnight. Mapai accused the Revisionists of murder; the incident poisoned relations between the two parties for many years thereafter.*

¶

* One of the odder decisions of the Begin administration was to establish an official commission of inquiry in 1982 to determine whether there was any truth to the claim, made anew in Shabtai Teveth's biography of Ben-Gurion, that two members of the Revisionist movement were partners in the murder of Arlosoroff. The commission concluded that the men named were neither murderers nor accomplices to murder. Yet the commission also held that the evidence did not allow it to determine the identity of the murderers or whether the death had been a political assassination.[47] The mystery remained unsolved.

Instead of dealing with the Nazis, the Revisionists proposed banishing Germany from the family of nations and imposing an international economic and diplomatic boycott. This idea was born in America; it was belligerent and proud but had no hope of toppling Hitler's regime. The Nazis, though, did not make light of the ability of the Jews to cause them damage; they threatened the Jewish leadership in America, organized a one-day counterboycott against Jewish stores in Germany, and speeded up the negotiations on the haavara agreement. One of their goals was to divide the Jewish world between the supporters of the haavara and the supporters of the boycott—and the division indeed occurred.[48]

When the Zionist Congress convened in Prague in August 1933, it in effect approved the haavara policy. Yet when it adjourned, many of the delegates and functionaries went on to Geneva for an international Jewish conference called by Rabbi Stephen Wise of the American Jewish Congress to make plans for the boycott of Germany.* The purpose of the boycott was to force the Nazis to halt their persecution, so that Jews could continue to live in Germany. Ben-Gurion and his associates, by contrast, wanted German Jews to settle in Palestine, and they saw the haavara policy as a means toward that end.

In Palestine too, the debate continued. "What's happened to you?" Ben-Gurion exploded when the haavara was challenged at a meeting of the Vaad Leumi (National Council) in 1935: "Have you lost your minds?"† What had happened to Judaism, he wondered, always so pragmatic and commonsensical? Did the members want to assist Hitler?[49] Years later, this same style, sometimes the very same words, shaped the debate over the reparations agreement between West Germany and Israel.

In his impassioned speech, Ben-Gurion called for the rescue of German Jewry, "a tribe of Israel," and their transfer to Palestine, rather than action against Hitler. "I do not believe that we can oust him and I am not interested in anything other than saving these 500,000 Jews," he said.[50] Ben-Gurion saw the debate between rescue and boycott as a debate between Zionism and assimilation, between the nationalist interests of Jewish settlement in Palestine and the international war against anti-

---

* This was the second meeting of its kind, the first having been convened the previous year, before the Nazis came to power; the third came a year later. These conferences, in part, laid the groundwork for the World Jewish Congress.

† The Vaad Leumi, the elected National Council of the Jews of Palestine, oversaw Jewish municipal governments, handled internal matters such as the school system, and, along with the Jewish Agency, supervised the Haganah, the clandestine Jewish defense force.

Semitism.[51] The assumption implicit in his words was that the war against anti-Semitism was not part of the Zionist mission. "The difference between the Exile [as the Diaspora was called] and Zion is that the Exile, fighting for its life, wishes to overcome the evil Haman in his country," explained Yehoshua Radler-Feldman, a well-known columnist who wrote under the pen name Rabbi Benyamin. The Exile, he continued, "wants the Jews to remain in Germany despite all the troubles and persecutions and victims. . . . Zion wants to uproot them. It washes its hands of a war with Haman, which in its eyes is but a Sisyphean task, its whole interest being only in illegal and legal immigration, despite all the anguish and sacrifice on the way to Zion."[52]

According to Ben-Gurion, there was within every Jew both a Zionist and an assimilationist. The struggle between the two, he said, was the "most urgent moral national issue" facing Jewry at that particular moment.[53] "The assimilationists have always declared war on anti-Semitism," he said.

> Now this is expressed in a "boycott" against Hitler. Zionism has always [advocated] the Jewish people's independence in its homeland. Now some Zionists have joined the chorus of the assimilationists: a "war" against anti-Semitism. But we must give a *Zionist* response to the catastrophe faced by German Jewry—to turn this disaster into an opportunity to develop our country, to save the lives and property of the Jews of Germany for the sake of Zion. *This* rescue takes priority over all else.

To concentrate now on a boycott, he concluded, would be a "moral failure" of unprecedented proportions.[54]

Ben-Gurion's words provoked strong reactions. "All this enthusiasm from the left would not have been were institutions affiliated with Mapai not benefiting [from the haavara agreement]," huffed *Doar Hayom.*[55] The more moderate right-wing *Haboker* described Ben-Gurion's speech as "banal, vain talk," both irresponsible and insulting. There would always be Jews living in other countries, the paper stated, describing the use of the term *assimilationist* as "the height of demagoguery."[56]

Even among the Zionist leadership, Ben-Gurion's position was not unanimously supported. Some Jewish Agency leaders charged that the agreement with the Germans was liable to encourage the Poles to attack their Jews as well. Yitzhak Gruenbaum, a member of the executive and formerly a Jewish leader in Poland, demanded an end to the haavara. "We must begin an open war against Nazi Germany without giving any consideration to the fate of the Jews in Germany," Gruenbaum said. He proposed examining the possibility of "smashing the windows in all their embassies" and organizing mass demonstrations. "German Jewry will obviously pay for this," he noted, "but there is no alternative. If we do not do it now, the fate of the Jews of Poland and Romania tomorrow will be like that of the Jews of Germany today."[57] Gruenbaum felt that settlement should not be rushed: "We need the Exile for at least another fifty years," he said, and warned that Jews should not be encouraged to flee their countries: "A nation in flight cannot build a homeland."[58]

Other Jewish Agency leaders continued to argue that there was no contradiction between the boycott and the haavara policies and that both had a part to play in a single strategy. This was, of course, illogical. Ben-Gurion was right: the movement to boycott Germany did in fact reflect a rather pathetic attempt to maintain Jewish rights wherever Jews lived, including Nazi Germany. To make his point, Ben-Gurion used harsh language that would in time be employed by anti-Zionists: "If I knew that it was possible to save all the children in Germany by transporting them to England, but only half of them by transporting them to Palestine, I would choose the second—because we face not only the reckoning of those children, but the historical reckoning of the Jewish people."*[59] In the wake of the *Kristallnacht* pogroms, Ben-Gurion commented that "the human conscience" might bring various countries to open their doors to Jewish refugees from Germany. He saw this as a threat and warned: "Zionism is in danger!"[62]

The haavara debate thus led to collective soul-searching among the Jews in Palestine and to a deep crisis of identity. Who are we, they asked—humans, Jews, or Zionists? What are our privileges and our duties? Each party found support for its own claims in Jewish history.

---

* Shabtai Teveth, Ben-Gurion's biographer, made a great effort to put this statement in a different light. Two years previously, Ben-Gurion had said the opposite, and he was in the habit of phrasing his positions with gross overstatement, in the form of a reductio ad absurdum, the loyal biographer explained. Ben-Gurion knew that he had no way of saving these children, either in Palestine or in England. He did not intend the horrifying connotation that future events would give to his words. All he wanted to say was that the only possible deliverance for the Jewish people was in Palestine, Teveth wrote.[60] In any case, the haavara agreement with the Nazis was based on the condition that the Jews go to Palestine.[61]

"History," *Haboker* said, "will always relate proudly and with admiration the story of an exceptional woman, Doña Gracia Mendes, who initiated (in the sixteenth century) the movement to boycott the adversaries of the Jewish people. Were she to hear speeches like those of David Ben-Gurion to the Vaad Leumi, she would hang her head in shame."[63] Others said that there was no reason not to negotiate with Adolf Hitler to save German Jews and bring them to Palestine; after all, Moses had had no qualms about negotiating with Pharaoh to take the children of Israel out of Egypt.[64]

In this struggle for control of the Zionist movement, the proponents of the haavara agreement prevailed. The next Zionist Congress, meeting in Lucerne in 1935, reaffirmed the policy. The Vaad Leumi, in the end, also rejected the boycott.[65]

ß

The haavara agreement would in the end shore up the Jewish Agency —then almost bankrupt—and grant it renewed momentum. But this victory was not without cost; it effectively isolated the yishuv from the dominant current of world Jewish response to the rise of the Nazis. Nevertheless, the pragmatists were convinced that the boycott of Germany could not advance the interests of Palestine, that their ends could best be accomplished through contact with the Nazis. Thus the leaders sought to keep relations with Nazi Germany as normal as possible: Two months after Hitler came to power the Jewish Agency executive in Jerusalem had sent a telegram straight to the Führer in Berlin, assuring him that the yishuv had not declared a boycott against his country; the telegram was sent at the request of German Jewry in the hope of halting their persecution, but it reflected the Jewish Agency's inclination to maintain correct relations with the Nazi government. Many years later, Menahem Begin revealed that the Zionist Organization had sent Hitler a cable of condolence on the death of President Hindenburg.[66]

There were further contacts with the Nazis over the years. Working in cooperation with the German authorities, the Jewish Agency maintained immigration agents in Nazi Berlin.[67] Georg Landauer, for example, carried a letter, in German, certifying that the Jewish Agency had authorized him to conduct negotiations with the Third Reich about vocational training for prospective immigrants and arrangements for the transfer of their capital. The letter was signed by Arthur Ruppin and David Ben-Gurion.[68]

The Zionists also cultivated public relations in Germany. In the spring of 1933, they invited Baron Leopold Itz von Mildenstein, an engineer and journalist of Austrian extraction and one of the first members of the SS, to come to Palestine with his wife, to write a series of articles for *Angriff*, Joseph Goebbels's newspaper. The von Mildensteins came, accompanied by Kurt Tuchler and his wife. Tuchler was active in the Zionist Organization of Berlin and was in charge of relations with the Nazi party. "Our goal," he would later recall, "was to create, in an important Nazi newspaper, an atmosphere that would advance the cause of Zionist settlements in Palestine." According to Tuchler, Zionist "authorities" approved his initiative.[69]

The goals were fully realized: Von Mildenstein toured the country from one end to the other, met large numbers of Arabs and Jews, and was also the guest of several kibbutzim. He was deeply impressed. His articles, titled "A Nazi Visits Palestine," exuded sympathy for Zionism.[70]

The *Angriff* attached such importance to this series of articles that it cast a special medallion to commemorate von Mildenstein's journey: one side displayed a swastika and the other a Star of David. Von Mildenstein also took several recordings of Hebrew songs back with him; Tuchler heard one of the records playing during one of his visits to Gestapo headquarters. Von Mildenstein did more than promote Zionism to the German public. From time to time he also passed on useful information to Tuchler. He kept in contact with the Tuchler family even after they settled in Palestine. Each year he sent them greetings, in Hebrew, for Rosh Hashanah, the Jewish New Year.[71]

Von Mildenstein headed the Office of Jewish Affairs; on his staff was the man who would be his successor: Adolf Eichmann. Eichmann himself set out to visit Palestine in 1937, but the British would give him only a transit pass good for a single night in Haifa. Traveling on to Cairo, he summoned a Jew from Jerusalem, one Feibl Folkes. A report Eichmann wrote of his trip and the record of his interrogation by the Israeli police decades later indicate that Folkes was a member of the Haganah—the clandestine Jewish defense force—and a Nazi agent. On one occasion he even met with Eichmann in Berlin. The Nazis paid him for his information, mostly rather general political and economic evaluations. Among other things, Eichmann quoted Folkes to the effect that Zionist leaders were pleased by the persecution of German Jewry, since it would encourage immigration to Palestine. During his meeting with Folkes, at the Groppi coffeehouse in Cairo, Eichmann asked about the absorption of German Jews in Palestine.*

The Reich annexed Austria in 1938. After the *Anschluss*, Eichmann was put in charge of Jewish affairs there and, in this capacity, met more than once with Jewish representatives and Zionist functionaries, including Teddy Kollek, later one of Ben-Gurion's chief assistants and mayor of Jerusalem. The meeting took place in the spring of 1939 in Vienna, where Kollek had grown up. Eichmann's staff was housed in a wing of the Rothschild mansion.

"My appointment with Eichmann was the first time I had ever visited the home of the Rothschilds," Kollek later recalled. "I walked through a large, elegant, wood-paneled room up to a desk, and there he was, a neatly dressed, clean-shaven young man in a black uniform with the swastika on his arm. He gave the impression of being a minor clerk— not aggressive, not loud, not impolite. But he kept me standing throughout the interview." Kollek notified Eichmann that he had entry permits to England for young Jews who were then in an agricultural training camp. He asked that they be allowed to leave Austria, with Palestine as their ultimate destination. "Eichmann was very businesslike and asked me a few technical questions," Kollek wrote. "How many English entry permits could I provide? How soon could the people leave? Would the permits include both boys and girls?" After about fifteen minutes Eichmann approved the request and sent Kollek on his way. "He did not make any special impression on me," wrote Kollek, who did not see Eichmann again until twenty-one years later, when he was in charge of arrangements for the trial in Jerusalem.[73]

Less than a month before the war started, Jewish Agency representatives were still talking with Eichmann about an agreement—never carried out—to allow ten thousand Jews to leave through the port of Hamburg.[74]

Other Zionist notables also had contact with the Gestapo, including its first commander, Rudolf Diels. They did not accomplish much, but

---

* It is hard to be certain what position Folkes held in the Haganah, if any. He claimed that the entire story was a fabrication and that he had met with Eichmann and his associates for business purposes, at his own initiative. The Haganah archives produce a note written by Shaul Avigur, a Haganah leader, to Yehuda Slotzki, the organization's official historian, stating that, based on an examination conducted with the assistance of the Israeli security services, Avigur had reached the conclusion that the Folkes-Eichmann meeting had been "a passing episode of no significance."[72]

sometimes they helped free prisoners and ease the work of the Central Organization of German Jews, which was established on the orders of the Nazis and which included German Zionists. A number of these contacts grew out of personal acquaintances made before the Nazis came to power, often between people who had gone to the same school.[75] Jewish Agency official Haim Arlosoroff once considered taking advantage of his acquaintance with Magda Friedlander, a classmate who had married Joseph Goebbels.[76]

Ironically, the Revisionists also had fairly wide-ranging links with the Nazis. The Betar youth movement was active in Berlin and several other German cities. About half a year before the Nazis came to power, the movement's leadership distributed a memorandum to its members that was both commonsensical and cautious. The Nazis should be treated politely and with reserve, the memorandum instructed. Whenever Betar members were in public, they should remain quiet and refrain from vocal debates and critical comments. Under no circumstances should anyone say anything that could be interpreted as an insult to the German people, to its institutions, or to its prevailing ideology.[77]

The Nazis allowed Betar to continue its activities—meetings, conventions, summer camps, hikes, sports, sailing, and agricultural training. Members were allowed to wear their uniforms, which included brown shirts, and they were allowed to publish mimeographed pamphlets, including Zionist articles in a nationalistic, para-Fascist tone, in the spirit of the times. The German Betar pamphlets focused on events in Palestine, and their exuberant nationalism targeted the British, the Arabs, and the Zionist left. They contained no references to the political situation in Germany. With this exception, they were similar to nationalist German youth publications, including those published by the Nazis. Jabotinsky decried the influence Hitlerism was having on the members of Betar.[78]

As the Revisionists pushed for a boycott, they could no longer openly support their youth movement in Germany. German Betar thus received a new name, Herzlia. The movement's activity in Germany required, of course, Gestapo approval; in fact, the movement operated under the Gestapo's protection. A group of SS men once attacked a Betar summer camp. The head of the movement complained to the Gestapo, and a few days later the secret police announced that the SS men involved had been disciplined. The Gestapo asked Betar what compensation would be appropriate. The movement asked that a recent prohibition forbidding them to wear their brown shirts be lifted; the request was granted.*[79]

Betar was active in Austria as well. Its members continued to meet even after the *Anschluss*. This required regular contacts with Gestapo representatives and with Adolf Eichmann. Betar leaders sent the German secret police a memorandum offering to organize the emigration of Austrian Jews. The assumption was that the Nazis and Betar had common interests, just as the Nazis and the Jewish Agency had. The Nazis allowed Betar to open an emigration office and even helped by supplying the emigrants with foreign currency. Most of these emigrants were meant to enter Palestine illegally on boats chartered by Betar.[80]

In the second half of 1940, a few members of the Irgun Zvai Leumi (National Military Organization)—the anti-British terrorist group sponsored by the Revisionists and known by its acronym Etzel, and to the British simply as the Irgun—made contact with representatives of Fascist Italy, offering to cooperate against the British. Soon the Etzel split, and the group headed by Avraham "Yair" Stern formed itself into the Lehi (from the initials of its Hebrew name, Lohamei Herut Yisrael—Fighters for the Freedom of Israel), also known as the Stern Gang. A representative of this group met with a German foreign ministry official and offered to help Nazi Germany in its war against the British. The Germans understood that the group aimed to establish an independent state based on the totalitarian principles of the Fascist and Nazi regimes.[82] Many years after he tried to forge this link with the Nazis, a former Lehi leader explained what had guided his men at the time: "Our obligation was to fight the enemy. We were justified in taking aid from the Nazi oppressor, who was in this case the enemy of our enemy—the British."[83]

All this indicates that the Revisionists were no less pragmatic than the Zionist leadership. They were simply more cynical. The inflammatory arguments the Revisionists used to condemn relations with Hitler's Germany were meant to advance their own political interests. To that end, they organized public rallies and processions and even a "referendum" against the haavara, a kind of mass petition condemning the agreement. The Jewish Agency responded with large, unsigned placards calling for "political maturity" and charging that the Revisionists were exploiting

---

* Other groups more loosely affiliated with the right wing also considered contact with Germany. As the Berlin Olympics of 1936 approached, the sports pages of the Hebrew press were full of debate over whether the Maccabee sport club in Tel Aviv should take part in a series of competitions with the Berlin branch of the organization. In the end, the athletes did not go.[80]

the tragedy of German Jewry: "Jews!" cried the Jewish Agency broadside. "Do you want to help them sacrifice German Jewry? Do you want to aid the extermination of German Jewry?" This was the first time in the nation's history, the placard stated, that the yishuv was being given a chance "to save an entire persecuted tribe."[84]

Zionist logic dictated that Jews needed their own independent country because they would always face discrimination and persecution anyplace else. The Zionist dream conceived of a "new man" in a new society, who would come to the Land of Israel in search of personal and national salvation. Those who came only because they had no other choice, however, did not fit this image and often found themselves objects of condescension and contempt. This paradox was built into Zionist ideology and colored the mentality of the yishuv. "There was this guy named Hitler, in Germany," Ben-Gurion once commented derisively. "Hitler appeared and the Jews began to come."[85] Though most of the immigrants from Germany, and their children after them, stayed in Israel, most did indeed come against their will, as refugees; they were not Zionists. As a result, they found themselves from the start in conflict with the fundamental values of the yishuv. They were called "Hitler Zionists."

2 | "A Son of Europe"

At the beginning of 1933 there were about half a million Jews in Germany, some 1 percent of the total population; another 200,000 lived in Austria. About a third of the Jews of these two countries were murdered; the rest managed to get out in time. They settled in the United States, in England, and in other countries around the world; only one out of every ten came to Palestine, a total of between 50,000 and 60,000 people, Hitler's first refugees. They were 20 percent of the total number of immigrants who arrived during the twelve years of the Third Reich, but during the two years that preceded the Second World War, they numbered half of all immigrants.[1] They came shocked and confused, having been uprooted from a country they had loved as their own. The awareness that they had erred in feeling at home, and the need to emigrate to a distant land, was a catastrophe for them—not an ascent, as in the literal sense of *aliya*, the Hebrew term for moving to Israel, but a descent. It was a sad story.

In Palestine they were called "yekkes." No one knows the origin of this word. It seems to have been used by eastern European Jews for some time before it became common in Palestine. It may derive from the smoking jacket, or *Jacke*, favored by German Jews. Or it may come from the German word *Geck*, "fop" or "clown," a cognate of the English "joker." In Palestine some said it was formed from the Hebrew initials of "block-headed Jew." Many German Jews took the term as an offense, as indeed it often was; but they also frequently used it to identify themselves. *

With the exception of the philosopher Martin Buber, the poet Else Lasker-Schüler, and the architect Erich Mendelsohn, none of the German Jewish community's best-known or wealthiest figures went to Palestine. Author Lion Feuchtwanger, composer Kurt Weill, philosopher Hannah Arendt (whose worldwide fame was still ahead of her), physicist Albert Einstein, and other leading scientists, artists, and intellectuals all took advantage of other opportunities. When the Nazis came to power, there were seven Jewish Nobel laureate scientists living in Germany. With one exception, they all emigrated; none went to Palestine. "My motherland is Germany," Richard Willstätter, a Nobel Prize-winning chemist, told Chaim Weizmann; he died as a refugee in Switzerland. Albert Einstein voiced—to Weizmann and in interviews with a number of newspapers—all sorts of reservations and arguments against the Hebrew University; he settled in Princeton.[3]

¶

Among the first yekkes to settle in Palestine was a writer who, while not the most famous of his generation, had been well known in German literary circles; his novels had been translated into other languages. His name was Arnold Zweig. In his first months in Haifa, he lived in the Wollstein House, a small hotel. Zweig was not content. His room was cramped, the desk too small for him to spread out his manuscripts. He had just smoked the last cigar he had brought with him from Europe. It was January 1934, and the hotel's central heating didn't work. The wind whistled annoyingly around the window sash. He was depressed.

Zweig poured out his misery in a letter to another Jewish intellectual, still living in Vienna. The engineer who had put in the heating system, he related, had not bothered to speak with the contractor, who first forgot to build a chimney and then added it as an afterthought. But the chimney turned out to be too narrow—wouldn't you know it!—and now, in the

* In 1979 Israeli television was planning to broadcast a documentary film on the Jews of Germany, *The Yekkes*. A citizen of German birth, insulted by the title, petitioned the Supreme Court for an injunction forbidding Israeli television to use the humiliating term. The court rejected the suit, ruling that "yekke" is not an insult but, on the contrary, a term of respect and even affection. One of the three judges who sat on the case was Haim Cohen, a former attorney general, one of the few yekkes who had reached a position of influence in Israel.[2]

pouring rain, it had to be widened. It still was not working as it should, because of the wind. "You will find, dear Papa Freud, that I am expatiating too much on the central heating," Zweig wrote, "but these questions of practical life, where the apparatus of civilization functions only creakingly, are the main problems in this country. We are not prepared to give up our standard of living, and this country is not yet prepared to satisfy it. And since the Palestinian Jews are justifiably proud of what does exist, and since we are justifiably irritated about what does not, there is much friction."[4]

The low quality of life was indeed an important component of the tragedy German Jews faced on returning to "the land of their fathers"— Zweig put the phrase in quotation marks. He would live in Palestine free of the illusions of Zionism, he wrote to Freud, and he would see things as they were—without self-deception, without derision. Having to live among Jews did not excite him. Palestine was not his home. Indeed, Zweig never acquired a sense of belonging. He did not put down roots; during his entire stay in Palestine he never really unpacked his suitcases. Like a vacation in the south of France, he wrote to Freud.[5]

Zweig and Freud were then corresponding for the seventh straight year. Zweig idolized Freud, and Freud respected Zweig. They wrote to each other about their work, exchanged manuscripts and opinions, as well as information about their health and everyday tribulations. Zweig was forty-seven when he emigrated to Palestine. He had visited the country as a tourist and had liked what he saw. For a time he had written for the Zionist newspaper *Jüdische Rundschau*, published in Berlin. His letters to Freud reveal that he was frequently in high spirits. He wrote much and published much. He loved the scenery of Palestine, the mountains, the sun, and the sea, and he formed friendships with other yekkes. He put out his own periodical in German, called *Orient*, part printed, part mimeographed. But he never stopped complaining. Aside from what he saw as Asiatic backwardness, there was the problem of language and the rising tension between Jews and Arabs. Zweig had trouble learning Hebrew; his politics were dovish. He was afraid of terrorism. His letters do not tell a happy story.

The managers of the Habima Theater did not respond to a play he sent them. He wrote once, twice, and yet again but received no reply.[6] "I do not belong here," he wrote a year later, annoyed after speaking at a peace demonstration where the organizers insisted on translating his German speech into Hebrew, even though all those present were speaking

Yiddish among themselves. "So we are beginning to think about leaving," he wrote.[7] His political and cultural influence was close to zero, he wrote, explaining: "The people demand their Hebrew and I cannot give it to them. I am a German writer, a son of Europe."[8] "I rebel against my very presence in Palestine. I feel I am in the wrong place. Human relations are narrow and are made narrower still by the Hebraic nationalism of the Hebraists who refuse to permit any other language to be used for publications."[9]

He dreamed that the Nazi regime would be overthrown and a liberal government set up in Germany, headed perhaps by the grandson of the deposed Kaiser. He knew, however, that this could not happen soon.[10] If, in the meantime, he had to grapple with a foreign language, why should it not be English, in Britain or America? His German passport was about to expire. He did not want to ask the Third Reich to extend it, but neither did he want to be the one to cut his ties with the German people; he still did not have a Palestinian passport—the dilemmas of an exile. He was a Jew, of course he was a Jew, he wrote, but his feelings about his Jewish nationality were uncertain. His children were already learning Hebrew at school, but the German intellectual was not happy: "They are learning almost nothing," he complained. "Wretched schools, narrow horizons."[11] He wrote of his financial straits more and more often. He exaggerated—he did have a car and a maid and enough money to vacation in Europe—but imagined money problems gave him yet another excuse to leave.[12]

Freud was understanding and sympathetic. When he heard that Zweig's library had been left behind in Berlin, he sent him his collected works in twelve volumes. It was not the first time he had heard of Palestine's cultural shortcomings, he wrote to Zweig; the Jewish people's past had not prepared them properly to create their own state. He advised Zweig not to leave Palestine yet, despite his financial problems, his loneliness, and the nationalistic atmosphere. In Palestine he at least enjoyed personal security and civil rights. In America it would be much harder—there, too, he would have to struggle with a foreign language. The day would come when the Nazis would be defeated, and while Germany would never again be what it once had been, it would at least be possible to take part in its rehabilitation.[13]

Yes, Zweig agreed, it would be horrible to have to pack his belongings again; if he could only leave but keep an apartment in Palestine to return to in time of need![14] In the meantime his political opposition to what was occurring around him increased. "Yesterday a bomb was thrown into the Arab market place [in Jerusalem] on a Friday," he told Freud, in 1938, "just when the streets were particularly full and the villagers from the surrounding countryside, who are already oppressed by terrorists, were doing their shopping." This bombing had been perpetrated by the Etzel a few days after the authorities had executed one of their men, Shlomo Ben-Yosef. "The whole country in its cowardly fear of Jewish nationalism has glorified an eighteen-year-old assassin, who has (unfortunately) been hanged," Zweig wrote. "A terrible vengeance will descend upon us all. . . . The Jews, who came to this country against the will of the Arab majority and who since 1919 have been incapable of winning the goodwill of the Arabs, had only one thing in their favor: their moral position, their passive endurance. Their aggression as immigrants and the aggression of the Arab terrorists canceled each other out. But if they now throw bombs, I see a dark future ahead for us all."[15]

With his nerves strained, his depression deepened and troubled him more than ever. He had attacks of panic and feared for his life and the welfare of his family. His maid's brother was shot and killed while riding a bus less than two weeks after arriving as a refugee from Hitler's Germany. Only Freud's theories could explain such mass psychosis, Zweig believed. In the meantime, just in case, he packed all his manuscripts in a large trunk.[16]

Freud, who had recently celebrated his eightieth birthday, was now facing his own troubles. His health was uncertain, and when the Nazis entered Vienna, he was forced to flee to London. From then on he wrote to Zweig as one exile to another. Zweig sent Freud an article that had appeared in the ultraorthodox Agudat Yisrael newspaper on Freud's book *Moses and Monotheism*. "Incredibly black and funny," Zweig commented.[17] Freud suggested that his friend not settle in England, for it was a strange country and difficult to adapt to.[18] A short while later, Freud died. War broke out; Zweig was trapped in Palestine for the duration.

"They charge that I still feel like an immigrant here," he wrote in *Orient* in 1942. As if this were an insult, he found it necessary to justify himself: he was not alienated from the country; the country was alienated from him. Ten years had gone by and not one of his books had come out in Hebrew translation, and with the exception of payment for articles he wrote for the *Palestine Post*, he had no local source of income. Not a single Hebrew newspaper had asked him to write on a regular basis.

No, he had not maligned the Hebrew language, he asserted in German, but had had difficulty mastering it because of an eye disease and a serious road accident. Zweig tried to leave the impression that he wanted to find a place for himself in Palestine. Perhaps he wanted to but could not; perhaps he both did and didn't want to.[19] Soon after the war, Zweig packed his bags and moved to East Germany. Under the protection of the Communist dictatorship, he became, at last, a national cultural hero.

¶

The Jewish Agency, the recognized representative of the yishuv, had received from the British the right to distribute, according to agreed-on criteria, the quota of immigration certificates that the British allocated every six months. Immigration, of course, increased the tension between Jews and Palestinian Arabs, and the British responded to the expanding Arab national struggle and the violent outbursts across the country by continuing to limit the number of Jews allowed into Palestine. The British only rarely handed out immigration certificates themselves, through their consulates. For the most part, it fell to the Jewish Agency officials in Palestine to divide the certificates among different countries. This often involved bargaining and deals between the parties belonging to the Zionist executive. The political divisions in the yishuv paralleled, more or less, the Jewish political parties in the Diaspora. Each party tried to get as many certificates as it could to distribute among its members and sympathizers. The selection of actual immigrants was in the hands of the Jewish Agency representatives abroad. As the situation in Europe grew more serious, demand for immigration certificates rose, and the shortage became acute. Distribution of the permits took on a Darwinian cast— those chosen lived; those not chosen were likely to die. There was little hope of relief.

The yishuv debated two subjects, both of them critical in principle and in practice: illegal immigration, or *haapala*, and the selection of candidates for immigration, or *selektsia*. In July 1934 a small boat named the *Vilos* sailed from Greece. On its deck were 350 passengers from eastern Europe who lacked immigration permits. The ship arrived in secret, the passengers reaching shore under cover of darkness. They were the first *maapilim*, "illegals." Up until the establishment of the state fourteen years later, more than 100,000 such illegal immigrants arrived on some 140 ships; about half came after the Holocaust, in the three years between the end of the war in 1945 and the declaration of independence in 1948. Sometimes the illegals outnumbered the legal immigrants.

David Ben-Gurion generally opposed illegal immigration, even when the lives of many European Jews depended on getting into Palestine. Until the end of the war, he and most of the Mapai leadership tended to view the Jewish Agency as a national, quasi-governmental institution that drew its authority from the British. Its capacity for action, then, largely depended on its cooperation with the authorities. The agency was also one instrument of Mapai's power and patronage. All these considerations led Ben-Gurion and his Jewish Agency colleagues to respect the laws of the British Mandate for the most part and to advance the goals of the Zionist movement through negotiations with the mandatory government. The majority of the yishuv supported this approach.

The push to bring Jews in clandestinely and illegally came from opposition circles within Mapai—primarily the kibbutz movement—and from outside the party, namely Jabotinsky's Revisionists. In fact, most of the maapilim boats were launched by the radical activists of the kibbutz movement or of Betar. Naturally, the haapala activists were more likely than not to take passengers who were close to them personally and politically. And though Ben-Gurion defended his opposition to illegal immigration on moral grounds—the illegals were taking immigration certificates from those waiting patiently for them—he did not conceal the political interest implicit in his position: Mapai was losing its control over the choice of immigrants.[20]

Control over the choice of immigrants was also at the center of another conflict between Mapai and the Revisionists, the debate between mass immigration of all Jews and selective immigration. Since 1932, Jabotinsky had been calling for the evacuation of European Jews in order to rescue them and to create a Jewish majority in Palestine. Evacuation, the term he used, connoted a state of emergency. He never worked out a concrete plan, though, and the details changed over time; in its most audacious version, the plan foresaw the immigration of a million Jews over two years. The call for evacuation was also politically motivated. The Revisionists charged that their followers, mostly of the urban lower middle class, were being discriminated against in the distribution of immigration certificates. "The land of Israel exists today only for a select class," Jabotinsky said in 1939, "and those chosen are young people whose color is red," that is, the socialist working class.[21]

After the Holocaust, members of Menahem Begin's Herut party, which

grew out of the Revisionist movement, charged Mapai with having sabotaged the evacuation. "We might have been able to save millions, or
at least hundreds of thousands, more Jews," said Yohanan Bader, a
leading Herut politician.[22] But in the early days of the Reich, when
immigration to Palestine was significantly less restricted and it might have
been possible to bring over large numbers of European Jews, most were
less than interested in coming; all efforts to persuade them failed. By the
time their situation worsened and many wished to escape, the British
forbade them to come to Palestine. The only way to save them at that
point was through haapala, largely before the war, perhaps during it also;
and yet, illegal immigration was very limited in scope—it could never
have brought in the numbers Bader claimed. Nonetheless, with Jewish
Agency support, haapala could have brought in more people than it did.
But it was not at the top of the Jewish Agency's priorities, partly because
of Ben-Gurion's opposition. In hindsight, the agency's policy seems to
have been a terrible mistake. *

The Jewish Agency, of course, agreed with the need to create a Jewish
majority in Palestine—but through selective immigration, not mass evacuation. The labor Zionists who dominated the agency believed that a
new society needed to be created, entirely different from the one that
characterized Jewish existence in the Exile. They proposed returning the
Jewish people to agricultural labor. Urban life was, in their eyes, a symp-
tom of social and moral degeneration; returning to the land would give
birth to the "new man" they hoped to create in Palestine. In parceling
out the immigration certificates, they therefore gave preference to those
who could play a role in their program for building the country. They
preferred healthy young Zionists, ideally with agricultural training or at
least a willingness to work on the land. They did not ignore the tribulations
of the Jews of Europe, and from time to time they told one another that
permits should also be given to people in need who might not advance

---

* Hindsight seems, however, to put Ben-Gurion on the right side of another debate with
the Revisionists. In 1937, as tension between Jews and Arabs rose, a British commission
proposed dividing Palestine into two countries, as a UN commission was to do ten years
later. Ben-Gurion leaned toward supporting the proposal; the Revisionists and some of
Ben-Gurion's colleagues in Mapai rejected it because, among other reasons, the territory
that the British had proposed for the Jewish state was too small, in their opinion. (The
plan was also rejected by the Arabs.) This episode left a frightful question in its wake:
how many of the Jews killed in the Holocaust could Israel have taken in had it been
created two years before the war, instead of three years afterwards?[23]

the Zionist enterprise; but when it came to actually choosing the immigrants, their chief consideration was how to best meet the needs of the new society.

The ideal settlers, then, were the "pioneers," or *halutzim*, that is, those who helped set up new agricultural settlements or joined existing ones. The term also had a manifestly political significance: not only did the Halutz movement in Europe give agricultural training to young Jews who planned to become farmers in Palestine, it instilled socialist ideology in its members. When immigration certificates were handed out to pioneers, the intention was to encourage agricultural development but also to strengthen the labor movement in the yishuv. Members of the distinctly urban Betar movement distributed the immigration permits allotted to them according to their own political criteria—they gave preference to immigrants who were willing and able to serve in the Etzel. Like the Jewish Agency, Betar also refused to help those who wished to go to other countries. [24]

The question was what to do with those refugees who were neither Zionist nor fit to help build the new society in Palestine. "Only God knows how the poor little Land of Israel can take in this stream of people and emerge with a healthy social structure," Chaim Weizmann wrote. [25] The German Immigrants' Association complained that the Jewish Agency's representatives in Berlin were giving immigration certificates to invalids. "The human material coming from Germany is getting worse and worse," the association charged after almost a year of Nazi rule. "They are not able and not willing to work, and they need social assistance." [26] A year later the association sent to Berlin a list of names of people who should not have been sent. [27] Henrietta Szold, who headed the Jewish Agency's social-work division, also frequently protested about the sick and needy among the immigrants. From time to time Szold demanded that certain of such "cases" be returned to Nazi Germany so that they would not be a burden on the yishuv. [28]

The Jewish Agency office in Berlin was also responsible for ascertaining the moral character and political affiliations of the immigrants it sent to Palestine. A Bornstein family had established a brothel in Jaffa—obviously a violation of the Zionist ideal—charged an official in the office of Agency executive member Werner Senator. [29] In 1937 the Joint Distribution Committee, an American organization that assisted needy Jews, negotiated with the German authorities for the release of 120 Jewish prisoners from the Dachau concentration camp. "I am not sure that from a political point of view it is desirable that all those released come to Palestine," a Jewish Agency official wrote to one of his colleagues.[30] Most were not Zionists; and there may even have been Communists among them.

Senator, who was active in bringing German Jews to Palestine, warned the Jewish Agency office in Berlin that if it did not improve the quality of the "human material" it was sending, the agency was liable to cut back the number of certificates set aside for the German capital. The immigrants from Germany enjoyed all sorts of special benefits, Senator wrote. They received immigration certificates after only six months of agricultural training, while in other countries up to two years was required. Requests for family reunification from Germans with relatives in Palestine were also quickly approved. All this required special attention to the quality of the immigrants, who should be true pioneers. Senator was not referring to occasional errors in judgment, he assured his colleagues; he was talking about a trend. More and more "welfare cases" were arriving from Germany, as well as too many "businessmen with children" rather than single men and women.[31]

At one point it was decided that candidates above the age of thirty-five would receive immigration certificates "only if there is no reason to believe that they might become a burden here." Accordingly, they had to have a profession. "Anyone who was a merchant," the decision stated, "or of similar employment, will not receive a certificate under any circumstances, except in the case of veteran Zionists." This was in 1935.[32] "In days of plenty it was possible to handle this material," explained Yitzhak Gruenbaum. "In days of shortages and unemployment, this material will cause us many problems. . . . We must be allowed to choose from among the refugees those worthy of immigration and not accept them all."*[33]

German Jews who were given immigration permits "merely as refugees" were also considered "undesirable human material" by Eliahu Dobkin, a Mapai member of the Jewish Agency executive. "I understand very well the special situation in which the overseas institutions dealing with German refugees find themselves, but I would like to believe that you would agree with me that we must approach this question not from a philan-

* In 1939 the world press followed the drama of the St. Louis, a boat carrying several hundred Jewish refugees from Germany. No country would give them asylum. The Joint Distribution Committee asked the Jewish Agency to allot the passengers several hundred immigration certificates from the quota. The Jewish Agency refused. In the end the refugees were allowed into Antwerp.[34]

thropic point of view but from the point of view of the country's needs," Dobkin wrote to one of his colleagues. "My opinion is that from among the refugees we must bring only those who meet this condition."[35] Leaders of the German immigrants in Palestine agreed. "As I see it, 90 percent of them are not indispensable here," one of them wrote to another.[36]

When the Jewish Agency executive discussed the allocation of immigration certificates, there were also frequent protests against the preference given to German Jews. Similar debates arose over the distribution of financial aid. Hearing of a special rescue fund for German Jewry established in London, one member objected, "Why have the Jews of Russia ceased to be privileged and the German Jews become privileged?"[37] The special collection for German Jews, like the haavara agreement, encouraged the Jewish Agency to assign more certificates to Germany. Arthur Ruppin explained that a decline in the number of immigrants from Germany would make it more difficult to collect money for the special fund. "But there are three million suffering Jews in Poland and only 400,000 in Germany," a member of the executive protested, suggesting that the permits be distributed proportional to the number of Jews in each country.[38] A German-born member complained about discrimination against German Jews: their situation was extremely grave, he said. A Polish-born member said that the situation in Poland was even worse.[39]

The tragic struggle to reconcile opposing but legitimate needs continued without letup. "The situation in Poland leads one to feel that Hitler's day there is approaching," Yitzhak Gruenbaum correctly predicted in 1936.[40] Two and a half years later, the Jewish Agency's immigration department apologized in a memorandum to all agency representatives abroad: "The terrible plight of the Jews of Austria and Germany has forced us to assign about half the quota to them. . . . We hope that the other countries will accept this necessary sacrifice for the Jews of Austria and Germany."[41] It was an incomparably cruel reality: every Jew who received an immigration certificate during those years lived in Palestine knowing that some other Jew who had not received that certificate had been murdered. This was the basis for the sense of guilt that would later trouble so many Israelis who escaped the Holocaust.

§

Some of those who came from Germany went to existing agricultural settlements or established their own—several dozen kibbutzim and farming villages. For the most part, they were new to working the land. They had lived in big cities and been doctors, lawyers, teachers, and civil servants. Some had discovered Zionism and decided to settle the land as pioneers only after the rise of the Nazis. Some were children sent to Palestine without their parents, under the Aliyat Hanoar (youth immigration) program. There were those who saw manual labor as an ideal and succeeded; the settlements and farms they established flourished and produced second and third generations of farmers.

The Jewish Agency, however, did not trust to the ideological steadfastness of the candidates for immigration. It instructed its offices abroad to obtain a written commitment from each candidate to work on the land in Palestine, wherever he or she was sent, for at least two years. This helps explain why so many German immigrants began their careers in Palestine as farmers. Some who signed the commitment reneged and, when they arrived, refused to work the land.[42] It was, after all, a difficult life. Even before arriving, they could read in the German Zionist newspaper *Jüdische Rundschau* that the farming conditions awaiting them were "primitive" in comparison to those in Germany and that they would succeed as farmers only if they "completely renounced" their former way of life. Close to half of them quit farming over the years.[43] Most settled from the start in the large cities—Haifa, Tel Aviv, and Jerusalem.

They brought their belongings with them in huge wooden crates, some of which saw further service as backyard tool sheds or as shanties for the homeless. The crates contained heavy mahogany furniture, grand pianos, and electric refrigerators that, overtaxed by the Levantine heat, quickly broke down and were demoted to simple iceboxes. They brought their crystal and china and bedspreads and pillows and lace napkins, the tailored suits they had worn in Germany, and innumerable other items that had made life there pleasant—the gadget that sliced the tip off one's cigar, another that pitted cherries, little scales to weigh letters before taking them to the post office, special wick-snipping scissors to keep candles from smoking, a miniature brush and dustpan to sweep crumbs from the table after a meal. Doctors and craftsmen brought sophisticated equipment and professional tools that were rare, even unheard of, in Palestine, all in the hope of maintaining the way of life they had known in the old country, of picking it up and transplanting it to Palestine. In planning their move, they assumed they would have housemaids; many brought private cars with them.[44] And they shipped over entire libraries, including classics and works of modern German literature.*

The first yekkes warned those who came after them of the dangers awaiting them in the new land. Under no circumstances should one eat uncooked fruits or vegetables unless they had been soaked for at least twenty minutes in purple calcium-hypermagnesium solution. Water had to be boiled before it was drunk. No one should buy the soft drinks that street vendors sold by the glass from large containers. Nor should ice cream be eaten outside. Nothing, in fact, should be eaten outside. One should wear loose white cotton garments, including white cotton shoes. Never go without socks—although, in places where there were no mosquitoes, the socks need not be knee-length. A straw hat was acceptable, but a tropical safari hat was recommended.

The greatest threat to one's health was fashion that sometimes dictated clothes inappropriate to the climate. One should not compromise: "In our country, clothing should be simple, practical, and logical." Children should wear large hats to protect them from the sun. Ideally, they should be forbidden to wear sandals, but under no circumstances should they be allowed to wear sandals without socks. It would be far better if they wore comfortable low leather shoes. Children should not be allowed to swim in the sea without a doctor's approval. During heat waves everyone should avoid going outside. Windows and shutters should be closed. An afternoon nap should be observed between the hours of two and four. Bodies, underwear, and homes should be kept scrupulously clean—floors should be washed daily with kerosene or Lysol; scraps of food should not be left around the house lest they attract flies, ants, and other disease-carrying pests.[45]

Some of this advice was wise. Some of it reflected fear of a distant Asian land that others had already learned to live in. The natives, after all, wore sandals without socks, swam in the sea, and bought soft drinks on the street; yekke children were conspicuously different.

Among the newcomers were young people without families, who were housed first in immigrant hostels or in tents without proper sanitation.[46] But almost half the immigrants from Germany were in their thirties,

---

* Many of these editions survived only in Palestine since the Nazis had confiscated and burned all the copies in Germany. Many years later, when the yekkes grew old and died, leaving behind native-born children who could not read German, buyers from West Germany descended on Israel to purchase and repatriate the valuable volumes.

married professionals and "capitalists" who had brought money with them.[47] Like the ones who decided to become farmers, those who settled in the cities were often forced to change professions. Generally, they had to earn a living at jobs with less status on the German social scale than their old ones. Many became construction workers. An architect became a carpenter, a judge founded a laundry, a dentist opened a dry-goods store.

Those were the days that produced, among countless other stories about the yekkes, one about the woman who went into labor on a bus. The passengers called "Doctor! Doctor!" and six of them, all new immigrants from Germany, rushed to help the woman. The driver, also a German immigrant and former doctor, brushed them off: "Excuse me, gentlemen, but in my bus, I deliver the babies myself."

One out of every two doctors who came to live in Palestine in the thirties came from Germany, a total of some 1,200. A survey in 1946 revealed that 35 percent of the doctors in the country had been born in Germany. Hundreds were unable to find work in their profession.[48]

The impetus for their emigration from Germany was the Nazi prohibition against Jews practicing medicine. They settled in Palestine because they found it hard to manage in other countries and because new regulations stipulated that they would only be licensed in Palestine if they arrived before 1936. Nearly 500 German doctors came to Palestine in October and November of 1935. "I had always been a good Jew," wrote Hermann Zondek, a prominent physician and hospital director from Berlin, "but hadn't I always been a good German as well? And a loyal European?" SA thugs broke into his office and threw him out. He resettled first in Manchester, England. Chaim Weizmann and Sir Louis Namier, the historian, persuaded him to come to Palestine. Others had told him that Palestine was too primitive for a doctor of his standing. Even though he eventually became director of a small hospital in Jerusalem, it seems that to the end of his days he remained uncertain he had made the right decision.[49]

The level of medical care in Palestine was much inferior to that in Germany. Many specializations were not known to the yishuv at all, while Weimar Germany had been a world center of modern medicine. Many of the doctors from Germany had worked in public-health clinics but had, at the same time, maintained private practices. They brought a clear political and class identity with them, one typical of professionals. In Palestine they were expected to practice as salaried workers in the tiny public-health clinics of the Histadrut's medical cooperative, the Kupat Holim, spread all over the country. There were no university medical centers and no large hospitals. Private practice was forbidden by Histadrut ideology. Patients paid only a tiny sum for the care they received—but they had to wait in long lines, clutching numbered tickets, and were not allowed to choose their doctors themselves. This placed an unaccustomed administrative burden on the doctors—one that conflicted with their social views.

There were those who took up senior positions in Kupat Holim hospitals. But when they tried to change the way the cooperative worked, they found themselves in the midst of an ideological struggle. It was a fight for political control of the cooperative and those it insured—doctors against bureaucrats, liberal individualism against socialist collectivism.[50] In 1946 the doctors at the Kupat Holim's Beilinson Hospital, many of them German-born, signed a petition demanding they be allowed to live in their own houses outside the hospital grounds and to open private practices. They also insisted on "the right to have a car and own paintings," in violation of the austere values of the labor movement.

The conflict caused much friction; each side fired off volleys of insults. The doctors complained of the Histadrut dictatorship, and Histadrut officials retorted sarcastically: "Oh, you really had it good in Germany!"[51] There were doctors who opened private practices in Palestine and offered care that, until then, could be received only abroad. Soon thereafter, they set up a private health-insurance organization and established a competing Kupat Holim, private hospitals, and pharmaceutical factories. The level of medical care, both public and private, rose swiftly, soon approaching that of Europe and the United States.

§

The difficulty of finding a place in the collectivist framework was faced not only by doctors. Similar difficulties led many yekkes to leave kibbutzim and made job-hunting through the Histadrut's labor exchange problematic. For them, dependence on the collectivist Histadrut bureaucracy was "a heavy emotional burden."[52] One Histadrut official complained that "the Germans" who applied to the employment service had "unsatisfactory" attitudes. They demanded special privileges, he claimed.[53]

But with their demanding individualism, their European ways, the yekkes were a seminal force. They helped change the face of the cities with the houses they designed and built, some in functional Bauhaus style, the latest word in architecture. Yekke businessmen changed the yishuv's economy in a similar way. They were among the founders of the Tel Aviv stock exchange. They opened stores and businesses unlike any known to the yishuv, some with wide display windows on either sides of the entrances: stationery shops and appliance stores, leather goods and cosmetics boutiques, stores specializing in children's shoes, sweets, tobacco; here and there the first small department stores appeared. European cafés sprang up on every corner. Yekkes organized lectures and chamber-music concerts. Arturo Toscanini himself came to conduct the newly founded refugee orchestra—later to become the Israeli Philharmonic—as a gesture of protest against the injustices of fascism. This is the irony of history. The rise of the Nazis, so destructive and murderous in Europe, much improved the quality of life in Palestine. Tel Aviv, which until then had been a provincial town, began to seem like a cosmopolitan city.

The yishuv establishment recognized the contribution of the yekkes but also saw them as an ideological, political, and cultural problem. "Those coming to us are not Jews filled with Hebrew culture," Berl Katznelson said to the Nineteenth Zionist Congress in Lucerne in August 1935, but rather people "severed from the roots of the national culture and the national existence, lacking the cultural glue that united the Jewish Diaspora over long periods and made them into a single entity." Katznelson spoke of "we" and "they," as did everyone in those days: "We are commanded to build the land of Israel with these burned and rootless Jews," he stated, "and the big question is—how can we make them into a nation? These masses are lacking Hebrew roots, most of them come with little [Hebrew] culture at all. What should we do so that they will not be a burden to us? What can we do so that they meld into the country and join the builders?"[54]

Countless anecdotes depicted the yekkes as conservative, blockheaded, and cold. "They don't understand Jewish humor," it was charged—an echo of the strained relations that had always existed, even in Europe, between Jews from Germany and those from eastern Europe. The Germans were also ridiculed for their attitude toward Jewish tradition. Among the eastern European Jews there were also many who were not religious, and the yekkes included many who were observant, even ultraorthodox. But German Jews were stereotyped as being alienated from Judaism. "There is something positive in their tragedy," Menahem Ussishkin said at a meeting of the Zionist executive, "and that is that Hitler oppressed them as a race and not as a religion. Had he done the latter, half the Jews in Germany would simply have converted to Christianity."[55] One newspaper reported with some bewilderment that a group of German immigrants had organized a celebration of Kaiser Wilhelm's birthday.[56]

The Viennese-born writer Moshe Yaakov Ben-Gabriel (Eugen Höflich) suggested that the immigrants "assimilate submissively" into the good land, and David Ben-Gurion demanded a "spiritual revolution."[57] One of the old-timers promised "to educate them to take responsibility for the needs of all."[58] The yekkes, of course, did not want to be educated; they considered themselves better able to teach: "We too want to take part in the reconstruction of our people's culture," said one of their representatives, and Martin Buber warned them not to think of the country as an American melting pot.[59] The question was who would assimilate whom.

The yekkes stood out, different from all previous immigrants. They were more familiar with Western culture than were most of the rest of the yishuv. Many, perhaps most, refused to adopt local ways, and their attitude greatly irritated the veterans in Palestine: new immigrants were supposed to try to be like the old-timers. The culture of the yekkes roused opposition from the start, partly because it was identified with Hitler's Germany. On occasion, they were identified simply as "Germans," with "German" characteristics. In a fight, an argument, or even a simple disagreement, they would often be called "Hitler."[60]

There were those who attacked them as a group for being what they were and for refusing to change, for refusing to disappear into the local society. This was taken as evidence that they thought themselves superior to the locals. "But a single group, thinking it has special glory, fears the melting pot; after ten years among us it still thinks itself 'new' because it still holds fast to a now shapeless identity—Germannness," charged a well-known German-born journalist, Azriel Karlebach. "They flock around the shallow water of the yishuv, lapping at it with the tips of their tongues, then turn away with expressions of disgust, muttering daintily about the stench."[61]

The yekkes were constructing "a thick wall between them and us," one newspaper complained. Among them were only "Adolfs, Richards, Arthurs, Hermanns, Wilhelms, and Philipps."[62] "They lack a Jewish outlook on the questions of the yishuv," another asserted. "There is not a whiff of spirituality in their attitude toward the Land of Israel." This was an attack from the right. And while the labor press decried the yekkes' selfish individualism, the Revisionist papers identified them with the social-democratic movement. One commented: "Germans are always a collective, never individuals. They have no independence, no private or personal characteristics; it's as if they were all born together. The German no sooner came into the world than he was a society." The writer demanded of the yekkes that they become closer to "the simple folk, the people of the Land of Israel who feel the pain of the nation and who shed tears on its destruction."[63]

Sometimes the yekkes were mocked for the values of formal education they brought with them, for their professional training, for their attention to the quality of their work. The yishuv attached greater importance to manual labor and the ability to improvise. The yekkes were attacked for the overly high standard of living they had brought with them, which clashed with an ideology that identified plenty with moral decay. They were criticized for the "many luxuries inappropriate to this place and 'conveniences' that we don't need and that will bring corruption and degeneration with them."[64] The increased imports from Germany resulting from the haavara agreement further fueled resentment against the yekkes. The issue of imports was presented, as usual, as a test of national and Zionist loyalty: the haavara, it was argued, was "consciously destroying young Jewish industry," all in order to make a profit and to pamper the German immigrants, who refused to accept local products. This meant closing factories and laying off workers and so led to the weakening of the Zionist enterprise, claimed representatives of the local industrialists. A group calling itself the United Committee for Boycotting German Products warned from time to time that it would not be able to restrain its members much longer, that there would soon be violence.[65]

§

The archives of the Tel Aviv municipality contain letters from German Jews who had settled in the city. They tell of a water main that had burst and had not been emptied, a property-tax assessment that was too high. They discuss all kinds of personal problems that the new residents of the first Hebrew city did not know how to solve, since they had just arrived, and for which they turned to their mayor. One needed work, another an operation, another was searching for a relative who remained in Europe, another was without a home—sad letters revealing helplessness, loneliness, alienation. It would seem that most of the writers were not young.

They all wrote in German because they knew no other tongue. They addressed the mayor as "His Excellency," as was the custom in Germany—in very formal language, with awe, with expressions of submission, subjects addressing their liege. The mayor never saw these letters; the city secretary, Yehuda Nedivi, filed them away. Some he returned to their senders with short formal notes instructing the writers to direct their inquiries to the city "in the official language of Tel Aviv and its municipal government, Hebrew."[66]

The same archives contain correspondence between Mayor Meir Dizengoff and the principal of the Gimnasia Haivrit high school, Haim Bograshov. The subject was an attack on, and threats against the owners of, the Rivoli café. Several Gimnasia students, incensed because the owners did not speak Hebrew, had broken the café windows and sent a threatening letter. Dizengoff condemned the act and warned that it was liable to spark street riots. But he promised nevertheless that he would give full support to the war against "the new Germanism" and to the organization of a united front "to suppress the attempts to implant foreign customs and languages among us."[67]

Some years later, the municipality itself sent strongly worded, almost threatening, letters to some of its German-speaking residents. "It has come to my attention that in your house, 21 Allenby Street, the Association for a Free Austria holds parties and balls entirely in the German language, including programs foreign to the spirit of our city," the acting municipal secretary wrote, adding: "I would be thankful to you if you would find a way to explain to these people that this will not be tolerated in Tel Aviv and that they must cease this activity of theirs."[68]

Most German immigrants continued to speak German among themselves—many of their children grew up with two languages: German, which they spoke at home, was their first, Hebrew their second. The German Immigrants' Association organized Hebrew courses and, outwardly, the yekkes all recognized the need to adopt the country's language as their own. Most, however, had great difficulty learning Hebrew, and many discovered they could get by without it. Nothing more clearly brought home their foreignness and alienation than their inability—sometimes their refusal—to learn Hebrew. Nothing else put them in such deep and painful conflict with the Zionist ethos of the yishuv.

The struggle for the primacy of the Hebrew language in general, and against the use of German in particular, had preceded the arrival of the yekkes. The first "war of the languages" had been fought at the beginning of the century. It was a long-running battle, part of the effort to renew the Hebrew identity of the nation in preparation for independence in its own country. The promoters of Hebrew succeeded in pushing through municipal ordinances that limited the use of foreign languages for store signs and for public lectures and other cultural activities, including in movie subtitles.

The Central Council for the Supremacy of Hebrew, an official Zionist organization headed by Menahem Ussishkin, praised itself for its work in German Jewish farming cooperatives in Palestine. At one of its meetings the following process was described: the director of a cooperative in Naharia had written to the mayor. The man did not know sufficient Hebrew, so he wrote his letter in German, and his secretary translated it into Hebrew. Unfortunately, the mayor did not know Hebrew, either, but he also had a secretary who translated the letter back into German. The Central Council for the Supremacy of Hebrew was satisfied: the files of the cooperative and the municipality would preserve only the Hebrew letters.[69]

As the number of German speakers in the yishuv grew, so did the German-language newspapers. These were legitimate commercial ventures, but they ran into opposition from the German Immigrants' Association and the competing Hebrew press. As usual, this was presented as part of the struggle for the Hebrew character of the nation.

In March 1939, Haaretz came out against the publication of the Jüdische Rundschau in Jerusalem, describing the German press as "an assault on the yishuv's soul," and warning in boldface that "the yishuv will not tolerate it."[70] Yet in two years some half a dozen German newspapers had sprouted up in Palestine. Haaretz once again took up the subject. Yes, there were countries that tolerated a foreign-language press, but things permitted in an established country whose independence was unquestioned could not be allowed in a community fighting hard for political rights, Haaretz charged. The newspaper demanded that the yishuv leadership "stop talking and start taking action to counter the destructive power of the foreign-language press."[71]

A few leaders did try to do something. They conducted long negotiations with the owners of four of the German newspapers and tried to persuade them to cease publication. When this failed, the presidium of the Central Council for the Supremacy of Hebrew discussed ways of forcing the newspaper publishers to accept "national discipline." The aim was "to get the German newspapers out of our lives." Some of the participants said it meant war. One of them proposed demanding of advertisers that they refrain from buying space in the foreign-language press—and demanding of Hebrew newspapers that they not accept ads from those who advertised there. Coffeehouses, barbershops, and hotels should also be told not to offer foreign-language newspapers to their customers.[72] But when the council discussed the necessity of wiping out the foreign-language press, one of those present dared to say that something should be done about the Yiddish and English newspapers as well. His colleagues quickly put him in his place. "English is the language of the government and Yiddish is the language of sentiment," Menahem Ussishkin ruled. And that was the end of the debate.[73] The yekkes, then, were expected to show a deeper sense of patriotism than the yishuv leadership demanded of itself.

But the greater the attempts to sever the yekkes from their culture and language, the greater their alienation. "This feeling the yekkes have," one of them said to David Ben-Gurion, "tells them that everyone hates them because they are yekkes; they feel discriminated against in every sense."[74]

The German Immigrants' Association wrote in its newsletter that the number of suicides in the German immigrant community seemed disproportionately high. The newsletter suggested that the phenomenon reflected the heavy material and mental burden that many yekkes had to bear because, among other things, of their concern for the fate of relatives left behind in Europe.[75] An editor of *Davar*, the Histadrut daily, sought to arouse readers' sympathy for the plight of the yekkes:

Every day I meet members of this tribe on the quiet streets of Jerusalem. Scientists and artists living among us as if on a desert island, cut off, silent, demanding nothing and requesting nothing: lonely old men and women, bent over, fearing for the fate of their children, feeling the claws of the satanic enemy with no one to comfort them; men and women of all ages fighting a war of survival, and with their last strength gripping the horns of life lest they trip and lest they lose their humanity.

I have seen them sell their belongings one by one—Sabbath candlesticks, a silver spoon or fork, or a clock that they saved from the land of their enemy. I have seen how they sell the only souls who loved them and who comforted them a bit—their puppies—

because they could not afford to pay the license fee. I have witnessed suicides out of loneliness, fear, hunger, from sorrow and anguish no longer bearable—delicate, sensitive souls who chose death over a life of degeneration. I have seen them and told myself: go to the city gates and cry—my brothers, do not this evil![76]

Among the yekkes were those who tended to be apologetic about the hostility surrounding them and who criticized themselves. "We are spoiled," the German Immigrants' Association wrote in its newsletter. "We are constantly recalling the greatest events of European history and comparing them with the things we see around us in Palestine."[77] When the war broke out, yekkes warned each other that the German language now had a much nastier ring than it had had. "People shout the latest news from the radio to each other from balcony to balcony in fluent and clear German," the newsletter reprimanded its readers. "On buses we greet each other over the heads of the other passengers in the loudest of voices. And there are places on the Tel Aviv beach where it looks as if there were an invisible sign that proclaims: 'The Hebrew language is forbidden here.' " Since many of the German immigrants knew no other language, the newsletter advised them to remain silent in public places, or at least to speak in a whisper.[78] The association did its best to broaden the scope of the Hebrew lessons it organized. It advertised and also established a kind of adult-education college, with the participation of some of the most respected scholars in the country, among them Martin Buber and Gershom Scholem. The greater portion of the lectures were still given in German, but they were part of the effort to bring the German immigrants closer to Judaism, to the country, and to its language. "This country has only one official language, and it is Hebrew," the German Immigrants' Association declared, demanding that its members recognize this fact.[79]

As the years went by, however, the yekkes learned to stand up for themselves and answer their critics—with resentment, sarcasm, and not a little disdain.

The yekkes believed that the hostility and ridicule that had greeted them were the products of envy and were no different from what they had experienced in the past. "They poke into everything, collect all the negative traits they can find about every ethnic group, and create the monster they need for the moment"—just as in Nazi Germany.[80] "J'ac-cuse," wrote Gustav Krojanker, a German-born Zionist activist, maintaining that the vituperative language used against the yekkes was not far from that used by anti-Semites.[81] The German immigrants' newsletter printed—although with a disclaimer—an extremely harsh article by one of its readers attacking the chauvinism exhibited in the battle against the German language. "We have seen Germany's nationalism gone mad and we trembled; we are on the road to a similar situation here," the man wrote.[82] The intolerance and fanaticism that characterized the campaign to promote Hebrew offended many, the German Immigrants' Association warned in its newsletter, adopting a heroine for itself: a fourteen-year-old girl, a pupil at a Jerusalem school, to whom a classmate had said, "Go back to Hitler." The brave and proud girl slapped her classmate on the cheek.[83]

In time, the yekkes learned to glory in their contribution to yishuv society. They learned to take pride in who they were and saw themselves as having a mission—as ambassadors of European culture. "The goal of our cultural work must be to create a new Hebrew humanism that will derive not only from man's greatness but also from his humility, one that will not bring about uncontrolled selfishness but will recognize and preserve man's relations with his fellowman, with the nation, and with mankind as a whole, so as to revive the past and, as part of this rebirth, to open the present toward the future," said one of their leaders. It was a message of humanistic openness that included veiled and cautious criticism of the nationalist insularity that had been fostered by the yishuv.[84] "An eastern European Jew has something to learn about being Jewish, too," wrote the German-born educator Ernst Simon.[85]

On the everyday level, the yekkes wanted only a large choice of wursts and *Brezeln*, and bookstores with proprietors who actually read the books they sold. They wanted quiet and order and good manners, respect for parents and consideration for one's fellowman. They did not want to hear radio programs blasting through their neighbors' windows.[86] Theirs was a struggle for the quality of life; the German immigrants saw it as their mission to save the country from its "primitive" way of life.[87] This Kulturkampf was also a struggle for a place among the elite. "You may tell the [British] government," Georg Landauer wrote to Moshe Shertok, "that lawyers from abroad raise professional standards. Lawyers from Germany, for example, have come and passed all the examinations and are much better than those who studied here."[88] In 1941, less than ten years after the yekkes began to come in large numbers, one wrote: "The question is not whether they adjusted to the yishuv but whether the yishuv, of which they are a part, has made the necessary corresponding adjustment."[89] Ten months later the German immigrants' newsletter stated: "There is no question whether we belong to the yishuv. To a large extent we *are* the yishuv."[90]

David Ben-Gurion summed up yekke psychology thus: German immigrants "have both a superiority and an inferiority complex. The superiority complex is 'We have been educated in German culture, we have Kant and Beethoven, the best novels, German philosophy and culture. . . . And here everything is eastern European.' But there is also an inferiority complex. They see that these people have done something. . . . [There is] jealousy as well—'Here are these Jews [from eastern Europe] and they've grabbed everything.' " Ben-Gurion added that he doubted whether all the world's best novels had, in fact, been written in German.[91]

¶

The yekkes developed their own system of community work and mutual aid, but more than anything else, until the establishment of their own political party, the one cause that most united them was the fight for the haavara agreement. They had a clear interest in this issue, and it fit in with Mapai's political interests. They contended that the haavara agreement reflected Zionism's true spirit and needs; they emphasized that Germany realized only a small advantage from it. The Revisionists, German immigrant leaders wrote, were exploiting the public's "primitive instincts"—that is, its hatred of anything German—for their own ends.[92]

In 1935, the German Immigrants' Association put up a candidate of its own for the Tel Aviv city council. Felix Rosenblüth promised the voters that he would work for more polite civil servants, a better-planned city, cleaner streets, improved education, and social services like those in other countries. He was elected.[93] From then on, the association began to function as a party. It participated in elections to various community institutions under the name Aliya Hadasha (new immigration). In the 1944 national elections to the Vaad Leumi, its slate of candidates received more than 20,000 votes, some 10 percent of the total, and its eighteen delegates made it the fourth-largest party in the country.[94]

Before the election, Ben-Gurion had assembled a number of Mapai activists of German origin in an effort to get them to campaign against the new party. This was in the fall of 1943, at Kfar Yedidya, a cooperative farming settlement in the Hefer valley that had been founded by German immigrants some ten years earlier. During the course of the conversation, the yekkes claimed that the yishuv had not made them feel welcome and that everyone assumed that, when the war was over, they would go back to Germany. This, they argued, despite the fact that among the old-timers who boasted of their national vision—including even the legendary Bilu settlers who had founded the first new Jewish settlements at the end of the nineteenth century—there were many who had come, as they had, not as Zionists but as refugees, in that instance from the Russian pogroms.

Ben-Gurion, out to please them, agreed with their opinion. He had much to say about the tension between the Zionism of "redemption" and the Zionism of "rescue," and affirmed that the Zionist enterprise in Palestine was based on both these forces: the national vision of the Land of Israel and the reality of Jewish suffering. The yekkes could take satisfaction in that: Ben-Gurion had brought them into Zionist history. He would never call them yekkes, he graciously promised. But Ben-Gurion himself did not hide his belief that the eastern Europeans were better Zionists. In speaking to the yekkes he too used the pronouns "we" and "you"—we from eastern Europe, the real Israel, and you, the yekkes, strangers who still have to prove yourselves.

In this session, Ben-Gurion repeated almost every negative stereotype that had been pinned on the yekkes. He ridiculed their longing for German culture, and needled them for being sticklers for the law. In Germany, he said, law was law, "and there, if you want to have a revolution, you have to get a permit from the *Polizeimeister.*" German obedience, a national characteristic, had made it possible for the Nazis to gain power, Ben-Gurion said. He implied that, had the German Jews not been persecuted for being Jews, they too would have supported Hitler. "Those of us who came from Russia . . . received something of the spirit of the Russian Revolution," he said proudly, as if he had not been born in Poland and as if the Soviet masses were even then rising up against Stalin's dictatorship.[95]

But the stereotype of obedience to the law was strong: there was a story at the time about a yekke who was traveling by train from Haifa to Naharia. He sat facing backwards, and this bothered him. By the time he arrived in Naharia, he was dizzy and had a headache—all because he had sat facing the wrong way. It had been horrible, he complained to his friends in Naharia. They asked why he had not asked the passenger sitting opposite him to trade places. But that's the trouble, the yekke responded —no one was sitting there!

And many yekkes were in fact painfully law-abiding. In 1938 the Nazis decreed that every Jewish citizen of Germany had to have a Jewish name. This was part of the effort to identify and isolate the Jews, like the requirement that they wear a yellow Star of David on their clothing and carry a special stamp in their passports. According to the new regulation, anyone who did not already have one of the names on a list published by the authorities had to add Jewish names to their existing ones: Israel for men and Sarah for women. The German Immigrants' Association noted that some of the acceptable Jewish names on the Nazi list, like Feibl, were not Hebrew names. Furthermore, some new Hebrew names, like Uri, were not included, and some of the names that did appear, like the biblical Hamor (Hebrew for "donkey"), were ludicrous.

The files of the German consulate in Jerusalem contain letters from local yekkes—some of whom were still German citizens—notifying the Reich that they meant to comply with the order by officially adopting the names Israel and Sarah, in accordance with the law. "I have added the name Israel to my name as required," Fritz Israel Stein from Kfar Yedidya wrote to the consulate. The consulate certified the change and Stein wrote to express his thanks. But the consulate addressed its letter to "Isidore Stein," and Stein wrote back asking whether his name was Israel or Isidore. He and others who wrote may simply have wanted to preserve their citizenship or pension rights. Either way, in the history of the painful relations between the yekkes and their old homeland, there is hardly anything more grotesque than this.[96]

Many yekkes had trouble coming to terms with what they saw as disrespect for government authority. The phenomenon must derive, they explained to themselves, from the oppression of Jews in the countries from which they came. The eastern Europeans had of necessity learned the art of cheating the local landowners and evading the measures that had been imposed on them. The Zionist enterprise similarly had to engage in a number of activities that violated British mandatory law, including spiriting illegal immigrants into the country. The leaders of the yishuv would soon apply themselves to the task of getting the British out of the country entirely, using terrorism, among other methods. "One of our central missions in this country is to improve this attitude over time and replace it with a positive one toward public institutions," the yekkes wrote in their newsletter.[97]

Ben-Gurion tried, nevertheless, to persuade the yekkes to play a role in the struggle against the British regime. If only he could manage to free them from their Teutonic tendency to obey every law and any regime, even an oppressive and evil one! If only the yekkes better understood the realities of Palestine, they would no doubt agree with him that the time had come to throw the British out and establish a Jewish state, even at the price of a war with the Arabs, he said. He saw the problem as mainly one of mentality. Ben-Gurion apparently had a hard time accepting that the yekkes had the ability to form political opinions opposed to his. At the very most, he said, he could "respect" the ethical foundations that deterred them from any activity that might inflict an injustice on the Arabs.[98]

§

The Jews in Germany had generally identified with the centrist, liberal national movement that had withered during the First World War and ceased to exist soon thereafter. German Zionism, similarly, represented an attempt to maintain a moderate, nonviolent nationalist sentiment in the face of the chauvinism that swept through Europe. In Palestine, the yekkes believed there was room for compromise between Zionist and Palestinian Arab nationalism. Several German immigrants, some of whom had settled in Palestine before the rise of the Nazis, were prominent in the circles that hoped to further cooperation between Jews and Arabs. The League for Jewish-Arab Friendship, Brit Shalom, Bar-Kochba, Ihud, and other such tiny dovish organizations believed that Jews and Arabs could live together in the same country under a foreign—British or international—regime. They advocated all kinds of arrangements, such as autonomy and cantonization. But in the main they supported a bi-national society and rejected the various plans for dividing the country into two independent states. In doing so, the yekkes rejected the basic aspiration of both the Zionist movement and the Palestinian national movement.[99] Their centrist position proved as untenable in Palestine as it had in Germany. Ironically, nationalism gained strength in Palestine on both sides, at least in part as a result of the mass immigration of the yekkes.

In his first speech after the election, Rosenblüth, to the surprise of his compatriots and party colleagues, accepted the possibility of establishing a Jewish state "on condition that it not entangle us in a Thirty Years' War with the Arab world."[100] The German Immigrants' Association news-letter and the internal documents of Aliya Hadasha had up till that point expressed the desire to reduce the nationalist tension characteristic of the

Zionist establishment, to halt acts of terrorism against the British regime, and to compromise with the Arabs over control of Palestine. Aliya Hadasha always took care to speak of a "national home," not of a "state."

The dispute within the party reached its climax when Aliya Hadasha decided to support the 1947 UN partition plan. An opposition group to Felix Rosenblüth believed partition to be viable only if Arabs were forcibly expelled from Palestine. They debated the point furiously. "I was shocked to hear that our faction supports partition and demands a Jewish state," a party member, Erich Goldstein of Jerusalem, wrote to Rosenblüth.[101] There were others who thought as he did, but the party did not adopt their opinions. "We must get used to the fact that we cannot say publicly everything we think," Rosenblüth noted.[102]

And in fact, he knew what he was talking about. When the yekkes established a political party, they opened themselves to attacks harsher than any they had yet been subject to. They claimed that establishment of the party reflected their efforts to integrate into society, but their opponents accused them of ethnic partisanship and described their conciliatory position toward the Arabs as treasonous. The yekke newsletter reported to its readers that, in an article published in one of the Hebrew papers, Aliya Hadasha was described as a "party of the master race" that had been approved by Hitler.[103] Once it became clear that the partition of the country into two states was an established fact, there was no longer any reason to oppose it, Felix Rosenblüth decided. To preserve Aliya Hadasha, he felt it best to fight for his beliefs from within. When Israel declared its independence, he founded the Progressive party and joined Ben-Gurion's government as minister of justice. Soon thereafter, he changed his name to Pinhas Rosen.[104]

For Georg Landauer, no such accommodation was possible. The establishment of a Jewish state at the price of an endless war with the Arabs was, to him, the downfall of Zionism. Landauer still believed in compromise with the Arabs and thought that the only way to achieve it would be with the help of a third, international force that would impose a solution on both Jews and Arabs. In a private letter to Rosenblüth, Landauer wrote in painful and frightened language: the dream of a humanistic Zionism was being smashed before his eyes and was turning into a violent, nationalistic, destructive force. Landauer had no place in the country's changed political climate. He resigned from his party and was soon forgotten.[105]

"We were neither here nor there," summed up Shimon Sigfried Kanowitz, one of the founders of Aliya Hadasha and the Progressive party, formerly vice-chairman of the Zionist Organization in Germany. "We were on neither this side nor the other; we were a bridge."[106] Kanowitz was a doctor and went on to serve as a member of the Knesset. He left his name ensconced in Israeli parliamentary terminology: a "Kanowitz law" is a good and proper but unenforceable law, like the law to prevent noise and air pollution that Kanowitz himself pushed through, with great effort. His story is to a large extent the story of all the yekkes. They had the right values but generally failed to impose them on Israel.

Their power never expressed itself in collectivist frameworks—not in politics, or in economics, or in the army. There were a few German-born government ministers; there were bankers and businessmen, generals and ambassadors. Real influence, however, remained the preserve of a handful—in particular the judges, including several supreme court justices, newspaper editors, here and there a few senior civil servants, artists, and professors.

As a group, then, the German immigrants did not live up to their full potential, but they played an important part in shaping and molding the society, culture, and mentality of the emerging state. In the conflict between the national insularity of Israeli Zionism and openness to world Jewry, most of the yekkes advocated openness and the values of universal humanism. In the conflict between the values of religion and the values of secular liberalism, most of the yekkes were among the secularists. In the conflict between socialist collectivism and liberal individualism, the yekkes were among the liberals. In the conflict between the needs of the country and the rights of the individual, most yekkes supported the individual. In the conflict between get-the-job-done improvisation and professional expertise, the yekkes were the professionals. In the conflict between insubordination and law and order, the yekkes sided with the law. In the conflict between violence, militarism, extremism, and hostility to the Arabs and the readiness to make peace, the yekkes favored tolerance and compromise.

The battle over the ethical and ideological character of Israel began before the yekkes arrived, but it was given a large push by their arrival. The yekkes played a major role in this battle. They lost; perhaps they never had a chance. Israel was born of terror, war, and revolution, and its creation required a measure of fanaticism and of cruelty. In its early days Israel was far from the dream of the yekkes. But the values that escaped with them from Hitler's Germany survived after them. The fight to preserve these values became one of the permanent features of Israeli life.

The yekkes were the first refugees from Nazi Europe to arrive in Palestine. One of them, Georg Landauer, documented faithfully, and from a rather detached point of view, the response of the yishuv to events in Germany and Austria. "The news from Europe shocked us all," Landauer wrote in 1938, after *Kristallnacht*, "but the yishuv is occupied with local problems—the political fate of Israel, immigration, security matters. The press responds with great vehemence to events in Europe, but there is no great awakening in the public."[107] Following the reports of the extermination of the Jews, Landauer wrote:

> As it becomes more clear that the yishuv leadership is helpless, lacking any ability to save the Jews of Europe, the organized rallies of mourning and protest multiply. They shout to the skies. Their cries become routine and their effect is dulled, loses its force, stops being a natural and spontaneous response. Mourning and anger become a kind of national duty, the speakers and columnists compete over who can best stir up emotion. It is horrible to see how the tragedy of the Jews is being transformed into an "issue." Only the first cry was a real cry that rose from within.[108]

That was written in March 1943; the extermination of the Jews was at its peak.

PART II

HOLOCAUST:
It Was in the Papers

3 | *"Rommel, Rommel, How Are You?"*

A few days after the Nazi army invaded Poland and World War II began, a Tel Aviv theater celebrated its 125th performance of Jaroslav Hašek's antiwar classic, *The Good Soldier Schweik*. The show was a wild success, yet the Hebrew press's leading theater critic did not like the sweetly bumbling Schweik. He was an imbecile, a defeatist, and a deserter, the critic fumed. His character was despicable and dangerous: "If, heaven forbid, the armies of the democratic nations contained many Schweiks, Hitler would have conquered the entire world by now." Only God in heaven knew, the critic complained, how it came to be that "this ridiculous and primitive pacifist" had become so popular with the public at a time when all now depended on the outcome of the war—"our future, our existence as human beings and as Jews."[1]

The Hebrew press could be very patriotic in those days. Britain's war against Nazi Germany was presented as the war of the Jews in Palestine. In September 1940, the Italians, at war with Britain, bombed downtown Tel Aviv, with over a hundred casualties. Consequently streetlights and headlights, store windows and house lights were blacked out. Food was rationed, as in Europe, and everyone was asked to conserve and to contribute to emergency funds. Thousands enlisted in the British army.

Those were cosmopolitan days for Palestine. City streets were packed with foreign soldiers—British, Australian, Indian, New Zealander, African, Free French, Polish, Czech. The store windows displayed huge signs: PORTUGUESE SPOKEN HERE, SERBIAN SPOKEN HERE, SENEGALESE

SPOKEN HERE. "A tower of Babel," a local policeman wrote in his diary.[2]

Palestine equipped the British army throughout the Middle East. It supplied bullets and mines, fuel, tires, and auto parts. It dressed and shod the soldiers, fed them, housed them, and entertained them when they were on furlough. "Shillings are rolling through everyone's hands," an observer wrote to a friend in amazement, and with a hint of self-righteous disgust.[3] Coffeehouses and bars, hotels and dance clubs sold an intoxicating fantasy complete with soldiers and adventurers, merchants and crooks, refugees, poets, dreamers, secret agents, and the prostitutes who serviced them all. Tens of thousands of people made a living from it. The transition from a peace to a war economy had its problems, but all in all the country did well by the war.

On the eve of the war, Palestine was still deep in the economic depression that had begun in 1936; from that time on, fewer immigrants had come, the Jewish-Arab conflict had grown more acute, and terrorism had increased. The Arab economy had shut down for an extended period as part of the great Palestinian revolt against Zionism. The war reduced citrus exports and halted construction work. In August 1940 the unemployed reached record numbers—some 27,000, about 15 percent of the Jewish work force. But then Britain began to take advantage of Palestine's industrial potential, and its economy blossomed. Unemployment almost completely disappeared; there was a labor shortage. It was in this period that the country's first real industries appeared: metal, rubber, cement, textiles, shoes, and food. A survey of Jewish industry in 1943 showed that in the previous five years more than five hundred new factories had been built—tripling the previous total—and that the number of workers in them had doubled. Tens of thousands of laborers were employed in building defense fortifications, mostly in the north, including a set of police citadels; the military employed 15 percent of the Jewish work force. During the war, some fifty new settlements were established, mostly kibbutzim—almost one a month.[4]

As the German army overran Europe and North Africa, it appeared possible that it would conquer Palestine as well. In the summer of 1940, in the spring of 1941, and again in the fall of 1942 the danger seemed imminent. The yishuv panicked; the anticipated invasion was described as an impending holocaust.[5] "Yesterday the church bells of Jerusalem rang for hours, and the day before, on the Sabbath, the Western Wall looked as if all the Jews of Jerusalem had come to cry before it," wrote the same policeman, Haviv Canaan, in his diary. "Crowds streamed toward the wall, thronged there, prayed, kissed its stones, and watered the brown moss in the cracks between the holy rocks with their tears."[6] People were convinced that the Nazis would exterminate all the Jews in Palestine, he reported. According to one rumor, the Gestapo had a list of their former opponents among the German Jewish immigrants, and these would die first. Many people tried to find a way out of the country, but it was not easy. There was a rumor that if the Germans invaded, the Old City, behind the walls, would be placed under the protection of the International Red Cross or the Vatican and would be declared a demilitarized zone. Jews from all around the country, as well as refugees from Egypt, started pouring into Jerusalem. Anxious and confused, they wandered among the convents and churches, trying to arrange hiding places. Canaan wrote that some of his friends were taking no chances; they carried cyanide capsules.[7]

In June 1941 the British army distributed questionnaires to its Jewish soldiers in Palestine, to see if their families wanted to move to South Africa. Some took up the offer, some rejected it. Others, less sure, asked for instructions. Moshe Sharett informed the Jewish Agency executive that, after consulting with Ben-Gurion, he had told the petitioners that the agency did not approve but that each soldier was free to decide for himself. At the same time Sharett complained to the British army commander in Palestine that the questionnaire was causing disquiet among the populace.[8]

The idea of evacuating civilians hung in the air—some advocated only bringing women and children from border settlements to the interior of the country; others suggested a general evacuation to other countries, including India and the United States. There was also a proposal that the retreating British army should take along the country's young people so that they could fight for liberation.[9] At least two yishuv leaders proposed sending Jewish Agency officials out of the country so that they could serve as a government-in-exile of the kind set up by other countries that had been occupied by the Nazis. Zalman Aran spoke of a "handful of important people" who would be "the Zionist nucleus that would maintain continuity.[10] A document presented to Moshe Sharett stated: "We should still seriously discuss if it would not be best to send the Zionist executive, including all its institutions and funds, out of the country— to America or South Africa . . . to enable its continued operation. If this is not done, there is a risk of losing the most valuable and most important Zionist forces."[11]

At the same time, blueprints were drawn up for various military actions to repel the German invader. Some suggested conducting guerrilla warfare and terrorism against the expected German occupation. Others demanded that all fighting be carried out, without exception, in uniform, so as not to give the Germans an excuse to take action against the civilian population. There was also a proposal to try to obtain prisoner-of-war status for the entire yishuv.[12] Moshe Dayan planned a network of secret radio transmitters for intelligence purposes. Apparently he was the first to think of training German Jewish immigrants with "Aryan" features to disguise themselves as Germans and carry out sabotage and commando activities. They became the "German unit" of the Palmach, the Haganah's special combat force founded in response to the danger from Germany and the fear that the Arabs would join forces with the invaders. *[13]

Some members of the Jewish Agency executive counseled surrender to the Germans. As long as there was the slightest hope, one of them said, he would prefer life, even if it was life in a ghetto. He therefore opposed all guerrilla activity. Another participant in the same discussion supported him. After all, it would hardly be difficult to destroy the entire Zionist enterprise in twenty-four hours, he noted dryly.[15] The continuous debate centered on the value of life at all costs versus death with honor: "As a Zionist I say: if we are destined to fall, let us fall here, with the women and children and all we have," said Yitzhak Tabenkin, a leader of Hakibbutz Hameuhad, the largest federation of kibbutzim. "I do not wish to see us die here, but I do wish not to see us leave, not to leave alive." This patriotism, to the death, expressed the self-image of the Zionist elite as a national vanguard: the shame of surrender terrified them no less than the invasion itself. "The Hebrew flag in the Land of Israel will be worthless if the Jews of Palestine do not rise up in a last heroic effort to defend it," Tabenkin insisted. The poet Natan Alterman had already composed an ode to their glorious end: "There is not a traitor among them, nor have they fear, and tomorrow they will perish to the last man." This was the honorable-suicide mentality, in the spirit of Masada. "Where will you stand when they come here and want, . . .

* The Zionist archives contain what purports to be a copy of a letter sent by a member of the Jerusalem anti-Zionist ultraorthodox community to the Arab High Committee: "There are quiet people from the old generation who have never taken part in politics and who have always opposed the politics of the Zionists and have treated the Arab nation respectfully and politely." He asked that they be spared when the Nazis arrived. Moshe Sharett noted, for his part, that not all the Arab public wished the Germans well.[14]

here in the land of the Hebrews, to make you wear the yellow Star of David?" asked a member of Kibbutz Ramat Hakovesh. "The answer is simple. I will not allow them to lead me to the slaughter. I may go to my death, but it will be in a battle to my last breath. There is no choice, I have nowhere to flee to, because this is the only, the last piece of land. Masada is not just a battle to the death; it is also the fighting spirit of the Jews, an expression of our refusal to surrender."[16] Those who advocated surrender said, in contrast, that Jewish honor was best expressed in Jewish ethics and in the fact that the Jews were not a "master race."[17]

Even in 1942, the Jews of the yishuv used this self-righteous doctrine of death with honor to excoriate their brothers in Europe who had not taken up arms against the Nazis. "The problem with the Jews in the Exile is that they prefer the life of a beaten dog to death with honor," said Yitzhak Gruenbaum. He reasoned that there was no hope of saving anything of the Zionist undertaking in the face of a German invasion. Given that, he said, "we must at the very least see to it that we leave a Masada legend behind us."[18]

The threat of invasion gave rise to a fantasy called the Northern Plan. The idea was to gather the last of the fighters, or perhaps the entire Jewish population, somewhere in the north—on Mount Carmel or perhaps elsewhere in the Galilee—and conduct a fight to the last drop of blood, a sort of Masada, Musa Dag, and Stalingrad all rolled into one. "A tremendous idea," one Haganah commander wrote to his wife. It is almost certain that this plan was never really operational. The Etzel also considered a symbolic mass suicide. It planned to smuggle a thousand fighters into Jerusalem's Old City, where they would declare a Jewish state within the walls and defend it to the last man.[19]

A file in the Central Zionist Archives preserves an unsigned memorandum that shows that someone, at least, was doing some practical planning for surviving the German invasion. "It is difficult to predict what the occupying regime's attitude towards the Jewish yishuv will be," the anonymous writer stated. He assumed, however, that there would be, as in Europe, a military government of occupation that would gradually develop a civil administration under the supervision of the Gestapo. The author expected an improvement on the present in one area: the Germans would restrain the Arabs because they would want to keep things quiet. On the other hand, he wrote, "it is most unlikely that the occupation regime would tolerate the Jewish Agency." He proposed, therefore, obscuring the political activity of the agency and presenting it as a communal institution dedicated to organizing the emigration of Jews from Europe to Palestine and to teaching the newcomers Hebrew. The plan would require eliminating some of the agency's departments; alternate jobs would have to be found for the affected employees, he said.

The Gestapo would, of course, try to destroy the Histadrut, the yishuv's labor federation—its socialism was evident to the Nazi secret police. It was thus necessary to present it, also, as a communal-economic institution. The various associations serving immigrants from Germany, Austria, Czechoslovakia, and Poland should be eliminated so that the Nazis would not be able to use them to hunt down people on its blacklist. The author of the memorandum supposed that there would be in Palestine, "as in every other country," people willing, for various reasons, to collaborate with the Gestapo. "Most of these are well known to us," he wrote, stating that it was essential to "transfer them immediately to internment camps in distant countries." Yet, of course, the yishuv would need people to represent it to the occupying regime. He recommended appointing them without delay to official positions on the Histadrut executive committee and other bodies: "The immediate appointment is essential to give these people authority in the eyes of the invading power and to prevent the possibility that they would be considered traitors here or overseas." Neither did the author forget to recommend sifting through archives and libraries to destroy incriminating material, such as photographs and posters of Marxist leaders and slogans.[20]

And so the yishuv might have chosen an honorable death, bequeathing to later generations a legend of Zionist heroism and eternal glory. Or perhaps they might have submitted to the authority of a local Judenrat, as the Jews in the ghettos of occupied Europe had done—leaving a legacy of shame and ignominy. There is no way of knowing. The Germans never reached Jerusalem. By the end of 1942, after the German defeats at Stalingrad and in the Sahara, it became clear that Palestine was no longer in danger of a German invasion; Schweik continued to play to full houses. Buried in the volumes of *Hapoel Hatsair*, the Mapai weekly, there is one comment that most clearly expresses the Zionist establishment's view of the relative importance of the Jewish communities in Palestine and outside it: "Had the enemy succeeded in striking us here," the newspaper said, "it would have been a blow to our very souls. This devastation would no doubt have been much smaller quantitatively than the devastation of the Jews in Europe, but qualitatively, and in its historical significance, it would have been the greater."[21]

¶

It was against this background that the first news of the extermination of the Jews was received. The news came not in a flood but in a trickle, and it did not immediately arouse all who heard it.

On June 30, 1942, the influential Histadrut daily, *Davar*, reported that a million Jews had been murdered in Europe.[22] The newspaper put the item on the front page but did not give it the main headline. In a sense, the article contained nothing new or startling—similar items had appeared in the paper before. Information about the fate of the Jews filtered into the West on a regular basis from a number of sources, arriving without great difficulty or delay by mail, wire, and phone. There were also firsthand reports, some from eyewitnesses who had escaped from the occupied countries: refugees, diplomats, businessmen, various messengers, journalists, and spies. Not all the reports were reliable. Furthermore, not all that was known elsewhere was known in Palestine; neither was all that was known to the leaders of the Jewish Agency known, immediately, to the media. But the accumulated data available to a daily newspaper editor in Tel Aviv were sufficient to enable him to report to his readers that the Nazis were murdering Jews systematically and that gas chambers were among the methods in use. The newspapers generally published such Jewish stories beside the major reports from the war fronts, as if they were only a local angle on the real drama. From a professional point of view, the newspapers missed one of the biggest stories of the century.

From time to time, the papers accused one another of overstating the horrors: "We have cautioned more than once against the unfortunate practice of some local newspapers that inflate every evil rumor about the spilling of Jewish blood, playing up the number of victims and dead and enclosing it all in a black frame to darken what is already black and make a stronger impression," one newspaper complained. "What for? Do the Jewish people not have enough problems?"[23] Other newspapers tended to agree: "We are printing this horrible report based on the above-mentioned source," *Davar* wrote, distancing itself from an eyewitness report of the murder of Jews in mobile gas facilities near the village of Chelmno, Poland. The article appeared on page 2.[24] A story on trucks used to gas Jews had appeared in the newspaper a few months earlier, without reservations but again without major play. The main headline that day was about the submarine war; the editorial criticized the British government's supervision of Palestine's health system.[25]

Other newspapers of the period published countless similar items. *Haaretz*, for instance, ran a story about atrocities in Kharkov, Ukraine ("The Nazi slave drivers herded masses of half-naked Jews down the streets of the city, whipping them and beating them with the butts of their rifles. Exhausted old people and children fell helpless along the way"). The item appeared on page 2, under a one-column headline. Immediately above it, in the same column, was news of a great victory won by the Jewish soccer team in Damascus ("Schachewitz's goals were executed with great originality").[26] After the war, newspapermen would claim they had doubted the information that had reached their offices, it was so horrifying and unprecedented: "I did not believe it and I called for others not to believe it, either," wrote a member of the *Davar* staff.[27]

It seems, however, that they also feared that their doubts would lead them to miss a story and get scooped by the competition. So they published the stories, but with disclaimers—to be on the safe side. Their reservations were often expressed by a question mark, as in one headline from *Davar*: "Half a Million Jews Exterminated in Romania?"[28]

A substantial amount of the information about the massacre of the Jews reached the newspapers through the Zionist Organization's news agency, Palcor. The yishuv's newspapers considered Palcor's releases to be semiofficial statements, not particularly reliable. But they published them anyway, since, after all, they saw themselves as part of the Zionist movement's communications system. They did not, however, highlight the releases—as if they feared that, as independent newspapers, they should not overplay official communiqués.[29]

¶

Toward the end of November 1942, the Jewish Agency executive made an official statement asserting that the murders were being carried out in accordance with a master plan to exterminate European Jewry and that a special state apparatus had been established for that purpose. "Multitudes of children up to twelve years of age have been killed with no mercy, and the elderly have been killed as well," the agency stated, adding that masses of people were also sent off to unknown destinations and all trace of them was lost.[30]

The statement emerged from a routine meeting. David Ben-Gurion was not present; Moshe Sharett surveyed diplomatic developments and left. The second item on the agenda was "the situation of the Jews in Europe." Three weeks previously, several dozen members of the yishuv had returned from Poland, where they had traveled on business or family visits. They had not been able to get out before the German invasion of September 1939 and had been trapped in the ghettos. Their return was made possible by a deal worked out between Britain and Germany: in exchange for them, Britain released German citizens held on its territory. Upon arrival in Palestine, they were questioned, and the information they provided indicated that the Nazis were murdering Jews systematically. Among other things, they reported that a locomotive engineer back from the Russian border had told them that Jews were being herded into special buildings, where they were murdered with poison gas. In a small village called Oświęcim (the Germans called it Auschwitz), there were three furnaces in which Jews were burned, the engineer reported, and another two were under construction.

This testimony confirmed a secret report that the Jewish Agency had received some weeks before. A spy named Eduard Schulte, a German industrialist opposed to the Nazi regime, had told Gerhart Riegner, representative of the World Jewish Congress in Switzerland, that the Nazis had drawn up a plan to exterminate every Jew in Europe—the "Final Solution."

When the information brought by the returnees was reported at the meeting, the members of the Jewish Agency executive were unsure what to do. "Perhaps we should issue a statement on the situation this time," one of them proposed. They decided to establish a committee. Then they talked a bit about the agency's next budget, and went on to consider the next item on the agenda—a labor dispute at the Assis cannery.[31] On receiving the same information, Rabbi Stephen Wise, president of the World Jewish Congress, immediately announced a press conference. The Jewish Agency's statement was made forty-eight hours before his conference.*

In the wake of the Jewish Agency statement, the leaders of the yishuv organized demonstrations and acts of public mourning, which continued, in one form or another, until the war ended. The yishuv's governing

---

* The Third Reich's "most closely guarded secret" leaked out almost immediately, apparently from Hitler's own staff. The Jewish Agency did not reveal its source. Wise received permission to claim the U.S. State Department as his source. He said that the Nazis were planning to destroy European Jewry as a whole and that they had begun carrying out their program. His statement was published, and it prompted a few comments from President Franklin Roosevelt and Prime Minister Winston Churchill. But nothing further happened: the extermination of the Jews continued according to plan.[32]

institutions held special meetings. There were rallies and public prayers in the synagogues and at the Western Wall. The chief rabbinate declared a fast day. Schools devoted special lessons to the slaughter of the Jews. Black flags appeared on apartment balconies. Newspapers framed their front pages in black (but the frames printed after the deaths of some local leaders were heavier). From time to time there was a commercial strike. Public entertainment was canceled, and toward the end of the war there was a one-day general strike and voluntary curfew.

All this was coordinated and agreed on, of course, only after lengthy debate. "The yishuv must do something," said one Jewish Agency leader, proposing a general strike and transportation standstill. But a colleague objected. A day off would turn into a holiday rather than a day of mourning, he said. Not only that, but "Hitler would be happy if we struck," because of the loss to the national economy. Another leader suggested expressing mourning over the Holocaust by adding two additional work hours to each day, for the war effort.[33]

It would later become accepted wisdom that the Jewish Agency announcement had significantly revised the public's attitude to the Holocaust. Until then, according to several students of this issue, people did not know what was happening to the Jews in the occupied countries, or they did not really know it because they had not "internalized" the information they had. Now they understood all at once that there was a vast plan to systematically destroy all the Jews of Europe; shocked, they responded accordingly.[34] But the truth is that the Jewish Agency statement contained little that was new. The editors of *Haaretz*, in fact, decided to give a banner headline in the next day's paper to the Stalingrad front.[35] And though, over the next few weeks, the newspapers devoted much space to the extermination of the Jews, even giving it major headlines expressing protest and lamentation, a few months later they bumped the subject back to the inside pages. From the second half of 1943 onward, the Holocaust was, again, no big news.

"I don't know if people want to hear about those things," *Davar* editor Berl Katznelson suggested. "Have you ever sat by a radio while people were listening to the news? As soon as the world news ends and they start to give 'our' news, their attention falls off completely. I'm not blaming them—maybe they just don't have the strength to listen."[36] It would seem, then, that there was no great demand for news of the Holocaust. "We read, sigh, and go on," wrote a Jewish Agency leader.[37] Everyone knows that they should get emotional over the news of the Holocaust,

Katznelson said. Everyone knows that the situation is horrible, but people have trouble understanding those stories as part of their personal experience.[38]

This was not, of course, true in every house. On the eve of the war, close to half a million Jews lived in Palestine. Two out of three had arrived during the preceding decade; one out of every five had been in the country five years or less. The vast majority had come from central or eastern Europe.[39] Many, perhaps most, had not yet broken their ties with their places of birth. To these immigrants, the cities and towns conquered by the Germans were not just names in the news, and the death camps were not distant planets. They received reports of friends and relatives who had been deported, lost, or killed—fathers and sisters, husbands, wives, and children. The Holocaust was their personal tragedy; they lived in fear, in mourning.

Many had rebelled against their "father's house," as they called the Jewish communities of eastern Europe, and had abandoned them. Spiritually and ideologically speaking, then, the rebels had sentenced them to destruction. Now that the home communities were in fact being destroyed, they felt terrible guilt. In a poem, Uri Zvi Greenberg quotes his nephew Shmuel:

> Uncle, oh, uncle, I loved you always!
> And yet you left us in the hands of the killer
> And went to Jerusalem, my uncle!
> And you did not waken King David for us. . . .
>
> How can you live without us, uncle?
> How can you eat and drink and get dressed?

Greenberg answers: "I have sinned, I have trespassed, I have transgressed, my martyr!" Greenberg apparently expressed the feelings of many when he wrote: "How can we live our lives? / Hell there with you, and paradise with us."[40]

Nonetheless, the life of the yishuv went on. The newspapers show an ebullient society: notices of sports events and fashion shows, of end-of-season sales and a wide range of other entertainments—all in the shadow of the horrors in Europe. "JEWISH CHILDREN KILLED WITH RIFLE BUTTS," the front page of *Haaretz* proclaimed, while the back page advertised the opening of *Pagliacci* by the Tel Aviv Popular Opera Company.

In March 1943, *Haaretz* ran an editorial with its headline in a black frame, like an obituary notice. It responded to a report that the number of Jews killed in Europe had reached three million. The same page included an article headed CRUMBS FOR PURIM. The Purim holiday, usually celebrated with wild abandon, was to be restrained that year as "a sign of mourning," *Haaretz* said. The traditional student ball was held as planned, but because of the Holocaust it had required a special permit from the Vaad Leumi. Walt Disney's *Pinocchio* was playing at a Tel Aviv cinema. *Davar's* film critic liked what he saw: "The Hebrew-speaking public will certainly take advantage of this unforgettable opportunity to enjoy a pleasant imaginary land from the world of fairy tales and to escape for a bit from a world in which the worst nightmares have come so horribly to life."[41]

There were those who used the war to commercial advantage: the large firm that produced Kiwi shoe polish apologized for the temporary shortage of its product. "All of us are willing to make this sacrifice, our contribution to the war effort," the company proclaimed, stating that it was "another reason to strive for victory, for the days when Kiwi will again be plentiful." Toy stores were selling a game called the Road to Victory. A Tel Aviv theater company presented a satirical revue in ten parts called *Rommel, Rommel, How Are You?*[42]

A few books on the Holocaust had already been published, but unlike books about the progress of the war, they did not sell well. Berl Katznelson, who put out a series of booklets about the war, related that one devoted to the London Blitz was a best-seller, while most copies of another, containing letters from the ghettos, remained piled in the warehouse. "That says more about the reality of our lives than many other things do," he said.[43] Golda Meir was angry at the people for not contributing more generously to a fund for the Jews in the ghettos because, among other reasons, they said they did not believe that the money would really reach its destination. "They won't do anything until they get receipts from the ghetto," she remonstrated.[44]

The opposition to Mapai claimed that the Jewish Agency had purposely reined in the public's emotion, lest the people demand more than the agency could or would do, and called its leadership into question. According to them, the agency had been careful to channel mourning into activities that were official, cold, and lacking in real emotion.[45] When the agency finally released its first statement on the Holocaust, the Revisionists charged that the Mapai leadership had known about the extermination of the Jews for months and had deliberately kept the public in the dark. Their silence had been intended to conceal their own failure, the Revisionists claimed: had they followed the advice of Revisionist leader Zeev Jabotinsky, they would have evacuated all the Jews of Europe to Palestine long before the war. Instead, they had evacuated only potential members of Mapai.[46]

The Jewish Agency's statement had, in fact, been incomplete: it did not mention that the agency already knew then about the gas chambers. Perhaps the agency was not certain that the information was correct, or perhaps it thought that publicizing it would make the announcement less believable. Perhaps the agency feared damaging the chances for rescuing more Jews. But it may indeed be that the agency concealed the information in an attempt to moderate the public's response.[47]

Whatever the case, the political storm created by the purported coverup was no less intense than the reaction to the announcement itself. Mapai's leaders defended themselves. "It is not true that [the people] did not know what European Jewry was enduring. [They] knew it all!" exclaimed one of them, and a colleague enumerated the reports of the murder of Jews that had been published at the agency's initiative. David Ben-Gurion said that no one needed official announcements to know that Hitler intended to exterminate the Jews—it was all in *Mein Kampf*. All that people had to do was read the book. The problem, Ben-Gurion added, was that the Jews had sadistic natures: instead of concentrating on what needed to be done in the future, they spent their time looking for someone to blame.[*48]

People responded when their leaders called for displays of mourning, yet their willingness to do so had limits. One of the notable characteristics of the yishuv, later to be one of the foundations of Israeli democracy, was the people's tendency to see their leaders unromantically, not as larger than life, and to regard them—and their dramatic speeches—with skepticism, even cynicism. When told to sign a petition, they signed.

---

* The truth was that neither the leadership nor the yishuv they informed knew everything. All information was partial, fueled by rumors and speculation. Eliahu Dobkin, of the Jewish Agency executive, once told the Mapai central committee that he had spoken that day with a man who had seen with his own eyes an order signed by Hitler directing that the Jews be exterminated by January 1, 1943. None of those present, Ben-Gurion included, had any doubts that their colleague, a local party official like they were, actually spoke with someone who had seen "with his own eyes" an order signed by Hitler. Scholars of the Holocaust know of no extermination order signed by Hitler.[49]

When instructed to stage a strike, they struck. Yet the attempt to orchestrate some collective expression of mourning was only partially successful. There was another, more intangible reason for the public's restrained reaction. The inclination to believe the worst is rooted deep in Jewish tradition; paradoxically, it serves as the basis for an intrinsic optimism. Both these traits derive from a long history of persecution, expulsion, and death, including the extermination of entire Jewish communities, and from an equally long history of survival and rebirth. The reports that came in from the occupied lands sounded, then, like a recurrence of Jewish persecution and did not go beyond what was already part of the collective memory of the Jewish people. They confirmed people's expectations of Nazi Germany, and people learned to live with the horrors that were reported stage by stage, each stage preparing them for the next.

Organized agony lost force over time, until it became just one of the many items on the national agenda, a public duty rather than a cry from the heart.[50] Cinema owners, for instance, objected to the suggestion that their theaters remain dark as a sign of mourning. "We hereby express our firm opposition to said proposal, which is liable to deprive the thousands of people employed by this industry of their livelihoods," they cabled the Jewish Agency.[51] There were negotiations, and it was finally agreed that the cinemas would remain open; but "mourning would be emphasized" by eliminating music during intermission. At the end of 1942, cabaret shows were halted for thirty days, during which the public was asked to keep celebrations to a minimum and to abstain from games and dancing. The rabbinate called on people to limit the refreshments and the number of guests at circumcisions and bar mitzvahs.[52]

At the end of 1942, a group of about twenty-five writers, historians, and intellectuals, among them philosopher Martin Buber and writer S.Y. Agnon, banded together to increase awareness of the Holocaust and to demand that the yishuv leadership give top priority to rescue efforts. The group called itself Al Domi ("Do Not Keep Silence"), taking the name from the first verse of Psalm 83: "Do not keep silence, O God: do not hold thy peace and be still." The group sent letters to yishuv leaders and to newspapers, published declarations, and tried to enlist well-known figures overseas. During the second half of 1943, they wrote to a number of prominent writers and asked them to call for the rescue of Hungarian Jewry. George Bernard Shaw cabled his response: "I can do nothing to help Hungarian Jewry. Do you suppose that I am Emperor of Europe?

Of course my sympathies are with the Jews; but the connection of my name with their cause would create as much hostile prejudice as friendly support."[53]

The members of the group had little success and few practical ideas about what should be done, but their hearts raged and their language was blunt. Fighting against apathy, complacency, and irresolution, they charged that not everything that should and could was being done for the Jews of Europe. They demanded the establishment of a "regime of national salvation" in the yishuv. One member of the group rose at an official memorial service, stood on the table, and began to shout. This was Yehoshua Radler-Feldman, the polemicist known as Rabbi Benyamin. He seems to have been the first to urge the yishuv leadership to demand that the Allies bomb the death camps. His was a voice of conscience, but, as often happens, his outburst itself became a subject of discussion. Instead of making people think about his arguments, his manners became the main subject of debate. He denied having jumped on the table.[54]

The establishment looked on Al Domi's radicalism as a nuisance. Most of the yishuv paid no attention.

4 | "Happy Is the Match"

The story of the yishuv leaders during the Holocaust was essentially one of helplessness. They rescued a few thousand Jews from Europe. They could, perhaps, have saved more, but they could not save millions. "This is one of the cases in which the historian feels that he wants to throw away all the rules he was taught—restrained language, precise examination of sources, cautious and supportable conclusions—and just sit down and cry," wrote Israeli historian Dina Porat on the failure of an attempt to rescue close to thirty thousand children.[1]

In the second week of the war, the Mapai central committee met in Tel Aviv and heard Ben-Gurion say that, since members of the party had no control over what was happening in Europe, there was no point wasting words on the moral aspects of recent developments. These, he said, should be treated as "natural disasters." The question was what to do. The Versailles Treaty after the First World War had taken Palestine from the Turks, and placed it under British rule. The British then gave the Zionists the Balfour Declaration—the recognition of the right of the Jews to establish a "national home" in Palestine. The second war should end by giving them their own state. That, according to Ben-Gurion, was the "political compass" that would guide the Zionist movement during the war.[2]

The movement's position has left a legacy of doubts and paradoxes, ambivalence, and, above all, nagging questions. For the leaders of the state-to-be believed it was not their job to save the Jews of Europe.

The Jewish Agency's business, David Ben-Gurion said at the height of the Holocaust, was to build the Land of Israel. He did not want to judge which was more important, building the country or saving a single Jewish child from, say, Zagreb. Sometimes, he added generously, it may well be more important to save a child from Zagreb. But the Jewish Agency's job was to save Jews by bringing them to Palestine; saving them where they were or sending them to other countries was the business of bodies like the World Jewish Congress, the American Jewish Congress, and the Joint Distribution Committee—all philanthropic, not Zionist, organizations, according to Ben-Gurion. Never was the distance between the Zionist establishment in Palestine and the Jews of the world greater than in those days.[3]

In 1939, shortly before the war began, the British promulgated a series of pro-Arab, anti-Zionist regulations called "the White Paper policy." These limited the number of Jews allowed to settle in Palestine during the ensuing five years, after which Jewish immigration would depend on Arab agreement. Britain's refusal to allow more Jews to seek refuge in Palestine meant sending many, perhaps millions, to their deaths. Yet, in his appearance before his party's central committee, Ben-Gurion's response to the new policy was his famous statement that "We shall fight with Great Britain in this war as if there were no White Paper, and we shall fight the White Paper as if there were no war." He assumed—correctly—that the British would allow the Jews of Palestine to serve in the British military, experience that would eventually help the Zionist movement found its own fighting force, the nucleus of the future Israeli army.

One of the participants in that closed debate advocated sending units of this "Jewish army" to reinforce the French front. Ben-Gurion hastened to caution him not to repeat his proposal in public. The Jewish people wished to see the victory of England and the defeat of Hitler, he agreed, and every Jew was obligated to do whatever he could to bring down the Nazi regime. But the yishuv would not benefit from having battalions on the French front. The task of the "Jewish army" was to strengthen the yishuv, a necessary step toward national independence.[4] "Every [Jewish] soldier is a future member of the Jewish army," Moshe Sharett said.[5] Enlistment in the British army was thus presented from the start as a service to the nation, similar to membership in the Haganah, the Palmach, and the other military organizations that preceded the establishment of the Israeli army. The newspapers were full of notices calling for people to volunteer for war duty. By the end of the war some thirty thousand had done so.

The Jewish Legion, which fought as part of the British army in the last stages of the First World War, had won the Zionist movement some standing in the peace talks after the war. So in the Second World War the leaders of the yishuv made a great effort to convince the British to establish a Jewish Brigade. The goal was to win the yishuv recognition as a belligerent, thus ensuring the Zionist movement a role in the shaping of postwar Europe. The British, understanding the political motives behind the proposal, rejected it. Only during the last months of the war was the Jewish Brigade set up. It consisted of five thousand men with their own banner and insignia: a yellow Star of David, symbol of the fight against the yellow star that the Nazis forced the Jews to wear. The brigade had time only to hear the war's last shots. During the weeks preceding the surrender it saw some action in northern Italy. Some of these soldiers remained in Europe after the war as Zionist representatives among the Jewish refugees. Many later served in the Israeli Defense Forces, some in senior command positions.[6]

¶

About fifty thousand Jewish refugees arrived in Palestine during the war; of these, approximately sixteen thousand were smuggled into the country by sea.

Each of the illegal immigrant ships created its own legend, an odyssey of daring, skill, international intrigue, and frustration, and, above all, a testament to the immigrants' wish for life. It was necessary to find crews and vessels, to fit the craft out for the journey, to provision it with food and medication, to obtain documents and flags. The passengers had to be brought together and taken to the embarkation points, often across national frontiers, over mountains and through forests—all this while the war was at its height. The Nazis tried to prevent the Jews from leaving, and the British tried to prevent their entry into Palestine. The operation demanded faith, courage, organizational ability, connections, talent, and money—money to bribe police officers, the heads of intelligence agencies, government ministers, and foreign consuls. The Mediterranean Sea was a battlefield, dangerous for any civilian craft. The refugees were more often than not transported on the decks of dilapidated boats, under the worst conditions. There was overcrowding, hunger, and shortages of water and sanitary facilities. Often the vessels were little more than sailboats with a few refugees on board; one boat set out from Romania with only a dozen passengers.

Some of the boats succeeded in reaching their destination, their passengers disembarking secretly, under cover of darkness or stormy weather, on deserted beaches. Refugees who managed to get into the country were generally allowed to stay. Some of the boats, however, were discovered at sea and forced to turn back. Some were sent to Cyprus, where the passengers were put into detention camps; others were escorted by British ships to the shores of Palestine, the passengers then transferred to other ships and deported.

The British Empire's war against the refugees took its toll. The *Patria*, a British craft about to deport a few hundred illegal refugees who had been captured on other boats, was sabotaged in a hasty and bungled action by the Haganah, which hoped to prevent it from sailing. Close to 300 people were killed. The *Struma*, with more than 750 passengers, sank near Istanbul after having been denied entry to Palestine. Some other ships also sank.

Over half the maapilim arrived through the help of the Revisionist movement and a number of other groups, including private travel agents. Almost eight thousand, slightly less than half the total, came on boats outfitted by the Haganah, which set up a special arm called the Mossad L'Aliya Bet to organize illegal immigration. The Mossad, a forerunner of Israel's intelligence organization, spent about $2 million to this end, about $250 per immigrant. However, between March 1941 and March 1944, the height of the war and the extermination of the Jews, the Haganah did not bring in even one refugee boat.[7] This was not only because of technical difficulties involved in the covert sailings during wartime, and not only because of the economic crisis in Palestine at the beginning of the war; it was also a result of the reluctance of the Jewish Agency leaders to engage in illegal activity. They had undertaken it in response to pressure from within—from kibbutz and Palmach circles— and in the face of continued Revisionist efforts. But if anything, the war reinforced the agency's inclination to cooperate with the authorities and to adhere to the immigration quotas. The British warned that if illegal immigration was not halted, legal immigration would be.

As it had before the war, the Jewish Agency leadership continued to defend its right to select immigrants in accordance with the country's needs and in keeping with the division agreed on by the political parties; illegal immigration circumvented the leaders' ability to monitor immigration. "There's no control," complained Moshe Sharett in his diary. "The wolves [the Revisionists] have renewed their activity and will keep going." They took everyone, Sharett wrote—the blind, the crippled, and "an entire old-age home." Sharett did not advocate cessation of illegal immigration, but even when the killing of Jews was at its peak, he protested that the organizers of the haapala were not taking care to bring desirable "human material." A short while after the war began, he formulated his principle of immigration, completely unaffected by events: bring the "good" and leave the "rabble."[8]

When the Haganah resumed an active role in illegal immigration toward the end of the war, it did so not only because the technical difficulties had diminished. The Jewish Agency leadership felt it necessary to prove to the Holocaust survivors that the Zionist movement had not abandoned them to their fate. This was the beginning of the struggle for the minds of the survivors—the Jewish Agency feared that most of them would prefer to return to their homes after the war and would not want to come to Palestine.[9] Haganah leader Eliahu Golomb warned of "anti-Zionist poison" that the survivors were likely to spread if they realized that they had not been helped. He proposed renewing illegal immigration without delay.[10] "The fact that the Jews of Palestine led the rescue operations is an important Zionist argument," David Ben-Gurion said, thinking, among other things, of the need to advance Zionist fund-raising drives.[11]

Over the course of the war, the Jewish Agency tried persuading the British to help it send commandos from the yishuv into occupied territory, where they could set up Jewish underground groups to fight the Nazis. The agency pictured about a thousand men. At least they could try to sabotage the railroads to the death camps. Ben-Gurion had no faith in the idea: "Jewish commandos in the war in Poland is ludicrous! If you want to have commandos, you have to have a state," he ruled.[12] The British rejected it for various reasons: they did not believe that such an operation would advance the war effort; they did not want to enhance the Jewish Agency's power; they did not want to be indebted to the agency. All such proposals were rejected or lost in bureaucratic channels.

Moshe Sharett asked Randolph Churchill to speak with his father about a plan to parachute agents from the yishuv into Yugoslavia to join Tito's partisans. Prime Minister Churchill responded favorably at first, but in the end this idea, too, came to nothing. Yet the Jewish Agency did not give up, and eventually thirty paratroopers, three of them women, set out on their missions. RAF planes parachuted them behind enemy lines in Romania, Hungary, Yugoslavia, and elsewhere, mostly between March and September 1944. The missions gave birth to a legend.

Most of the paratroopers were kibbutzniks in their twenties who had left Europe only a few years before and were now volunteering to return. They had been selected from over two hundred candidates, then trained; they had no previous experience and could trust only themselves and their faith in the mission. Most of them were enlisted as soldiers in the British army. The British, hoping to gain intelligence from them, equipped them with radios and instructed them to aid the partisans. A few were sent to save Allied fighter pilots who had been taken prisoner.

On the eve of their departure, the paratroopers met with the leaders of the yishuv, among them Berl Katznelson, David Ben-Gurion, and Golda Meir. They tried to learn what was expected of them, but instead of operational instructions they received only words of inspiration and encouragement. Ben-Gurion told them to make sure "that the Jewish people recognize the Land of Israel as their land and fortress," so that after the war they would come by the thousands. Eliahu Golomb told them that the goal was to show the Jewish people how to "stand proud." One Jewish Agency official told them to bring the "Messiah" to the Jews of the Exile; Golda Meir just wept, paratrooper Yoel Palgi later recalled.[13]

By the time the British agreed to the Jewish Agency proposal, it was too late to save any Jews, the number of paratroopers too small. There was not much left to do, yet by this point it was impossible to back out. As with illegal immigration, the paratrooper operation grew out of a feeling that it would soon be necessary to persuade the survivors of the Holocaust that the yishuv had not abandoned them.[14] It was, therefore, a mission of national, Zionist reawakening, to save the souls of the remnant of the Jewish people, rather than a military mission to save their lives. "Happy is the match that, burning, sparked the flames," wrote the most famous of the paratroopers, Hannah Senesh, a Hungarian-born poet of twenty-three who was captured after she landed, then tortured, tried, and executed: "Happy is the flame that burned secretly in the heart."[15]

The paratroopers were not necessarily welcomed as rescuers. Haike Grossman, a partisan fighter from Bialystok, later a member of the Knesset, wrote: "I was once asked what I would have done had paratroopers from Palestine arrived at the place where the partisans were fighting. I answered: 'The first thing would have been to find them a place to hide.' "[16] Egon Rott, a Jewish rebel leader in Slovakia, castigated the paratroopers who reached him: "Really, why did you come? Did you think this was a child's game here? You wanted to be heroes? . . . You came here to play soldier. . . . Didn't you think of the responsibility you were giving us? Until now we were responsible only for our own lives, but now you are weighing on our consciences." He told them to get on the first flight out and return to the Holy Land.[17]

The official historian of the Haganah wrote in an afterword to paratrooper Yoel Palgi's memoirs: "The paratroopers' mission revealed in its full strength the spirit of voluntarism that animated the Hebrew pioneer movement and the Haganah from the very beginning, a spirit of self-sacrifice for the people and readiness to fight and, if necessary, to die. . . . The paratroopers' mission became an example and a stimulus to Israeli youth. Their deeds, letters, and memoirs became part of the heroic heritage of Israel. New settlements were named after those who fell. They became a link in the chain of Jewish heroism of all generations." Palgi himself did not like such idolatry: "The people yearned for a heroic legend," he noted, reluctantly, in his book.*[18]

Here was a legend more powerful than its heroes. Some of the paratroopers fought in the ranks of the partisans; some performed intelligence and sabotage missions. Some made contact with Jewish communities, mostly in the last stages of the war. Some found themselves embroiled in local politics: the Zionists fought the Communists with their help. Almost half the paratroopers from Palestine fell prisoner, and seven were executed.

The Jewish Agency and a few other yishuv organizations sent rescue missions to Turkey. Other groups tried to help from Geneva, Tehran, Sweden, and—when it was too late—from Spain and Portugal. Chaim Weizmann and other Zionist leaders tried to work out of London. The agents in Istanbul, most of them young people, helped refugees who passed through Turkey on their way to Palestine. From time to time they led refugees across closed borders, and sometimes they sent secret messengers into occupied countries. "The great days for us were when couriers returned from behind enemy territory," Teddy Kollek later recalled. Some

---

* When the war broke out, seven representatives of Hakibbutz Hameuhad were stranded in Poland. They were all home within three months. Berl Katznelson was furious: "I would prefer to see ten representatives martyred in occupied territory." The yishuv needed symbols.[19]

of the couriers were Jews, some not; most were double agents who worked more or less openly for the Gestapo. Kollek described with some romanticism the espionage community that worked out of Istanbul in those days: everyone sat in hotel bars, plotting international intrigue and spying on everyone else. Yet, he wrote, "we saved only a small number of people, microscopic in comparison to the number killed."[20] Historian Dina Porat asked Venya Pomerantz, one of the agents in Turkey, what they had done there. "Nothing," he answered.[21]

When the war broke out the Jewish Agency set up a committee in Jerusalem to help support refugees who came to Palestine from Poland. The effort involved contacts with the Polish government-in-exile in London. When Germany attacked the USSR in 1941, the committee tried to help evacuate Jewish refugees who had fled from Poland to Russia. This was the Polish Affairs Committee, or the "Committee of Four," headed by Yitzhak Gruenbaum, a member of the Jewish Agency executive, previously a leader of the Polish Jewish community and a member of the Polish parliament. In the wake of the agency's announcement about the Holocaust in November 1942, there were demands that someone work full-time on the rescue of the Jews. Gruenbaum—a rather pathetic bureaucrat, with strong opinions and a sharp tongue, but without true authority, influence, or talent—was chosen to head the new body, which became the scene of much infighting over its political composition and its affiliation with the agency, and even over its name. One of its members claimed at one point that it was nothing but a fiction.[22] The Rescue Committee, as it was called in the end, from time to time held meetings that generated the usual verbose bureaucratese rather than imaginative action. The committee sent money, food packages, and letters to Jewish communities in Europe, and sometimes gold, diamonds, and forged identity papers. It tried to obtain exit permits, travel papers, and immigration permits; it made efforts to rouse public opinion in Palestine and overseas. Gruenbaum once hosted the U.S. consul general in his home and asked that the American air force bomb the death camps.[23] "It would be impossible to say that our work met with even a small measure of success," he later wrote.[24] Ben-Gurion, for his part, spent most of his time on other matters.

Three times during the war there were, it seemed, opportunities to save thousands of Jews in exchange for money. The Transnistria affair, the Europa Plan, and the Trucks-for-Blood episode have been investigated in detail again and again, and every shred of evidence has been examined with a magnifying glass from every angle. The sad result is this: there is no way of knowing whether an opportunity was missed. Only one thing can be said with certainty: each of the three episodes demanded capability and imagination beyond those possessed by Ben-Gurion and the other leaders of the yishuv.

Transnistria is an area north of Odessa, in the southern Ukraine, between the Dniester and Bug rivers. The Nazis gave it to Romania in exchange for Romania's support during the invasion of the Soviet Union. In October 1941 some 200,000 Jews were deported from Romania to Transnistria; within a few months, two out of every three had died or been murdered. About 70,000 were left alive.

A year after the deportation the phone of a Jewish Agency representative in Istanbul rang. It was a leader of the Bucharest Jewish community, who informed the agent that a messenger would soon come to him with a proposal for saving the Jews of Transnistria. Several details remain unclear, but the essence was that the Romanian government was offering to exchange the remnant of the Jews for a sum that, according to different calculations, ranged between $14 million and $28 million—that is, between $200 and $400 a head. The agency thought the price was high and did not believe that the operation could be carried out, but it did what it had to do: it ordered its representatives in Istanbul to check out the offer. It also informed the British authorities. Nothing came of the offer: the British opposed it, as did the Germans, who were the de facto rulers of Romania.

The British were acting under pressure from the Arabs; they feared strengthening the yishuv at the expense of the Arab population. The possibility that the Jews of Transnistria might come to Palestine was described by one official as "a frightful prospect." The proposed deal, it was said, was apt to burden the British with even more Jews than it already had on its hands.[25] The British also opposed in principle allowing citizens of enemy countries into Palestine, a position that, over the years, cost the lives of many Jews. The Americans supported the British opposition to transferring money to enemy states, and this also made assistance to the Jews very difficult. The Allies stood firm on their somewhat sanctimonious principle of refusing to give in to blackmail. This left only the unlikely possibility that the Jewish Agency might have reached a secret agreement with the Romanians, behind the backs of the Allies.[26] But then the whole story was leaked to the press—and that was the end of it.

In Bratislava, capital of the Nazi puppet state of Slovakia, a man and a woman with little in common came up with another rescue plan, of much larger dimensions than any other. He was an ultraorthodox rabbi known for his scholarship and virulent anti-Zionism; she was a wealthy widow, active in WIZO, the women's Zionist organization. Rabbi Michael Dov-Ber Weissmandel and Gisi Fleischmann left behind many poignant letters, largely despairing pleas for help. They needed money. In the summer of 1942 they had succeeded in making a deal with one of the SS officers working under Adolf Eichmann. Dieter Wisliceny received tens of thousands of dollars from them, apparently with the knowledge of his superiors. In exchange, the expulsion of Jews from Slovakia was halted; up until then, some sixty thousand had been sent away, most to extermination at Auschwitz. Another thirty thousand remained alive. The ransom paid to the Nazis delayed resumption of the expulsions for another two years. The Nazis assumed that the money came from Switzerland, on the orders of "World Jewry," an echo of their ideological conviction that the Jews ruled the world. In fact, Weissmandel and Fleischmann raised the money themselves. They had to iron some of the bank notes so they would look new, as befit Jewish dollars from Switzerland.

The success of the first deal led Weissmandel, Fleischmann, and several others to initiate a second round of negotiations with the Nazis. Weissmandel wrote himself a letter on stationery he had brought from a Swiss hotel on a prewar trip. He used a Swiss typewriter and authorized himself, in coded language and in the name of "representatives of the rabbis of the world," to open negotiations with the Nazis to halt the expulsion and murder of the Jews in all Nazi-controlled territory, in exchange for several million dollars. This was the Europa Plan. The Nazis apparently believed the fake letter of authorization the rabbi presented; in any case, they conducted serious negotiations. Adolf Eichmann was informed of the plan's progress, as was, it seems, SS chief Heinrich Himmler himself. There is reason to believe that Himmler saw the negotiations with the Jews as an opening toward negotiating a separate peace between the SS and the Allies in anticipation of Germany's expected defeat in the war. The Nazis demanded a $200,000 advance. Weissmandel appealed to the Geneva representative of the Joint Distribution Committee, who referred the matter to his superiors in New York. The organization's directors at first rejected the plea, as did the Zionist movement.

During the following months the deal swung back and forth, girdling the world—from Bratislava to Geneva to Jerusalem, from Jerusalem to Geneva to London, from Bratislava to Berlin, from Geneva to New York to Washington. Weissmandel and Fleischmann continued to bombard the West with desperate petitions: the deadline the Nazis had set for receiving their advance would soon arrive. Weissmandel wrote in the Hebrew of a Torah scholar, Fleischmann in German. In Jerusalem and Geneva, in London, New York, and Washington, their correspondents could not decide whether the offer was genuine or merely a German bluff. The documents that survive display political, legal, and bureaucratic temporizing and unhurried complacency, in grotesque contrast to the cries for help in the letters of Weissmandel and Fleischmann. Ben-Gurion believed that the Jewish Agency could not contribute to the cost of the bribe: it would soon have to fund the absorption of five thousand children, and that demanded a large investment. "There are Jews in Palestine, too," he explained.[27] Two officials of the American Jewish Congress succeeded in obtaining President Roosevelt's agreement in principle to depositing the advance in a trust fund at a Swiss bank, for use after the war. The people in Bratislava said they could not go back to the Nazis with that kind of legalistic sleight of hand—and time was running out.

About half a year after the matter was first brought to its attention, the Jewish Agency decided to smuggle most of the money—more than $150,000—into Bratislava by courier. The representative of the Joint Distribution Committee in Geneva agreed to transfer the remainder, in cash. It is not clear what happened then: it seems likely that all or part of the money did in fact reach its destination. The Nazis, however, announced in the meantime that they were suspending negotiations; the expulsions continued.

Gisi Fleischmann and Rabbi Weissmandel were themselves sent to Auschwitz. She was murdered there; he succeeded in jumping from a moving train and settled in the United States after the war. Later he published a terrible indictment of the Zionist movement. The Zionists had abandoned him and his people because they were ultraorthodox non-Zionists, he charged, as if Gisi Fleischmann had not been his partner. He based his arguments on letters he quoted from memory; they are unavailable in any archives. They may have been lost or spirited away, or they may never have been written.

There is no way of knowing if the Europa Plan ever really had a chance. Perhaps not. The only thing we may be sure of is that, had the leaders of the Jewish Agency been quicker about sending the money to Bratislava, they could at least have bought themselves the right to look following generations in the eye and say without hesitation: We did what we could, we did not miss any opportunity. [28]

On May 19, 1944, a Jewish rescue envoy sent by the Nazis in Hungary landed at Istanbul airport in neutral Turkey. He carried a proposal that had been put together in a series of meetings with Adolf Eichmann and other German government representatives in Budapest; one of them was the same Dieter Wisliceny who had been involved in the Europa Plan. Again, the Germans proposed to leave a number of Jews alive, perhaps a million, but this time they demanded not money but ten thousand trucks and several hundred tons of commodities: coffee, tea, cocoa, and soap. Like the Europa Plan, this deal was also meant to lead to a separate peace between Himmler's SS and the Western powers, without the knowledge, and perhaps only after the death, of Hitler and without the Soviets—perhaps even against them. This was the infamous Trucks-for-Blood proposal; within days, it was the subject of high-level diplomatic correspondence between Jerusalem, London, Washington, and Moscow. Within a few months it was leaked to the press, and then it died. Perhaps it never offered a real chance to save lives. "It was a heartbreaking and depressing affair," Moshe Sharett said. [29]

The messenger from Budapest was Joel Brand, thirty-eight years old, a salesman for his wife's glove factory. Raised in Germany and a Communist in his younger days, he had crisscrossed the world as an agent of the Comintern; the war found him in Budapest. He used his acquaintance with agents of various intelligence services to organize a network for smuggling Jews from Poland into Hungary, in cooperation with the leaders of the Zionist Organization in Hungary. He was a tragic figure, courageous and naïve. Apparently he never fully understood the significance of the episode in which he played a leading role.

Everything went wrong from the start. He was not greeted in Istanbul by Chaim Weizmann, as he had in his innocence expected to be. Instead, there were Jewish Agency representatives, Turkish detectives, and British secret agents. The first days were mostly spent overcoming the difficulties in getting him a visa that would allow him to stay in Turkey. Then came a tangle of events that led to endless accusations and counteraccusations. Brand was arrested by the British, taken to Egypt, and thrown in jail. He attributed his arrest to the Jewish Agency's mismanagement of the affair; he also accused Jerusalem of undermining his mission.

The Jewish Agency executive discussed the German offer within a week of Brand's arrival in Istanbul. One of those who had met him at the airport flew to Jerusalem with details of the offer hidden in a tube of shaving cream. Gruenbaum, the chairman of the Rescue Committee, saw the plan as a "diabolical provocation." Indeed, the whole thing was fantastic, Ben-Gurion said, but that should not detract from its seriousness. Even if there was only one chance in a million, the risk should be taken. He proposed sending Moshe Sharett to Turkey—and informing the British authorities. One participant in the discussion wondered whether that was wise. Ben-Gurion ruled that they could make no move without the help of the government.[30] A full account of the matter was given to the British high commissioner, Sir Harold MacMichael. But the British, and the Americans as well, already knew about it from their own sources. Both Winston Churchill and Franklin Roosevelt were aware of the German offer. They saw it as an attempt to sabotage the West's alliance with the Soviet Union.

Brand in fact had not arrived alone in Istanbul. The Nazis had sent one of their agents with him, a Jewish adventurer and swindler who told anyone willing to listen that the ransom deal was meant to be only a sideshow to negotiations for a separate peace between the SS and the West. The American and British ambassadors in Moscow were ordered to report the proposal to the Russians, and the Kremlin, of course, opposed negotiating any separate peace with the Germans: the Red Army was already making preparations for the conquest of Hungary. "The Joel Brand episode was finished off in Moscow," a Jewish Agency leader later remarked.[31] The United States and Britain were therefore left with no course but to ensure that, in the future, they would not be accused of having missed an opportunity to save what remained of the Jews. All parties—Jerusalem, Berlin, London, and Washington—seemed to be preparing alibis for the day of judgment after the war. The latter two pretended they were interested in drawing out the negotiations with the Germans as long as possible. Yet, like the offer to sell the Jews of Transnistria to the Jewish Agency, the Trucks-for-Blood deal, if carried through, would have meant a mass exodus of Jews to the West and raised the question of where they would go. No one knew what to do with a million Jews. The British, therefore, did what they had done with the Transnistria affair: they leaked the story to the press, which effectively scotched the negotiations. But then, it may well be that the Germans would not have concluded the negotiations, either.

The turpitude and cynicism of some British government officials can be compared only to that of the Germans themselves. In its efforts to prevent the entry of illegal immigrants arriving on visitors' visas, the British government demanded that the Yugoslavian government stamp Jewish passports with a "J," just as the Nazis did. Before the *Struma* sank with over 750 refugees aboard, the British high commissioner wrote to his superiors in London that the ship should not be allowed to anchor in Palestine because there might be enemy agents among the passengers. Aside from that, he wrote, most of the passengers were professionals, and the country had no way to absorb more unproductive immigrants— provisions were short, and there was a threat of a locust plague.

The Jewish Agency still saw itself as a branch of government. Even the opportunity to save the Jews of Hungary did not motivate it to take any independent action, if only to play for time. At one point there was discussion about sending an agency envoy to Budapest to continue the negotiations, since Brand was in jail in Egypt. Chaim Weizmann and Moshe Sharett contacted British Foreign Minister Anthony Eden and presented the idea to him, statesmen to statesman. Eden consulted his advisers, who told him to reject the proposal. No British subject should be allowed to conduct separate negotiations with the enemy, they argued. The Jewish Agency complied, and the envoy did not go.

The Jewish Agency was unable, by itself, to deliver ten thousand trucks to the Nazis and accept a million Jews in return without Allied approval. On the other hand, it would seem that the agency did not do all it could to lead on the Germans behind the backs of the British. The Zionists already knew that the British were not interested in saving Jews and that no help could be expected from them. It was time for a great bluff. The yishuv leadership could have disobeyed the British orders and negotiated secretly with the Nazis; they could have sent someone from a neutral country to represent them. They could have offered the Germans money instead of trucks, or at least an advance—anything to gain time, since the Russians were not far from Hungary. It seems that they thought of this at one point, but nothing was done.* They emerge from this affair

---

* The negotiations with the Germans continued on another track, beginning with a meeting between Saly Mayer, a Swiss representative of the Joint Distribution Committee, and several SS officers. They spoke while standing on the Sankt Margarethen Bridge, which connects Austria with Switzerland. There were further meetings as well. Mayer tried, and succeeded in, buying time. At one point he even obtained a few tractors for the Germans as a goodwill gesture. Himmler directed that no more Jews be deported from Budapest. Mayer deserves history's praise. Eliahu Dobkin later claimed that the Jewish Agency had set up these negotiations, but Mayer was not acting in its name—in fact, he was not a Zionist.[32]

as small people, unimaginative, whose self-image as respected statesmen hampered their ability and willingness to get involved in fraud and clandestine activities.

The whole Trucks-for-Blood affair is but a footnote to the history of the Holocaust, but it occupied Israeli politics for years to come, never ceasing to haunt the country. Adolf Eichmann would later testify that he had been absolutely serious about the proposal he sent to the Jewish Agency through Brand.[33] And the idea of trading Jews for ransom was not, apparently, foreign even to Adolf Hitler himself. A memo Heinrich Himmler wrote on December 10, 1942, states that Hitler agreed to the exchange deals, on condition that they bring Germany large amounts of foreign currency.[34]

§

There had been about nine million Jews in Europe on the eve of the war; about six million were killed, leaving three million alive. Most of them were saved by Germany's defeat in the war. Some were spared thanks to help they received from various governments and organizations such as the Joint Distribution Committee and from thousands of good-hearted people in almost every country—the "righteous gentiles." There were dramatic rescue operations such as the flight across the Pyrenees from France to Spain and the convoys of Jews that sailed from Denmark to Sweden. Only a few survivors owed their lives to the efforts of the Zionist movement.

5 | "A Warm Jewish Heart"

Early in 1943, David Ben-Gurion went to Haifa to see a young woman who had recently arrived from Poland and hear firsthand what she had endured. He was deeply disturbed, to the point of tears. "I can't escape from the nightmare," he wrote afterwards. For three hours the girl told him of the horrors she had suffered and, said Ben-Gurion, "no Dante or Poe" could imagine such things. He felt helpless, he wrote. It was a rare outburst of emotion on his part—he seldom spoke of the suffering of individuals—and even here he quickly regained his composure: "The sun is rising in all its might and one must go on with one's work."[1]

He meant the creation of the Jewish state, and that is the key to understanding Ben-Gurion's perspective on the extermination of the Jews. For him it was, above all else, a crime against Zionism. Obviously he saw the deeds of the Nazis as a crime against humanity and against the Jewish people, but more than anything else he feared that the murder of the Jews would prevent the establishment of the State of Israel. "The extermination of European Jewry is a catastrophe for Zionism," he said in December 1942; "there won't be anyone to build the country with!" He repeated such sentiments on other occasions, as well.[2]

The founding fathers of the Zionist movement had not envisioned the furnaces of Treblinka, but their ideology assumed that, in the long run, Jews would not survive as Jews in the Diaspora; they would disappear, sooner or later, in one way or another. "The nations among which the Jews live are all alike, whether covertly or overtly: anti-Semites," Theodor

Herzl had argued in 1896.[3] "The Zionists do not mean to exploit the horrible tragedy of the Jews of Europe," Moshe Sharett said now, sounding a recurrent theme, "but they cannot refrain from emphasizing the fact that events have totally proven the Zionist position on the solution of the Jewish problem. Zionism predicted the Holocaust decades ago."[4] *Davar* published an article describing the extermination of the Jews as "punishment from heaven" for not having come to Palestine.[5]

In fact, Zionism suffered its own defeat in the Holocaust; as a movement, it failed. It had not, after all, persuaded the majority of Jews to leave Europe for Palestine while it was still possible to do so. And, in time of need, the Zionist movement was too weak to help them. The Holocaust also put an end to the dream of the Zionist pioneer who would be a new kind of Jew in a new kind of society—"a new man" out of choice and ideology rather than necessity and flight. Dismay over this failure explains the tone of rebuke that could often be heard in Ben-Gurion's voice when he spoke of the victims of the Holocaust. "They did not want to listen to us," he complained; in their deaths they had sabotaged the Zionist dream.[6]

Ben-Gurion identified rescue almost exclusively with immigration to Palestine and realized that there was no chance of saving many this way. Later, some would charge that his attitude toward the Holocaust had been one of complacency—partly because he rarely spoke of it. His biographer explained it differently: "Ben-Gurion had nothing to propose to ease the suffering or save lives, and perhaps for this reason he preferred silence to empty talk and no action."[7] It may also be that, since the rescue effort was doomed to failure, Ben-Gurion, a seasoned politician, preferred to leave it in the hands of others. "The disaster facing European Jewry is not directly my business," he once said.[8] He frequently said that "everything should be done" to save the Jews but sounded much like the newspaper editorials on the subject. "I was not well-informed at the time in the matter of saving Jews under Nazi occupation," he later wrote. "Although I was then chairman of the Jewish Agency executive, the enlistment of the Jewish people in the demand for a Jewish state was at the center of my activity."*[9]

---

* Ben-Gurion was not alone in his single-minded concern with state building, to the exclusion of all else. Jewish Agency executive member Dov Yosef recorded his response to a reporter who told him that the journalists' union had called for the world's leading press unions to give maximum publicity to the atrocities of the Holocaust. "I warned .

¶

The files of the Rescue Committee contain a five-page memorandum titled "Comments on Aid and Rescue." It was apparently written at the beginning of 1943 by Apolinari Hartglass, a Zionist activist from Poland who coordinated the committee's work and here reflected its opinions. The basic assumption was that there really was not much that could be done for the Jews of Europe—their fate was sealed; there was no chance of saving many. "My feeling was that we had been appointed to witness death," said Yitzhak Gruenbaum, chairman of the committee.[12] Hartglass examined the question of whether the yishuv could, nevertheless, get anything useful out of the Holocaust, including in the area of public relations. The memorandum was meant for Zionist eyes only, he wrote at its head. Excerpts follow:

> In the parts of Europe through which the war has passed—in Germany, the occupied countries, and the Axis countries—we may expect the extermination of more than 7 million Jews. . . . It is clear to us today that we cannot dream of saving more than twelve thousand or some tens of thousands of Jews. . . . What this committee can do is only a drop in the sea; it is self-delusion or conscience-salving and not real action. We must hope that despite all the atrocities, a large part of European Jewry, many more than the committee is able to save, will be saved by the force of the will to live. . . .
> If the efforts of the committee are likely, therefore, to lead to only the most minimal of results, we must at least achieve some political gain from them. From a Zionist point of view we will achieve this political gain under the following conditions:
> a) if the whole world knows that the only country that wants to receive the rescued Jews is Palestine and that the only community that wants to absorb them is the yishuv;

him not to exaggerate the number of Jewish victims," Yosef wrote, "because if we begin declaring that millions of Jews were murdered by the Nazis, they will ask us, rightly, where the millions of Jews are for whom, according to us, we need to find a new home in Palestine after the war."[10] Labor leader Berl Katznelson was also not involved in any rescue efforts. His silence concerning the Holocaust was almost complete, his biographer noted.[11]

b) if the whole world knows that the initiative to save the Jews of
   Europe comes from Zionist circles;

c) if the Jews that are saved from extermination know during the
   course of the war or after its end that the Zionist movement and
   the yishuv tried to save them.

If this recognition exists also in political circles, in non-Jewish public
opinion, and within the Jewish public in all the free countries, it
will reinforce the image of Zionist Palestine internationally . . . as
the country to which all the masses of Jews expelled from Europe
should be sent. This will increase the assistance of the Jewish world
in building the land and will direct the exodus of Jews that survived
the worldwide massacre to Palestine. . . .

Whom to save: . . . Should we help everyone in need, without
regard to the quality of the people? Should we not give this activity
a Zionist-national character and try foremost to save those who can
be of use to the Land of Israel and to Jewry? I understand that it
seems cruel to put the question in this form, but unfortunately we
must state that if we are able to save only 10,000 people from among
50,000 who can contribute to building the country and to the national revival of the people, as against saving a million Jews who
will be a burden, or at best an apathetic element, we must restrain
ourselves and save the 10,000 that can be saved from among the
50,000—despite the accusations and pleas of the million. I take
comfort from the fact that it will be impossible to apply this harsh
principle 100 percent and that the million will get something also.
But let us see that it does not get too much.

Going on from this assumption, we must save children first, because they are the best material for the yishuv. The pioneer youth
must be saved, but specifically those who have received training and
are spiritually able to perform Zionist labor. Zionist leaders must be
saved, since they deserve something from the Zionist movement in
return for their work. . . .

Purely philanthropic rescue, such as the rescue of German Jewry,
. . . can only cause damage from a Zionist perspective, particularly
if the possibilities are so limited and the disaster so large. We were
able to use this method for the German Jews, since they had one
advantage—they brought property with them. The current refugees
lack this advantage, since they arrive without anything. They therefore do not give anything to the yishuv and we can only expect

more of what we've already seen from a large portion of German Jewry: complete alienation and sometimes hostility to the Land of Israel, a disrespectful attitude toward everything that is Jewish and Hebrew. . . .

The immigrants who have come via Tehran also demonstrate what distressing results arise from immigration without proper selection. Along with the pioneers and Zionist leaders come masses of people who have no connection with Zionism, people who are completely demoralized in the national sense. . . . They want to educate their children in Polish and English schools. This is not true of the Zionist activists who live under the same conditions— they are happy with their lot, have patience with the many difficulties, and give thanks for all the help given them.

Had we the means to save them all there can be no doubt that we would have to accept these things. But, sadly, we do not have sufficient means to save even the good elements, so we have no choice but to give up on saving the bad elements.[13]

The leaders of the Jewish Agency generally agreed with the principle that the few that could be saved should be selected in accordance with the needs of the Zionist enterprise in Palestine. They argued mostly over details. Almost everyone agreed that preference should be given to children and youth, since the chances were good that they would remain in the country. Ben-Gurion did not agree with most of the others that preference should also be given to Zionist activists.[14] There were occasional complaints about the practice of saving only those who were considered useful to Zionism, such as children, who could be educated in the Mapai spirit. As one of the opposition newspapers charged: "They don't care about the fate of old Jews."[15] Here was a terrible decision: more than anything else, of course, the need to choose between those to rescue and those to abandon underlined the powerlessness of the yishuv. The issue was the subject of a frenzy of negotiations, both in Palestine and within Jewish communities overseas, involving all manner of political intrigue, mutual accusation, and deception.[16] At one point it was decided to help everyone possible: "It is clear that under conditions of war there can be no question of selecting the material. We brought those whom we could bring," a member of the agency informed Ben-Gurion.[17]

Golda Meir said at one meeting that, in the face of the Holocaust, there was no Zionism other than rescuing Jews. This raised another question for debate: was it proper to use money earmarked for developing the yishuv to rescue Jews from Europe?[18] Rabbi Yitzhak Itshe Meir Levin, a leader of the ultraorthodox Agudat Yisrael, thought so: "Take the Jewish National Fund money. . . . Won't you halt the work in Palestine during such a period, when they are murdering and slaughtering Jews by the hundreds of thousands, even millions? Don't establish new settlements; take the money for those needs."

But Yitzhak Gruenbaum felt the yishuv's needs had priority: "I think it is necessary to state here—Zionism is above everything," he said.

Yosef Sprinzak objected: "What do we need at this moment? Not a Zionist program but something very simple: *a varm Yiddish hartz* [in Yiddish: a warm Jewish heart]. That's what we must have. Long speeches will not help us here. A *varm Yiddish hartz* should beat in all our houses, in the Jewish Agency, in the Histadrut, and everywhere."

"They will say that I am anti-Semitic," Gruenbaum responded, "that I don't want to save the Exile, that I don't have *a varm Yiddish hartz*. . . . Let them say what they want. I will not demand that the Jewish Agency allocate a sum of 300,000 or 100,000 pounds sterling to help European Jewry. And I think that whoever demands such things is performing an anti-Zionist act."[*][19] At the time of these exchanges—January 1943—Jews were being exterminated in great numbers.

It is difficult to compute how much money the yishuv actually spent on saving Jews; the total comes to several million dollars, according to one reckoning—about a quarter of the entire Jewish Agency budget. Significantly more was spent on buying land and establishing new settlements.[21]

§

From the earliest days of the war, there was a tendency in the yishuv to distance the present and concentrate on the needs of the future. Four

---

* Gruenbaum was torn at the time between ideological rigidity, which he considered obligatory in a Zionist leader, and a personal tragedy; his son had disappeared in Poland, and it was some time before Gruenbaum learned that he was at Auschwitz. Ironically, at one meeting of the Jewish Agency executive, Gruenbaum asked for an appropriation of 100 Palestinian pounds (about $400) to pay for cables he had sent to Europe in an effort to receive information on the condition of the Jews. "It seems to me that 50 pounds would suffice to send the telegrams," responded the agency's treasurer, and his recommendation was accepted.[20]

weeks after the Nazi invasion of Poland, the Mapai political committee discussed the question of what should be done "after the Holocaust that has come upon Polish Jewry."[22] This was not a slip of the tongue: even then, at the beginning of November 1939, the Holocaust was often spoken of in the past tense. Perhaps this was the yishuv's way of dealing with the news of the murder of the Jews and with their own powerlessness to save them. Instead of thinking of the Holocaust in terms that would require effective and immediate action, they exiled it from real time into history. Thus the first press report of the murder of Jews in mobile gas chambers was worded as though it were a story that happened long ago: "They would put them in a truck, the driver would put poison gas in pipes specially prepared for this purpose. . . . Voices and dull pounding would be heard from the truck, but after a while all would go quiet. . . . One of the drivers would turn on a flashlight and peek into the truck. . . . Then came the turn of the Jewish gravediggers."[23]

With the Holocaust still raging, the leaders of the yishuv and opinion makers indicted themselves for apathy and for their failure to rescue the Jews. "Our silence is a sin against the education of the younger generation," one newspaper stated, and another proclaimed, "We are all guilty!"[24] One Mapai leader said, "We heard and knew about the atrocities . . . but we paid no attention." A colleague seconded him: "I do not feel that we did all we could do. We thought that the difficulties were so great that they could not be overcome and that we had no possibility of making contacts or offering assistance. Only this, perhaps, excuses the fact that we did nothing, or almost nothing, for such a long time." One of the newspapers stated: "We have asked ourselves again and again: did we do everything possible?" A member of the Mapai executive committee blamed the press: he had made a speech about the murder of the Jews, but *Davar* had not covered it. His colleagues agreed: "None of us have any doubt that we have not done our duty in this area." "We are full of sin," summed up one of them, and another predicted that after the war the Jewish Agency would find itself in the dock. "Shame on us," said Golda Meir.[25] Apparently, the yishuv preferred to take historical responsibility for inaction and negligence rather than admit their powerlessness. Reuven Shiloah, one of the founders of Israel's secret intelligence services, mused, about a year before the end of the war, "Who knows if the fate of European Jewry might not have been otherwise if the first Nazi attempts to exterminate Jews had met with resistance?"[26]

They spoke as if these dark days were already behind them, part of their past. There was of course something purifying in this willingness, this enthusiasm almost, to confess their collective guilt: when everyone is guilty, no one is.

The inclination to ease the murder of the Jews out of the present and into the past—and so to move beyond it—was apparent in other realms as well, particularly in a tendency to benefit from the historical lessons of a tragedy that had not yet occurred and to apply them to an uncertain future. Some were already planning memorials for the victims. Others, David Ben-Gurion among them, contemplated the demands for reparations that the Jewish people would submit to Germany after the war.

It is uncertain who was the first to suggest that the Germans would have to pay reparations for the property they had expropriated from Jews and for the suffering they had caused. The idea seems to have been in the air from the time the war started, apparently sparked by the punitive reparations payments imposed on Germany at the end of World War I. Ben-Gurion received a memorandum on the subject as early as 1940. Berl Katznelson spoke of it publicly toward the end of that year.[27] By December 1942, there was already a private organization in Tel Aviv called Justicia that offered to help Nazi victims draft compensation demands.[28]

A former delegate to several Zionist congresses, Mordecai Shenhabi, proposed in September 1942 that the Jewish National Fund establish a memorial to the victims of the Holocaust, "the war dead and heroes of Israel." Not long thereafter, the projected memorial received the name it would bear when it was built some years later: Yad Vashem. Shenhabi's proposals led to discussions and letters, and a committee was set up to examine them. There was no clearer, more grotesque, even macabre expression of the tendency to think of the Holocaust in the past tense: while the yishuv discussed the most appropriate way to memorialize them, most of the victims were still alive.[29]

The newspapers protected the public from the Holocaust, in their own way. Instead of confronting their readers with the information and forcing them to face up to it, they packaged it in biblical laments and poetic slogans, printed above their logos: "Cry, Jerusalem, for the fallen of your exile; shout, Zion: save your sons and daughters, be refuge to my children and little ones," read one. Newspapers reported events that took place in "the vale of tears," in "the valley of death," or "the vale of sorrows." Everything happened in "hell" or in "the inferno," not here and now, in the political climate that the newspapers chronicled. "SATAN'S PLOTS

AND EVIL DEEDS," *Davar* said in a headline. In this way, the newspapers distanced the Holocaust from day-to-day life and absolved their readers of the obligation to see it as part of reality.[30]

In the political realm, the debates in the yishuv continued to take precedence over the events in Europe. At a meeting of the Mapai central committee in December 1938, a few days after *Kristallnacht*, Moshe Sharett spoke of the "Holocaust" that was consuming German Jewry. A few minutes later, Ben-Gurion asked for the floor. "I confess my sin," he said. "In these terrible days of the beginning of the disaster that threatens European Jewry, I am still more worried about the elections at the [Mapai] branch in Tel Aviv."[31] The destruction of European Jewry was at its height when Ben-Gurion resigned from the Jewish Agency executive over a political dispute that he described as "hell."[32] His preoccupation with party politics was not unique; his colleagues, too, were passionately immersed in the relentless politicking that would cause a split in Mapai before the war was over.*

At the same time, the hostility between the labor movement and the Revisionist right continued unabated. The Haganah would kidnap right-wing terrorists and turn them over to the authorities; *Davar* printed British "wanted" notices, including offers of rewards for whoever brought about the capture of rightist terrorists. Among the wanted was Yitzhak Jezernitzky, who would later change his name to Yitzhak Shamir and serve as prime minister of Israel.[34] This was an ideological and political battle, as well as a struggle for control of the state-in-formation. The Holocaust and the rescue efforts were reduced to mere arguments in the debate. *Davar* accused the Revisionists of attempting to sabotage the rescue fund. The Revisionist paper *Hamashkif* responded, "You came late and missed the opportunity," referring, again, to Jabotinsky's evacuation plan.[35] Earlier, *Herut*, another Revisionist paper, had complained that "it is possible

---

* The conflict between David Ben-Gurion and Chaim Weizmann, who lived in London, also greatly agitated the yishuv. The first evidence about the "final solution" was already known to him when Weizmann dropped all his other work to describe Ben-Gurion in a long letter as "a petty dictator." The letter, never sent, was addressed to the Jewish Agency executive in Jerusalem. Weizmann did not mention Adolf Hitler by name but, when he compared Ben-Gurion to European dictators, he left no doubt as to whom he meant. "They all fit a definite pattern: they are humorless, thin-lipped, morally stunted, and stubborn, apparently frustrated in some ambition, and nothing is more dangerous than a small man nursing his grievances." According to Weizmann, "it would be a calamity to have to fight a new and more dangerous brand of fascism under the leadership of Ben-Gurion."[33]

to save, but there are no saviors." The paper further charged: "The leadership clique in the yishuv denies the urgent need to start a real and unrelenting war to open the country's gates immediately." The "real war" it advocated was a war against the British. [36]

Refugees were at the center of one of the first skirmishes between the religious and the secular factions—a conflict that would only intensify in years to come. During the first half of 1943, the yishuv's politicians launched a grand battle for the souls of the "Tehran children." [37] The children were among those who had managed to escape from Poland in the first days of the German occupation. They crossed the border into the Soviet Union and were sent from there to Iran without the assistance of the yishuv. Almost all of them had horror stories to tell. One boy related that all the Jewish men in his village, including his own father, had been herded into the school building, where the Germans had shot them through the windows. He had been nine at the time. His mother had taken her three children by foot over the border. It was cold; they were hungry, frightened. They walked and walked through the forest for weeks on end. The two smaller children died one after the other; their mother buried them in the snow. In the end she, too, could go on no longer. In her last moments, she told her son how to get to a Christian orphanage in the Central Asian city of Samarkand. She warned him not to reveal to anyone that he was a Jew. The boy found the orphanage and was allowed to stay there, but he had difficulty hiding his Judaism. It was especially hard in the shower. The other children tormented him. Nearly two years passed and, by the time he reached the refugee camp in Tehran, he was eleven. There were some seven hundred Jewish boys and girls there. All had seen death.

In the Tehran transfer camp, the children were prepared for immigration to Palestine by counselors from the Jewish Agency. Already there were fights over kosher food, prayers, and Sabbath observance. Some of the counselors, particularly those from kibbutzim, were virulently antireligious; others were observant. They spent much time fighting among themselves and accusing each other of trying to force their own beliefs and opinions on the children. The religious counselors accused the secular ones of forcing the boys to cut off their sidelocks; the secular counselors accused the religious ones of inciting the children against Zionism.

The children left the transfer camp in late 1942, and after journeying by land to India, by boat to Egypt, and by train to Palestine, they finally arrived six months later, in February 1943: seven hundred boys and girls in identical woolen sweaters, oversized short pants, and safari hats. They were weak, some of them sick, almost all of them deep in depression and shock. In the meantime, the politicians fought over whether they should receive a secular or a religious education.

The dispute was the subject of countless meetings, some of them involving Ben-Gurion. Tempers flared and produced many newspaper editorials and public demonstrations, and at least one violent incident: several people beat one of the administrators of the Tehran camp as he walked down the street, on the ground that he had forced religious boys to go bareheaded. The Tel Aviv police hustled him to safety in a nearby house, while passersby commented that this was how the Nazis attacked Jews in Germany.[38] The leaders of the ultraorthodox community threatened the leaders of the Jewish Agency with a rabbinic ban on Zionist fund-raising drives in the United States if the children were not handed over to them.

This was an ideological battle over the religious and cultural character of the yishuv and a political fight for control of the educational system that would train the next generation of voters. All the participants realized that they were setting precedents for the arrival of the Holocaust survivors after the war. In the end it was decided that the children would be educated in accordance with the way their parents had lived. They were brought one by one before a special board that interrogated them about the level of religious observance in their parents' houses. Had their fathers prayed every morning? Had Mother lit candles for the Sabbath? Where there was doubt, the children were sent to religious schools. Children over the age of fourteen were allowed to choose for themselves where they would study. They found themselves caught between pressures and counterpressures before they had even got out of the Jewish Agency transfer camps. Counselors tried to convince them, persuade them, to entice them with promises or frighten them with threats, all in the name of the ideologies that divided the yishuv. *Haaretz* was not surprised: "Had they managed to absorb the children without causing partisan conflict, it would have been something of a miracle."[39]

Prisoners of politics, the leaders of the yishuv persisted in partisan, factional, and personal disputes, most of which had their roots in the years before the Holocaust. Their thinking was always on a small scale. A discussion of rescue efforts at a meeting of the Mapai central committee quickly turned into a debate over procedure: one of the members fretted that his colleagues had not taken an interest in the subject earlier. "I never heard it come up at any meeting," another defended himself. "It came up, but as the nineteenth item on the agenda," the first speaker shot back. Golda Meir rejected his argument, as if it was some pet peeve of the speaker: we met with him only a week ago and he didn't say anything about it, she said. She herself had been asked to work on the rescue efforts, she said, but had refused, because she suspected that the committee was not serious. "You can find better-looking window dressing," she had told them.*[40]

Those who were involved in the actual rescue efforts also spent much time fighting along party lines. "It was one of the most terrible disappointments of my life," wrote one member of the Rescue Committee. He was referring not to the committee's poor results, but to the fact that the members of his party did not win the standing he felt they deserved and that the agents in Istanbul had no respect for the members of the committee in Jerusalem.[42] The envoys in Istanbul represented contrary partisan interests and didn't care about each other, either. They wasted much time arguing over how to parcel out the little aid that they could extend. As with the immigration certificates, both money and packages were sent to the needy behind enemy lines according to political quotas.

In Geneva, too, one committee member commented, "Everyone hated everyone else."[43] Their enmity exacerbated the existing competition between the Jewish Agency and other Jewish aid agencies, mostly American ones. One file contains a long report of the disagreements between the Jewish Agency and the Joint Distribution Committee in Tehran, which sent packages of tea, soap, butter, and sometimes candy to the refugees. One subject of debate was which organization would sign the greeting contained in the packages. In the meantime they were delayed for months. "The refugees will give up the ghost before they arrive," the report stated.[44]

All of this factionalism and infighting reflected not only the inability of the yishuv to save European Jewry, but also the great spiritual distance between Palestine and the tragic events unfolding in Europe. Certainly the Jews of Palestine saw themselves as part of the Jewish people, denying neither Jewish history nor religious tradition. They were committed to Jewish solidarity and aid to the Jews of the Diaspora. They maintained that the Zionist project in the Land of Israel was a project for all Jews;

* The agenda for a May 1943 meeting of the Histadrut executive committee listed "rescue efforts" as the sixth of eight items. Among those that preceded it were Dead Sea development and May Day celebrations.[41]

they lavished love and even nostalgia on *Beth Abba*, "father's house"—
the Jewish home in the old country. But there was at the same time a
strong countertendency to "negate the Exile," an aspiration to create a
new, proud Hebrew race that could stand up and defend itself, part of
a new, healthy, just, national society. The years of the Holocaust saw
the coming of age of the second and even the third generation of young
people who had been educated in this spirit, raised to be "proud and
generous and cruel," as Jabotinsky put it.

Negation of the Exile took the form of a deep contempt, and even
disgust, for Jewish life in the Diaspora, particularly in eastern Europe,
which was characterized as degenerate, degraded, humiliating, and morally corrupt. In their tragedy, Diaspora Jews seemed even more repellent.
"Our children read and hear much about the destruction of the Exile,
about the atrocities committed against our brothers and the suffering of
the Jews under occupation, yet their hearts are hard and uncaring about
it all," wrote one educator in a teachers' magazine. From time to time,
he related, he asked his students to write compositions about the Holocaust. Their writings reflected alienation rather than spiritual identification with those who suffered. No wonder, the teacher noted. "Our
youth are proud and upright in stance and spirit. They believe in their
strength and know its value. They love freedom, desire space and liberty,
and will not tolerate humiliation or repression."[45] Berl Katznelson
agreed—unwillingly—that the Land of Israel had produced "an entirely
different tribe."[46] This was the "new man" that socialist Zionism had
prophesied.

The Holocaust came to be seen as a Jewish defeat. Its victims were
censured for having let the Nazis murder them without fighting for their
lives or at least for the right to "die with honor." This attitude in time
became a sort of psychological and political ghost that haunted the State
of Israel—reflecting scorn and shame, hubris and dread, injustice and
folly. Yitzhak Gruenbaum said, while the Holocaust was still at its height,
that the fact that the Jews of Poland "had not found in their souls the
courage" to defend themselves filled him with a feeling of "stinging
mortification." Gruenbaum, who came from Poland, described his erst-
while compatriots with repugnance: "Thousands of Jews waited calmly"
until they were loaded onto the railway cars that carted them off to their
deaths, he said. He had not imagined that they would not defend themselves "in such instances," that there would not be even a single leader
who would summon them to die in self-defense. Six months after saying

that the Jews of Poland had preferred "the life of a dog over an honorable death," he commented: "People have turned into dishrags."[47]

This disparagement of European Jewry was heard often, even when everyone already knew everything and when Auschwitz had become a household word. "Why are the Jews of Hungary not defending themselves?" *Davar* asked in a front-page headline in June 1944.[48] Another newspaper exclaimed: "We have been disgusted by the cries of the oppressed who are unable to fight back."[49] The resentment against the victims of the Holocaust recalled the way Zionist poets, such as Haim Nahman Bialik, had depicted the victims of an earlier pogrom: "They fled like mice, hid like bugs, and died like dogs over there, wherever they were found." Even then, the emphasis was on *there*. Had they come *here* earlier, it would not have happened to them.[50]

In December 1941 another poet, Abba Kovner, distributed a leaflet to his comrades in the Vilna ghetto, calling on them not to go to their deaths "like lambs to the slaughter." He apparently borrowed the expression from Isaiah 53:7, as others had before him. The phrase came to express a national trauma. It was meant to define how Zionist heroism in the Land of Israel differed from Jewish humiliation in the Exile.[51] Ironically, the new Jews, standing tall in Palestine, did just what the persecuted Jews of the Exile had always done, and were as powerless as they had been. They presented petitions to the authorities, always careful not to rebel openly. They "raised a great cry" in the press. "Hurry to halt the massacre," said a notice from the National Committee that described the Nazis as "armed bandits." They sent envoys to other Jewish communities; they tried to get donations from philanthropists. They prayed, they fasted as a sign of mourning, and they imposed restrictions on their family celebrations in accordance with rabbinic injunctions from the seventeenth-century pogroms against the Jews of the Ukraine.[52] Thus the Zionist Jewish community in Palestine comes out looking just like any other Jewish community in the world. Only their better fortune and their hubris distinguished them from their brothers.

Somewhere in the minutes of one of those innumerable meetings are the words of one of the Jewish Agency's rescue emissaries in Istanbul. They saved only a small number of people, compared to the huge number murdered, the emissary reported. But there was this consolation: those saved emerged from the inferno as Zionists and saw Israel as their home. "We have saved their souls," another emissary agreed.[53] Uri Kesari, a columnist for *Yediot Aharonot*, wrote with self-irony rare in those days: "We have mourned. Now we can go on."[54]

PART **III**

ISRAEL:
The Last Jews

6 | "At First I Thought They Were Animals"

By September 1944, everyone was prepared for the German defeat. Said David Ben-Gurion, "We are now on the brink of the end of the war, with most of the Jews destroyed. Everyone wonders: where will we find the people for Palestine?"[1] He would later write, "Hitler harmed more than the Jewish people, whom he knew and hated: he caused damage to the Jewish state, whose coming he did not foresee. He destroyed the country's main support and central force. The state appeared and did not find the nation that had awaited it."[2] The fear that after the war there would not be enough Jews who would want to emigrate to Palestine continually plagued the yishuv leaders. Ben-Gurion called it a "nightmare."[3] Now more than ever, people lived with the sense that the time for Zionism was running out, that each missed opportunity was lost forever. Toward the end of the war, Ben-Gurion proposed that the Zionist movement commit itself to bringing in "immediately" a million Jews, double the number of Jews then in Palestine: "[Another] million Jews— [and] the conflict with the Arabs will be over," he declared.[4] This was, at that point, a declaration of purpose rather than an operational plan, but members of the Jewish Agency executive reacted with alarm, charging that the country could not absorb so many all at once. One member said that the very thought made his hair stand on end, and another said that such a thing could be carried out only "the way Hitler did things," with military organization and the methods of dictatorship. A third viewed such immigration as conditional on the expulsion of the

Arabs—in his words, their "transfer." Ben-Gurion admitted that the immigrants would suffer, but he was not deterred. "It's all right," he said. "They suffered a lot in Europe."*5

Several months later, in December 1944, Ben-Gurion visited Bulgaria and met with Holocaust survivors. "Horror, shame, . . . terror," he wrote in his diary.7 On May 8, 1945, he recorded: "Victory day. Sad, very sad."8 Not long after, Ben-Gurion drew up "a postwar Zionist reckoning." He was then on the deck of the *Queen Elizabeth*, heading back to Europe from the United States. His entry for that day looks like a page from an accountant's ledger, all numbers: so many Jews lived in Europe before the war, so many were murdered, so many remained alive. Ben-Gurion listed them by country; not a single one of the sums he recorded was correct. He divided the Jews in the world into five blocs, altogether some 10 million people. The conclusion: "We must immediately bring all of bloc 5 (some 855,000 Jews from the Islamic world), most of bloc 4 (the 253,000 Jews of western Europe, not including Great Britain); all we can from bloc 3 (some 3 million Jews from eastern Europe) and the pioneers from bloc 2 (some 6 million Jews from the English-speaking world and from Latin America)."9

On arriving in Europe, Ben-Gurion first set out to see some of the displaced-persons camps in Germany. "The feeling in Bergen-Belsen is depressing," he wrote, "as if they were still living in a concentration camp." He copied into his diary two songs he heard in the camp, the "Partisans' Song," in Hebrew, and "The Burning Town," in Yiddish. One inmate at the camp was a cousin of his from Lodz. Ben-Gurion recorded his barracks number. With similar attention to detail, he recorded the precise composition of the food packages being sent to the DPs. At Dachau, he wrote, "238,000 were burned in the crematorium. . . . I saw the crematorium, gas chambers, the dog pens, the gallows, the prisoners' camps, and the SS camps. There are now some 10,000 SS men imprisoned there."

The next day he was saved from death—miraculously, as he noted with the same dry practicality. A truck collided with his car on the way

* Ben-Gurion did not in principle oppose the idea of expelling the Arabs through what was called "voluntary transfer," that is, with the agreement of Arab rulers (but not necessarily with the agreement of all those to be deported): "I do not reject transfer from a moral point of view, nor do I reject it politically, if there is a chance for it. . . . But it must not be a Jewish proposal. . . . If we propose it, the Arabs will reject it and the gentiles will say that there is no room for Jews in Palestine."6

from Munich to Frankfurt. In the afternoon he reached Heidelberg. In his diary he wrote: "They are putting us up in the Schloss Hotel. This is the first time in Germany that I have a big room with a private bath and, even more wondrous, towels. . . . They told me there is nowhere to get Greek books. Sold out."*10

The first members of the yishuv to reach Europe at the end of the war were the soldiers of the Jewish Brigade, who had fought under the command of the British forces. By the time they arrived, several thousand victims of Nazi persecution had already managed to flee and find asylum in Palestine. Nevertheless, the horrors they recounted hardly prepared the brigade's soldiers for the sight of those who had survived the Nazi camps. In many cases, Jewish soldier met Jewish victim in the liberated camps—like Buchenwald, Bergen-Belsen, and Dachau, where the survivors were still living—within the very fences that until recently had been wired with a deadly electric charge. Some of the brigade soldiers heard there for the first time what had happened to their loved ones; many found relatives who they had thought were dead. For the survivors, the Jewish soldiers from Palestine seemed to have some mystical presence: "If the soldiers had told them to walk into the sea they would have gone, with the certainty that the water would part before them," one of the Jewish Agency envoys later said.12

In the first weeks after liberation, many thousands of inmates died. "The situation in the camps is horrifying," wrote Yehezkel Sahar, then Major Sakharov, later to be the chief of the Israeli police force. "There are no blankets or warm clothing for the people, who live mostly in wooden barracks, without heat. The weather here is wintery, with frost at night . . . and there are large numbers of pregnant women and children, and no one is doing anything for them. The authorities are ignoring it intentionally. Recently, an anti-Semitic atmosphere has penetrated all

---

* Even on his first visit to Germany after the Holocaust, Ben-Gurion did not suppress his compulsive passion for collecting books. Ruth Klieger Aliav, in Germany to arrange for the immigration of Jews to Palestine, accompanied him. She recalled how he made her drive him in her jeep through the ruins of Frankfurt, evading American military police barriers, to see if any books remained there. In one store he found, she said, "treasures": ancient Haggadahs, a nineteenth-century Bible, and loose pages from old books. He delved through them with an expert hand, saying "this yes, that no," loading what he found into the jeep. "In the meantime it began to rain," Aliav related. "German women sat, dressed in black, on mounds of rubble and began to place stone on stone, brick on brick. And he said: 'What's this?' I said: 'That's Germany's new future.' "11

the offices dealing with refugees, and my impression is that they are trying to make the refugees' lives as bitter as possible so that they will agree to return to Poland." The food given to them was bad, often inadequate. People slept on the same shelves, in the same barracks, where the Nazis had forced them to sleep. Many slept on the floors. It was overcrowded. There were not enough toilets or showers.[13]

Other sources also reported the harsh living conditions in the camps. The best known is a document drafted by Earl G. Harrison, a representative of the U.S. State Department. Dean of the University of Pennsylvania Law School and the American representative on the Intergovernmental Committee on Refugees, he told President Truman that the American army's treatment of the Jewish refugees in the displaced-persons camps differed from that of the Nazis only insofar as the Americans were not exterminating the Jews.[14]

The survivors told bloodcurdling stories. Aharon Hoter-Yishai, an officer in the Jewish Brigade, later a well-known attorney, met women who had been saved after being herded into a gas chamber. They had been forced to stand there a day and a night, with men and children, all of them naked, awaiting death. But the number of victims in the chamber was less than the minimum required; the Germans did not want to waste an entire dose of gas on an inadequate number of people, so the victims were taken out to await an additional shipment of Jews. In the meantime the camp was liberated.[15]

Ruth Klieger Aliav discovered forty-seven small children who had been hidden in the cellar of a building that had once been a synagogue, on Grenadierstrasse, in the Russian sector of Berlin. By the time she reached them, she reported, mice had begun to gnaw at them.[16] *Haaretz* described an incident in southern Germany. The residents of a camp there were making preparations for the wedding of a survivor—a Jewish man whose wife and two children had perished at Auschwitz. The bride was also alone in the world. "As usual in such cases, there was much fuss in the barracks where the bride lived. Everything was ready for the ceremony." But the groom didn't come. Witnesses found him "wandering the camp grounds, staring into space, walking around and around. From time to time he stopped by children at play. He followed them around, picked them up, romped around with them, while his lips moved silently— 'Hanele, my Hanele, you aren't mad at me, are you? For betraying you? For marrying?' " The man was sent to a mental hospital.[17] One of the first envoys from Palestine to see the DP camps described them as cemeteries.[18]

"I have seen the Tehran children, I have seen other refugees, but I have never seen a picture as horrifying as this one," reported Eliahu Dobkin of the Jewish Agency executive. "These are torn and broken shadows of men, plagued by lice and boils and eye diseases." Dobkin told of one child who stole toothpaste and a toothbrush from a man who slept in the next room. "I asked him, 'Aren't you ashamed of yourself?' The boy replied, 'They're taking him to the crematorium anyway. He's an old man.' " The man was about thirty-five. It was, Dobkin said, "God's own horror."[19]

The envoys sent frequent reports. Before long, the reports ceased to reflect the initial shock. Instead they took on a very critical tone. These reports reflected not just the situation of the Holocaust survivors but also the social and political values of the socialist Zionist establishment that had sent the envoys to Europe, values that shaped their expectations about the "remnant."* The reports generally described the refugees as a formless, faceless mass, "human debris," "a huge community of beggars," degenerate, backward, diminished not only physically and psychologically but also morally.[21] Again and again, the envoys expressed their amazement that so many of the survivors quickly married and had children. Haim Yahil estimated that there was no rate of natural increase higher than that in the DP camps.[22] A psychologist who studied the survivors called the alliances "marriages of despair." They were a way for the survivors to rise up against the attempt to deny them their humanity. Many were not happy marriages, but there were few divorces, as if the couples felt that separating would be a final victory for the Nazis.[23] Yet the life wish of the DPs, just like their extermination, was foreign to the envoys from Palestine. "At first I thought they were animals," one related. "There were families that lived five, six couples in one room, their entire sex life and everything together." But since "they were always in camps" and had suffered greatly, he concluded that "for them it was natural."[24]

Other envoys were equally harsh: The survivors had lost their self-respect, all faith in their fellowman and in altruism, to the point of cynicism, nihilism, and lawlessness. The observers attributed this not only to the survivors' experience in the camps and to the atmosphere of

---

* The expression *remnant* (*sheerit hapleta*) is found in the Bible. "And God sent me before you to preserve you a remnant in the earth, and to save your lives by a great deliverance" (Genesis 45:7). "For out of Jerusalem shall a remnant go out, and they that escape out of Mount Zion" (Isaiah, 37:31, 32). The term was first applied to persecuted European Jewry immediately after the Nazis came to power.[20]

degeneracy that pervaded Europe after the war but also to their life in the Exile, before the Holocaust. For many of the envoys, the encounter was their first with what they, as proud Zionists and socialists, had always detested as "Exile mentality"; they were shocked.[25] The survivors are not willing to work, one reported. Some of them leave the camps, marry German women, and open stores or do business in the German black market. "An empty materialism has overtaken the people," lamented Haim Yahil. According to him, many of the survivors had become accustomed to "making an easy living" and to a much higher standard of living than they had enjoyed before the war. They tended "to allow themselves luxuries," specifically jewelry and silk dresses. But "even more dangerous than the love of luxuries" was the employment of German maids and nannies in the homes of Jewish refugees who had settled in German towns. The "moral danger" seemed obvious to Yahil. He also feared that the more the survivors got used to a comfortable life in Germany, the harder it would be for them to adjust to the demands of life in Palestine. They were "desecrating the honor of Israel," he declared, as if the yishuv had no black marketeers or women in silk. He called them "trash" and accused them of the worst thing of all—support of the right-wing terrorist organizations, Mapai's opponents.[26]

David Shaltiel, later an Israeli army general and an ambassador, reported on his journey with several survivors to Palestine. "Horrible things" happened along the way, he related. Young people tried to eject old ones from their berths; the boys and girls wanted only to fool around. "They are in a state of demoralization," he declared. "We had to be policemen. The boys would go to the girls' bedrooms in the evenings and at night. We kicked them out, but they went back. The girls went around with sailors and soldiers and showed no sense of virtue, and it was not easy to do our job of preserving a certain standard." Shaltiel proposed a theory to his party: "I believe that those who remained alive lived because they were egotists and looked out for themselves first." A lot of them, it seemed, had had "time to make a lot of money" under the Germans. His conclusion: "The fact that a person was in a camp is not reason enough to send him to Palestine."[27]

The chairman of the meeting of the secretariat commented that its members had never before heard such things.[28] This was not accurate; Shaltiel was only using blunter language. His report, with its suggestion that, to survive, one had to be corrupt, was no different from the reports of other envoys; it reflected common opinion. "Among the survivors of the German concentration camps," Ben-Gurion said, "were those who, had they not been what they were—harsh, evil, and egotistical people —would not have survived, and all they endured rooted out every good part of their souls."[29] "We have to see things with open eyes," *Haaretz* wrote. "The few that remain to us in Europe are not necessarily Judaism's best. The nation's jewels were destroyed first," and many of the survivors "are suspected of low morality."[30]

Haim Yahil tried to be objective:

The Jewish prisoners who remained alive were not the chosen of the people and were not saved because of their superior gifts. But it would be a great injustice to them if we were to think . . . that the remnant is "a result of negative selection," and that it is composed mostly of the worst elements of the Jewish people. The facts contradict such an assumption. . . . To the extent that there was a selective criterion at all, one can say that those who remained were those with a strong character and an overwhelming desire to live, whether the urge to live chose a positive channel or whether it found a negative and asocial expression. What is true is that the more sensitive were in special danger, because their minds could not face the terror. It is also true that the enemy persecuted the intelligentsia relentlessly, more than it did any other group. But despite all this, people of various groups survived, people with different human and social values.[31]

The yishuv felt morally and ideologically responsible for the survivors. Everyone knew that, without them, there was no chance of achieving statehood. During Ben-Gurion's visit to a former Nazi prison camp near Frankfurt, a blonde girl with long braids had approached him. Her name was Malkele; she asked him in Yiddish, "Are you the king of Israel?" Ben-Gurion patted her on the head and said he was not the king. But the girl insisted: "Yes! They told me that you are the king! Take me to the Land of Israel right now!"[32] Everywhere Ben-Gurion went he heard that people wanted to come to Palestine. He estimated their numbers at between 60 and 70 percent of the residents of the camps. Everywhere, he asked them if they were ready to accept the difficulties involved in waiting for immigration certificates, and everywhere they said yes. On his return home, then, he reported to the Jewish Agency executive that most of the residents of the DP camps were "loyal Zionists."*33

Leaders of the yishuv heard such reports from other envoys as well. Some explained that Europe, as far as the survivors were concerned, was one huge graveyard; they could not rebuild their homes or lives there. Others emphasized that everywhere in Europe, especially in the East, anti-Semitism was on the rise, pushing Jews to leave. But most of the returning envoys had grave doubts as to whether many of the survivors would want to make their homes in Palestine. "The majority do not want to settle here," reported a member of the Jewish Agency executive. "They want quiet, they want rest. They are not made for a war of ideals." More than anything else, said another envoy, they were just tired; they had no strength to be uprooted yet again.35

At the same time, the yishuv made it clear that the survivors were not ideal "human material." One of the envoys warned that 5,000 Jews of the type he had met in Europe would turn Palestine into "one big mad-house."36 There were those who said that the survivors were liable to "poison" Zionism, democracy, and progress and to obliterate the country's socialist agricultural foundation, until it became, as Meir Yaari said while the Holocaust was still in progress, "one big Tel Aviv."37

There were those who feared for Mapai's future. As long as selection for immigration reflected relative party strength, Mapai could ensure its majority. Uncontrolled immigration was liable to bring a "terrible holo-caust" on the party, one of its leaders said.38 One envoy to the displaced persons told Ben-Gurion that, if a hundred thousand of them indeed

---

* In Germany Ben-Gurion met with Gen. Dwight Eisenhower and proposed an original idea: concentrating all the Jewish refugees in Bavaria—in villages to be evacuated of their German residents—and granting them self-government. The refugees would be taught agricultural skills and given paramilitary training until they were allowed to come to Palestine. Ben-Gurion told his colleagues that he had, in fact, proposed to Eisenhower the establishment of a Jewish state in Bavaria. The startled general said that it was "a new idea." In principle, he supported concentrating the Jews in one place, he said, because their dispersal made it more difficult to care for them, and it upset the German population. The Bavarian Jewish state was not established, but Eisenhower promised to improve living conditions in the camps, and even gave the Zionist movement use of an airplane to fly in Hebrew books for distribution in the camps. Most importantly, he agreed to accept the entry of tens of thousands of Jews from eastern Europe into the American zone of occupation. "Eisenhower is one of the most decent types I've met," Ben-Gurion later noted. "He did not seem like a general, just an incomparably fair-minded man."34

came to Israel, they would cause a disaster; he called them "scum." Ben-Gurion responded that it was best for "scum" to live in Palestine. "We will have troubles," he granted, "but at least the troubles will come from Jews."[39]

After the war, the envoys still tried to encourage the immigration of helpful and desirable "human material" and to delay the immigration of undesirables, especially right before Israel's War of Independence. During those months they sent the yishuv almost exclusively young people fit for combat. In the 1950s they again debated this point, and for a while even reinstituted what was then still called *selektsia*—that is, choosing candidates for immigration according to their country of origin, age, professional training, family status, and even, as in the past, party affiliation. Yet the dream that guided the Zionist movement before the Holocaust, of an ideal society that would in time create a new man out of the very best of European Jewry, was dead. The slaughter of the Jews forced the Zionists to recognize that it was necessary to bring all those who remained alive to Palestine immediately. One of the organizers of the immigration said that, in practice, they would have to take "everything that comes along," excepting only "absolutely antisocial types and un-reformable criminals."[40]

Once the Holocaust had forced the leaders of the Zionist movement to give up the principle of selection, they began to discover, for the first time, the Jews of the Islamic world. Until word of the extermination in Europe had begun to arrive, the Zionist movement had taken little interest in the Jews of North Africa and the Arab countries. "We were used to thinking of the Oriental Jews mostly as subjects for historical and anthropological research," one leader said.[41] The movement's roots were in Europe, and its activists, as Ben-Gurion said, "did not notice" the Jews of the Arab world.[42] The Holocaust dictated a new outlook. When one member of the Jewish Agency executive reported to Mapai on the Nazi exterminations, he immediately noted that some three-quarters of a million Jews lived in the Middle East and North Africa and that these henceforth would be Zionism's reservoir of immigration.[43]

The efforts to reach the Jews of the Moslem world and organize them for immigration were intensified as the dimensions of the European Holocaust became known. While there was also concern about the physical safety of these communities, as after the 1941 pogrom in Baghdad, the Jews of Islam were seen mainly as a replacement for the manpower lost in Europe. This, then, was the most dramatic effect of the Holocaust on the composition of Israeli society, culture, and politics. Hitler's rise to power had brought German Jews to Palestine; the extermination of European Jewry in the Holocaust brought Israel the Jews of the Arab world.

Records of the discussion of this issue reflect a certain regret among the leadership for not having discovered the Oriental Jews earlier, and a feeling, too, that more should be done for them than was done to save the Jews of Europe. "There's no need to wait until they slaughter them," Ben-Gurion said of Iraq's Jews. "We don't have to wait until 'Poland' repeats itself there."[44] Others agreed. "These Jews, at the slightest reversal of fortunes, are likely to become victims just like the Jews of Europe," said Moshe Shapira, a member of the Jewish Agency executive and later Israel's minister of the interior. Steps should be taken to rescue them immediately, he said. "In Europe we came too late," another member concurred. "Our reach was too short for us to come to the aid of millions of Jews and save them in time when it was still possible."[45]

The mass immigration satisfied the need for "working and fighting hands," as one Israeli leader said, and it was, after all, what the Zionist dream was all about.[46] At the same time there was a sense of guilt over the yishuv's failure to save Jews during the Holocaust. The Jews of the Arab world were brought to Israel in large numbers and at a rapid rate, with no selection and before anyone had any idea what to do with them. The main reason they were brought in so hastily was not only because it was feared that they were in immediate danger, but also because Israeli politicians knew that some day they themselves might be held accountable for the loss of another Jewish population. The same was true for the remaining Jews in Europe. The government of Israel paid some eastern European countries hundreds of dollars for each Jew allowed to come to Israel. When these payments came up for discussion, one member of the Jewish Agency executive said: "We have to live with our consciences. For that reason, we must know that we did everything that could be done!"[47]

7 | "A Certain Distance"

At the end of the war, Europe became a huge traffic jam. Some fourteen million displaced persons were trying to get home. They traveled in trains and cars, horse-drawn wagons and oxcarts. They rode bicycles and animals. Millions went by foot, crossing border after border in endless caravans. It was a period of twilight and chaos. Vast swaths of the continent were ruled by foreign armies, without proper administrative procedures. It was a paradise for smugglers, counterfeiters, traders, speculators, adventurers, and swindlers of all nations, many preying on the migrating refugees.

All told, there were about a million Jews remaining in the territories that had been under Nazi rule, most of them in Romania, Hungary, Czechoslovakia, Bulgaria, and Poland; many were on the road.[1] The migration began spontaneously, without plan. The Nazis were defeated. The concentration camps were liberated, and people set out, first of all, to search for their families; the hope of finding them alive had been a source of strength in the camps. Most of the wanderers turned east; others returned from the Soviet Union, to which they had fled during the war. Although in some places there were anti-Semitic attacks, most Jews were not in danger—they could have stayed where they were had they wanted to. Tens of thousands did in fact stay, at least for a time, even in Poland. Many who returned found their houses and property destroyed, plundered, or handed over to others. In a few countries there was talk of returning property, but the chances were almost nil. The Communist regimes did not look with favor on the small businesses and private enterprises that were the traditional trades of the urban Jews, and most of the Jews did not favor communism.

The heaviest blow for the refugees was not finding lost loved ones; and once they realized they were alone in the world, they no longer saw any reason to stay where they were. They began to return west, to look for a new life, far from the lands of devastation. Many of them mingled with the waves of German refugees expelled from the East.

Most of the Jews who reached central Europe from the East were forced to steal over the borders. Some progressed under cover of night, through forests and over mountain paths. For the most part illegal—and dangerous—this migration became known as the *briha*, the flight; the term refers both to the migration itself and to the apparatus that soon began to organize and aid the refugees. In the history of Israel, the briha is surrounded by a heroic halo, as if it had been an operation to save Jews during the Holocaust; nearly two years after the war was over, an article in *Davar* argued that the Holocaust was still raging.[2] In fact, the briha was initiated by the survivors themselves. Its first leaders had fought with the partisans. It is difficult to know how many of those streaming westward intended from the start to reach Palestine; tens of thousands went to the United States, Latin America, and other countries. Many were directed by soldiers of the Jewish Brigade stationed in Italy with the British army to settle near their bases or proceed to DP camps in Austria and Germany. The briha agents sent by the yishuv only arrived some months later and took it as their task to accelerate the briha to the West. Over the next two years this became, in fact, their exclusive operation, occupying about four hundred people.

The goal was to make the world aware that the future of the Jewish DPs was inseparably bound up with the future of Palestine—and that the two problems had a single solution: an independent state for the Jews. The more people in the camps, the greater the pressure on Great Britain to allow the inmates to go to Palestine. The pressure came from a number of sources: from New York and Washington, via public opinion and the lobbies of Jewish organizations, and from within the camps themselves. An Anglo-American commission that investigated the state of affairs in Palestine early in 1946 visited the DP camps as well. It recommended allowing 100,000 DPs to go to Palestine. When the recommendations were published in April 1946, one member of the Jewish Agency executive said that, in the five previous months, more than 68,000 Jews had been smuggled into the camps from the East, which, he believed, had had a decisive impact on the commission's conclusions. "Had there been only 40,000 there, I don't know what the results of the demand for 100,000 [immigration] certificates would have been," he said.*[3]

Before people could be sent west, though, it was necessary to identify travel routes and safe crossing points on the borders—not only between countries but also between zones of occupation. Along the way, the refugees had to evade all kinds of national and military officials trying to prevent their exit or entrance. Yet everywhere they found border guards and police who let them pass—officials who thought everything was legally in order, or who were bribed, or whose hearts went out to the refugees, or who wanted to get rid of them, or who simply were indifferent.

The success of the briha depended on taking advantage of every possibility. This required agreements with trustworthy guides and gave birth to an entire industry of document forgery. On one occasion, someone managed to obtain a Red Cross certificate declaring him a refugee returning to his homeland. Tens of thousands of copies were made of this certificate, in three languages—Hungarian, English, and Russian—all with the Red Cross seal. They identified the bearers as refugees from Greece returning from the East. Greece was not chosen by accident. The route to Greece went through Austria and Germany, where the DP camps were located.[5]

Before setting off, the refugees had to be gathered together; meeting points were conveyed by word of mouth. In general, these were abandoned warehouses or factory halls in the industrial zones of cities in central Poland. There, the travelers were organized into groups called "kibbutzim" and told what to bring with them, what not to bring, and what precautions to take along the way. Then they were brought to the border in trains or cars. They needed transport schedules, boarding arrangements, food, clothing, and blankets, and often medical treatment as well; the travelers included old people, pregnant women, and day-old babies. Often, the briha agents had trouble imposing discipline. Sometimes they assigned the refugees ID numbers.

---

* The 100,000 figure apparently grew out of a conversation between Chaim Weizmann and Winston Churchill in November 1944, some five months after Ben-Gurion had spoken of "a million immediately." Weizmann spoke with Churchill about a million and a half Jews who would immigrate to Palestine over the coming fifteen years—100,000 a year. A year later Earl Harrison, the American representative, visited the DP camps and also recommended giving the refugees 100,000 immigration certificates. President Truman accepted his recommendations, but the British rejected them.[4]

The journey from Poland sometimes took several days. In the North, movement was in the direction of Berlin via Szczecin (Stettin). The southern route crossed the Slovakian border; up to a thousand people a day went that way.[6] They continued by train to Bratislava, and from there via the Russian zone in Austria to Vienna. In Vienna they passed through a medical diagnostic center in a building that had once been the local Jewish community's Rothschild Hospital. From there they were taken by military trains to the American occupation zones in Austria and Germany. This leg of the journey was coordinated with the American military authorities, in the open. Most of the refugees were housed in two tent camps, one near Hamm, in central Germany, and the second next to Landshut, in the south. Each had space for 6,000 to 8,000 people. From here, they were transferred to other camps. At first these were run by the American army, but control was later handed over to the United Nations refugee agency, UNRRA. In the spring of 1947 the total number of Jewish DPs had approached a quarter of a million. Close to 160,000 were in the American zone in Germany, 40,000 in Austria, and nearly 20,000 in Italy.[7]

The briha operation required cash. During the war, the Sachsenhausen concentration camp had produced counterfeit British bank notes for the use of the Nazi secret services. After the war, many of these bills came into the hands of a Jewish businessman in Holland, who made them available to the briha. These bank notes served as one of the operation's first sources of funding.[8] In Poland, the briha was funded from the money of Jews who had managed to hide gold and jewelry during the war or who had already made profits in the black market. Some refused to part with their money, and briha agents had to come and take it by force.[9] Later, expenses were covered by contributions from Palestine and the American Jewish community, part of which came through the Joint Distribution Committee. The briha's success was largely determined by its agents' discernment, courage, and audacity. Dov Gur, a briha operative and Jewish Brigade member, then called Robert Grossman, related a story about smuggling refugees from Austria into Italy, en route to Palestine. His group would send trucks to a camp in Austria, where the British army was holding the refugees who had crossed the Soviet border. They would pick up the refugees and take them to the brigade's absorption camp. "For all intents and purposes we did this with the consent of the British, since the British commander did not know that he was forbidden to give us the people." But then one day, the camp commander was ordered not to allow the refugees to be taken away. Grossman persisted, however, arranging for the escape of four hundred people.

A week later he was called up before the brigade commander, who notified him that he had been accused of taking the refugees from the camp and asked what he had to say for himself. "I told him: 'I stole the people because I had no other choice,' " Grossman recalled.

> To his question as to whether I knew that I could be court-martialed, I answered in the affirmative and added: "But you yourself knew about my activities and conspired with me to keep it quiet." Upon hearing this, the commander removed his monocle and asked: "How do you spell 'Grossman'—with one 's' or two?" I said with two. He looked at the paper in front of him and said: "Then it's not you. Here they've written 'Grosman' with one 's.' " So he informed his superiors that he did not have an officer by that name.[10]

When the British began to demobilize the Jewish Brigade and send its men home, some of the men decided to stay on to continue organizational and propaganda activity among the refugees. This is how it was done: A few men from the brigade volunteered to disguise themselves as refugees, borrowing identities and documents from real DPs. To keep the British from noting their absence, they decided to infiltrate refugees in British uniforms into the brigade. This was not simple. At first, it was necessary to locate resourceful men among the refugees who looked more or less like the soldiers who were to remain in Europe. They had to be given some minimum training so that their British officers would not notice that they were out of place—"present arms," "shoulder arms," "yes, sir," "no, sir." The right uniforms had to be found—not too new—and, finally, the men had to be transferred from the DP camps in Germany to the brigade's base, which had moved in the meantime to Belgium. A special operation was required.

One day, a soldier in the brigade died while he was, by chance, in the British occupation zone in Germany. The regimental commander ordered the body brought to the base in Belgium. Three soldiers were sent to accompany it. This was the opportunity the Jewish soldiers had been waiting for. First, they changed the number on the pass from 3 to 30, allowing them to sneak 30 disguised refugees into the brigade's base. They found candidates among the survivors of Bergen-Belsen. Then they discovered that there were five possible border crossings. So they formed five different funeral processions that went through each of the five points at the same time, each with an honor guard of 30 (all of them imposters), each with a casket containing another imposter playing dead, for a grand total of 154 playacting soldiers and one real dead body.

The result was that over a hundred men from the brigade were able to remain in Europe. Each borrowed the identity of a refugee, and the refugees arrived in Palestine in the summer of 1946, disguised as soldiers.[11]

Ruth Aliav has related another story that belongs in that gray area between courage and impropriety, perhaps between reality and imagination: When Ben-Gurion was in Germany, she was assigned to arrange the meeting between him and Eisenhower. While she was waiting for the general in his office, she suddenly noticed a document lying on his table. It was a top-secret copy of the Harrison report. "Somehow, it got into my purse, I don't know how," she said years later. Chaim Weizmann gave her a kiss on the forehead when she brought him the document, and Ben-Gurion told her: "Our history will not forget you."[12]

§

About seven months after the end of the war, in December 1945, a Jewish Agency delegation from Palestine arrived in Europe. Haim Yahil, who led it, later recounted that its original purpose had been "to extend basic assistance to the few twigs that had been saved from the furnace fires." The delegation was organized, he wrote, as an "aid force," but in fact he soon came to feel that history had charged it with enlisting the refugees in the great Jewish revolution.[13] To do this, he had to ensure that the refugees, instead of settling in Europe, waited until they could be taken to Palestine.

A certain amount of "tension, disquiet, and ferment" was necessary, he believed, if the refugees were to be turned into a "great popular movement" and an "active Jewish force." The moment was unique. Sensing, as Yahil wrote, "that the window of opportunity for the creation of such a force was liable to close very quickly," the delegation decided that its most important activity was to accelerate Jewish migration from eastern Europe to the American occupation zone and from there to the embarkation points for illegal immigration to Palestine.[14]

Yahil took one side in a dispute between two groups with opposing views. One group held that everything should be done to keep Jews from settling where they were, in Germany and other countries. The opposing group favored rehabilitating the prewar communities. Thus the Joint Distribution Committee continually came under attack in the Zionist executive for helping Jews build new lives in Europe. "I fear the danger of the Communist vermin uniting with the Joint," Ben-Gurion said. He called the Jewish Communists of eastern Europe "the dregs of Judaism." Another Jewish leader hypothesized even earlier that a "common front" against Zionism, combining the Joint and the Communists, could come into being. Ben-Gurion set forth the following rules: "1. The Jewish Agency does not deal in aid and reconstruction in the Diaspora; it works to strengthen the Zionist movement in Palestine. 2. We must, to the extent we can, keep the Joint from taking over and prevent the reinforcement of anti-Zionist trends within Judaism by its sole control over the distribution of aid. 3. [We must] concentrate immigration and all auxiliary activities in the Jewish Agency." Some time later, Ben-Gurion said to one of the movement's envoys to Europe: "It is the job of Zionism not to save the remnant of Israel in Europe but rather to save the land of Israel for the Jewish people and the yishuv." Eliahu Dobkin warned that the refugees were facing a decision about what to do with themselves. Their desire to come to Palestine was "hanging by a hair." Much depended on the Zionist movement's ability to appear among them "with all its strength."[15]

By the end of the first year after the war, there were yishuv envoys in most of the camps, working as teachers, counselors, nurses, doctors, lecturer-propagandists, and administrators. Soon offices would be set up in various locations, something like embassies of the state-to-be. Their goal was to attract as many DPs as possible to the Zionist movement and its struggle, to instill in them a desire to settle in Palestine, and to distribute the few immigration certificates available. Tens of thousands of refugees without certificates became maapilim.

On Friday, July 18, 1947, just before the Sabbath twilight settled over Palestine, a passenger ship arrived in Haifa: *Exodus 1947*. Like several other haapala ships, this one had been purchased in the United States; its original name was the *President Warfield*.* It had spent its early days

* The ship was named for the president of the company that built it, not after the American president James A. Garfield, as many journalists mistakenly thought. The man who proposed the name *Exodus 1947* was Moshe Sneh, a Haganah commander and future leader of the Israeli Communist party. Moshe Sharett would later say that it had been "a name of genius." A Hebrew translation was to have been added but was never painted on the ship. Signs carried by the passengers displayed only the name *Exodus*, in English. One photograph of the vessel was later doctored to make it look as if the boat had been inscribed with the Hebrew name as well.[16]

on the Baltimore-Norfolk line, carrying vacationers and honeymooners. During World War II the ship was given to Britain as part of the Lend-Lease arrangement. Ironically, it was the British who armored it, thus preparing it for its Zionist mission after the war. On the verge of being sold for scrap iron, it was bought by a front company for the Haganah's Mossad—the haapala organization—for $50,000 and reincarnated as a symbol of the haapala.

Its purchase, outfitting, the swearing in of its crew, even the details of its mission, were no secret. American newspapermen were invited to cover the story, which included ceremonies and celebrations preceding the sailing. From the very start, it was intended as a public-relations tool for the Zionist movement. Among those who read about it was the British ambassador to the United States. He sent press clippings to London. By the time the ship reached Port-de-Bouc, the port near Marseilles, France, where its passengers boarded, the British knew everything they needed to know about the boat and its journey, including the names of its crew members, almost all of them American Jewish volunteers. The British made a series of diplomatic contacts in an effort to prevent the launching of the ship; Foreign Minister Ernest Bevin was personally involved. In the meantime, the Mossad had removed about 4,500 displaced Jews from camps in Germany and had brought them to France, sometimes by using counterfeit immigration certificates. French officials either actively helped or conveniently looked the other way.

Historian Aviva Halamish has suggested that the passengers were chosen hastily and that for this reason there were relatively fewer people with "pioneer" political training and identity than there had been on previous ships. There were pregnant women and hundreds of infants. Halamish was trying to repudiate the charge that the haapala activists included them intentionally to add to the human drama and symbolism of the journey. Yet there is good reason to believe that they were also thinking of the press; when the first baby was born on board, the news was telegraphed to the entire world.

The British committed every possible error. Ben-Gurion once said that "The best British propaganda for Zionism is the [DP] camp at Bergen-Belsen. They behave like Nazis there."[17] Their harshness in the *Exodus* affair also played into Zionist hands. While the *Exodus* was still outside Palestinian territorial waters, it was surrounded by six battleships of the Royal Navy. One of them rammed the hull, and its sailors took the ship by force, using live ammunition. The passengers threw bottles and cans at the British soldiers, attacking them with iron rods and hatchets and trying to spray them with boiling oil. The British opened fire. Three passengers were killed, including a fifteen-year-old boy, and dozens were injured, some seriously. These were not the last victims; before the journey was over there would be more dead, including a one-day-old baby who was buried at sea in a tin box lowered into the Bay of Biscay. The poet Natan Alterman made the baby into a national hero.[18] Among those who came to greet the *Exodus* when it reached the port of Haifa were two members of a commission of inquiry sent by the UN to Palestine to make recommendations for a solution to the Jewish-Arab conflict. Golda Meir later wrote that in attacking the *Exodus* the British made a notable contribution to the commission's final recommendations.[19]

Even after they attacked the ship, in violation of the accepted rules, the British could have minimized the propaganda value of the *Exodus* to the Zionist movement had they diverted the passengers to Cyprus. But instead they transferred them to three British ships and sent them back to Port-de-Bouc, from which they had originally sailed. The French did not allow the passengers to be disembarked against their will, and the passengers, except for a few dozen, refused to leave the ship. The drama lasted three weeks, the Zionist movement making the most of it. Journalists from around the world, dispatched to the port, described the would-be immigrants as prisoners in a "floating Auschwitz." The world had not been swept by such a wave of sympathy for Jewish suffering since the day the first reporters entered the concentration camps.*

Then, when it looked as if the media were losing interest in the story, the British made another mistake. They announced they would return the illegals to the British zone of occupation in Germany. This was foolish; the Jewish Agency did not miss the story. Only Chaim Weizmann, it seemed, was tempted to spare the passengers the shock of returning to Germany. He was concerned about the suffering that awaited them and urged them to disembark in France. But Ben-Gurion succeeded in neutralizing Weizmann's efforts in another one of those clashes that broke out between the two from time to time. The agency had an interest in

---

* Each of the three ships had representatives of the yishuv on board, some of whom had succeeded in sneaking on after the ship arrived at Port-de-Bouc. One disguised himself as a bread deliveryman, another hid in a crate of food that was loaded onto the deck. The haapala agents rented motorboats that circled the three ships and broadcast encouraging slogans and instructions over loudspeakers; they managed to smuggle letters to and from the boat nearly every day.

the sentimental and symbolic aspects of deportation to Germany. In September 1947, two months after leaving the DP camps, the people of the *Exodus* found themselves on the shores of a "cursed" country, as they called Germany, in two fenced-in camps not far from Lübeck on the Baltic seacoast.

David Ben-Gurion and the leaders of the Jewish Agency continued to object, in principle, to flagrant violation of the Mandatory immigration laws. Yet they now had to support the haapala in order not to seem helpless, idle, and unpatriotic and so as to give the Haganah, which carried out much of the briha and haapala activities, an outlet for the national revolutionary sentiment that erupted during those days of creation. It was necessary, too, to counter the intensive illegal activity of the right-wing underground factions. The haapala also created ferment in the DP camps and rallied people together around the Zionist struggle in general and the haapala agents in particular.

In the three years between the end of the war and Israel's declaration of independence, some 140 ships sailed from Europe, carrying more than 70,000 maapilim. Yet most of the vessels were apprehended before reaching the shores of Palestine. The British commandeered them and put the passengers in prison camps, first in Atlit, near Haifa, and then in Cyprus. About half these prisoners were eventually allowed to enter Palestine as part of the monthly quota of legal immigrants. The illegal operation did not, then, bring the yishuv many more people than would have come legally; from that point of view it was futile. It also did not ensure better "human material." The British authorities rarely interfered with the choice of candidates for immigration, leaving it to the Jewish Agency. The same people could have been sent legally. The Jewish Agency and the Haganah did not generally try to use force to resist the apprehension of the ships and their passengers; the detention of the illegals in the internment camps and their deportation to Cyprus were carried out more or less in accordance with established rules, generally without violence. The deportations did not cause any real difficulties in relations between the Jewish Agency leadership and the authorities. In general, these continued to be, as before, practical and correct. The reason was that smuggling people into the country was no longer the operation's major goal. The major purpose of illegal immigration after the Holocaust was the operation itself—as a weapon in the struggle for the creation and control of a Jewish state.

The Mossad, which was in charge of the haapala, operated, like the Palmach, as an arm of the Haganah. Like that militia, it developed its own values and operating methods, which did not always mesh with the instructions it received from the Jewish Agency and the Haganah command. Haapala activists bought ships, manned them, took care of the technical and legal preparations for sailing, brought the people through the briha to the port of embarkation, gave them instructions for their voyage, put them on the ships, accompanied them and protected them along the way. Sometimes they not only commanded the boats but navigated them. On arriving at the Palestinian coast, they smuggled the passengers ashore. If the British discovered and arrested the refugees, the haapala agents went with them to the prison camps. They worked in coordination with the Palmach, sometimes also disagreeing with them.

The ships bore carefully chosen, imaginative, hope-inspiring names. One or two of the names were meant for international consumption, but most were meant to raise morale in the yishuv: *Af Al Pi Chen* ("Despite It All"), *Lo Tafihidunu* ("You Will Not Frighten Us"), and *Lanitzahon* ("To Victory"). Some of the names memorialized the Israeli-Arab war for control of the country, like *Yerushalaim Hanetzura* ("Jerusalem Besieged"). None of the names was taken from Jewish religious sources or from the Bible, and only a few from the Diaspora, mostly names of heroes of the Zionist movement, like the *Theodor Herzl*. One name that symbolized Israeli heroism was notable by its absence: Masada. This was because the ships were supposed to broadcast a message of struggle and life, not defeat and suicide. The Holocaust was also absent from the names, as if it had never happened or as if it were somehow shameful. One ship was called *Mordei Hagetaot* ("The Ghetto Rebels"). [20]

The founders and leaders of the Mossad were mostly kibbutz members, idealistic men and a few women who could count on their kibbutzim to support their families while they volunteered for a national mission. In contrast to most of the Palmach, they had been born overseas and came to Israel as young Zionists. Most were in their forties and fifties, considerably older than the members of the Palmach. They were married, and many had been involved in public activity at their kibbutzim, in their political parties, or in the Histadrut. They had only limited formal education, but they were experienced, knew languages, and valued secrecy.

At their head stood Shaul Meirov (Avigur) from Kvutsat Kineret, born in Russia, who was among the first members of the Haganah's intelligence service and a Ben-Gurion loyalist. A dry, humorless type, he was imbued with a sense of mission and addicted to secrecy; people found him charismatic.

The haapala activists knew and enlisted one another, linked not only by the labor movement and a single, somewhat Spartan ethic but also by mutual loyalty and a sense of the nobility of national service. Aside from organizing the briha and immigration, both legal and illegal, they also enlisted soldiers and purchased military equipment needed by Israel in the War of Independence. These operations often required secret diplomacy and covert activities. The future state's top leadership came from their ranks—managers, diplomats, generals. Some of them were among the founders of Israel's security and intelligence services, part of which would also be called Mossad. The briha, illegal immigration, and arms purchases during the prestate days prepared them well for the tasks they assumed after independence.[21]

Before the *Exodus* refugees arrived in Germany, Shaul Avigur proposed that Ben-Gurion instruct them to violently resist being landed on German soil. Ben-Gurion answered that the passengers had done enough, that they should not be ordered to act in a way that could lead to bloodshed. From Ben-Gurion's point of view, the haapala had served its purpose: it had persuaded the world that the Jewish people needed their own state. With the United Nations Special Commission on Palestine (UNSCOP) drafting its recommendations, it was now important to maintain the lowest possible profile.

But someone in the haapala command refused to obey. One of the three deportation ships was sabotaged with a bomb smuggled onto it while it was still in France. Ben-Gurion demanded an investigation; both the attack on the ship and the haapala itself now seemed to him a challenge to his authority, damaging to the political interests of the Zionist movement. At that time, he was trying to persuade UNSCOP that the Jews in Palestine wanted only peace and stability, that, if given the opportunity, they would know how to manage the country's affairs wisely.

At the end of August 1947, UNSCOP recommended the partition of Palestine into two states, one for Jews and one for Arabs. The UN General Assembly accepted the recommendations on November 29. For the first time, the way was open for fulfillment of the Zionist dream. It had not been easy to get the necessary majority in the UN. The lobbying, pressures, inducements, and intrigues before the vote put the Zionist movement's diplomatic skills to an unparalleled test. Meanwhile, it became known that the haapala agency was about to launch two more ships, the *Pan York* and the *Pan Crescent*—in Hebrew, the *Kibbutz Galuyot* ("Ingathering of the Exiles") and the *Atsmaut* ("Independence"). The two ships together carried close to 15,000 immigrants, three times the number that had been on the *Exodus* (which had itself been larger than any of its predecessors)—almost 25 percent of all the maapilim who had set out from the end of the war until the establishment of the state. In response to pressures from the American State Department, the launch of the *Pans* was delayed until after the vote on the partition resolution. Yet, even after the UN made its decision, the Jewish Agency leadership believed that the ships should not sail. "Statehood is not in our pockets," Ben-Gurion said to justify his objection to the operation, in opposition to Shaul Avigur. It was a very dramatic dispute. Some 15,000 people had been taken from their homes and were sitting on bundles of their belongings, ready to set out, Avigur reported. They had fled hunger and snow; they could not be sent back now. Gathered by special trains from all over Romania, they were waiting in special camps set up after protracted and complex negotiations with the Romanian and Bulgarian governments. Any further delay in their trip would lead to a violent uprising. Who knew what might happen? Perhaps the entire immigration operation would be destroyed.

Ben-Gurion refused to change his mind. He had always warned against large contingents of illegal immigrants, he asserted, but no one had listened to him. He did not want to decide what was more important, he said: bringing the immigrants to Palestine or the political struggle of which the illegal immigration movement was a part. Either way, the goal was to discomfit the British, and a large number of small boats was more annoying than a small number of large ships. No one had openly disagreed with him; they had just gone and done the opposite, Ben-Gurion complained. Now the state-to-be was facing a decisive moment: a war was about to begin. "I don't know what will be next week," Ben-Gurion said. So this was not the time to provoke the rest of the world; the country could not afford tension or war now. Here Ben-Gurion lashed out at Avigur: "At this delicate moment, when our entire existence in this country is in danger, [you come] with such a provocation. Are you willing to take responsibility? I'm amazed at your self-assurance!" Avigur said that he was thinking of the immigrants in terms of his kibbutz, Kineret. Each of the two ships carried enough people to set up twelve to thirteen new Kinerets. But Ben-Gurion responded in what seems to have summarized his entire worldview: "Security is even more important than immigration!"[22] In the end, of course, it was not possible to abandon 15,000 people after they had been uprooted. The British also understood this. They agreed to allow the *Pans* to sail straight to Cyprus.

Most of the yishuv remained indifferent to the plight of the maapilim. Only a small number attended demonstrations against their deportation. Even fewer contributed to funding the struggle: a special collection proclaimed for this purpose had failed. Most of the maapilim were the kind of "human material" the yishuv wanted, but each one allowed to remain in the country meant one less immigration certificate for others, at a time when thousands were applying for permits for relatives in the camps. The British rejected these applications, saying they had had no choice but to grant the certificates to illegals who had forced their way into the country.

The hundreds of Zionist envoys and briha agents had not arrived in Europe only in the name of the land of Israel. Most came also in the service of a political party. The great majority saw the "remnant" not just as potential soldiers or future citizens but as eventual voters. The envoys came to Europe to fight for their souls in uncompromising combat that at times turned violent. Each party tried to put its people in control of the committees that governed the DP camps and assumed that the refugees would continue to support them once they arrived in Palestine. "The movements hand out money, supplementary allowances, gifts, in order to kidnap people," Eliahu Dobkin told members of his party, Mapai. He reported fights with fists and knives, even exchanges of gunfire. People were sent to specific camps to influence the political composition of the DP population. "There is one god," Dobkin said, "the party. Nothing else exists; there is no common interest."[23]

Dobkin was not a disinterested champion of Jewish unity: at that time, unity happened to be of vital concern to Mapai. About a year before the end of the war, in March 1944, internal tensions there had reached the breaking point, and the party split. The faction that walked out founded a new, more radical, more rebellious, more militant, younger party. Ahdut Haavodah ("Worker Unity") was more hawkish in its attitudes toward the conflict with the Arabs and in its Zionist policy and further left in its socialist ideology. It represented, for the most part, the kibbutzim that belonged to Hakibbutz Hameuhad, the largest of the kibbutz movements.[24] Mapai called the split "treason."[25] People's deep involvement with their parties and their perception of every political dispute as a life-or-death battle had not changed as a consequence of the war—the Holocaust had not given the yishuv a different sense of proportion or new criteria for judgment.

Competition among the movements gave rise to harsh accusations. Hashomer Hatsair activists charged that Mapai envoys were impeding their people in the DP camps and discriminating against them in housing allocation and food distribution.* This was, they said, "a holdover from the totalitarian methods of Germany." Ben-Gurion wrote to his wife, Paula, that "some mistakes" had indeed been made and that Hashomer Hatsair's claims were, to some extent, justified.[26] Mapai activists feared the charisma of Hashomer Hatsair counselors, as that movement called its envoys. "The counselors are little Stalins," complained one party leader. Another said the DPs considered the counselors "Führers."[27] Parties also accused one another of "kidnapping children"—that is, attempting to gain control of the educational system.

With yishuv Zionists expanding their influence over life in the DP camps, the religious parties also began demanding their fair share. As in the fight over the Tehran children, they demanded religious education, prayers, public Sabbath observance, and kosher food in the camps. A dispute ensued: "We are teaching hypocrisy and lies to the children," fumed Golda Meir.[28] The religious parties made a considerable effort to locate Jewish children who had been given to Christian foster families or hidden in convents during the war. This "redemption of the children" also offered a way to influence the voters of the future.

Most of the envoys from Palestine were from the labor movement. With the briha becoming a quasi-official operation, the Revisionist movement demanded its fair share, too. Some Revisionists organized their own haapala convoys. The enmity between the two groups sometimes took on the character of a gang war. In September 1947 several dozen young people, led by members of the Revisionist youth movement, Betar, entered a briha transit camp in Gnadewald, not far from Innsbruck, Austria, apparently intending to capture it and thereby win control of one of the briha routes. But perhaps they simply wanted revenge for the time when camp residents arrested and beat some people they believed were exploiting the briha route from the East for smuggling. The suspects may not have belonged to Betar, but the Betar men used them as a pretext to force their way into the camp. They broke into the radio room, where the radiomen surrendered without a fight. One, though, was sleeping. They woke him, but apparently he did not immediately comprehend

* Hashomer Hatsair: Socialist Zionist group with its own kibbutz federation and, after 1948, its own political party, Mapam. More Marxist and generally more ideologically socialist than Mapai, Hashomer Hatsair was at that time in sympathy with some parts of the international Communist party line.

what was happening. When they told him to put his hands up, he groggily said something like "leave me alone," and they shot and killed him. The victim was Eitan Avidov from Nahalal, son of a well-known labor-movement figure. The murder reflected the great tension between left and right: Haim Yahil maintained that at one point the DPs were close to civil war.[29]

Within months after the war's end a whole network of political groups operated in the DP camps, running a number of representative and organizational bodies. Elected committees spoke for the displaced persons, represented them to the occupying armies and welfare organizations, and accepted responsibility for preserving the public peace in the camps. Here and there, internal courts were established in accordance with interparty agreements. There were groups that organized cultural and educational activities and provided religious services and vocational training, including "pioneer" training on German farms close to the camps. In time, the assignment of places and beds in the camp barracks and the distribution of blankets, clothing, food, mail, and even medical care were accomplished under arrangements that reflected the relative strength of the different parties in the camps. From time to time there were elections and referendums, more or less democratic, all as part of Zionist politics. *[30]

Life in the detention camps in Cyprus was also run by the parties, strictly according to quotas. Some 20,000 people stayed in these camps. On entry, inmates were required to state the party they belonged to or the one they wished to join. Then that party saw to all their needs. They lived with their party comrades, ate food from a party kitchen, participated in cultural activities organized by their party, and chose their party's representatives to the camp's administrative bodies.

David Shaari, a Jewish Agency envoy, wrote that in Cyprus, as in the DP camps of Europe, the politicization of life was inescapable. Hardest was the fate of the "solitaries," the refugees who refused to accept a party label. The party agents treated them as foreigners. "They live the life of

* It was, perhaps, the high politicization, the sense of history, or an appreciation of the value of the collective morale that made the envoys pay special attention to the symbolic aspects of their work in Germany. They once held an assembly in the same famous Munich beer cellar in which Hitler had staged his abortive putsch; another time they gathered in the village of Berchtesgaden, at the foot of Hitler's "Eagle's Nest." One group of DPs was intentionally sent to receive agricultural training at the farm that had belonged to Julius Streicher, editor of *Der Stürmer*.[31]

the past," one of them observed. "How will they manage in Israel? They have no direct contact with anyone. . . . They have ceased to see themselves giving to the public. They want only to receive."[32]

"Our attitude toward the remnant," wrote Haim Yahil, "was determined not by humanitarian motives alone but above all in accordance with an evaluation of the role they were to play in our struggle. For this reason, we were not always gentle. Despite all our sympathy for the survivors' plight and their fundamental demands, we have kept a certain distance between them and us. . . . We have not declared that the remnant and the Land of Israel are one and the same; rather, we have emphasized that the remnant must exert great mental and physical effort in order to unite with the yishuv."[33]

8 | *"Six Million Germans"*

A few months after the war in Europe, a Holocaust survivor arrived in Palestine with a plan for vengeance. Abba Kovner, then twenty-seven years old, had been a ghetto defender, a partisan fighter in the forests, an activist in the socialist Hashomer Hatsair movement, a poet, and a visionary. He was short, with sharp, ascetic, melancholy features, flashing eyes, and wavy hair. "A classic specimen of the Jewish intellectual," an acquaintance wrote.[1] People attributed to him compelling power to influence people, and many regarded him as a living symbol of Jewish resistance to the Nazis, a spiritual and moral authority. It was he who wrote that the Jews should not go like lambs to the slaughter.

Many years later Kovner admitted that any normal person should have seen madness in his plan. And he was quite correct, because what he had done was to enlist a group of other young Holocaust survivors to poison the drinking water of several major West German cities; they hoped to murder six million Germans.[2]

"The force that motivates them is the desire for revenge," reported a Jewish Agency leader returning from a mission among Holocaust survivors.[3] Ample testimony confirms this. Years later, eight out of ten young survivors recalled that at war's end they longed for vengeance: no other emotion was so widespread among them—not agony nor anxiety, happiness nor hope.[4] Tzivia Lubetkin, a leader of the Warsaw ghetto uprising, remembered her first surprised reaction when she heard that in the city of Lublin, Poland, 15,000 Jews had survived but did not know what to do with themselves now that the war was over. "We knew what to do," she declared. "If we could find people and if we had the means, there was only this to do: to avenge! We did not then feel the urge to build; rather we felt the desire to destroy, to destroy all we could, as much as we could!"[5] It was in Lublin, on the outskirts of which lay the Majdanek extermination camp, that Abba Kovner and his comrades founded their avenging force.

The idea was born among young Jews serving in the ranks of the Ukrainian partisans. "There were many debates," Yitzhak Avidov, then called Pasha Reichman, would later remember. The question was: What would happen "the day after"? No one was thinking yet of a grand operation against the entire German people, only of a revenge scheme against local populations. Some joined the Soviet secret police, the NKVD, and found opportunities to liquidate Nazi collaborators. Others tried to organize the westward flight of Jews from the Soviet Union. At one point they went to Lublin to meet other young partisan veterans, among them Abba Kovner.[6]

Kovner had joined the partisans after the collapse of the resistance in the Vilna ghetto. He had been a leader of that uprising. Toward the end of the war, he argued that the Jewish partisans should continue to fight as a guerrilla force that could be parachuted into Prussia. He presented the plan to the Jewish Brigade, which rejected it. His comrades from the forest did too, demanding that all efforts be concentrated on evacuating people to the West, and thence to Palestine. Kovner was active in such work for a time, helping people "escape from the land of the Holocaust to the land of the living," but soon became possessed by the idea of revenge.[7]

Reichman's people had heard of Kovner before they met him in Lublin. He won their hearts in an instant. "It was love at first sight," Reichman, now Avidov, recalled. Kovner was older; he radiated leadership. The group lived together in an apartment. One evening they were sitting and drinking, and the conversation turned to revenge. "It came of itself," Avidov said in a deposition he recorded for the Hebrew University's Institute for Oral Documentation. "We sat with our glasses and the idea flew out of us and suddenly it was no longer in the air but on the table. . . . Everyone wanted revenge."

Then someone said it: mass murder of the Germans, by the millions. This person knew of a plant that grew in India from which poison could be produced. "We were very excited," Avidov related. "We were young and reckless." Kovner also liked the idea.

Thus the Nakam (Revenge) organization was born, with a command echelon of five members. Each enlisted additional members. At one point they moved to Bucharest. One day, according to Avidov, they gathered clandestinely as if to celebrate the birth of their organization. There were already more than forty people. Kovner spoke and swept everyone away, as always. "There was no doubt that we were taking action that God himself, were there a God, would have taken," Avidov related.[8]

Kovner would later recount that the idea obsessed the group and that they "sanctified" themselves to it. He said they saw themselves as messengers of fate. Kovner described their mental state in those days: "The destruction was not around us. It was within us. . . . We did not imagine that we could return to life, or that we had the right to do so, to come to the Land of Israel, to establish families, to get up in the morning and work as if accounts with the Germans had been settled."[9] This was, in essence, an accounting between two nations. To be true revenge it had to precisely equal the dimensions of the crime. Kovner therefore set six million German citizens as his goal. He thought in apocalyptic terms: revenge was a holy obligation that would redeem and purify the Jewish people. The group divided into cells, each with a commander. Their primary goal, Plan A, was "to poison as many Germans as possible." Plan B was to poison several thousand former SS men in the American army's POW camps. Reichman succeeded in infiltrating some members of the group into the Hamburg and Nuremberg water companies. Kovner went to Palestine to bring the poison—and, he hoped, to receive the blessing of the Haganah.

Kovner was well known in Palestine and was invited to address the Histadrut central committee. He spoke of the Holocaust and the survivors. He did not even hint at his plan for revenge.[10] Apparently, he confided in only a handful of individuals, none of whom shared his enthusiasm for revenge.

The idea also aroused opposition within his movement, Hashomer Hatsair. Kovner and his comrades came out of the Holocaust with a feeling that the political divisiveness that preceded the war was outdated. They did not disavow their previous affiliation; yet they now identified more as survivors than as members of any particular party. They saw themselves as "a party of witnesses" whose duty it was to proclaim ceaselessly that the Jewish nation was still in danger. Pointing to the hatred of Jews in the Soviet Union, he said that there was no future for Jews outside Palestine, and that national unity was all-important.

This last idea brought down on them the anger of Hashomer Hatsair's leader Meir Yaari. Yaari did not want unity; on the contrary, he wanted to rebuild Hashomer Hatsair as an independent political entity. He refused to accept the possibility that the movement would cease to exist in Poland, where it had been born and where, he believed, its political reserves still lay. He rejected criticism of the Soviet Union. Kovner, with his past as a terrorist and partisan, his involvement in covert revenge operations, and his charisma, aroused Yaari's suspicions. Yaari said that Kovner suffered from the same syndrome that afflicted demobilized soldiers after World War I—that of trying "to start history all over again" by continuing in peacetime to live the life of the front and the underground, unable to relearn "the heroism of everyday routine." The worldview that Kovner and his men brought with them from the forests was based, according to Yaari, on "parafascist" concepts. He proposed sending them for "reeducation."[11]

Soon after arriving in Palestine, Kovner wrote to Pasha Reichman that the Haganah would never approve Plan A but that it might be possible to find someone who would look the other way if they carried out Plan B. Kovner would later relate that he had succeeded in obtaining a large quantity of poison and that the man who helped him get it was none other than Chaim Weizmann, leader of the Zionist Organization, who would become the first president of Israel. Professor Weizmann was a chemist by training.

Kovner described Weizmann as listening, deep in thought, to the plan. At first he was silent. Finally, Kovner related, Weizmann, then seventy-one, rose and said: "Were I younger and in your place, I might do the very same thing." Kovner did not say whether he told Weizmann of the plan to poison six million Germans or only about the "small plan" to poison prisoners of war. According to Kovner, Weizmann sent him to a scientist whom he asked to prepare the poison. In his recorded testimony, which he demanded be kept secret, Kovner identified the scientist as Ernst David Bergman, later a father of Israel's nuclear project. Bergman knew only that the substance was needed for action against former Nazis, and he did not ask for details. Kovner packed the material in milk cans. Weizmann also sent him, he claimed, to someone who gave him money. This, Kovner said, was Hans Moller, founder of Ata, a major textile concern. Kovner bought gold with the money and hid it in toothpaste tubes. Then he began to plan his return trip.

Kovner has remained the sole source for this part of the story. The

Weizmann archives contain no mention of a discussion with Kovner; Weizmann was out of the country at the time. It is possible, then, that the poet dreamed up the meeting. He may have wished, after the fact, to claim official support for his plan of revenge. But the rest of the story can be confirmed from other sources.

In December 1945 Kovner disguised himself as a soldier in the Jewish Brigade and sailed for Europe on a ship of the British fleet, pretending, with the help of the Haganah, to be returning to his unit from a furlough. In his recorded testimony, he said he assumed that the Haganah command was well aware of who he was and the nature of his mission. But again he did not say, and was not asked, whether he meant the "big plan" or only Plan B. He mentioned two names: Yitzhak Sadeh, the legendary commander of the Palmach, and Shaul Avigur of the Mossad. Yisrael Galili, who would later be a senior minister in Golda Meir's cabinet, was also informed. Kovner received forged transport documents and the brigade uniform he needed, as well as an escort from the Haganah, to help him in time of need. Had he succeeded in carrying out his plan, then, it would not have been possible to say that he had acted on his own.

His trip was a failure. Just before the boat entered the port of Toulon, in France, Kovner heard his name being paged over the ship's loudspeaker. He was ordered to present himself to the captain. "The call was repeated several times," Kovner related. "I immediately went to the soldier who was my escort from the Haganah and asked him, 'What does it mean?' He said, 'It's probably a call for guard duty, as usual.' I knew only a few words of English, but the tone of the voice on the loudspeaker sounded suspicious to me."

Up to that point, his escort knew only that Kovner was not a brigade soldier. He knew nothing of the mission. Kovner decided to tell him. He showed him the poison and told him that if anything happened, he should take it to such and such a place or, if necessary, destroy it. He also gave him the gold. Then, on second thought, he decided not to trust the young man. Before reporting to the captain, he threw half the poison out the bathroom porthole, into the sea. He went up on the deck—and was arrested immediately.

Kovner was jailed in a military prison in Cairo for about four months. The British apparently never asked him about his revenge plan. They did not know about the poison; actually, it seems that they did not really know why they had arrested him. His imprisonment remains a mystery.

Kovner was convinced to the end of his days that someone turned him in to sabotage his mission. The rest of the poison was lost, too: his escort, afraid to keep it, threw it into the water. He did, however, get the gold to its destination.[12]

Pasha Reichman was now alone. He felt responsible to history and to his people, and he worried about the safety of his men. They continued to work in the Hamburg and Nuremberg waterworks, in a state of almost intolerable tension, pretending to be part of a German society they abhorred and plotted to destroy, always in danger that their true identities would be revealed. They had already pinpointed where they would mix the poison into the water mains. In Nuremberg they even succeeded in locating the valves of pipes that led to the residential neighborhoods where American military personnel and their families lived. The avengers planned to spare those lives. All was ready. All they needed was the poison.

When Reichman learned that Kovner had been arrested and the poison lost, he decided to proceed with Plan B. It was not easy to explain the change to his people, he later recalled. They all believed they were going to kill six million Germans and now were being told to satisfy themselves with a thousand. "It was a tragedy," Reichman related. He promised them that the big plan had simply been postponed for a while.[13] Reichman had earlier turned to Yitzhak "Antek" Zuckerman—a leader of the Warsaw ghetto uprising and husband of Tzivia Lubetkin—and proposed that Zuckerman now lead the avengers in place of Kovner. Zuckerman refused. "If I thought we could destroy the German people, nation against nation, I would have joined," he later recounted. "But to poison wells or a river? To cause a plague? Say we liquidated ten thousand—what would be the point? . . . Despite it all, a little Jewish humanism remained within us, even after all they did to us." He saw among Kovner's band "counterfeit romanticism," "false messianism," and madness.[14]

On April 13, 1946, some members of the organization stole into the bakery that supplied bread to the Stalag 13 POW camp, not far from Nuremberg. They spread flourlike white arsenic powder on the bottoms of a few thousand loaves of bread but were interrupted as they worked and had to flee. The police, assuming a burglary attempt, did not notice that the bread had been poisoned, so it was shipped to the camp. A few days later, the Associated Press reported that close to two thousand of the fifteen thousand prisoners in the camp had come down with food poisoning. Some were "seriously ill," but none died.[15] Kovner consoled himself with that vague language. "There were conflicting reports from the army and the press," he said years later. "In any case, hundreds of American army ambulances were called in. There were reports that four hundred died, and the rest were in critical condition. There were reports of two hundred, there were reports of a thousand. There were reports that most of them were out of danger." It may have been that the poison was not good, he ventured—Reichman had managed to get it in Paris.[16] In any case, the operation received no great publicity; it made no waves in Palestine.

It was not, then, the "shocking deed" that Kovner and his followers had dreamed about, and Kovner, who had in the meantime been released, demanded that they come to Palestine for consultations. As far as he could determine, the failure of the operation had plunged them deep into depression. He had reports that some of them had considered suicide. Most of them had difficulty giving up the plan; some accused Kovner of having betrayed the idea of revenge. They suspected he was plotting to tempt them into a normal life—an unforgivable sin, in their eyes.[17]

They came unwillingly, staying at Kibbutz Ein Hahoresh, where efforts were made to train them to work in the beet fields and banana groves. "Growing bananas meant nothing to them," Avidov later noted. They wanted revenge and demanded to be sent back to Europe.[18] Kovner tried to convince them that they had lost the mental strength needed for revenge, that conditions in Europe had changed, that Plan A could no longer be executed. One reason was the risk that it might harm the many Jews who had settled in German cities. Some members refused to listen to him; they returned to Europe. Among them were a few so overcome by disappointment and despair over the "betrayal" by the man they had admired that they never returned to Israel. Others played a role in what was called Plan C: individual, direct attacks on identified Nazi war criminals. This operation was carried out with the knowledge of the Haganah high command, and soldiers from the Jewish Brigade also participated.

Many in the Jewish Brigade had relatives who perished in the Holocaust. Some of these soldiers were among the first to enter the Nazi concentration camps after liberation, and they brought descriptions of the horrors back to their comrades, a few of whom had met with Abba Kovner. They were impressed by his thirst for revenge, and helped procure the poison for the Stalag 13 operation and transport it from Paris to Nuremberg.[19] Writer Hanoch Bartov re-created their sentiments:

Not a lot . . . a thousand burnt houses. Five hundred dead. Hundreds of raped women. . . . That's why we're here. Not for Roosevelt's freedoms. Not for the British Empire. Not for Stalin. We're here for blood revenge. A single wild Jewish revenge. Just once like the Tatars. Like the Ukrainians. Like the Germans. All of us, all the bleeding hearts, . . . we'll all go into one city and burn it, street by street, house by house, German by German. Why should it just be us remembering Auschwitz? Let them remember the one city that we'll destroy. [20]

At the end of the war they hoped to be sent to Germany as part of the occupying army. This was necessary, according to Moshe Sharett, not for military reasons, but "before all else" for symbolic and moral reasons—"to give satisfaction to the Jewish people."[21]

By the time the Jewish Brigade reached Italy, the war had already been decided. The soldiers took part in only a handful of battles. It was disappointing. Afterwards, they sat idle. Some took out their anger on German prisoners of war and vandalized civilian property. These acts, of course, reduced their chances of being sent to Germany. The longer they remained in Italy, the more bored they were. "Our patience is running out," one of them wrote. "I'm afraid that something will explode. Such an explosion is liable to harm us, because it will be difficult to channel properly."[22] At one point, the youngest of them got together and decided to begin revenge operations by searching out Gestapo and SS agents in the border area between Italy and Austria. This was, in the words of one soldier, "an act of rebellion." Their officers, however, probably viewed it as a useful outlet for the soldiers' frustration.[23]

One officer, Yisrael Karmi, would later describe them as "the best men of the brigade, the most loyal of the loyal."[24] By chance, they succeeded almost immediately in discovering a senior Gestapo official. The man cooperated with them and provided a list of names. Karmi recalled that the list was submitted, neatly typed, in exemplary order: names, biographical details, past activities, addresses. It served as their list of targets.[25] "We have reached the source," brigade officer Meir Grabovski reported to Moshe Sharett at the Jewish Agency executive. "All the investigations are in our hands. We have obtained the card file and we know who they are and where they are. . . . We are the only ones who can find them and turn them over [to the avengers] without having to take into account the tangles of world politics, just the right to avenge the blood spilled." Grabovski (later Argov), a Mapai leader, put revenge at the top of the brigade's goals after the war. In his letter to Sharett he wrote that he meant not "a mob's revenge" but rather retribution against the SS men who had participated in the slaughter.

Their method was simple. They disguised themselves as British military policemen and appeared at their victims' houses in a military pickup truck, its license plates obscured with mud. They would knock on the door, ascertain the identity of the man, and ask him to come with them for some sort of routine procedure. In general, there were no problems. They would take their victim to a predesignated location, identify themselves, and shoot him. On occasion, they would not venture far from the house. "Our truck was closed on all sides with a canvas cover," one of them related. "The floor was lined with mattresses. One or two of us would lie in wait in the dark. The minute the German's head appeared, the ambusher would lean over him, clasp his arms under the man's chin and on the throat and then throw himself backwards on the mattress, which muffled all sound. The fall, with the German's head in the grip, would suffocate him and break his neck vertebrae instantly."[26]

One of the avengers who had come from Palestine for this purpose was Shimon Avidan, formerly commander of the German unit of the Palmach. Avidan took upon himself, among other things, the task of locating Adolf Eichmann. According to Kovner, he succeeded in penetrating the Nazi's hideout, but, unfortunately, he killed someone else. "It was a man who called himself Eichmann," Kovner related. A woman who they thought was Eichmann's wife also said it was her husband. There were many external similarities. The avengers were convinced that Avidan had killed Eichmann. Kovner also believed it—until Israeli agents arrested Eichmann in Argentina in 1960. According to Kovner, Avidan himself, though, had always said that he was only 50 percent sure that he had killed Eichmann.[27]

The Haganah officer responsible for the brigade, Michael Ben-Gal, sanctioned their actions only unwillingly. He saw revenge as desirable and positive and believed that those who had participated in the murder of Jews deserved to be liquidated. But he rejected what he years later termed the "guerrilla nature" of the operation. "It was a guerrilla operation because there is a lot of the guerrilla in the Jewish character, and the character of the Haganah men who came from Palestine was more than a little guerrillalike." When they came to get his approval for the liquidation of a person, he would demand evidence of the target's guilt. If they killed the victim without Ben-Gal's approval, he would infer that the evidence had not been sufficient.

Some deeds of revenge were, in his eyes, no more than "acts of hooliganism." Thus, for instance, a few avengers once waited in ambush alongside a road and shot at anything that moved. In at least one instance, Ben-Gal related, they killed a Jewish woman, a Holocaust survivor, by accident. There was also the problem of what to do with the bodies. The avengers liked leaving them to be discovered. But Ben-Gal feared that doing so would endanger the soldiers of the brigade. He demanded that the bodies be thrown into lakes in the vicinity but was not always obeyed. He complained of the lack of discipline.

As a military man, Ben-Gal wanted precise instructions before acting. Once he asked Moshe Sharett for guidelines. Sharett replied that revenge in the name of the Jewish people ought to be "revenge worthy of the name." It should be directed at a prominent target, to "make an impression on the entire world, so that the world will realize that Jewish blood does not come cheap." Ben-Gal came to the conclusion that Abba Kovner and his group, "with their special zeal," were more fitted to the mission than were soldiers from the brigade. He agreed, therefore, to assist them. [28]

Some of the soldiers who participated in the vengeance operations would, in the years that followed, be promoted to senior ranks in the Israeli army. Among them were generals and a chief of staff, Haim Laskov. Years later, Laskov said: "They were not 'nice' acts. They were acts of revenge. When it comes down to it, we lost the war. We lost six million Jews. Anyone who hasn't seen those places, the concentration camps and crematoriums, can never understand what they did to us. Because we were weak, and did not have our own country, and did not have power, we avenged. It was not a nice act." In any event, it was not done on a large scale. "I'm sorry to say that we did not liquidate very many," Laskov said. [29]

§

The calls to wreak vengeance on the Nazis heard in Palestine during the war grew ever louder as information about the extermination of the Jews became widespread. In slogans, editorials, and statements by various organizations, the press gave frequent voice to the desire for revenge. These expressions of the public's emotions were also somewhat pathetic attempts to deter the Nazis. The war against the Nazis was "a war of honor and revenge," and enlistment in the British army was an act reflecting "pent-up anger and the fury of revenge."[30] "Any one of us might have been there," *Haaretz* wrote, "and whoever was saved—his life is dedicated to war and retribution. No mourning and no weeping: revenge!" A few days earlier, the newspaper had said: "One must assume that no cry will hold the German murderers back from their deeds. But the murderers will know that revenge will come, as is written: 'an eye for an eye, a tooth for a tooth.' "[31] "May every hand in Israel stretch out boldly to avenge our victims," declared the central committee of the Writers' Association."[32] The Etzel announced that it was establishing avenging battalions "that will renew the tradition of revenge from the days of Samson," that is, the tradition of redemption by blood. "The Etzel in the Land of Israel will take revenge on the Germans wherever they are. . . . A jealous and avenging God will be our aid, amen."*[33]

When the extermination of the Jews was at its height, *Haolam*, the principal newspaper of the World Zionist Organization, then published in Jerusalem, ran an article demanding "real revenge" and "concrete retribution." For every Jew that the Nazis killed, a Nazi prisoner of the Allies should be killed. The call for revenge prompted sharp reactions, leading the paper's editor, Moshe Kleinman, to attempt to express the consensus of opinion. The desire to avenge, he wrote, was "a holy human emotion, like every human feeling." But, he said, it did not express a plan of action. It reflected, rather, abysmal despair—"the desperate cry of the miserable and oppressed, those powerless to protect themselves, [who] demand vindication for their blood and humiliation from the conscience of the world and long, at least in their imaginations, to see 'the revenging of the blood of thy servants.' " Had they the ability to avenge, they would not do so, the editor of *Haolam* added: "It may be said with absolute certainty that there would not be one of us, not even among those who shout ceaselessly for revenge, who would cleave a skull with his own hands, dismember the young and the old, cut open the stomach

---

* The God of Israel is described in the Bible as a "God of revenge" (Psalms 94:1), avenging those who attack him and combating his enemies (Nahum 1:2). Yet there is also the verse "Thou shalt not avenge, nor bear any grudge against the children of thy people, but thou shalt love thy neighbor as thyself" (Leviticus 19:18). The Midrash resolved this apparent contradiction in the name of the Holy One himself: "I wrote in the Torah 'Thou shalt not avenge, nor bear any grudge against the children of thy people,' but I take revenge and bear grudges against pagans" (Bereshit Rabba 55:3). The opponents of revenge against the Nazis quoted this interpretation to support their claim that revenge is in the hands of heaven, not in the hands of man.

of a pregnant woman. . . . No, such things were never done by Jews and will never be done. A Jewish person is unable to do them, even if all day he screams and shouts 'Revenge! Revenge!' " Here the editor distinguished between the individual German and the German nation: "Under no circumstances would I cleave the skull of an individual German who came into my hands. But I am prepared to impose on the German people a boundless measure of suffering and torture to be endured for hundreds of years, until their heavy sins are burned away and purified."[34]

The desire for vengeance is a basic emotion, like fear and happiness and perhaps also like hunger and thirst, wrote a columnist in *Davar*, but "the supreme European-Jewish ethic classifies it as a base instinct that ought to be rooted out of the heart."[35] The proper response to the crimes of the Nazis, *Haaretz* maintained, cannot be a simple act of retribution or revenge, but only "a full and just punishment" after a trial.[36] The socialist *Mishmar* stated: "Revenge for Jewish blood has been accomplished largely by the Soviet Union," through the Red Army and its victory in the war.[37]

Pasha Reichman recalled how he tried to get David Ben-Gurion to support revenge, but Ben-Gurion listened for only a few minutes before he ruled: "Revenge in history is a very important thing indeed, but if we could bring back six million Jews, rather than kill six million Germans —this would be even more important." He refused to support Reichman's group.[38] The dominant state of mind in the yishuv while the war was in progress was, then, to suppress the urge to avenge. This predilection grew after the war, when the immediate mission was to accelerate the briha from eastern Europe into the American occupation zone of Germany, in order to force Britain to revoke the immigration restrictions. The revenge fantasies of the Holocaust survivors belonged, like the Holocaust itself, to a different, very foreign world. The death of millions of Germans could not advance the Zionist struggle. On the contrary, like the adventurism of the haapala, the revenge operation was likely to harm the Jewish Agency's efforts to create goodwill and support for its major goal—the establishment of the state.

This was the consensus after Israel was founded, too. Meir Argov, formerly Grabovski, of the Jewish Brigade, now a member of the Knesset, quoted Haim Nahman Bialik during a debate over Israel's relations with Germany: "Not even the devil has devised a fitting revenge for the blood of a small child." There was no absolution for the blood of the millions murdered, Argov explained. On another occasion, Argov said in the Knesset that, had Hitler seen the Israeli flag flying in Bonn, he would have shuddered. This was real revenge, he said.[39] Rozka Korczak, who served in the partisan forces with Kovner, believed that the proper response was the victory of the living in Israel: "Building, the idea of building, the value of building, will form our revenge."[40] Even Menahem Begin, who led the opposition to recognizing Germany, stated that a war of revenge was no longer appropriate.[41]

Most of the avengers, in the end, chose to keep their stories to themselves. Some were interviewed on condition that their names not be revealed, while others deposited their memoirs in historical archives, also on condition of anonymity. Most preferred to remain silent, and there is no way of knowing what they wanted to hide—what they did, little as it was, or the fact that they did not do more. Some used their anonymity to live out their fantasies in their testimony. Their mission was not possible to carry out and morally dubious from any perspective. Ultimately their activities were limited, and made hardly any impression. Hence the avengers were not awarded a place in Israel's pantheon of glory, occupied by the ghetto rebels, the paratroopers, gunrunners, and those who participated in the briha and the haapala. The avengers saw themselves as history's agents, but most of the Zionist leaders saw them as a nuisance and a political liability. The avengers wanted justice; the leaders wanted statehood. The avengers spoke for the last Jews; the future belonged to the first Israelis.

9 | "A Barrier of Blood and Silence"

Toward the end of the war, Miriam Weinfeld turned seventeen. In the days before the German surrender, she was taken on the death march from Auschwitz to Bergen-Belsen. Her mental anguish, particularly her inability to help her mother, had been harder to bear than the physical hardship, she later recalled. Conditions in Bergen-Belsen in the weeks before the camp was liberated were even worse than they had been in the past. Her mother died before her eyes. When the British soldiers finally arrived, wearing gas masks against the stench of the tens of thousands of corpses strewn around the barracks, Weinfeld's first thought was, "Too bad they came so late." There was nothing left to save.

Then came the hope, the hatred, the shock, and the struggle to return to life. More than anything else, she hoped to find her brother. They had left their house together when he was seventeen and she fourteen, and somewhere, in one of the forests close to Lvov, she had lost him. She tortured herself: Why had she survived when he had not? But after Bergen-Belsen, when her senses returned to her, she grasped at the hope that perhaps he was still alive. Every young man she saw from a distance reminded her of her brother. She held on tightly to her memories—he had been a nimble, bright boy. Yes, perhaps he was still alive: why not, after all? The hope nurtured her all through the first days after liberation. It was her only strength: she weighed less than sixty pounds and suffered from tuberculosis; she was bald and her body was covered with sores.

Although still disoriented, she believed that the time had come to square accounts. The thirst for revenge was her strongest feeling, and she thought that the Germans should be exterminated. All of them—women, children, everyone. A while later she was sent, with other survivors, to convalesce in northern Sweden. There she saw life proceeding as if nothing had happened: boys and girls her age, healthy and properly dressed, went to school. This threw her into shock again. Somehow, she had imagined that the earth would stop in its course when Bergen-Belsen was discovered, yet it went on as it always had. The Swedes tried to make the survivors feel welcome, but Weinfeld's return to life was not easy. She had to sleep on paper sheets, she remembered—cold, always rustling, impossible to wrap oneself up in. Next to her lay a girl who broke into hysterics, laughing and crying, crying and laughing, day and night.

Weinfeld lived deep within herself. She wrote poetry in Polish. Despite her depression and indifference toward everything around her, she wanted to be pretty. She knew she looked like a walking skeleton, that no man would want her. She would never have children; perhaps she was not fit to bring children into the world.

Later she met Hanan Yakobowitz. He knew only Hungarian, she only Polish. Their language of love was German, picked up in Auschwitz and Bergen-Belsen. One day he was hurt while working in a carpentry shop, and two of his fingers were severed. She took care of him; that brought them closer. The camp had counselors from Palestine, who gave them a dream—to live in a free land. They received legal immigration certif-icates. She felt her spirits rise but was afraid: she longed for renewal but felt deeply inferior, isolated from all that had happened in the world. On the boat to Palestine there were counselors from Kibbutz Degania Bet. They were nice. Miriam Weinfeld and her boyfriend went there.

In the second half of 1945, some 90,000 Jewish refugees came to Palestine from Europe.[1] All had lived under Nazi occupation; some had been in concentration camps. In the next three years, another 60,000 survivors came, and in the first year of statehood, nearly 200,000 more.[2] At the end of 1949 there were, then, close to 350,000 Holocaust survivors living in Israel—almost one out of every three Israelis. On arrival, they faced a difficult struggle.

It was very hot in the banana groves of the Jordan Valley kibbutz, and life was hard for Miriam Weinfeld and Hanan Yakobowitz. In the first weeks they slept outside, under mosquito nets. At night the wails of the jackals brought back memories of Bergen-Belsen. Weinfeld's memories and her longing for home were stronger than her ability to adjust to the kibbutz. And the kibbutz did not encourage individual soul-searching; members were told to put aside the past and become part of the group.

Weinfeld felt shunned by the young people at Degania Bet. Although she did not speak Hebrew, their cliquishness hurt; she sensed arrogance, sometimes even mockery and hostility. The older members were more welcoming; they tried to adopt the new couple, but did not know how to make life easier for them. She sensed in their kindness guilt, even shame. She wanted to be asked about herself; her story was the only thing she had to contribute to her relationship with the new country. But no one asked.

For many of the survivors, telling their story seemed a patriotic duty: Many said that in the postwar months, they felt as though they were the last living Jews, who alone knew what had happened to their communities. Each had a moral and historical obligation to preserve the memory of all the others. Yet trying to tell the story also expressed the intense need to share with others the crushing emotional burden. It was a very personal, individual need. But the survivors discovered that people did not always want to listen to them, or could not.

Often, the stories were simply not believed. In 1943, at the forced-labor camp that the Nazis set up near the town of Przemyśl, Poland, a seventeen-year-old prisoner named Michael Goldman was brought before the camp commandant, Franz Schwammberger. The commandant whipped and beat him. Goldman fainted. When he woke, the commandant kept on beating him—eighty lashes, until Goldman broke. His back was torn and bloody but he was alive. He survived and came to Israel. When he told his relatives what had happened to him, they refused to believe it. They were sure he was imagining things or exaggerating. "That disbelief was the eighty-first blow," Goldman later said. The story became a symbol.* "They didn't believe me!" wrote Yaakov Kurtz, who arrived at the end of 1942. "They asked me questions and interrogated me as if I were a criminal who wanted to mislead people."[4] This was the survivors' first difficulty in their new country.

---

* The Eighty-first Blow became the name of a well-known film, made by Haim Guri and Zako Erlich. Fifteen years after being rescued, Michael Gilad (Goldman), a police officer, was one of Adolf Eichmann's interrogators, and he was present at the execution. In 1987 the Argentine police arrested an elderly German who had been wanted since the end of the war: Franz Schwammberger. Eventually he was extradited to Germany. Gilad, then a senior official of the Jewish Agency, read about the arrest in the newspaper. "Too bad he was able to live so long," he said.[5]

Weinfeld's new direction in life, at the kibbutz, turned out to be a blind alley. She felt trapped. Then she married her Hanan. They had a modest wedding, on a flatbed trailer, by the Sea of Galilee. Someone lent them a ring. They received three presents: a tablecloth, a vase, and a Bible. It was not how she had imagined her wedding as a child, a nice, middle-class girl from Poland. What would her mother have said? After the ceremony Miriam and Hanan Yakobowitz crossed the banana grove and went to the neighboring kibbutz, Beit Zera, where relatives gave them a room for a night. Years later, she would say that she began her family too early, before she was ready, perhaps before she really wanted to. But back then, she had no one to ask for advice. The first baby died soon after it was born: another reminder of the trauma of the concentration camps.

After the wedding, they moved to another kibbutz, Ginegar. She did not feel at home there either, but she worked, took part in the community's social life, learned how to shoot a rifle, and did guard duty during the War of Independence. She felt that she was contributing something to life at the kibbutz but that the kibbutz was giving her less than she gave. Other members of the group that she and her husband had been part of in Sweden arrived in the country, having set out on a maapilim ship and spent two years in Cyprus. The experience had given them a group identity. Miriam and Hanan Yakobowitz joined them in founding Kibbutz Nahsholim on the coast, near Mount Carmel, where an Arab village, Tantura, had previously been. The two years that had passed since they had last seen the group set them apart, but their seniority in the country gave them a certain advantage. Hanan Yakobowitz became the treasurer of the new kibbutz.

After a time, they left Kibbutz Nahsholim as well. They bought a tiny apartment in Neve Amal, near Herzlia—without doors, door frames, or shutters. They were no longer newlyweds, so they did not qualify for the gifts the state gave to young couples—a pressure cooker, a broom, and the like. Living alongside them were immigrants from Yemen and Persia, as well as other Holocaust survivors, struggling young couples. They helped each other. They showered at the neighbors' houses, where there was hot water. Someone brought them a few orange crates for furniture. They had no connection with the old-timers in the country and knew only a few. After a series of medical and psychological complications, Ronit was born. Miriam Yakobowitz's first response was, "She looks like Mama." Suddenly the thought came to her that she was older than her mother had been when she died. A while later, they had another daughter. They earned salaries as employees of public and government organizations; she was a nurse in the Histadrut health collective, while he somehow found a job with the internal security service. Once or twice, the government sent them overseas, so in accordance with official regulations they Hebraized their family name. Forty years after Bergen-Belsen, Miriam Akavia writes books, mostly for young people, which have also been published in several European countries, including Germany and Poland. She writes in Hebrew but has never lost her Polish accent: always something of an outsider, always a Holocaust survivor.[5]

Like Miriam Akavia, thousands of Holocaust survivors settled in the country's cities, villages, and kibbutzim, served in the army, learned trades, worked, married, bought apartments, had children, and spoke with them in Hebrew, a testament to the life wish that had helped get them through the war. Many of them very much wanted to be Israelis and so adopted the mores and way of life of their new country. Thousands Hebraized their names—taking on, as it were, a new identity.

From one perspective, their encounter with Israel was an amazing triumph. People who had been dead to the world, at Auschwitz and Bergen-Belsen and Dachau and the rest of the camps, ghettos, and hiding places, returned to life in Israel. This is the significance of a story that appeared in *Maariv* one day early in 1949. On that day Rivka Waxman went out shopping on Herzl Street in Haifa. It was also one of her first days in Israel, she had just come from Poland. Near the Ora cinema she suddenly noticed a young soldier get out of a jeep and go to the ticket booth. She froze in place. "Haim?" she called. The soldier turned to her, and for the next few seconds they stared at each other in disbelief. Then the woman held out her arms, close to fainting, and fell on the youth's shoulder. She was his mother. They had last seen each other eight years before, when he was fourteen. Until she met him in the street, Rivka Waxman believed that her Haim had been killed in the Holocaust.[6] Thousands of people had, like the Waxmans, been torn from their loved ones—in the ghettos, during the deportations, at the death camps, and in the forests—and here in Israel they found one another by chance or through notices published in newspapers and on a heartrending radio program called *Who Knows*. They were new immigrants, on the verge of a new life.

Yet if they found it difficult to start a new life, or if they wanted to preserve their previous identity, they were often in conflict with their new country. Israel was apprehensive about them and wanted to change them. The task the country's leaders set for themselves was to give the survivors a new personality, to imbue them with new values. "They must learn love of the homeland, a work ethic, and human morals," said a Mapai leader, and another added that they should be given "the first concepts of humanity." One said, as if they were a huge ball of dough, that it was necessary to "knead their countenances." At one meeting of the Mapai secretariat it was said that they should be "reeducated."[7] Such statements did not only give voice to the negative political and social stereotype of the survivor. People sincerely feared meeting the survivors face to face, with their physical and psychological handicaps, their suffering and terror. How will we live with them, they asked themselves over and over again—and their fears were justified. The Holocaust survivors came from another world and, to the end of their days, they were its prisoners.

Four months before the war ended, Rozka Korczak made an appearance at a Hashomer Hatsair kibbutz and told the gathered membership of an incident in the village of Punar, not far from Vilna, in Lithuania. After the Nazis shot everyone, the bodies were burned. Among the bodies was one of a pregnant woman. When the body grew hot in the fire, the fetus was expelled from the body and burned together with its mother. Korczak said that this was "a symbolic fact"—not only those who were there but also their descendants had been sentenced to extermination.[8] Indeed, liberation came too late for many of the Holocaust survivors, and they did not succeed in rehabilitating themselves. Thousands left Israel, especially in the 1950s.[9] Many needed psychological care, and some continued to need it for years. They did not escape the nightmare of their pasts.

Over the years they wrote thousands of books about that "other planet" they had left yet not left, but all they could do was enumerate the atrocities. Those were part of their story that could be told. The rest remained inside. "Even if you studied all the documentation," Elie Wiesel has said, "even if you listened to all the testimonies, visited all the camps and museums and read all the diaries, you would not be able to even approach the portal of that eternal night. That is the tragedy of the survivor's mission. He must tell a story that cannot be told. He must deliver a message that cannot be delivered. . . . In this sense the enemy, ironically, realized his goal. Since he extended the crime beyond all bounds, and since there is no way to cross those bounds except through language, it is impossible to tell the full story of his crime."[10]

Miriam Weinfeld was sometimes asked about the blue number tattooed on her arm. She felt that the question reflected only casual interest, not a real desire to hear the true story. So she evaded it. She knew people who had undergone plastic surgery to have the number removed. She did not; but she generally kept it hidden from strangers and never looked at it herself, never learned it by heart. Michael Gilad used to tell his son that it was his telephone number at work.

During the stay in the DP camps before the journey to Palestine, the survivors recuperated; by the time they arrived, they were no longer the walking skeletons the Allied forces discovered in the concentration camps. While still in Europe, they had time to gather themselves and give thought to their futures. There was nothing they wanted more than to return to normalcy: "It is hard to describe their longing for a normal life," commented one of the envoys from Palestine.[11] But they suffered from anxieties, nightmares, and attacks of depression, fury, and apathy; from difficulties in concentrating and in establishing relations with others; from suspicion of strangers, introversion, overwhelming worries about their personal, economic, and professional security, great fear and great aspirations for their children.

Many raised their children with the feeling that their own lives were barely worth living, that their only purpose in living was to ensure the good, the welfare, and the future of their children. Many forced the children to bear the burden of memory by giving them the names of relatives who had died in the Holocaust. Many, perhaps most, could not, and did not want to, tell their children what they had experienced, and the children did not dare ask, as if the answer were a terrible, threatening family secret. Holocaust anxieties could suddenly break into daily life, triggered by routine events at home or at work or on the news. An illness, losing a job, or a border incident—everything took them back to "there." For many, the past continued to intrude years after the end of the war.

There were those who became ambitious and tough, able to endure suffering and adjust to crises. Others had trouble dealing with even minor setbacks. Many feared dependence, failure, separation. They were often sick, or thought they were. Many experienced inchoate feelings of grief and violence that had never found release. They were ashamed that they had not been able to resist what had been done to them. They blamed their parents for abandoning them and suffered guilt at having survived their loved ones. "My conscience torments me," one survivor said. "I left children on the way, and they fell into the hands of the Germans."[12]

This was a common feeling; and though most survivors owed their lives to chance, not to another's sacrifice, they still felt guilt for having survived. The feeling often served a psychological and moral purpose: It acted as a cover for the powerlessness of the victims. It allowed them to think they had had a choice, and had chosen to live. The sense of guilt had a contrary purpose, too. It was for the survivors a kind of pledge of allegiance to humanistic ethical values, another bid, after the fact, to counter the attempt to rob them of their humanity.[13] The few who had resisted had it easier; many of them tended to set themselves off from the other survivors, even displaying a measure of arrogance. But they too tortured themselves; perhaps they could have done more. "When the Germans entered Poland, had we immediately recognized the danger and started to act," Tzivia Lubetkin said, "perhaps the whole thing would have looked different."[14] In August 1949, the state prosecutor brought the minister of justice's attention to the disturbing rise in the number of new immigrants, among them Holocaust survivors, who were taking their own lives.[15]

Like the survivors, the entire country was in the throes of an emotional crisis. Thousands of those who had come to Palestine before the war had also lost relatives; they too were in mourning. Many tortured themselves with the same guilt feelings that plagued the survivors. Shouldn't they have died in place of a loved one? There were, of course, many who felt an obligation to help the survivors, as if the survivors were their lost parents and siblings. But many others blamed the survivors, as if these had survived at the expense of their relatives and so shared part of the guilt for their deaths. One survivor, Simha Rotem, wrote, "In almost every contact with the inhabitants of the country, the question would come up of how we had remained alive. It was asked again and again and not always in the most delicate way. I had a feeling that I was being blamed for having stayed alive."[16] The conflict pitted the victims of one trauma against the victims of another.

The earliest immigrants spent their first days in the country in transit camps; later immigrants spent their first weeks and months there. Each received a "primary needs" package from the Jewish Agency. First came cash, 7 to 10 liras (up to $40), which had to suffice for immediate needs in the transit camp or in a Jewish Agency residence while the immigrant looked for work and a permanent place to live. The immigrants were also given iron beds and mattresses. These "agency beds" became an Israeli symbol.

Until they found apartments, immigrants might stay with relatives. But such arrangements could be difficult. Those responsible for absorption complained that few Israelis were willing to accept their immigrant relatives into their houses. There were Israelis who instructed newly arrived relatives not to let the Jewish Agency know that they had family in the country, lest the agency make the local family responsible and not assist the immigrants further.

Someone proposed declaring a national voluntary campaign—every family would take an immigrant into its house. Ben-Gurion dismissed the idea. He believed that few people would respond to the call. Later, there was talk of a special law that would allow the confiscation of rooms for immigrants, but it was obvious that it could not be enforced—people would find ways of cheating the government.[17] Many did in fact live in crowded conditions that did not allow them to take in immigrant relatives.

The Jewish Agency and other public bodies built rental apartments for the immigrants—one room and a kitchen. Some apartments were even sparsely furnished. But construction could not keep pace with demand, and the shortage grew month to month, year to year. Neither were jobs created for everyone, nor schools for the children, nor clinics for the ill.

The failure was principally due to the lack of funds. But the yishuv also tended to scorn organized planning. The Jews, having lived under foreign rule for centuries, had learned to act outside the law, to improvise, and this ability became a valued part of the yishuv's self-image. As one leader said: "We just need to throw the immigrants here and there and they will be absorbed somehow."[18] Furthermore, the yishuv was unsure many survivors would come; after all, they had not come in droves before the war and there were indications that most of them would not come now either. Why build them houses before they arrived?

Then the War of Independence broke out, and tens of thousands of homes were suddenly available. This was what Shaul Avigur called "the Arab miracle": Hundreds of thousands of Arabs fled, and were expelled from their homes. Entire cities and hundreds of villages left empty were repopulated in short order with new immigrants. In April 1949 they numbered 100,000, most of them Holocaust survivors.[19] The moment was a dramatic one in the war for Israel, and a frightfully banal one, too, focused as it was on the struggle over houses and furniture. Free people—Arabs—had gone into exile and become destitute refugees; destitute refugees—Jews—took the exiles' places as a first step in their new lives as free people. One group lost all they had, while the other found everything they needed—tables, chairs, closets, pots, pans, plates, sometimes clothes, family albums, books, radios, and pets. Most of the immigrants broke into the abandoned Arab houses without direction, without order, without permission. For several months the country was caught up in a frenzy of take-what-you-can, first-come, first-served.[20] Afterwards, the authorities tried to halt the looting and take control of the allocation of houses, but in general they came too late. Immigrants also took possession of Arab stores and workshops, and some Arab neighborhoods soon looked like Jewish towns in prewar Europe, with tailors, shoemakers, dry-goods merchants—all the traditional Jewish occupations.

Soon, though, unemployment, want, and hunger spread among the new settlers. Arab neighborhoods had been damaged during the war, and municipal and community services had not yet been restored. There wasn't enough electricity and water; sewage flowed in the streets. There were no telephones, clinics, or schools. In villages, matters were more organized. To hand outlying villages over to Jewish settlers was, in part, to meet a strategic political need; settlement of the countryside. Most of the abandoned houses in the villages needed renovation, having been damaged or despoiled during the war. Many were far from other Jewish settlements, cut off from the water, electricity, and sewage networks.

The Arab houses were all occupied within a few months after the War of Independence. At the same time, the state of the immigrant camps grew worse from day to day. "If we compare the objective situation—housing, food, family life—in the DP camps with the situation in our camps in Pardes Hannah, Benyamina, or any other place," said Giora Yoseftal, chief of the Jewish Agency's absorption department, "the conditions in Bergen-Belsen are better, because there, 3,000 people live in a camp built for 13,000, while in our camp built for 8,000 there are 10,000 people."[21] When he wrote, 22,000 immigrants lived in transit camps. A few months later, their number had risen to 100,000, about half of them survivors. In later years, the tribulations of the transit camps would be associated with the absorption of immigrants from the Islamic world. In fact, the beginning was also very difficult for the Holocaust survivors. Here and there, they received preferential treatment, but they went through the same stages of absorption, the same humiliating mass disinfecting with DDT, the same intolerably crowded conditions, meager food, fetid blankets, doorless, sometimes dividerless latrines. Not surprisingly, they felt despondent and unsure of the future.

Members of the Jewish Agency, the Histadrut, and Mapai frequently blamed themselves for the continuing immigrant housing problem. As the months went on, they were seized by a sense of failure, of despair. They described the situation in the camps as "a crime," "a catastrophe," and "God's own horror," and complained, justifiably, that the leaders of the party, with Ben-Gurion at their head, had not put the welfare of the immigrants higher on their list of priorities. Ben-Gurion responded that he unfortunately could not find the time to see to immigrant absorption. He reprimanded his colleagues, telling them not to spoil the immigrants: "People can live in tents for years," he said. "Anyone who does not want to live in a tent shouldn't come here."[22]

The files of the immigration departments of the Jewish Agency, the Histadrut, the municipalities, Mapai, and the other parties are full of reports that document the misery of the immigrants. Officials generally took note of the applicant's past in the forms they filled out and the letters they wrote trying to help individual survivors. They often recorded, after the names of the applicants, the names of the concentration camps the applicants had been in, as if these were their country of origin. The Holocaust was reason enough to assist them, the letters indicated. But, as is the way of bureaucrats, the officials were loyal to procedure, and they tended to think the immigrants were demanding too much. "They want the yishuv to set them up in the same situation and same position they had before the Nazis came," one writer for *Haaretz* complained. He thought this an unreasonable demand.[23]

Regina Hitter, "an immigrant from Bergen-Belsen," was thirty-one when she arrived in Palestine in September 1945, widowed, the mother of a baby girl. She was sent to Beit Hahalutzot, a hostel for immigrant women in Haifa. Genia Shvadron, director of the hostel, wrote on Hitter's behalf to the Jewish Agency's Haifa immigration department, which forwarded a copy of her letter to the main office in Jerusalem. "The above-mentioned woman wants very much to learn a trade," Shvadron wrote: girdle making. She had begun to learn this skill in Belgium, after her release from Bergen-Belsen. The Tel Aviv office of WIZO (the Women's International Zionist Organization) had given her a 40-lira grant (about $160) for that purpose. Now she needed 50 liras to support herself while taking the four-month course. The Histadrut had given her 20 liras. Beit Hahalutzot was applying on her behalf for a grant of 30 liras that would enable her to complete her training and make an honorable living. The

Haifa immigration department's first application to the main office on Hitter's request was made on November 11, 1945, and is marked with a large, official-looking stamp and with the number 6253, file number E-914. In Jerusalem the letter was given the number 218/28098. Three weeks passed. Jerusalem sent a questionnaire to Haifa. Haifa filled it out and returned it to Jerusalem. Jerusalem asked for details about the woman's file to the present date: Who was caring for her daughter? Who was paying for her? Haifa responded. Regina Hitter had received 22.5 liras. Her daughter was in a day-care program. Jerusalem checked this information and discovered in its files that Mrs. Regina Fertig-Hitter was supposed to receive 10 liras, with another 10 for her daughter. Four more weeks went by. Now there was the question of whether Comrade Regina had received something in advance. In any case, Jerusalem directed that she be paid an additional 10 liras and assumed that this would help her "a great deal" and that therefore "the matter is no longer current." The serial number given to the young woman's affairs had in the meantime grown to 7142/5/405/914. Here the matter ended: Regina Fertig-Hitter of Bergen-Belsen was one of tens of thousands of immigrants who managed to find a place for themselves in one of the country's cities. Golda Meir said of them that they had "disappeared"—no one noticed them, no one knew what they were doing.[24] Whether or not Regina Fertig-Hitter managed to get the rest of the money she needed and found happiness as a girdle maker in Israel we shall never know; perhaps she did.[25]

Some of the aid to immigrants, such as education, medical care, and housing, was given on the basis of political party affiliation. The parties set up special divisions for immigrants. Mapai, which controlled most of the absorption machinery, had the greatest potential to benefit—but also the most to lose. The discussions in party councils reflected great anxiety about the party's future, but also a sense of national responsibility. Characteristically, no distinction was made between the two. "In my opinion," wrote the director of the Bnei Brak immigrant camp to the head of the Mapai immigration division, "every camp director interested in the good of the country and the party must ease the hardships of the immigrants and improve, to the extent possible, their housing conditions; this will necessarily increase sympathy with the party and with the government, both of which are responsible for everything done in the country." The director of the Bnei Brak camp had doubts, apparently, about whether to favor party members, "since that is our job and that is what we were sent here for," or whether to avoid favoritism, because it might harm the party.[26]

The task was impossible. In a time of shortages, putting the care of immigrants in the hands of people who saw it as a party mission necessarily led to preferential treatment and discrimination, or as it was called then, *protektsia.* The Labor party archives contain a file with dozens of brief letters from one Mapai official to another, each a request for help for "our people." This was called the "note system."[27]

Sometimes the Holocaust past of the "protectionee" was cited in the notes: "The bearer of this letter, Comrade Aharon Kutzik (Kamelnitzki), one of the surviving Warsaw ghetto fighters and one of their leaders, is applying with regard to his housing and is deserving of support."[28] Most of these notes were directed to a special committee of the Jewish Agency, the Functionaries Committee. "Please approve an apartment for Comrade Baruch Vinograd from Poland. The above-noted is an activist in our party. Recently he has been a member of our party's central committee in Poland." Activists of the Zionist parties outside the country received special privileges. Sometimes it was enough for a man to be among the senior members of the party, in which case he was directed to the Jewish Agency's Senior Members Committee: "Please approve an apartment in the Tel Aviv area for Comrade Shmuel Brenner, a senior member of our party in Poland." This note was the 1,715th of its type in the file.[*29]

¶

On October 12, 1932, a small crowd of German Jews gathered on the platform of the Anhalter train station in Berlin. They came to see off twelve youngsters who were about to set off for the Ben Shemen Youth Village in Palestine. Everyone was very emotional; the parents cried. One of the community leaders turned to the woman who had campaigned for

---

* It is almost certainly impossible to determine precisely which parties won the immigrants' support in the end. Even a sampling of the election results provides no basis for anything but speculation. Some 200,000 voters participated in the 1944 elections to the representative assembly. Mapai won 36 percent of the vote. In the elections to the first Knesset in 1949, there were more than 400,000 voters; Mapai again won 36 percent of the vote. In the elections to the second Knesset, in 1951, nearly 700,000 voters took part. Mapai won 37 percent of the vote. The other political blocs also preserved, more or less, their relative strength. Most of the new voters were immigrants from Europe, Holocaust survivors. It would seem, therefore, that they voted along the same lines as the rest of the population.[30]

the youths to go and who had made all the arrangements and told her: "Frau Freier, this is a historic moment." Ten weeks later, the Nazis were in power; in hindsight, those young people could say that Recha Freier had saved their lives.[31] By the time the war broke out, the organization she set up had helped 5,000 children and young people leave Germany. During the war, close to 10,000 more went, and between the end of the war and the establishment of the state, another 15,000 arrived—a total of 30,000.[32]

The program was the Aliyat Hanoar, or Youth Aliya (immigration). Most of the children came without their parents; many were orphans. Recha Freier, a rabbi's wife with an interest in music and folklore, gave the beginning of the operation a mystic air. The first teenagers who had come to ask for her help had been "sent to her," she liked to say, as if destiny had brought them. She was a unique combination of humanistic romanticism, heavenly visions, organizational determination, and solid performance, fragile, almost transparent, but hard as a rock.

"One night," she wrote in her memoirs, "I was illuminated by a simple and clear idea, a solution to the problem: the children must go to Palestine, to the settlements of the labor movement, where they would be trained for work and for life."[33]

Yet Aliyat Hanoar's primary mission was to be a rescue operation, and it sent children and teenagers not just to Palestine but also to countries of refuge in Europe. The program avoided illegal activity, taking care to obtain immigration certificates for the young people it brought to Palestine. It invested greatly in education, particularly vocational education as opposed to the agricultural training favored by the socialist Zionist establishment. Some members of the Aliyat Hanoar leadership had been brought up in the liberal spirit of German Jewry, yekkes who themselves were still cultural outsiders in the yishuv. The files in the organization's archives reflect compassion and sincere, rather middle-class efforts to look after the individual welfare of the charges, and not just in kibbutzim.

The Aliyat Hanoar officials knew the history of each and every one and were often personally acquainted with the boys and girls. "The boy may be receiving all the supplies he should be," wrote one official to a colleague, "but we have now discovered that he is in great need of an additional pair of sandals for two reasons: first, his old shoes are small on him and he has cuts on his feet. Second, for health reasons—he sweats a lot."[34] Another file has a similar entry: "We have sent a package for Moshe. The package includes a raincoat and boots. The boots are small for him, but we don't have any other size, so you are to exchange them in some store for a larger size. We promise to pay any difference in price."[35]

Often Aliyat Hanoar continued to follow the children for years after they had left its care. One boy from the program later enlisted in the army. In 1952 he deserted from his unit and was arrested and court-martialed. Aliyat Hanoar wrote to the general in command, explaining that the boy's case was typical of Holocaust survivors. The letter explained that, despite what his ID card said, there was no way of being sure what his name and age were; he might not even be of military age. "He knows almost nothing about himself. And he has not a relative nor a guardian in the world," the program director wrote to the general. "You must ensure that this fruit of the Holocaust not be crushed between the mill-stones of life." The army acceded to the request. The deserter was trans-ferred to a different unit.[36]

Aliyat Hanoar would later become a division of the Jewish Agency. Recha Freier was eased out of the project she had initiated, to be replaced by Henrietta Szold. In time, the organization became less concerned with the individual welfare of each child and increasingly emphasized its part in the realization of the Zionist vision. One member demanded adherence to "a national settlement-oriented approach," averring that Aliyat Hanoar was not a rescue operation. "We are not motivated solely by humanitarian considerations," he said, as if these were somehow inferior. "The educational goal of Aliyat Hanoar," one of its leaders stated, "is to train youth for agricultural settlement rather than to care for in-dividuals who refuse to conform."[37] Six out of seven children in the program were sent to kibbutzim. The small children studied. From age fifteen and a half, the youngsters worked half a day and studied for four hours. Many had trouble adjusting to the work; they were simply too weak.

The kibbutzim tried to help the Holocaust children in the only way they knew: they made an effort to erase the children's past, obliterate their otherness, and teach them to be better people—Israelis. They taught the children Hebrew, told them about Zionism and socialism, took them on trips and organized games. A counselor named Tsvi entered his first impressions in his diary: "The children are saturated with hate of Russia, of the red flag, of socialism. They don't want to hear about the kibbutz because it reminds them of the kolkhoz." So he set himself a task—to make them like the kibbutz. The problem was, he noted, that the children "did not think the right way" about the relations between the individual and society. The world they came from did not educate them for social life. On the contrary, it imbued them with individualistic traits. In the meantime, Tsvi was encountering a problem he had difficulty dealing with. The children were suspicious of their environment. They did not want to work. They stole food from one another and hid it under their mattresses. The counselor called them "corrupt." They all wanted sunglasses; perhaps they suffered from what Aharon Appelfeld later described as "searing light." The counselor regarded this as part of their strangeness. Many waited constantly for letters from their relatives, and when these did not arrive, they cried. Many of them had attacks of hysteria. "It is hard to look at them," Tsvi recorded in his diary. "The distribution of clothes is always difficult. They want nice new clothes and shoes exactly their size. We are not used to such demands from kibbutz children."[38]

The children were short for their ages, another counselor noted— independent, prematurely adult, selfish, and antisocial.[39] The children brought the horrors of their past with them and imposed them on the kibbutz. One counselor described a disturbing game she saw several fourteen-year-old girls playing. They dug a little grave, decorated it with flowers, and buried a doll.[40]

Nine out of ten of them had fled from their homes, most with their parents. Six out of ten had lost contact with at least one parent in their wanderings. Nine out of ten had seen their parents, brothers, and sisters beaten or tortured. About half knew that one or both parents were dead. Many had seen their parents and siblings die, from sickness or starvation or cold. They had seen their families beaten to death, or shot, or burned, or drowned in rivers. A quarter of Aliyat Hanoar children had been in concentration camps. Many had been taken in by strangers; some had been mistreated. A large number were alone in the world. Asked years later, 80 percent said their childhoods, before the Holocaust, had been happy. They had grown up in middle-class houses; their parents had worked as merchants or professionals. The spoken language of the house was that of the country they lived in; only a handful had known Hebrew. Eight out of ten were between the ages of seven and seventeen when they came to Palestine; more than half were between twelve and seventeen.[41] Their personal files yield a picture of melancholy and depression, problems in developing personal relationships, loneliness, learning difficulties, nightmares, anxieties, stuttering, bed-wetting, nail biting, mistreatment of kittens, and other signs of anguish.

Several hundred of the charges were sent to a special institute in Jerusalem for psychiatric evaluation. Some members of the institute came from the United States and knew only English; some knew only German. All were orthodox Freudians. They diagnosed "Oedipal complexes," "inferiority complexes," "weak egos," "latent homosexuality," and the like. Their diagnoses were frequently impressionistic: "He seems like a *tembel* [blockhead] and looks like a big teddy bear," they wrote of one boy, while of another they wrote that he "performs all sorts of sadistic pranks" and that he was "good-natured but dull, like Lenny in *Of Mice and Men.*" Of one child it was said that he was "overattached to his mother"; she had been killed in the war. Another was termed "disturbed" because he spoke too much Polish.[42] They diagnosed one boy as having "a large impediment in listening ability," and then noted, casually, that they had not even succeeded in speaking with the child because, unfortunately, he knew only Hungarian.[43]

The kibbutz counselors who had no formal education in this field frequently described their charges as "retarded" and "disturbed" and as exhibiting "strange and alien" behavior. In one case this was because a boy was not interested in agriculture or in animals. Another boy was described as "a hysterical type," the reason being that "Yosef has excessive demands regarding his standard of life, which he contrasts with the comfortable standard of his parents' home." A group of young people from Germany, all born in 1934, were continually referred to as "the Germans": "Is there any hope of educating this youth, who have something of the gleanings of Nazi education?"[44] Another counselor described the typical charge—apparently with some measure of self-parody: "His eyes are not ready to see, and his ears are not ready to hear and learn. He does not accept the hand stretched out to help him or the friendship offered him. He comes with clenched teeth and a locked heart, his eyes to the ground, darting stubbornly to each side; sometimes he brings with him no small portion of cynicism toward what is sacred to us, even toward our outstretched hand. Neither romance nor beauty excites him, neither the prophet Amos nor the country's landscape."[45]

The encounter between the children of the Holocaust and their Israeli counselors was described as "an all-out war between the old and the new," a mythic battle between the sons of light and the sons of darkness. The goal was "a primal formation of a new pioneering Jewish personality from elements of chaos, disfigurement, and both spiritual and physical castration." The struggle was "for a complete change of values: the breaking of invalid and selfish habits, concepts, and moral norms and the putting of positive values in their place."[46] In general, the newcomers did not live together with the kibbutz children. Yet if they found it hard to change and adjust—or did not want to do so—their behavior was termed "deviant," "regressive," and "ungrateful." If they criticized the educational framework or the kibbutz itself, they were called "nihilists" or "relativists."[47]

The files of Aliyat Hanoar also reveal that there was often no coordination between the young people's aspirations and the kibbutz's needs. Many of them wanted to study. The kibbutz wanted them to work, fearing that, if they learned a trade, they would leave for the cities.

At one point, three boys asked to be transferred from the agricultural school at Ayanot to a vocational school. "We are young," they wrote. "There is no one to help us and only you can help us, because we don't have any other way and we are turning to you because we have no one else to turn to. Our parents remained in the Transnistria camps and we are substituting you for our parents."

Someone in the main office smelled a mutiny. "Of course, we have no intention of responding to this request of theirs, especially since it appeared in the form of a collective demand," wrote one official to a colleague, asking for the agricultural school's opinion. These boys are stubborn shirkers, the kibbutz replied; "they smoke!" In the meantime, they were called up for an "explanation," at the end of which they admitted they had erred in asking to learn a trade. To be sure, Ayanot proposed that they be separated. Two were transferred elsewhere.[48]

Something of this sort occurred also at Givat Haim. A group of boys asked to be transferred to Kfar Vitkin, to study metalworking at the ORT vocational school there. Many other teenagers had also applied for admission, and it was impossible to satisfy them all. But the rejection of their request was also based, not unexpectedly, on ideology. The ORT school system gave the boys a chance to leave the kibbutz and make their livings as craftsmen in the cities. Commented one official,

There are tendencies within the yishuv that are beginning to cast doubt on the primacy of the principle of agriculture and cooperative education. . . . When a young person is educated in the Aliyat Hanoar movement, he learns necessarily to burn a number of bridges. Up until now we have taught them to burn the bridge to the social milieu in which a profession is the most important element. If they realize that the way to vocational training is open to them and exempts them from the difficulties of adjusting to . . . rural life, they will not make the moral effort . . . and there will be no psychological revolution. . . . They will think that it is possible to be a good citizen of the country as a professional alone and will content themselves with that.

But then, it seems to me, we will cease to be what we are.[49]

Forty years later, most graduates of the Aliyat Hanoar program gave the project good marks. They praised their teachers and counselors, many kept in touch with them. They said the education they had received instilled in them a sense of belonging and shaped their worldview as Israelis. A comparison of statistical data on their lives with data on an Israeli control group shows that few of them became officers or volunteered to continue in the army after completing their mandatory service. They produced fewer managers and college graduates than the control group, but the statistics indicate that their lives were stable—they did not change homes or jobs frequently. Nine out of ten said their marriages were good. Their children tended to live close by and to maintain contact.[50] Their histories reveal a great human drama. The boy thrown into the Danube with his father, who drowned, became a production engineer at a factory in the Galilee. The boy who was described as an asocial type who should be expelled from the program reached the rank of lieutenant colonel in the army. The boy whose file contains the remark that "he gives the impression of being retarded" became a school principal. This was the Israeli dream.[51]

The ability and willingness of the kibbutzim to absorb the survivors was conditioned on the ability and willingness of the survivors to change. If they wanted to remain what they were, they had to look for a more open and tolerant community. The kibbutz framework demanded that everyone adjust to a single system of values, norms, and sensibilities; it could not accommodate the needs or respond to the personal anguish of any one individual. The ideological and social elitism of the kibbutz members led them to sacrifice personal comfort and invest their money in helping the immigrants they absorbed. But it also made them demand that the immigrants sacrifice, almost denounce, their past in the Exile and recognize the moral superiority of the kibbutz way of life.

The kibbutzim needed new members for their development and for shoring up the economic and political status of their movement. To get new members, they fought for the right to absorb immigrants. They even "kidnaped" immigrants from other kibbutzim. Kibbutz Givat Brenner once protested to the Histadrut that in the immigrant camps someone was spreading "atrocity rumors" against it and that, as a result, a group of immigrants it had wanted had been "snatched" by Degania.[52] Mapai leaders described the strengthening of the kibbutzim as the party's "innermost desire" and expressed concern that too few immigrants were joining the kibbutzim.[53] "The greatest tragedy of this wave of immigration is that the settlement movement is not being built up by it," one of them said. They frequently discussed how to encourage immigrants to join kibbutzim. "We know that this wave of immigration lacks a [good] attitude towards rural settlement," said one member, "but if we speak to the immigrant's heart, once or twice, if we show him the facts, then to the extent that he wants to be active and to assimilate well into the country, he must in the end reach the conclusion that, for him, going to a settlement is imperative." That is not enough, said Shmuel Dayan, proposing to "force" immigrants to go to agricultural settlements. "What's so horrible about that?" Moshe Dayan's father asked. "After all, we're not sending them to Siberia." The Histadrut immigration division proposed all kinds of administrative tricks to make it difficult for immigrants to leave the kibbutzim.[54]

In 1949 David Ben-Gurion toyed with the idea of sending immigrants to work on development projects under a military or "paramilitary" regimen, in order to get rid of "the demoralizing material" among them and to give them occupational training, mastery of Hebrew, and "national discipline," as well as to create "social cells" for agricultural settlement. The plan, never activated, was often discussed. Eight out of ten Israelis polled in 1949 said that the concentration of immigrants in the cities endangered the country's economic and social structure; nine out of ten said the immigrants should be "directed" to agricultural settlements, and slightly more than half said they should be "forced" to go to settlements.[55] Immigrants were often censured for refusing to be farmers. "To the city, to the city," jeered *Haaretz*, "to a place where café lights beckon and cinema posters glare." The newspaper contended that the immigrants were "not taking seriously the obligations they took upon themselves before their immigration" and accused them of not feeling any "personal responsibility for the Zionist enterprise."[56] Yet at that time, at least 90 percent of Israelis lived in cities.

The kibbutzim saw themselves as the social elite of Israel and of Zionism, the ideological vanguard. Their commitment to living the national revolution infused them with a sense of personal duty. Thus the kibbutzim paid for new members' housing, meals, clothing, and sometimes travel and medical expenses. In those days the kibbutzim had not yet reached the economic pinnacle of a generation later, and the immigrants were often a burden to them. At Ein Harod, members volunteered to care for immigrants after their regular work hours, and some took in foster children for months at a time. At Shaar Haamakim, the members evacuated their rooms and gave them to the immigrants. The members themselves slept under the open sky until the Jewish Agency sent them tents. Kibbutz members often cited this duty: "We took it upon ourselves to absorb these immigrants, and we will continue to do so."[57]

The letters that the kibbutzim sent to the Histadrut's immigration center and to the immigration department of the Jewish Agency spoke of the practical difficulties involved in absorbing the newcomers. The kibbutzim complained that these institutions were not aiding them. "Our collective does not have the ability to bear all the necessary costs of setting up an immigrant who lacks everything, to the extent of helping him feel good and assuring his successful absorption," Kibbutz Ayelet Hashahar wrote to the Jewish Agency. The absorption of forty-two immigrants from Romania had strained the resources and patience of Kibbutz Elon:

It has raised many difficult questions that we cannot solve by ourselves. . . . These people arrived without anything. Without even minimal possessions. From the very first day we had to equip them with clothing, shoes, and housing. We received zero help from you. Two and a half liras [$10] for each person. Most of the people are too exhausted and weak from the trials they have been through in the Nazi inferno, and they are not able to work. We have had to nurse them and let them rest. Among them are ten serious chronic invalids who are not able to work at all and who need special care and training. We have been grappling with all these questions continually, out of appreciation of the role we have been assigned. But there is a limit to our abilities. We are a mountain community, not yet on our feet, and the burden that has fallen on us is too heavy . . . and with all our understanding and willingness to absorb immigration, we cannot handle it. The winter is coming. In our difficult climate we will have to provide the people with winter clothes and warm bedding, or they will not last. How can we do it on our own?

Enclosed with the letter to the Jewish Agency were receipts showing medical expenses for the immigrants.[58]

The dispute was, in essence, financial. The kibbutzim demanded an increase in the allowance they received for each immigrant they absorbed. They demanded to be permitted to keep the "primary needs" package given to each immigrant, including the "agency bed," even if the newcomer left the kibbutz. Furthermore, they charged, no one took any interest in the immigrants after they were sent to the kibbutzim, as if placing them were enough. The kibbutzim were to make sure they maintained good health, learned Hebrew, became part of the community, and overcame the trauma of the Holocaust. But the kibbutzim could not perform this task, they said.

The kibbutzim were small, extremely insular communities in which people lived in very close quarters. They could not and did not want to accept just anyone. Kibbutz Afikim did not want Yehudit Kahane, "an immigrant from Bergen-Belsen," because she demanded special treatment. Kibbutz Usha made the problem a matter of principle, informing the Histadrut that it would send back, forthwith, any person sent to it without its consent. The Histadrut responded that "in certain instances" it was allowed to send immigrants to a kibbutz "temporarily," even if prior permission had not been given. Usha's announcement that it would return people was unbecoming to a kibbutz, "which is founded on the principle of concern and assistance for the absorption of immigrants," the Histadrut chided. But Usha had the last word: "We know that you have not sent the neighboring kibbutzim any people, or at most just a handful, not more than a score of them. You therefore have no right and no grounds to lecture us."[59] The argument was not just about money or authority; it was a battle for "the quality of human material." The kibbutzim, and the other types of agricultural settlements, did not want sick people or "social cases," small children or old people. Malka Shlein from an agricultural settlement called Kfar Kish complained that the Immigration Center had sent people in their fifties, "on the verge of old age." She explained why her community could not accept them, saying that its members were interested in people their own age, twenty-eight to thirty or so, who could be integrated into the community and who would strengthen it. Kfar Kish was not interested in setting up a golden-age community, she wrote.[60] This phenomenon was not, however, limited to kibbutzim and other agricultural settlements. Levi Eshkol once justified the policy of selection in immigration: "Israel can't absorb all the crazy Jews of the world."[61]

Some Holocaust survivors came to Israel with the goal of joining a kibbutz. Many had received appropriate training while they were still in Europe, and they settled happily into kibbutz life. Often, the kibbutz replaced the family they had lost and provided hope and security, sometimes common memories. For those who had belonged to the socialist Zionist youth movement before the Holocaust, kibbutz life was a kind of delayed victory over the Nazis. And if, moreover, the kibbutz flourished and their sons became officers in Israeli army combat units, these too were compensation for the defeat and humiliation suffered in Europe. Paradoxically, the kibbutz—so Israeli, so different from the Exile—was, in its insularity, similar to the small eastern European Jewish towns that had been destroyed in the Holocaust. The resemblance was especially notable in kibbutzim where most of the members had endured the Holocaust.

There were also survivors who, with no advance training, adjusted easily to kibbutz life. Yet, in the end, it was a solution for only a few. By the end of 1949, about 10,000 immigrants had been taken in by the kibbutzim; half of them later left.[62]

Many immigrants who reached kibbutzim rejected the collective idea in principle. After years in concentration camps, DP camps, British detention camps, Israeli immigrant camps, and Israeli army camps, most of the survivors wanted nothing more than a room of their own and attention to their personal troubles. "They have a preconditioned negative reaction to any place where there are a lot of people together," explained a Mapai leader to his colleagues. "They claim that the collective communities remind them of the concentration camps. So they can't adjust and they look for some way to live individually."[63] Life in the kibbutz did not shield the survivors from mental anguish: they often had the same nightmares, the same anxieties, the same feelings of guilt and shame. One of the immigrants sent to Kibbutz Mishmarot related: "When I sat down at a table in the dining room, waiting for the server to come to my table, I was shaking. I was afraid that there wouldn't be enough food and that my table wouldn't get any."[64] Many suffered mental crises, generally after two or three years at the kibbutz, when they began to grasp that their families were lost and would never return. The crisis frequently began with the birth of their first child and brought on hallucinations and suicide attempts.[65]

Kibbutz members often found the presence of the immigrants disturbing. "We can't see our own members for all the immigrants," some complained; they proposed setting up separate dining halls, "to distance them a little bit, so that we can live our own lives." At Kibbutz Alonim, the members were asked why the relationship between the two groups was so difficult. They listed the causes in the following order: the immigrants' unwillingness to adjust to kibbutz life; the shortage of girls among the immigrants; their lack of desire to live at the kibbutz; their impatience in the face of crises; the fact that most of the immigrants had arrived alone. The number of members who believed that they, too, were guilty of the lack of communication was much smaller. Only a few said the kibbutz might not be caring for the immigrants properly. Even fewer said that there was not a sufficiently welcoming atmosphere at the kibbutz or agreed that the kibbutz did not provide for the immigrants' minimal needs. Most of the members, then, tended to blame the immigrants themselves for their difficulties in adjusting to kibbutz life and often regarded them as a nuisance. At the same time, the members believed that they should continue to absorb more immigrants: it was their ideological duty, and it was essential for the future of the kibbutz.[66] Comparatively, the kibbutzim absorbed fewer immigrants than the rest of the country. A year and a half after the establishment of the state, 7 percent of the country's population lived on kibbutzim, but the kibbutzim absorbed only 4 percent of the immigrants.[67]

¶

A year and a half after World War II ended, the Haganah commander in Europe, Nahum Shadmi, began to sign up young men from the DP camps for military training. The immediate goal was not to enlist them in Israel's fight for independence but to turn them from "human debris" into "upstanding" young people, to make them indistinguishable from the "sabras," the native Israelis. Only with difficulty did Shadmi convince his superiors, among them Ben-Gurion, to encourage this overseas enlistment (called *gahal* in Hebrew). But when the War of Independence broke out, the leadership changed its mind.[68] About two months before the declaration of independence, with the war raging, Ben-Gurion wrote to one of the immigration envoys:

The war depends on immigration, because the manpower in Israel will not suffice. The Arabs have huge reserves and we need people from overseas for the war now. Immigration that is not directed entirely, from start to finish, to the war's needs is no blessing. You must understand that your operation, like the life of the yishuv, must accommodate itself to those needs, and this means sending only people from the ages of 18 to 35 or, in exceptional cases, to 40, trained to carry arms.

"First [send] all the young people who can help us with the war," demanded a member of the Jewish Agency executive. One haapala activist, unenthusiastic about the new order, told his men that the Jewish Agency had threatened to "cease funding our operation if the immigration does not serve the war."[69] The envoys presented enlistment as the duty of every man and woman. "I require the Jews of the camps to enlist. They are like citizens of Israel," Shadmi reported.[70] Haim Yahil wrote that there was "an atmosphere of enlistment" in the camps, noting that parents of enlistees won respect, and evaders were publicly disgraced. A young man who did not sign up had trouble walking through the camp. Later, Yahil would write: "The remnant's volunteering for the War of Independence was perhaps the most wonderful episode in its history."[71]

A total of 22,000 Holocaust survivors took part in the war—one out of every three fighters. Most enlisted while they were in DP camps or detention camps in Cyprus. Some received basic training before arriving; but most were taken into the army within days of arrival, without proper training and without any knowledge of the country they were being sent to defend. Most did not know Hebrew and so could not be assigned to administrative roles, in the rear. Instead they were sent to the front. One out of three of the war's casualties was a Holocaust survivor.[72] As a group, the survivors tended to be older than the rest of the soldiers. To the native-born men, they were refugees, foreigners, "of the Exile." The army was not prepared for them.

It was frustrating. Army psychologists found the newcomers' morale poor and feared that their presence lowered morale among other soldiers as well. Low-ranking commanders often humiliated and insulted the new recruits, who had a reputation for being melancholy, cowardly soldiers, prisoners of their past. "The men fled at the decisive moment," it was said of them. "Difficult, stubborn, and cowardly men." In his war diary, Ben-Gurion quoted Yitzhak Rabin, who attributed the demoralization in his battalion to the immigrants.[73] Many of them had enlisted in the war partly under the influence of agents from Israel who promised they would find a warm home in their new country. But they generally had trouble finding a place for themselves in the legendary brotherhood of arms—it was too Israeli, too closed. They differed conspicuously from both the sabra soldiers and the foreign soldiers who came to help the Israeli Defense Forces (IDF). These foreign volunteers were not refugees; they came mainly from the United States, spoke English, not Yiddish, and were greatly appreciated.

In addition to the memories of the previous war that plagued the immigrants, they also agonized over not having had time before enlistment to locate their relatives; neither did they know what they would do with themselves after being discharged. An internal IDF report stated, in a tone of concern, that many described themselves as "cannon fodder." This was a widespread expression.[74] Soon thereafter a myth was born:

> Ben-Gurion threw human debris
> Into the enemies' eyes.
> On the bones of boys from the Holocaust
> A new road to Jerusalem was built.

Statistical evidence indicates that there is no foundation to this claim.[75]

The IDF was aware that its Holocaust-survivor soldiers needed special help, both material and psychological, and it formulated various plans to make it easier for them to locate relatives, learn Hebrew, tour the country, and visit in the houses of other Israelis. In July 1948, the chief enlistment officer ordered that the soldiers be called out immediately and that the commanders should "explain the special approach to new immigrants who come from the Nazi inferno and from long years of life in concentration camps. . . . The immigrants should be treated generously and considerately and be given the feeling that they are coming home."[76] Another document states that, to raise their morale, "it is imperative to eliminate the feeling that they are meant to be no more than cannon fodder."[77]

Military service gave the soldier who had survived the Holocaust a part in the victory, compensating him at least for some of what he had endured in Europe. In the army he gained a certain acquaintance with the country and its people and a sense of belonging. The army did little, however, to advance the immigrants' social integration. The general opinion was that the human quality of the natives was higher than that of the immigrants, that the natives, not the immigrants, were making the Israeli revolution. This perception was the "strange wall" between the Holocaust survivors and the native Israelis diagnosed by a member of the Jewish Agency executive. Ben-Gurion called it "a barrier of blood and silence and agony and loneliness."[78]

On top of all this, there was the ideological dispute. The yishuv was permeated with a deep, almost mystic faith in its superiority, as symbolized by a hardy cactus whose fruit was spiked on the outside and sweet inside—the prickly pear, the sabra. Author Yehudit Hendel once said on Israeli television:

> To put it bluntly, there were almost two races in this country. There was one race of people who thought they were gods. These were the ones who had had the honor and privilege of being born in Degania, or in the Borochov neighborhood of Givataim, and I belong, as it were, to those gods. I grew up in a workers' neighborhood near Haifa. And there was, we can certainly say, an inferior race. People we saw as inferior who had some kind of flaw, some kind of hunchback, and these were the people who came after the war. I was taught in school that the ugliest, basest thing is not the Exile but the Jew who came from there.[79]

"This people is ugly, impoverished, morally suspect, and hard to love," Leah Goldberg said in a meeting Ben-Gurion held with a group of writers. Like Dostoevsky and Gorky, who were unafraid of ugliness, stench, and lowness, the poet added, the Israeli writer had to see in the Holocaust survivor the human image, and not only the man hiding dollars in his belt. Of course, she said, this was a task that required "a tremendous effort."

Itzhak Sadeh, commander of the Palmach elite militia, wrote an often-quoted essay called "My Little Sister." He describes meeting a young woman who has just arrived from Europe. Her body bears a tattoo "FOR OFFICERS ONLY." It later emerges that the Germans not only forced her into prostitution but also sterilized her. "Why am I here? Do I deserve to be rescued by these strong, healthy young men, who risk their lives to save mine?" she asks. Sadeh responds: "Be our sister, be our bride, be our mother," and he sums up: "For the sake of my sisters I'll be brave. For the sake of my sisters I'll also be cruel: everything, everything!" It was no coincidence that the Holocaust was symbolized by a prostitute; the metaphor was a continuation of a common stereotype that depicted the Exile as weak, feminine, and passive, and the yishuv as strong, masculine, and active.[80]

The sabra represented a national ideal, and the Holocaust survivor its reverse. Moreover, the survivors threatened that ideal at a time when sabras were still fighting their parents' generation for preeminence in Israeli society. The country fostered the sabra image, seeing in it the fulfillment of the Zionist and labor movement dreams of national renewal and return to a "healthy" social structure. Yet most people could not live up to this ideal. They had not lived long in the country, and many had not yet rid themselves of their "Diaspora mentality." Holocaust survivors imposed on earlier immigrants a past that many had not yet succeeded in putting aside, and their disdain of the survivors often reflected a desire to distance themselves, to deny what they themselves were. The survivors forced the Israelis to realize that the vision of the "new man" was not to be. Most came as refugees, not as visionary Zionists. "Many of them are nothing but migrants who have come because they have nowhere else to go," wrote a *Haaretz* reporter scornfully.[81] The same was true, of course, of many who had come before.

The dissonance between ideal and reality made the Israelis harsher with the new immigrants. The newcomers were expected to identify with the sabra stereotype and transform themselves in its image; the effort to do so was seen as a pledge of loyalty and a rite of entry into the tribe. Aharon Appelfeld wrote of a boy newly arrived from Poland whose fellows beat him because he could not get a suntan like theirs. He assured them that he was trying as hard as he could to make his skin darker, but they told him that, if he really wanted it, it would have happened long before. His pallor forced them to confront the Diaspora and the Holocaust, so they hit him.[82]

Even Rozka Korczak, who had fought the Nazis in the Vilna ghetto and who was received as a heroine, found herself under attack. She arrived in Palestine in December 1944 and soon thereafter appeared at a Histadrut convention. She spoke in Yiddish. David Ben-Gurion complained that "Comrade Refugee" was speaking "a foreign language" (or, according to another source, "a foreign, discordant language") instead of speaking Hebrew.[83]

Each new arrival was a reminder that the Zionist movement had been defeated in the Holocaust. The leadership could reiterate that the extermination of the Jews occurred before the Zionist movement had enough power to save them. It could repeat that the Holocaust was proof of the need to establish a Jewish state. It could recall that the British were to blame for having blocked entry to the country, and that the Arabs were to blame for making them do so, and that the entire world was at fault for standing aside and not coming to the aid of the Jews. It could glorify and extol the few rescue attempts that were made. But none of this could change the fact that the Zionist movement had been helpless. Not only did the yishuv not come to the rescue, but it now found itself in a position where its existence and future depended on the willingness of the Holocaust survivors to settle in the country and fortify its army against the Arab threat.

There were those who were inclined to blame European Jewry itself for its extermination. If they had only recognized the truth of Zionism. "Did we not warn them?" wrote author Moshe Smilansky. "Build yourself a home in your country, your homeland, soon, so you will not be lost." But the warning did not help: "The people heard but did not act."[84] Avraham Shlonsky wrote:

> The storm jolted them with a shower of sparks,
> With a fiery rune,
> Omens, omens, omens,
> And the inferno had already engulfed the forest
> And they fell deaf, they shielded their eyes.[85]

Haim Yahil took this idea one step further: "After all, we cannot forget that the war against the Jews served the Nazis as a major springboard for capturing and maintaining control," he wrote; the implication was that if the Jews had come to Zion, the Nazis would not have gained power in Germany.[86] An article that appeared in *Haaretz* less than four weeks after the German surrender asked: "Did the Jews also have a hand in the horrible bloodshed committed against our nation?"[87] Such sentiments too were a way for native Israelis to defend themselves against the survivors' accusations and to salve their consciences, tormented by impotence, complacency, and above all, psychological detachment from the Jews of Europe while the Holocaust raged.

Many survivors, for their part, resented, even blamed the yishuv. "You danced the hora while we were being burned in the crematoriums," said Yosef Rosensaft, a DP leader at Bergen-Belsen, who settled in America.[88] Usually such things were said only in private. But even unsaid, the accusations poisoned relations between the survivors and the yishuv. "The question lurks in our hearts," said Dov Shilansky, who would later serve as speaker of the Knesset. "What did our brothers outside of hell do?"[89]

Yitzhak "Antek" Zuckerman, speaking at a Zionist conference in London, complained that several months had elapsed between the end of the war and the arrival of the first yishuv envoys in Poland. "How could we have gotten into Poland?" Moshe Sharett asked in self-defense. Zuckerman retorted that they could have entered the same way the refugees got out. "I will forgive you everything," he said, but "I won't forgive that for those last eight months you did not reach us."[90] Zuckerman spent the first thirty-two years of his life in Poland, but from the day he was old enough to think for himself, he knew he would live in Israel, on a kibbutz; yet, for his next thirty-four years, in Israel, up to his death in June 1981, he continued to live the Holocaust as if it had never ended. He settled at Kibbutz Lohamei Hagetaot, devoting most of his time to memorializing the Warsaw ghetto uprising; he had been the deputy to Mordecai Anielewicz, the uprising's leader. His comrades said he had a talent for raising their morale. Haim Guri, who described him as "a towering giant" and attributed to him "a rare combination of strength and beauty," wrote this of him: "More than once, in the middle of a meeting here, I saw that he was there, with the people that were and are no longer. He and the power that was in his silences, as if he refused to say outright what he would say some day and what was choked inside him." Zuckerman indeed had accusations to make against the yishuv, but as a loyal party and kibbutz member he remained silent. Only toward the end of his life did he record his testimony, on condition that it not be published while he was alive. "Israel did not search for us. We felt that we had been abandoned." When Zuckerman said "Israel," he meant the leadership of the kibbutz federation, Hakibbutz Hameuhad.

He was incensed that during the war the movement had made no real effort to send an envoy to Warsaw with greetings and words of encouragement. He spoke of smuggler-envoys who arrived from the Jewish rescue mission in Istanbul. They brought money, sometimes a letter. They were not Jews, not comrades; they brought no advice. He believed that the movement could have sent Jewish emissaries as well. The fact that fellow Jews did not come was, in his eyes, testimony to the psychological abyss between his party's leadership in Palestine and its members in Poland. Guri once asked Zuckerman what would have happened had the party sent 500 paratroopers to the ghetto. Zuckerman replied, according to Guri, that 490 would have been killed and the 10 remaining would have been an additional burden on the ghetto. "When Antek said that the movement had abandoned the ghetto," Guri concluded, "he did not mean an operational failure. He was raising a metaphysical cry. They did not need 500 paratroopers. They needed only one man who would bring them a word of goodwill from the Land of Israel. Just one man. And he did not come."[91]

§

A few days after he came home from his mission to Hungary, paratrooper Yoel Palgi went to a veterans' club in Tel Aviv. It was June 1945. Everyone received him warmly and with admiration, he later wrote. They all wanted to hear what had happened over there. But no one was interested in accounts of Jewish suffering. They wanted a different story, about the few who had fought like lions. "Everywhere I turned," Palgi wrote, "the question was fired at me: why did the Jews not rebel? Why did they go like lambs to the slaughter? Suddenly I realized that we were ashamed of those who were tortured, shot, burned. There is a kind of general agreement that the Holocaust dead were worthless people. Unconsciously, we have accepted the Nazi view that the Jews were subhuman. . . . History is playing a bitter joke on us: have we not ourselves put the six million on trial?"[92]

The bluntest expression of this was in yishuv slang. At some point the word *sabon*, "soap," came to be used to refer to Holocaust survivors. There is some dispute as to when it first appeared, but there is no denying that it was widespread. It reflected the general belief that the Nazis used the bodies of murdered Jews to produce soap, a charge that was constantly repeated and became an accepted truth that also found its way into Knesset speeches, textbooks, and Israeli literature ("On the shelf in the store, wrapped in yellow paper with olive trees drawn on it, lies the Rabinowitz family," wrote Yoram Kaniuk in *Man, Son of Dog*). It seems unlikely that anything could better express the contempt that native-born Israelis felt toward the survivors.*

---

* The Holocaust memorial in Jerusalem, Yad Vashem, has received many letters from people asking about bars of soap left over from the war years. Some offered to contribute the soap to the museum, while others asked whether the soap ought to be properly buried. Yad Vashem always officially replies that the Nazis did not make soap out of Jews. During the war, Germany suffered a shortage of fats, and soap production came under government supervision. Bars of soap were imprinted with the initials RIF, a German acronym for "pure industrial fat." Some mistakenly read the letters as RJF, or "pure Jewish fat." The rumor spread quickly, particularly in the ghettos. There is evidence that senior officials

The attempt of the last Jews of the Warsaw ghetto to "die with honor" and leave a heritage of Jewish heroism, and to take some Germans with them, contradicted the stereotype of the Diaspora Jews going passively to their deaths. It robbed Israel of its monopoly on heroism. The embarrassing truth was that the rebels had not received any help from the yishuv. The yishuv envoys stationed among them before the war had all gone home in due course. Yishuv mythology took care of this problem in its own way—it adopted the uprisings as if they had been its own operations. "The initiative for active self-defense came from our movement," Moshe Sharett said proudly.[94] Most of the rebels in fact belonged to Zionist youth movements, but that did not make their organizations "our underground," as they were later termed in Israel.[95]

The paratrooper mission was similarly presented. The young men and women who parachuted behind the Nazi lines had in fact lived for a short while in kibbutzim, and some of them belonged to the Palmach. But most had arrived in Israel after the war began, when they were already over twenty years old. Their bravery was a product not of the yishuv but of the Diaspora. Only rarely was the role of the refugees themselves in the haapala given its due. Thus the poet Natan Alterman celebrated the heroism of "our boys, who carry the nation on their shoulders," but described the maapilim as the Diaspora's tailors, cobblers, and money changers, "a huddled and despairing throng," "without a man's face or a woman's image."[96]

Palestine's heroism during the war was also lauded. Yitzhak Gruenbaum told a group of survivors how the country had protected and strengthened itself in preparation for the fateful hour of decision. "Don't think it was easy," Gruenbaum said.[97] The yishuv had to believe this to be able to look the survivors in the eye, perhaps to look in the mirror, too.

§

Within a short time after the survivors began to come, a kind of ideological-emotional compact was settled between the Israelis and the

---

in the Nazi regime, among them the governor of Poland, Hans Frank, also believed that the soap was indeed produced from human fats.

A few months before the end of the war, a laboratory in Danzig began conducting experiments to find out whether human fats could be used in food production. Yad Vashem has concluded that Jews were not murdered for this purpose. Here, then, is the history of a myth.[93]

"remnants," built on four basic assumptions that united them during the war effort of 1948, the depression of the 1950s, and the mass immigration from the Islamic countries. The first assumption, enshrined in the Declaration of Independence, stated that the Holocaust had proven once again that the only solution to the Jewish problem was an independent state in Israel. The second assumption was that the rest of the world—literally every nation—was hostile and had done nothing to save the Jews during the Holocaust. "This is the most terrible lesson, perhaps, that we have learned in the present generation," wrote a columnist for *Haaretz*.[98] The third assumption was summed up in the phrase "Holocaust and heroism" and held that the two were of equal moment, "two flames burning in one heart." This assumption was also the ideological basis for the memorial culture that developed over the years.[99] The fourth assumption said that the less everybody talked about the Holocaust, the better. Thus the great silence was born; it continued for years and was broken only in 1951, at the time of the Kastner trial. The assumptions were not the product of conscious deliberation; rather, they arose spontaneously from a recognition that without a consensus of this sort, it would be very hard to live together.

In 1949 the composition of the incoming immigrants began to change. Instead of Holocaust survivors, Jews from Asia and North Africa arrived. The result was that the Holocaust survivors experienced what past immigrants had: they suddenly became "old-timers." Like the German Jews and the Holocaust survivors before them, the immigrants from the Islamic world had to deal not only with practical difficulties but also with a hostile atmosphere. "We need to teach them the most elementary things—how to eat, how to sleep, how to wash," a member of the Jewish Agency executive remarked.[100] Many of them were abandoned upon their arrival in miserable conditions, without proper housing, without education for their children, without medical care, without work. Many lived for a while in front yards, public parks, even on the streets; many went hungry. Their situation was so difficult that one Mapai leader who dealt with them said the worst thing any real Zionist could say: "Had I known what awaited them here, I would have voted in favor of leaving them in Syria."[101] Their distress lasted for years, passing on to their children and even grandchildren, and has become a central, painful issue in Israeli history. Yet at base their experience was very similar to that of the Holocaust survivors.

With the arrival of the immigrants from the Arab countries, a new kind of social struggle came into existence. It was no longer old-timers versus Holocaust survivors, sabras versus "debris," but European Jews versus Oriental Jews, Ashkenazim versus Sephardim. Soon the survivors were part of the European establishment that ruled the country. Anticipating the arrival of more immigrants from Poland, the Jewish Agency executive in 1949 considered a proposal to house them in hotels, reserving the transit camps for immigrants from Arab countries. After all, explained one participant in the discussion, the Europeans belong to our tribe.[102] Soon, the Holocaust survivors would begin receiving payments from Germany, compensation for their suffering and the property they had lost. This, too, widened the gap between them and the newcomers from the Islamic countries and helped bring them, finally, into the tribe.

PART IV

RESTITUTION:
How Much Will We Get for
Grandma and Grandpa?

10 | "Add a Few Moral Arguments"

On a November day in 1951 an SAS passenger plane landed at Tel Aviv airport, on a stopover between the Far East and Europe. Among the passengers was a German citizen who had boarded the craft after a last-minute change of plans: He had at first intended to fly KLM, with a stopover in Cairo. Upon finding himself in Israel, he became greatly agitated; his wife too was upset. They feared they would be arrested. The man was Hjalmar Schacht, formerly minister of economic affairs in Hitler's government. The international tribunal in Nuremberg had acquitted him; a court for denazification sentenced him to eight years in prison but he was released soon thereafter.

Fifteen months prior to Schacht's unexpected arrival in Tel Aviv, the Knesset had passed the Nazi and Nazi Collaborators (Punishment) Law, which authorized the death penalty for war criminals, but now no one called the police. Some people in line at the airport cafeteria recognized, and spoke with, Schacht; a cafeteria worker asked for his autograph. Journalists approached him and asked him, as an economic expert, whether Germany would pay reparations to the Jews. "In an airport filled with hundreds of Jews, some of them armed, no one wanted to claim the crown of Frankfurter and Schwarzbart," Knesset member Yohanan Bader of the right-wing opposition party later complained, noting, rightly, that their reluctance "was proof of a peculiar attitude."* Prime Minister

---

* In Paris in 1926, Shalom Schwarzbart assassinated Simon Petlura, whose men had massacred thousands of Jews in the Ukraine; David Frankfurter had killed the Swiss Nazi leader Wilhelm Gustloff in 1936.

David Ben-Gurion said that he would not have recommended killing Schacht, but he admitted he was stunned and ashamed at how the ranking Nazi had been received, and he ordered a reexamination of the rules regarding passengers in transit.[1] Yet the incident was typical. In those days all agreed that the legacy of the Holocaust imposed certain rules of behavior, but it was hard to establish specifically what was permissible and what was taboo.

Many Israelis still identified Adenauer's Germany with Hitler's, rejecting any contact with it as contact with the devil. That was what personal loss, revenge, and national honor required; that was their duty as survivors, they believed. Their hearts burst, their blood boiled, their souls raged; Nazi Germany was liable to rise again, they warned.

"It is unthinkable that we should have any contact or any communication with the murderers," said Knesset member Mordecai Nurok of the national-religious Mizrahi party. "It would be a horrible betrayal of the memory of our holy martyrs."[2] In his view, all Germans were and always would be murderers. Nurok was an elderly rabbi who served for a few weeks as postmaster in Ben-Gurion's cabinet. A dignified man whose habitual tailored suit gave him a European appearance, he had been a Jewish community leader and member of parliament in Riga, Latvia. When addressing the Latvian Sjem, Nurok liked to speak in German, a right granted to representatives of national minorities. In the Knesset, too, he always began his speeches with the words "Eminent House," as was customary in German parliaments. During his fourteen years in the Knesset, Nurok spoke almost exclusively about the Holocaust. With few exceptions, he delivered virtually the same speech, demanding a permanent boycott of Germany. He was the Knesset's Cato the Elder; he had lost his wife and both his children in World War II.

Hatred of Germans and the call to ostracize them echoed everywhere. "The Germans cannot be redeemed except through total destruction or total sterilization," citizen Yermiah Yafeh wrote to the prime minister.[3] "We must impress hatred of the Germans upon our young children and their descendants," wrote a columnist for the popular independent paper *Yediot Aharonot*; she demanded that "not even a hairpin or shoelace of German manufacture be allowed in the country" and proposed that "if we meet a German in our travels, on a boat or a train, we should spit in his face, or at his feet, so that he not forget."[4] The editor of *Haaretz*, Gershom Schocken, proposed a special law barring Israelis from any social contacts with German citizens, including incidental contacts, such as between tourists in a hotel. The law would also forbid Israeli citizens to travel to Germany except as government representatives sent for a specific purpose.[5] The foreign ministry stamped on every Israeli passport, in English, a notification that the document was not valid in Germany. The Government Press Office announced that Israelis who settled in Germany permanently would not be allowed to return.[6]

During its first months, Israel did indeed seem likely to forbid all contacts with Germany and to boycott it for generations. The boycott that, according to tradition, the Jewish people had imposed on Spain as retribution for the expulsion of the Jews in 1492 was taken as a model. This reaction was largely instinctive: It expressed what most Israelis believed was the right thing to do. The boycott was considered a national duty.[7] A year and a half after the Declaration of Independence, Israel was still, in principle, unbending; as a senior foreign ministry official wrote to an Israeli envoy overseas, "the government will not enter into any legal or economic negotiations with any German body."[8]

But, in fact, it was hard to boycott Germany—and counterproductive. As a result, there were many deviations from the boycott policy, although as long as it was accepted as a guiding principle, the deviations were seen as unique and exceptional. "Export to Germany is a commercial link with that country and, as a rule, is undesirable," the Committee for Foreign Trade acknowledged to the foreign and finance ministers. But then there was the possibility of exporting citrus fruit to Germany, as had been done before the war, even under Nazi rule. The Germans were willing to pay hard currency. So, perhaps, this matter "should be judged separately."[9] Exceptions were very frequent.

Most Israelis, including policymakers, felt a sense of obligation to emotion and conscience, to morals and history. Yet, when forced to decide, most gave priority to state, economic, and personal interests. The man who led the way was David Ben-Gurion. Cold, pragmatic, and powerful, he forced Israel to make up with "the different Germany," as he liked to describe the Federal Republic. He did this with determination, and perhaps too quickly. He brought Israel into the Western bloc led by the United States at a time when many other countries played with the idea of remaining neutral between East and West. The United States, for its part, was not immediately enthusiastic about including Israel in its sphere of influence. But Ben-Gurion understood that the Cold War and Israel's needs required Israel to declare itself; had it been possible, he would have brought the country into NATO.[10] Hence Ben-Gurion pushed to strengthen relations with both France and Germany; neither moral nor emotional qualms blocked this move. Indeed, his moral and emotional standards were determined almost exclusively by the interests of the State of Israel, as he saw them. And he often identified the country's interests with those of Mapai, and vice versa. So it had been before the Holocaust, so it had been during the Holocaust; it was only natural that the pattern continue once an independent state was established. From time to time it seemed as if the young Israeli democracy would not be able to withstand the division that Ben-Gurion's German policy created. In hindsight, however, that was an illusion. Most Israelis supported the prime minister.

Israel's international aspirations were difficult to reconcile with boycott. The United States and other countries were endeavoring to bring Germany back into the family of nations just as Israel was battling for its international position against the efforts of the Arab countries to isolate the Jewish state. Clearly, then, Israel could not afford, for instance, to walk out of international organizations that accepted Germany as a member. In general, Israel voted against accepting Germany, but later, as a member of these organizations, it could not avoid contacts with Germans. Moreover, Israel could not very well promote itself as a potential host for international conferences and then forbid Germans to attend.

Israel's diplomats frequently found themselves face to face with their West German counterparts at cocktail parties and other events where they had to decide whether to respond to a German greeting or to act as if the person facing them were transparent. And what if the German were to extend his hand? Could he be ignored without insulting their mutual host? What should the Israeli representative do if the German diplomat tried to engage him in conversation? "He should extend his hand politely, converse for a minute or two, and take advantage of the first opportunity to talk to someone else," the foreign ministry instructed its people. What if a German telephoned his Israeli counterpart? Once, twice, even three times it was possible, with the help of one's secretary, to avoid taking the call, but what could be done if the German was insistent and called again and again? "He should be told politely that, since there are no relations between the two countries, the Israeli consul is not available," the foreign ministry ordered. But this raised another possibility: "If the German comes to visit the Israeli consulate, he should be told the same thing, politely, if possible by a low-ranking official, and in any case not by the head of the consulate.[11] Something of the sort happened in New York. But when the Israeli representative was the dean of the diplomatic corps, as was the case in another capital, it was impossible for him to ignore his German colleague.[12]

When the state was established, the Jewish Agency office in Munich became an Israeli consulate, accredited to the occupying powers. In December 1949, with occupied Germany moving toward de facto independence, it was decided to keep the consulate functioning "for the time being." The consul was instructed not to have contacts with any German institution, only with the occupation authorities.[13] The instruction was, of course, unrealistic. Eliahu Kurt Livneh functioned in Germany as a diplomatic representative in all respects, but, as much as possible, he tried to keep a low profile. The secrecy of his contacts was often the condition for allowing them. Once the consul reported that the eminent Jerusalem scholar Gershom Scholem was negotiating the transfer of the German Jewish archives to the Zionist archives in Jerusalem and that the Germans were "apt to make the transfer of the archives an occasion for a public, semiofficial ceremony." He suggested a solution. Better to change the name of the institution that received the archives and to call it, for purposes of the ceremony, the Central Jewish Archives, omitting the overly national term *Zionist*. (The foreign ministry rejected the proposal.)*[14]

The papers in the foreign ministry archives reveal much thought and professionalism, and no little intellectual snobbery. Israel's first diplomats loved long, pompous reports full of scholarly allusions and sophisticated convolutions. Most of them had been born in central Europe; a number were yekkes. Many others came from English-speaking countries. Most had a university education and a talent for expressing themselves, orally and in writing. They spoke foreign languages. They often preferred to correspond among themselves in English or French—perhaps because their Hebrew was not good or perhaps because they believed that real diplomacy could be practiced only in European tongues. Or perhaps they simply didn't have enough Hebrew typewriters and telex machines.

The great majority relied on the limited experience they had gained in the days of the "state-to-be," when the Zionist movement's strength

---

* The first German films to be screened in Israeli cinemas were passed off as Austrian or Swiss. The same was done at times with German periodicals. At the end of 1950, the government censorship office forbade a foreign opera star to sing arias by Mozart, Schubert, and Brahms in German.[15]

depended on the measure of goodwill and support it could enlist in worldwide public opinion. The movement's diplomats tended to equate its aspirations, most importantly the establishment of a state, with the great moral debt that the free world owed the Jewish people, especially after the Holocaust. Fostering this connection required careful, realistic, rational diplomacy and a democratic, peace-loving, cultured image. Israel's first diplomats identified, as a group, with this image. They tended to think of themselves as liberal men of the world. They avoided extremism; most supported Mapai, at least in public. Most also pondered the prospect of relations with Germany in these terms. They played a large part in establishing, shaping, and advancing these relations.

At the end of 1950, Gershon Avner, the director of the western European division of the foreign ministry, inquired of several senior officials, "What must the Israeli government's attitude to Germany be in the light of Germany's impending entry into the family of nations with the West's support? Should we continue the diplomatic boycott of Germany, or should we change our policy, and is a change of policy required by political realities?"[16] So began a discussion that was part existential anxiety and hostility verging on revenge, part historiography and ethics, but mostly cold pragmatism. "We must decide immediately," responded Shlomo Ginossar, Israel's chargé d'affaires in Italy, to his superior in Jerusalem, "because at this point the Germans are coming to us, but soon they will not need us and if we want reconciliation then, we will have to pursue them. . . . Extended wavering on our part could easily mean that in the end we will make up with the Germans without getting any benefit out of it and will even need to ask it of them as a favor after having rejected their overtures today."[17]

Mordecai Reginald Kidron, Israel's chargé d'affaires in London, had recorded his evaluation a few months earlier. Referring to the writings of the Prussian general Karl Maria von Clausewitz, Kidron predicted that Israel's days of freedom were numbered—that in ten to fifteen years Germany would once again "let loose the dogs of war" against the Jewish people, to complete what Hitler had begun. The sad thing, the diplomat wrote, was that everyone agreed that his prediction was accurate, but no one was doing anything and no one was protesting. He assigned that role to his country: "The world needs a new Jeremiah," he declared, "and where will it find one if not in Israel?"[18] Gideon Rafael, adviser to the Israeli delegation at the United Nations, was also overcome with fear, mostly because of the aid West Germany was receiving from the United

States. "The American policy regarding Germany is leading all of us to destruction," he wrote to his superior, Ambassador Abba Eban, "and we have no right, as representatives of Israel, to face this holocaust lying down."[19]

Elyashiv Ben-Horin, of the foreign ministry's western European division, described his "sense of revulsion at any contact with the heirs of the Nazis" and argued that softening the line with Germany would only encourage them to evade paying reparations. "The deep truth in the words of Professor [Lewis] Namier on the German character should not be ignored," Ben-Horin wrote. "The individual, unaffiliated German may be no different from the Englishman, the American, or a member of any other cultured nation. The great danger with the German begins the minute he appears in a group."*

The most sober analysis came from Brussels. "Being a heretic, I express my opinion openly—that we have erred in our policy with regard to Germany," wrote Michael Amir, Israel's chargé d'affaires for the Benelux countries.

> I would like to express my unreserved opinion, and forgive me if it is formulated too sharply. To persist with the pariah and boycott policy is to persist with a nice and moral Don Quixote policy, but it means jousting with windmills. It is pretty and consistent, but it brings no benefit, only harm.
>
> I don't support establishing relations for their own sake. I assume that Germany, in order to atone for the crimes of Hitler's regime, is interested in entering negotiations with us over a declaration that condemns the injustice done in the name of the German people to the Jewish people as a whole and that assesses the material and moral responsibility of the German people for the atrocities its leaders committed against the Jewish people. Germany will want, on the basis of this declaration, to conduct negotiations for comprehensive reparations.
>
> Do not say that I am trading in blood and that I am haggling over the cruel crimes of which humanity has never seen the like. . . . I do not make light of reparations from one nation to another, from

---

* This paragraph was omitted from the version of Ben-Horin's letter published in 1988 in the official collection of the foreign ministry's records. In the meantime, Ben-Horin had served as Israel's ambassador in Germany.[20]

one state to another. At the stage of historical decisiveness at which we now stand, they may be able to aid, to a great extent, the building of our land.

There is a great struggle within me as I write these lines. I see before me at this very moment the tragic marches to the gas chambers and I ask myself, of course, if I am not alienating myself from those millions of victims. Yet I always come back to the opinion, expressed by [Ernest] Renan: 'Whoever wishes to make history is obligated to forget history.' I do not forget, but we, in the State of Israel, are obligated to take a realistic political line. . . . I will admit without shame that it grates on my deepest emotions, but policy is not a matter of emotion.[21]

The foreign ministry's director-general, Walter Eitan, agreed with him. Nothing would be achieved without direct ties with Bonn, he wrote.[22] It is hard to determine when, precisely, the first official contact between the two countries was made. Some historians have pinpointed it as December 30, 1951, the day the government decided to enter negotiations on reparations.[23] In fact, a long series of unofficial and semiofficial contacts preceded this decision.

Jewish organizations in the United States had begun examining, as early as 1941, the legal and political ramifications of claiming reparations and compensation from Germany.*[24] At the end of the war, the leaders of the Jewish Agency also began giving the subject attention. They reviewed proposals, memorandums, and position papers they had received over the years from jurists and economists, most of them of German origin; some had specialized in the 1930s in the haavara agreements. A few wrote in German, and one introduced, while the war was going on, the conciliatory and irksome legal term *Wiedergutmachung*—literally, "to make good again," to right the wrong, to rectify.[25] The Jewish Agency was mostly interested in the private assets that remained without heirs

---

* The distinction between these two terms is of great importance. The Hebrew term for reparations, *shilumim*, was coined by Moshe Sharett, who based it on a term from Jewish legal tradition that denoted punitive payments. The term *compensation*, *pitsuim* in Hebrew, connotes the payment of a debt and the satisfaction of a claim, so correcting the original injustice. The two terms have been used interchangeably by some, but here *reparations* is used for the money Israel received and *compensation* for the money individuals received. A general term, referring to both public and individual claims, is *restitution*.

and in the community property that was left without communities—
synagogues, yeshivas, *mikvahs*, schools, libraries of valuable manuscripts,
art museums, hospitals, old-age homes, charitable establishments, apartment houses, office buildings. It was not easy to find the proper legal
basis for claiming restitution, since much of the property had been confiscated from its Jewish owners in accordance with German law. It was
difficult for many to prove their claim to the property in question, and
no one knew how to assess its value. There were other problems as well.
The Jews were not a recognized entity in international law; ironically,
since they were not considered a belligerent nation, they found it difficult
to make a claim for collective restitution during the peace negotiations.
It was not clear who had the authority to draft their claim for them, to
represent them, or to receive property in their name. The question was
a challenge for the Jewish Agency and, later, for the State of Israel.

In September 1945, Chaim Weizmann sent the four occupying powers
a demand that title to all Jewish property without heirs be transferred to
the Jewish Agency.[26] Weizmann valued this property at 2 billion pounds
sterling, or about $8 billion. Money was not his only concern—he de-
manded that the Allies recognize the right of the Jewish Agency to speak
in the name of the Jewish people, both the living and the dead, both
Zionists and non-Zionists. The move was not well received. On the eve
of the decisive struggle for Palestine, there was no chance that the British
would lift a finger to enhance the Jewish Agency's status. Other Jewish
organizations, mostly from the United States, also rejected the Zionist
movement's claim to represent all Jews. The Allies agreed to allocate
only $25 million, to be divided between the Jewish Agency and other
Jewish welfare organizations, to fund humanitarian efforts; years went by
before they paid what they had promised.[27]

With the end of the war, a number of people, especially those of
German origin, began renewing their personal connections with the old
country. Many yekkes visited Germany as soon as it was possible. Some
went on business, some to visit friends. Twelve years of Nazi rule had
not expunged the memories of childhood and youth.* Some returned
permanently. Others went to Germany only to locate property they had

---

* Philosopher Martin Buber accepted the Goethe Prize from Hamburg University. He
explained that he did so to encourage those Germans who had fought for the principles
of humanism. His acceptance raised a storm in the press and the Knesset, and in the
end Buber decided not to travel to Germany to receive the prize.[28]

left behind, to collect old debts, to arrange for pensions or insurance, and to demand compensation.

Some eastern European survivors also ignored the calls for boycott. They did business in Germany, some building on contacts they had made in the DP camps. They also demanded compensation. So it happened that the first law concerning Nazi crimes to be considered by the Knesset was a technical one, aimed at making it easier for Israeli citizens to file for compensation from Germany. The Certification of Documents (Special Purposes) Act permitted the officials of the Association of Central European Immigrants and similar organizations to certify the personal documents of people demanding compensation. The minister of justice, Pinhas Rosen, estimated that the law affected between 30,000 and 50,000 people, each of whom would need an average of three notarized certifications within the next four months. "The question before us is how to organize this huge amount of paperwork with the greatest possible speed and with minimal costs to those eligible," he explained. One Knesset member said, "Were we not such a poor people, we would not have to accept even one of the crumbs thrown our way." Another said, "No money and no ideology can wash the blood from the hands of the German people," and "Our historical accounts with Nazi Germany will not be closed with the demand for and receipt of compensation." Despite the objections, the law was approved, without opposition, ten days after it was introduced in December 1949.[29] That same month, Walter Eitan, the director-general of the foreign ministry, wrote to the cabinet secretary: "There is a feeling that the position on Germany demanded by Israeli honor is growing less firm."[30]

In March 1950, Minister of Finance Eliezer Kaplan wrote to Foreign Minister Moshe Sharett: "In my opinion . . . we should send someone to Germany for the preliminary negotiations" on reparations and compensation. "I do not believe that the state can trust to others and delay action when the matter touches on protecting its interests and those of its citizens."[31] The emissary chosen was Kurt Mendelsohn, the finance ministry's director of customs and stamp taxes. Formally the initiative came from Levi Eshkol, then a member of the Jewish Agency executive, not yet a government minister; still trying to adhere publicly to its position on the requirements of Israeli honor, the government preferred to camouflage its contacts with Germany. "When the matter reaches the stage of transferring funds or goods, the Jewish Agency will be responsible," the foreign ministry stated.[32]

Yet Mendelsohn went to Bonn as a representative of Israel, in the first official mission of its kind. There, he met with the German finance minister, Fritz Schäffer. Mendelsohn brought a detailed memorandum with him, but the Germans gave him the runaround. He also got into disputes with representatives of other Jewish organizations, who were also demanding money and who had arrived in Germany before him.[33]

A few months later, in the summer of 1950, President Chaim Weizmann went to vacation in Bürgenstock, a resort on Lake Lucerne in Switzerland. Among the other guests in the hotel was Chancellor Konrad Adenauer. The two passed each other in the garden but, to the chancellor's dismay, never had a conversation—the Israelis maintained that their president was not feeling well. However, Adenauer's assistant Ernst Ostermann and Israeli chargé d'affaires Shmuel Tulkowsky did speak. The Israeli asked what was happening with the reparations, apparently referring to Kurt Mendelsohn's memorandum and to the subsequent contacts between representatives of the World Jewish Congress and the chancellor's office in Bonn. Ostermann promised a reply.

A few months later, Tulkowsky sent a reminder, noting that "it is the intention of the Israeli government, immediately after receiving the response of the government of the Federal Republic, to raise the issue in direct contacts with the chancellor of your government." Ostermann's answer was evasive.

When Foreign Minister Moshe Sharett came across this exchange of letters, he couldn't believe his eyes. "I was in shock," he wrote to a ministry official. "Here was an official Israeli communication with Germany—and also an explicit announcement that we were prepared for direct negotiations. Was such a thing ever decided on?" It turned out that Sharett had missed the development because he was out of the country. Tulkowsky's letter had been sent with the knowledge of the foreign ministry's director-general and with the approval of Finance Minister Kaplan, but without a formal discussion of the principle at hand.[34] One may suppose that, when the foreign minister recovered from his shock, he was pleased—since a few months previously he had written to Kaplan that he was extremely worried. "We hear each day about the rising fortunes of the Germans—political, economical, and moral," he wrote. "Time is against us in this matter, and I fear we may have missed the hour."[35]

At the end of December 1950, the foreign ministry suggested that the government send an official delegation to Germany to pursue the demands for reparations and compensation. The cabinet was split: Dov Yosef, minister of transportation, opposed all contact with the Germans, even if this meant receiving no money. (Not long before, Chancellor Adenauer had mentioned to a Jewish newspaper in Germany a sum of 10 million marks, about $2 million—a ridiculous sum by any account.[36]) Moshe Shapira, minister of the interior, health, and immigration, said everything depended on how much money was at stake: It was pointless to soil oneself with the taint of German contact for a pittance, but if the sum was substantial, it might well be worthwhile.

As the debate continued, Ben-Gurion suddenly proposed that Israel declare war on Germany, retroactive to the day Israel was founded, three years after Germany's surrender in World War II. The idea was, apparently, just another of the wild inspirations Ben-Gurion sometimes had. Yet it was enough to startle the foreign ministry's director-general, who immediately tried to persuade the prime minister to shelve his war plans until the legal aspects of the issue could be examined. In the meantime, the cabinet rejected the idea of sending a delegation to Germany, instead instructing the foreign ministry to address its demands to the occupation powers.[37]

And so it was in January 1951 that Israel asked the United States, the Soviet Union, Britain, and France to impose $1.5 billion in reparation payments on Germany. Washington, London, and Paris responded politely that they were doing their best and suggested that Israel contact Germany directly. Moscow made no reply. In March, Israel wrote again to the three Western powers, but by the time their replies came, in July, relations between the Jews and the Germans had taken a dramatic turn.[38]

¶

In the afternoon hours of April 19, 1951, two Israeli government officials arrived at the Crillon Hotel in Paris. David Horowitz, then director-general of the finance ministry and later governor of the Bank of Israel, and Maurice Fischer, Israel's chargé d'affaires in France, took care to arrive and leave separately, so as to minimize the risk that their presence in the hotel would arouse attention. Before the Israelis parted from their negotiating partner, he promised to observe the condition Israel had stipulated—namely, that if the press should discover the meeting had taken place, he would deny it. Fischer suggested to his superiors in Jerusalem that they forgo, for reasons of secrecy, a written report, that they wait until Horowitz returned to brief them in person. The government had approved the meeting, but Horowitz wrote in his memoirs that Ben-Gurion instructed him to conceal the contents of the conversations from the other ministers.[39]

As always, a leak occurred. "All the rumors that have been spreading about this matter are incorrect," Foreign Minister Moshe Sharett lied, and the press did not pressure him. The story seemed almost fantastic.[40] For the man David Horowitz and Maurice Fischer had come to see at the Crillon was Chancellor Konrad Adenauer. It was the first meeting at such a high level between representatives of the two countries—a decisive step toward reconciliation between the Jewish and German nations. The Israelis demanded $1.5 billion.

They spoke in German; the conversation was tense, Horowitz later recalled. Adenauer said he wanted to repair, in some small way, the great injustice the Germans had done the Jews. Horowitz replied that there was no way to repair the injustice. As instructed, he maintained a calm reserve, without hostility. Before the two countries could proceed with financial negotiations, he stated, Germany had to condemn the crimes of the Nazis. The chancellor said he had condemned their crimes on many occasions, but Horowitz demanded that an official declaration of contrition be made "in a ceremonial act." Adenauer accepted the condition: "It will be done," he said, adding that his country would like to help Israel. Horowitz interrupted him. He had not come to ask for help, he said. The subject was the return of stolen property, and the sum that Israel was demanding was but a tiny part of the value of the property the Germans stole from the Jews. The Germans had previously indicated their willingness to negotiate on the basis of the Israeli demand. Adenauer did not demur, but he avoided an outright yes. Fischer felt he was facing a cold, calculating man. The old German tried, however, to demonstrate his goodwill: Time after time, he asked his Israeli guests not to be in a rush to leave and told them that some of his best friends were Jewish, that at least one Jew had been saved from the Nazis thanks to his personal intervention. Horowitz responded with a chilly silence. "I had instructions to preserve a proud and honorable bearing, to fight for our demands, but not to humiliate ourselves and not to let the negotiations descend into street bargaining," he wrote in his memoirs.[41]

On September 27, 1951, Chancellor Adenauer made a historic declaration in the Bundestag in Bonn. World opinion, he said, had concerned itself repeatedly in the recent past with the Federal Republic's attitude toward the Jews. "Doubts have been expressed here and there as to whether the new state has been guided on this momentous question by principles that do justice to the frightful crimes of the past and put the relationship of the Jews to the German people on a new and healthy basis." German Jews were now equal citizens under law, as stipulated by the constitution, which forbids discrimination on the basis of ethnic origin, race, religion, and other such factors, Adenauer noted. West Germany had signed the European Convention on Human Rights. Legislation, however, was not enough, the chancellor continued. It was necessary to educate people in human and religious tolerance. To prevent disruption of this educational work, the government had decided to fight "circles that are still engaging in anti-Semitic agitation."

At this point Adenauer had read about half his declaration, having spoken for about ten minutes. Then he said:

> The government of the Federal Republic and with it the great majority of the German people are aware of the immeasurable suffering that was brought upon the Jews in Germany and the occupied territories during the time of National Socialism. The overwhelming majority of the German people abominated the crimes committed against the Jews and did not participate in them. During the National Socialist time, there were many among the German people who showed their readiness to help their Jewish fellow citizens at their own peril—for religious reasons, from distress of conscience, out of shame at the disgrace of the German name. But unspeakable crimes have been committed in the name of the German people, calling for moral and material indemnity, both with regard to the individual harm done to the Jews and with regard to the Jewish property for which no legitimate individual claimants still exist. In this field, the first steps have been taken. Very much remains to be done. The Federal Republic will see to it that reparation legislation is soon enacted and justly carried out. Part of the identifiable Jewish property has been restored; further restitution will follow.

Here the chancellor stated a reservation. Not only the great injury done to "the values of Judaism" should be taken into account. Consideration should also be given to Germany's ability to pay, since the country now had to care for those hurt by the war and for the innumerable refugees and exiles who had found sanctuary on its territory. The Federal Republic was prepared to reach a solution to the problem of material restitution "jointly with representatives of the Jewish people and the State of Israel, which has admitted so many homeless Jewish refugees."[42]

This, then, was the statement of contrition that Horowitz had demanded from Adenauer five months earlier, the "ceremonial act." The Bundestag signaled its assent by standing in silence, in memory of the victims of Nazism. Adenauer chose his words carefully and—as was learned a generation later, when Israeli diplomatic records were opened to research—he had not been alone in choosing them. Some of the words had been dictated to him from Jerusalem. Adenauer had sent drafts of his declaration to Maurice Fischer in Paris, using a special envoy, Jacob Altmeier, a Jewish member of the Bundestag for the Social Democratic party. Altmeier had also been involved in arranging the Adenauer-Fischer-Horowitz meeting. Fischer passed the draft declaration on to Nahum Goldmann, president of the World Jewish Congress. Goldmann edited it in red ink, as though a teacher correcting a composition, and sent the corrected pages to Jerusalem, where they were further amended and returned, via Fischer in Paris, to Bonn.

Jerusalem obviously attached special importance to this declaration. "There is no longer any doubt that the cabinet will decide on direct negotiations, if the German declaration only gives it some thread to hang on to without losing face," the director of the western European division of the foreign ministry wrote to Israel's ambassador in Washington. "The prime minister, finance minister, foreign minister, and others are certain that there will be such a decision, but it will come only after the declaration. So it is essential that the declaration be as good as possible." The foreign minister thus instructed the Washington embassy to request that the Americans put pressure on Adenauer.[43]

David Ben-Gurion needed the declaration to justify direct negotiations with Germany. He therefore demanded that Adenauer acknowledge the guilt of the German people and say explicitly that Germany was willing to compensate the State of Israel and the Jewish people. But Adenauer refused to say that the German nation was guilty of the extermination of the Jews; in one early draft, he even explicitly rejected the thesis of collective guilt. The most it was possible to extract from him on this point was that the German people were responsible for the crimes "committed in [their] name." In the same early draft, Adenauer also said that the Federal Republic was a partner in the defense of the Western world against the march of communism. The foreign ministry in Jerusalem suggested soft-pedaling this point: it "will not help us at home," noted one senior ministry official, thinking of the parties of the Stalinist left, Mapam and Maki.[44] The sentence was left out of the final version. In the draft, Adenauer declared his willingness to enter negotiations with "representatives of the Jewish people"; Israel was not mentioned. The name of the country was inserted in Jerusalem.

Both Jerusalem and the World Jewish Congress weighed every word. Where Adenauer wanted to say that people had been killed, they demanded that he say "innocent people." The draft said that the majority of the German people "had not wanted any part" in the crimes of the Nazis and noted that this was a fact "known to anyone of unbiased opinion." The Israelis, however, struck these phrases. Instead of "had not wanted," Jerusalem suggested "abominated," a fuzzier term; this was accepted. Jerusalem had wanted Adenauer not to speak generally of "circles" still engaged in anti-Semitic agitation but to say specifically "groups." Bonn rejected this demand but gave in on its original intention of saying "limited circles." One of the drafts that reached Jerusalem spoke of crimes committed in "territories occupied by the German army." The words "German army" were subsequently deleted—in the opinion of the Israeli foreign ministry, to satisfy those Germans who wished to minimize the guilt of the Nazi army.

Jerusalem wanted it specified that compensation would be paid not only for property but also for "general injury done to the Jewish people." Bonn rejected the demand. Where Adenauer wanted to say that, unfortunately, his country could pay only within the bounds of its limited ability, Israel insisted that the word "limited" be omitted, and Adenauer agreed. Adenauer wanted to say that "much remains to be done" in the matter of restoring property to its rightful owners. Jerusalem demanded that, instead of "much," he say that "most" still remains to be done. Adenauer agreed to say "very much."[45]

So they drafted and revised and redrafted and revised again: "I hope that the big boss in Bonn accepts this," Nahum Goldmann wrote to Moshe Sharett.[46] In August, a foreign ministry official noted that the version taking shape was better than they had hoped.[47] Chancellor Adenauer's statement was expected any day; Jerusalem had already drafted a largely favorable response, to be released after the speech to the Bundestag.

But there were pressures on the big boss in Bonn, as well. The drafts of his declaration had now changed for the worse, from Israel's point of view. Two days before the speech in the Bundestag, Ben-Gurion noted in his diary: "There is a modification in Adenauer's declaration—he won't speak of guilt or of responsibility."[48] Walter Eitan dashed off an urgent cable to the Israeli consul in Munich: "You must base yourself on the first draft and notify them that if the declaration is not revised, we cannot promise a favorable reaction on the part of the Israeli government and world Jewry, and the Germans are, after all, interested in a favorable response."[49] In the meantime, the foreign ministry began recasting its response: "Add a few moral arguments," the director-general ordered.[50] This last-minute pressure worked: Adenauer reverted to the previous version. Israel reacted with restraint. The foreign office promised, perhaps sarcastically, "to study" the declaration.[51] "There is some doubt to what extent the declaration may be seen as an expression of a prevailing mood of repentance," *Haaretz* wrote.[52]

In early December 1951, Nahum Goldmann arrived in London and met with Adenauer for the first time. Goldmann came as president of the Conference on Jewish Material Claims against Germany, a coalition of Jewish organizations that had been formed in coordination with the Israeli government. The Claims Conference, as it came to be known, was supposed to represent the claims of Jews from all countries for personal compensation. Goldmann did not come, therefore, to further the Israeli government's demand for reparations, but he received from Adenauer a letter containing a statement that Germany was willing to negotiate with both the Claims Conference and the Israeli government. "The honor of the German people requires it to do all it can to compensate the Jewish people for the injustice done to it," said the letter—also drafted by Goldmann himself. Germany would welcome the possibility of aiding in the building of Israel through the supply of goods, the chancellor wrote, and noted that negotiations between the two countries would be conducted on the basis of the letters Israel had submitted to the occupying powers in early 1951—that is, on the basis of its demand for $1.5 billion.[53] According to Goldmann, the German chancellor told him that he heard the beating of history's wings.[54] Adenauer, a devout Catholic, who had not been a Nazi, found himself in an enviable position; his conscience and morality coincided precisely with his country's political interests. The reparations and compensation treaties with Israel and the Jewish people would make it easier for Germany to reintegrate itself into the family of nations. For many Israelis, though, the opposite was true—their country's needs conflicted with their consciences.

A few days later, on December 13, the Mapai central committee convened in Tel Aviv. Everything was in place for negotiations with Germany. All that was needed now was the agreement of the Israeli people, which obviously could not be achieved in secret. "This is the penalty one always pays for the inefficiency of democracy," Moshe Sharett later commented.[55] Most members of the central committee came to the meeting to vote in favor, not needing a debate to help them form an opinion. In fact, no one changed ground as a consequence of the debate. Some expressed concern about how future generations would view their actions. "I do not want Jewish and world history to record that we received compensation from Germany, just as I do not accept the Torah's stricture that for a rape one pays compensation to the father," said Yosef Sprinzak, speaker of the Knesset. "I think it's morally absurd." Sprinzak was also concerned about his party's image. Mapai's history would look better if members were not compelled to vote the party line in the Knesset and raise their hands in support of accepting compensation, he said.[56] Delegates worried how the press would play the debate, although it was supposed to be closed. Ben-Gurion tried to ease their fears by telling them that most of what the press wrote was "demagoguery." But they were right to be worried.

Most of the daily papers were associated with opposition parties that rejected negotiations with Germany, particularly the right-wing *Herut* and the Communist *Kol Haam. Yediot Aharonot* and *Maariv*, two independent evening papers, conducted an anti-German campaign no less shrill than that of the party papers. "What will I say to my loved ones, my burned ones, my murdered ones when they come to me at night, and as they continue to come forever?" asked Azriel Karlebach, editor in chief of *Maariv*. In writing about relations with Germany, the papers often launched into flights of biblical language, just as they had when writing about the Holocaust. They quoted Hebrew poetry, painted vivid portraits of Jewish village life in eastern Europe, and fostered an overheated rhetorical style designed to whip up anti-German feeling. "How will I bear my shame when my country is exposed to the nations—a grocery store whose shelves are all empty, and yet here, in one corner, someone finds a jar of martyrs' ashes, and even that is up for sale?" Karlebach wrote. "And where will I hide my shame when I see that the single drunken customer who chanced by hesitates to buy my father's ashes and that a nimble hand takes the dusty tablets of the covenant from under the counter and breaks off the piece inscribed 'Thou shalt not kill!' and, with a shaky hand, holds this out, too, to the drunken goy, enticing him to have pity and buy?" Some day, the editor of *Maariv* wrote, "a true peace movement will arise in the world, and it will ensure peace in Europe by eradicating Germany from the face of the earth."[57]

As the hour grew late and the central committee session dragged on, many in attendance lost their patience. Some demanded an immediate vote; others simply went home. For the most part, however, the debate was thoroughgoing and honest. People said what they thought and felt, since they were not yet restrained by an official party position. They spoke of politics and morals, weighed the country's needs against the demands of conscience, honor against utility, emotion against rationality. Everyone referred to the Bible: "Remember what Amalek did unto thee" versus "Hast thou killed, and also taken possession?"* In doing so, they found themselves weighing their Jewish identities against their Israeli identities. Some looked to their personal experiences as Nazi victims for guidance. Yet even here there was conflict: their pasts demanded of them both a commitment to remember and a commitment to ensure the future. Mapai was a distinctly centrist party: the debate in the central committee reflected what most Israelis thought.

The two main opponents of the restitution agreement, Meir Dworzecki and Arieh Sheftel, were both Holocaust survivors. Knesset member Sheftel spoke of his memories:

In the Vilna ghetto, when the winter reached minus 39 degrees centigrade, when Jews died in the streets of cold and hunger, the Germans brought us the garments of hundreds of thousands of murdered Jews and told us: Go ahead, take them, cover your nakedness. The Jewish representatives refused to accept clothing stained with

---

* The prophet Samuel, in the name of God, ordered King Saul to kill all the Amalekites and "utterly destroy all that they had in retribution for their violence against the children of Israel." But Saul and his people had mercy on Agag, the Amalekite king, and, coveting the Amalekite's wealth, they spared "the best of the sheep, and of the oxen, . . . and all that was good." Samuel killed Agag with his own hands; for his sin, Saul was stripped of his kingdom. Saul's sin—his choice to disobey God and take halfhearted revenge out of greed—and the commandment to "remember what Amalek did unto thee" appeared many times in the debate over relations with Germany. So did the expression "Hast thou killed, and also taken possession?"—the prophet Elijah's indictment of King Ahab, who murdered Navot the Jezreelite and took his vineyard. (Deuteronomy 25:17, 19; I Samuel 15; I Kings 21.) Whereas Samuel's commandment was used as a call for revenge, Elijah's injunction was taken to mean: Now that the Germans have killed all the Jews, shall they be allowed to profit by keeping all their property as well?

their brothers' blood. I sat there then—Dworzecki was there and many others—and we said we will not accept this, . . . because they want to exploit us when we receive the clothes. . . . They wanted to take our pictures as we dressed in the garments of our brothers and sisters. . . . Yes, it's irrational. After the war, there was another irrational event. In the fields of Treblinka, gold hunters started to search for severed fingers and take the gold rings off them. The Jews of Poland went to the Polish government and asked that the practice be halted, and they fenced Treblinka in and did not touch the gold that was buried in the earth. That's the height of irrationality, but it is a moral and historic thing.[58]

Dworzecki, a doctor and a historian, had been a concentration-camp prisoner in Estonia and a member of the Vilna ghetto underground. He lost most of his family in the Holocaust. "If you ask me what I want to receive from the German people," he said, "I would say, a mother for a mother, a father for a father, a child for a child. My soul would be at rest if I knew that there would be six million German dead to match the six million Jews. If we do not have the ability to do that, then at least we have to do a historic thing that will pain them like the pain of blood—to spit in their faces."[59]

David Ben-Gurion answered with a blunt and revealing outburst. You have a ghetto mentality, he said to the opponents of restitution, adding that sovereign states deal in security, economic strength, and the well-being of their peoples but do not "spit on anyone." He then touched on all the contested issues:

National honor:

I see national honor in the existence of the State of Israel. I see national honor in that we brought 50,000 Yemenite Jews here from their dark and terrible exile. That is national honor. If national honor is for spitting and demonstrating, I despise that honor.

Konrad Adenauer:

I do not intend to take responsibility for Adenauer. Maybe he'll cheat us. I should guarantee Adenauer's honesty? But why should we give up what is ours?

Revenge:

> If I could take German property without sitting down with them for even a minute but go in with jeeps and machine guns to the warehouses and take it, I would do that—if, for instance, we had the ability to send a hundred divisions and tell them "take it." But we can't do that, because even if we could, I would do it first against Iraq. But even there I can't do it. We can't do everything. Even the Russians and the Americans can't do anything they want.

The opposition:

> Those who oppose us politically . . . want to make the government fail, but I know that they will make the country fail as well. And they don't care about making the country fail so long as the government fails.

Amalek:

> If the Amalekite nation were still in existence and had universities, the Jews would be studying at them. I won't argue with the prophet Samuel, if he was right about Agag or not. But "blot out the remembrance of Amalek" is a meaningless verse for us. Is that what you bring as evidence of how we should behave in our time?

Memory:

> What we have to say on the things they did to us we'll say if we need to say it. And I doubt if we'll feel the need day and night. But . . . better not to say it for a long time, because . . . if you repeat it too often, the world will get sick of you—and in that world there are Jews, too. If a new Jeremiah arises, he'll speak his part.[60]

A few central committee members requested waiving party discipline, even after the committee vote, to allow Mapai's representatives in the Knesset to vote their consciences. The chairman, Meir Argov, quickly suppressed the dangerous initiative. "I do not favor such freedom," he said. "Until the decision [in the central committee], freedom. After the decision, no." He did not conceal his reasoning from his fellows: "If we do not obligate our members, our motion will fail in the Knesset." That was Ben-Gurion's concern, as well, but he knew the limits of the possible. Even though what was at issue, he said, was a feeling he regarded as "totally invalid," it was incumbent on him to respect it, because it was sincere. For that reason, he permitted party representatives to absent themselves from the Knesset vote, on condition that their absence would not put the end result at risk. No one would be allowed to defeat the Jewish people, the country, or the government, Ben-Gurion said.[61]

The central committee voted. Five opposed negotiations with Germany, forty-two favored them. At the end of that month, the cabinet also approved negotiations, and then the issue was presented to the Knesset.

11 | *"Gas against Jews"*

Storms of dissension buffeted the country during the weeks that followed. The governing coalition led by Mapai would probably carry the vote in the Knesset, but it was impossible to be certain. In several parties, opinions were split. More and more Knesset members were demanding that they be allowed to vote their consciences, free of party strictures. Against this background, lobbies and pressure groups appeared in every corner. There were public meetings and rallies and demonstrations. Posters appeared on walls, advertisements in newspapers. Intellectuals were called on to support one side or the other. The left-wing Mapam enlisted former partisans and ghetto fighters to oppose restitution, including such near-mythological figures as Antek Zuckerman, Tsivia Lubetkin, and Haike Grossman. There were writers and poets, too, who opposed contact with Germany, among them Moshe Shamir and Avraham Shlonsky. A delegation of writers and public figures met with Ben-Gurion and were told he had no moral, only a practical, dispute with them; they later denounced him at a press conference.[1] In support of the negotiations, Mapai trotted out poet Natan Alterman. Martin Buber also said something in support of beneficial links between the two countries. But Alterman and Buber sounded unsure of themselves; they acknowledged the necessity of negotiations with Germany, but not the moral validity of such a step.[2] A similar ambivalence was also evident in the moderate, independent *Haaretz*, and even in *Davar*, the Histadrut-sponsored daily that usually expressed the positions of Mapai.

As the Knesset debate approached, *Maariv* conducted a survey, as an alternative to the plebiscite that the right-wing Herut party was demanding. The paper's readers were asked to fill out a form printed in the newspaper and return it to the newsstands or to the paper by mail. A stamp was unnecessary, but the readers were asked to note their names and addresses. A question was printed twice on each form in order to allow the participation of "the wife or other respondent." Readers were asked if they were for or against direct negotiations with Germany. According to *Maariv*, 12,000 answers were received, of which 80 percent were opposed.[3]

A week before the debate, Knesset member Menahem Begin published a statement calling on his followers in Herut to "enlist and act" against negotiations with Germany. "We have resolved to frustrate this horrible plot with the help of the masses," he said.[4] The great dramatist of Israeli politics put much thought into his direction of the fight against negotiations; he considered each act, each scene, and played the lead role himself. At the climax, he appeared at a mass rally in Jerusalem, in pouring rain, calling Ben-Gurion "a tiny despot and great maniac."[5]

Begin was a relative newcomer to Israeli politics. He had only arrived in the country in 1942; Ben-Gurion had settled in Palestine in 1906, seven years before Begin was born. Ben-Gurion came as a socialist pioneer, Begin as a soldier in the Free Polish army, almost a refugee. He had studied law in Warsaw, headed the Betar movement in Poland, and spent two years in a Soviet prison camp. Prior to the establishment of the state, he commanded the Etzel and led a series of terrorist operations against the British. After independence, the Etzel formed itself into the Herut party, the standard-bearer of Jabotinsky's Revisionist movement, the antisocialist nemesis of the labor Zionists. Begin was a naturally fluid speaker with smooth Polish middle-class manners and an extreme tendency to see things legalistically. But he also knew how to inflame the masses with his populist harangues, all the while surrounded by uniformed henchmen. He addressed people's patriotism and exploited their chauvinistic impulses. Begin was a demagogue, all majestic gestures and historical symbolism. Contrary, however, to what his opponents charged and to the impression he himself sometimes gave, he was no fascist. By the time he was elected prime minister, he had played an important role in consolidating Israel's parliamentary democracy. It was not easy to head a loyal opposition to Ben-Gurion: many Mapai leaders made no distinction between their party and the state, and saw any attempt to unseat Mapai as an attack on the state itself.

In those days Begin was no political or ideological threat to Mapai but he thought himself better able to defend the national honor. His attitude was an insult to Mapai and to the entire generation of founders, and it rankled. Begin described Mapai's rule in prestate Palestine as "collaboration with the British"—just as he described the haavara as collaboration with the Nazis. When the state was founded, Begin accused Mapai of ceding to the Arabs territory precious to every Jewish heart, including the Western Wall and the Old City of Jerusalem. Now Begin was preparing to declare a monopoly on the memory of the Holocaust: He accused Mapai of failing to rescue Jews from Europe. He, too, had been in Palestine during the extermination, but he somehow gave the impression that he had come "from there." Occasionally he recalled how the Nazis had drowned his father in the Bug River.* Ben-Gurion despised him.

As the Knesset debate approached, Herut published a declaration saying that any hands raised in favor of negotiations with Germany would be "treasonous hands." Therefore, "whatever the decision is, the nation will not reconcile itself" to those who voted for Germany.[7] At a rally in Tel Aviv, Begin said, "I warn you, Mr. Ben-Gurion, warn you publicly: if you dare do this thing, be aware of the conclusion that every Jew will reach: if this is permissible in the State of Israel, everything is permissible in the State of Israel!"[8] His message smacked of rebellion, and not by chance. Begin was trying to revive the days when he headed the Etzel, and to do this he had to identify the Israeli government with the despised British regime—which he used to compare to the Nazis. Later he called negotiations with Germany a "holocaust" and identified Mapai with the Nazis. Party posters screamed: "The bones of our martyred parents—to the Mapai-Nazi Blood Market."[9] Begin claimed that the impure money of the "Teutonic pack of wolves" was intended to shore up Mapai's economic position, as the haavara had in the 1930s. "Acting in the name of all of us," Begin cried in his Tel Aviv speech, "in the name of my father, in the name of your mother, in the name of his son, in the name of six million slaughtered and burned, they, the men in power, tell

---

* Begin liked to say that his father had led a procession of five hundred of the city's Jews and that the river had turned red with their blood. In fact, he did not know this for certain. His sister, Rachel Halperin, told his biographer, Eric Silver, that her brother's version of the events was a "tall tale." She believed that their father had been shot to death by a soldier. Their mother was murdered while being treated at a hospital. Begin claimed that both his parents had been murdered "before his eyes," but in fact, he was no longer in the city when they were killed.[6] He had made his escape in time.

Adenauer and his government: give us five percent of the Jewish property [to establish] another Solel Boneh [a Histadrut-owned company]."[10] The money from Germany was to be compensation for the property stolen by the Nazis and for the physical and economic damage suffered by the Holocaust survivors, but Begin created the impression that it was a kind of fine imposed as punishment for the murders themselves. "The reparations money is dipped in Jewish blood," his party claimed.[11] *Herut*, the party daily, began to print slogans of alarm and mourning over its logo, as the papers had done during the Holocaust.

On the morning of January 7, 1952, the day of the debate, the Herut daily printed, to the right of its logo, a quotation from the section of Maimonides's legal code devoted to murderers. "And one should take care not to take ransom from a murderer even if he gives all the money in the world and even if the blood avenger wishes to absolve him, since the soul of the victim is not the property of the avenger but the property of the Holy One, Blessed Be He." To the left of the logo was a picture said to have been taken at a death camp by a soldier of the Jewish Brigade; it showed two words in Yiddish, purportedly written in blood: *Yidn nekome*—Jews, revenge. Across the page, in a banner over the news story, appeared the legend: "Remember what Amalek did unto thee." The main story revealed that Adenauer's conciliatory declaration had been drafted after a prior agreement with Israel.* A subhead linked two symbols of evil: "The British Are Pressing for Normal Relations between Israel and Germany." In the right-hand column the paper said: "An end to the rule of the people of the British Agency of yesterday, who are today turning into the Nazi German Agency." The day of the Knesset vote was termed "the day of judgment." In the left-hand column was a direct call, in poetic form, to each member of the Knesset: "They are watching you," it said, "from the great, wide, deep mass graves, red with blood/From the chimneys of the furnaces of death, from Majdanek, Mauthausen, and Auschwitz/They are watching you: six million pairs of hollow eyes." At the bottom of the page was a notice calling for a mass demonstration that afternoon at Jerusalem's Zion Square.[13]

The police had taken precautions but they soon proved insufficient. Hundreds of policemen were brought to Jerusalem, armed with pistols,

---

* That same day, Knesset member Moshe Sneh (Mapam) revealed that, ten days before Adenauer made his speech of repentance, Sneh had seen the speech in the hands of Nahum Goldmann in Paris. Sneh concluded that "the story of Adenauer's repentance is nothing but a lie."[12]

steel helmets, shields, clubs, and gas masks. Ambulances and fire engines were on alert; the army was ready with reinforcements. The Knesset, then meeting in a building in the center of town, a short walk from the demonstration site, was surrounded with barriers and barbed wire. Streets were closed off; only residents and local shopkeepers were allowed to pass. Jerusalem had not known such tension since the siege during the War of Independence. In the early afternoon many of the city's residents went to Mount Zion, the holiest place in Jerusalem and the site of the first Holocaust memorial. They were responding to a call from the chief rabbis, who had declared the next day, the traditional fast of the tenth day of Tevet, as an annual memorial day for the victims of the Holocaust. That the fast coincided with the Knesset debate gave Herut an incomparable opportunity, which it exploited to the fullest. Many people came straight from Mount Zion to Zion Square, to hear Menahem Begin.

The Knesset session began a few minutes after four o'clock. Before regular business could proceed, there were some administrative matters that required attention. One such matter was the swearing in of Knesset member Begin, who had not made an appearance for five months. "I swear to remain loyal to the State of Israel and to faithfully fulfill my mission in the Knesset," the oath was read to him. Begin responded, "I do."[14] Almost all the members of the Knesset and all the government ministers were in their seats. The visitors' and press galleries were packed. People stood in the aisles, and hundreds of others massed around the entrance to the building, hoping for passes to enter. A few parliamentary questions needed to be answered and then the prime minister took the floor. Ben-Gurion spoke for a little more than twenty minutes. Once again he detailed, somewhat hoarsely and dryly, Israel's demands on Germany, explaining that the government felt obligated to make every effort to recover, as speedily as possible, the greater part of the spoils the Germans had stolen from individual Jews and the Jewish nation. The statement was matter-of-fact, devoid of pathos, except for the words with which it concluded: "Let not the murderers of our nation also be its heirs."[15]

Ben-Gurion was permitted to speak without interruption. But the discussion that followed erupted with emotion. The first speaker, Elimelech Rimalt of the centrist General Zionist party, told the Knesset of an incident in his home. "My little son came to me and asked, 'How much will we get for Grandma and Grandpa?' "[16] Both his parents had been murdered, Rimalt explained. And that was only the beginning.

Menahem Begin, in the meantime, left the Knesset and made his way to the balcony of the Aviv Hotel, overlooking Zion Square. Thousands had gathered there. People had come from all over the country by chartered bus. They wore yellow Stars of David, like the ones Jews in the ghettos had been forced to wear; under the word *Jude* were the words "Remember what Amalek did unto thee." Begin told them about the drowning of his father, adding: "They say that a new German government has arisen with whom we can talk, conduct negotiations, and sign an agreement. Before Hitler came to power, the German people voted for him. Twelve million Germans served in the Nazi army. There is not one German who has not murdered our fathers. Every German is a Nazi. Every German is a murderer. Adenauer is a murderer. . . . All his assistants are murderers."

When he reached the halfway point in his speech, he suddenly waved a piece of paper, as if it had only then been handed to him. He had just been informed, he said, that the policemen stationed around the square were equipped with tear-gas grenades—made in Germany. He shrieked: "The same gases that asphyxiated our parents!" He told the people to protest by not paying taxes and promised that the opponents of reparations would not be frightened even by the "torture chambers." He termed the struggle "a war to the death." Finally, he called on the crowd to raise their hands and swore them to a biblical-style oath "in the name of Jerusalem, in the name of those who went to the gallows, in the name of Zeev Jabotinsky: If I forget the extermination of the Jews, may my right hand lose its cunning; may my tongue cleave to the roof of my mouth if I do not remember thee, if I do not set the extermination of the Jews over all my sorrows."[17] It was very cold and it rained.

The question that arose the next day was whether Begin had incited the crowd to storm the Knesset. *Davar* quoted him as saying, "Rise up against the Knesset, surround it, and if they do not let you in—break through!" *Haaretz* had him declaring: "Today I will give the order— blood!"[18] According to his own party's newspaper, Begin said, "Today I will give the order—yes [to resistance]," and continued, "Go, my brothers, and do not fear the gas grenades. Tell the Jewish policemen that you, also, are a Jew. There is no way we can agree to this. . . . We are not fighting for bread. . . . We are fighting for the soul of the people and the honor of the nation. Go, with the flag of the nation's purity in your souls."[19] Begin himself later admitted that he had told the crowd, "Go, make a stand, surround the Knesset." He meant, he argued, that "they should do as in Roman times. When the Roman governor wanted

to put an idol in the sanctuary, Jews came from all over the land, surrounded the temple, and said, only over our bodies will you pass."
According to Begin, he demanded a "thundering silence" from his supporters and warned them not to interfere with the proceedings. [20] In any
case, at the end of his speech Begin returned to the legislative chamber,
his people marching behind him.

On the way up Ben-Yehuda Street, halfway to the Knesset, the demonstrators encountered a police barrier, which they pushed aside. When
the policemen did not resist, the protesters continued on their way. A
little further up, a fire engine turned its hoses on them, but the demonstrators marched on. A correspondent for the *Jerusalem Post* reported
that some carried army packs filled with stones they had brought with
them from Tel Aviv and Haifa. [21] There is no way of knowing exactly
how many demonstrators there were—certainly fewer than had attended
Begin's rally. Most were young—veterans of the Etzel, Herut party
activists—and not all were Holocaust survivors. The list of those arrested,
published in the press, indicates that many were Oriental Jews.

The Herut protesters were joined later by participants from another
rally, one organized by the Committee for Peace—a group sponsored by
Mapam, the Communist party (Maki), and student activists.

In those days, Mapam and Maki toed the Soviet line. Yaakov Hazan,
one of Mapam's leaders, described Stalin's country as his "second homeland."[22] These two parties accordingly adopted the Soviet distinction
between the two Germanys: West Germany was unclean, East Germany
pure. The millions of East Germans who had supported Hitler, and the
several government officials that the Communist regime inherited from
the Third Reich, did not exist, as far as these parties were concerned.
Only the West Germans fell heir to the Nazis' guilt, and as such had to
be ostracized. In October 1951, Mapam had sent two of its members to
participate in an international conference in East Berlin. One was Hanan
(Hans) Rubin, who had been a member of the German Social Democratic
party in the Weimar Republic. Rubin was one of the first Israelis to visit
East Germany. But like his schizophrenic party, he voted obediently
against negotiations with West Germany. Ben-Gurion called him "vile"
for this. [23]

At some point, the police climbed up to the roofs and hurled smoke
bombs and tear-gas grenades into the crowd. But the wind blew the
suffocating fumes back in the direction of the police and the Knesset.
The protesters advanced further, armed with sticks, throwing stones, and,

according to Ben-Gurion, carrying tear-gas grenades.[24] They overturned parked cars. One went up in flames. Store windows were shattered. People were wounded, some in fistfights, some trampled by the crowd. In one case, an injured man was dragged out of an ambulance and beaten again.

§

In the meantime, the Knesset continued its debate. But during the second speech, by Yaakov Hazan of Mapam, the riot outside was clearly audible—the shouts, the cries, the sirens. Suddenly, Herut's Yohanan Bader shouted: "Gas against Jews!" Speaker Sprinzak struggled to maintain order. During the next speech, by Yitzhak Rafael of the national-religious Hapoel Hamizrahi, two members of the Knesset—Meir Vilner and his former wife, Esther Vilenska, both Communists—burst into the chamber shouting: "We're sitting here chattering and outside people are being murdered!" At this point the first windows were broken in the Knesset chamber, which was on the ground floor, facing the street. Stones smashed through them, one after the other. Splinters of glass littered the legislators' desks and the floor. The speaker said for the record: "All I can do is state the fact that stones have been thrown into the Knesset and that the Knesset is not shooting."[25] Everyone was shouting; the stenographers stopped trying to record the speeches.

Shalom Rosenfeld of *Maariv* reported the next day that he had heard the words *murderer, madman, scum,* and *fascist.* Clouds of gas billowed into the chamber through the shattered windows. Rosenfeld wrote, "At first you feel a slight itch in the eyes, but the effects of the gas increase slowly and soon everyone could be seen wiping their teary eyes with handkerchiefs." People began pushing toward the exits. Chaos reigned. Suddenly there was a scream—someone was wounded. A stone had hit Hanan Rubin of Mapam on the head. Ben-Zion Harel, a General Zionist and a doctor by profession, rushed to tend to him.[26]

There were dozens of wounded—policemen and demonstrators. Many were brought into the Knesset building to receive first aid. Ben-Gurion's wife, Paula, a nurse, helped. Amos Ben-Gurion, their son, deputy chief of police, commanded the police action outside. At one point, Prime Minister Ben-Gurion ordered the army called out to prevent the mob from penetrating the building. The demonstrators were only a few yards from the entrance, but the prime minister, who also was defense minister, forbade opening fire on them. Yohanan Bader wrote in his memoirs: "Begin and I remained in our places and, as the stones fell right and left,

Begin said to me in Polish, 'Yashu, sit down. Mother would have been happy.' "[27]

Begin was the next speaker. There was nothing new in his speech, except for a call to the Arab members of the Knesset, among them members of Mapai's satellite factions, to abstain from the vote: "This is a matter for us; the blood of our mothers, brothers, and sisters is involved in it; let us decide this matter."*[28] Just before Begin concluded, Ben-Gurion shouted something at him about the "hooligans" outside. Begin replied, "You're a hooligan." The chairman demanded that Begin withdraw his words. Begin demanded that Ben-Gurion take back his own words. At that point the members of Mapai began shouting, "Don't let him speak! Don't let him speak!" Begin said, "If I don't talk, no one will talk. You'll take me out only by force." The chairman adjourned the session.[30]

By the time the Knesset reconvened, it was dark and the demonstrators had gone home. About 200 of them, plus 140 policemen, had been wounded; dozens had to be hospitalized. Close to 400 had been arrested. Begin withdrew his attack on Ben-Gurion and was allowed to conclude his speech. "It may well be that this is my last speech in the Knesset," he began. Then he launched into the subject of martyrdom. This is what he had learned from his father, he said: "There are things in life more precious than life itself. There are things in life that are worse than death itself. And this is one of those things that we will give up our lives for, for which we are ready to die. We will leave our families, bid our children farewell, and there will be no negotiations with Germany."

The Knesset listened in silence. It had never heard, and would never again hear, such a speech:

Nations worthy of the name have gone to the barricades for lesser matters. On this matter, we, the last generation of slaves and the first of the redeemed; we, who saw our fathers dragged to the gas chambers; we, who heard the clatter of the death trains; we, before whose eyes the elderly father was cast into the river with five hundred Jews from the glorious community of Brisk in Lithuania, so the river ran red with blood; we, before whose eyes the elderly mother was

* A day earlier, a worried Ben-Gurion had also calculated how the vote would go with the Arabs and how it would go if they abstained. But in the end, their votes were not decisive.[29]

murdered in the hospital; we, before whose eyes all these events unparalleled in history occurred—shall we fear risking our lives to prevent negotiations with our parents' murderers? . . . We are prepared to do anything, anything to prevent this disgrace to Israel. . . .

This, then, is my last cry to the Knesset: Prevent another Holocaust of the Jews!

I know that you have power. You have jails, concentration camps, an army, police, detectives, artillery, machine guns. No matter. In this case, all that force will shatter like glass on a rock. For this, we will fight to the end. Physical power is useless; it is vanity, striving after wind.

I warn, but I do not threaten. Whom could I threaten? I know that you will drag me to the concentration camps. Today you arrested hundreds. Tomorrow you may arrest thousands. No matter, they will go, they will sit in prison. We will sit there with them. If necessary, we will be killed with them. But there will be no "reparations" from Germany.

May God help us all to prevent this Holocaust of our people, in the name of our future, in the name of our honor.

At the end of his speech, Begin asked to inform "the state authorities" that, if the law of parliamentary immunity applied to him, he saw that law as "null and void."[31] The next day's headline in *Yediot Aharonot* was "THE KNESSET WEPT."[32] Ben-Gurion wrote in his diary that "Begin's putsch" ended in "tragic and ludicrous" failure.[33]

The day after the attack on the Knesset, Ben-Gurion spoke to the nation on the radio. "The first attempt has been made to destroy democracy in Israel," he said, "to wrest control of policymaking from the nation's elected representatives by the people of the fist and of political assassination." The attack was, in his words, "a criminal and treasonous plot." He described the demonstrators as "a wild mob" and "a gang of rioters." The leader and organizer of this "rebellion" was Menahem Begin, Ben-Gurion said, and with him marched "the former members of the Etzel," aided and supported by the Communists. As prime minister and minister of defense, Ben-Gurion declared, he could reassure the people that all means necessary had been taken to protect democracy, the sovereignty of the Knesset, and the rule of law, security, and peace. To remove any doubts, Ben-Gurion emphasized the words "all means."

"Do not be alarmed and do not fear," he declared. "There are enough forces and powers in the country's hands to defend Israel's sovereignty and freedom, to prevent thugs and assassins from taking over the country, and to prevent further acts of terror. The army, the police, and the people, desiring freedom and independence, are the most trustworthy guarantee that the criminal and insane plot of the Herut thugs and their communist supporters will never succeed." He condemned "the impure ideology of fascism in its various incarnations, on the right and on the left," and declared: "The State of Israel will not turn into Spain or Syria."[34]

All this was enough to justify outlawing Herut and possibly even Maki. Rumor had it that this was indeed Ben-Gurion's intention and that he reversed himself only at the last minute—a wise decision, not just because the vote on negotiations with Germany was yet to come, but also because Herut would, if outlawed, continue to exist underground, acquiring the halo of the persecuted.[35] Begin would have played such a situation to the hilt. He was plotting a drama, not a coup. He did not mean to die on account of this vote, nor even to go to jail, but he stretched democracy to its limit. Ben-Gurion's dramatic reaction added danger to the explosive situation.

In the meantime, cables expressing support from his party's branches and from citizens all over the country poured into Ben-Gurion's office. "To the architect of the State of Israel—congratulations, and keep it up," someone telegraphed from Ramat Gan, while the message from Kfar Saba was: "We will stand as a living wall in defense of the country, the law, and democracy." The residents of the Holon old-age home sent greetings in a shaky hand to "our dear and beloved prime minister," and from Haifa and other cities came reports that workers were demanding to be bused to Jerusalem "to defend the Knesset."[36] The chief of the security services, Isser Harel, encouraged these demands.*[37]

For the moment, the debate over negotiations with Germany was shunted aside. It was not restitution that was up for debate, *Haaretz* stated, but the question of whether the country would be able to defend itself from a mob that wanted to force its own dictates. Begin, in the meantime, lost the support of the evening papers. Even *Maariv*, founded

---

* One party member later told Michael Bar-Zohar, Ben-Gurion's biographer, of unofficially calling up a reserve brigade of kibbutz members, planting them in the crowd at Herut's next demonstration in Tel Aviv, and seeing to it that Begin was informed that "there are in this crowd a thousand guys who've come from the valleys with weapons in hand—ready to attack at the first provocation."[38]

by a group of his followers, attacked him. Azriel Karlebach wrote fervidly: "With this action, the members of Herut have done more than anyone to advance the agreement with Germany."[39]

The vote took place two days later, on January 9, 1952, in an atmosphere of great tension. The Knesset was surrounded by rings of policemen and armed soldiers. Opponents of negotiations worked until the last minute, trying to convince members to vote their consciences, against party discipline. But Mapai agreed to forgo a decision expressly favoring negotiations and satisfied itself with an evasive resolution according to which the Knesset authorized the Foreign Affairs and Defense Committee (on which Mapai had a majority) "to make a final determination, in accordance with circumstances and conditions." Each of the Knesset's 120 members was called on to vote for this proposal or for a resolution rejecting negotiations. Except for four absentees, all the members sat in their places; Arieh Ben-Eliezer (Herut), who was sick, was brought in on a stretcher. Five members abstained, fifty voted against—chiefly the opposition parties—and sixty-one were in favor—Mapai and the five Arabs from its satellite factions, most of the members of the religious Mizrahi and Hapoel Hamizrahi parties, and most of the Progressives.[40] Except for a handful, all voted in accordance with their political parties. In Mapai, some who opposed negotiations voted in favor; among the General Zionists—who also had conducted stormy debates in the preceding weeks—there were those who favored negotiations but voted against. Among the ultrareligious, those who opposed negotiations abstained or stayed away.

Three weeks later, the Knesset decided to suspend Begin for more than three months, as punishment for threatening violence. That decision required another debate, and again the words were harsh. "Hitler is the democrat who serves as your example," said Haim Landau (Herut) to Mapai. Earlier, Meir Argov (Mapai) had compared the attack on the Knesset to the burning of the Reichstag.[41] Herut continued its fight, holding more rallies and demonstrations and initiating Knesset debates. There was nothing new to say, so all involved competed over how they said it. Herut outdid all comers in macabre inventiveness. In March 1952, just days before the negotiations with Germany began, Yohanan Bader said: "Suppose they pay you for six million Jews, but when the reparations period is over, . . . where will you get six million more Jews so that you can get more money?"[42] This comment completed the question that Arieh Ben-Eliezer had presented to Mapai a few months before, when it became known that Germany was going to pay Israel not in cash but in the form of goods. "Will these German products include soap produced from human bodies?" Ben-Eliezer asked. [43] Haim Landau called out in Yiddish to Shmuel Dayan (Mapai): "A *glik hot unz getrofen* (lucky us!)—six million Jews were murdered and we can get some money." [44]

The fight against negotiations with Germany rescued Menahem Begin from a period of depression and lifted his party from a low point. Begin acted euphoric; his party took on new life. In every Herut branch there was an assembly, and in many cities there were demonstrations. Activists were called up for "mandatory service" and were commanded to be ready for the party's call twenty-four hours a day. The party offices looked almost like military headquarters, with runners coming and going, volunteers working the telephones to enlist members and sympathizers.

During the stormy weeks before the Knesset vote, Begin acted as if he and his party had always opposed accepting reparations and compensation. But this was not true. In December 1949, two Herut representatives had participated in the Knesset debate on the Certification of Documents Act, which was intended to facilitate claims for compensation from Germany. Even though it was clear that direct contact with German government authorities would be involved, neither of the two Herut Knesset members had expressed any opposition in principle. On the contrary, Haim Landau attacked the government for not having submitted the bill earlier. "After all, we are talking here about an opportunity to rehabilitate tens of thousands of Jews in their homeland," Landau said. "We will stand guard, insist on and demand the full amount of compensation to which we are entitled." [45]

In early 1951, the question of compensation had again come before the Knesset. Foreign Minister Sharett read to the parliament the letter Israel had sent to the occupying powers. In the first half, Israel detailed the extermination of the Jews, citing the verdict of the Nuremberg tribunal. The second half set out the monetary demands—$1.5 billion. "No progress toward restoring Germany to its place in the family of nations can be possible as long as this basic debt is not paid," the letter concluded. [46]

This time, it was Begin who criticized the government. He saw the letter as evidence of Israel's willingness to establish relations with Germany. He also took exception to the structure of the message—it was not proper for the story of the Holocaust to appear in a document that also dealt with money; rather it should go in a letter protesting the shortening of sentences imposed on Nazi criminals in Germany. But Begin did not oppose the reparations on ideological, moral, or national grounds, as he would later. Indeed, he had a revelation to make: "More than half a year ago," he related, "I proposed to Mr. Sharett at a meeting of the foreign-affairs committee that he demand compensation for Jewish property plundered by the Germans." According to Begin, Sharett had replied that the matter was under government consideration. Begin did not object to applying to the Allies. He attacked the government for having been slow to act and for having demanded too little. "We came too late," he said. "I have no proof that if we had submitted the claim two years ago it would have been met. However, in submitting the demand for a billion and a half, while the estimate of the value of Jewish property is six billion, you are conceding the claim for three-quarters of the plundered Jewish property. Why did you concede the claim? In whose name did you concede the claim?"[47]

That was in 1951, more than a year before Begin announced he was ready to die in an Israeli concentration camp in order to prevent negotiations for restitution.

In the first Knesset, elected in 1949, Herut had 14 of the 120 members. In the local elections of November 1950 it lost some votes.[48] "The expectations were great and the disappointment even greater," Yohanan Bader, a senior party member and a friend of Begin's, later recalled.[49] Begin's opponents in his party attacked him fiercely. One, Shmuel Tamir, screamed at him, "Why is the word *resignation* in the dictionary if you don't resign?" According to Bader, Begin decided to go but put off his resignation until after the elections to the second Knesset in 1951. "I visited Begin often," Bader wrote, "so that he would not feel alone in his low spirits."[50]

Begin worked hard during the second campaign, but again disappointment awaited him. Bader brought him the results: Herut had gone down from fourteen seats to eight. Even though the number of voters had doubled, the party received a few thousand votes less than in the previous elections.[51] Mapai was "the party of victory" in the War of Independence; Ben-Gurion was "the architect of the state."

Many voters were new immigrants; they admired Ben-Gurion, identified him with the country, and depended on his party for their livelihoods. Begin was tired and sad, Bader recalled. He went for a vacation in Italy with his wife, Aliza. When he returned, he again found himself facing opponents from within. During one of Tamir's attacks, Begin shut himself up in the next room with some of his close associates. After a while he came out and announced he had decided to take an extended vacation. His colleagues understood this to mean that he had decided to leave politics.

For the next several months, Begin lived in a rented room in Jerusalem and prepared for examinations in criminal law. He attributed the decline in his party's strength to the mood of the first Israelis: those were days for routine, not for heroism. The revolution and the war had ended, and now people were thinking about their half-stocked refrigerators. Begin's Herut needed a great national issue, something to spark emotions. [52]

Then came Adenauer's declaration of repentance, and the matter of reparations was brought before the Knesset for approval. "I have no doubt that the Knesset will go wild over this issue," Ben-Gurion said, and he was right. Begin returned to the fray. [53] Yohanan Bader told him that he must resume his political activity; it was "his duty to his mother" and other family members killed in the Holocaust. According to Bader, this was the argument that persuaded Begin. [54]

In the first Knesset, the issue had been whether or not to talk to the occupying powers. Now the country was contemplating direct negotiations with Germany, and that perhaps explains the change in Begin's position. But to revive his party and his career as its leader, he had to electrify the masses. It was not enough to quibble over a diplomatic text, over whom to negotiate with, over the amount to be demanded. Begin needed "an abomination with no parallel in our history since the concubine of Giva." [55] He identified this abomination as the money itself, denouncing the very idea of accepting any money at all. His demand of just over a year before, that the government act quickly to get reparations, was never mentioned: in the heated atmosphere that surrounded Begin, it was conveniently forgotten.

Begin was striving to bring down the Mapai coalition so that he himself might govern. But he was also involved in another struggle, which engaged his deepest convictions—the ongoing struggle to shape the memory of the Holocaust and formulate its lessons. Begin placed the Holocaust at the center of a system of values, emotions, and ceremonies and saw it as the source of all norms of good and evil, purity and impurity, permitted and forbidden, reward and punishment. It was not by coincidence that he described the victims of the Nazis as "holy martyrs"; Begin sought to develop the heritage of the Holocaust into an almost religious dogma. The lessons of the Holocaust were to guide national policy, to serve as a political ideology and emotional alternative to Ben-Gurion's pragmatism.

As the high priest of this new religion, Begin not only put emotion above national policy, the "soul of the nation" above financial interest, but put the lessons of the Holocaust above the state itself—just as the ultraorthodox parties challenged it with God, and just as, for a short period, Mapam and the Communists challenged it with Marx. All identified themselves with history, held fast to absolute and all-embracing dogmas, and tried to force their dogmas on the country—and all failed, including Begin.

Begin failed not just because Herut conducted its struggle against the treaties with Germany as part of its battle for power or because he demanded that people give up the prospect of money. He failed primarily because he could only conceive of the Holocaust as a collective experience. But during that period, the Holocaust was still first and foremost a part of the individual biographies of its survivors; it was their personal catastrophe. Begin did not understand this. He may have been ahead of his time; years later the Holocaust did indeed develop into a sort of civic national religion. But in the early 1950s, the memory of the Holocaust was sharp and fresh, and Begin's operatic anti-German rhetoric never succeeded in expressing the force of personal suffering or touching the depths of individual tragedy. For this reason, the survivors had little difficulty ignoring what he demanded of them and accepting their share of the compensation money. The money changed nothing within them, nor was it particularly relevant to their identity as survivors; at most it allowed them to buy larger apartments. Only a handful of them refused to take the compensation they had coming to them. The survivors' decisions were the true plebiscite for measuring Israel's attitudes toward this question.

12 | *"The Baby Went for Free"*

The negotiations between Israel and Germany began on March 20, 1952, in Wassenaar, a town in Holland near The Hague; in six months there was an agreement.[1] The two countries bargained over every dollar in a tough atmosphere that Nahum Goldmann described to Chancellor Adenauer as "a cattle market."[2] Both sides acted in accordance with numerous considerations; both were subject to pressures and both made concessions.

The Israelis and the Jewish people appeared at the talks as two delegations, but, at least to the Germans, they spoke with one voice. The Israeli delegation was headed by Giora (Georg) Yoseftal and Eliezer (Felix) Shinar, and among its prominent members was Georg Landauer; all three were German-born and had been involved in the haavara. Yoseftal was a Mapai functionary, the head of the Jewish Agency's absorption department, and later a government minister. Shinar (formerly Schneebalg), a doctor of law, was employed by the millionaire Zalman Schocken and managed *Haaretz*. He had over the years been a financial expert, the government fuel supervisor, and an adviser to the Israeli embassy in London. He later served as head of the Israeli purchasing delegation in West Germany and, until the two countries established diplomatic relations, was Israel's ambassador there in all but name. Georg Landauer, active in the German immigrant community in Israel, was a senior official of the Jewish Agency. In addition to the Israeli delegation, there was Nahum Goldmann, who represented the Claims Conference; in fact, he conducted the negotiations with Germany in the name of Israel as well.

The German delegation, by contrast, spoke with at least two voices. The head of the delegation was Franz Böhm, rector of Frankfurt University. His deputy was Otto Küster, a former classmate of Shinar's at the Stuttgart gymnasium; Shinar described him as a paragon of honesty and justness. Shinar also praised Böhm for his warm personality, purity of heart, and superior moral sensibility.[3] Alongside these two men of goodwill and others like them, there were some in Bonn who did their best to sabotage the negotiations in order to delay the agreement or abort it entirely. First among them was the finance minister, Fritz Schäffer, who apparently was not aware of the promise Adenauer had made to Goldmann and who, at first, did not properly understand what was under discussion. A note found among his papers, referring to Adenauer as a source of information, states that when the chancellor was in London "a Mr. Goldstein came to him and claimed that the Jews had suffered greatly under Hitler."[4] Over the next few months an open power struggle developed in Bonn between those who supported making good on Adenauer's promise and those who demanded that he repudiate it. The reparations agreement expressed, to a great extent, the ability of the Israelis and the Jews, especially Goldmann, to navigate between the two camps.

Nahum Goldmann, a statesman without a state, liked to describe himself as an "international Jew"; in his old age he related the story of his life in terms of the multitude of countries that had issued him passports, even diplomatic papers: Russia, Germany, Lithuania, Poland, Honduras, the United States, Israel, and Switzerland. Born in 1884 in Lithuania, Goldmann had studied at Heidelberg University and married into a wealthy family. He was, from the time of his earliest memories, an active Zionist. In the 1930s he represented the Zionist Organization at the League of Nations in Geneva. His brand of Zionism was worldwide Jewish solidarity, not only and not always in the service of Israel. He played a part in the diplomatic efforts that led to the establishment of the State of Israel, but the country was too small for him. As long as Ben-Gurion was alive, he had no chance of leading it, Goldmann said, and he had no interest in being just a government minister. Like Bruno Kreisky and Henry Kissinger after him, he found himself in constant conflict with what seemed to him an all too nationalistic and power-oriented Israeli policy. "One can admire the Israelis, but it is impossible to be fond of them," Goldmann once said.

He was a liberal—a man of humor, polish, and overwhelming charm—a sharp romantic, and an incorrigible egotist. Life pampered him, and he, as he himself said, did not take it too seriously. "I never identify 100 percent with anything. Not with a man, not with a woman, not with an idea, not with a movement," he said of himself. He liked good conversation and good meals, books, cigars, women, politics, opera, and gossip. But more than anything else, he loved the company of famous people—world leaders and financial barons, popes, kings, presidents, prime ministers, and cabinet members from every country. In every capital he was received as though he were the king of the Jews. Benito Mussolini tried, in 1935, to arrange a meeting between him and Adolf Hitler, but Goldmann refused; to the end of his days he was plagued by doubts over whether he had done the right thing. Had he known then about Auschwitz, he said, he would have gone to meet Hitler.[5]

He admired Talleyrand, the French diplomat and veteran political survivor, and liked to boast of his ability to think, as Talleyrand had, in a broad historical context. He once said to Ben-Gurion: "You see the world from Sde Boker [the kibbutz Ben-Gurion retired to]. I look down on it from 12,000 feet, from an airplane. That's the difference between us."[6] Beginning in 1953, Goldmann was president of the World Jewish Congress. His personality and style brought the congress a degree of prestige and respect that its real influence did not warrant; in that sense, he was an imposter.

§

The reparations and compensation agreements with Germany were largely the fruit of Goldmann's ability to impress Konrad Adenauer. The German chancellor respected him, used him, suspected him—and feared him as well. He seems to have believed that Goldmann had as much influence on the American government and on American public opinion as he pretended to have. Adenauer's memoirs, written fifteen years after the fact, mention their first meeting. Adenauer said that Goldmann had brought with him Israel's ambassador to London, but had introduced him under an assumed name to conceal Israel's willingness to speak with him directly.[7] He was incorrect: the man who accompanied Goldmann was Noah Baru of the World Jewish Congress, who had helped correct the draft of Adenauer's declaration to the Bundestag. The fact that, after so many years and after the innumerable meetings he had since held with Goldmann, the German chancellor still believed that the Jewish leader had tried to mislead him says something about the relations between them.

In another context, Adenauer noted in his memoirs that he knew better than to underestimate the ability of "Jewish banking circles" to bring his country harm.[8] Goldmann, a tireless dissembler, exploited his image as one of "the elders of Zion," sometimes to the point of making threats bordering on extortion. A file in his archives contains information on the Nazi backgrounds of key members of Adenauer's government. Some in Bonn believed that Goldmann had the power to destroy them unless they could ensure his silence about their pasts. He was much helped by Hans Globke, one of the chancellor's close advisers and formerly a high official in the Nazi interior ministry, where he had been an expert on the Nuremberg laws.[9]

The Israeli delegation came to Wassenaar with Adenauer's commitment to the sum of $1.5 billion. The Claims Conference demanded an additional $500 million, for a total of $2 billion—a quarter of the amount Chaim Weizmann had demanded immediately after the war. But when the talks began, the Germans, claiming that they did not have that much money, contended that it was necessary to wait for the outcome of an international conference convened in London to discuss Germany's debt to other countries. The Germans feared that, if they took on large obligations to Israel and the Jews, the sums demanded in London would balloon. The Israelis and Jews, on the other hand, feared that, if they linked their demands with the discussion in London, they would receive much less than they were asking for. It was not a good start.

A week after the opening of negotiations, a stranger in downtown Munich asked two boys to take a package to the nearest post office for him. The man acted under instructions from Eliahu Tabin, an Etzel veteran, who was then living in Paris. The package was addressed to Chancellor Adenauer. It caused some suspicion, and two security men were summoned. As they were examining the package, it exploded; one of the men was killed. The bomb had been hidden in a copy of Knauer's dictionary. Tabin believed that Adenauer's assassination would halt the talks with Israel and lead to the fall of Ben-Gurion's government.[10]

As the negotiations proceeded, Israel made clear officially what it had previously indicated to Adenauer unofficially—that it would, in effect, concede half a billion dollars, because the original sum it had named was its demand from both Germanys. A third of that, or half a billion, was to have come from East Germany. Eliezer Shinar had recommended this apportioning in 1951.[11] It was probably a mistake—East Germany refused to pay anything, and West Germany claimed to be the only Germany, though justifying that claim, apparently, was not worth half a billion dollars. In Wassenaar, everyone assumed from the start that Bonn had to pay only its own portion. Yet the Germans did not want to pay $1 billion, either, even in kind. They proposed goods worth only $750 million. They seem to have estimated that Israel's economic situation was so severe that it would accept almost any offer. Israel said no, and the talks were cut off, some six weeks after they began.

When the Israeli and Jewish representatives walked out of the formal negotiations, Nahum Goldmann's great hour as a lobbyist and manipulator began. Goldmann organized and coordinated a worldwide network of activities aimed at persuading the Germans that it was in their best interests to reach an agreement. As part of this effort, he monitored, and even took part in, the ceaseless haggling in Bonn. He went to see cabinet ministers, senior officials, and members of parliament, making his way through the corridors of power and into the inner chambers. He saw everything and heard everything. He plotted intrigues. He shared secrets with supporters, thwarted opponents, collected promises, made threats: a man of a thousand faces. Before long, the research department of the foreign ministry in Jerusalem was reporting that in Bonn "people are saying" that Goldmann's men had bribed Herbert Blankenhorn, one of the chancellor's assistants. [12] From time to time, Goldmann went to speak with the chancellor himself. "Here are two old foxes," Franz Böhm said, "but when they are together, they purr at each other like kittens."[13]

Goldmann and his team also mobilized officials in Israel, the leaders of Jewish organizations in the United States, and the American media. Ambassador Abba Eban asked Secretary of State Dean Acheson to put pressure on Germany. "An unsatisfactory answer from Bonn would be one of the darkest events in the annals of human morals," Eban said, getting carried away.[14] Acheson spoke with Adenauer. Some American Jewish leaders spoke with President Truman.[15] The American high commissioner in Germany, John J. McCloy, also intervened.[16] At one point, Gen. Julius Klein, head of the Jewish War Veterans organization in the United States, was sent to Adenauer. Klein told Adenauer that, if the talks were not resumed, he would campaign for shelving the "Germany Agreements," which were meant to return Germany to the community of nations and clear the way for membership in NATO. Klein dropped the name of influential senator Robert A. Taft, who was known as a friend of Israel. "Adenauer was impressed by Klein's brutal position and promised to do everything to renew the negotiations," Maurice Fischer reported from Paris. "Klein advises that we behave stubbornly and roughly with the Germans, and see to it that the subject of reparations remains on the front pages of the American newspapers," so that the Germans will receive the impression that keeping their promises plays a major part in their admission to NATO.[17]

A few days before the signing of the "Germany Agreements," Eliezer Shinar met with Hermann Abs, an influential banker who was both the head of the German delegation to the debt conference in London and an adviser to Chancellor Adenauer in the reparations negotiations. Abs now proposed, informally, about $200 million—a quarter of the sum that the Germans had previously offered.[18] That was the signal to switch gears. Goldmann immediately contacted Adenauer and notified him that he was "surprised and disappointed" by Abs's proposal, which he contended contradicted Adenauer's declaration of repentance and his written commitment to conduct the negotiations on the basis of Israel's original demands.

"When I consider Mr. Abs's proposals in the light of these earlier declarations, without which we would never have agreed to the opening of talks," Goldmann wrote, "I am convinced that the Jewish public cannot see them as anything but—and excuse me for the harsh word—an insult." Abs's claim of the Federal Republic's inability to bear such a heavy financial burden, Goldmann added, would convince neither the Jewish people nor world opinion, given the economic miracle of Germany.

Despite his "deep disappointment," Goldmann declared, he still had faith in Adenauer's fundamental approach to the question of Germany's moral obligation to compensate the Jewish people. For this reason he did not believe that Abs's proposals represented the chancellor's views. If, however, it became clear that the sum Abs had mentioned really represented the Federal Republic's official position, then Israel, and the Jewish people, would be forced to halt the talks. "Such a failure," Goldmann wrote, "will deeply shake the faith in the new Germany's sincere desire to repent the crimes of its predecessor, particularly in the eyes of those who wish to see in you, Mr. Chancellor, the spokesman and representative of this Germany. An angry reaction from the Jewish world and from the wide non-Jewish circles that were horrified by the Holocaust inflicted on the Jewish people by the Nazi regime will be inevitable and totally justified." This was an open threat.

Goldmann left Adenauer an honorable way out: "At this critical juncture," with the talks "on the brink of failure," he called on him to raise the discussions once more "to the high moral level" where they had started. He urged Adenauer to invoke his full personal authority and to ensure the speedy submission of a proposal that would allow the official talks to be reopened.*

Now developments came quickly. The deputy chief of the German delegation, Otto Küster, resigned, and the head of the delegation, Franz Böhm, threatened to resign as well. Adenauer was preoccupied with preparations for the signing of the Germany Agreements, but, having no choice, he found time to bring the reparations and compensation issue up for discussion in his cabinet. He then instructed Böhm to revert to the previous offer. Three days before the signing of the Germany Agreements, the American high commissioner in Germany, John McCloy, telephoned Goldmann's home in Paris and notified him that he would shortly receive an important call. The next day Böhm called and asked for a personal meeting. He was now authorized to go back to the proposal that had brought about the cessation of the talks, he said—goods worth $750 million, to be supplied to Israel over eight to twelve years. Goldmann promptly said he could recommend that the Israeli government accept this offer "in principle" but immediately noted that the Germans would have to do better on some points. The members of the Israeli delegation cabled to Jerusalem that there had been "a serious and solid" achievement, especially given the fact that Germany's steadily improving international position gave it less incentive to offer more. Even though they hadn't got a billion, the sum they would receive was "in keeping with the character of the claim and with the honor of the State of Israel."[20]

The moment was significant not only in the history of Jewish relations with Germany but also in Jewish history as a whole. For the first time, Jews were to be compensated, even if only partially, for the suffering an anti-Semitic regime had caused them. All told, the German government committed itself to paying 3.4 billion marks, about $820 million. About 70 percent of the money was earmarked for goods made in Germany, and about 30 percent for the purchase of fuel. The agreement was to be carried out over a period of twelve to fourteen years. Of the agreed sum, $750 million was to go to Israel. Regarding the rest, the Israeli government served as a sort of trust company. It would receive payment, also in the

---

* Both men included this letter in their memoirs. In the Israeli edition of his memoirs, Goldmann sharpened the original wording a bit: the apology for the use of the word *insult* was omitted from the Hebrew translation. Adenauer omitted the entire paragraph containing the threat, replacing it with a discreet ellipsis.[19]

form of goods, and would transfer it—partly in the form of goods, partly in foreign currency, and partly in Israeli currency—to the Jewish organizations participating in the Claims Conference, among them the Joint Distribution Committee and the Jewish Agency. These would use the money in part to fund their activities in Israel. The upshot was that most of the money paid to the Claims Conference remained in Israel or returned to it. The choice, purchase, and shipping of the goods were to be accomplished by a "purchase delegation" that Israel would establish in Germany and which would enjoy diplomatic status.

Germany also obligated itself to compensating Nazi victims for their lost property, for imprisonment, and for the slave labor they had been forced to perform, as well as for damage to their health and for a long list of other injuries they had suffered.[21] These provisions, too, were largely the work of Nahum Goldmann. During the negotiations, he yielded on about 80 percent of the sum he had originally demanded in the name of the Claims Conference. His strategy paid off in the end. He induced the Germans to enact, in lieu of immediate payment, laws that guaranteed compensation to hundreds of thousands of survivors, mostly from eastern Europe, some of whom now lived in Israel. Over the years, Goldmann succeeded in adding more and more groups to the list of those with standing to demand payments. He also arranged increases in the size of the payments and improvements in the regulations governing compensation. And he brought about the establishment of funds for special cases and of various sorts of loans and grants. All this was thanks to the promises he secured from the Germans during the initial negotiations in exchange for forgoing the right to immediate payment. Over the years the number of recipients of these personal pensions rose steadily, as did the size of the payments—from $6 million in 1954 to $100 million in 1961.[22]

The signing ceremony was set for September 10, 1952, at eight in the morning, in the Luxembourg city hall. For security reasons, the authorities lied to the press, announcing a different location and a later hour. Foreign Minister Moshe Sharett urged his people to arrive early. When they reached city hall, no one was ready for the ceremony. An employee opened the wedding hall for them, after wasting considerable time looking for the key. They waited for the Germans. Adenauer came at the prescribed hour. "I have waited for this day in anticipation and joy," he told Sharett, who responded in German, "It is a special and most significant day for us as well." After the formal introductions, Moshe

Sharett, Nahum Goldmann, and Konrad Adenauer signed the agreements. Sharett had prepared a major speech; he had gone through the "seven circles of hell," he said, before the speech was approved by the Israeli government. Some ministers had criticized it for being too subdued; Ben-Gurion, by contrast, had demanded that it be softened even more by omitting the assertion that there was no forgiveness for spilled blood. "He thinks it is overly cruel to say this straight out to the other side," Sharett related, but he himself wanted to make an "Israeli" speech, he said. "I am the foreign minister of the State of Israel and not just a Jew they slaughtered." He wanted "Jewish fervor" over the blood that had been spilled, "ten times stronger" than in the speech expected of Goldmann. When the speech was completed, it was passed on to Chancellor Adenauer, who refused to approve it. "I am ready to hear this," he told Sharett, "but Germany is not." In the end they agreed there would be no speeches.[23]

Adenauer was right—it took half a year for the German parliament's two houses to confirm the treaty. In the process, Nahum Goldmann's talent for political maneuvering was tested and retested, and Israel was forced to make an embarrassing emotional concession. Someone drew the attention of the German ministers to a section of the agreement that forbade using German vessels to ship the merchandise Israel was to buy. Adenauer sent Walter Hallstein to Shinar. Perhaps it would be possible to change that stipulation, the German suggested, and Shinar understood that this minor annoyance was liable to delay the confirmation of the entire treaty. He flew to Israel and presented the issue to the prime minister. Ben-Gurion brought the matter to the cabinet. "This we cannot swallow under any circumstances; we will choke on it," warned Zalman Aran, one of the heads of Mapai and soon a member of the cabinet. The Knesset again broke into an uproar. "The German flag, the flag of murder, will fly over the territory of our homeland!" cried Herut's Haim Landau, and Ben-Gurion responded that "we heard that style in another country, from a fellow whose bones, to the world's happiness, are already rotting in the grave." More to the point, Ben-Gurion explained that, even with the change the Germans were asking, the preferred status of Israeli ships in carrying the merchandise would be preserved. What would be eliminated was the prohibition against using German ships when there were not enough Israeli ones.[24]

The six months between the signing of the agreement and its confirmation by both houses of the German parliament were crammed with events that had no connection to Israel's relations with Germany. Israel suffered a series of crises that buffeted the country's political system. As a wave of anti-Semitism swept eastern Europe, a bomb exploded outside the Soviet delegation in Tel Aviv, and Moscow severed its diplomatic relations with Israel. This move escalated the political and ideological tension within the Israeli left and between the left and the right. Relations between Mapai and the religious parties grew worse as a result of the debate over mandatory military service for women and the education of immigrant children. In this atmosphere, the debate over Germany lost some of its vitality. German products and German books were on sale everywhere in the country. "We no longer feel the pain; the struggle of those who rose against the reparations is fading, and their voices are growing silent," said Dov Shilansky. This bothered him a lot; he couldn't take it. "I walked about like a lunatic," he later said. So he went to the foreign ministry.[25]

The story of Dov Shilansky, the son of a prosperous leather merchant from Lithuania, was the story of an entire generation of Holocaust survivors aligned with the political right, whose encounter with Israel was marked by outrage and betrayal, feelings that continued to erupt even as diplomats shook hands. The anti-German fanaticism that burned within Shilansky was a reflection of his experience, not of political ambition. Herut exploited him for its purposes; yet even years later—when many Israelis had learned to accept the changing times, when even Prime Minister Menahem Begin received German guests in his office—Shilansky remained faithful to his past. A small man with a boyish smile, a nasal voice, and a noticeable Yiddish accent, he described himself once, in a moment of good humor, as a *tembel,* a dummy.[26]

This is his story, as it emerged in a Tel Aviv district court on October 5, 1952: "I was born [in 1924] in Siauliai, Lithuania, a city in which Hebrew culture flourished. I studied at the Hebrew gymnasium. In 1937 I joined the Betar youth movement and in 1939 I joined a Diaspora cell of the Etzel. I was about to emigrate to Palestine . . . but the war broke out, and the great deluge of blood descended on our city as well." He saw mass arrests and murders and witnessed the hanging of a member of his underground ghetto group. He saw German soldiers rounding up ghetto children for extermination. "I still keep in my home the undershirt of a one-year-old child, an undershirt with a yellow star that was found in the ghetto," he related.

After his abortive attempts to organize a rebellion in the ghetto, he was sent from one concentration camp to another until he arrived in Dachau.

> I saw thousands of Jews cold and bloated with hunger . . . My family and I were unexpectedly lucky; I was able to find my mother and sisters, who had managed to stay alive. My mother's agony caused me the deepest pain. She was the oldest woman in the camp. She was not quick enough, and everyone hit and insulted her. . . .
>
> And then came the Death March. . . . I remember the thirtieth of April, the most terrible day of all. It was a winter day. In a snow-covered grove, many breathed their last breaths, of hunger and exhaustion; twilight came, and the snow continued to fall. . . . That night, the snow covered us completely. We no longer felt anything. The thousands of people lying under the snow were almost invisible. Those who still had a little strength to shake the snow off their faces, lest they be buried alive, fell asleep from exhaustion; they did not even hear the roar of the hundreds of fleeing German trucks.
>
> When we opened our eyes on the morning of May 1, 1945, frozen, skeletons, there was no SS guard around us, and the villagers who found us told us that the Americans would be coming in a few more hours. We struggled toward one of the villages. On the way, there was a dead horse, killed in the battles. We all pounced on it. Within a few minutes, nothing remained but bones. So came the liberation.

Shilansky felt as if he had been reborn:

> That morning, when I woke and saw that the Germans had fled, I felt a great urge to chase them down and destroy them. But reality was otherwise, and that overwhelming urge turned in my heart into an immense desire to realize the dream of my life—a Hebrew state that would, on a national scale, bring about that great revenge.

During the War of Independence, Shilansky commanded a platoon that reached the Lebanese border; had it not received an order to halt, it would have continued northward, Shilansky maintained. Afterward, the army sent him for officer training. For the next four years he worked as a clerk and an accountant. He and his wife lived in poverty but, he said, after ten years of horror, these were happy years. They had a son, Yossi.

Then Shilansky heard of the negotiations with Germany. At first he refused to believe it. Slowly, he realized what was happening, and his life became hell. "I found no rest. Whatever I did, that fact pierced my brain and pierced it again. I was a citizen of a treasonous nation; my inaction was one endorsement of that treason. In an instant I was torn from my quiet life and thrown into an unending battle against the great madness, the cruel crime of negotiations with Germany. I began to organize my friends, and through them I contacted larger groups of people. I found many willing to listen. I spoke with hundreds, perhaps thousands of people." Herut heard of him and invited him to take part in their activities. He organized a traveling exhibition on the Holocaust and proposed screening pictures from Buchenwald and Auschwitz in the movie theaters, "to wake people out of their sleep." At one point he toyed with the idea of organizing a group of writers and intellectuals to climb to the top of Mount Zion, where they would commit collective suicide, as on Masada.

He took part in Begin's rally in front of the Knesset and was jailed for ten days. The Knesset vote shocked him. No, he was not the only Holocaust survivor who felt this way, he said, but others seemed to want to be normal, to forget or repress their pasts. At most, they went to memorial ceremonies. Shilansky wanted to do more. So he prepared a time bomb with six pounds of explosives, put it in his briefcase, and brought it to the grounds of the foreign ministry in Tel Aviv. The police arrested him before anything happened, although it was unclear whether he was a terrorist, intent on activating his bomb, or simply a protester wishing to be noticed. He was sentenced to twenty-one months in prison.

After his release, Shilansky studied law and became a successful attorney. He had two more sons. Yossi, his eldest, fell as a soldier in the Galilee, not far from the place where Shilansky had fought in the War of Independence. Later, Shilansky entered politics and became speaker of the Knesset. He continued to believe that he did what he had to do and regretted only that his bomb did not change the course of history.[27]

In April 1953, while Dov Shilansky was still in jail, the violinist Jascha Heifetz came to Israel for a series of concerts. He included in his program a piece by Richard Strauss, who had been a supporter of the Nazi regime during its first two years. Heifetz received several letters warning him not to play Strauss in Israel; he ignored them. Two government ministers requested, in writing, that he omit the Strauss piece. But Heifetz insisted: he rejected musical censorship, he explained. His concerts proceeded in a tense atmosphere. Yet the audiences in Tel Aviv, Haifa, and Jerusalem received him warmly, despite the Strauss work. After the concert in Jerusalem an unidentified youth accosted him near the King David Hotel. He swung at Heifetz with an iron rod, hitting him on the hand.

Two days later, Heifetz went to visit Ben-Gurion, his hand still bandaged. The prime minister wrote in his diary: "I told him that if the people had asked me whether to allow Strauss to be played, I would have advised judging the music only by its quality. But had Heifetz asked me whether to play Strauss, I would have advised him not to play. His visit here is an event for many, including for those who do not go to concerts, and many of them will be upset if he plays Strauss, and for their sake he should not do it, because man is not a rational creature, and emotions play an important role in life." Now, though, Ben-Gurion persuaded Heifetz not to cut his visit short in the wake of the attack and indeed "to play Strauss as well." He promised police protection. "He asked me if I would come," Ben-Gurion noted. "I said yes, although I do not understand music."[28] The man who attacked Heifetz was never apprehended. Years later, Shilansky claimed to know his identity but would never reveal it.[29]

In September 1953 the police prevented an attempt to sneak a bomb into the Haifa port, a protest against the importation of the reparations goods.[30]

§

Nahum Goldmann liked to repeat Ben-Gurion's comment that the two of them had witnessed two miracles: the establishment of the State of Israel and the signing of the treaty with Germany. "I was responsible for the first and you for the second," Goldmann quoted Ben-Gurion.[31] If Ben-Gurion did indeed compare the agreement with the Germans with the establishment of Israel, only Goldmann heard it—Ben-Gurion never made such a comparison in writing. In July 1952 Ben-Gurion wrote: "My dear Goldmann: There can be no doubt that your part in this important project is a great one, but it seems to me that you are not in need of compliments." That was an error—Goldmann needed compliments, and he needed them in English. As a result, Ben-Gurion signed a second letter that reads as if Goldmann drafted it himself: "Your energy, wisdom, tact, and also your courage played a decisive role in the negotiations," Ben-Gurion wrote to "Dear Nahum," and glowingly depicted the moral stature of the agreement. Even so, the prime minister expressed his doubts that the Germans would execute the agreement in full. It was too early to say, he noted cautiously.[32] In the meantime, he gave instructions that the treaty include a provision ensuring that only a single Israeli company would receive merchandise from Germany, to prevent "Jewish profiteers" from flooding the German market. "I know no other nation with so many thieves, con men, and profiteers lacking all conscience as this tiny nation called Israel," the prime minister wrote.[33]

As far as the Germans were concerned, his suspicion turned out to be groundless. They paid up to the last mark. From time to time they agreed to improve the terms, adding various considerations and discounts, even granting the Israelis interim funding that allowed them to order merchandise against payments due in years to come. The agreement led to daily contacts between the head of the Israeli purchase delegation, Eliezer Shinar, and German officials. There were endless bureaucratic, financial, and legal matters that demanded clarification and attention. Shinar and his staff of several hundred created a businesslike atmosphere. They took care to act like men with three-quarters of a billion dollars to spend, expecting appropriate treatment. All in all, they found no reason to complain: generally they were treated as preferred customers. The Bank of Israel reported later that the purchase delegation had worked with professional efficiency and had bought good merchandise at competitive prices.[34]

The reparations agreement passed the political test, too, when Israel invaded the Sinai peninsula in October 1956. Shinar was in Israel for consultations at the time. The United Nations considered a proposal to impose economic sanctions on the Jewish state. Shinar flew immediately to Bonn late at night, in a darkened plane under military escort. He took with him a letter from Ben-Gurion to Adenauer explaining the reasons for the war. "Once again," Shinar later wrote, "I was struck by something in Adenauer's manner, something that had impressed me in previous conversations with him. After he had read the letter and asked a few questions about the Sinai campaign, he decided on the spot, with a clear and unequivocal response, with no ifs or buts. I could notify Ben-Gurion that the Federal Republic would continue in the future, as it had done in the past, to carry out the agreement and supply the agreed-upon goods for the peaceful development of Israel."[35]

The Israeli purchase delegation established its headquarters in Cologne. It received the money, in annual installments, from the German government and then bought goods and shipped them to Israel. The delegation received the orders from a company set up for this purpose in Tel

Aviv that decided what to purchase in Germany and for whom. The Reparations Company was headed by Hillel Dan, an old Mapai hand and a prominent figure in the management of large Histadrut organizations such as the Solel Boneh construction company. About 30 percent of the German money went to buy fuel. The greater part of the rest went to purchase equipment and raw materials for companies owned by the government, the Jewish Agency, and the Histadrut.* Some 17 percent of the total money received, more than $100 million, went to purchase close to fifty ships—freight carriers and two passenger liners. By the end of 1961, these reparations vessels constituted two-thirds of the Israeli merchant fleet. The Haifa port purchased new cranes, including a floating one named *Bar Kochba*.

During the first ten years of the agreement, from 1953 to 1963, the reparations money funded about a third of the total investment in Israel's electrical system, which tripled its capacity, and nearly half the total investment in the railways, buying German diesel engines, cars, tracks, and signaling equipment. Equipment for developing the water supply, for oil drilling, and for operating the copper mines in Timna was bought in Germany, as well as heavy equipment for agriculture and construction—tractors, combines, and trucks.

During the twelve years the reparations agreement was in effect, Israel's gross national product tripled; the Bank of Israel reckoned that 15 percent of this growth, and 45,000 jobs, could be attributed to investments made with reparations monies. Yet in estimating the influence of the reparations on the country's economic development, the bank concluded that, without this money, Israel would have nonetheless succeeded in raising the funds it needed—through loans and probably also through grants from

---

* About 8 percent of the reparations money—a total of $66 million—went to purchase equipment for more than 1,300 industrial plants engaged in optics, rubber, textiles, medical equipment, canning. It provided everything from printing presses to machines for making sausages. Two-thirds of this sum went for buying equipment for just thirty-six factories, most owned by the Histadrut. Hillel Dan observed in his memoirs that there was "a complete correspondence between the interests of Solel Boneh and those of the state."[36] Only $22 million went for equipment for the hundreds of other factories, mostly privately owned, that wanted it.[37]

Israel paid for about 68 percent of all its imports with foreign capital, more than almost any other country.[38] Most of the money came from contributions solicited by the United Jewish Appeal, from loans from foreign banks, and from U.S. aid. The reparations agreement and the personal compensation funds constituted some 23 percent of imported capital; by 1961 it supplied 40 percent.

other sources. The reparations did not, then, save Israel from economic collapse. But they did expedite development that was already under way, and they had indisputable psychological and political importance.[39]

For these were difficult times—less than ten years after the Holocaust, less than five years after the War of Independence. The country was flooded with hundreds of thousands of new immigrants, many still homeless. Under an austerity program, food and other necessities were rationed; a black market developed. Unemployment led to emigration. The constant tension along the borders added to the depressing atmosphere. Israel's survival was never really in doubt; the question was, rather, whether the country could provide its citizens with a better life, and when. The reparations certainly helped. Hence they were beneficial to Mapai. The new industrial and agricultural equipment created better conditions for the worker and the farmer. Soon, display windows began showing merchandise long absent—fruits, vegetables, and various food products. People were able to enjoy apples again and spread their bread with butter instead of margarine. Now it was possible to choose from a variety of clothes, shoes, furniture, paper goods, and electrical equipment. The supply did not equal what was available in developed countries, but it was enough to give the impression that the country was finally emerging from austerity. Construction began in every city; there were modern cranes and cement mixers; suddenly there was momentum. New power stations arrived, and there were fewer electrical outages. People could now have their own telephone lines and travel on railroad cars offering almost European comfort and luxury. None of this was essential, but it made people feel better in their country.

¶

Tens of thousands of people—later hundreds of thousands—began to receive personal compensation. The first claims were filed by the yekkes, under the compensation laws imposed by the occupying powers in Germany even before the signing of the agreement with Israel. In general, these were lawsuits for the return of property that had been expropriated under Nazi laws or sold at great loss—factories, shops, department stores, lots, houses, apartments, furniture. Claims had to be submitted in German; any accompanying documents had to be translated, and the translation notarized or certified by someone authorized to do so by the Certification of Documents Act. The complicated procedures required familiarity with a tangle of frequently revised orders and regulations that were not necessarily identical in each of the occupation zones. These claims provided work for many lawyers, among them Israelis of German origin who had previously been unable to make a living at their profession—one of the best known was Hans Grünbaum, who had worked until then as a gardener. Most took a percentage of the money they succeeded in getting from the Germans. To help people save money in pursuing these claims, a nonprofit international organization of lawyers was established—the United Restoration Organization (URO)—which charged a fee of not more than 12 percent of the compensation received. At one point it employed more than a thousand attorneys in Israel, Germany, the United States, and other countries; in 1967 the organization pursued more than 125,000 claims.[40]

The German authorities demanded documents of proof and examined them carefully—titles, rental contracts, bills of sale, receipts, balance sheets, as well as sworn statements from relatives and business partners, suppliers, customers, neighbors: "The family lived on our floor, on the other side of the stairs. They were very quiet people and I recall that they had a Biedermeier cabinet in their dining room"[41]—things like that. Over the years, the yekkes sent thousands of inventories of their property to Germany, detailing everything down to the flower embroidered on a kitchen towel. Taken together, these testimonies form a memorial to a lost way of life. Every letter expressed sadness, every number nostalgia.

"We had heavy modern furniture then, built to order for us by the Braun firm of Nuremberg," wrote an engineer from Ramat Gan, formerly a businessman in the city of Bamberg. "The study was furnished in varnished walnut: a large desk (diplomatic style), a large bookcase, a leather armchair and four chairs (upholstered), a large table (expandable), a corner bench (a custom design, with a hand-carved scrolled back), and also green curtains (velvet) and a chandelier (crystal)—for a total of 2,500 marks. In the bedroom (light birch) stood two beds (the wide model, by special order), night tables (with lamps), a large clothes cabinet (three doors, with mirror), a dressing table with two chairs—for a total of 1,800 marks."

There was also the factory that produced insulating material, and it was necessary to determine for sure who owned it—the claimant from Ramat Gan or his Uncle Emil. And so the years went by; the Germans were in no hurry. 1957, 1960, 1961. Further forms and letters and inquiries were added to the file: testimony from relatives and acquaintances arrived from Berlin (West) and from Amersfoort (Netherlands);

from Cilote (Chile), from Huntington Park (California), and from Hadera (Israel). All these brought the file up to 1964, when the Germans asked if perhaps the family could locate Uncle Emil, after all. It would be best if he himself could testify before an authorized notary so as to clarify once and for all who owned the firm. But no, unfortunately Uncle Emil perished in Theresienstadt, as was noted at the time the original claim was made, in early 1951. All that remained of him was a postcard he sent to Horst, his nephew, on August 23, 1942, greetings for the Jewish New Year. And Horst, the claimant from Ramat Gan, who was now called Ilan, had attached a copy of the postcard to his original claim, at the beginning of 1951, as noted, and he respectfully attaches another. Sometime in 1967 an order to pay 20,627 marks (a little more than $5,000) appeared in the file. At the end of the year it was determined that a bit more was due, and eventually another payment was made, of 2,422 marks—about $600.

There was also life insurance. Uncle Emil, may he rest in peace, had taken out a policy shortly after returning from the front in World War I. It had not expired. The insurance company still existed (the Vienna branch) and, miraculously, it still had Uncle Emil's file. At the beginning of 1963 the company (the Frankfurt branch) responded that it had done its figures and was happy to notify its old and respected customer that the value of the policy, $5,000 in 1919, now entitled his heirs to 714 marks and 23 pfennigs, about $200.

Eventually, it became possible to demand compensation for the cessation of studies and the loss of a professional career. Anyone forced to leave Germany while studying—law, for example—could claim that he would have supported himself as a German attorney or government employee and thus would have earned more than in a comparable position in Israel. If he had excelled at his studies (and produced as proof the grades he received then), he could argue that he had been deprived of a career as a judge in a German municipal court, and perhaps, who knows, as the chief justice of the district court. The Germans took such claims into account and awarded pensions accordingly.

Here is a piece of Zionist irony: The money from Germany was supposed to express the victory of Zionism and revenge against the Nazis, but many of those who filed for compensation based their claims on the argument that they would not have left Germany had they been allowed to stay. Hence, they should be seen as political refugees whose life in Israel was something less than what they would have had in Germany.

"Hitler appeared and the Jews began to come"
Jaffa (1933)

"The New Man"
European newcomers at an
agricultural settlement near Haifa

The same couple after a few days

"The best human material"
The "Tehran children" arrive in Palestine (1943)
CENTRAL ZIONIST ARCHIVE

לשחרור מעונים,
לנקמת טבוחים,

התגייסו !

"Everybody wanted revenge"
Poster calling for enlistment in
the British army (1943):
"Liberation for the tormented.
Vengeance for the slaughtered"

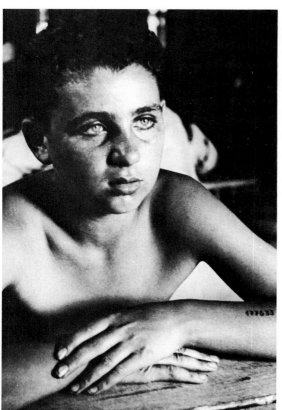

"A million immediately"
Briha refugees on the way (1945)

"Like Lenny in Of Mice and Men"
Haifa (1945)

"The remnant"
Holocaust survivors arrive in Haifa (July 15, 1945)
KLUGER COLLECTION, ISRAELI GOVERNMENT PRESS OFFICE

Holocaust survivors arrive in Israel (1946)
ISRAELI GOVERNMENT PRESS OFFICE

"The best propaganda for Zionism"
The *Exodus* in Haifa (1947)

Immigrants on the *Pan York* (1948)

עסקת הנשק עם "גרמניה האחרת"
בעיני שמואל כץ (על המשמר, 10.7.59)

Arms deal with the "other Germany" as
seen by Shmuel Katz
Al Hamishmar (July 10, 1959)

"Moral satisfaction"
Konrad Adenauer and David Ben-
Gurion in New York (March 14, 1960)
HAARETZ ARCHIVES

"You are a wandering Jew"
Nahum Goldmann (1979)
HAARETZ ARCHIVES

"If this is permissible in Israel—everything is permissible"
Menahem Begin at an antireparations rally in Tel Aviv (February 25, 1952)

"Six million times No!"
Demonstration against Rolf Pauls, first German ambassador to Israel, in
Jerusalem (August 19, 1965)

At least one of the claimants gave some thought to Israel's lost honor. Dr. V. Falk, a pediatrician from Haifa, wrote to the director-general of the foreign ministry for advice. The Germans had granted him less than he had asked for. He could appeal. To do so, he had to prove that the salary of the director of a ward in a government hospital in Israel was not enough to live on. "I have no doubt that it is possible to prove this, but I have doubts about whether it is desirable to engage in such a debate before a German court." The foreign ministry, less sensitive to such matters, told the good citizen that it had no objections to his appeal.[42]

Many claimants even demanded that Germany pay for expenses incurred in moving to the land of their fathers.

> We had to sell the heavy furniture at unfair prices, because we could not take it with us, since it was not appropriate to the size of apartments in Palestine (an average room is between 40 and 50 square feet). For this reason we took only the piano and some small pieces of furniture, the crib, three rugs (one large), household implements, clothing, bed linens, and several hundred books, a total of 15 crates and suitcases packed by the firm of Philip Guttmann of Lichtenfels (Upper Franconia), which is no longer in existence, but the bill has been preserved and the price stated thereon (packing, insurance, and shipping) is 498 marks. We traveled via Munich to Trieste by train, second class, and sailed for Haifa on the *Martha Washington*, tourist class, and we have preserved the tickets, which show a price of 200 marks. The baby went for free. My total claim is 4,200 marks.

These were marks of the Reich, equal to 488 marks of the Federal Republic—about $100. The Germans paid up.

Many Israelis of German origin thus began to receive both lump-sum compensation payments and pensions in the middle of the 1950s. Most received more than one payment, on separate claims. The compensation arrangements were discriminatory from the start: Israelis from Germany were allowed to claim more than those from elsewhere. The Bank of Israel calculated that 10 percent of those who received compensation received between 31 and 43 percent of the total sum paid out; many in this group were yekkes.[43] Among them were businessmen, hoteliers, storekeepers, doctors, professionals, and others of relatively high income. Few got rich from the compensation, but many were able to live well, free of financial anxieties. Many were no longer young. These were the people who went to chamber-music concerts at the Hebrew University's Wise auditorium. They arrived in Volkswagens and, during intermission, they would tell each other about the previous summer and the summer to come—in Interlaken, Switzerland, or Zell am See, Austria. The compensation payments further set them apart from other Israelis. Not surprisingly, many refugees claimed that their parents had spoken German with them and sent them to German schools, and as a result they were part of "the sphere of German culture." The Germans recognized this claim, but often demanded proof, sending the claimants for language tests.

Holocaust survivors from eastern Europe also had to endure the German bureaucracy, not infrequently encountering small-minded, arbitrary, insensitive, and malevolent officials. The Germans paid them for their days of imprisonment in concentration camps at the rate of five marks per day, beginning after the first month. A year in Auschwitz thus entitled a survivor of the camp to 1,800 marks, some $450. To prove that they had indeed been in Auschwitz, the claimants were required to explain under what circumstances they arrived there. In doing so, they had to submit the stories of their lives in German, on a special form, and attach proof. The Germans generally demanded two sworn statements from witnesses who were with the claimant at the camp. They also requested the former prisoner's number. The witnesses were asked to note whether they had also submitted claims; the Germans then cross-checked the information in the different documents. For some camps, the Germans had documents listing the serial numbers given to prisoners there; for other camps they had lists of prisoners by name. "You cannot have been in Buchenwald on the date you cited, since your name appears on the list of the prisoners at Gross Rosen and at Gross Rosen this number was already in use," they responded to one claimant. They compared dates that appeared in various documents and discovered contradictions. "We have taken note of your claim that, when you arrived at the camp, you said that you were older, in order to save yourself from the extermination of the children, but your vita indicates that you were in fact 18 months older and as a result it is not clear to us why you had to give a false date when you registered at the camp." Or in another case:

In computing the period of imprisonment that entitles you to compensation, we cannot take into account your imprisonment in Hungary. Even if we accept the claim that you arrived in Budapest as a refugee, as a result of the invasion of Slovakia, the claim is unsupported in your file by anything except your declaration. You should remember that Hungary was at this time an independent country, not a country under occupation, and that the German government does not take responsibility for that country's laws. It should also be emphasized that, aside from your declaration in this matter, there is no support for your claim that the Hungarians arrested you because you were a Jew.

Things of that sort.

At one point the Germans paid compensation for having forced Jews in the ghettos to wear a patch, generally yellow, sewn onto their outer garments. Claims for offense to "Jewish honor," as the documents termed it, occasionally exposed inconsistencies and inaccuracies in compensation requests. "If you were forced to wear the Jewish star on the date you mentioned, it cannot be that you were in a camp on the date you mentioned, because according to the information in our possession, the Jewish star was imposed in the ghetto where you allegedly lived only after the date that you allegedly arrived in the camp."

Some survivors were eligible for compensation for injury to their health, if such injury resulted from persecution by the Nazis. It was not always possible to prove this. To do so, the victims had to be examined by Israeli doctors approved by the Germans. The results were transmitted to German doctors for a second opinion. "We have taken note of your claim that the injury to your spinal cord was caused in Buchenwald camp, when an SS officer whose name you did not mention, because you allegedly do not recall it, kicked you with his boot and allegedly also stomped on you. But it appears from your curriculum vitae that in 1951 you enlisted in the Israel Defense Forces. We therefore request that you produce for our examination a copy of your army medical file, translated, signed, and certified by a notary, so that we may clarify your claim, since if you were found fit for military service, it may be that the damage to your spinal cord was not severe or may have resulted from your army service."

As the years went by, it was possible to claim money for rest cures at the hot springs near Tiberias and other such places, and to request increases in the level of payments on the basis of a worsening medical condition. In time, the Germans began to recognize psychological trauma as well. Instead of X-rays and blood and urine tests, intimate documentation of anxieties, mental anguish, sleep disturbances, and sexual difficulties had to be sent to Germany. Thus, claimants were often compelled to relive the terrors of the Holocaust for the benefit of medical personnel. Frequently, it was necessary to hire an attorney to convince the authorities in Germany that "it was all true," and to bargain with them on the percentages of dysfunction.

Once a pension claim was recognized, the level of payment had to be determined. The Germans demanded certification from the Israeli income-tax authorities on the income of claimants and their spouses retroactive to the day the claim was submitted, sometimes ten to fifteen years earlier. It was not easy to obtain such documentation. The Israeli finance ministry had an interest in making it easy for the claimants and, at one stage, even issued the information they asked for on special forms, in German. But Israeli officials also shunted claimants from one clerk to another, for months and years. The Germans picked through the Israeli documentation, looking for the smallest discrepancies. "In the breakdown of your income for the period between 1 April 1954 and 31 March 1971, details of your income between 1 April 1957 and 31 March 1958 are missing. Please notify us if during this period you also supported yourself from your haberdashery shop and what the level of your income was during this period. We cannot process your claim until it is completed." And in another case: "We understand that your son Yoram is currently studying chemistry at the University of California, Berkeley. Please produce for us an explanation, with documents translated into German and certified by a notary, of the source of funding for his residence in the United States (including scholarship, loans, etc.)." German law allowed the claimants to appeal the decisions. If their appeals were rejected, they could go to court. Often, the levels of the lump-sum compensation and the monthly pension were set only after extensive bargaining and compromise. Then the difference between what the Germans initially approved and the final sum agreed on would be paid—sometimes 25,000 marks, sometimes 40,000, sometimes even 80,000 or 100,000 marks (about $25,000)—all at once.

The Germans assumed that those claiming compensation were trying to cheat them. It was a reasonable assumption—the claimants had every reason to do so. From time to time people were unmasked—in Germany, Israel, and a host of other countries—who made their living fabricating testimony and counterfeiting documentation. The office of one Tel Aviv attorney was described as "a claims factory."[44] A member of the Knesset described the typical claims-chasing lawyer: "He migrates between Germany and Israel, to the point that you don't know if he is a German lawyer with an office in Israel or an Israeli lawyer with an office in Germany."[45]

Estimates are that more than 250,000 Israelis received compensation from Germany. The lump-sum payment to survivors equaled, on the average, a year's income.* Many used the money to move into better apartments. The monthly pension from Germany raised the typical recipient's income by about 30 percent over that of an Israeli who did not receive compensation.[47] It was a major factor in widening the ethnic gap between Ashkenazim and Oriental Jews.

A few thousand of those entitled to personal compensation lived in kibbutzim. Members who wished to take advantage of their rights were required to give the kibbutzim power of attorney to pursue their claim. The kibbutzim cooperated among themselves to collect the money as a group. Eligibility for compensation put many kibbutz members to a cruel personal and ideological test. People could live on a kibbutz out of habit, or because they had no choice, and consider themselves more or less happy—since the question did not arise on a daily basis. Now, with their newfound economic resources, they had to tell themselves that they were staying at the kibbutz by choice. And if they stayed, they had to transfer the money to the kibbutz. This often meant giving up not only what was theirs but also what they could pass on to their children and relatives outside the kibbutz. Many found it difficult to make that choice, and they were under intense pressure to do so.

In September 1956, the assembly of Hakibbutz Hameuhad, meeting at Kibbutz Kabri, decided that a member who received compensation payments and hid them from "the institutions of his settlement," nullified his membership in the kibbutz. The regulations governing these funds, the assembly ruled, were no different from those governing money or property that a kibbutz member received from any other source: The entire sum belonged to the kibbutz. The assembly decided, however, that this money would be used not for ordinary expenses but for some "public purpose" as decided by the membership of each kibbutz. Apparently, they wanted to make it easier for the members to hand over their money by allowing them to at least see it serving a public need. Many kibbutzim used the payments to build swimming pools, athletic fields, new dining rooms, and lounges for the members. A year later, though, Hakibbutz Hameuhad decided it was permissible to use the compensation payments to raise the standard of living of the members. Thus the kibbut-

---

* According to the agreements with Germany, some survivors were to receive their pensions directly from the Israeli government. But the government paid only half what the Germans paid, though the sums were updated from time to time.[46]

zim could buy new furniture for members' rooms. The condition was that everyone benefit, not just those who received the payments.

In many kibbutzim, the German money provoked envy and suspicion, as well as tension between the yekkes and the Holocaust survivors from eastern Europe. Most kibbutz yekkes were among the senior members of their communities and lived there out of ideological conviction. As in the cities, they received more money than Holocaust survivors did. They handed it over to the kibbutz without hesitation. Many survivors had, by contrast, come to the kibbutzim unwillingly. Even though they had suffered more than the yekkes, they received less. They often had doubts over whether to give the money to the kibbutz. Many did not ask for much for themselves, but the kibbutzim were unresponsive even so. Givat Brenner rejected a member's request to purchase the *Hebrew Encyclopedia* for himself. Several kibbutzim rejected requests to pursue hobbies, to study, or to travel overseas. By the time the kibbutzim became wise enough to give consideration to their members' personal wishes, they had often lost both the members and the money. In some kibbutzim, the issue of compensation payments released previously submerged social tensions. Kibbutz Hahotrim lost 50 of its 150 members as the result of such friction.

Some kibbutzim knew it was best to be cautious: "We should avoid putting a member of the kibbutz to an overly difficult test on the matter of property that comes to him from the outside, because most of the public will not stand for it," declared one kibbutz periodical. "Let us not force members to evade, and sneak around, our rules. If we act with extremism, we will cause them to live with a divided soul and ethic."[48] The religious kibbutzim agreed to treat the compensation payments as interest-bearing deposits—a member who decided to leave was allowed to take his compensation money with him—with the exception of the monthly pension. The Hashomer Hatsair kibbutzim apparently spent little time debating the subject, though some received large sums through the yekkes who were their members. All in all, the kibbutzim learned to adjust their ideological and ethical demands to the welcome change in their financial position—just as most other Israelis did.

¶

Those who predicted that the reparations and compensation agreements would involve humiliation to the state and its citizens proved right. Israel made many concessions—ideological, political, and financial. First, it yielded on its declared refusal to conduct direct negotiations with Germany. Then it abandoned its claim that it had the standing to speak for all Holocaust victims and survivors. "The Israeli government," Moshe Sharett said in the Knesset, "claims the reparations for itself, because it sees the State of Israel as bearing the rights of the millions who were slaughtered and as empowered and commanded to demand their satisfaction, being the only national embodiment of the people who, because of their association with it, were sentenced to destruction."[49] In fact, the reparations agreement did not recognize Israel as the representative of the Jews who were murdered by the Nazis: the money Israel received was explicitly allocated to cover the cost of absorbing and rehabilitating the survivors of the Holocaust. Israel's opening position was based on the assumption that the cost of absorbing a single refugee was $3,000. Some 500,000 were absorbed, for a total of $1.5 billion. This agreement depicted Israel not as the homeland of the Jewish people, the realization of the Zionist dream, but rather as a state accepting immigrants for money. The Germans bargained well. They examined the Israeli figures and found that the price was exaggerated, that it was possible to absorb a refugee-immigrant for only $2,500. At that moment, Israel hardly resembled its ideal image.

Most of the money was paid to private individuals. But only one in four recipients lived in Israel. They received their money for being Jews persecuted by the Nazis, not for being Israelis. Together, they received more than the country received in reparations. This was, then, a distinctly individualistic success story for the Jews of the world, not a collective Israeli success.

The Germans did not pay much. Eliezer Shinar computed that, to support the reparations and compensation payments, every citizen of Germany paid out about 40 marks a year ($10) for fifteen years.[50] That was true as of 1967. The Germans later figured that, by the year 2030, they would have paid out 120 billion marks (between $30 and $60 billion, in keeping with changes in the exchange rate). This was the sum that approximately 60 million Germans would pay out over 75 years, the average per person coming to 26 marks a year—about half a mark (25 cents) a week. A large part of that money was intended as payment for property confiscated by the Germans that remained in their hands. Some who received pensions would have been eligible to receive them anyway, as German citizens. There is no reason to divide the total sum the Germans paid by the number of Jews they murdered, but neither does such a formula give an impressive result in actuarial terms: 120 billion marks for six million victims comes to 20,000 marks per person, between $5,000 and $10,000. The reparations to the State of Israel totaled no more than 15 percent of this sum.[51]

Those who predicted that the reparations and compensation agreements would bring about a reconciliation between the Jewish and German peoples, and lead to a normalization of relations between Israel and West Germany, were also right. Thus the Israeli consul in Munich, Eliahu Livneh, could not forever refuse the repeated invitations of German president Theodor Heuss. After avoiding him for several months, Livneh went to Bonn—although not in a black suit, to make it clear that he was not on an official visit. Heuss was exuberant. He told Livneh about his links with the Zionist movement, reminding his guest that he had a Jewish relative. Before they parted, the German president chided the Israeli consul for not having enriched his store of Jewish jokes. The consul was quick to acquiesce with a story about two Hasidim. "The enthusiasm and the understanding with which Heuss heard the joke marked the conclusion of this warm and friendly conversation," the consul reported.[52]

Ben-Gurion's German policy triggered stormy emotions. But only a few objected with true sincerity. Mordecai Nurok and Dov Shilansky, and others like them on the right and left and in the center, campaigned passionately to halt the tide. Theirs was a lost cause, even a pathetic one, but they spoke from their hearts, felt what they said, and said what they felt. Others—cynics and hypocrites—exploited the issues for the sake of rhetoric and gave up their positions as soon as it was politically expedient to do so. Thus in December 1952, the General Zionists joined the government. Three of the four ministers had, only a year before, voted against negotiations with Germany, and one of them, Yisrael Rokah, was so bothered by his conscience that he had even threatened to stage a hunger strike. Now the General Zionist ministers demanded more influence over the commercial contacts with Germany. Similarly, Mapam's Yaakov Hazan praised the Hashomer Hatsair kibbutzim for the noble manner in which they had used their money; four years before he had described the negotiations with Germany as "selling our souls."[53] "Even the members of parties that opposed reparations have avidly enjoyed the reparations goods," Ben-Gurion gloated.[54]

Ben-Gurion had won. But his adversaries were already preparing for the next battle: the battle over the memory and meaning of the Holocaust. During one Knesset debate, Eri Jabotinsky, the son of the great Revisionist leader, demanded the establishment of a special court to investigate the history of the Holocaust and, in particular, the Jewish Agency's failure to save more Jews.[55] A special court was never established, but soon Mapai found itself standing accused in the Jerusalem district court.

PART V

POLITICS:
The Kastner Affair

13 | *"It Is Hard for Us, the Judges of Israel"*

In the early 1950s, there lived in Jerusalem an elderly, God-fearing stamp collector of Hungarian birth who ran a ten-room hotel on Zion Square. He had once been a low-level diplomat in the service of the Austro-Hungarian Empire. In Vienna he had tried to make a name for himself as a journalist but found it hard to sell what he wrote. Supporting himself with other work, he occasionally got tangled up in various kinds of fraud and crookedness.

He entered Israeli history as the sole defendant in the first great Holocaust trial held in Israel, though ultimately he played only a supporting role in this drama, in which his name is no more than a footnote. One day, when he was late for his trial, the judge ordered the sergeant-at-arms to go out to the corridor and call him. "Excuse me," the sergeant replied. "What did you say his name was?" The judge fidgeted for a moment, then cast a questioning glance at the defense attorney. "Gruenwald, your honor," the lawyer reminded him. "Malchiel Gruenwald."[1] *Time* magazine, which liked to call him simply Malchiel, computed that the Nazis had murdered more than fifty members of his family.[2]

Divided Jerusalem, wounded in the War of Independence, was in those days a sleepy, poor provincial town, a magnet for tens of thousands of homeless, jobless immigrants who lived in tent camps on the outskirts, waiting for better times. But behind the city's misery and its gray stone face there was a vigor and vitality that nourished philosophers and politicians. The Hebrew University, still housed in the Terra Sancta monastery, the Jewish Agency, the prime minister's office, the Central Synagogue, and the Knesset all stood along one shaded boulevard that still bore the name given to it by the British authorities—King George V Street. The prime minister, many cabinet ministers, almost everyone who was anyone, lived side by side in Rehavia, a neighborhood within walking distance of Zion Square. Not far from there, in a building constructed a century earlier to house pilgrims from Russia, were the courts. Tel Aviv was the home of the central committees of the major parties, of the Histadrut, the stock exchange, and the army general staff; the north was where industry and agriculture developed; but the intellectual and political center of the country, intense and intimate, was in downtown Jerusalem. There, politicians and thinkers, prophets and poets, reformers and lunatics all knew one another; all frequented the same sidewalk cafés, espousing philosophical systems and founding social movements in a maelstrom of vision and zealotry, genius and madness. In Jerusalem, words ruled, and their power was immense.

Gruenwald, a frail man of seventy-two, with a black yarmulke and goatee, had been a supporter of the Etzel; his son had fought in its ranks and had been killed in the War of Independence, on Mount Zion. It was then that Gruenwald changed the name of his hotel from the Austria to the Mount Zion. Gruenwald liked to write. From time to time he put out a newsletter, *Letters to Friends in the Mizrahi*, an angry brew of political commentary that revived forgotten conflicts, old grudges, and all kinds of dusty scandals from the pre-Holocaust Jewish communities of Budapest and Vienna. Gruenwald especially liked to lash out at certain leaders of the Mizrahi and other religious Zionist groups, as well as politicians from other parties, including members of the Knesset and ministers. More than anything else, he hated Mapai. After writing an essay in German and finding someone to translate it into Hebrew, Gruenwald would have several hundred copies run off, three pages each. Then he would stuff them into envelopes, address them, stamp them, and take them to the post office. Dogged, tireless, he did it all himself, at his own expense, asking nothing of his correspondents except that they read what he sent.

On his mailing list were the names of several journalists: many of them threw his pamphlet into the wastebasket where it belonged. Every so often someone would threaten to sue him for libel, and Gruenwald would make a public apology. In general, these episodes never went any further than the clientele of the Café Vienna, on the ground floor of Gruenwald's hotel. The same could just as easily have been the fate of newsletter no. 51.

It was issued in August 1952. Continuing a topic raised in a previous issue, Gruenwald attacked one of the heads of the Hungarian Jewish community in Israel, Israel Rudolf (Rezso) Kastner. "The smell of a corpse is tingling in my nostrils!" Gruenwald wrote in that pamphlet. "It will be a funeral of the very best kind! Dr. Rudolf Kastner must be liquidated!"[3]

Kastner, trained as a lawyer but working as a journalist, had been a Zionist functionary in Budapest, associated with Mapai. During the war, while he was in his early forties, he headed the Rescue Committee in Hungary. He negotiated a deal with Adolf Eichmann and SS officer Kurt Becher to release a million Jews in exchange for 10,000 trucks. That was the deal that failed with the arrest of Joel Brand, the envoy Eichmann sent to Istanbul in May 1944. Kastner, in the meantime, was involved in other rescue operations; there were many people who owed him their lives.

When Gruenwald's inflammatory pamphlet came out, Kastner was serving as press spokesman for the Ministry of Commerce and Industry. He hoped to become a member of the Knesset, having been on Mapai's list of candidates in the first and second elections. His name appears several times in Ben-Gurion's diary.[4]

Gruenwald wrote: "For three years I have waited for this moment in order to bring to justice . . . this careerist, who benefits from Hitler's theft and murder. On the basis of his criminal machinations and because of his collaboration with the Nazis, . . . I see him as the indirect murderer of my dear brothers." As though addressing Kastner directly, Gruenwald went on: "For whose sake and at whose expense did you travel in 1946 —secretly, like a thief in the night—to Nuremberg, in order to testify at the trial of the greatest war criminals in the history of the world, appearing as a defense witness for SS Obersturmbannführer Kurt Becher, murderer-thief who exploited our brothers in Hungary and sucked their blood? . . . Why did you save Becher from the hanging he deserved?" Gruenwald's answer:

> He wanted to save himself, so that Becher would not reveal to the international court their deals and their joint acts of robbery. . . . Where now is the money of the Jews of Hungary, millions for which no accounting was given? . . . He saved no fewer than fifty-two of

his relatives, and hundreds of other Jews—most of whom had converted to Christianity—bought their rescue from Kastner by paying
millions! That's how Kastner saved the members of Mapai. . . . He
saved people with connections, and made a fortune in the process.
But thousands of senior Zionists, members of the Mizrahi and the
ultrareligious parties—these, Kastner left in the valley of the shadow
of death.[5]

It was a confused and pathetic tirade. District Court Judge Benyamin
Halevy later commented, correctly, that it was not easy to sum up the
accusations against Kastner, but he placed them under four headings: (1)
collaboration with the Nazis; (2) "indirect murder," or "paving the way
for the murder" of Hungarian Jewry; (3) partnership with a Nazi war
criminal in acts of thievery; (4) saving that war criminal from punishment
after the war.

Kastner was aware of the accusations against him. A Mizrahi functionary in Hungary had registered a complaint against him as early as
the 22nd Zionist Congress, in Basel, in 1946. He accused Kastner of
having misused half a million dollars earmarked for rescuing Jews. Kastner
responded with a libel suit in the congress's court of honor; he also wrote
a long account of his actions during the war. The hearing of this suit
was never concluded. Years later, in Israel, a native of Kastner's city
appeared several times at election rallies in the Israeli Hungarian community and interrupted Kastner with shouts and accusations when Kastner
spoke for Mapai. Kastner tried unsuccessfully to calm the man. After the
Knesset passed the Nazi and Nazi Collaborators Law in 1950, Kastner
was questioned by the police, but no charges were filed. Kastner never
denied having negotiated with Nazi Germany's representatives in Hungary, Adolf Eichmann among them. But he claimed consistently that
everything he did had been aimed at saving Hungarian Jewry and that
he had in fact succeeded in rescuing thousands.[6]

Kastner was the best-known Israeli ever accused of collaboration with
the Nazis, but he was not the only one. There were other cases after the
war, when Holocaust survivors—walking down the street, lying on the
beach, riding a bus, or standing in line at the cinema—suddenly found
themselves face to face with "Jewish traitors who lent a hand to the
extermination of their nation," as Knesset member Mordecai Nurok put
it.[7]

A reporter for *Haaretz* described such a scene at an intersection in Tel

Aviv at the beginning of 1946. An agitated crowd surrounded a well-dressed young man, and several people beat him on the head while shouting "Murderer!" and "Gestapo!" "The man stood there, white-faced, and then tried to escape," the reporter wrote. Two young men explained to the throng that the man was Shmuel Wishlitsky from Ostrowiec, Poland, and denounced him for having collaborated with the Gestapo while serving as a policeman in the ghetto. They suspected him of turning in members of their families who had managed to escape the ghetto. Injured, the man fled down a side street. "People continued to gather on the site discussing the incident," the paper said.[8]

Many collaborators thus identified had been kapos during the war—concentration-camp inmates to whom the Nazis had assigned various supervisory positions in the camps and workplaces, such as enforcing discipline and cleanliness. The kapos had authority to impose punishments; many were notorious for their cruelty. "Every one of them murdered," Dov Shilansky related. "The Jews who worked for the Germans, and almost every Jew with even the ribbon of a deputy kapo on his arm, murdered—all but an exceptional few."[9] In the camps, and in the ghettos as well, various police and administrative functions were assigned to Jews. Some of these were under the authority of the local Jewish Council (*Judenrat*) the Nazis set up in many cities they occupied.

After the war, the collaborators mixed in with the refugees, trying to hide their pasts. Many, however, were identified while in the DP camps. Once, when David Ben-Gurion visited a camp in Europe after the war, he witnessed a group that suddenly identified and beat a kapo. In Ben-Gurion's words, the three attackers had "eyes red with blood, capable of killing a man."[10] The incident shocked him. "I thought he would collapse," related Ruth Aliav, who accompanied the Jewish Agency chief. It was, she recalled, the first time Ben-Gurion had encountered this embarrassing aspect of the Holocaust.[11]

A few months later, Eliahu Dobkin, a member of the Jewish Agency executive and a leader of Mapai, told his colleagues of an "inner disquiet" that had not left him—something that, had he not seen it with his own eyes, he would not have believed: there were lynchings. In Munich, Dobkin said, he had been told that hundreds of Jews had been murdered by other Jews after the liberation. He saw one man beaten "until he was driven insane." The attackers insisted that he had been a sadist of the most horrible kind. Here Dobkin commented: "I think it is no secret that the son of one of our best Zionists was accused of the same crime. I sympathize with the tragedy of his old father." He was referring to Yitzhak Gruenbaum, a member of the Jewish Agency executive, later minister of the interior under Ben-Gurion. His son had been a kapo at Auschwitz.[12]

One newspaper demanded that collaborators be "liquidated." But it warned that it was not enough for someone to point at someone else in the street and shout "Kapo!" The suspect's guilt should be established with certainty. Even then, he should not be lynched but be punished by the "institutions in authority."[13] Yet the British Mandatory authorities were uninterested in the problem and the Jewish Agency was busy at the time with more pressing concerns. Dobkin thought it was now more important than ever to attend to the saying of the Jewish sages: "Do not judge your comrade until you stand in his place." He told his colleagues about a newly released prisoner he had met: the man had been in a death camp, where he worked transporting people to the gas chambers. Once, his mother was in the van he drove. "Many good Jews then did all kinds of jobs like that. It's not so horrible," the man had argued. "I would not take it upon myself to judge his case," Dobkin said. "I don't know who can judge it."[14]

After the state was established, people would report collaborators to the police. But the police were powerless—there was no law that covered this situation or allowed them to arrest the suspects. As a result, the Ministry of Justice introduced an Act against Jewish War Criminals in August 1949 but did not push for immediate enactment.[15] Like the Jewish Agency, the ministry preferred to avoid such delicate matters and deal with other things first. Mordecai Nurok brought the issue before the Knesset. Minister of Justice Pinhas Rosen gave assurances that his ministry was working on the issue but needed more time. Half a year went by. "The State of Israel is the only country in the world in which it is impossible to try and judge Nazi murderers and their helpers," Nurok complained. "Eminent house," he said, "were Göring and Goebbels, may their evil names rot, walking among us today, the hand of the law would not reach them."[16] Four months later, the proposed Nazi and Nazi Collaborators Law was finally introduced. It took nearly five months to win the Knesset's approval. In the meantime, the Knesset was able to deal with more abstract issues, and it debated and passed an act for the prevention and punishment of genocide.

Minister of Justice Rosen told the Knesset that the Nazi and Nazi Collaborators Law could not be expected to lead to the execution of many

Nazis; it would be invoked primarily against Jewish collaborators.* By the mid-1950s, about thirty Jews suspected of collaborating with the Nazis were under investigation; the impression was that the police were showing no enthusiasm for these cases, and pursued them only when citizens filed detailed complaints and pressed for action. Only a few of these investigations led to indictments. The government prosecutor tended not to indict Israeli citizens for "crimes against the Jewish people," as permitted under the law, preferring instead to accuse them of having caused specific injuries to identifiable individuals. Sometimes they were also accused of "crimes against humanity." Some of the accused were acquitted. As for the guilty, their sentences tended to be lightened on appeal, generally to two or three years but even as little as a few months. The Nazi and Nazi Collaborators Law stipulated the death penalty, yet in 1951, the death sentence of one Israeli citizen convicted under the law was commuted by the high court to ten years.[18] After the abolition of capital punishment, in 1954, the death penalty remained in effect for those convicted under this law, but it was not clear whether it was mandatory.

The law provided considerable leeway for subjective evaluations by each judge. The judges knew only one way of determining the truth— as did their counterparts in West Germany, whose methods more than once aroused the ire of witnesses and foreign observers. Like the Germans, Israeli judges insisted on delving into the tiniest details of a case. Else Trank, for instance, had been responsible for keeping order in a barracks at the women's camp at Auschwitz-Birkenau. The question for consideration: did she beat the prisoners with a stick, a whip, a belt, or only her hands? It was determined that she beat them with her hands. Now the court had to consider whether she struck the prisoners with an open hand—that is, did she slap the prisoners, or did she beat them with the bony part of her hand? Or perhaps with a clenched fist? Did she hit the prisoners on the face, the back, or the shoulders, or all of these? All of these, the court found. On one detail she was acquitted because the judges had doubts. They were persuaded that the defendant forced one prisoner to kneel down, but they could not determine if she had hit the prisoner. One witness said she had not seen blows.

---

* *Haaretz* reported that one of the proposed "laws against Jewish war criminals," as it called them, would mandate the punishment of all those who sabotaged immigration to Palestine through "collaboration with the enemy." In the end, however, the cabinet did not submit this legislation, and the Knesset did not demand it.[17]

Forced to consider the reality of life in the camps, the judges, unintentionally and perhaps inevitably, fell into using Nazi terminology in their rulings. Their verdict against Else Trank distinguished between "innocent prisoners" and others who broke the rules of the camp. It stated, twice, that inmates had belonged to "the Jewish race."[19]

The trials required the judges to make extraordinary ethical and historical decisions that often fell outside their areas of expertise. They had to decide whether a man could refuse to accept the post of kapo, and to what extent the job required cruelty. They tended not to punish a person for simply being a kapo, only for not having been a decent one. They cited Exodus 5:14: From among the Pharaoh's slaves, several children of Israel were assigned to supervise the others. According to the commentator Rashi, these foremen did not oppress their fellow Israelites, so Egyptian taskmasters had to be placed over them. "There were kapos in our day that also . . . did not fear the Hitlerist taskmasters and did not oppress the prisoners," one verdict stated.[20]

"It is hard for us, the judges of Israel, to free ourselves of the feeling that, in punishing a worm of this sort, we are diminishing, even if by only a trace, the abysmal guilt of the Nazis themselves," wrote Supreme Court Justice Moshe Silberg.[21] More than anything else, it seems that the judges shared the unwillingness of most Israelis to deal with the Holocaust in general and with Jewish war criminals in particular. Generally, only Holocaust survivors connected to the case at hand visited the courtrooms. Sometimes there were violent outbursts against the defendants and their attorneys. Only a few trials were covered by the press, some not at all. A kapo trial was a filthy and embarrassing story, and the papers did not want to get caught up in it.

Thus, when the Gruenwald case came to trial, Shmuel Tamir, attorney, and Uri Avneri, editor of the weekly magazine *Haolam Hazeh*, needed to use every rhetorical device and journalistic trick to attract the public's attention. Yet eventually the trial became the most important and painful one ever held in Israel, with the possible exception of Eichmann's.

Herut had been the only newspaper to take notice of Gruenwald's newsletter, in a short item written by Yoel Marcus, who later became a political columnist for *Haaretz*. "For three years," Marcus wrote, "many Hungarian Jews have been accusing a man with an official position of having testified in favor of a Nazi criminal, of shady dealings, and of fat profits at the expense of operations to rescue Jews. Why does he not exonerate himself?"[22] Marcus's little scoop might have remained merely that, soon forgotten. It required no action. "The accusations against Dr. Kastner had no bearing on Kastner's position in the ministry," wrote his boss, the minister of commerce and industry, Dov Yosef, in his memoirs. "It was his personal matter to decide if he wanted to take action against Gruenwald." Yosef told Kastner that he doubted it was worthwhile suing Gruenwald for libel, especially in the light of the way such trials were conducted in Israel. But the attorney general, Haim Cohen, notified Kastner that, given the serious nature of the accusations, he must either take action to clear his name or resign.[23] "Rezso did not want the trial," his widow related. "But he was in an impossible situation. He was presented with a merciless dilemma. He was told he had to agree to the government's submission of a libel suit on his behalf or resign from his position under Dov Yosef. I told him, 'Resign!' But he answered that he had no choice, that he had to agree to initiating procedures."[24] "Kastner told me that under no circumstances did he want it," Cohen himself said. "He wanted to push that entire period out of his memory and consciousness. He did not want to remember. But Kastner's personal interest was of no interest to me. What interested me was the matter itself."[25]

Haim Cohen concluded his career in the early 1980s as one of the most liberal justices on the Israeli Supreme Court, a staunch advocate of human and civil rights. But in the 1950s, as attorney general, he served the government—including the military administration imposed on Israel's Arab citizens—and tended to restrict freedom of expression and the press. "They were years in which I was convinced that the press was endangering national security," he explained later. "I was a bit influenced on this subject by Ben-Gurion. He was certain that the press was mankind's number one enemy. As attorney general, I saw one of my roles as restraining the press. . . . I then believed, rightly or wrongly, that they were sabotaging the building of the state with sensationalism or, what was no better, out of political blindness. I thought it my job to prevent that. It seems I was wrong."

Cohen, a yekke born in Lübeck, was well versed in Jewish studies, having grown up in a family of famous rabbinic scholars. He radiated a cold intelligence. Sarcastic and condescending, he could also be tearfully sentimental. When he first arrived in Jerusalem, in 1930, he still wore the sidelocks and beard of an ultraorthodox Jew, and he worked for one of the leaders of Agudat Yisrael. Later, he abandoned religion in a painful process accompanied by an extended personal and intellectual crisis. "I despaired of the Lord of the universe and rebelled against him," he recalled.

> It was a process that began with the Holocaust. I had a brother with whom I was very, very close. A genius. He died in very, very tragic and horrible circumstances. He was in the French resistance (the Maquis) and refused to come to Palestine until the Nazis were defeated. He was taken prisoner and sent to Auschwitz. Emotionally I was unwilling, unable, to accept such a thing. But it made me conscious of the enormity of that huge catastrophe. And in those days I felt it as if each one of those millions were my own flesh. One could say, a bit poetically, a bit dramatically, that I myself became a victim of the Holocaust. Something was killed inside me. I was not "liberated" from religion. It wasn't "liberation." It was murder. It took me many years to recover from it.[26]

Some officials warned Cohen against suing Gruenwald. Among them were Minister of Justice Pinhas Rosen and Erwin Shimron, the state prosecutor, both also yekkes. But Cohen, the formalist, insisted. "No one can be allowed to say that a senior government official collaborated with the Nazis without there being a response," he later maintained. He had no way of knowing then, he asserted, that a lawsuit would put Mapai itself on trial. "With all his sharpness of mind," Moshe Sharett wrote in his diary, "he lacked all public sense."[27]

Malchiel Gruenwald's trial opened on January 1, 1954. The first prosecution witness was Rudolf Kastner. The next day's papers gave no indication that the events in District Court Judge Benyamin Halevy's small courtroom were worth following. There were no articles in advance of the trial, and the first few days were covered only in brief. *Haaretz*, for example, merely noted—in a small, single-column item at the bottom of the last page—that Kastner had begun his testimony. Another libel trial was in progress at the time, concerning the endless debate over who was responsible for the murder of Haim Arlosoroff; it, too, aroused little excitement. Statehood had opened a new era in the people's history, and times were hard. Editors sensed they could not burden their readers with grievances from the past; the Holocaust was then still, to a large extent, taboo.

In his testimony, Kastner set out the background to the destruction of Hungarian Jewry, a community numbering 800,000. Close to half a million of them, mostly from the provincial towns, were murdered by the Nazis during the ten months between the Germans' occupation of Hungary in March 1944 and their expulsion by the Soviets in January 1945. More than a year before the Germans invaded, several Zionist party functionaries in Budapest met and established a Rescue Committee, with Kastner as executive director. Using money smuggled to them by the Jewish Agency and other Jewish organizations, as well as funds they collected on their own, the Rescue Committee assisted Jews from Poland and Slovakia to cross the border into Hungary. There, the committee provided for the refugees' basic needs, mostly in Budapest.

When the Germans came, they summoned the Jewish leaders, as they had in other occupied lands, assuring them that they had no intention of harming the Jews. They asked the leaders to prevent panic. Nonetheless, arrests and deportations began almost at once. Still Kastner maintained contact with the Germans, in an effort, he testified, to save the Jewish community from certain destruction. He described his various efforts to bargain with the Nazis, including the dramatic story of Joel Brand and the failed trucks-for-blood deal.*

Kastner related how, while the trucks-for-blood deal was still a live possibility, he succeeded in negotiating his own deal with Eichmann. He was allowed to put 1,685 Jews on a special train to Switzerland. It became known as the "VIP train," and all its passengers were saved. Kastner had selected them. Among the passengers were several hundred people from his hometown, Cluj, and a few dozen members of his family, including his mother, wife, and siblings. The story was grotesque, repellent; the papers began to take notice. The man who made the financial arrangements for the train was SS officer Kurt Becher. Toward the end of the war, relations between Kastner and Becher became still closer. Their dealings branched out; at one point Becher even sent Kastner to Berlin to meet Heinrich Himmler; Kastner went, but the meeting did not take place. Even when all his family, and he himself, were safely in Switzerland, Kastner returned to the Reich to continue his efforts to save more Jews, in coordination with Becher. After the war, Kastner testified in Becher's defense.

When he appeared as a prosecution witness in the Jerusalem court-

---

* Even Brand's story—which most Israelis had not yet heard—was first reported in only a two-column item on the back page of *Haaretz*. Among the stories on the front page were reports on the basketball game between the Israeli army and French all-stars, with pictures (the Israelis lost), and detailed reports of the transfer of the remains of Baron Edmond de Rothschild for burial in Israel (two pictures).[28]

room, Kastner spoke quietly, believably, convinced he had done right. He came across as a bold man who saved the lives of hundreds in his community, perhaps thousands. He seemed more a tragic hero than a scoundrel. When he concluded his testimony, Justice Halevy suggested to Gruenwald that he retract his accusations. Gruenwald refused, and the cross-examination by defense attorney Shmuel M. Tamir began.

Of the leading figures in the affair, only Tamir grew up in Israel, with Hebrew as his native tongue. Born into the Katznelson family, part of the "Rehavia aristocracy," he went to the highly regarded Gimnasia Haivrit high school, then to the Hebrew University. His father was deputy director of the Hadassah hospital. The family, old-line Zionists from Russia, liked to flaunt its Revisionist credentials, though some Katznelsons found their way into the Mapai hierarchy as well. Tamir ("tall") was the code name Shmuel Katznelson had taken in the Etzel, where he served as deputy commander in Jerusalem. The British arrested him and deported him to a prison camp in Kenya. On his release in 1948, he helped found the Herut party. From the start, he was at odds with Menahem Begin. Journalists attributed the tension between the two to the difference between the worldview of a native-born Israeli of twenty-five and that of a thirty-five-year-old man from Poland. Begin emphasized foreign and defense issues; Tamir argued that all effort should be concentrated on removing Mapai from power. "Liberating the Kirya [the government office complex] from Mapai takes precedence over liberating the Temple Mount," he was quoted as saying. He spoke also of the need to create "a new Hebrew nation."[29]

In January 1952, a few months before Gruenwald put out his notorious newsletter, Tamir published an article in Herut in which he termed Ben-Gurion the "Minister of Treason and Minister of Abomination." He accused the prime minister of criminal and immoral acts, including "direct partnership" in the extermination of the Jews of Europe and establishment of relations with West Germany. Tamir wrote:

As a native of this country, as one who was never in the Exile, as one of the happy ones who lost no close family members in that horrifying Holocaust, precisely as such I feel that Israel's stance toward Germany is one of the most basic tests of our people's ability to survive. It is a test of the very question of whether the Hebrew nation exists at all, and if it has the right to exist. In a single sentence: Are we a people, or was this nation truly nothing more than a rotting excretion and a stinking scrap that remained alive? In a single question: Are we a great nation, or was Hitler right in his definition of the Jews and their character?[30]

Tamir's worldview, however, could only have been the second most important motivation for his career—his personal ambition came first. He wanted to be the number-one man in his party. Later in life, when he served as minister of justice in Begin's government, he dreamed of inheriting the prime ministership. He was a crafty politician, an attorney with a quick eye and a sharp tongue, with a craving for dramatic intrigues and media attention.

Tamir first gained fame when he defended Yaakov Heruti, the leader of a group that supported the establishment of an "Israelite kingdom" that would reach from the Mediterranean Sea to the Euphrates River. The group's members were nationalist-religious fanatics who hated Arabs, Communists, Christian missionaries, and foreigners in general. They were accused of planting a bomb near the Soviet legation in Tel Aviv and of a series of violent acts—some aimed at preventing the signing of the reparations agreement with Germany. The group was called the Tsrifin Underground, after the name of the army camp where the trial was held before a military court. The prosecutor at the Tsrifin trial was Haim Cohen, the judge Benyamin Halevy, who had been returned to active duty especially for the trial and given the temporary rank of colonel for a period of two months.

It was an unfortunate proceeding. The prosecution hoped to prove that this group of lunatics was an organization that endangered the national security. In fact, they had not even threatened Mapai's hold on the government. The government had a difficult time finding a judge willing to take part in such a show. The justices of the Supreme Court refused; the public had no confidence in military proceedings, they explained to Ben-Gurion, so it wasn't desirable for them to be involved. But they suggested to Justice Minister Rosen that he take Halevy. "Yekke, religious," Ben-Gurion noted in his diary, and he could have added "somewhat eccentric" as well.[31] Halevy and Tamir had trained under the same Jerusalem lawyer. Halevy did not allow Tamir to subpoena the prime minister, foreign minister, or defense minister. And, even though he found no proof of the link between the "underground" and the attack on the Soviet legation, Halevy ruled that the Tsrifin group on trial was "a criminal underground organization whose very existence and kind of activity constitute a severe danger to state security." He sentenced Heruti to ten years in prison—a sentence he deemed light—"out of consideration of his being married, and father to a child."* Tamir argued that the law allowing such a proceeding was a greater danger to the state than all the underground organizations in the world. From that point onward, he was the foremost political lawyer in the country. He defended the *Herut* newspaper in a libel suit, then he also defended Dov Shilansky. When Malchiel Gruenwald approached him, Tamir realized the political potential of the case. Gruenwald offered his stamp collection in exchange for legal services; Tamir sent him away after fifteen minutes, demanding only that the old man spare him his idle talk and just let him run the trial as he saw fit. Gruenwald himself was of no interest to him. Tamir, then thirty-one years old, set out to topple the regime.

At the trial, Tamir did not deny that Gruenwald wrote the offending newsletter. Quite the contrary—he intended to prove that everything in it was the truth. This seemed impossible at first. But even before Tamir called his defense witnesses, before he laid the foundations of his version of Mapai's culpability, he caught Kastner in what seemed to be a bald lie, though actually it was no more than a foolish attempt to fudge the truth. Kastner declared: "What is written in the defendant's article, that I went to Nuremberg to testify and save Becher, is a lie. . . . It is not true that I helped him evade punishment. In Nuremberg I gave no formal testimony in his favor." Technically, Kastner was right. His declaration in support of Becher was in fact given not in the international tribunal but before a local denazification court. Moreover, Kastner insisted, the testimony was neither in Becher's favor nor against him but merely a factual description of negotiations between them.

But the next day, Tamir showed Kastner a letter and asked if he recognized it.

---

* The eleven other defendants were given prison sentences of one to twelve years. They had planted a bomb at the Czechoslovakian legation and tried to set fire to the legation's car; they succeeded in burning the Soviet legation's car, as well as a butcher shop that sold pork. They collected weapons and explosives. Acting Defense Minister Pinhas Lavon decided immediately to commute some of the sentences. Within two years, Ben-Gurion pardoned them all, "so that they might participate in the Independence Day celebrations as free citizens of the State of Israel, seven years after it was founded."[32] Apparently, Halevy alone believed that the fantasy of an "Israelite kingdom" endangered the country's security.

KASTNER: Yes, this is the letter I wrote to Finance Minister Eliezer Kaplan regarding Becher's deposit.

TAMIR: Dr. Kastner, in this letter you write: "Becher has been freed for the time being thanks to my personal intervention." Do you confirm that you wrote this?

KASTNER: Yes.

TAMIR: A moment ago you said that it was a lie that Becher was freed at Nuremberg thanks to your personal intervention. Do you still maintain that?

KASTNER: I maintain what I told the court. . . . If I was guilty of the careless wording of a letter, I am willing to admit it. I take responsibility for errors in my wording. . . . What I wrote to Kaplan was overstated. [33]

At this point, Tamir did not yet have the affidavit that Kastner had submitted in Becher's favor, but he had managed to demonstrate one thing: Kastner was acting like a man who had something to hide.

A few months later, Tamir managed to find a copy of the affidavit, which was in a file at the Pentagon in Washington. "There can be no doubt that Becher was one of the few SS leaders who had the courage to take a stand against the extermination program and who made an attempt to save human lives," Kastner had written, adding that Becher's intervention had helped save 85,000 Jews from the Budapest ghettos. During the final stage of the war, the affidavit said, Becher fought with Himmler to hand the inmates of the concentration camps over to the Allies and to avoid bloody battles near the camps. "Becher did everything he could, given his position, to save innocent lives from the blind, murderous rampage of the Nazi leadership," Kastner testified. "For this reason I never for a minute doubted his good intentions, even if the form and basis for our negotiations were of an objectionable character." At the end of his affidavit, Kastner wrote that in his opinion Becher deserved "the fullest possible consideration" when his matter came before the Allied or German authorities. [34] During his stay in Nuremberg, Kastner also testified against two leading Nazi figures in Hungary, and the two were given long prison sentences.

Becher was freed. He had been involved in the murder of half a million Hungarian Jews; he had acted to slow down the deportations in order to create an alibi for himself. There is no way of knowing why Kastner testified in his favor. Perhaps because he thought Becher worthy, for having saved tens of thousands of Jews. Perhaps to buy Becher's silence. One of Kastner's acquaintances thought Kastner helped Becher so as to experience again, one last time, the power he had held during the war, when he had decided who would live and who would die.[35] Either way, Tamir described Kastner's willingness to aid Becher as a "national crime." Kastner was caught in Tamir's snare, tangled in excuses, contradictions, and little lies. The final, most damaging sentence in his affidavit perhaps suggests why Kastner shifted about so much: "I make this statement not only in my name but also on behalf of the Jewish Agency and the World Jewish Congress." So it was not just Rudolf Kastner but the leaders of the Jewish people—or, as Tamir always emphasized, the leaders of Mapai—who had defended Kurt Becher. Witness Eliahu Dobkin of the Jewish Agency denied that he had allowed Kastner to sign his affidavit in the name of that institution. Clearly, someone was not telling the truth. Tamir was skillful enough to leave the impression that both were lying, that the Jewish Agency, and perhaps the State of Israel as well, had been party to dark dealings with SS officer Kurt Becher. After the war, Becher became a wealthy grain merchant and, according to reports that were denied, did business with Israel as part of the reparations agreement.[36]

Somehow, another intriguing mystery got mixed up in all this: the whereabouts of an alleged "treasure" of money and valuables that Becher had collected from Jews—suitcases full of diamonds and gold coins worth millions of dollars. After the war, Becher returned at least some of what he had taken, but a large part of it vanished. Its disappearance was the subject of Kastner's letter to Finance Minister Kaplan. "It seems to me that it is too late now to chart the circumstances of the disappearance of these valuables. In my opinion, the fault for neglecting effective oversight falls on those Jewish Agency representatives whose job it was to carefully guard the suitcase," Kastner wrote to Finance Minister Kaplan.[37] Becher and Kastner could have divided the treasure between them, but Kastner did not go to his grave a rich man. Tamir preferred to imply that Becher's treasure found its way into the Mapai treasury: that certainly would explain why Kastner prevaricated so over this matter instead of simply saying, with a clear conscience, that he had defended Becher because it was his human and Jewish duty to tell the truth about a man to whom thousands of Jews owed their lives. Perhaps he assumed that in the Israel of 1954 he had no chance of justifying such a position. Perhaps he believed that his affidavit would never be discovered. Apparently, Haim Cohen did not properly prepare his witness, whose testimony made him his own worst enemy. From time to time Kastner lost his temper, shouted, became flustered. Tamir made him the defendant; and so the Gruenwald trial became the Kastner trial.

Once Kastner was tainted with the suspicion that he was involved in the theft of Becher's treasure, Tamir turned to his main task—proving collaboration with the Nazis. He presented the following thesis to the court: Kastner knew the Nazis intended to exterminate Hungarian Jewry but kept the information from the members of his community. Had he warned them in time, they might have been able to flee to Romania or organize armed resistance. Since they did not know what awaited them, they boarded the death trains without resistance. Tamir's witnesses, natives of Kastner's hometown, confirmed what Tamir said: Kastner had not told them the truth. Had they only known, they would have escaped or resisted. Kastner maintained that he had not known for certain that the Nazis would murder the Jews. Furthermore, even if he had given a warning, it would only have spread panic, and would thus have prevented him from saving those he was able to save. That was just the point, Tamir shot back. He had been given the VIP train in exchange for his silence. Tamir also badgered Kastner with the question of how the passengers were chosen.

But Tamir did not aim at Kastner alone. In Hungary, Kastner had belonged to the Ihud party, identified with Mapai. He acted in coordination with Mapai and under its instructions, Tamir asserted. He argued that Kastner's collaboration with the Nazis in Hungary was just like Mapai's collaboration with the British in Palestine. Mapai had earlier collaborated with the Nazis in the haavara agreements, and was now collaborating with the Germans through the reparations agreements. Mapai's leaders also, like Kastner, suppressed reports of the Holocaust. Had they revealed the truth to the public, the yishuv would have risen up and might have rebelled against the British, forcing them to do something to save the Jews of Europe. But then Mapai would have lost control of the situation and would have had to give up power. Apparently, that was more important to the party, Tamir said—there was no other explanation. The Jewish Agency was depicted as the Judenrat of Palestine. Kastner, who had chosen the passengers for his train, now looked like the "doctor" who had stood on the train platform at the death camps and, with a wave of his finger, performed the selection—who would be sent to work, who to the gas chambers. There were collaborators there, and here as well—

Mapai in Budapest, Mapai in Tel Aviv—a single party with a single mentality.

With this thesis, Tamir presented his own version of a series of affairs, including Joel Brand's mission; Kastner had taken part in the meetings with Adolf Eichmann that had led to the mission. Tamir brought up the story in order to smear Mapai. Moshe Sharett, who in January 1954 had replaced Ben-Gurion as prime minister, along with Ehud Avriel and Teddy Kollek, both close associates of Ben-Gurion, were depicted by Tamir as traitors who as executives of the Jewish Agency had deliberately sabotaged the mission that could have saved hundreds of thousands of Jews, perhaps even a million. They did so in the service of the British, Tamir argued—the British, after all, had not wanted any more Jews in Palestine.

Tamir called Katarina Senesh, mother of the legendary paratrooper Hannah Senesh, to the witness stand. She told how Kastner ignored her all through her daughter's capture, torture, and execution: The implication was that Kastner preferred obedience to the Nazis over assistance to the Jewish agent from Palestine. Tamir also had paratrooper Yoel Palgi recount how Kastner made him and his comrade, Peretz Goldstein, turn themselves in to the Gestapo, thus preventing them from organizing resistance within the Jewish community. According to Palgi, Kastner assumed that the Nazis knew about the presence of the paratroopers in Budapest. He feared that unless they turned themselves in, he and probably the entire Jewish community would be held accountable and punished. So he informed the Germans and persuaded Palgi to contact them. Pretending he had come to deliver a message from Brand, Palgi went to the Gestapo. Although he was arrested, he managed to survive. Goldstein perished in a German concentration camp. Sometime before the beginning of the trial, Palgi had published his memoirs, glossing over these events; he was considered an Israeli hero. Tamir forced him to admit he lied in his book to cover up for Kastner, his party colleague. Palgi emerged from the court looking like a coward, almost a deserter. Mapai, according to the thesis, sent the paratroopers to Hungary in coordination with the British, and Kastner turned them in to the Nazis, so as not to endanger his position. Kastner sent Brand to Palestine in coordination with the Nazis, and Mapai turned him over to the British, so as not to endanger its position. By now the Kastner trial had become the trial of Mapai.

Benyamin Halevy had good reason to be angry at Mapai. Shortly before the Gruenwald trial, he was passed over for appointment to the Supreme Court. He took an unusual step in response. He appealed directly to David Ben-Gurion, then out of office. Reminding him of the Tsrifin trial, he asked for assistance in furthering what he described as a struggle within the court system for a "national approach" to the country's problems. "If you believe, as I do, that there is a great need to enhance the national approach of our judges and that I have the ability to act in this interest on the Supreme Court, I ask you to help me," the judge wrote to the Mapai leader. Two days later Halevy submitted his resignation. Ben-Gurion did not assist him, expressing only his hope that Halevy would reconsider his resignation. Halevy decided to stay.[38] In the meantime, the Gruenwald-Kastner trial began.

Halevy allowed Tamir almost every trick and caprice, including irrelevant testimony on matters in which Kastner was not involved. The judge accepted hearsay—including that of a man who was no longer alive—and did not halt the incessant interrogations on trivial matters. The chief justice of the Supreme Court, Yitzhak Olshan, noted afterwards that Kastner was called to the stand no fewer than eleven times during the trial. In this regard, Olshan wrote, Halevy behaved as if there were no rules of judicial procedure. His taking part in the questioning at times was "most improper," Olshan contended, in censure exceptional for its fierce language. "While it created a forest, one could hardly see it for all the trees."[39] In the midst of all this judicial drama, Malchiel Gruenwald himself was almost forgotten.

From time to time Tamir would return to a motif he was particularly fond of—the contemptible wretchedness of the Jews of the Exile as compared to the "stalwart" character of the Israelis. "Excuse me for the question," he said to a Hungarian Jewish community activist who was testifying, "but I would like to ask you, sir, if my definition would be correct if I said that your mentality and that of your group is the mentality of Jews of the Exile. I apologize for using the term. But it seems to me that this is the case."

"Is there such a thing at all?" responded the witness, Pinhas Freudiger.

TAMIR: I think so.

FREUDIGER: I was a religious Jew in the Exile and I am a religious Jew in Israel as well.

TAMIR: That was not what I meant. I mean to say that the mentality, the form of life, accepted the reality of the Exile and the need, in time of trouble, to resort to bribery and special pleading.

FREUDIGER: It is written explicitly: "Seek the peace of the city."

TAMIR: That is why I ask: was that your mentality?

FREUDIGER: Yes.

TAMIR: Did Dr. Kastner propose that you and your group form an underground?

FREUDIGER: No.[40]

This was also Mapai's mentality, Tamir declared, which was why it had obeyed the British, turning in members of the Etzel and Lehi organizations. "While your comrades collaborated with the British and you with the Nazis, we were out fighting to save Jews," Tamir berated Kastner. "Do you know about an Etzel leaflet of 1944 concerning the rescue of Hungarian Jewry?" he asked one witness. "Do you know that in 1944 members of the Etzel and Lehi were arrested by the Haganah?"[41] He submitted entire volumes of *Davar* to the court to prove that the newspaper that represented Mapai had been more interested in the war against the Etzel and Lehi, in the service of the British, than in the war against the Nazis. Tamir made no secret of the fact that the leadership of the yishuv interested him more than the dispute between Gruenwald and Kastner.

From time to time, Halevy forced the witnesses to comment on complex moral, ethical, and philosophical dilemmas beyond their grasp—or that of anyone else in the courtroom, including, apparently, Halevy himself. *Haaretz*, with no little astonishment, printed Halevy's examination of the witness Hillel Danzig, a leader of the Jewish community in Kastner's hometown:

HALEVY: Had you known that the train on which you were to travel was going straight to Auschwitz, and had you known what Auschwitz meant, what the real meaning of Auschwitz was, would you of your own free will have got on that train? . . . What would you have done with regard to your family and yourself?

DANZIG: I don't know, your honor. I can think about it today and give an answer. But that has no connection with those circumstances, with what I would have done in that situation.

HALEVY: Why is there no connection?

DANZIG: Because we are sitting here today in a completely different situation. What is being asked and answered today, here, in the State of Israel, ten years later, has no connection with the situation then. . . .

HALEVY: You would not, for instance, have tried to escape? . . . You could not have gotten your mother and wife out?

And so the trial of Mapai became the trial of the victims and survivors of the Holocaust.[42]

14 | *"His Soul to the Devil"*

A few months after the trial opened, it became necessary to transfer the proceedings to a larger courtroom. Crowds began to flock to the doors, including reporters from Israel and overseas. Previously, most newspapers had used the reports put out by the Israeli news agency, Itim. But as the trial went on, the newspapers allotted it more space. Only two saw the story from the start as a political affair: *Herut* and *Haolam Hazeh*. Both were under Tamir's influence, and they played up his side of the story. The other side was left, in the meantime, without any press backing. Though Tamir was not a member of the Herut party during the trial, the party and its newspaper supported his line of defense. His accusations against the Jewish Agency and Mapai were covered in great detail, on the front page, and were described as "shocking revelations": "THE JEWISH AGENCY QUASHED NEWS OF THE EXTERMINATION IN HUNGARY"; "WEIZMANN SAID—MILLIONS OF JEWS WILL BE EXTERMINATED, WHAT'S IMPORTANT IS THAT ENGLAND WILL BENEFIT."*

Haolam Hazeh was a weekly news-photo magazine, founded in the late 1930s as a family publication with the motto "The rhythm of life, the pulse of time." Purchased in 1950 by Uri Avneri and Shalom Cohen, it acquired a new motto: "Without fear, without bias." *Haolam Hazeh* was the first Israeli newspaper to expose the corruption and folly of public officials, matters that until then had been taboo in the Israeli press. Most

---

* The quote from Weizmann was distorted.[1]

of the newspapers at the time saw themselves as partners in the Zionist struggle for establishment of the state, and their editors considered themselves part of the leadership. Thus though *Haolam Hazeh* was not the only periodical to oppose Ben-Gurion's rule, it was the first to back up its views with investigative journalism. As such, the magazine and Avneri, its editor, performed a service to Israeli democracy.

Avneri has written millions, perhaps tens of millions, of words over the course of his life—words he combined into concise, clear, direct, flowing sentences. Much of his writing, though, was too rigid, his arguments too judgmental, too arrogant, too simplistic, humorless, sometimes foolish, often unfair. Those who were good were completely good, the bad were utterly bad, both good and bad were larger than life and unambiguously defined. Avneri was not always consistent, but he never left any room for doubt. He did not formulate a carefully considered alternative to Zionist ideology, as he on occasion took credit for doing, but his articles were stimulating, thought-provoking, and intriguing. No one else could write as he did. He was often correct. A believer in secular democracy, he called for a compromise with the Palestinian Arab nation many years before others did. Yet in the 1950s he was carried away by an almost mystical admiration for the army and the war wounded. In his teens, he had preached the "renewal of the Hebrew race" and other parafascist ideas and had joined the Etzel.[2]

Avneri's magazine was meant to speak for the generation that had fought, as Avneri had, in the War of Independence. It fostered and marketed the Ashkenazic sabra mentality that Avneri himself tried to adopt when he arrived in the country with his parents in 1933. Originally Helmut Ostermann, he was born in Germany, the youngest son of a banker, and went to a school that produced at least one other famous journalist—Rudolf Augstein, publisher and editor of *Der Spiegel*.

Haolam Hazeh was more than a news magazine. It rallied its readers and reinforced in them a sense of being a select group. The impression was created that those who read *Haolam Hazeh* knew more than those who read other periodicals. This was sometimes true, though not always. But no other periodical was so adept at flattering its readers. It told them that the very fact that they were leafing through it meant that they were among the good and the righteous, the wise and the bold. It made them into the magazine's defenders, gave them the sense that they were the forces of light doing battle with the forces of darkness, the few against the many. Over the years, *Haolam Hazeh* created a set of myths and images that lived only in its own pages, in the language and style that existed only between its covers, an imaginary world of heroes and villains, objects of admiration and abhorrence, of fondness and fear. *Haolam Hazeh* led the way toward the Americanization of Israeli life and mentality. The secret of its allure was in the Tel Aviv ambience that it invented and that its readers so much wanted to be part of.

Despite his efforts to become what he and his magazine regarded as "Israeli," Avneri was different from the myth he created. He read more and thought more than most sabras did, and he never managed to get rid of his yekke accent. His conception of the world was shaped largely by the Weimar Republic's collapse and the Nazi seizure of power. Over the years he often compared the situation in Israel to that of Nazi Germany; he was one of the first to do so.[2]

Many years after the Gruenwald-Kastner trial, Avneri wrote that it would have been no more than a libel case against an eccentric old man from Jerusalem had *Haolam Hazeh* not given it maximal coverage from the very first.[3] His claim is not entirely warranted. *Haaretz* played it on the front page before *Haolam Hazeh* made it a cover story. But Avneri did sense, before anyone else, the historical drama and political ramifications of the trial. And once he latched on to it, he did not let it go for years. In retrospect, his coverage of the trial looks like a wild campaign of incitement that did nothing but express the hatred that Avneri and Shmuel Tamir had for Mapai and possibly hint at both men's future political ambitions. The Zionist movement led by Mapai did not collaborate with the Nazis in order to enable them to exterminate the Jews. Rudolf Kastner saved hundreds, perhaps thousands, of people. The rest were unable to escape. Avneri was in a position to know all that. The impression, then, is that *Haolam Hazeh*'s position during the trial was not an error—it was demagoguery. In his later years, Avneri maintained that Shmuel Tamir actually wrote many of the magazine's articles on the trial—including much of the praise for Tamir.[4]

In his first cover story on the affair, about ten months after the trial began, Avneri wrote: "The court has become a battlefield in the struggle for establishing the visage of history. Not only is this a fight for historical truth, it is a struggle for the shape of the Israeli regime in the future." Conjuring up the past, Avneri continued:

Six million Jews were slowly exterminated over long years. There is no doubt that it was possible to save a great many of them. . . .

In Palestine there was a center of Hebrew power, organized Hebrew power, national authority that could decide and act. . . . Had such a center declared a holy war to save Jews, it might well have changed the situation. But nothing of the sort happened. . . . Thus, a great guilt hovers over the politicians who set the course of the yishuv.

Their behavior, Avneri stated, "was astoundingly similar" to that of the Jewish ghetto leaders.[5]

Avneri saw the struggle between Shmuel Tamir, the young lawyer from Jerusalem, and Rudolf Kastner, Jewish functionary from Budapest, as a struggle between the "Israeli" and the "Exilic." In his eyes, Hebrew Israeliness was youthfulness and steadfastness and rebellion; the Exilic Jew was old, downtrodden, and groveling. The struggle, he wrote, was between Mordecai of the Book of Esther and Judah Maccabee—the former a supplicant, the latter a rebel. In Avneri's "Hebrew" view, life was worth less than national honor and the historical image of the nation. National pride was, he said, "the most fateful issue that faces the Israeli." Would the country continue to bow to foreign masters—he apparently meant the United States—or would "the sovereign nation attempt to take its fate in its own hands, to fight its own fights"?[6]

All this was sanctimonious, unfair, and contradictory. Tamir and Avneri condemned the Jewish Agency for having cooperated with the British but also attacked it for having sabotaged Brand's cooperation with the Nazis. Inconsistent as they were, Avneri and Tamir nevertheless supplied simple answers to a whole range of horrible questions that the Holocaust had left hanging in the air. For anyone who said "The leaders are guilty" was saying simultaneously "We were OK": We, the yishuv—had we only known about the Holocaust, we would have rebelled, we would have forced Britain to act, we would have roused the conscience of the world. But we didn't know, because the Mapai leadership hid the truth about the extermination of the Jews from us. We, the Hebrew youth—had we only been called to action, we would have enlisted immediately. We, the victims of the Holocaust—had we only known they were leading us to Auschwitz, we would have rebelled or fled. We would not have gone "like lambs to the slaughter," as Avneri wrote.[7]

These arguments were attractive but flawed. The Jews of Europe were murdered not because they were ignorant of what awaited them but because they were powerless to resist. The yishuv knew about the Holocaust as it was happening. No one suppressed or denied the reports.

Yet the yishuv continued to live its life, helpless and complacent. Avneri and Tamir, part of this truth, had trouble living with it; they also had a political interest in distorting it.

Avneri liked to say that *Haolam Hazeh* was "the most-read paper in the country." Whether or not it was, the weekly enjoyed great popularity during the 1950s, especially among the young. Many of them knew about the Kastner affair and its offshoots only from Avneri's coverage; many adopted his historical and political perspective. A book on the affair written years later by Isser Harel, a former head of the Mossad, Israel's intelligence agency, revealed how deeply the *Haolam Hazeh* articles troubled the government and Mapai.[8] As Teddy Kollek later wrote, "I believe that the Kastner trial was such a central issue because it was the first time that a large number of Israelis lost confidence in the establishment—in this case, certainly, for unjustified reasons. This was the first major blow to the leadership of Mapai."[9] From time to time, Kollek took part in consultations with Moshe Sharett about the trial. In the nine months that elapsed between the reading of the indictment and the summations in September 1954, the prime minister recorded thirteen discussions of the trial in his diary; the diary reflects grave concern, almost panic.

Early in the trial, Attorney General Cohen had assigned the prosecution to one of his assistants, Amnon Tel. This was a mistake, as would soon become clear. "The attorney general took the trial lightly and appointed as prosecutor some nobody who lacks any grasp of the political and public issues," Sharett wrote. "In the unending clashes with that thug, attorney Shmuel Tamir, he is always at a disadvantage." Sharett's advisers seconded his evaluation. "The attorney general apparently had no conception of the public and political nature of this trial and of its sensational effect," Sharett went on. "Tel, the prosecutor, is an utter failure. . . . There is no course other than to demand of Haim Cohen that he himself take up the prosecution." In his diary, Sharett continued to list his grievances against the attorney general. By the time Cohen took over the prosecution, six months after the trial had begun, his relationship with Sharett was strained, although there were other issues as well. The two exchanged many an angry letter. In the end, the prime minister had to invite the attorney general to his home to mollify him.

More than anything else, Sharett feared the testimony of Joel Brand. "If he appears as a witness, the whole thing will get very complicated," he wrote, "because in the period after the failure of his mission he went into a frenzy of sending accusatory memoranda to the leaders of the Jewish Agency, blaming them for the slaughter in Hungary, and now all that will serve as incriminating material in the hands of Shmuel Tamir." At one point, Sharett considered appearing as a witness. His advisers explained to him that such a thing could not be allowed. They worried, apparently, that Tamir would break him. Instead, Sharett decided that, after the trial, he would hold a press conference where he would tell "the whole truth" about the Brand episode.[10]

As the examinations and cross-examinations continued, Sharett's men tried to disseminate their version of history outside the courtroom. Two days after Joel Brand concluded his testimony, *Maariv* printed, very prominently, a secret report on the episode that Moshe Sharett had submitted to members of the Jewish Agency executive in London, in June 1944. The document assured his colleagues that he, Ben-Gurion, and other leaders of the Jewish Agency had done all they could to work out a deal that would save the Jews of Hungary and therefore carried no blame for Brand's arrest by the British or for the failure of his mission. "Ehud [Avriel, one of the prime minister's aides] gave the report to the newspaper, and its publication made a great impression," Sharett wrote in his diary. The publication was a clear violation of the laws of sub judice.[11]

About six weeks later, with Yoel Palgi's damaging testimony just concluded, Sharett planned to give his own version of the paratrooper affair at a mass memorial ceremony at Kibbutz Maagan. The ceremony seems to have been designed specifically for this purpose. Once again, the mission of the paratroopers was to be described as a heroic rescue operation initiated by the leaders of the Jewish Agency. Sharett put much effort into preparing his speech, dictating for hours, erasing and correcting and editing. A few minutes before the speech, a light plane was to shower the guests with printed greetings; it plummeted into the crowd, only a few feet from where Sharett was sitting. There were casualties, among them four of the paratroopers who had managed to return from their wartime missions in Europe ten years earlier. The prime minister's great historic speech turned into a memorial message.[12]

§

Judge Halevy sat at home for nine months and mulled over the evidence. There were close to 3,000 pages of transcripts, containing the words of some sixty witnesses in six languages. More than three hundred documents had been submitted as exhibits—memoranda, reports, even entire books. The verdict was announced on June 22, 1955, with an opinion that ranged over 274 pages. Reading it aloud in court took an entire day and on into the night. Halevy found that three of Gruenwald's four accusations in the original newsletter were justified and therefore not libelous; on the one remaining count of libel, he imposed a symbolic fine of one lira and ordered the state to refund Gruenwald a portion of his legal expenses, 200 liras. The opinion was one of the most heartless in the history of Israel, perhaps the most heartless ever. The Supreme Court would term it "lethal."[13]

"Masses of ghetto Jews boarded the deportation trains," Halevy wrote, "in total obedience, ignorant of the real destination and trusting the false declaration that they were being transferred to work camps in Hungary." Although he doubted that the Jews were in a position to resist, Halevy determined that the Nazis "could not have deceived the Jewish masses with such great efficiency had they not disseminated their false rumors through Jewish channels."[14] But some Jews were saved: "The organizers and executors of the extermination operation," Halevy continued, "allowed Kastner and the members of the Jewish council of Budapest to save their relatives and friends." The Nazi protection was "an inseparable part of the maneuvers in the 'psychological war' to destroy the Jews," he wrote.

> The temptation was great. K. was offered the opportunity to save six hundred souls from the impending Holocaust and a chance to somewhat increase their numbers through payment or further negotiations. And not just any six hundred souls, but those very people who were most important and deserving of rescue in his eyes, for whatever reason—if he wished, his relatives; if he wished, members of his movement; and if he wished, the important Jews of Hungary. . . . He had the opportunity to rescue his wife and mother from Budapest, his brother and father-in-law from Cluj, and all the rest of his relatives and friends. He was dazzled by the chance to save prominent figures, from provincial towns and even from Budapest. To rescue them would be both a personal achievement and a Zionist victory. . . . K. was extremely pessimistic about the odds that Jews could escape on their own from the Nazi extermination machine, which had already liquidated almost all the Jews of Europe, and he saw the main hope for rescue in an agreement with the Nazis. No

wonder he accepted the offer without hesitation. But *"timeo Danaos et dona ferentis"* [Beware of Greeks bearing gifts]. In accepting the offer, K. sold his soul to the devil.[15]

Halevy determined that Kastner assisted the Nazis' extermination of the Jews of Cluj in two ways:

> by deliberately encouraging the leaders of Cluj to collaborate in the deportation of members of their community to Auschwitz and by deliberately avoiding his duty, as head of the Rescue Committee, to reveal to the Jews the fate awaiting them and to organize their flight over the Romanian border. . . . The benefit the Nazis received from the agreement with K. was a facilitation of the extermination of the Jewish masses, and the price they paid was to forgo the extermination of the privileged few. With the agreement about the privileged, K. accepted the extermination of the ordinary people and abandoned them to their fates.

Then Halevy summarized the ancient law:

> Even in a case where his life is in danger, a Jewish person is forbidden to save himself by spilling the blood of an innocent man ("Now have you seen that your blood is redder, perhaps the blood of that man is redder?"); likewise it is forbidden to save one man by spilling the blood of another innocent man ("One does not put one soul over another"). It is also forbidden to save one man or even many by turning another innocent man over to a murderer ("All should die but not deliver them a single soul from Israel"). Even to save the majority of the community it is forbidden to hand over an innocent minority, or even "one soul from Israel," to murderers. Even more so, then, the opposite case, of turning over an innocent majority to murderers to save a few individuals. The violator of this principle deserves to die. . . . It seems to me that from a public, moral, and even legal point of view, K.'s behavior . . . is the same as turning over the majority of Jews to their murderers to benefit a few.[16]

Halevy went on to state that Kastner's collaboration with the Nazis led him to order the two paratroopers who had reached Budapest to turn themselves in to the Nazis and to abandon Hannah Senesh to her fate. Had he allowed them to organize the Jews for resistance, as they intended to do, their activity might have been the match that Hannah Senesh sang of before crossing the Hungarian border—"Happy is the match that, burning, sparked the flames." Kastner claimed that he had done all he could to help the paratroopers. On this matter, as well as on that of his testimony on behalf of Kurt Becher, Kastner had lied in court, Halevy ruled. As for Joel Brand's mission, the trial's major revelation—presented, with the judge's acquiescence, at sensational length—Halevy ruled that the matter was not germane to the trial and declined to address it. He acquitted Gruenwald of libel on his three major accusations: that Kastner had collaborated, had "paved the way for the murder of Hungarian Jewry," and had saved the war criminal Becher from punishment after the war. All that remained was Gruenwald's claim that Kastner had been in cahoots with Becher and took some of the valuables that the Nazis stole from the Jews of Hungary. This accusation had not been proven, Halevy ruled. Had Gruenwald written only that one, there would have been cause to impose real punishment on him, the judge continued. But given Gruenwald's acquittal on the other, decisive counts of libel, justice required imposing only a symbolic fine.[17]

Moshe Sharett saw the ruling as "a heavy blow." That same day—in fact, before Halevy finished reading his opinion—Sharett ordered Minister of Justice Rosen to appeal to the Supreme Court. "A nightmare, a horror," the prime minister wrote in his diary. "How could the judge dare! Strangulation for the party. Chaos."[18] And elections were only weeks away. Kastner's name had disappeared, as if by magic, from the Mapai slate of candidates.

15 | "The Walls Are Beginning to Crack"

The newspapers announced the verdict with huge headlines and devoted entire pages to it. Unsurprisingly, they gave prominent play to the judge's claim that Kastner, in dealing with Eichmann, had "sold his soul to the devil," an assertion that was generally reported as fact. *Herut* printed Kastner's picture with the caption: "Eichmann's partner." Under Tamir's picture was: "The main force for the discovery of the truth." For Herut Knesset member Yohanan Bader, the rescue of the prominent and the abandonment of the masses reopened the old debate between Weizmann and Jabotinksy. This was the debate between the backers of the selective immigration of pioneers and those who demanded the swift evacuation of all Jews to Palestine, including the independent merchant class, so despised by the establishment. Weizmann, Bader now recalled in *Herut*, had called the Jewish masses in eastern Europe "human debris." Businessmen had not received enough immigration permits and, for all intents and purposes, were abandoned to their deaths. Kastner, Bader maintained, followed in Weizmann's footsteps. The newspaper neglected, however, to tell its readers that the Revisionists in Budapest had also supported Kastner's efforts at mediation. The Communist *Kol Haam* said the negotiations between Kastner and Eichmann reflected the Nazi collaboration of the entire Zionist movement, as if there had never been a Hitler-Stalin pact. The religious parties saw Kastner as a representative of secular Zionism, as if there had been no observant Jews in the Judenrats. The leftist opposition parties Mapam and Ahdut Haavodah now identified themselves with the ghetto rebels, though during the Holocaust their people had been Mapai's partners in running the yishuv under the British.[1]

Haolam Hazeh wrote that the verdict revealed a political leadership without any feeling for the homeland, devoid of spiritual independence—in short, a ghetto leadership. The leadership's interests, Avneri wrote, stood in opposition to the sense of life of the new nation, growing in the Land of Israel, of the generation that had established the state with its blood and that would preserve it in the face of the trials of tomorrow. Regarding Judge Halevy, Avneri wrote: "Every honest man will salute this brave man in his heart, this man for whom being true to himself was more important than career, who spoke the truth, knowing that he was bringing the anger of the entire regime down on him."[2]

The Mapai press was paralyzed, trapped. It did not, of course, want to acknowledge that the judge was right, but neither did it want to attack the verdict, lest it give the impression that the party was thus defending its own interests. In the end, all it had to say was that on such a matter one should not trust to a single judge, and therefore it was best to wait for the results of the appeal to the Supreme Court. *Hapoel Hatsair* compared the task that Kastner had faced with that of Noah, before the flood.[3] Minister of Justice Rosen, naïve or sanctimonious—in any case, totally unrealistic—declared it would be best if everyone would refrain "for the time being" from expressing any opinions about the verdict. It certainly would have been pleasant and convenient for the government had everyone agreed to table the subject for a few years.

Two days after the verdict, Moshe Sharett wrote in his diary that he had "briefed" Moshe Keren, a prominent Berlin-born political commentator for *Haaretz*.[4] The newspaper had, that very day, severely criticized Judge Halevy. "A cautious and not overconfident verdict would certainly have been closer to justice than this verdict, which allows for only two shades, black and white." The newspaper disparaged the "shallowness" of the judgment, asserting that Halevy "refused to understand" that the people whose deeds he was judging had lived a nightmare.[5] During the following weeks, Keren wrote a series of articles containing the period's most intelligent analysis of the convoluted logic and unfairness of Halevy's opinion. Kastner had acted in conjunction with the community leaders, and if he was guilty, all of them were guilty, Keren wrote. Even had he warned his fellow townspeople about what awaited them, there was no reason to assume they could have escaped or would have been willing to do so. There was no evidence that they would have been able to organize a resistance. In contrast to what was implied by the judgment, Kastner did not face a free choice between two alternatives—to enter into negotiations with the Nazis or not. The negotiations with the Nazis were imposed on him. Had he refused to participate, he would have abandoned to their fates all those who in the end were saved on the VIP train. "Talk of a duty to sound the alarm, of the need for rescue on a larger scale, and of other such notions is nothing but empty words," Keren wrote. "One of the many astonishing things in the opinion is that the judge explicitly admits there was no hope of organizing a Jewish resistance at that point in the war. . . . If that is the case, what does he want, for God's sake?"[6]

Keren also argued that improper management of the prosecution required Haim Cohen's resignation. He doubted whether it was worthwhile to appeal the verdict to the Supreme Court, proposing instead a national commission of inquiry, with the agreement of all political parties. "The repercussions of the Kastner trial," Keren wrote, "will continually poison the air we breathe. In that, it is like other famous historical trials in the wake of which governments rose and fell—such as the Dreyfus trial in France, the Alger Hiss trial in the United States, and the 'knife in the back' trials in Germany, which sought to undermine the Weimar regime. Israel is not, after this verdict, what it was before."[7]

Four days after the verdict, Menahem Begin convened the Herut central committee to plan the impending election campaign. The party was pleasantly surprised—Herut had not expected a verdict before the elections. Halevy confirmed everything Herut had argued over the years— and it had not expected that, either. "I was astonished!" said one member, Arieh Ben-Eliezer. Herut's members had long been making such accusations against Mapai, and suddenly it became clear that they were right. Furthermore, Ben-Eliezer gloated (probably mistaking Halevy's voting habits), they had been vindicated not by "one of us" but by "one of them." Everyone agreed that the election campaign should make use of the judgment; the discussion was mainly about placards, slogans, and campaign spots to be screened in the movie theaters. "There's no need to get into specifics," one campaign expert suggested. "It's enough to say: 'When you vote Mapai, you vote for a Jew who turned Jews over to the Gestapo.' " Someone suggested dividing the judgment into sections and presenting it "in small portions" to separate target populations. To the new immigrants, Herut would emphasize Mapai's silence during the

Holocaust. Someone else coined the disparaging term *Kastnerism.* "This development could end Mapai's influence," another central committee member said with relish. "They identify and have identified with Kastner."

Begin agreed it was a difficult moment for Mapai. "The party is in a predicament," he said: "The walls are beginning to crack." He suspected that Kastner knew secrets that Mapai was anxious not to have revealed. Nevertheless, Begin said, the party should not get carried away by past scandals; Mapai could only benefit if people wasted their time arguing about Kastner, instead of being mad about the water pipe that had burst in front of their houses. He proposed, therefore, attacking Mapai largely for the criticism it had leveled against the verdict. As an example, he quoted the Mapai secretary general, Meir Argov, to the effect that only a judge with no conscience could have written such an opinion. Here was an opportunity to defend the judicial system, Begin maintained. "We are on the same side as Israel's judges," and we should put Mapai on the other side. Herut decided to distribute a placard with the headline "PUT THOSE WITH CONTEMPT FOR THE COURTS ON TRIAL" and to demand the revocation of Argov's parliamentary immunity.[8]

The cabinet met that same morning in Jerusalem. Minister of the Interior Yisrael Rokah (General Zionists) and the religious ministers opposed appealing the verdict. But in the end it was decided to leave the matter in the hands of the minister of justice, Pinhas Rosen. In the meantime, the subject came up in the Knesset. Herut and the Communists submitted no-confidence motions. Yohanan Bader spoke for Herut, whose central committee had decided it must defend the judge. Whoever said that Halevy took it upon himself to judge a matter that could not be judged was arguing against the punishment of all Nazi war criminals, Bader argued. There had been no reason to sue Gruenwald in the first place, he maintained. But now that Gruenwald had been acquitted, Mapai was rousing "the entire country" in order to appeal the verdict. All this just because Kastner belonged to Mapai.

Some went so far as to say that, instead of appealing, the government should try Kastner. "The government's refusal to try Kastner under the Nazi collaborators law," declared Esther Vilenska of the Communist Maki party, "is part of a government policy of defending the reestablishment of the Nazi Wehrmacht in exchange for the bribe of reparations. [It] is part of a government policy to bring Israel into a military alliance with the United States that is, indirectly, an alliance with the Hitlerist army of West Germany being established by the Americans."

Prime Minister Sharett explained that the serious nature of the verdict required the government to appeal it "in order to allow Kastner to defend himself." The original charges against Gruenwald had been filed by the government; having been no more than a witness at the trial, Kastner had no standing to appeal himself. But beyond that, Sharett said, it was necessary to review the judge's historical conclusions, "lest the trial linger in the public consciousness as a condemnation of the efforts for rescue in every possible way." To avoid this misconception was, perhaps, the most important thing, Sharett noted.

The transcripts are replete with vilification of the type that was heard almost every time the Knesset discussed the Holocaust: "You're selling your soul to the devil"; "Liar"; "Communist parrot." But the day's surprise came from Haim Ariav (General Zionists): "There is an impression that the government is continuing to protect Kastner." And that impression, he said, was based on "sorry and painful" fact. As a result the General Zionists—who were members of the ruling coalition, with three ministers—would abstain rather than vote confidence in the government.[9] "Suddenly in crisis," Sharett recorded in his diary.[10]

The Mapai Knesset delegation met that same night to determine how to respond. Ben-Gurion, "ready for battle," proposed that Sharett resign immediately, form a new government without the General Zionists, and prepare for general elections. It might well be that on the Kastner matter Mapai would lose votes in the coming election, Ben-Gurion said. "A party must sometimes be ready to lose votes. . . . The party has to do what it thinks is for the good of the country."

Mapai decided to let the government fall.[11] The next day Sharett formed another, without the General Zionists. After an edifying debate —during which Begin asserted that he knew who had, during the Holocaust, decided to keep the extermination of the Jews quiet, in response to which Golda Meir shouted at him that he was lying, to which he responded that the lady was not known for telling the truth—the government won the confidence of the Knesset and the parties got started on their election campaigns.[12]

§

The public debate that raged during those days seems almost surreal. Ten years after the Holocaust, seven years after the War of Independence, the founders had not yet gone into retirement, and the existence of Israel was not yet taken for granted. A year and a half later, it would find itself embroiled in a second war with Egypt. Israel was facing an entire range of real problems that required immediate decisions. Yet, instead of talking about the reality of their country and its future, the party leaders were agonizing over—and torturing one another with—horrible accusations that had their roots in the Jewish Europe that was no more. The closer the elections came, the deeper they dug into this pit, drawing forth more and more dark affairs. The leaders of each party were intent on proving to themselves and to the voters that it was not they but their opponents who were the villains of the Nazi period. In this free-for-all the Nazis and their crimes became no more than symbols or allegories. More than mere political opportunists, the party leaders come out looking like people enslaved to sorrow, gnawed at by doubts and guilt, the offspring of a helpless nation that groveled before the past, ignored the present, and left the future to the vagaries of faith and fate.

A scene from the theater of the absurd: Sitting in a coffeehouse in the town of Rehovot are Prime Minister Moshe Sharett and the head of the Mossad, Isser Harel, and their wives. The men are considering how to respond to "the coordinated hostility" of the newspapers *Lamerhav* (Ahdut Haavodah) and *Haboker* (General Zionists). Both newspapers had charged that, when it looked as if the Nazis were about to invade Palestine, members of Mapai had tried to make contact with them. The reason: to reach an agreement on the kind of regime they would impose on the country. "*Lamerhav* told of unnamed yishuv leaders who tried to get to Japan so that they would recommend us to the Nazis," Sharett wrote in his diary that evening, "and *Haboker* came out impudently reproaching Mapai for remaining silent in the face of such an accusation." The Mossad chief had had a few of his men pore over old files. They came up with evidence that what Sharett called the "Stern gang," the right-wing Lehi, had made contact with Nazi Germany and Fascist Italy. Harel proposed that the prime minister hand over for publication in *Davar* the material his men had culled from the files, and Sharett agreed.[13]

The next day, the prime minister continued to preoccupy himself with investigating the past. Ehud Avriel told him that several leaders of Ahdut Haavodah—one of the parties now criticizing Mapai for its lack of wartime zeal—had themselves been lukewarm in their support for sending the paratroopers to Europe, objecting that the operation demanded coordination with the hated British. Their objections had caused long and pointless debate with Mapai, and the paratrooper operation had been delayed. That same day, the prime minister found time to draft an official denial of an item that appeared in *Haboker*. No, it was not true that he had disturbed the justice minister, during his vacation at a Haifa hotel, to urge him to appeal the Gruenwald verdict. *"Haboker* is taunting me," Sharett recorded in his diary. "Why am I silent in the face of all the accusations being leveled at me about the Holocaust in Hungary?" He was "bursting" to call a special press conference immediately to present the entire story. But Isser Harel "expressed firm opposition." Avriel also counseled him not to do it, lest he add fuel to the fire.[14]

Nonetheless, Sharett decided to reply to his opponents at length at an election rally in Netanya. The party was not pleased with the prime minister's voluble efforts. "To the extent that there were consultations among us on this matter," said Knesset member Yonah Kesse, the consensus was that the Kastner affair should disappear until after the elections, "on the assumption that the main struggle on the matter would begin after the elections." He spoke at a special meeting with some of those involved in the Kastner affair, including Yoel Palgi and senior foreign ministry official Ehud Avriel, who had appeared as witnesses in the trial, to discuss how to remove the stain that the verdict had left on the party's image in history, how to assist the appeal argument, and what to say in the weeks that remained until the elections. "There is one failing we are not completely innocent of, and that is that during recent years we did not investigate many affairs for ourselves, including this one," said Avriel. "Part of the punishment has come down on us because of that sin." He proposed inviting "an important, well-known historian from overseas" and giving him all the material he needed to investigate the Hungary episode. "The idea is that it should be done for its own sake, without political ends," Avriel said. The other members agreed. Kesse promised to put the party archive at the historian's disposal.*

Yoel Palgi said that he was greatly concerned that no one in the party leadership had lived through the Holocaust. The party was not aware of the powerful public response to the affair. It went beyond all reason, Palgi said. He presented a concrete proposal: "Someone has to say openly: 'If [on appeal] Kastner is found to be a collaborator with the Nazis, he is to be sentenced to death.' In my opinion, such a statement will give

---

* For the duration of the affair, there was a watchdog committee in the prime minister's office, one of whose members was Teddy Kollek. Kollek later wrote in his memoirs that he met the American journalist Arthur Morse and encouraged him to investigate the free world's attitude to the extermination of the Jews. The result was the book *While Six Million Died.* Herut's version of events appeared in a book by another American writer, Ben Hecht.[15]

the party several Knesset seats." The other members responded with discomfort.

Everyone agreed, however, that it was necessary to get Natan Alterman to address the issue—which, it turned out, the poet had already promised to do.[16] Alterman, loyal to his party, lived up to his word. In the weeks just before the elections, he wrote three of his weekly columns in defense of Jews who had not rebelled during the Holocaust: "Other peoples, fettered by the enemy in their homelands, did not react differently," he wrote.[17]

The conjunction of the elections and the Kastner affair did not encourage a high level of discussion of the fundamental questions raised by the trial. The debate continued, however, after the elections and often reflected the guilt of a society looking for moral direction. Many Israelis took it on themselves to judge the Jews of the Holocaust as if it were within their abilities and as if it were their right to do so. These are the heroes, these are the cowards, these are worthy of glory, these of disgrace.

As an old member of the yishuv establishment, Natan Alterman was hardly the right person to establish criteria for the behavior of the Jews in the Holocaust. The war and the Holocaust went by as he sat at the Kasit coffeehouse in Tel Aviv, a gathering place for the yishuv literati. Yet years after the war he invited Abba Kovner to his house and questioned him at length about life in the Vilna ghetto and about the rebellion that Kovner had helped lead. He listened attentively, then pronounced: "Had I been in the ghetto, I would have been on the side of the Judenrat."

In his poems and in the notebooks published after his death, Alterman did not reject rebellion as a form of response. He wished, however, to defend the legitimacy of the other response, that of the Jews who tried to survive at any price. Rebel leaders also sent members of their communities to death, Alterman wrote, just as the Judenrats had in turning Jews over to the Nazis. Rebellion only hastened their deaths. In effect, rebel leaders were ordering the ghetto Jews to commit suicide. In their eyes, it was death with honor, but Alterman questioned whether they had the right to demand it of the entire community.[18] This was a debate over the value of rebellion as a symbol to be handed down to future generations.

Alterman frequently emphasized that the rebels did not have the rescue of Jews as their goal. Their object was an all-out war against fascism. In defending the Jews of Europe who opted for survival and rescue, Alterman was also defending the actions of his own Jewish community, the one in Israel, and its leaders. He was a poet in the service of his party. Like Haim Cohen, the attorney general, who enlisted the law in the party's interests, Alterman enlisted words.

Although Mapai was the main target of the attacks in this election campaign, its opponents also lashed out at one another. *Lamerhav* recounted that members of the Revisionist movement, the Herut party's progenitor, had served as officers in the Nazi-mandated Jewish police forces in the ghettos. *Lamerhav* and *Al Hamishmar* competed for the endorsements of the Warsaw ghetto rebel leaders. *Lamerhav*'s party, Ahdut Haavodah, had a certain advantage—Antek Zuckerman and Tzivia Lubetkin were among its members. Mapam could invoke the name of Mordecai Anielewicz, commander of the uprising, but could not send him off on the campaign trail, since he had been killed during the uprising. The Communist *Kol Haam* tried to steal the glory of the dead hero from Mapam—Anielewicz had supported an alliance with the Polish Communist underground to bolster the rebellion's chances of saving its survivors. The people who now headed Mapam, the Communists charged, had opposed this alliance out of political vindictiveness. *Al Hamishmar* responded that the Communists collaborated with the Grand Mufti of Jerusalem, Hitler's ally. It also attacked Moshe Sneh, a Mapam leader who had defected to the Communists. "Sneh abandoned Polish Jewry during the Holocaust to save his own skin," *Al Hamishmar* charged.[19] The election campaign was the most grotesque in Israel's history.

The elections were held on July 26, 1955. Mapai remained the largest faction, but its strength fell from forty-five to forty seats in the 120-member Knesset, its worst showing until the political upset of 1977. Herut almost doubled its strength, mostly at the expense of the General Zionists. It jumped from eight to fifteen seats, one more than it had had in the first Knesset. From this time on, its strength increased steadily until it became the ruling party in 1977. Mapai, analyzing its setback, cited a number of causes, like the reparations agreement and the Kastner episode. The most visible outcome of the election was that Ben-Gurion reassumed the position of prime minister.

Ben-Gurion tended in those months, as well as thereafter, to keep his distance from the Kastner affair. It was as if he had no part in it, as if it were, from beginning to end, merely a chapter in Moshe Sharett's biography, not his own. "I know almost nothing about the Kastner matter," he wrote to one of his acquaintances. "I did not follow the trial and did not read the verdict, except for a few sentences that appeared in the headlines."[20] Yet he was in fact no outsider: As chairman of the Jewish Agency executive during the Holocaust, Ben-Gurion had been involved in Joel Brand's mission. Kastner had testified that before going to Nuremberg to appear at the war crimes trials, he had consulted Ben-Gurion, who told him to go. Kastner visited Ben-Gurion at Sde Boker during the trial and related, upon returning, that Ben-Gurion promised that one day he would clear Kastner's name. But when Kastner's brother requested a statement to that effect, Ben-Gurion refused, even though he agreed that Kastner's good name had been "trampled by scoundrels." He knew well the disgusting plots of those muckrakers who had latched on to Kastner, he told the brother, but he could not recall having promised to clear his name. In fact, "several members of the Jewish Agency executive are much better informed than I am on what was done then to save European Jewry," Ben-Gurion wrote, as if it had all been a matter in the care of some other department.[21] "I would not take it upon myself to judge any Jew who was there," Ben-Gurion wrote to a member of the *Davar* staff; the Judenrat affair (and perhaps the Kastner affair) should be left to the judgment of history. "The Jews who lived in safety during the time of Hitler cannot judge their brothers who were burned and slaughtered or those who were saved. I saw some of the survivors in the German concentration camps just after the war, I heard of several atrocities, and I saw ugly behavior in some of the camps—but I did not see that I had the right to be judge and accuser, knowing what they had been through."

Ben-Gurion also believed there was no point establishing a public commission of inquiry into the incident, since "the political-party interests that exploit the Holocaust for their own purposes" would distort its work. For the time being, there was absolutely no danger that Israel's younger generation would adopt the Judenrat as a model to be imitated. They, after all, were being educated in the heritage of the Israeli Defense Forces and the military organizations that had preceded it, Ben-Gurion wrote, adding a rare expression of emotion: "The tragedy is deeper than the abyss, and the members of our generation who did not taste that hell would do best (in my modest opinion) to remain sorrowfully and humbly silent. My niece, her husband, and her two children were burned alive. Can such things be talked about?"[22]

Kastner had also testified in favor of SS officer Hermann Krumey, an aide to Adolf Eichmann. In the wake of the Eichmann trial, Krumey was tried in Germany. He submitted Kastner's testimony in his defense. Shmuel Tamir did not let the moment pass—he sent Ben-Gurion a long letter, on behalf of Malchiel Gruenwald, demanding a denial that he had authorized Kastner to be witness for Krumey. Ben-Gurion answered with a single sentence: "I refuse to have anything to do with any matter of Mr. Gruenwald's or of his representatives'." Tamir rushed with his letter to the offices of *Herut*.[23]

16 | *"Jeremiah the Prophet, for Example"*

Two and a half years would pass before the Supreme Court reached its decision on the appeal. In the meantime, the controversy set off by the affair continued to rage, although with less force and more rationality. But even in this more considered form, with its poetic language and moral arguments, it was more than a debate about the past. It was an attempt to shape the current image of Israeli society and to set the country's course for the future. When people debated the value of life in the Polish ghettos, they were actually debating the value of life in Israel. Soon there was another war and they were forced to examine themselves once again. Then came a new political crisis, over relations with Germany. Again, as in the days of the dispute over the reparations agreement, Israelis had to decide between morals and national interest, between emotion and reason.

On October 29, 1956, the Israeli Defense Forces invaded Egypt and, in just a week, occupied the entire Sinai peninsula. Nearly two hundred Israeli soldiers and several thousand Egyptians were killed. The Israeli invasion was justified as an act of self-defense, and indeed it came after a series of attacks by terrorists who had crossed into Israel from Jordan and Egypt, a country whose military strength was growing rapidly. In hindsight, however, this war smacks embarrassingly of adventurism, the product of a fantasy about a new order in the Middle East and a military intrigue between Israel, Britain, and France. The two European powers, unwilling to accept the end of the colonial era, wanted to topple the

Nasser regime and regain control of the Suez Canal. They did not achieve their ends. The Israeli press, like that of Britain and France, often compared Nasser to Hitler in both articles and cartoons. Israeli politicians, like their counterparts in Britain and France, did the same. David Ben-Gurion described Nasser as a "fascist dictator," and Begin claimed he was surrounded by Nazi emissaries.[1] Ten days before the occupation of the Sinai, *Maariv* devoted an entire page to an article with the headline "SWASTIKA IN THE LAND OF THE NILE," telling of a former SS officer, Otto Skorzeny, whom it described as "the man behind Nasser." (In fact, Skorzeny probably also worked as an Israeli agent.) A short time after the conquest of the Sinai, *Maariv* published a photograph of an Arabic edition of *Mein Kampf*, which it claimed had been found in Egyptian army camps. Elsewhere in the same issue, the newspaper stated that "the French-British action prevented Nasser from turning into the Hitler of the East. It overwhelmed him before the verbiage of his speeches was translated into a campaign of murder and extermination." *Yediot Aharonot* reported that the expulsion of Egyptian Jewry after the war was planned by a former SS man; the article was written by Eliezer Wiesel, later to become known as writer and Nobel Peace Prize laureate Elie Wiesel. The poet Uri Zvi Greenberg described the Arabs as "the haters of my race."[2]

In the face of international condemnation, several Knesset members used the Holocaust to justify the Sinai operation. "A million and a half young people and children were slaughtered in broad daylight, and the world's conscience was not moved," said Yitzhak Itshe Meir Levin (Agudat Yisrael). "But now that the Jews are gathered in to the State of Israel, the outside world cannot give its consent. Its conscience bothers it, apparently because they refuse to go to the slaughter, but defend themselves courageously."[3] Others spoke similarly, including Israel's ambassadors in foreign capitals. "You know as well as I do what they did to us fifteen years ago," Ben-Gurion wrote to one of President Eisenhower's associates, Gen. Walter Bedell Smith, in support of the thesis that the Sinai invasion was an act of self-defense, and an associate of the chief of staff said that the decision to act against the Egyptians was made out of fear.[4]

All these arguments were meant to score debating points. In fact, deep existential anxiety was not evident before the war, nor was it what led Israel to attack. It came in the wake of victory, when the United States and the Soviet Union joined forces and applied heavy pressure—accompanied by blunt threats—to force Israel to retreat. The Americans threatened to cut off financial aid to Israel, and the Russians threatened to send troops to Egypt. Ben-Gurion believed them. "It was a nightmare," he recorded in his diary. "Messages from Rome, Paris, and Washington come one after the other about a flow of aircraft and Soviet 'volunteers' to Syria, about a promise to bomb Israel—airfields, cities, and more. . . . There is, perhaps, much exaggeration in these messages, but [Premier Nikolai] Bulganin's letter to me—a letter that could well have been written by Hitler—and the madness of the Russian tanks in Hungary testify to what these Nazi Communists are capable of doing."[5] Education Minister Zalman Aran was quoted as saying: "I am a Jew of the Exile, and I am frightened. It will be outright extermination." Pinhas Sapir, minister of commerce and industry, explained to Ben-Gurion what would happen if the United States imposed all the economic sanctions it had the ability to impose. "It's death," he said.[6] Ben-Gurion accepted this evaluation. "We couldn't take it," he asserted a few months later in a speech to officers of the Israeli Defense Forces. "It would have turned into a catastrophe for the State of Israel."[7] The prime minister had said many times that Israel was in danger, but this appears to have been the first time that he thought of the danger concretely, in terms of destruction, obliteration, and Holocaust. By the beginning of March 1957, Israel withdrew from all the occupied territories, including the Gaza Strip.

¶

Israel's Arab citizens had been under military rule since the establishment of the state. The military government restricted their freedom of movement, made administrative arrests, and promulgated a variety of arbitrary regulations. The government contended that this type of control was necessary because the Arabs were a security and political risk. There was another benefit, too—military law also made it easier to confiscate Arab land. In the "triangle," an area bordering on Jordan with many Arab villages, the Arabs lived under a permanent curfew that began, generally, at nine P.M. On the first day of the Sinai campaign, the curfew was moved up to five P.M. A short while after the curfew went into effect that day, several dozen residents of Kfar Kassem appeared on the outskirts of their village. They were returning from work elsewhere and were not aware that the curfew had been changed. They arrived via the main road, in trucks and wagons and on bicycles. At the entrance to the village they met a detachment of the Border Police. The soldiers ordered them to halt. After identifying them in a general way as residents of the village, the guards lined them up and shot them to death, in compliance with the order they had been given: "Cut them down." Villagers continued to arrive in small groups, and they too were shot. Close to fifty people were killed, among them seven children and ten women. A few of the wounded played dead and survived.[8] "My God, what will become of our little country!" Moshe Sharett wrote in his diary; he had by then been ousted from the cabinet.[9]

The government at first tried to cover up the incident. And since the newspapers did not immediately demand the military censor's permission to publish the story, the first reports of the massacre were spread by word of mouth. A Mapam activist, Latif Dori, went from hospital to hospital and took testimony from the wounded. Communist party officials did the same. It was seven days after the incident that the newspapers began to submit brief and inaccurate items about the slaughter to the censor. The censor forbade publication. *Kol Haam* alone appealed the decision but was refused. In the days that followed, newspapers—most prominently *Kol Haam, Al Hamishmar, Haaretz,* and *Haolam Hazeh*—began to pressure the censor. Knesset member Esther Vilenska (Maki) mentioned the slaughter in one of her speeches but was immediately told to stop; her words were stricken from the record. Tawfik Tubi, also a Maki Knesset member, described the incident in a pamphlet he distributed. Ultimately the government, unable to withstand the growing pressure, was forced to publish an official statement. Earlier it had set up a commission of inquiry. After lengthy negotiations between the Knesset factions, it was agreed that Ben-Gurion would make a statement about the slaughter. The Knesset would rise for a moment of silence, and it would forgo debate. "There is no people in the world that values human life more than does the Jewish people," Ben-Gurion said in his statement. "We have learned that man was created in the image of God and no one knows what color skin Adam had."[10] That was about six weeks after the massacre. Most Israelis did not yet really know what it was all about.

Once publication of the story was permitted, the Israeli press voiced deep shock and led the country in some collective soul-searching. "How Could This Have Happened?" asked Shlomo Gross in *Haaretz* and Natan Alterman in *Davar*. What was the source of this hatred for minority groups? they wondered. What is the internal mechanism that brings a man to obey an order to murder? What are the limits of obedience, and what is an illegal order? Everyone seemed aware from the start that they were agonizing over the same questions that had been raised in Germany after the war, but no one dared say so explicitly at first. "We are no better than others," Uri Avneri intimated. "Things that happen to other nations can happen to us as well." But, at this stage, still trying to preserve his image of the purity of Israeli youth, Avneri complained: "Has the Hebrew youth in uniform ever been told when a legal order turns into an illegal one?" In other words, the politicians were guilty, not the army.

As details of the atrocity came to light, the newspapers explicitly compared the massacre of Kfar Kassem to the crimes of the Nazis. "We must demand of the entire nation a sense of shame and humiliation . . . that soon we will be like Nazis and the perpetrators of pogroms," wrote Rabbi Benyamin—the man who, during the Holocaust, had tried to call the yishuv and its leaders to action. He added: "May the leaders of the nation rise. May the rabbinical leaders rise and publicly confess this great crime, go to Kfar Kassem to beg forgiveness, exoneration, and atonement." Yeshayahu Leibowitz wrote in *Haaretz* with the biting sarcasm for which he was known: "For the sake of the justice that the State of Israel proclaims, we must organize in this country a mass petition addressed to the governments of the United States, Britain, France, and the Soviet Union and demand a revision of the Nuremberg laws and the rehabilitation of the officers, soldiers, and officials sentenced there to death and hanged, because all of them acted in accordance with explicit orders from their legal commanders." *Haaretz* later devoted an entire page to letters that agreed or disagreed with Leibowitz. Author Yehoshua Bar-Yosef, by contrast, tried to reassure the readers of *Davar*: "This is not the time for a mournful lament that the Nazi beast has wakened within us." And Uri Avneri patted himself on the back for the legal action taken against the murderers: "This is the decisive difference between the State of Israel and the German regime of atrocities," he wrote. *Davar* summed up: "How can it be, then, that normal people, our own boys, would commit a criminal act of this sort? There is no escaping the truth: not enough has been done to inoculate this nation against the dulling of the moral sense, against the tendency to ignore the holiness of human life when speaking of an enemy or a potential enemy."[11]

The other papers, *Yediot Aharonot* and *Maariv*, tended to play down the slaughter. They treated the murderers with understanding, attacking the reactions of the other newspapers and of the Knesset. *Yediot Aharonot* criticized the Knesset for having observed a moment of silence. "It is, of course, a scandal," the paper commented. "But to stage a public show like that in the Knesset means not only showing we are sorry but giving the impression that we are uncertain and perpetually terrified." The newspaper's parliamentary correspondent commented that no one had apologized for the expulsion of Iraqi Jewry. The reporter used the Nazi term for expulsion—*Aussiedlung. Yediot* reporter Eliahu Amikam attacked the "repentance hysteria" that had come over the country. He computed that, over the previous 2,000 years—some 730,000 days or 17 million hours—at least one Jew had been killed every hour. "The knights of the pen who slept while Jews were murdered by the millions began to pound the drums of morality to the sound of Maki's trumpets," he wrote, noting derisively that even Danny Kaye's visit to the country had not won such wide coverage. *Maariv* reported the incident for the first time under the headline "KFAR KASSEM TO RECEIVE A QUARTER MILLION LIRAS," compensation to the families of the victims.[12]

The Kfar Kassem killers were sentenced to prison terms of between seven and seventeen years. The verdict contained one of the most important, noble, and imprecise paragraphs ever formulated by an Israeli court. It defined the nature of an illegal order that is not to be obeyed: "The hallmark of manifest illegality is that it must wave like a black flag over the given order, a warning that says: 'forbidden!' Not formal illegality, obscure or partially obscure, not illegality that can be discerned only by legal scholars, is important here, but rather, the clear and obvious violation of law. . . . Illegality that pierces the eye and revolts the heart, if the eye is not blind and the heart is not impenetrable or corrupt—this is the measure of manifest illegality needed to override the soldier's duty to obey and to impose on him criminal liability for his action."[13]

The man who wrote these lines, after again donning his uniform to serve as president of the military court, was Benyamin Halevy. The "black flag" opinion was integrated into the army's educational program.

The comparison of the Kfar Kassem massacre with the crimes of the Nazis reflected an attempt to present the Holocaust as a source of ethical imperatives with regard to human rights in general and, specifically, the Israel-Arab conflict. There was a precedent. At one of its earliest meetings, the first cabinet discussed atrocities committed by Israeli soldiers against civilians during the War of Independence and thereafter. The information presented to the ministers was appalling and elicited one of the harshest statements ever made at the cabinet table. Aharon Zisling (Mapam), minister of agriculture, said: "I have not always agreed when the term *Nazi* was applied to the British. I would not want to use that expression with regard to them, even though they committed Nazi acts. But Nazi acts have been committed by Jews as well, and I am deeply shocked."[14]

However, as the letters that reached the newspapers attest, most Israelis rejected the comparison. *Maariv* and *Yediot Aharonot* reflected popular sentiment better than did the moralizing *Davar* and *Haaretz*. And ultimately, the official position also moved in that direction. The compensation paid to the families of the victims was miserly; the military government was revoked only years later. An appeals court reduced the murderers' sentences; the chief of staff and the president pardoned them and, three years after the massacre, they were all free. The commander of the regiment to which the soldiers belonged, Col. Yisachar Shadmi, was tried only in the wake of pressure from the newspapers. He was acquitted of murder and found guilty only of having overstepped his authority. Moshe Dayan, army chief of staff at the time of the incident, was a defense witness. The court imposed a fine of one grush—the smallest coin of the realm. The state did not appeal.

¶

Before the Supreme Court took the Israeli public back once more to the days of the Holocaust in Hungary, Ben-Gurion's government fell again —and was again reconstituted—this time over the government's plans to buy two submarines from West Germany. At the height of this crisis, three Israelis found themselves stuck in their car in the snow somewhere on the way to Bavaria. One of the three would later be appointed Israel's first ambassador to Germany, the second would be army chief of staff, and the third, minister of defense and prime minister.

It was December 1957, and Arthur Ben-Natan, Haim Laskov, and Shimon Peres were on their way to the home of Franz Josef Strauss, the German minister of defense. "We left Paris towards evening and arrived at Strasbourg, on the German border, after midnight," Peres wrote. "The winter was at its worst. The road was covered with snow and there was a heavy fog. Even before we came to the border we strayed off the road and the motor stopped running. By the light of a flashlight, we tried to restart the motor and find the way." When the car began to move, it almost ran over Laskov. "He was saved by a miracle," Peres wrote.

It took them until afternoon to reach Strauss's house in Rott am Inn, a small village about thirty miles south of Munich. Strauss was twenty minutes late for their meeting, having been out running with his dogs. Peres described him as a young, red-cheeked man overflowing with health and energy, who instantly grasped the subject at hand and often came up with brilliant formulations of the problem. His wife cooked lunch. "We said that America was helping us with money but not with arms and that France was helping us with arms but not with money," Peres wrote. "Germany could make a significant move in building bridges over the past were it to help us with arms for free. . . . We proposed that there be relations between us like the relations with France—relations based on trust, a broad perspective, and direct contact." They spoke for three hours, and Strauss promised to help. "We felt that, in fact, a foundation had been laid for special relations between the two countries," Peres wrote.[15] Ben-Gurion noted in his diary: "In Shimon's opinion, Strauss's attitude derives from (1) hatred and fear of the Russians; (2) admiration for the Israeli Defense Forces; (3) recognition of Europe's interests, as a power involved in the Middle East and Africa." Strauss oversaw German-Israeli relations, in coordination with Adenauer: "He attaches special importance to the secrecy of the contacts," Ben-Gurion noted.[16]

The initiative for military relations with Germany came, apparently, from Shimon Peres, and Ben-Gurion approved it. There was no formal discussion or decision in the cabinet. Earlier, the Mapai leader Giora Yoseftal had gone to Bonn and requested military aid from Adenauer.* Peres, too, had seen Strauss at least once prior to that winter visit to his home. According to the original plan, Peres was to have taken Army Chief of Staff Moshe Dayan with him. But then the inevitable had happened—the secret leaked out. At a cabinet meeting, Minister of Health Yisrael Barzilai (Mapam) asked Ben-Gurion if it was true that "a high-ranking person" was being sent to Germany. When Ben-Gurion confirmed the rumor, Barzilai demanded a discussion. Ben-Gurion agreed. He disclosed to the government that the person in question was the chief of staff. Six ministers—representing Mapam, Ahdut Haavodah, the Progressives, and the National Religious party—opposed the trip. But the seven Mapai ministers voted in favor, and the mission was approved on December 15, 1957. This was apparently the first formal decision about military links between Israel and Germany. The Ahdut Haavodah ministers decided to carry on with their campaign against the

---

* Nahum Goldmann also put out feelers in Bonn to find out whether Adenauer would be prepared to sell military equipment to Israel. On his return, he related to Ben-Gurion a bit of gossip: "Adenauer, eighty-one years old, intends to serve for ten more years. There are shots in Germany, first discovered in Russia, that rejuvenate old men." The pope took them, too, Ben-Gurion noted in his diary.[17]

trip. They referred to Strauss as one of the leaders of the "Nazi army of murderers," and had a story published in their newspaper, *Lamerhav*, without mentioning the name of the "high-ranking person." Characteristically, while everyone knew what was up, they all pretended it was still a secret. Thus when Ben-Gurion spoke on the matter in the Knesset, he did not say "submarines" but rather said "equipment that cannot be seen from land, sea, or air." "Arab spies," Menahem Begin retorted sarcastically, "figure out for yourselves what he meant."[18]

In the wake of the uproar, Ben-Gurion canceled Dayan's trip and sent the man appointed to be the next chief of staff—Laskov. The decision to purchase arms from Germany was another step toward full normalization between the two countries, and it required, as one might expect, crossing another emotional barrier. But, in fact, the crisis did not go beyond political charges and countercharges, and did not take on any real emotional proportions. Ben-Gurion tried to divert the debate from relations with Germany to security—specifically the extent to which the prime minister could trust his ministers not to reveal secrets. "Relations of mutual trust have now become a vital question," he said. "Is it possible to ensure secrecy or isn't it? This is a matter not between husband and wife but between us and fate."[19] The crisis went on for two weeks, and then Ben-Gurion and his government resigned. A week later, he formed a new cabinet with the same ministers. The Ahdut Haavodah representatives, duly dressed down, promised not to leak any more secrets.

In a "secret and private" letter to Yitzhak Ben-Aharon, one of the leaders of Ahdut Haavodah, Ben-Gurion stated that, to the best of his knowledge, Strauss had never been a Nazi. It was not proper, then, for Ben-Aharon to refer to him as one of the leaders of "the Nazi army of murderers," the prime minister protested. Ben-Gurion attached to the letter his notes of a conversation with the head of the defense ministry's purchase delegation in Germany. "Are there known Nazis holding important positions?" Ben-Gurion had asked the ministry's emissary. "No," the man had responded.

Q: And in the army?
A: In army circles not at all. Strauss appointed a committee that examined past records, and in every case, even the most doubtful, he removed former Nazis from their offices. . . .
Q: Do you have any idea which way the winds are blowing among German youth?

A: German young people today are interested in one thing—how to get on with their lives.

Q: Is there Nazism among them?

A: No. Their reaction to the play *Anne Frank* is one of deep interest.

Q: Is Nazism felt at all in Germany?

A: No.

Q: What happened to the Nazis?

A: They went underground.

He could neither confirm nor refute this evaluation, Ben-Gurion noted. But he knew the speaker as an intelligent and honest man and had heard similar impressions from other people.[20]

The affair gave birth to a rule laid down by Ben-Gurion and, in effect, accepted by all: "I will not hesitate for a moment to receive equipment from any country; and no country is ineligible, as far as I am concerned.*[21]

§

In January 1958, a few days after the arms crisis was defused, the Supreme Court handed down its verdict in the state's appeal of Malchiel Gruenwald's partial acquittal. Four of the five judges ruled in favor of the appeal, clearing Kastner of most of the accusations against him. They censured him only for the testimony he had given in favor of SS officer Kurt Becher after the war. One of the judges, Moshe Silberg, favored rejecting the appeal and accepting Benyamin Halevy's verdict. "Anyone

* A few years later, Ben-Gurion conducted a unique correspondence with twenty-nine-year-old Yariv Ben-Aharon, Yitzhak Ben-Aharon's son, who had published an article asserting that it was permissible to accept weapons from Germany despite the fact that it had not changed since it murdered six million Jews. "I was shocked by your article," Ben-Gurion wrote to the young man, "and I was shocked by your immoral approach. . . . Where did you get this Hottentot ethic?" Ben-Gurion was no longer satisfied with having his German policy recognized as a political, economic, and military necessity. He now wanted it to be recognized as a moral policy. Using the Bible, Ben-Gurion defended the thesis that the Germany of Adenauer and Willy Brandt was "a different Germany," just as Nikita Khrushchev's Soviet Union was not that of Stalin. "I have absolutely no doubt that Khrushchev did not protest or oppose Stalin's atrocities," he wrote, "yet were Khrushchev today to extend his hand in friendship, I would accept it." Likewise, he would be happy if the poet Yevgeny Yevtushenko would come for a visit. To refuse to have contacts with Germany simply because it was Germany "gives off a Hitlerist, or more politely, a racist scent," Ben-Gurion wrote. The young Ben-Aharon's feelings were hurt.[22]

who, after the fact, saved or helped to save Becher from hanging," Silberg wrote, "showed thereby that the acts of that great criminal were not all that despicable and abominable in his eyes."*

Supreme Court Justices Shimon Agranat, Yitzhak Olshan, Schneur Zalman Heshin, and David Edward Geutein wrote with compassion, awe, humility, and incredulity—all the virtues that were lacking in Halevy's judgment. "In coming to an evaluation of Dr. Kastner's behavior, we must be very, very cautious lest we fall victim to prejudgment," Agranat wrote. The moral and historical judgments they were being forced to make should never have reached the courtroom, they ruled; the proper forum, if there was one, was a public commission of historians. "It is strange that at a time when the nations of the world are trying the murderers themselves, and even executing them for the cruel murders they performed, we, the brothers of the victims, whose arms are too short to bring the murderers to trial, are preoccupying ourselves with gossips and rumormongers," Heshin wrote. He marveled at "these hotheads" who moved "the authorities" to choose, from among all the libelers and slanderers, none other than the pathetic Malchiel Gruenwald and put him on trial in such an exceptional, unorthodox procedure. Heshin attacked Halevy for the extraneous matters he allowed into the trial, some of them "the fruits of illusion and imagination." He also assailed him for weighing Kastner's moral quality rather than restricting himself to the legal question of whether Gruenwald had proven that Kastner collaborated with the Nazis.

The majority opinion, nearly two hundred pages long, was courageous, since clearing Kastner required the judges to take a most unpopular— and, to many, unpatriotic—view of the Holocaust, including the Warsaw ghetto uprising. This was not easy to do. Like Halevy, the Supreme Court justices chronicled the Holocaust in Hungary in detail but ruled that, at every juncture, Kastner did what he should have done. Therefore, it could not be said that he abandoned either his community or the paratroopers from Palestine. He did not collaborate with the Nazis; he did not sell his soul to the devil.

On the main question, Justice Agranat wrote that Kastner continued negotiating with the Germans until the end with the sole purpose of

---

* Uri Avneri got carried away. "It will be remembered to the credit of the living tradition of Jewish religious morality that Justice Silberg, just like Judge Halevy, is a man of deep religious convictions," he wrote. [23]

saving the largest number of Jews possible, given the conditions of the time and place. The VIP train was a by-product of these negotiations, Agranat found. He accepted as "a rational principle" the preference given to Zionist leaders in awarding places on the train, since these travelers were headed for Palestine, and ruled that Kastner should not be taken to task for putting his mother and wife on the train. The judge noted that about a hundred of Kastner's relatives had not been put on the train and had died. Cautiously, as if walking on hot coals, as if weighing every word, Agranat also noted that all the leaders of the Jewish community at the time, including the representatives of the Revisionist movement, supported Kastner's line of action.

Justice Heshin risked a clearer, sarcastic phrasing:

[Shmuel Tamir] cries excitedly that if Kastner's deeds are justified, there is no future for the people of Israel, since every leader will act in difficult times as he did. He also says, in addressing the reasons why Kastner did not call for a rebellion, that "the lack of arms should not have been a reason for not rebelling." This means that the Jews of the provincial ghettos in Hungary should all have fought and died as martyrs for the people's honor. In this context he points to the Warsaw ghetto rebels, who were publicly martyred. This is one way to look at it. The bloody history of the people of Israel tells of many such heroes. But there is also another point of view, different and opposite, and this view also has roots in the pages of our history. Jeremiah the prophet, for example, preached surrender to the enemy and an alliance with him, while Rabbi Yohanan Ben-Zakkai chose to save what could be saved in a time of trouble. Despite this, no one accused them of selling their souls to the devil.

On the charge of "collaboration with the Nazis," Heshin wrote:

Even the victims themselves, the Holocaust dead—the men, women, and children who dug their own graves under the rifle's glare, who were forced to enter the gas chambers and fiery furnaces—these, too, collaborated, inasmuch as their actions aided the Nazis and helped them carry out their plans. There is no need to go to great lengths to prove, from this point of view, that Joel Brand intended to collaborate with the Nazis. Had he succeeded in obtaining for the Germans a given number of trucks and a given number of tons of foodstuffs, he would have extended them real assistance and helped them continue their intrigues against the Jews, and perhaps have lengthened the war as well. Yet no one would dare cast a stone at him had he succeeded by this collaboration in saving so many thousands of Jews, since his thoughts were directed to good and not to evil, to rescue and not to extermination. . . . What this indicates is that there is collaboration that deserves praise and that, in any case, if it is not accompanied by malicious and evil intentions, it should not be condemned or seen as a moral failing.[24]

Here, then, were Alterman's two ways, now set out in a Supreme Court opinion—one leading to "death with honor," the other to rescue.

For Kastner, the ruling came several months too late. On the night of March 3, 1957, a few minutes after midnight, he returned from his work at the daily Hungarian-language newspaper *Uikelet*, one of a range of foreign-language newspapers published by Mapai; he had resigned from his post as spokesman for the Ministry of Commerce and Industry. He parked his car by his house, 6 Sderot Emanuel, Tel Aviv. At the entrance to the building, a young man approached him and asked if he was Dr. Kastner. Kastner answered in the affirmative—and then the stranger shot him three times. Kastner died of his wounds three days later.

Within a few hours of the attack, the police arrested three suspects. The speed with which they were apprehended gave rise to speculation that they were known to the police and the security service, the Shin Bet. It turned out that one of them, Zeev Eckstein, had indeed worked for the Shin Bet in the year before the murder. The security service had planted him in what was thought to be an extreme right-wing illegal underground movement. Ideologically, it was supposedly heir to the Lehi and to the Tsrifin Underground, which advocated the establishment of an "Israelite kingdom" between the Mediterranean and the Euphrates. The two other suspects were Dan Shemer and Yosef Menkes. All three suspects were convicted, partly on the basis of their confessions to the police, and sentenced to life in prison.

It was the first political assassination in Israel since that of Haim Arlosoroff, almost twenty-five years earlier. In that case, suspicion also fell on extreme right-wing circles, against the background of contacts with Germany. In both cases, mysteries remained. *Haolam Hazeh* suggested that Kastner was murdered by the Shin Bet to silence him. Since, at the time of the murder, legal proceedings in the Gruenwald-Kastner case were still in progress, on the face of it there was always a possibility that Kastner would choose to reveal secrets about contacts between the Mapai leadership and Nazi Germany.

Haolam Hazeh's interpretation would later receive support from an unexpected corner. Isser Harel, by that time retired as head of the Shin Bet and the Mossad, published a book with the sole purpose of proving that the Shin Bet did not murder Kastner. The source for Uri Avneri's version of events, Harel wrote, "should be located in the bounds of the writer's mental illness or, alternatively, in his malice and insistence on defaming the Shin Bet in every way and at any price."[25] Yet the book was not entirely convincing, leaving the reader with the impression that what Harel and the state prosecutor's office called an "underground" never existed, or at least had never gone beyond being a transient fringe group. During the Gruenwald trial and for more than a year afterward, Kastner was under police protection. A short time before his murder, the protection was lifted. Harel gives no better explanation in his book than this: "Who in the security forces had the inclination and time, in the period of the Sinai campaign, to deal with Kastner or assign personnel to guard him"?[26] The pardon eventually granted the assailants also seems strange; here were three dangerous murderers, members of what the authorities had described as a terrorist organization. Yet five years after they were sent to prison for life, Ben-Gurion approached Kastner's widow and daughter and asked them to consent to pardons. The widow refused, but the daughter agreed, and the men were freed.[27]

¶

Somewhere in the volumes of the literary weekly *Masa*, there are these lines written by Aharon Megged: "Kastner—a Jewish tragedy. It was foolish to bring his case to court. The law's involvement in this incident is like the involvement of gossip in a tragedy of love. What does gossip know: the details of the spats, the fights? The insults hurled at each other? The tears that were seen through the keyhole? What does it know of what took place inside the two people who fought for their lives on the narrow bridge between hope and despair?"[28]

Pinhas Rosen wrote to Haim Cohen "upon the end of the nightmare" to congratulate him on his success. His ever-so-tactful letter contained a note of censure: "Even you yourself did not always judge Kastner fairly, influenced as you were by his shortcomings as a witness, his occasional failure under the pressure of a confusing and lengthy interrogation," the minister of justice wrote. "But fundamentally Kastner was a simple man, in whom there was more good than evil and whose honor you saved and whose name you cleared—a great deed." Rosen wondered if it might not have been better, after all, to have ignored the tale-mongering of a man like Gruenwald. Either way, he disagreed with the judges' opinion that the best course would have been to put the whole matter in the hands of a public commission of inquiry. "It is sufficient to read the last issue of *Haolam Hazeh* to understand that this group of malicious prosecutors would have torn to pieces any public commission that, say, would have come to the same conclusion that the Supreme Court reached. And in the end, what kind of country is it in which you can accuse a high official of murder, and you have to tell him, 'The courts cannot protect you'?"[29]

Shmuel Tamir continued to stoke his political career with the Kastner affair and its offshoots. Now and then he would claim to have uncovered new evidence. He gave many interviews on the incident and from time to time published articles about it. He once demanded reopening Gruen-wald's trial. Much later, in 1969, he found himself serving in the seventh Knesset with Uri Avneri and Isser Harel. The three could be seen fighting over the episode in the cafeteria and in the chamber, slandering one another in unending enmity but also, it appeared, with much pleasure and nostalgia. Benyamin Halevy was also a member of the Knesset then, for Herut. He had risen as far as the Supreme Court and then retired to a career in politics. In the ninth Knesset, Halevy and Minister of Justice Tamir represented the same party, the Democratic Movement for Change. In an interview he once gave to the Israeli Defense Forces radio station, Halevy confided that he regretted the words "sold his soul to the devil" and would not use them were he to write his opinion again. They had been an unnecessary flourish that was not understood correctly, he said.[30]

17 | "There Is No Certainty That Our Children Will Remain Alive"

About a year and a half after the first weapons crisis came a second one. It was June 1959, four months before the elections to the fourth Knesset. The previous time, tempers had flared when it became known that Israel was buying arms from Germany. Now the West German weekly *Der Spiegel* reported that Israel was also selling arms to Germany. The Bundeswehr, the magazine reported, would be fitted out with a quarter of a million mortar shells made by Soltam, a plant owned jointly by a Finnish company and the Histadrut's Solel Boneh firm. The sale, according to *Der Spiegel*, was valued at DM 36 million, about $9 million.[1] The information, largely correct, hit Israel like a bomb.[2] David Ben-Gurion considered publication of the news a most serious matter, since he saw the arms deals with Germany as "a matter of life or death" and believed that it was vital to keep them secret.

It was a standard opening for a standard scandal. Many an Israeli political uproar has begun, as this one began, when a foreign newspaper published defense-political information that the government tried to hide for one reason or another.* Most of the newspapers in Israel reacted negatively to the arms deal. This time, even the moderate *Haaretz*, which

---

* Ben-Gurion had not heard of *Der Spiegel* until this incident. His staff explained to him that it was the German equivalent of *Haolam Hazeh*.[3]

generally supported Ben-Gurion's defense policies, sided with the papers that sympathized with Herut.[4] Herut submitted an urgent proposal for discussion in the Knesset, and Maki raised a no-confidence motion. Nonetheless, Ben-Gurion had the upper hand in managing the crisis. He engineered the publication of more and more secret documents and internal memoranda. At the height of the crisis, he resigned his post— and won the fight. The result was that another taboo was broken.

The decision to sell arms to Germany had emotional, moral, and political aspects. It was one of those decisions that require nations to define their relation to their histories and often, therefore, to define their national identities as well. It appears that the cabinet was committed to a Knesset resolution of five years earlier, expressing "deep fear" of the rearmament of the two Germanys. As Moshe Sharett had said in that debate, "The rearmament of Germany ought to waken the most serious concern and deepest bitterness of the Jewish people, whose memory is like a plastered well that loses not a drop."[5] Yet, when arms deals with Germany were considered, Ben-Gurion did not bring the matter before the cabinet in a formal way. Instead, he made the decision himself after consulting several of his men in the defense establishment, most importantly the director-general of the defense ministry, Shimon Peres.

Keeping the agreement from the cabinet saved Ben-Gurion the necessity of defending its wisdom and morality. But it did not prevent an unexpected inconvenience—the treaty turned out to be illegal unless the cabinet approved it. Having no other alternative, Ben-Gurion reluctantly presented the issue to his ministers and asked, in as general a way as possible, for their retroactive approval. Germany was mentioned only in passing, as though it were not the major issue. There was no opposition.

Three months later, on March 29, 1959, the cabinet was discussing fiscal policy. In the course of the discussion Ben-Gurion noted, with conspiratorial pride: "The defense ministry will bring in $7 million this year. We've signed a contract with West Germany." Minister of Finance Levi Eshkol responded: "I know that you're making me rich." Then came the following exchange, between Ben-Gurion and Yisrael Barzilai, the minister of health (Mapam):

BARZILAI: I have a question about that.
BEN-GURION: You think it's forbidden to sell arms to Germany? In which religious code is that written?

BARZILAI: It's not written in any code, but I think that we shouldn't be selling arms to Germany.

BEN-GURION: I disagree.

BARZILAI: I would like to discuss it.

BEN-GURION: Fine, next week. Is it just West Germany, or is East Germany forbidden, too?

BARZILAI: The East, too.

BEN-GURION: Why did you go to East Germany? I refused to respond to a German professor about a book on Spinoza, even though he's one of the world's most righteous men. I said that had he been a professor in Switzerland, I would have written happily.

BARZILAI: In my opinion, it is possible and necessary to go to all international conferences in East and West Germany. Everyone goes. You went to West Germany before us.

BEN-GURION: West Germany is permissible. Not East Germany. They are murderers and robbers who have not returned their loot. West Germany, at least, wants to compensate us. The East murdered and inherited, too. There is a difference between West and East Germany.

The arms sale to Germany was not mentioned again during that meeting.[6]

Six weeks went by. The cabinet held seven meetings, but not one of the Ahdut Haavodah or Mapam ministers brought up the arms sales—until news of it was published in *Der Spiegel*.

On the eve of the Knesset debate, Ben-Gurion appeared before the Mapai central committee. He brought with him a briefcase full of documents, including minutes of cabinet meetings that were not meant to be made public for at least fifty years. Thus the delegates received a fascinating lesson in cabinet decision-making procedures. In his speech, Ben-Gurion presented a political-strategic lecture designed to instill in his comrades the sense that Israel would be in danger if it did not sell weapons to Germany. We must do so, he said, not only because we need foreign currency but also to reinforce the Germans' willingness to sell us the military equipment we need for the future. The central committee members could have got the impression that the very existence of the country depended on the goodwill of the Germans. Ben-Gurion reiterated his credo regarding links with Adenauer's Germany, even waxing sentimental:

No country has helped Israel as America has—and yet it refuses to sell us weapons. Not many countries manufacture arms: America refuses to sell; Russia and her satellites are out of the question. The only possibilities are in Western Europe. It could someday be a matter of life or death for the State of Israel if we don't have the basic equipment for the army. . . . I believe that I have Jewish emotions. I am as shocked by the Holocaust as everyone else. . . . But if anyone concludes that the Holocaust forbids us to negotiate with Germany, I say that person lives in the past and not the present, cares more about his feelings than about the existence of the Jewish people. And if anyone says, "Let us not forget the dead," I say, "Let's concentrate on keeping the Jews living in this country from being slaughtered." In my opinion that could happen. I say that from a knowledge of the way things are. It won't be in the next few years, but I can't say that it might not happen in five years. . . .

Germany has become a central power in Europe not because we gave our stamp of approval. We gave no such approval. . . . Only idiots or political charlatans . . . fail to see that it would harm Israel's position in the world, its future, and perhaps even its existence were we to turn a huge power whose political and economic weight is constantly growing, into an enemy of ours and an ally of the Arabs. . . . There are vital things that have no chance without German cooperation. And I don't see any moral, emotional, or other proscription, just as I don't see any moral or emotional proscription against talking with England, even though England once expelled Jews from its land, and I don't know of any nation in the world that did not do that. Adenauer is not Hitler. Were he Hitler he would act like Hitler.

The longer he talked, the more worried Ben-Gurion sounded, and the more personal he became. "If certain things are not done on time," he said, "there is no certainty that our children and our grandchildren will remain alive." By his own admission, he bore a responsibility that would crush even a stronger man, and he could not shoulder that responsibility without full support.[7]

The members rose one after the other to encourage him. There were seventeen speakers in the debate, and all of them took his side. At a late hour, the Mapai central committee accepted the government's opinion regarding the export of weapons to foreign countries, including West Germany.

Now all that remained was the struggle in the Knesset.

Members of the Mapai central committee believed that the debate over the arms deal would be as emotional as the debate over reparations had been. Seven and a half years had passed since that debate, and the relationship between Israel and Germany had occupied the Knesset on no fewer than fifty occasions. Generally, the issue had been raised by the small anti-German lobby headed by Rabbi Mordecai Nurok, which closely followed every development, submitted endless parliamentary questions, and demanded debates. From time to time the lobby moved no confidence in the government; the government was forced to defend itself again and again. In the meantime, relations between the two countries grew closer in almost every area, and hundreds of thousands of Israelis received compensation payments. As the years went by, it looked as if the Knesset's anti-German lobby was treading water, far from shore, finding it difficult to get headlines. So it began to concentrate more and more on the obvious symbolic manifestations of Jewish-German collaboration, such as cultural events and visits of prominent Germans to Israel.* But the newspapers demanded big stories, and the revelation that Israel was selling arms to Germany was a big story. It now seems that, in the main, the crisis was an election-spurred political one. The slogans were the same as earlier, but they had lost much of their power to move people.

"This impure arms deal with those who continue in Hitler's ways casts a black and vile stain on our country," asserted Shmuel Mikunis (Maki). "Israeli weapons to Hitler's generals. . . . Only Ben-Gurion and his lackeys are capable of being the devil's advocate." Defilement was also Menahem Begin's theme: "All those who washed their hands with Jewish soap," he exclaimed, "are they to carry Jewish weapons as well? . . . Our arms are holy . . . should holiness be defiled? These holy Jewish weapons—should they be entrusted to the hands of a German soldier who perhaps himself led the clutch of Jews to the river, among them an

---

* One was banker Hermann Abs, director-general of the Deutsche Bank. Minister of Finance Levi Eshkol said that Abs and his wife had come to visit the holy sites. In fact, during his stay in Israel, Abs conducted economic talks in the name of the Bonn government and met with Ben-Gurion. Eshkol declared that "as far as is known," Abs had not been a Nazi. In fact, Abs was a leading figure in the German economy during the Third Reich.[8]

elderly father singing 'Hatikvah,' and who threw them into the river as they recited their confessions and prayers, and the river turned red with blood? Should these holy Jewish arms be put in the hands of this German soldier?" And, of course, national pride had its day: "Arming German soldiers with Israeli-made weapons is abhorrent from the aspect of national honor, from the aspect of Jewish sentiment," said Yigal Alon (Ahdut Haavodah). "Is there no value to national pride? . . . The attitude of our youth to arms is not a militaristic attitude. It is an attitude of holy awe for means of defense. Will our youth not learn from this that we have forgiven the Nazis? . . . The Germans have purchased these weapons not because the weapons are good, but because they are Jewish. The Germans desperately need rehabilitation."

Ben-Gurion replied to the opponents of the agreement in a speech that was all provocation, a contrast to the restraint that had characterized his speech on reparations. Sarcastically, he quoted at length from Mena-hem Begin's speech on that subject, including the paragraph in which Begin promised to go to a "concentration camp" if that was necessary to prevent an agreement with Germany. "Here is a hero and martyr whose ideology is dearer to him than life itself," Ben-Gurion said. "But if a year passed and there were negotiations with Germany, and you suddenly met this pathetic speaker and holy martyr and found he had not given up his life, not left his family, not bid his friends farewell, and if seven years later he still sang the same song—this time not with shouts but in a tiny voice drowned in tears—then you would be no longer impressed but, rather, overcome by repugnance and disgust for this false and theatrical rhetoric that had not even a smidgen of inner truth." He went on to take potshots at the rest of his opponents; the record notes at one point "laugh-ter in the chamber." In conclusion Ben-Gurion said: "One may favor or oppose reparations from Germany. One may favor or oppose buying weapons from Germany and selling weapons to Germany. But let no one here presume to speak in the name of the six million martyrs. This most horrible Holocaust in our history cannot be used as window dressing in the political shop of any party." A few minutes later, Ben-Gurion himself used the victims of the Holocaust as an argument: "If the six million slaughtered people were able to see, from their graves or from heaven, what was being done in Israel, they would no doubt cheer and rejoice and find comfort for their deep sorrow at the sight of the reestab-lished Israel, the Israeli army, and our military industries, whose value is recognized even by the Germans."[9]

Then the Knesset voted. Only the General Zionists had still to determine their position. After an internal debate, its members decided to support Ben-Gurion. Their decision saved the government, since Mapam and Ahdut Haavodah voted against it. The two parties of the left found themselves in a rather indefensible position: their ministers had known about the arms sales to Germany but had ignored the matter until it was made public; then they insisted that they could not remember or had not heard. Their discomfort was only increased when it was disclosed that both parties were represented on the board of directors of Koor, the company that ran all the industrial plants belonging to Solel Boneh, including Soltam. The Mapam and Ahdut Haavodah directors of Koor had actively participated in the negotiations with the Germans. The representative of the latter party had himself gone to Germany to negotiate the sale of Soltam mortar shells.

Having voted against the government, the Mapam and Ahdut Haavodah ministers had to resign. Their resignations were not only dictated by political logic but also required by the coalition agreement they had signed with Mapai. The four ministers refused to resign, however, and there was no way to remove them. So Ben-Gurion himself resigned, bringing the government down. Since, in the weeks that followed, he was not successful in finding partners for a new government, the old one, including the four disloyal ministers, continued to serve until elections could be held.

¶

The weapons deal with Germany was one of the main issues in the election campaign; Mapam trotted out the legendary Rozka Korczak, one of the leaders of the Vilna ghetto uprising. It is hard to say to what extent the issue affected the voters—perhaps not much. Ben-Gurion, then seventy-three years old, embarked on the campaign with the slogan "Say yes to the old man." Mapai won forty-seven seats in the Knesset, seven more than it had had in the previous parliament, one more than its highest showing until then. The arms deal with Germany had obviously done it no harm.* In the meantime, Ben-Gurion prepared for the next German scandal.

On Christmas Day in 1959, vandals painted swastikas and anti-Semitic

---

* Later, Israel would also sell Germany Uzi submachine guns and military uniforms produced by the Ata textile plant.[10]

slogans on the walls of a synagogue in Cologne, on the banks of the Rhine. The pattern repeated itself in other German cities; a total of four hundred such incidents were reported. From Germany, the phenomenon spread to other countries around the world. This sudden explosion strengthened those who opposed ties between Israel and Germany and they used it as proof that Ben-Gurion was wrong in describing the Federal Republic as a different Germany. The Israeli press was replete with reports and articles on neo-Nazi activity in Germany and elsewhere; organizations and institutions published condemnations and called for action.[11] The Communist party submitted a motion of no confidence in the government, plus a proposal calling for cancellation of the arms deal. Even though many individuals in Germany, among them President Heinrich Lübke and Chancellor Konrad Adenauer, condemned the anti-Semitic acts, it was not easy for Ben-Gurion to defend his policy. He declared boldly that he would not take back a word of what he said in the past—after all, such anti-Semitic acts had occurred in more than twenty-five countries, not just in Germany—and announced that he had instructed "one of our services that has the means to do so" to investigate the source of the phenomenon.

The mission was assigned to the Mossad. Isser Harel revealed years later that, in the wake of the worldwide outbreak of anti-Semitism, Israeli agents had embarked on operations against organized Nazi groups and had even trained Jews in various countries in self-defense and counterattacks.[12] In the meantime, the prime minister's office was busy with secret preparations for the first Ben-Gurion–Adenauer meeting. Despite the wave of neo-Nazism sweeping Germany, the prime minister ordered that the preparations continue.

The two men met—not by coincidence—in the largest Jewish city in the world, on May 14, 1960. Adenauer was in New York on his first official visit to the United States. The meeting with the Israeli leader was to create an atmosphere favorable to Germany in the Jewish community, the business world, and the press. Both of them lodged at the Waldorf-Astoria Hotel; Ben-Gurion honored the chancellor by descending to his suite, two floors below his own. To evade the photographers who lay in ambush at the elevators, he used the stairway. "He's older than I am," Ben-Gurion later explained when he was accused of excessive courtesy toward a German. The meeting was carefully prepared in both Bonn and Jerusalem. Ben-Gurion had come to ask for money and weapons. During preliminary talks with banker Hermann Abs and others, it was determined that Ben-Gurion would ask Adenauer for a $250 million loan for the development of Israel's southern Negev region. Germany would transfer the money to Israel in ten annual payments. Earlier, Shimon Peres had settled with Franz Josef Strauss that Germany would "loan" Israel—actually hand over without receiving payment—military equipment from NATO surpluses. Strauss said Adenauer's approval was needed, and Ben-Gurion decided to ask for it himself. It was decided that the two leaders would not speak of establishing diplomatic relations; the Germans, concerned about their relations with the Arab world, were not interested in that.

The conversation lasted nearly two hours. Adenauer spoke in German, which Ben-Gurion understood. Ben-Gurion spoke in English and his words were translated. They spoke of the new Israel and the new Germany, of the Nazis and the extermination of the Jews. Ben-Gurion explained to the German chancellor that the murder of European Jewry, Israel's largest pool of potential immigrants, had almost prevented the establishment of the Jewish state. Their absence is felt to this very day, the prime minister said. Adenauer inquired about the birthrate in Israel. Immigrants from Arab countries have an average of eight children per family, Ben-Gurion replied, but immigrants from Europe average only two. Adenauer said that it was not enough.

Then Ben-Gurion asked for the loan to develop the Negev. That same morning, when he was dressing for the meeting, his aide, Yitzhak Navon, later to be Israel's fifth president, had entered the room and remarked that $250 million spread over ten annual payments was a negligible sum for the Germans. He proposed that Ben-Gurion ask for a billion. The prime minister noted to his aide that, with everything agreed on in the preliminary talks with the Germans, he could not now ask for such a fantastic sum. Well then, Navon said, maybe it's worth asking for $750 million. Ben-Gurion rejected this proposal as well. But a moment later, when he was at the door, Ben-Gurion spun around to his aide and said he would ask for half a billion, twice the planned sum. This he did. "The economic argument," Ben-Gurion later wrote, "was that the Negev should be turned into a great industrial center for export to the countries of Asia and East Africa, through Eilat and the Red Sea." He gave Adenauer a moral argument as well: "I do not know if the youth of Germany today know what Nazi Germany did, but I have no doubts that one day they will know the horrifying truth—and every young German will feel sorrow and disgrace for these terrible crimes. I want to establish, with your help, productive projects in Israel that—when German youth see them or read about them—will impart a sense of moral satisfaction about the Germany of Adenauer that, to the extent that it was possible, made up for the sins of Hitler's Germany."[13]

Adenauer promised Ben-Gurion the loan, also approving the agreement reached by Peres and Strauss. Then the two leaders invited the reporters and photographers in and publicly displayed their friendship and, for a moment, even their high spirits as well. One of the photographs taken then was later used in a Herut election poster. It showed Ben-Gurion amicably laying his hand on Adenauer's arm. Adenauer told reporters that aid to Israel would bring dividends in the future; Ben-Gurion reiterated that the Germany of today was not the Germany of yesterday. The atmosphere was one of historic reconciliation.*

Back in Israel, Ben-Gurion was greeted with angry editorials, with censure even from Natan Alterman, and with a no-confidence motion in the Knesset. Again, as so often in the past, it was argued that Ben-Gurion's German policy constituted a gross insult to the victims of the Holocaust. Yet by that time Ben-Gurion already knew that Isser Harel would soon be bringing him Adolf Eichmann.

---

* In contrast with Nahum Goldmann, who took care whenever possible to get written agreements from Adenauer, Ben-Gurion satisfied himself with the chancellor's oral commitment. Over the next few months, lengthy correspondence was necessary to clarify what, in fact, had been concluded between the two leaders. The two men exchanged no fewer than nineteen letters. The result was satisfactory. The Germans kept most of Adenauer's promises.[14]

PART VI

TRIAL:

Eichmann in Jerusalem

18 | "Let Them Hate, and Let Them Go to Hell"

On the evening of May 11, 1960, a man known to his neighbors as Ricardo Clement returned from work to his home on Garibaldi Street in a suburb of Buenos Aires, Argentina. Two cars waited at the street corner. When the man approached, one car blinded him with its bright lights. Two men jumped out, knocked him down, and pushed him into the second car. They gagged him, tied his hands and feet, put dark glasses over his eyes, shoved him onto the floor, and covered him with a blanket. He was not given a knockout injection; the doctor they had brought with them warned that a drug could kill him. The car sped to a hideout forty minutes away, one of several the abductors had rented.

There the abductors asked Clement who he was. After first trying to deny it, he quickly realized that there was no point. "My name is Adolf Eichmann," he confessed. He understood immediately who his kidnappers were—agents of the Mossad. "I know Hebrew," he told them and, to their astonishment, began reciting the first verses of the Bible: "*Bereshit bara Elohim et hashamaim veet haaretz. . . .*" They talked; later he signed a statement that he was prepared to stand trial in Israel. Then they dressed him in the uniform of an airplane steward, supplied him with the necessary papers, sedated him with drugs, and boarded him on a special El Al plane waiting at the international airport. The aircraft had brought an Israeli delegation headed by Abba Eban to Argentina's sesquicentennial celebrations; Eban would return on another plane.[1]

¶

Eichmann had been born fifty-four years earlier in the city of Solingen in the Rhineland and had grown up in Linz, Austria. He had joined the Nazi party in 1932, a few months after Hitler came to power, and volunteered for service in the SS a few months after that. When the Nazis established the Third Reich, Eichmann moved to Germany. He first worked for the security services and then in the Central Office for Reich Security, which controlled, among other things, the police force and the Gestapo. Eichmann dealt with Jewish matters, including the emigration of Jews from the Reich. As anti-Jewish restrictions multiplied, the job grew more important, and Eichmann was promoted to head of the department. In his work, he dealt with the leaders of the resident Jewish community and with Zionist functionaries in Berlin, Vienna, and Prague. He read books about the history of Zionism, followed the Jewish press, and learned snatches of Yiddish and Hebrew.

During the war, Eichmann was involved in the deportation, expulsion, and extermination of Jews. In January 1942 he took part in an interdepartmental meeting in the Berlin suburb of Wannsee to discuss the organization of the extermination program. Eichmann did not make policy—he carried it out. By war's end he was an *Obersturmbannführer*, the equivalent, in the U.S. army, of a lieutenant colonel. He played a central role in organizing the transport of Jews to the death camps, and he visited some of the camps himself.[2] He was not the most senior officer in the program, but in general he was the highest Nazi official who had direct contact with Jewish leaders. To them he seemed omnipotent, and his name came up frequently during the Nuremberg trials.

After the war, Eichmann was held in an American army prison camp, but he succeeded in escaping before his identity was discovered. He eventually reached Argentina with his family, thanks to the help of fellow SS veterans. Two Holocaust survivors, Simon Wiesenthal from Vienna and Tuvia Friedman from Haifa, spent years gathering every scrap of information on his location; from time to time he was mentioned in the press.[3]

One day in September 1957, Fritz Bauer asked to see Eliezer Shinar, Israel's representative in Bonn. Bauer, a German Jew who had been arrested several times by the Nazis but had managed to escape, was now the chief prosecutor for the West German state of Hessen. Bauer gave Shinar information that had just reached him—Eichmann was living in

Buenos Aires. Bauer was giving Israel the information, he explained, because he feared that, if he put the matter in the hands of his own government, someone would make sure that Eichmann wasn't extradited or might even warn him. Only one person knew of Bauer's contacts with Israel—Georg August Zinn, Hessen's premier and, like Bauer, a member of the Social Democratic party.

Isser Harel sent a Mossad man to the German prosecutor, who gave him the name of his informant in Argentina. Harel sent an agent to confirm the information, but the informant and the agent were unable to locate Eichmann. The Mossad did not pursue the matter.* Two years later Bauer again contacted the Mossad; this time he could not reveal the name of his informant, he said, but he had a name and address for Eichmann. Harel consulted Attorney General Haim Cohen, and the two of them went to Ben-Gurion. They told him that, if Israel did not act, Bauer would pass the information on to his government and propose that it ask Argentina to extradite Eichmann to Germany. "I suggested asking him not to tell anyone and not to ask for his extradition, but to give us the address," Ben Gurion wrote in his diary. "If it turns out that he is there, we will catch him and bring him here. Isser will take care of it."[5] The name was correct, but when the Mossad agents reached the address Bauer had obtained, they learned that Ricardo Clement and his family had moved; one of the neighbors directed the agents to Garibaldi Street.

The mission was complicated and dangerous; Harel directed it himself. Ben-Gurion was kept informed on the progress of the operation. While

* Harel is almost the only source for the history of the Mossad, about which he has written extensively. But his books have to be read carefully. When he assumed responsibility for the intelligence organization in the early 1950s, he claims he put Eichmann at the top of his "most-wanted list," along with Josef Mengele. But the hunt for Nazi criminals was not really a high priority; the Israel-Arab conflict and the organization of the mass immigration were both much more urgent, and Harel's energy went into tracking down spies, terrorists, and sundry opponents of the Ben-Gurion–Mapai regime. His book about Eichmann's capture indicates that the leads came from Fritz Bauer; apparently, the Mossad had not been actively searching for the man.

One of Harel's autobiographical books includes a chapter called "Why Didn't We Catch Mengele?" The question is not really answered. It is not clear whether Josef Mengele, who conducted the horrendous "medical experiments" at Auschwitz, managed to evade Israel despite the Mossad's efforts to capture him or whether the efforts were minimal. In another book Harel criticizes Israeli army intelligence for failing to catch Gestapo commandant Heinrich Müller. It seems that Israel did not see hunting down Nazi criminals as an overriding national mission, just as the leaders of the state-to-be had not given vengeance high priority.[4]

Eichmann was still being held by his kidnappers in Buenos Aires, the prime minister wrote in his diary: "If there is no error in identification, this is an important and successful operation." Even when Harel notified him that Eichmann was in Israel, Ben-Gurion reacted with caution and demanded that someone who had known Eichmann personally confirm the identification. Harel found Moshe Agami, formerly a Jewish Agency representative in Vienna, who had met Eichmann in 1938 and was able to identify him.[6] Harel then notified Fritz Bauer of the mission's success.

Two hours later, on May 23, 1960, Ben-Gurion made the most dramatic announcement the Knesset had ever heard, pronouncing only two sentences: "It is my duty to inform you that a short time ago the security services apprehended one of the most infamous Nazi criminals, Adolf Eichmann, who was responsible, together with the Nazi leadership, for what they called 'the final solution to the Jewish problem'—in other words, the extermination of six million of Europe's Jews. Adolf Eichmann is already imprisoned in this country, and will soon be brought to trial in Israel under the Nazi and Nazi Collaborators (Punishment) Law of 1950."[7]

Israel was stunned. "The evening that Eichmann's capture first became known," Natan Alterman later wrote, "a Jewish woman walking down a Tel Aviv street was surprised to see people standing together reading newspapers fresh off the presses. The entire street seemed to be still, everyone reading something from hastily grabbed pages—as when war is declared. She approached one of the groups and saw what was written in large letters at the head of the page. Adolf Eichmann has been captured and is already in Israel. She saw it. She stood for a moment, wavered, and fell in a faint." But this was the moment to stand tall and proud: "Rise to your feet, Jewish woman," Alterman wrote.[8] "It is hard to remember any other instance of emotion and shock like the one that hit us this week," one of the newspapers said.[9] The key word in all that was said and written in those days was "we"; the Israelis had not known, since the Declaration of Independence, so deep a sense of national unity.

The immediate enthusiasm was for the operation itself. The phrase "the Israeli security services" had a mystery that sparked the imagination, that conjured up exploits of daring and sophistication. In the preceding weeks, Bauer and Harel had encouraged the rumor that Eichmann had found haven in Kuwait, like other Nazi criminals who were said to be hiding in Arab countries and working from there to destroy Israel.[10] The day after his announcement in the Knesset, Ben-Gurion stated in a letter:

"In Egypt and Syria the Nazis' disciples wish to destroy Israel, and this is the greatest danger awaiting us."*[11]

Many saw Eichmann's capture as a victorious moment in Israel's eternal struggle for survival. "Putting Eichmann on trial before a Jewish court in Israel will compensate for the inhuman and chaotic emptiness that has marked Jewish existence from the day the Jews went into Exile until now," Natan Alterman wrote.[13] Yet beyond the momentary pride, and deeper than the need to see a just punishment and to take revenge, were the horrifying memories and the pangs of shame and guilt. Memory tormented many Holocaust survivors, both old and young, imprisoned as they were behind a wall of silence. The trial of Adolf Eichmann, they knew, would force them to confront their memories, to recount them for the first time, parents to children, children to parents. The emotional explosion set off by the sudden announcement of Eichmann's arrest expressed their almost unbearable anxiety over what they would discover.

In his letters and interviews during the year between the arrest and the trial, Ben-Gurion often emphasized that the man Adolf Eichmann was of no interest to him; he was concerned only with the historic importance of the trial itself. "It is not the punishment that is the main thing here but the fact that the trial is taking place, and is taking place in Jerusalem," he stated, adding that not only Eichmann and his deeds but the entire Holocaust would come before the court.[14] Ben-Gurion had two goals: One was to remind the countries of the world that the Holocaust obligated them to support the only Jewish state on earth. The second was to impress the lessons of the Holocaust on the people of Israel, especially the younger generation. In an interview with the *New York Times*, a draft of which he apparently approved before publication, Ben-Gurion explained that the world must learn from the trial where hatred of the Jews had led— and then it must be made ashamed of itself. He called the extermination machine "a soap factory." He also noted that not only Germany was guilty—Britain's refusal to allow Jews to immigrate to Palestine had led to hundreds of thousands of deaths. The trial, he said, could unmask other Nazi criminals and perhaps, also, their links with several Arab rulers. He claimed that the anti-Zionist propaganda coming out of Egypt was anti-Semitic and inspired by the Nazis. "They generally say 'Zionists,' but they mean 'Jews,' " he maintained. This led to the obvious conclusion

* In the first days after the announcement, Israel did not say that Eichmann had been taken from Argentina; this secret, also, was first published in a foreign magazine, *Time*.[12]

that the enemies of the State of Israel were the enemies of the Jewish people and that supporting Israel was equivalent to fighting anti-Semitism.

Ben-Gurion was then at the height of his power as prime minister. He did not need the Eichmann trial to shore up his political position. But as a man who thought in terms of history and philosophy, he realized that the Israeli revolution had left a number of basic problems unresolved. The future of the state was not guaranteed. Most Jews of the world had not come to live in Israel—the country had not become the center of the Jewish people. The retreat from Sinai four years earlier, under joint pressure from the United States and the Soviet Union, was still described as a shameful capitulation; it was proof of the limits of Israel's sovereignty and security. The younger generation was to learn that Jews were not lambs to be led to the slaughter but, rather, a nation able to defend itself, as in the War of Independence, Ben-Gurion told the *New York Times*.[15] In the early 1960s, young Israelis were losing their pioneer spirit, and only a handful settled in the Negev; their center of gravity already seemed to be somewhere between Tel Aviv and New York. The trial was meant to inspire them with national pride, to remind them that for them there was only one country in the world, that only one country could guarantee security for Jews, and that was the State of Israel.

In the summer of 1959 there had been riots in Wadi Salib, a poor neighborhood in Haifa inhabited mostly by immigrants from Morocco; the riots had spread from Haifa to other locations. For the first time since the mass immigration from the Arab countries began, there seemed to be a threat to the hegemony of the Ashkenazic establishment led by Mapai. The Holocaust was foreign to the Sephardic immigrants. "They lived in Asia or Africa and they had no idea what was being done by Hitler, so we have to explain the thing to them from square one," Ben-Gurion later remarked.[16] Something was required to unite Israeli society—some collective experience, one that would be gripping, purifying, patriotic, a national catharsis.

The Eichmann trial would also enable Mapai to reassert its control over the heritage of the Holocaust, which it had lost to Herut and the parties of the left. The trial was meant, therefore, to expunge the historical guilt that had been attached to the Mapai leadership since the Kastner trial; it was to prove that—despite the ties with Germany, despite the reparations agreements and the arms deals—the Ben-Gurion administration was not insensitive to the Holocaust.

Thus, Ben-Gurion was incensed when Nahum Goldmann, president of the World Zionist Organization, echoed several foreign newspapers in proposing that Eichmann be tried not by an Israeli court but rather by a special international court. Martin Buber was of a similar mind: "I do not think that the victim should be the judge as well," the philosopher said.[17] Ben-Gurion considered the proposal a challenge to Israel's sovereignty and gave Goldmann a dressing-down in an open letter: "The publication of your proposal in a newspaper aimed at world opinion is, whether you intended it or not, a harsh and serious blow to the sensibilities of the people in Israel (and I think not only in Israel) and to the country's honor." Goldmann responded immediately:

In the interview [in *Haboker*] I said that I have no doubts of Israel's right to judge Eichmann, and I expressed my faith in Israeli justice. I simply thought, and continue to think, that since Eichmann and the Nazis exterminated not only Jews, it would be worthwhile to invite those countries, many of whose citizens were also killed by him, to send their own judges. I emphasized that the president of the court must be an Israeli judge and that the trial itself must take place in Israel. What kind of injury is this to the nation and the state? In my opinion it is a great honor to the country if other countries send judges of their own to participate in a court whose president is an Israeli judge.*[18]

It was yet another historiographical and political dispute. "The Holocaust that the Nazis wreaked on the Jewish people is not like other atrocities that the Nazis committed in the world," Ben-Gurion wrote to Goldmann, "but a unique episode that has no equal, an attempt to totally destroy the Jewish people, which Hitler and his helpers did not dare try with any other nation. It is the particular duty of the State of Israel, the Jewish people's only sovereign entity, to recount this episode in its full magnitude and horror, without ignoring the Nazi regime's other crimes against humanity—but not as one of these crimes, rather as the only

---

* Goldmann was in Israel for a meeting of the Mapai central committee that dealt in part with relations between Israel and Jewish communities overseas, especially American Jewry. When Ben-Gurion noticed Goldmann he called out to him, "You are a wandering Jew!"[19] Ben-Gurion was equally sarcastic in writing: "In Israel there is complete freedom of speech, not just for the residents of the country, but also for tourists."[20] Goldmann did not put up a fight—if his proposal was not to be accepted, he responded, perhaps it was worthwhile at least to invite foreign observers to the trial.

crime that has no parallel in human history." According to Ben-Gurion, the Holocaust happened because the Jews did not live in their own country. "Anti-Semitism is caused by the existence of the Jews in the Exile," he wrote in this regard, in another letter. "When they are different from their neighbors they awaken fear or derision, and when they try to be like them, and as usual become more Catholic than the pope, they are repulsed."[21]

A few days after the exchange with Goldmann, Ben-Gurion received a letter from Joseph M. Proskauer, a New York judge and honorary president of the American Jewish Committee. The AJC was fighting Ben-Gurion's tendency to arrogate to Israel the right to speak in the name of world Jewry. Many questions were involved: What is Judaism? Who is a Jew? To what extent is the State of Israel a Jewish state? Is the life of a Jew in Israel more complete than the life of a Jew in any other country? All this had been gone over in a lengthy and agonizing correspondence between Ben-Gurion and the leaders of the American Jewish community. As the Eichmann trial approached, these questions came up again. Proskauer, too, called on Ben-Gurion not to try Eichmann in Israel but rather to hand him over to West Germany or to some international body. Attached to his letter was an editorial from the *Washington Post* arguing that Israel was not authorized to speak in the name of Jews from other countries. Proskauer warned that the Eichmann trial would hurt Israel's image in the United States. It would thus make it difficult for Israel's friends to persuade the administration to supply military aid. He also feared that the trial would reawaken anti-Semitic feelings. "What do you gain by it?" he asked, stating that the "emotional urge" to conduct the trial in Israel did not justify the damage it would cause.

Ben-Gurion responded with a long letter. He would admit only that Israel did not speak for Jews living in other countries. He would not, however, forgo Israel's claim to speak in the name of the Holocaust's victims; by insisting on that claim, he made them all into Zionists.[22] As in his conversation with Adenauer, he described the Holocaust victims as people lost to the State of Israel: "The Jewish state (which is called Israel) is the heir of the six million who were murdered, the only heir; for these millions, the opinion of the *Washington Post* notwithstanding, ·regarded themselves as sons of the Jewish people and only as sons of the Jewish people. If they had lived, the great majority of them would have come to Israel. The only historic prosecuting attorney for these millions is Israel, and for reasons of historic justice, it is the duty of the Israeli government, as the government of the Jewish state, whose foundations were laid by millions of European Jews and whose establishment was their dearest hope, to try their murderers."[23] Ben-Gurion repeated this argument in an interview with the *New York Times*.[24] He could not, of course, have known for certain that the victims would have gone to Israel. In fact, most of the victims were murdered because they remained in their countries and did not emigrate to Palestine, while it was possible to do so. There is no way of knowing how many of them thought of themselves as Zionists. The Nazis murdered them regardless of whether they considered themselves Zionist, anti-Zionist, or even Jewish. Ben-Gurion tended to ignore such subtleties.

As for the danger of anti-Semitism, the Israeli prime minister assured the honorary president of the American Jewish Committee: "There are anti-Semitic manifestations in America—we find these in all countries —but the American people are not anti-Semitic. I am not even prepared to accuse Sen. [J. William] Fulbright [a well-known critic of the Israeli government and then chairman of the Senate Foreign Affairs Committee] of an anti-Semitic attitude."[25] In a letter to an acquaintance in Israel who expressed similar fears, Ben-Gurion wrote: "If the anti-Semites want to hate—let them hate, and let them go to hell."[26]

In that same letter Ben-Gurion described himself as "a Jew who has no concern for what the Gentiles say."[27] Yet in his letter to Proskauer he quoted at length from editorials published around the world supporting Israel's right to try Eichmann; he was especially impressed with an article in Spanish published in a Dutch newspaper on the occasion of a state visit by the president of Argentina, Arturo Frondizi. The article that Proskauer had sent Ben-Gurion clearly discomfited the prime minister: "I take it that the *Washington Post*'s comments express not only the views of one of that important paper's writers but also those of a section of American public opinion," he wrote.

> But I do not believe that the writer speaks in the name of the United States or expresses the attitude of the American people. . . . The editorial contends that the government of Israel is not entitled to speak in the name of Jews in other countries or act on behalf of "an imaginary Jewish ethnic unit." The *Washington Post* is certainly not authorized to speak in the name of the Jews, and as for the existence of a "Jewish ethnic unit"—I am well aware that there are differences of opinion on this matter among many American Jews as well. But

it is a question of six million Jews who were murdered in Europe; they believed and felt with every fiber of their being that they belonged to a Jewish people and that there is such a thing as a Jewish people in the world.

He cited Chancellor Adenauer: "When Adenauer's Germany recognized the moral responsibility of the German people for the crimes of the Nazis, it undertook to pay reparations to the government of Israel. It did not accept the theories of the *Washington Post* [but] recognized that this state speaks on behalf of all the murdered Jews."[28] He was incorrect: Israel did not receive reparations from the Germans because it spoke "in the name of the murdered Jews," but because it had taken in survivors.

The whole thing obviously upset Ben-Gurion. "Israel does not need the moral protection of an international court," he said to the *New York Times*. "Only anti-Semites or Jews with an inferiority complex would say that it does."[29]

In Israel, the prime minister enjoyed unanimous public and political backing on the Eichmann question. In their enthusiasm, the newspapers immediately ruled that Eichmann should die. "There is but one sentence for genocide—death!" proclaimed *Maariv* the day after the announcement of his capture; a few days later it added, "Eichmann is not a human being." *Yediot Aharonot* wrote, "The fact that this arch-cannibal has finally been captured should raise our spirits and reaffirm man's faith in his creator." Even the normally restrained *Haaretz* accompanied its report of Eichmann's arrest with a drawing of a noose, the first in a long line of variations on that theme printed over the months that followed in the Israeli press.

"I hope I will not be accused of having religious tendencies if I say that the moment the news of Eichmann's capture was announced, the angel of death immediately prepared him a place in hell beside Hitler and Himmler. That is where he belongs," declared Communist Knesset member Moshe Sneh. "There is no room for legal considerations. There has to be a judicial procedure, and we will have it with all due order and process. But the verdict has already been determined." Earlier, Sneh had called Eichmann "a two-legged beast of prey." Shmuel Tamir published an article entitled "The Trial of Satan," evoking Judge Benyamin Halevy's characterization of Eichmann as the "devil" to whom Rudolf Kastner had sold his soul. The justices of the Supreme Court also referred to Eichmann as a "scourge," a "hangman," and a "monster."[30] Newspaper editors, as well as police stations, were flooded with proposals of methods for inflicting horrible tortures and cruel death on Eichmann; there were some who volunteered to kill him with their own hands, in public.

"The trial is not necesary for this defendant, whose name we need not soil our mouths by pronouncing too often," Moshe Sneh said. "This trial is necessary because we need to remind the world of what happened during World War II, something many would like to consign to oblivion."[31] When Israelis referred to "the world," they generally meant the press; in those days many Israelis had an almost mystic faith in the power of the international media to harm Israel or help it, and they deeply desired to win its support and favor. When Argentina protested the violation of its sovereignty and brought the matter up for discussion in the UN Security Council, the Israeli press responded with a real sense of injury. The Israelis were not satisfied with having laid their hands on Eichmann. They also demanded that "the world" recognize their moral and historic right to kidnap and try him.

In the light of these attitudes there was something naïve and unrealistic in Justice Minister Pinhas Rosen's request that the press observe the restraints of sub judice. The president of the Supreme Court, Yitzhak Olshan, also tried to halt what he saw as "the incitement of the masses." "A few weeks ago," Olshan wrote to Rosen, "I was shocked to read in several newspapers headlines along the lines of 'Eichmann to be killed with an ax or a rope? And if with an ax then by hand or mechanically?' And last Friday, *Maariv* printed a discussion under the headline: 'SHOULD EICHMANN BE EXECUTED?' . . . Were it not for the duty assigned them by law, [most judges] would refuse to sit on this trial given the atmosphere that is being created by the press."[32] Rosen spoke with the editors; the newspapers responded with sarcasm: "Are we to write, until the verdict, 'the suspected murderer of millions'?" *Davar* asked. Several members of the Knesset assailed Rosen for his warning.[33]

The legal basis for the trial of Eichmann had been laid ten years before his capture: the Law against Genocide and the Nazi and Nazi Collaborators (Punishment) Law were among the first laws enacted in Israel; both of them led the Knesset into moral and historical reflections on the lessons to be learned from the Holocaust. "The principal danger threatening the future of mankind, and of human culture, is the possibility that the precedent of Auschwitz will merge with the precedent of Hiroshima: if that happens, mankind is doomed," one member declared, adding that Israeli schools must "educate citizens of the world," who will be aware of their personal responsibility for crimes of the state and demonstrate concern for the fate of man and world peace. Another member said that she could not forget the horrible brutalities committed against the Armenian people. "The nation must be educated to tolerance from the day of birth," she stated. "Not just 'love thy neighbor as thyself,' but tolerance, that the yellow or black man is equal to the white man."[34]

In debating the Law against Genocide, the Knesset focused on two critical issues that were to recur as part of the endless debate over the lesson to be learned from the Holocaust: the death penalty and the limits to obedience. Golda Meir said that she rejected the death penalty in principle, but in this case she would vote in favor. "We, the Jewish people, we should be the last to act as exemplars of generosity with regard to these criminals," she said. The law finally passed by the Knesset adopted the provisions of the international convention on genocide drafted by the United Nations: it mandated the death penalty. Yosef Lamm, a Mapai Knesset member, proposed considering as an extenuating circumstance the fact that a man accused under the law acted "in obedience to an order or to a law, so long as he did all that was in his power to mitigate the serious consequences deriving from the crime." Menahem Begin opposed this: "Acting in obedience to a genocidal law cannot diminish the degree of responsibility for the genocide committed: every man has the duty to rebel against such a law." Lamm immediately withdrew his proposal.[35]

The anti-Nazi law listed a series of acts committed during the Second World War and classified them as crimes against the Jewish people, crimes against humanity, and war crimes. When the minister of justice submitted the legislation to the Knesset, he was hard put to explain why, in fact, it was needed: no one then thought it possible that Adolf Eichmann would be tried in Israel. Apparently, apart from answering the need to punish Jews who collaborated with the Nazis, it was to a large extent a declarative law, enacted because of a widespread feeling that it was "inconceivable" not to enact it. The Law against Genocide, Rosen said, was meant to prevent genocide in the future. It was intended to provide protection to minorities, a matter of particular interest to the State of Israel, "in consideration of the special position of the Jewish people in the Diaspora." The Nazi and Nazi Collaborators Law, by contrast, "made a statement about the past," Rosen said: it declared that "we will not forget or forgive." The law also gave expression to the revolution that had taken place in the political status of the Jewish people, the minister added. Previously, the Jewish people had not had the authority to judge Nazi criminals in their own courts; thus the need for "the Jewish people and the State of Israel to respond to the injustice committed against the Jewish people." This rationale was not accurate: courts in other democratic countries had convicted Nazis in the name of their own Jewish citizens. Rosen himself mentioned Britain and Holland. In saying that the "Jewish people" had not previously been able to bring Nazi criminals to justice, Rosen once again expressed the tendency to identify the Jewish people with the State of Israel.[36] Members of the Knesset competed to reinforce the declarative and symbolic elements of the law and to make it more severe. Several members demanded that the law apply solely to the extermination of the Jews.[37]

On the face of it, the wording of the law does seem to render crimes against the Jewish people more serious than crimes against humanity. A person could be convicted of crimes against the Jewish people for having done less serious things than those required to convict him of crimes against humanity: thus, the primary crime against the Jewish people is "manslaughter"; the primary crime against humanity is "murder." This issue was addressed in the opinion of the Tel Aviv district court, which determined that such a discriminatory interpretation was not what the law intended.[38]

In submitting the bill to the Knesset, Rosen commented that it included a series of deviations from "established principles" of justice and due process. First, it was a retroactive law: it set out to punish deeds that were not necessarily defined as crimes when they were committed; in fact, the State of Israel had not even been in existence at the time. Second, it was an extraterritorial law: it was meant to punish criminals for deeds committed outside the borders of the state. Third, though one of the defining elements of a criminal act is criminal intent, the Nazi and Nazi Collaborators Law declared it sufficient to prove the act itself, without consideration of criminal intent. Fourth, while an established principle holds that a person cannot be punished more than once for the same crime, the proposed law allowed for the trying of criminals who had already been punished for the same offense in other countries. Fifth, the proposed law allowed the prosecution to deviate from accepted rules of evidence, permitting, among other things, hearsay evidence. Sixth, criminal law generally recognizes a period of limitations, after which it is no longer possible to bring a person to justice for a crime, but the Nazi and Nazi

Collaborators Law contained no statute of limitations for crimes against the Jewish people and crimes against humanity, though it did for war crimes and membership in criminal organizations, such as the SS. The chairman of the Knesset's Constitution, Law, and Justice Committee said that these deviations were meant to express the Jewish people's "bitterness and protest" against what it had suffered during World War II.[39]

A member of Mapam, Moshe Erem, demanded changing the law's name, using the word "Fascist" instead of "Nazi," since the Nazis were only one manifestation of the "poison and impurity" that also produced colonialism, imperialism, and so on. Here yet another debate ensued over the question of whether the attempt to exterminate the Jewish people was unique. Erem also wanted to expand the law to include racist provocation, and provocation to war in general—that is, to take the meaning of the Holocaust beyond the borders of Zionism and the Jewish people.[40] Similarly, there was a dispute about whether the history of Nazism contained a period of legitimacy: the proposed law stated that the Nazis and their accessories were to be punished only for acts committed after the enactment of the Nuremberg laws in 1935, as if the Nazi dictatorship had not harmed Jews before that. At the initiative of Zorach Warhaftig (National Religious party), the Knesset broadened the application of the law to include the entire Nazi period, beginning on 30 January 1933.[41]

§

About two weeks before Ben-Gurion announced Eichmann's capture, a new attorney general, Gideon Hausner, had taken office. A well-known Jerusalem lawyer, then forty-five years old, he was born in Lvov, Poland. He had arrived in Israel at the age of twelve, when his father—who had previously been a member of the Polish Sjem and had served briefly as secretary to Theodor Herzl—was appointed the Polish consul in Palestine. Hausner, a leading member of the Progressive party, had been one of its candidates for the Knesset. He understood—and shared—Ben-Gurion's goals for the trial.

In his memoirs, Hausner recounted his preparations for the trial, describing them as a production far more elaborate than what was necessary to convict Adolf Eichmann in court. Hausner sought to design a national saga that would echo through the generations. To do so, he had to make a series of decisions, some of them historiographical, some educational, some political, some almost dramaturgical. From time to time he received specific instructions from Ben-Gurion.

The police were assigned to interrogate Eichmann. They set up a special division called "Bureau 06" for this purpose (the force had had five bureaus until then); at one point the bureau employed more than fifty people. Eichmann cooperated. He was questioned in German; his words were recorded, transcribed, and submitted for his approval. He signed the pages after carefully correcting their wording. The first difficulty facing the investigators was clarifying the twists and turns of the far-flung bureaucratic apparatus that the Nazis had established to exterminate the Jews and identifying Eichmann's precise place within it: All this was necessary because Eichmann was to base his defense largely on the argument that he had not been responsible for the crimes attributed to him. Thus it was necessary to discover who was in charge of what, who was subordinate to whom—names, ranks, offices, divisions, branches, major departments. Eichmann's division was called IV-B-4. The police were almost overwhelmed by what was expected of them; officer Avraham Zeliger, who directed the investigation, later wrote, "We weren't even sure we knew what a historic trial was."[42]

The investigators were assisted by archives and research institutions in a number of countries; their main resource was the material that had been gathered for the Nuremberg trials—a huge mass of paper. "I soon began to 'gulp down' the sagging volumes of the Nuremberg trials at the rate of one volume per day," Hausner wrote. "I had to learn Eichmann's statement forward and backward and had to digest the huge piles of documents—thousands of multipaged documents gathered by Bureau 06. It was necessary to decide finally which of them would be submitted to the court as exhibits. In addition, I had to become deeply acquainted with the literature of the Holocaust, to prepare the opening statement, and to go over the legal arguments. All this demanded a supreme effort. I locked myself up in the Sharon Hotel in Herzlia with two carloads of books and files and began to work almost without stop, in total isolation." This part took six weeks.

He discovered that the police had prepared a good case, from a legal point of view; they proposed to base the major part of the prosecution on documents. To do so was a great advantage, Hausner admitted: "What is written in a document speaks for itself, in black and white, unlike a person giving testimony. There is no need to depend on memory, years after the event. A document cannot be cross-examined and cannot be broken under interrogation." The use of documents was the principal prosecution strategy of the Nuremberg trials as well. "Everything went smoothly and efficiently there," Hausner wrote, "but that is also one of the reasons the trials did not shock the heart."

To convict Eichmann, it would have been sufficient to present the documents: "Even a fraction of them would have been enough to convict him ten times over," Hausner wrote. But he wanted to shock the heart: "I wanted people in Israel and the world to come closer, through the trial, to this great catastrophe." Like Ben-Gurion, he thought about affecting younger people. "This is a generation with no grandfathers and grandmothers. It does not understand what happened, because it has not gone into the facts. The gap between the generations has turned into a chasm, creating repugnance for the nation's past. 'How did they allow themselves to be led like lambs to the slaughter?' is the common question." To bring the youth closer to the nation's past would require more than just paper, Hausner felt: "We need a massive living re-creation of this national and human disaster." That role fell to the witnesses. In his memoirs, Hausner emerges as the impresario of a national-historic production. Proving guilt and exacting punishment were not the only objects, he wrote; there was also the need to teach. Any trial must capture attention, reflect an event, and impart a lesson. "This is all the more true of a special trial like this one. It was clear to me that it was possible to achieve that goal and to give the information to people in Israel and to the entire world . . . through the words of witnesses." The prosecutor thus found no need for the witnesses to prove a direct connection between the defendant and a specific crime. "I wanted them to talk about the various stages of the extermination from the beginning, about the large Jewish cities and what had happened to them, about the communities and people who tried to resist the disaster, and about the extermination camps themselves. More than anything else, I wanted people to report what they had seen with their own eyes and experienced with their own flesh." He found a large number of witnesses through the testimony-gathering division of Yad Vashem, the Holocaust memorial. At the head of the division stood Rachel Auerbach, a historian and survivor of the Warsaw ghetto; over the years the division had interviewed hundreds of Holocaust survivors. The list of witnesses that Auerbach prepared for Hausner largely determined the character of the trial.

When, years later, she described her part in the preparations, Auerbach spoke in the plural, apparently expressing a feeling that prevailed among the survivors. At first they feared that the authorities wanted to concentrate on Eichmann's personal guilt, holding a small criminal trial instead of a great historic trial. "It looked as if we would have to work hard to persuade the people in charge . . . to expose the full extent and unique character of the extermination of European Jewry," Auerbach wrote. But when it became clear that Hausner also wanted a large trial, with witnesses, Auerbach proposed focusing immediately on the extermination itself, without losing too much time on the early stages of the persecution of the Jews. She also proposed that the witnesses be led to point out "special phenomena" that would underline the Nazis' "odiousness and satanic cruelty." She listed such examples as the torture inflicted on victims before extermination; the special mistreatment of women, children, the elderly, the ill, and religious Jews in traditional dress; the purposefully drawn-out suffering of those condemned to die in the gas chambers with an insufficient quantity of gas; the brutal smashing of babies to save ammunition; burning people alive; and finally, "that greatest of all earthly horrors—the mass graves, in which the injured shifted and whimpered for entire days and nights after the executions." The survivors also insisted on prominent mention of deeds of self-sacrifice, resistance, rebellion, revenge, and flight, Auerbach wrote. Righteous gentiles and the non-Jewish victims of the Holocaust should be cited also, they advised.

In the end, Auerbach was not satisfied. Too much time was devoted, she thought, to the administrative aspects of the crime as reflected in the documents, and too little time to the human agonies of the extermination itself.[43] The transcript shows, however, that in general the trial was conducted according to Auerbach's suggestion, including emphasis on the details of the horrors and on the resistance to the Nazis. Most of the witnesses were those she had suggested: "I chose from among them those with a talent for expressing themselves," Hausner related. He was also attentive to the overall social profile, so that the story would come "from all parts of the public," he wrote. "Professors and housewives, craftsmen and writers, farmers and merchants, laborers and doctors, officials and industrialists. The Holocaust was inflicted on all parts of the nation, and people from all walks of the nation came to testify about it." Actually, Hausner tended to favor well-known witnesses whose stories had already been published.

At the start, Hausner encountered reluctance: Many Holocaust survivors feared the encounter with the unspoken terrors of the past, some also feared that they would not be believed. The closer the date of the trial came, though, the more people asked to testify. "We were flooded with offers," Hausner wrote. The urge to tell began to overwhelm the need to remain silent. "I invited a metalworker to testify on the events and on the underground in one of the large ghettos in Poland," he related. "After his testimony was recorded, I received an offer from a famous public figure to testify about events in that same place. But I wanted the metalworker to tell the story in his simple words, so I left him on the list of witnesses and was forced, unfortunately, to do without the testimony of the public figure, who has not forgiven me to this day." David Ben-Gurion demanded that Hausner call up Zalman Shazar, formerly minister of education and later Israel's third president. Ben-Gurion thought that Shazar was the right person to speak generally about European Jewry, before the Holocaust and after it. But Hausner feared "the extreme emotionalism characteristic of that exceptional and dear man"; when he decided to assign the historical testimony to Salo Baron of Columbia University, Ben-Gurion was hurt.

There was something about which the prime minister was even more sensitive—West Germany. Shortly after Eichmann was arrested, Adenauer contacted Ben-Gurion and asked him to take action to ensure that the trial did not waken a new wave of anti-German sentiment in the world; Franz Josef Strauss spoke of this in a secret conversation with Ben-Gurion in Paris.[44] The Germans had grounds for their fears: the countries of the Communist bloc, led by East Germany, wished to exploit the trial to identify the Federal Republic with the Nazis, as if East Germany had no share in the guilt. An East Berlin attorney named Friedrich Kaul appeared in Jerusalem with documents, some of them useful to the prosecution, demanding to participate in the trial as a civil prosecutor. When it was explained to him that Israeli law did not allow for such participation, Kaul called a press conference to protest. The focus of the matter was that West Germany had not done enough to arrest Nazi war criminals and had even employed some of them in the government. The man everyone was talking about was Hans Globke, one of Adenauer's close advisers; he had been involved in establishing links with Israel, including the reparations agreement. During the Nazi period, Globke had been employed by the interior ministry and had written one of the authoritative interpretations of the Nuremberg statutes. Together with Eichmann's men, Globke had had a hand in the deportation of Germany's Jews and the expropriation of their property.

"Kaul's documents were extremely incriminating," Hausner recalled. "I notified Ben-Gurion that I intended to submit them to the court. Ben-

Gurion did not want to hurt Adenauer and asked if it was possible to do without them. I responded that perhaps it was but that I would then be concealing important legal material relating to the charges and that I had no intention of doing so. Ben-Gurion felt uncomfortable and expressed his displeasure. . . . An unpleasant conversation ensued." Before allowing Hausner to use the material, Ben-Gurion sent Eliezer Shinar, Israel's representative in Bonn, to explain to Adenauer that from a legal point of view one could not keep these documents from the court. Adenauer, Shinar later reported, "did not show enthusiasm" but "responded with understanding." During the trial, Hausner took care to avoid attracting attention to Globke's role. On the other hand, he gave great prominence to the testimony of Heinrich Grüber, a Protestant clergyman who had been involved in efforts to help Jews and had even gone to Eichmann to plead for the lives of some of them. In the end, he was arrested and sent to a concentration camp. At the trial, he represented the good German. The message that Hausner assigned to the testimony was that "it was not necessary to be like Eichmann in Germany. It was possible to be like Grüber." The tactic was a matter of discretion—Israel could cause Adenauer great embarrassment, and discussions were still in progress over carrying out the promises Adenauer had made to Ben-Gurion in New York.

Proceeding cautiously, Hausner sought the advice of two leaders of the Warsaw ghetto uprising, Antek Zuckerman and his wife, Tzivia Lubetkin. The story of the uprising, like many other incidents Hausner was to bring up during the trial, was extremely sensitive. The question was how much weight the uprising should be given, what to bring into the open, and what to leave untold. The ghetto fighters had experienced considerable moral qualms and engaged in political struggles over their role in the ghetto and their responsibility for its eventual annihilation. The acrimonious dispute over the "two ways," which had started during the Kastner affair, had not yet been resolved. Obviously the ghetto fighters demanded that the trial endorse their way, not that of the Judenrat.

Finally, Hausner had to decide whether to limit the charges to specific actions of Eichmann's or to include the entire extermination campaign. This decision, too, was one of national proportions. "There were advantages to limiting the charges," Hausner later wrote, "to emphasize the incidents in which Eichmann acted with malice and evil beyond what was required by the orders he received"—for instance, in the extermination of Dutch Jewry. And such an approach would immediately controvert Eichmann's claim that he had only carried out orders. The disadvantage to the approach was that it would confine the evidence to those specific incidents at the cost of an opportunity to present the entire story of the Final Solution. But were he to submit broad charges, the prosecution would have to bring evidence that linked Eichmann to the entire range of crimes. Hausner was doubtful: if he didn't succeed, the defendant would "be acquitted of charges that were unproven or drafted too generally." In a regular trial, he explained, no great damage was caused when a defendant was acquitted on one count or another; even if Eichmann were acquitted on some counts, there would be enough proof to convict him of other crimes. "But then," Hausner wrote, "there would be room for the argument that he is not as bad as we described him and that we inflated the extent of his crimes. Then it is only one step to another fallacy, that the description of the Holocaust itself was inflated and exaggerated."

The decision was one of Hausner's most difficult; in the end he decided to submit broad charges that included crimes against Jews throughout the Nazi-occupied lands, judging that it would be possible to obtain conviction. Eichmann's "particular satanic deeds would be lost in the story as a whole and would not stand in the limelight," Hausner wrote, "but I thought it would be better that way."[45]

Before the trial could open, it was necessary to overcome another problem, more political than legal. According to the law, Eichmann had to be tried in the Jerusalem District Court. The composition of the panel of judges was in the hands of the court's president, and he could, if he saw fit, appoint himself. The president of the Jerusalem District Court was Benyamin Halevy, who had earlier compared Eichmann to the devil. Yitzhak Olshan, president of the Supreme Court, thought that for this reason it would be best if Halevy was not one of Eichmann's judges. Pinhas Rosen, the minister of justice, concurred. Olshan summoned Halevy to his chambers; Halevy announced that he indeed intended to appoint himself presiding judge. "Our conversation went on for more than an hour, and all my efforts to persuade him to abandon his intention came to naught," Olshan later recalled. "I pointed to all the objections around the world to hearing Eichmann's case in Israel. . . . . I brought up many similar reasons. I asked him what he would do if, at the beginning of the trial, the defense counsel proposed that he step down. Judge Halevy responded, without any hesitation, that he would refuse." Olshan explained that although he understood why Halevy wanted to preside over such a historic trial, the judge should put the country's interests first. "I could only imagine what the world's reaction, let alone Israel's, would be in the light of the principle that it was not enough for justice to be done, it had to be seen to be done," Olshan wrote. "All my efforts at persuasion were useless."[46]

Many years later, Halevy said that his verdict in the Gruenwald-Kastner case had earned him enemies in the Israeli establishment and that the government did not want him to sit on the Eichmann trial out of fear that he might probe too closely into the behavior of Jewish leaders during the Holocaust.[47]

When Halevy also refused to accede to pressure from the minister of justice, Olshan suggested passing a special law that would transfer the authority to determine the panel of judges in such cases from the president of the District Court (Halevy) to the president of the Supreme Court (Olshan himself). Rosen supported the proposal, but when it was made public, it caused a scandal. Herut's representatives in the Knesset came out in defense of Halevy's "right" to judge Eichmann and protested the "discrimination" against him. Olshan encouraged Rosen to hold his own, but Rosen was forced to accept a compromise—the presiding judge would be appointed by the president of the Supreme Court but the remaining judges by the president of the District Court.[48] So it was. Presiding over the bench was Supreme Court Justice Moshe Landau. Benyamin Halevy appointed himself as one of the judges and Yitzhak Raveh of the Tel Aviv District Court as the third; all of them were German-born.

The appearance of Eichmann's chosen defense attorney, Robert Servatius of Cologne, also demanded special legislation, since until then only Israeli citizens could appear in Israeli courts.[49] The Israeli government paid part of his fees, a total of $30,000.

The practical arrangements for the trial were made by the director-general of the prime minister's office, Teddy Kollek. His job included responsibility for the Government Press Office, so he had to provide technical support for the more than six hundred foreign correspondents who wished to cover the trial. They were offered simultaneous translation into several languages, as well as complete translations of the court records. Contrary to normal practice, the court allowed the Government Press Office to photograph court sessions, and for the first time in Israel a television camera was allowed into the chamber. Since the court had no hall large enough to seat so many reporters, it was decided to hold the trial in the auditorium of the new Beit Haam theater. Construction had to be accelerated so that it would be ready in time. "Not a bad place for the show trial David Ben-Gurion had in mind when he decided to have Eichmann kidnapped," Hannah Arendt noted in the important and provocative book that she wrote in the wake of the trial. [50]

19 | *"Six Million Times No!"*

The trial began in April 1961, about a year after Eichmann was brought to Israel; the charges were headed by the accusation that, "together with others," he had caused the murders of millions of Jews. Eichmann pleaded not guilty—"in the spirit of the charges," he was careful to say, as if he felt guilty in some other spirit. He sat within an armored glass cell built specially to protect him. Gideon Hausner, who first saw him when the trial opened, later wrote that he had "disconcerting eyes," which during the cross-examination "burned with a bottomless hatred." A closer look, the attorney general wrote, revealed that he also had "hands like talons"—a photograph of his fingers was published in the press and was, Hausner said, "frightening." In fact, the glass booth contained only a bland and balding man in a suit and eyeglasses, with a nervous tic at the corner of his mouth, leafing endlessly through the stacks of documents in front of him. But Hausner wrote that Eichmann was putting on a show: "The prince of darkness is a gentleman," he quoted from *King Lear*.*[1]

The trial got off to a slow start. The German defense attorney, round and red-faced Robert Servatius, had preliminary arguments. Israel, he said, had no authority to try Eichmann after having kidnapped him from Argentina; the law under which Eichmann was being brought to trial

---

* During the trial, Hausner tried to prove that Eichmann had murdered a Jewish boy with his own hands. The boy had stolen fruit from a cherry tree in the yard of Eichmann's house in Budapest. The court ruled that the charge was not proven.[2]

was invalid; Jewish judges could not judge him impartially. His arguments took up an entire exasperating week. The newspapers expressed their disappointment—this was not the way they had imagined the opening of this historical drama. One of Hausner's acquaintances warned him that he needed to be as brief as possible in responding to the defense's preliminary arguments: "Realize that there are six hundred reporters here from overseas. Most of them will stay here only for about a week. They won't even see the beginning of the trial proper. The legal dispute bores them. Think of what they will write in their newspapers." Hausner responded that this was a trial, not a show, but admitted that the man was right. He had momentarily forgotten the press, he wrote, as if in apology. In the meantime, he continued to work on his opening speech, which he intended to be a fundamental declaration of Israel's official attitude toward the Holocaust. When he completed it, he sent it to the prime minister for inspection and asked for comments. This was unusual procedure, another indication that the legal aspect of the event was not primary.

Ben-Gurion read only the first part, since the other sections, he later wrote, seemed to have no "special political significance." He requested three corrections, all aimed at protecting West Germany's image and diminishing the guilt of the German people; here was a leader dictating the historiography of his people. He even dictated the wording: "Every time reference is made to the crimes of 'the Germans,' it should, in my opinion, say 'Nazi Germany,' " the prime minister wrote to the attorney general.

He also suggested omitting the thesis that Nazism was inevitable. In general, Ben-Gurion wrote, it is doubtful whether anything in history was inevitable. Moreover, "it is almost clear to me," Ben-Gurion wrote, "that had Europe, and particularly France and England, not been blind and had it immediately risen up against Hitler when he entered the Rhineland in violation of the Versailles Treaty, when he entered Austria, and when he attacked Czechoslovakia, Hitler would have fallen and we would not have seen the Second World War and the Nazi atrocities against the Jews." The thesis that Nazism was inevitable seemed to Ben-Gurion a "pseudo-scientific excuse" for the Nazi regime, and he regarded it as weakening the prosecution. He also feared that the thesis would lead to a debate—"not necessary for our purposes"—over developmental trends of German history generally or even over the German character and whether there could really ever be such a thing as "a different Germany." Hausner eliminated the paragraph.

The third change that Ben-Gurion suggested was meant to emphasize

Hitler's guilt—apparently in contrast to the collective guilt of the Germans. "In my opinion Adolf Hitler should be given precedence over Adolf Eichmann, even though Eichmann is the defendant," the prime minister instructed the attorney general. "I think that you should mention first the main and central factor, Hitler, and only then Eichmann."[3]

Hausner was himself not yet satisfied, and he continued to look for an opening that would encapsulate the real content of the entire trial. The night before he was to speak in court he did not sleep at all. In the end, he scribbled a few sentences on a sheet of paper and woke his wife up. "It's OK," she said.[4] So his speech began:

> As I stand before you, judges of Israel, to lead the prosecution of Adolf Eichmann, I am not standing alone. With me are six million accusers. But they cannot rise to their feet to point an accusing finger toward the glass booth and cry out at the man sitting there, "I accuse." For their ashes are piled up on the hills of Auschwitz and the fields of Treblinka, washed by the rivers of Poland, and their graves are scattered the length and breadth of Europe. Their blood cries out, but their voices cannot be heard. I, therefore, will be their spokesman and will pronounce, in their names, this awesome indictment.
>
> The history of the people of Israel is steeped in suffering and tears. . . . Pharaoh in Egypt tortured and oppressed them and threw their sons into the river. Haman ordered them destroyed, murdered, and obliterated; Chmielnicki slaughtered them in masses; Petlura launched pogroms against them. But along this people's entire bloody way, from its emergence as a nation to this day, no other man has inflicted what Hitler's evil regime inflicted, through Adolf Eichmann, its agent sent to exterminate the Jewish people. No other example in the history of nations calls for an indictment like the one being heard here. Even the most bloodcurdling and grisly malefactions of Nero, Attila, and Genghis Khan—archetypes of barbarity and blood lust, watchwords of evil and infamy—pale beside the atrocities and terrors of the destruction that will be described in this court.*

---

* In the summer of 1947, Agudat Yisrael leader Yitzhak Meir Levin appeared before the UN commission of inquiry that later recommended the partition of Palestine into two states. Levin said that he was not appearing before the commission alone: "Six million Jewish souls are standing and crying out before you," the rabbi said. "Their blood is

This prologue set the stage for the entire trial: the proceedings were designed as an emotional experience more than an informative one. Even though Hausner tried to set apart the extermination of the Jews as a unique crime—genocide—he nevertheless presented the Holocaust as but one link in a long chain of anti-Semitic persecutions, which began in ancient times and went on through the Ukrainian pogroms of Bogdan Chmielnicki in the seventeenth century and of Simon Petlura in the twentieth. This view reflected the Zionist movement's conception of history and undoubtedly found favor with the Germans. The trial would, in the end, touch only in passing, if at all, on the factors that led to the Nazis' rise to power, the characteristics of their regime, and the causes that led millions of people to believe in and support them. The prosecutor did not analyze the nature of racism or what made it possible for the Nazis to use the state bureaucracy to murder Jews. "People have asked and will continue to ask themselves, 'How could it have happened? How was it possible in the twentieth century?' " Hausner said. "I fear that even we, at this trial, will not succeed in exposing the roots of this affliction." He charged that it was Adolf Eichmann who "planned, initiated, organized, and ordered others to spill the ocean of blood." But the first sentences of his speech clearly showed what was already known—it was not Adolf Eichmann's deeds that were at the center of the trial but rather the sufferings of the Jewish people. The opening speech also showed that the trial would not put any special emphasis on the duty of the individual to remain committed, even in wartime, to the basic principles of human morality. It would also almost completely ignore the ambiguities and dilemmas posed by the need to obey the law versus the responsibility to disobey "manifestly illegal" orders. The trial would emphasize both the inability of the Jews to resist their murderers and their attempts to rebel. Hausner would almost completely ignore the Judenrats.

At the same time, Hausner peppered his speech with distinguished names—Heinrich Heine and Sigmund Freud, Albert Einstein and Marc Chagall. In the Zionist part of the speech, he mentioned Prime Minister Ben-Gurion. This section was written in a spirit of national unity that was not, in those days, much evident in Israeli politics. Hausner invoked

---

churning and will not be silent." In the winter of 1952, Dov Shilansky told the Tel Aviv District Court that he had not gone alone to the foreign ministry with that bomb in his briefcase. "Six million skeletons" had gone with him, he said. The ceremonious, biblical-sounding expression "judges of Israel" appeared in a verdict handed down by Moshe Silberg against a kapo.[6]

the religious and the nonreligious, the left and the right. The history of the Jews in Europe was presented as the history of the entire Jewish people, ignoring the Jews of the Arab world.

From a Jewish point of view, European Jewry was, before the Holocaust, the heart of the nation, the source of its vitality. The vast majority of great thinkers and Jewish leaders lived or came from Europe: the renowned Torah scholars, the heirs of the Gaon, Rabbi Eliahu of Vilna in the famous Volozhin yeshiva; the Slobodka yeshiva was there, in a suburb of Kovna, continuing the tradition of Lithuanian scholarship in the spirit of Rabbi Yitzhak Elhanan. From there came Rabbi Kook and the Hafetz Haim, from there came the visionaries of statehood, the shapers of Jewish nationalism, its leaders, thinkers, and writers. This was the Jewish community that in recent generations gave the people Herzl and Nordau, Ahad Haam and Pinsker, Bialik, Chernikowski, Sholem Aleichem and Shneur, Weizmann, Ben-Gurion, and Jabotinsky. From there came the bold pioneers who made their way to Israel, the people of the First and Second waves of immigration, who laid the foundations for the establishment of the state. From there came the dreamers and fighters who shaped the way of life, thinking, and image of the new Jew, men like A. D. Gordon, Berl Katznelson, Kurt Blumenfeld, Shmaryahu Levin, and many, many others. *

Then Hausner, like Ben-Gurion, described the Holocaust's victims as Zionists: "The millions who were exterminated were those who awaited the Jewish state and were not privileged to see it," he stated.[8] Twice during the course of his speech Hausner quoted poetry translated from the Yiddish.

* Of the people Hausner invoked, only two were still alive: Ben-Gurion and Kurt Blumenfeld. Blumenfeld, formerly a Zionist activist in Germany, was a close associate of Justice Minister Rosen.

The identification of Jewish history with that of the Jews in Europe characterized Ben-Gurion's thinking as well. "God's presence has left the Oriental Jewish community, and their influence within the Jewish nation has been reduced or ceased entirely," he once wrote. "In recent centuries, European Jewry has been at the nation's head, both in quantity and quality." European Jewry, he added, "shaped the image of the Jewish people throughout the world," while the Jews of Arab countries had played, during the previous centuries, "only a passive role in the people's history."[7]

His speech lasted eight hours. "I felt, in an actual physical way, that the trembling that went through me was also going through the audience that filled the hall, even though I stood with my back to the hall and my face to the judges," he later wrote. "When I finished, I heard quiet weeping in the audience."[9] The speech did indeed make a deep impression: Haim Guri, the poet who covered the trial for the newspaper *Lamerhav*, called Hausner one of "the great lamenters," and added: "Never has a man born of woman said to another man born of woman the things that Gideon Hausner said today to Adolf Eichmann."[10]

The trial became, from this point onward, the central event in the lives of many Israelis. People waited in line for hours at Beit Haam's doors for entrance passes. A television camera in the courtroom relayed the proceedings to a hall in the nearby Ratisbonne convent, which was also generally full. In those days Israel still had no television broadcasts, but much of the trial was carried live on radio; everywhere, people listened—in houses and offices, in cafés and stores and buses and factories. The stories of terror mixed in with the sounds of routine. Many schools canceled regular studies to allow students to listen. Some of the broadcasts were translated into Yiddish. Natan Alterman wrote of this: "You shivered on hearing the words of the language of the slaughtered and the burned: '*Mir transmitern die ershte zitsung fun Eichmann protses*' ('We present the first session of the Eichmann trial'). . . . In the history of the partnership and rivalry of these two tongues—Hebrew and Yiddish—there has been no moment so deep and exalted as this."[11]

Then came what Hausner in his memoirs called "the parade of the Holocaust witnesses"—more than a hundred men and women. Most were called as "background witnesses." The extermination of the Jews was a fact of history, and there was no need to prove it legally; the defense did not deny that it had taken place. The judges more than once evinced discomfort with the weak connection between the testimony and the defendant standing before them. Time after time they demanded that the prosecution concentrate on the deeds of the defendant himself, yet Hausner continued to call up the witnesses he had chosen, one after the other, representatives of countries, communities, ghettos, camps, even political factions. Once the witnesses were on the stand, it was almost impossible to stop them or demand that they be brief. For it was not the mass-murder policy that was at the center of their stories, not the general organization or the timetables of the trains for which Eichmann was responsible, but the terrors of death itself. The witnesses told their own stories, and that is what lent power to their words. Unlike Menahem Begin, who had early on presented the Holocaust as a collective experience in the history of the nation, Hausner understood its significance as a chapter in the life of each individual survivor. In encouraging them to unlock what had been sealed within their memories and to relate their personal stories, he redeemed them and an entire generation of survivors: Thus the trial served as a sort of national group therapy. This was the significance of the appearance of writer Ka-Tzetnik, Yehiel De-Nur, who fainted on the witness stand.

Hausner instructed the witnesses to recount every horrifying detail of the atrocities they had endured, including acts of sexual abuse. He had set the tone in his own opening statement: "In a cell for those sentenced to die of hunger, a dead prisoner was found with a second prisoner slumped over him—also dead—who had managed to tear the liver out of the first man's body. Death came to him as he consumed a human liver."[12] Testimony on sterilization was heard in closed session only when the witnesses themselves requested privacy. "Listening was torture," Hausner wrote. "I felt almost as if I were breathing the gases and the stench of the burnt flesh."[13] From time to time, people in the audience fainted and were taken out by first-aid crews. Haim Guri wrote: "Not one of us will leave here as he was before."[14]

Rivka Joselewska of Ramat Gan testified how SS soldiers had shot the people of her village after ordering them to undress and stand at the edge of a deep pit; her parents and sister were shot before her eyes by a single SS soldier. Then it was her turn. She held her daughter in her arms. The German asked her which to shoot first, her or her daughter. She did not answer. He shot the girl. Then he shot her and she fell into the pit. "I thought I was dead," she related. She was under a pile of bodies; many of them were still dying. She began to suffocate: "People were dragging, biting, scratching, pulling me down. Despite this, with my remaining strength, I rose upwards. . . ." Joselewska testified in Yiddish. At the time of the trial she was married and had two sons.[15]

At least twenty-five of the witnesses spoke of the abuse of children. Many years later Hausner said in an interview in *Maariv,* "I wanted testimony about the fate of young men and women, so that our own young people would hear what happened." He believed, he said, that it would be easier for them to identify with those of their own age, and he wanted them to see themselves in the place of the victims.[16] This did not happen immediately. The first witnesses induced revulsion rather than identification. Morris Fleischman, formerly a Zionist official in Austria, described the humiliation of Jews in the streets of Vienna. Haim Guri wrote of him: "I do not want to hear this short, broken man go on at length about his sufferings, his illnesses, his humiliation, or the cheers of the mob at the sight of the men of his community: 'We were beaten, we were hungry, we were wet like the walls of a urinal.' . . . I do not want to see him and I do not want to hear him. I would prefer today to be at the Nahal [army unit] parade, at the stadium, seeing handsome and strong people."[17]

A few months later the time came to bring up the matter of Hungary. "Now the shadow of another trial fell over the courtroom," Hausner wrote. First, Hausner took upon himself a political mission. "I asked all the groups of Hungarian immigrants to abstain from recriminations among themselves. This is the trial of the exterminator and not of his victims, I said." They promised restraint, but he knew that the issue involved accounts to be settled not only among the Hungarian immigrants but also among the entire Zionist leadership. "We had, then, to move carefully," he wrote. "The Hungarian part of the prosecution was prepared with great care, and every suggestion was examined from different points of view. Gabriel Bach (the deputy prosecutor) prepared the material. I told him that I disqualified in advance any witness who would exploit the trial to polemicize for or against Kastner." At least two witnesses were rejected on that basis. "Bach," Hausner wrote, "called up most of the witnesses in the Hungarian part and treated them with his usual tact. He succeeded in avoiding the traps." But during the testimony of one of the leaders of the orthodox Jewish community of Budapest, someone got up and shouted at him in Hungarian: "You reassured us so that we wouldn't flee, so that you and your families could save yourselves!"

Joel Brand was also called to testify. In his memoirs, Hausner recreated Brand's testimony with a mixture of compassion and reserve: "I realized that the man was a store of memories and no more. He had no present or future. His life had been cut off long before. . . . All he could do was to go back and retell the story of his failed mission, like a broken record, endlessly playing a single note."[18]

But the subject was again being aired, so Hausner could now do what his counterpart in the Kastner trial had not done: he submitted to the court a collection of documents from the Weizmann Archives setting out in detail the efforts that the Zionist leadership had made to convince the British authorities to enter into negotiations with the Nazis over the

proposal Brand had brought from Eichmann. The documents were meant
to prove that the leaders of the Jewish Agency had done their best.* "I
vehemently condemned the leaders of Britain and the United States,"
Hausner wrote later, quoting newspaper headlines from around the world:
"THE ENTIRE WORLD IS ON TRIAL HERE."[20] Hausner also submitted documents that set out the opposition of Arab leaders, chief among them
the Grand Mufti of Jerusalem, to the rescue of the Jews. The Mufti had
even gone to Berlin, where he had been received by Adolf Hitler. Hausner
wished to prove that there had been "firm links" between the Mufti and
Eichmann himself. The court ruled that the two had indeed met once,
but it could not determine whether this had been in Eichmann's office
or at a social gathering.[21]

Occasionally Hausner asked witnesses to tell why they had not organized resistance to the Nazis; Judge Halevy often asked the same. The
witnesses explained that, to the very last minute, they had not believed
that they were being led to their deaths, because the Nazis engaged in
all kinds of tricks to mislead them; besides, they had no weapons. Hausner
also called witnesses who had been involved in attempts at resistance.
"The truth about the underground and the resistance was important in
and of itself," and also desirable "for the education of our youth. Lacking
information, they constantly asked why there hadn't been more uprisings," he wrote. "Here was an opportunity to bring before the entire world
the hundreds and thousands of heroic deeds that were not generally
known." Hausner's attempts to convince the court that the story of Jewish
resistance was part of the story of Jewish extermination were only partly
successful. The court reluctantly allowed him to call Tzivia Lubetkin
and Antek Zuckerman, who told about the Warsaw ghetto uprising. It
also allowed him to call Abba Kovner, who submitted to the court the
well-known broadside he had written in the Vilna ghetto, in which he
had called on the Jews not to "go like lambs to the slaughter." Lubetkin,
Zuckerman, and Kovner came with prepared statements, and Hausner
seldom interrupted them with questions. The story of the revolt was
presented in court as its leaders wished it to be remembered.

During Kovner's testimony it was evident that the presiding judge,

---

* Eichmann testified that the "trucks-for-blood" offer had been a real one. Based on this
testimony and the historical material submitted to the court, attorney Shmuel Tamir
asked the Supreme Court to reopen the Gruenwald trial. Attorney General Gideon
Hausner opposed the request, and the Supreme Court accepted his opinion and rejected
Tamir's petition.[19]

Moshe Landau, was losing patience. When the witness reached his conclusion, the judge reprimanded the prosecutor.[22] Though Hausner wished
to expand even more on the revolt, he realized that the court would
forbid him—giving the undesirable impression that it doubted the truth
of the evidence he wished to submit. So he gave in—"with sorrow and
displeasure," he wrote.[23] He managed, nevertheless, to call up one more
witness who told about the Jewish partisans and another who told about
the Jewish Brigade. Shalom Holavski, of the partisans, presented the
court with a playing card he had found in the possession of a farmer not
far from his own town; it was made from a piece of Torah scroll that had
remained when the ghetto was destroyed. Attorney Aharon Hoter-Yishai
of the Jewish Brigade, the last witness, testified about his first encounter
with survivors of a concentration camp—all of them had crowded around
to kiss the Star of David he had fastened onto the brigade's car, he related.
"This story," Hausner wrote, "of a Jewish emblem arriving in blood-
soaked Europe to save the survivors, concluded the prosecution's testimony." The prosecution had presented 121 witnesses and several hundred
documents.[24]

Defense attorney Robert Servatius kept his cross-examination of the
witnesses to a minimum; their testimony did not directly touch on his
client's actions. He asked to call up a series of German witnesses, most
of them war criminals, but the attorney general refused to promise them
immunity, so they could not come to Jerusalem. Some of them were
interrogated overseas, but most showed no eagerness to help Eichmann.
The main defense witness was Adolf Eichmann himself. "It was strange
to hear the devil taking an oath in the name of God," Hausner wrote.[25]

As a witness, Eichmann did himself little good. He spoke like someone
who had been caught up in some sort of bureaucratic misunderstanding
that had to be cleared up. No, it was not his division that had decided
about the murder of the Jews but rather another division, and the things
that had been decided in his division his superiors, or his subordinates
—but at any rate not he—had decided. He had only done what he had
been told to do, to the letter. So there was no point to the question of
whether he had regrets. Of course he recognized that the extermination
of the Jews was one of the most horrible crimes in human history. But
he had only been a small cog in a big machine, merely following orders,
a tool in the hands of forces far more powerful than he. As such, he
washed his hands of the affair, like Pontius Pilate.[26] He spoke in long,
convoluted sentences, in the bureaucratese of the Nazi government. The

trial took on a grotesque dimension; the translators had difficulty understanding him and the judges preferred to speak to him directly in German.

"The notion that I was among the fanatics in persecuting the Jews is
greatly mistaken," Eichmann said.

> During the entire period after the war the fact that all my superiors
> have placed all the guilt on me has bothered and upset me. In fact,
> I never expressed myself in any terms that could indicate any fa-
> naticism on my part and there is no blood on my hands. Witnesses
> here have created an utter fabrication. The accumulation of testi-
> mony and documents in court seems very persuasive at first glance,
> but it can mislead. . . . I was asked by the judge if I would like to
> make a confession, as did the commandant of Auschwitz, [Rudolf]
> Höss. . . . Höss was the man who actually carried out the mass
> executions. My position is different. I never had either the authority
> or responsibility to give orders. I never carried out executions as
> Höss did. Had I received an order to carry out those executions, I
> would not have tried to simply evade it with a lame excuse. As I
> declared in my interrogation: with no choice but to obey orders,
> I would have shot a bullet into my head to resolve the conflict
> between conscience and duty.[27]

"He goes on spewing, in his Austrian accent, prepared answers to
prepared questions that make him out to be very small," Haim Guri
wrote. "Soon we will need a magnifying glass." Without, for all intents
and purposes, any sub judice restrictions on the coverage of the trial,
Guri could describe Eichmann's testimony as "an exhibition of fantastic
lies," and he also wrote, "If his testimony lasts another week we will burst
out in bitter weeping and ask that he be released, compensated, and given
a heartfelt apology for our groundless suspicions against him."[28]

Then came the cross-examination. Hausner often raised his voice; he
had a somewhat nasal, penetrating tenor. He laced his questions with
hostile sarcasm. Sometimes he stretched out his arm, pointing at the
defendant, his black robe forming a triangle from his wrist to his belt.
He looked like a huge raven—dark, frightening, very theatrical.

In his summation Hausner again quoted poetry. Of Rivka Joselewska's
testimony he said: "She frustrated the evil plan. They wanted to kill her
and she brought new children into the world. The dry bones took on
sinews and flesh, rose and covered themselves with skin, and the breath

of life came among them. Rivka Joselewska symbolizes the entire Jewish nation."[29]

The trial took four months, from April to August 1961; the verdict was handed down in December. It was concise, almost dry, notably different from the prosecutor's style. The judges based themselves largely on the documents and made little use of the witnesses' testimony. They seldom cited the suffering of the victims, concentrating instead on the crimes themselves. They were more methodical than the prosecution, more matter-of-fact, careful to avoid emotion and ideology.

First the judges ruled that the State of Israel had standing to try Eichmann because

> the terrible slaughter of millions of Jews by Nazi criminals, which almost obliterated European Jewry, was one of the great causes of the establishment of a state of survivors. The state cannot be disconnected from its roots in the Holocaust of European Jewry. Half the citizens of the country immigrated in the last generation from Europe, part of them before the Nazi slaughter and part afterwards. There is hardly one of them who did not lose parents, brothers, and sisters, and many lost their spouses, sons, and daughters in the Nazi inferno.

Gideon Hausner wrote of this: "So the State of Israel spread its protection, through its judicial arm, over the entire Jewish people."[30] That was one of the purposes of the trial.

Eichmann was convicted of crimes against the Jewish people and crimes against humanity. Only some of his acts against the Jews were also included among the crimes against humanity; the Final Solution was not. Among the crimes against humanity of which Eichmann was convicted was the deportation of hundreds of thousands of Poles, Slovenes, and Gypsies, and of several dozen children from the Czech village of Lidice. He was not found guilty of their deaths, and he was also acquitted on the charge of membership in the SS, because of the statute of limitations in the law. The judgment set out the story of the extermination of the Jews, but it did not analyze the historical uniqueness of the crime, nor did it solve the riddle of Adolf Eichmann's personality. "We halt, defeated, before this conundrum," Haim Guri wrote.[31]

Before the sentence was read, Eichmann was allowed to speak. "I see that my hope for a just trial has been disappointed," he began. "I did not want to kill; . . . my guilt is only in my obedience, my dutiful service in time of war, my loyalty to the oath, to the flag. . . . I did not persecute Jews with eagerness and passion. That the government did. . . . I would now like to request the forgiveness of the Jewish people and to confess that I am ashamed at the memory of what was inflicted on them, but given the arguments of this verdict this would most likely be interpreted as hypocrisy. . . . I am not the monster that was depicted here. . . . I am convinced to the depths of my heart that I must give account here for deeds done by others. I must shoulder what fate has imposed on me."[32]

The judge, in his sentencing statement, responded to Eichmann's speech. "Even if we were to find that the defendant acted out of blind obedience, as he claims, we would still say that a man who participated in crimes of these dimensions, over years, must suffer the greatest punishment known to the law, and no order can mitigate this punishment. But we have found that the defendant acted out of internal identification with the orders given him, and with a great desire to achieve the criminal object, and it makes no difference, in our opinion, in imposing punishment for such horrifying crimes, how this identification and this desire were born or whether they were the product of ideological education given the defendant by the regime that appointed him, as the defense counsel claims."[33]

Eichmann was sentenced to death. *Maariv* published an editorial the next day, on its front page, with the headline: "DO IT!" To kill a man, the newspaper wrote, was difficult under any circumstances, but here it was a national duty: "Not because we are bloodthirsty or hungry for revenge . . . but because if there is justice in the world, this is the dictate of justice. . . . This is a thing we must do, so that the holy and pure souls of Eichmann's victims will know, in the places where they lie, that there is justice."[34]

Eichmann appealed the judgment, and the process kept him alive for another five months.

¶

At the time that she sat among the hundreds of journalists who covered the Eichmann trial, Hannah Arendt was already known for her works of history and philosophy; she was numbered among the most important intellectuals in the United States. Her book on the trial appeared first as a series of articles in the *New Yorker*. Throughout, Arendt wrote in a tone that was critical of, and occasionally even hostile to, the political and ideological aspects of the trial. She also criticized Hausner's style— it was too operatic for her taste. Arendt never disavowed her Jewish origins; after leaving Germany, she had even worked for a time in the offices of the Zionist Organization in Paris. As the years went by, however, she was among the intellectuals, many of them Jewish, who felt uncomfortable with, and even alienated by, David Ben-Gurion's Israel. It was overly nationalistic, for one thing, and there were those who labeled it racist, too religious, unwilling to make concessions on the Israel-Arab question, not sufficiently liberal in its treatment of the Arab minority, arrogant in its attitude toward Jews who chose to live in other countries, and all too quick to ascribe to itself special moral virtue. Arendt did not deny Israel's right to exist, but she had no sympathy for some of Zionism's ideological assumptions. All these factors informed her articles on the Eichmann trial; she described the poor quality of the simultaneous translation into German as proof of Israel's discrimination against the yekkes.

Arendt wrote that the trial should have been limited to Adolf Eichmann's part in the extermination of the Jews and should not have recounted the entire history of the Holocaust. Eichmann's crimes were sufficient to convict him according to the law and sufficient to justify his execution, she wrote. In her opinion, his murder of Jews should have been termed a crime against humanity. But what Arendt seemed to ignore was that to punish Adolf Eichmann from section IV-B-4 it was not necessary to bring him to Israel—he could have been liquidated on Garibaldi Street. The trial was only a medium, and Eichmann's role was simply to be there, in the glass booth; the real purpose of the trial was to give voice to the Jewish people, for whom Israel claimed to speak in the ideological spirit of Zionism. The state did not aspire to speak in the name of all humanity: Israel, in fact, rejected efforts to categorize the Holocaust as a universal crime, seeing them as attempts to diminish the significance of the Final Solution and to deny the Jewish people's unique right to demand the support of other nations. Arendt couldn't accept that position. When Golda Meir told her that, as a socialist, she believed not in God but in the Jewish people, Arendt was shocked. The greatness of the Jewish people was that it believed in God, she later wrote, as if this were her real dispute with the State of Israel.[35] Indeed, she rejected the Zionist foundation of Israel and its failure to separate church and state. She returned from Jerusalem with a heavy burden of anger, which did her book no good.

The importance of Arendt's book is contained in its subtitle: "A Report on the Banality of Evil." This concept also, inevitably, led to a fight with Israel. A monster was needed to make sense of the horrible memories of the Holocaust survivors and to justify the politicization of those memories. But for Arendt, Eichmann was no monster: her thesis was that Eichmann was not really different from countless other people—that he was completely normal. This was the nature of the Nazi evil: it was typified not by the sadistic perversions that were let loose under its sway but rather by its ability to corrupt man's moral qualities. Arendt's view of human nature was profoundly pessimistic. It was not easy to comprehend her thesis, and many rejected it. The book created a worldwide debate, and that was the Eichmann trial's contribution, albeit indirect, to the century's political thought.

The somewhat hysterical reactions that the book awakened in Israel focused largely on Arendt's discussion of the Judenrats. Had they not collaborated with the Nazi occupiers, she stated, the Nazis would have found it difficult to carry out the extermination program. Arendt did not bewail Jews going like lambs to the slaughter; on the contrary, she attacked Hausner for repeatedly nagging his witnesses about their lack of resistance. This was a cruel and baseless tack, Arendt said. She did not expect European Jewry to rise up against the Nazis; other peoples had not done so. Rebellion was not possible and would not have saved them. Many of them would have been saved, however, had their leaders not helped the Nazis organize the concentration of Jews in the ghettos, their deportation to the east, and their transport to the death camps. In other words, the proper thing to have done, Arendt believed, would have been to do nothing. That would have increased the chaos and so would have made mass extermination difficult and, in the end, reduced the number of victims. This speculation on her part fit her theory on the banality of evil. So all-encompassing was the Nazi evil, so deep its penetration, that even the victims were not immune, time and again choosing cooperation rather than inaction.

Accusations about the collaboration between the Judenrats—as well as the Zionist leaders—and the Nazis had until then been the province of the Israeli right wing. There was something ironic in the right's receiving support from Hannah Arendt, but that was only one side of the paradox. The Judenrats were always described as a shameful phenomenon, the antithesis of the ghetto rebellions. The Eichmann trial almost completely ignored them, while it set out the history of the rebellions at great length. Rebellion symbolized Zionist "stalwartness," the Judenrats the "spiritual degeneracy and the Jewish submissiveness of the Exile." But Hannah Arendt rejected this distinction: she attacked not only the Judenrats but also the Zionists.

Arendt's position made it very difficult for those who supported the point of view that received such clear expression in the Eichmann trial. They did not want to defend the Judenrats, but Arendt left them no choice, since her argument encompassed Zionists as well. Some of them distorted her words and attacked her personally. The Hebrew University in Jerusalem approved a master's-degree dissertation that contained a statement to the effect that the central lines in Arendt's thought were "invisibly influenced" by anti-Semitic thinking: Mein Kampf, it said, was echoed in her opinions about the relations of the Jews to the state and their influence in society.[36] There were those who said she wished to minimize Eichmann's guilt and that of all Nazis, and to accuse the Jews themselves. This she did out of "masochism" and "self-hatred," they wrote. Speakers at Yad Vashem tried to divert the debate from the actions of the Judenrats to the "honor of the dead," which, they said, Arendt had sullied.

An article in the Yad Vashem journal stated that Arendt's method and conclusions were liable to give aid and comfort to neo-Nazis. Arendt's most vocal critics in Israel included Martin Buber and his circle, who were upset by, among other things, her pointed attacks on the leaders of the Jewish community in Germany. The scholar Gershom Scholem denounced her for not having displayed enough "love for the Jewish people." Despite its being one of the most important books written about the Holocaust, and a work most worthy of intelligent debate, Eichmann in Jerusalem did not appear in Hebrew, aside from a few chapters that were printed in Haaretz. A book written to prove that Arendt had distorted the truth was, however, translated.[37]

Somewhere in one of the archives lies the manuscript of a book that was never published: Adolf Eichmann's autobiography. Gideon Hausner explained to David Ben-Gurion that Eichmann's book was meant to contest the verdict and, if published, would give rise to doubts about the correctness of the verdict. Eichmann had received an appropriate opportunity to tell his side during the trial, and the State of Israel had no obligation to allow him any more publicity, he said. The prime minister ordered the manuscript sealed.[38]

Unlike several members of his cabinet, Ben-Gurion did not attend a single session of the court, but he rightly called that year the year of the Eichmann trial.[39] Never had Israel lived the horror of the Holocaust as it did in those months—not after the war, not during the Nuremberg trials. The Eichmann trial marked the beginning of a dramatic shift in the way Israelis related to the Holocaust. The terrifying stories that broke forth from the depths of silence brought about a process of identification with the suffering of the victims and survivors. Haim Guri, who at the beginning of the trial had felt ashamed of the witnesses' stories, wrote toward the end: "We must ask absolution from untold numbers whom we have judged in our hearts, we who lived outside that realm. We often judged them without having asked ourselves what right we had to do so."[40] Many young people also began to take an interest in the Holocaust.

¶

About two weeks before the summations in the Eichmann trial, a seventy-eight-year-old scholar named Shmuel Hugo Bergmann, an admired professor of philosophy at the Hebrew University, received a letter from three of his former students, who had read in a newspaper that Bergmann was organizing a petition urging the court not to sentence Eichmann to death.* The report was premature but substantially correct. Born in Prague and a childhood friend of Franz Kafka's, Bergmann had, in his early days in Jerusalem, been among the members of Brit Shalom, an organization that preached the mutual acceptance of Jews and Arabs on the basis of compromise and coexistence. Now he responded to his students: "I utterly oppose the death penalty in any form."

> That people learned in law would sit together tranquilly and decide, with cold and objective consideration, that a man should be hanged—and that not they, but some other man paid a fee for it, would hang him—that is in my eyes the utmost cruelty. Who gave them permission to take life, and in so doing to take from the defendant the possibility of doing penance for his sins while he is still in this world? Only he who creates life has the authority to take life. . . . The horrible deeds were performed by the defendant nearly twenty years ago, in entirely different historical and psychological

---

* Bergmann's letter identifies his three students only by their first names—Leah, Rina, and Geula. The last of these was Geula Cohen, later a member of the Knesset for the Herut and Tehiya parties.

circumstances. In the meantime the man has lived nearly twenty years in other circumstances, more or less normal ones, and there is grave doubt whether the man being judged today is the same one who in his youth committed crimes in an entirely different world, even though I do not know if he has indeed repented. I do not want to say that there is a statute of limitations on his crimes, but a great change has occurred in the world since then. . . .

As for the man himself, the death penalty is a much more lenient punishment than lifetime imprisonment in an Israeli jail. Given the horrible crime he committed, there is no fit punishment for him; but in any case, the death penalty is the most lenient. The main point in my eyes: I am concerned for the soul of Israel. The horrible experience of the Holocaust has already made its impression on us and on our souls. All the complexes that have plagued us these hundreds of years, which I will call for short the "Amalek complex," have reawakened. I believe with perfect faith that the Holy One, Blessed Be He, has chosen us to be a light unto the gentiles. This mission perhaps justifies our being "a people that shall dwell alone," as long as we do so out of love for mankind, out of a sense of responsibility for those to whom we have been called on to show the way to our Father in Heaven, Who is the Father of all of us. But here is the terrible dilemma and danger for our souls and our purpose: that we will choose our isolation for its own sake, that we will dismiss other people as "uncircumcised," "impure," and so on, and that by this action and this attitude we will abandon our role among the nations.

I believe with perfect faith that clemency for this man will halt the chain of hatred and bring the world a bit of salvation. Equally certain am I that a death sentence carried out will increase the hatred in the world—hatred against us and our hatred against other people—and will help the devil with a great victory in the world.[41]

Earlier, Bergmann had recorded his thoughts on this matter in German, in his diary. "There have always been in Judaism, from time immemorial, two strains grappling with each other in a duel. One is the isolationist. It hates the stranger, fosters the Amalek complex, and at every opportunity emphasizes 'Remember what they did to you.' And there is another Judaism, which I would characterize perhaps with the verse 'Love thy neighbor as thyself.' This is a Judaism whose prayer is

'Allow me to forget Amalek'—a Judaism of love and forgiveness." Here is the key to understanding the basic division in Israeli politics: nationalistic isolationism versus humanistic openness. In another place in his diary, Bergmann wrote simply: "There are two peoples of Israel."[42]

From time to time Bergmann would visit his neighbor, friend, and colleague Martin Buber, who lived in a little stone house surrounded by cactus plants. Buber, then eighty-three, liked to receive his guests in a dimly lit, book-lined study. In winter a kerosene heater diffused a yellow heat; a cat lay curled beside it. When Eichmann's death sentence was pronounced in December 1961, Buber assembled several Jerusalem scholars to consider how to prevent the execution. Most of them were elderly European-born veterans of Brit Shalom. The call to have mercy on the life of Adolf Eichmann reflected a certain intellectual detachment from the emotions that moved the hearts of most Israelis, but it also demanded no small measure of daring and courage: Buber's estate preserves dozens of threatening letters he received after his initiative was made public.[43]

Bergmann described in his diary how the group gathered in Buber's house and drafted the letter they planned to send to President Yitzhak Ben-Zvi, asking him to commute Eichmann's sentence. Among others, they talked to Pinhas Rosen, who did not wish to join their initiative openly, but advised them on what to say and not to say in their request to the president. He, too, objected to Eichmann's execution.[44]

The version that was finally sent to the president read,

> We are not pleading for his life, because we know that no man is less worthy than he is of mercy, and we are not asking you to pardon him. We ask your decision [to commute the execution] for the sake of our country and for the sake of our people. Our belief is that concluding Eichmann's trial with his execution will diminish the image of the Holocaust and falsify the historical and moral significance of this trial.

> We do not want the nemesis to bring us to the point where we appoint a hangman from among us; if we do so it will be a victory for the nemesis, and we do not wish such a victory. The haters of Israel around the world want us to be caught in this trap. Carrying out a death sentence will make it possible for them to claim that the crime of the Nazis has been paid for, that blood ransom has been paid to the Jewish people for the blood that was shed. Let us

not lend our hands to this; let us not agree, or even imply that we agree, that it is possible to ransom the sacrifice of six million by the hanging of this evil man.[45]

In addition to Buber, Bergmann, and Gershom Scholem, seventeen other people signed the letter, most of them professors from the Hebrew University. The poet Leah Goldberg also signed, as did the Jerusalem painter Yehuda Bacon, who had been a prosecution witness at the trial. He had been a boy of fourteen when he arrived at Auschwitz with other children; they were given all sorts of tasks to do, including scattering human ashes on the snowy paths of the camp to keep people from slipping. From time to time, Bacon testified, they were allowed to warm themselves in the crematories or even in the gas chambers; the prosecution submitted sketches he had drawn that showed the gas chambers from the inside.[46] Bacon once heard Martin Buber lecture on Job. Afterwards he accompanied Buber home. Along the way they discussed the possibility of faith after Auschwitz. "I will never forget that night," Bacon wrote on a postcard he sent Buber. "When I returned to my room I cried from happiness."[47]

Much as Gideon Hausner had found in Rivka Joselewska's indomitability a symbol of the fate of the Jewish people, so Shmuel Hugo Bergmann saw national symbolism in Yehuda Bacon's willingness to plead for Eichmann's life. "This was, in my eyes, proof that the Judaism of love and compassion still lived and breathed even after the Holocaust," Bergmann later wrote in his diary. "The other Judaism, that of Amalek and revenge, won this time, and Eichmann was executed. Eichmann alive was nothing. But now, with our own hands we have created a myth around which hatred of Israel will take form. The Judaism of love and compassion was defeated. But Yehuda Bacon's signature on the petition to the president initiated by Martin Buber also means something. And our struggle for the purity of Israel will continue, with yet greater dignity and power."[48]

Buber's initiative, supported by few and vilified by many, is worthy of note also because the man whom *Time* described as the greatest Jewish philosopher in the world and whom *Maariv* compared to "an ancient prophet" did not satisfy himself with drafting a petition. He also called the prime minister's office and asked for a meeting to argue against the hanging of Eichmann. At seventy-five, Ben-Gurion deemed that, since he was younger than Buber, it was only fitting that he should go to the philosopher's house. He sat there and listened for close to two hours—

but he was not convinced. Attorney General Hausner also went to Buber.

The press rejected the petition with near unanimity. "A pardon for Eichmann?" *Maariv* asked—and answered, "No! Six million times no!" But the question was a real one, partly thanks to Buber's campaign, and the cabinet held a special meeting to discuss it. Ben-Gurion presented the ministers with the contents of a letter he had received, apparently at Buber's initiative, from an American Jewish scholar, Morris S. Friedman; it proposed that Israel declare that there was no fit punishment for Eichmann and that he be set free. Hausner urged the ministers to decide to carry out the sentence. "We owe it to the Holocaust survivors to impose the punishment," he said. There was a vote, and the majority favored hanging. The minority then asked for a second vote, so that the record would show that the decision to execute Eichmann had been unanimous. President Ben-Zvi needed only a few hours to reject the various requests to grant Eichmann clemency, including that of Eichmann himself. In the margins of Eichmann's petition Ben-Zvi wrote the prophet Samuel's words on Amalek: "As thy sword has made women childless, so shall thy mother be childless among women" (I Samuel 15:33).[49]

Adolf Eichmann was hanged in the Ramla prison in the evening hours of May 31, 1962. He had earlier requested and received a bottle of white wine and had rejected the offer of a Canadian pastor, William Hall, to say a final prayer. "Long live Germany, long live Argentina, long live Austria; I will never forget them," he called out to the clutch of reporters allowed to be present. In that moment he was completely himself, Hannah Arendt wrote: "Nothing could have demonstrated this more convincingly than the grotesque silliness of his last words."[50] A few seconds later he was dead. His body was burned and the ashes scattered at sea, outside Israel's territorial waters.

§

Many years later, Yeshayahu Leibowitz, a Jerusalem scholar known for his exceptional opinions and sharp tongue, said: "The Eichmann trial was a total failure; Eichmann really was a small and insignificant cog in a big machine. I think it was a conspiracy by Adenauer and Ben-Gurion to clear the name of the German people. In exchange they paid us billions. In my opinion, when we caught Eichmann and brought him here, we should have put him on trial and given him the best defense attorney we have, who would explain that this man was not guilty and not responsible for anything. . . . because he was the product of two thousand years of Christian history, the whole end of which is the destruction of the Jews. . . . He did, in fact, just carry out orders—a matter of importance to us—but the main thing is that he carried out mankind's will with regard to the Jewish people!"[51]

During the trial the Israeli press kept close watch on reactions in the West German press and political parties; the impression was that the Germans were following the trial with a large measure of sympathy for Israel, awareness of their guilt, and desire for absolution. Ironically, then, the Eichmann trial moderated anti-German sentiment in Israel.

20 | *"Gloom Shall Not Prevail"*

In December 1960, six months after *Time* first revealed that Israeli agents had captured Eichmann in Argentina, the magazine again came out with an Israeli scoop. It reported that Israel was building an atom bomb. David Ben-Gurion immediately denied the report but confirmed in the Knesset that Israel was indeed building a second nuclear power plant, in the Negev, outside Dimona. It was being built with France's help, and had been, until then, top secret: the residents of the region had been told it was a textile factory. Like the first nuclear reactor, in the Soreq River area south of Tel Aviv—known to insiders as the "small reactor"—the "big reactor" near Dimona was, Ben-Gurion said, to be used for peaceful purposes only. He compared it to a plant that Canada had helped build in India.*

Ben-Gurion had always been interested in scientific research, for both civilian and military purposes. Science was an important component of his vision of Israel; he tended to think of it as linked to biblical prophecies. "My lot is not with those who despair of mankind's future because of the terrible use that has been made of the discoveries of physics and of the forces hidden in the atom," he said at the opening of the nuclear-physics

---

* Israel always denied reports that it possessed nuclear weapons. The official line from the 1960s on was that Israel had no such weapons and would not be the first to bring them into the Middle East. This line remains unchanged, having been reasserted by the government in 1986, when a worker at the nuclear-research park at Dimona, Mordecai Vanounou, smuggled photographs and documents from the reactor out of the country.[1]

center at the Weizmann Institute of Science. "I am more inclined to believe that there is a blessing in the progress of nuclear science." Basing himself on the Bible, Ben-Gurion said that he trusted in "the cosmic union of science and ethics": "The State of Israel would not have come into the world had our people not believed in the superiority of the spirit, . . . and we could not have continued to exist after the frightening Holocaust brought upon us by the Nazis only fifteen or sixteen years ago had we not believed in the human conscience and in its final victory."[2] Immediately after the establishment of the state, Ben-Gurion ordered a search for uranium in the Negev. By the beginning of the 1950s, the Weizmann Institute was refining uranium from phosphates; it also made heavy water. The institute's achievements in these fields created a foundation for nuclear cooperation between Israel and other countries, France and Germany in particular.[3]

Ben-Gurion's revelation of the nuclear reactor outside Dimona led to no real public debate, partly because military censorship strangled every attempt to write about it. Two years later, Mapam and Maki demanded a Knesset debate on their proposal to create a nuclear-weapons-free zone in the Middle East. In speaking of the danger that the Israel-Arab conflict would lead to a nuclear confrontation, the representatives of these parties used the word *holocaust*. At Ben-Gurion's request, the Knesset removed the subject from its agenda.[4]

A small circle of intellectuals tried to interest the public in the need for nuclear disarmament in the Middle East. The group, headed by Yeshayahu Leibowitz, included Ernst Akiva Simon, an associate of Martin Buber's who had signed his Eichmann petition and had been involved in efforts to create understanding between Jews and Arabs. They gathered in a Jerusalem apartment, drafted memoranda, sent letters to newspapers, spoke with members of the Knesset. They received a letter of encouragement from the British philosopher Bertrand Russell. But they had no real influence: "We weren't taken seriously," Yehuda Ben-Moshe, the group's coordinator, later wrote. Among their opponents were many Holocaust survivors. "Who did anything to help us during the war?" they would ask Ben-Moshe. "You have no idea what it means to live in existential fear." But as far as Ben-Moshe could remember, only Shimon Peres thought they were endangering the country's interests.[5]

Peres, then deputy minister of defense, was very much involved in the nuclear project. He made no distinction in principle between conventional and nuclear weapons—the difference was only semantic, he claimed. He opposed declaring a nuclear-free zone prior to signing peace agreements with Israel's neighbors. He once debated this issue with Knesset member Uri Avneri: "How many wars have broken out in the world because of the arms race?" Avneri shouted during one of Peres's speeches. Peres responded with an example: "After World War I people began to think that if they disarmed Germany, there would be peace in the world. They said: 'Little boat, little war; big boat, big war.' What good did it do? Did it prevent Hitler's rise?"[6]

Israel's nuclear project was born, then, out of a vision of scientific development, out of global and regional strategic considerations, and out of the uninhibited desire for action on the part of a younger generation, who now ascended to power under the aegis of the omnipotent Ben-Gurion. In retrospect it seems as if the project was almost inevitable. A decision not to launch the project would have required a large measure of imagination and daring—perhaps more than the decision to go ahead did. Abandoning the project would have required a sense of security and a fundamental confidence in the country's ability to survive, neither of which the leaders had or, perhaps, could have had. Ben-Gurion could speak about faith and survival and about the historical vision that brought about the miracle of the Jewish state, but alongside such fervent affirmation, a basic pessimism and anxiety dwelt within him, and within many others as well. These reactions, too, derived from the Holocaust. "They could slaughter us tomorrow in this country," Ben-Gurion said to the members of his party during a debate over the reparations agreement; he emphasized this point to Holocaust survivors in particular. "We don't want to reach again the situation that you were in. We do not want the Arab Nazis to come and slaughter us."[7] During the great debate over selling Israeli arms to Germany, Moshe Dayan said: "The historical heritage of the six million—the historical imperative they left us—is to make sure that such a thing won't happen again." The people of Israel have a greater responsibility in this, he said, than any other Jewish community, not only because they must safeguard the state, but for a simpler reason: they are the only group of Jews today whose enemies are actively planning to destroy them.[8] These men were not just making points in a debate but articulating fundamental components of Israel's existential self-conception, and therefore of Israel's defense doctrine: anything can happen, and when it does, Israel will stand alone. Therefore, Israel cannot afford to pass over any weapon it has the ability to obtain.

The founding father of Israel's nuclear project was Ernst David Bergman. * Formerly an assistant to Haim Weizmann and among the founders of the institute that bore the first president's name, the Berlin-born chemist was among the most senior Israeli scientists. Even before Israeli independence, Bergman devoted much of his time to military research; he was close to Ben-Gurion and served as his principal adviser on nuclear policy. One of his colleagues later wrote: "I believe that Ben-Gurion accepted Bergman's opinion without question. Every proposal that came up had first to receive Bergman's support; if Bergman was convinced of its value, Ben-Gurion would accept it."[9]

For years, Bergman served as chairman of Israel's Atomic Energy Commission, which was part of the prime minister's office. Shortly after retiring from this position in the summer of 1966, Bergman sent a long, very pessimistic letter to Mapam leader Meir Yaari. In contrast to those demanding a nuclear-weapons-free Middle East, Bergman assumed that many countries, probably even Arab countries, would achieve nuclear capability. The conclusion he drew, Bergman said, was influenced by the lessons of the Holocaust. "The spread of nuclear weapons is unavoidable," he wrote. He remarked that there was no chance that the nuclear powers would reach agreement on disarmament and reminded his reader not to believe the denials of several countries, including India, that had nuclear reactors but claimed not to be producing nuclear weapons. "Any development in the field of atomic energy for peaceful purposes inevitably brings the country with atomic energy closer to nuclear weapons," Bergman stated. He chided Yaari:

I was surprised that a man like you, one of the shapers of our policy, is prepared to close his eyes and assume that reality is how we would all like to see it. There is no person in this country who does not fear a nuclear war and there is no man in this country who does not hope that, despite it all, logic will rule in the world of tomorrow. But we are not permitted to exchange precise knowledge and realistic evaluations for hopes and illusions. I cannot forget that the Holocaust came on the Jewish people as a surprise. The Jewish people cannot allow themselves such an illusion for a second time. †[10]

---

* No relation to philosopher Shmuel Hugo Bergmann.
† In October 1964, a senior German government official told reporters in Bonn that Israel and his country had for years cooperated on nuclear research for peaceful purposes. The daily newspaper *Frankfurter Rundschau* added that Israel would soon have an atom

On July 21, 1962, Gamal Abdel Nasser's Egypt celebrated the tenth anniversary of the officers' revolt that toppled the monarchy. The military parade through the streets of Cairo displayed twenty ground-to-ground missiles. The Egyptian authorities had previously invited reporters to see the launching of four of them, two of the model called al-Zafer ("the Victor") and two of the model al-Qaher ("the Conqueror"). A year earlier, in July 1961, Israel had launched a home-produced missile called the Shavit-2—for meteorological purposes, it was claimed. Ben-Gurion was photographed next to the Shavit before it was launched, and a confident wave of patriotic enthusiasm swept the country. When, however, Nasser presented his Victor and Conqueror, and defined their targets—"any point south of Beirut"—the danger seemed real and present.

The political and intelligence communities were in an uproar. Deputy Defense Minister Shimon Peres and Meir Amit, chief of military intelligence, accused Isser Harel, the head of the Mossad—whom they saw as a rival and competitor—of having neglected the problem. Harel, a man of great power, was a confidant of the prime minister, and their meetings were always private. Ben-Gurion had absolute faith in him. After Egypt tested its missiles, Harel produced documents proving that they had been built with the guidance of German scientists, some of whose professional experience dated from the Nazi period. Harel recommended that Ben-Gurion contact Chancellor Adenauer directly and ask him to call the scientists home; Ben-Gurion feared that Adenauer would do nothing and that the request would poison the delicate relations between the two countries. Instead he had Shimon Peres talk to German Minister of Defense Franz Josef Strauss; Ben-Gurion was proven right: Strauss did nothing. At the same time, Ben-Gurion permitted Harel and Amit to send their men out on direct action against the German scientists. At least two scientists were kidnapped and disappeared; others were wounded when they opened booby-trapped packages sent to them in the mail. Still others received threats.

---

bomb and that German scientists had helped in its construction. The report prompted two no-confidence motions in the government. Minister of Education Abba Eban denied the allegation: "There is no activity of German scientists in Israel in general and none in the nuclear field in particular." But the newspapers mentioned the names of Hans Jensen, a Nobel laureate in physics, and Wolfgang Gentner, director of the nuclear-physics branch of the prestigious Max Planck Institute in Heidelberg. Both of them had been in Israel and had been mentioned in Knesset debates. The government confirmed that they had visited the Weizmann Institute.[11]

¶

One day in March 1963, a man named Otto Jokelik telephoned the home of Heidi Görke in Germany and asked that she meet with him and with a man from Israel to talk about her father's work. Görke was the daughter of Paul Görke, who worked in Egypt. Jokelik was an Austrian adventurer who had previously worked for the Egyptian missile project and who was now working for the Mossad. They agreed to meet at the Three Kings Hotel in Basel, Switzerland (where, seventy years earlier, one of the best-known photographs in Zionist history had been taken—Theodor Herzl on a balcony, gazing at the Rhine). Heidi Görke, a lawyer, tricked the two Mossad agents as deftly as the heroine of a spy movie. She called the Swiss police, who planted a microphone under the table and another in a vase. Everything was recorded. A few hours later the two Mossad agents were arrested and charged with making threats.

The ensuing scandal would plague Israeli politics for two years and more. Among other things, it revealed a tangle of intrigues within the secret intelligence services. The newspapers devoted banner headlines and entire pages to the subject, emphasizing the Nazi pasts of the scientists in Egypt and their expertise in the development of chemical and bacteriological weapons. The key word was *gas*. Isser Harel encouraged this line of reporting. He presented the Mossad's activities against the German scientists as a war against an active plot to destroy Israel, a direct continuation of the Holocaust. This vision of a coordinated, far-reaching plot helped him account for the failure of his men in Basel and helped, too, unsettle one of Shimon Peres's power bases—his web of contacts with the German military establishment. In his memoirs, Harel related how he fed details about the scientists' work to the press. He went so far as to send three Israeli reporters to Europe, supplied with names, addresses, and background information; their stories were printed as investigative journalism. [12]

The reports of the German scientists in Egypt dealt the harshest blow ever to Ben-Gurion's German policy; at the time, the prime minister was entertaining, for the umpteenth time, the hope that West Germany would soon establish full diplomatic relations with Israel. Harel did not intend to harm the prime minister; he intended to harm Peres. But the blow to Ben-Gurion's German policy was inevitable. And perhaps Harel truly believed that the German scientists endangered Israel's security, as he later claimed in his books.

Ben-Gurion had his doubts and tried to keep a low profile, but as the furor in the press grew, he was forced to have his foreign minister, Golda Meir, make an official statement in the Knesset. Meir called the German scientists a gang of criminals and stated that there was no doubt that they were in Egypt not only to make money but also out of anti-Semitic motives. "There have been close links between Cairo and the Nazis since Hitler's time, and it is no secret that Cairo today serves as a center and refuge for Nazi leaders," Meir said. It was a sharply worded statement. While it included a nod to "the masses of German people who are repelled by Germany's Nazi past and who want a different Germany," Meir made it clear that "eighteen years after the fall of the Nazi regime that brought about the extermination of millions of Jews, members of this nation are again associated with deeds meant to destroy the State of Israel, where the refugees of the Holocaust and the extermination have gathered."

Although all factions agreed to accept the foreign minister's statement, there was nevertheless a debate:

MENAHEM BEGIN (HERUT): Look at the paradox before your eyes: you invite German education experts here, and Germany sends death experts to Nasser. You sew uniforms for the German army, and the Germans give them know-how about gases they can use against the Jewish people. You send our Uzi to Germany, and the Germans give our enemies bacteria. Please, now, at the very least, search your souls. How long will you continue this system of servility, this inconceivable friendship?

ELIMELECH RIMALT (LIBERAL): The citizens of West Germany . . . are again busy producing gases, bacteria, and radioactive material intended for use against Israel, against the population of the Jewish state. . . . We do not want to accuse the entire Egyptian nation, . . . but the rulers and leaders of that country have inherited the spirit of Nazism. . . .

YISRAEL BARZILAI (MAPAM): They say that German scientists and experts in Egypt are inventing the most terrible kinds of weapons ever conceived by the human brain—the famous "death rays." Dozens of Nazi scientists worked on this in Hitler's time with only partial success, and now they are trying to complete the job.

Mapai and Herut agreed on a common resolution—a first in Israeli politics. Ben-Gurion did not attend this session, as if he wished to demonstrate that the situation did not justify interrupting his vacation. He was at his favorite hotel on the Sea of Galilee and then at his kibbutz, Sde Boker, in the Negev. Harsh words were spoken in the Knesset against his German policy, and Golda Meir did not rise to defend it.[13]

Shimon Peres had in the meantime received the new intelligence evaluation he had ordered from Meir Amit, and it indicated that the information disseminated by Harel was, in Amit's words, "a bunch of baloney." Some of the reported plans of the German scientists in Egypt turned out to be imaginative fictions, most of them very far from execution. There was, then, no basis for the public's hysteria, and certainly not for a renewed excoriation of Germany.[14] Ben-Gurion leaned, of course, toward accepting this new intelligence evaluation, and Harel resigned after a lengthy and rather painful conversation with Ben-Gurion over the question of whether West Germany was indeed "a different Germany." Ben-Gurion could not publicly disavow the statement his foreign minister had made to the Knesset, but when he explained Harel's departure a few days later, he said: "The deep concern awakened in us by the Egyptian leader's plot to destroy Israel and by the assistance given to him by German and other scientists and technicians should not make us lose our sanity."[15]

Ben-Gurion's leadership was in its twilight hours. Another prolonged intelligence scandal, known as the Lavon affair, had strained his nerves. "He lost something of his self-confidence and his ability to make contact with people, his knack for talking with them," Teddy Kollek, his close associate, later recalled. "He knew that his position was correct, but when he realized that he could not convince others, despair took hold. So great was his frustrated anger that he began to attack his opponents personally, and this in the end led to his fall. . . . No one liked to hear him talk that way. No one liked to see him stoop so low. It was embarrassing. . . . I think that he finally retired in 1963 because he felt that he had lost the support of his old political friends. This was the basic reason. But what brought about his resignation at that time in particular was largely connected to Isser Harel."[16]

Two very spiteful, very Ben-Gurionish provocations preceded his resignation.

In May of 1963 he suddenly latched onto an article published thirty years earlier by Revisionist ideologue Abba Ahimeir. The article included words of praise for Hitler. If Herut's forerunners had been wrong then, it proved that Herut was also wrong in its current opposition to reconciliation with Adenauer's Germany, Ben-Gurion said; as expected, he stirred up a storm. The speaker of the Knesset ordered his comment expunged from the record.[17] Two weeks later, Ben-Gurion received a visitor: Franz Josef Strauss. Strauss had recently been dismissed as minister of defense for trying to use state force to break the weekly *Der Spiegel*. A right-wing nationalist, Strauss did not typify what most people thought of as the new Germany. But he and Shimon Peres were central to the relations between Ben-Gurion's Israel and Adenauer's Germany. At that time Germany was supplying Israel with aircraft, tanks, artillery, and antitank missiles—gratis, all from NATO surpluses. It had also helped Israel obtain French helicopters and British submarines. The German air force trained Israeli pilots; Israeli officers trained at the German army's officers school. The national budget submitted to the Bundestag in 1962 contained an item with a vague heading: "Aid for Military Provision— DM 240 million" (about $60 million).[18] This was the cost of the aid to Israel. Strauss had made it possible; nonetheless, his visit to Israel angered many. That Ben-Gurion would invite Strauss, in provocative disregard of public reaction, was also characteristic of his final days. *

On the night of Saturday, June 15, 1963, Teddy Kollek brought Golda Meir to Ben-Gurion's residence. The foreign minister had learned that the German news agency was about to release a report that Israeli army personnel were training in Germany. Meir demanded that Ben-Gurion forbid the publication of the report in the Israeli press. Ben-Gurion rejected the demand. That evening they spoke of the German-scientists affair and about the whole web of relations between Israel and Germany. Meir, emotional as usual, found it hard to accept the pragmatism of Ben-Gurion's German policy. Her character, her heart, and her political instincts led her to trust Isser Harel's pessimistic evaluations more than those Ben-Gurion had received from Peres. "I saw how dejected he was

---

* A letter that was only later made public reflected Ben-Gurion's state of mind in those days. "Begin is clearly a Hitler type," the prime minister wrote to Haim Guri. "Racist, ready to destroy all the Arabs for Greater Israel, willing to sanctify all means to achieve the holy purpose—absolute rule; I see him as a serious danger to Israel's internal and external situation." Ben-Gurion predicted that if Begin took control of the country, he would "replace the command of the army and police with his thugs, rule as Hitler ruled Germany, suppress the labor movement with force and cruelty, and destroy the country by launching foreign adventures. . . . I have no doubt that Begin hates Hitler—but this hatred does not prove that he is any different. . . . When I first heard Begin speak on the radio, I heard Hitler's voice and howls."[19]

at not being able to convince Golda on this matter," Teddy Kollek wrote. "The dispute over this subject was as sharp as it was because there was already a rift between them, not specifically because it was impossible to overcome this particular problem. Their conversation did not end with a bang—it seemed more like a mutual distancing, a rupture between their ways of thinking."[20]

The next day Ben-Gurion resigned. There seems to be something symbolic in his political career's coming to an end over the single most painful and repugnant issue of his years as prime minister.

The German scientists in Egypt continued to preoccupy the Israeli public for another two years, with varying degrees of emotional and political force. Again and again the subject came before the Knesset— no less than seventeen times all told. Ben-Gurion summed up his political legacy: "We have done everything and will do everything to prevent assistance by German scientists to the Hitler of our time. . . . But we will not fool the people. . . . A scientist from another country who assists Nasser in his Nazi plot to destroy Israel is no less dangerous than a German scientist who does so, and the actual foreseeable danger from Egypt is from conventional weaponry." Menahem Begin warned, how- ever, that Nasser's German missiles threatened to eliminate "the biolog- ical existence of this nation." Such a disaster could occur, for example, Begin said, if Nasser should one day suddenly lose his mind. As on many occasions in the past, Begin expressed the deepest fears of many.[21]

Reports of German military aid to Israel appeared in many newspapers, in various countries, during those weeks. Adenauer had retired a year earlier; Strauss was also out of office. The assumption was that the pro- Arab lobby in the German foreign ministry had leaked the reports in order to halt the military ties with Israel. The Arab states reacted, pre- dictably, with a wave of condemnation but, in doing so, set in motion a series of far-reaching diplomatic events that led, a few months later, to the establishment of full diplomatic relations between Israel and Ger- many.

Prior to the exchange of ambassadors, relations between the two coun- tries went through two periods. During the first, Germany exhibited interest in establishing diplomatic relations, and Israel shied away; during the second, Israel was interested but Germany refused. David Ben- Gurion, Moshe Sharett, and the foreign ministry leadership supported relations as early as the beginning of the 1950s. "In my opinion, we would have had to seek links with Germany even if there had not been reparations payments," wrote diplomat Haim Yahil to Moshe Sharett shortly after the reparations agreements were signed. "There is no ignoring the fact that Germany is advancing quickly into the status of the most important power on the European continent."[22] Nahum Goldmann made the same assessment in July 1954, and a few months later Ben-Gurion brought the subject before a special cabinet meeting. Two years later he addressed the subject publicly with foreign correspondents and in the Knesset. "The government has still not decided in favor of establishing normal relations with Germany. For now, at least, it is not practical. But my opinion is that it is possible and that it would be a blessing for the country—and that is the one criterion, at least for a Jew like me. We must, in my opinion, prepare the public for this, both in Israel and in the Jewish world."[23]

The public was indeed far from ready for diplomatic relations. The reparations and compensation agreements were meant to return stolen property; many Israelis profited personally and the country had been in distress and in need of money: even so, those treaties had been violently opposed. An exchange of ambassadors could be seen only as a symbol of reconciliation, and it would bring no real benefits. Ben-Gurion and Sharett assumed that most Israelis still opposed reconciliation. "The wound remains deep, even if on the outside it looks as if it has healed," *Haaretz* wrote in an editorial opposing full diplomatic relations, for the present. The newspaper's editor, Gershom Schocken, sent Foreign Minister Sharett a paragraph he had deleted on the advice of two members of the paper's editorial board: It said that it would be impossible to guarantee the safety of German diplomats in Israel."[24]

The subject occasionally came up in the Knesset; again and again the government had to give assurances that it had not decided on full diplomatic relations with Germany. In July 1956, Chancellor Adenauer hinted that he would like to see an exchange of ambassadors; in response, Golda Meir told the Knesset that Israel's government did not consider itself responsible for the declarations and sentiments of other countries' leaders. Israel's ambassador to France, Yaakov Tsur, tried to persuade the foreign minister that there was no avoiding an exchange of ambassadors with Germany. "Golda sat there pale and tense," the ambassador wrote in his memoirs. She responded: "What you say makes sense. But what can I do? I can't discuss it in any logical way—I who have fought for so many years against any approach to Germany." Then she sighed and repeated what Tsur called "the usual refrain": "Why did Ben-Gurion take me away from the labor ministry, which I liked so much and which didn't require me to do anything but build houses?"[25]

Ben-Gurion's way of circumventing the opposition to relations with Germany was to send an ambassador under another title. Eliezer Shinar was in Bonn ostensibly as the head of the reparations delegation, but in fact he functioned as ambassador in all respects. Shinar described in his memoirs how he tried, beginning in the mid-1950s, to bring about full diplomatic relations. But in this period, Germany no longer needed this Jewish connection; it had gained sufficient international recognition and preferred its relations with the Arabs. Time after time Shinar thought relations were on the verge of being consummated, and time after time the Germans pulled back at the last minute, without hiding their fears of reaction from the Arab states. The major task of West German diplomacy in that period was to isolate East Germany and to prevent other countries from recognizing its independence. The Arab countries did not recognize the Communist state—but might, if they wished to retaliate for West German recognition of Israel. Relations with Israel grew steadily closer in every area, but were always conducted in secret. As Knesset member Elimelech Rimalt put it, Israel had a "common-law marriage" with Germany.[26] The same people who had in the past attacked the government for its willingness to maintain relations with Germany now attacked Germany for its unwillingness to establish relations with Israel. It was odd: "A country of Hitler's heirs, the heirs of the murderers of the Jews, does not deign to establish diplomatic relations with the country of Hitler's victims!" thundered Maki leader Moshe Sneh.[27] After the German-scientists affair and the establishment of relations, the Knesset several times debated the German statute of limitations on Nazi crimes, which was expected to expire soon but was then put off, partly thanks to Nahum Goldmann's lobbying in the Bundestag. There were articles in the Israeli press, there was a rally, but all in all it was a fairly calm debate. The emotional energy that had impelled anti-German activity in the past was running out.[28]

In the wake of the reports of military cooperation between the two countries in February 1965, Germany announced that it had decided to stop providing Israel with military equipment and offered money instead. As the Israeli media and the Knesset were busily magnifying the incident into an issue, Nasser invited Walter Ulbricht, the East German leader, to Egypt. West Germany retaliated with a punitive move—it offered to establish diplomatic relations with Israel. All this happened quite suddenly and required an immediate decision, lest Germany change its mind. There was no time for the opponents of reconciliation to organize a campaign, and most Israelis were in favor by then. The decision was made first within the individual parties, after which the cabinet decided and then the Knesset. There were some doubts within the parties, there were opponents, but in contrast with the debate over the reparations, this struggle lacked fervor. This time, judging by the party minutes and the Knesset record, the opposition seemed more like a worn ritual than an expression of emotion. Menahem Begin quoted a poem in which Jews were described as scraps of soap; a member of the Knesset for Mapai said that an Israeli ambassador living in Bonn was the best possible revenge against the generations of murderers. Deputy Prime Minister Abba Eban, his language as polished as ever, gave the legislature the benefit of his erudition: when the German ambassador arrived, his country's national anthem would indeed be played in Jerusalem. The words to "Deutschland über Alles" had, however, actually been written by a liberal poet of the previous century by the name of Hoffmann. It had been adopted as the anthem during the term of a socialist president, Ebert. The opening line had been in use until the anthem was suspended in 1945. In 1952 the song was reinstated as the national anthem, but without the opening verse; indeed the only verse sung from then on was one expressing sentiments of unity, freedom, liberty, and brotherhood. Menahem Begin sarcastically cut Eban off: "Perhaps we should all sing it together: 'Deutschland, Deutschland über Alles'?" and his colleague Arieh Ben-Eliezer called out: "Yes, maybe we should all stand up and sing it together?"

Then the vote was recorded, by roll call, as it had been on the reparations agreement thirteen years earlier. Sixty-six members voted in favor of establishing diplomatic relations, twenty-nine opposed, and the rest abstained or were absent. In the vote on the reparations agreement, only sixty-one had been in favor and fifty had voted against. About a third of the members participated in both votes. Eight of those who had opposed the reparations agreement voted in favor of diplomatic relations.[29]

For a while the Israeli press and some Mapai leaders entertained the illusion that Israel could dictate to Germany the terms of the agreement: that Germany not halt the arms shipments, that it take action against the scientists in Egypt, that it revoke the statute of limitations on Nazi crimes, that it establish its embassy in Jerusalem rather than in Tel Aviv. Germany rejected these demands with a quite evident tone of impatience, as if

Israel should politely thank it for having deigned to exchange ambassadors. Israel would have liked the first German ambassador to be a man who would, in his person, symbolize Germany's repentance for the Nazis' crimes. Germany sent a professional diplomat who had lost his right arm in the Second World War: Rolf Pauls had been an officer in the Wehrmacht. The number-two man in his embassy, Alexander Török, was alleged to have been a member of the Arrow Cross, the Hungarian Nazi party.

While on his way to Jerusalem to present his credentials, Pauls saw buses taking thousands of demonstrators to the capital. "Gloom shall not prevail," President Shazar declared at the ceremony, "and even the darkest of nights yields to the dawn." Forty-eight Israeli soldiers from the tank corps saluted, and the police band played the anthem in which the verse starting with the words "Deutschland, Deutschland über Alles" was no longer included, but outside, the organizers of the demonstration lost control of their people and there was yet another violent clash: people were thrown to the ground and trampled by mounted police. Among the wounded were handicapped people, survivors of concentration camps; some of them needed to be hospitalized. Heartbreaking pictures appeared in the next morning's newspapers. The ambassador's car was extricated with great difficulty from the crowd that pressed around it, banging on its roof and windows; someone threw a rock. Poet Abba Kovner returned his Independence Medal to the president, accompanied by a letter that concluded with the words: "Would you believe it? I never, even there, knew so terrible a sense of helplessness as I felt on seeing Jerusalem receive an officer of the army of murderers." Antek Zuckerman of the Warsaw ghetto uprising said that the demonstration saved Israel's honor, but he asked why tens of thousands had not come. [30]

§

Only once more were Israelis to demonstrate violently against ties with Germany. In May 1966, former chancellor Konrad Adenauer, who had recently celebrated his ninetieth birthday, came to Israel. His visit was carefully planned. He was received everywhere with the greatest honor, in some places even with fondness.

But at a dinner with Prime Minister Levi Eshkol, there was a diplomatic incident—"Yes," Nahum Goldmann later said, "and what an incident!"

Eshkol invited him to his residence, in Rehavia, and made a huge faux pas. Adenauer was no longer chancellor. The meal, with twelve guests, was unofficial. Nevertheless, suddenly, before the dessert, Eshkol rose and gave a speech, for at least twenty minutes. And in the speech he said—I think he spoke in English—he said, "I hope and am convinced that, under your wise leadership, the German people will find the way back to the family of cultured nations." I was sitting at Adenauer's right. I immediately saw that something had happened. Except for Ben-Gurion, I never met a man so able to control himself. After Eshkol finished, Adenauer said, "Mr. Prime Minister, I thank you, but I am leaving the country tomorrow morning." He said to his aide, "Prepare the airplane." Everyone was shocked, and Eshkol asked, "What did I do?" Adenauer replied, "I am not here as chancellor, but I am a German and you have insulted the German people. Tomorrow I am leaving the country." There was actual panic around the table, and Eshkol stuttered, "But, sir, I praised you!" Adenauer, who could be forceful and cruel, said, "What you think of me is of no interest to me; we are speaking of the German people." In the meantime several dozen other guests had arrived, invited for coffee, and they waited in the adjoining parlor. I went into the parlor. Everyone asked where Eshkol was. I tried to reassure them, but they heard the voices.

I returned to the dining room. The atmosphere was horrible. It was like ice. Everyone sat quietly. I sat down next to Adenauer and I said, "Mr. Chancellor, prove that you are smart and not just intelligent." He began to laugh and asked, "What do you want from me?" I said, "Look, there are in this country hundreds of thousands of Jews who, justifiably, hate the Germans. There is Herut. There is Mapam. There are, especially, the victims of the Nazis. The fool of an aide who wrote the speech—Eshkol apparently did not know what was written in it—thought that he had to please the opposition. So he wrote that insulting sentence." Adenauer said, "I understand, but a solution must be found." I said to Eshkol, "Listen, it is now ten-thirty; when do the morning papers go to press?" Eshkol inquired and said, "About two in the morning." So I suggested that we send an urgent notice to the newspapers that this passage, which was indeed in the transcript, had been crossed out by Eshkol. And so it was. It did not appear.[31]

At least with regard to the final detail, Goldmann's memory led him astray—the entire incident was written up at length in the newspapers. It was the first time that Germany reprimanded Israel for mentioning its

Nazi past. Adenauer and Eshkol apparently made up, but the prime minister denied that he asked his German guest not to get mad at him.[32]

Two days later Adenauer visited the National Library on the Hebrew University campus. A few dozen students came to demonstrate against his visit, and little by little others joined them. A large contingent of police, clubs in hand, charged the students. "I saw one of them with his face bloodied, and it was David Naor, my son," related Herut Knesset member Esther Raziel-Naor. A few of the demonstrators had to be hospitalized. It seemed that the police had used far more force than necessary, but a commission of inquiry later exonerated them. The students, the commission determined, had provoked the police, calling them "dirty Moroccans" and "morons," as well as "Nazis." Adenauer commented before leaving the country that he had expected far larger demonstrations. "The small number of people participating in these demonstrations is what stands out," *Haaretz* noted.[33]

Ambassador Rolf Pauls brought with him a great deal of goodwill, wisdom, and tact, which helped him enter Israeli society. He had come, furthermore, with a sense of history and expected to be ostracized. His main role, as he himself defined it, was to break the interdict. To his surprise, he found himself in much demand. The yekkes befriended him as if he were their own ambassador.[34] The embassy handed out generous support to a long list of scientific and cultural institutions. Among other things, it encouraged Israeli publishers to bring out Hebrew translations of novels by Günter Grass, Heinrich Böll, Siegfried Lenz, and others, in addition to the wide selection of German literature already available in Hebrew, from Goethe to Thomas Mann to Erich Kästner, who had always been popular with Israeli children. The German embassy also made a great effort to improve its country's image in the Israeli press by offering journalists free trips to Germany. And with the inauguration of television broadcasts, Germany funded part of the cost of keeping Israeli correspondents in Bonn. Tens of thousands of Israeli high school students went to visit Germany, mostly at the expense of the German government. All this was carefully planned, step by step.

The closer the economic, military, and diplomatic relations between the two countries became, the more the opponents of reconciliation focused on cultural relations. Culture was an easy target—it was conspicuous, and not vital to the country's welfare or security. Esther Raziel-Naor had made a specialty of protesting the infiltration of German culture. She was particularly concerned with music: a Schubert *Lied*, in German, broadcast over the radio (Ben-Gurion apologized for the mistake); another broadcast, of Mozart's *Marriage of Figaro*, conducted by Herbert von Karajan (Education Minister Zalman Aran promised that it would not be played again); indications that the boycott of the music of Richard Wagner and Richard Strauss was being broken.[35] Prime Minister Levi Eshkol was once asked to comment on what was described as an attempt to force a radio announcer, Yael Ben-Yehuda, to broadcast, against the dictates of her conscience, an advertising jingle for Volkswagens.[36] Some Israeli artists, writers and performers who published or appeared in Germany found the Israeli media closed to them; satirist Efraim Kishon was fiercely attacked for his success in Germany. But the fight against cultural ties was almost the last battle; times had changed.*

The minister of education, Abba Eban, gave voice to the feeling that, with the Eichmann trial, the government had done its duty in this area and had no more need to justify itself. He commented on "the tendency to turn the Holocaust into a profession" and informed the Knesset that a ministerial committee had composed a set of guidelines for cultural relations with Germany. The committee wished to respect the deep emotions involved in this matter, Eban said pointedly, but also took into account the fact that Hitler had been defeated in 1945. He outlined what was permitted and what forbidden: Israelis were allowed to participate in international conferences in Germany, as well as in exhibitions, displays, and so on; Germans would be permitted to participate in similar events in Israel. The government would not forbid Israelis to study in Germany but would not allot scholarships for this purpose; German students, young workers, and professionals would be allowed to visit Israel. Israeli performers who wished to appear in Germany would need advance permission from an interministerial committee that would discuss each case individually; government permits would not be granted for German artistic performances in Israel. Israelis would be allowed to pursue their studies at German universities and research institutions "in fields vital to the country." Israeli institutions would be allowed to accept contributions from Germany provided the donors were not granted any control over the institution. "We stand here between the past and the future," Eban summed up, and the Knesset officially acknowledged his announcement.[37]

In the history of relations between nations, the story of the reconcil-

---

* Israeli cinemas were flooded with films set in the Austrian imperial court, starring Romy Schneider as "Sissi." Shortly before the end of the Eichmann trial, actress Marlene Dietrich visited Israel.

iation between Israel and Germany holds a special place. It is doubtful whether bridges were ever built so quickly over so deep an abyss. At the beginning of the 1980s a hand grenade exploded on the grounds of the German embassy in Tel Aviv; an organization that called itself Bal Nishkah—"Lest We Forget"—took credit.[38] Whoever coined that name did not understand reality: German-Israeli conciliation did not lead to the forgetting of the Holocaust. Quite the opposite: consciousness of the Holocaust became deeper and stronger. This is yet another of the paradoxes that so arrestingly characterize the story of the Israelis and the Holocaust.

PART VII

GROWING UP:
From War to War

21 | *"Everyone Thought about It"*

An early 1967 issue of *Nitsots*, the student newspaper of the Hebrew University of Jerusalem, had a completely black cover. At the bottom was the legend: "The current situation." This was a sophomoric generalization, of course, but it came from the guts and reflected the public mood: many Israelis were floundering in desolation and hopelessness. The depression hit the country late in 1966. The symptoms were alarming and severe and included a wave of black humor; one typical joke quoted a sign supposedly hanging at the Tel Aviv airport: "The last person out is kindly requested to turn off the lights." Author Natan Shaham later wrote, "We were like a walking cadaver at its own funeral, telling dirty jokes to the undertaker."[1]

The reasons were many. The days of creation had come to an end; David Ben-Gurion had resigned. His successor as prime minister and minister of defense was Levi Eshkol, a shrewd politician with a farmer's intuition and an avuncular sense of humor. Ushering in a new era of democratic dullness after the almost totalitarian turbulence of the Ben-Gurion years, he radiated a somewhat unpolished, grinning Yiddish-folksy affability. Eshkol was a man without charisma, not awesome in any sense. The public perceived him as hesitant, indecisive, and irresolute. While his administration defused some of the country's internal tensions—between Mapai and Herut, between Jews and Arabs, between the religious and the secular—his first historical responsibility was to impose routine without glory on his people. They never forgave him for it. Many of them still thought in the first-person plural, conceiving of themselves as a nation set apart working to make a vision real. Yet the great Zionist enterprise, the heroic, inspiring revolution, had run its course. The final challenge facing the country was the creation of a normal, everyday kind of life that had no further need for pioneers. Members of the generation that had founded the country were disappointed and frustrated, as were their children—they, too, had been raised to achieve great ends, and now it seemed as if all missions were accomplished. The country was forcing them to grow up too quickly. It was depressing.

The economy entered disheartening recession. Unlike the period of austerity in the early 1950s, when the dream was alive and immigrants came in masses, the recession of the 1960s seemed to have no purpose. In Tel Aviv there were violent demonstrations by the unemployed, most of whom were from the Oriental community; in Jerusalem there were demonstrations by ultraorthodox Jews. Israel, it seemed, was in a social crisis that could not be resolved; people spoke of leaving the country. And on top of all this, the borders were tense. The Syrians shelled the Hula Valley from the Golan Heights and apparently could not be stopped. Life in the northern settlements became intolerable. Not long before, Ben-Gurion had founded his own party, the Israel Workers' List—"Rafi," for short—and was joined by members of the younger generation who had advanced under him, among them Shimon Peres and Moshe Dayan. The effort was fairly pathetic. Among other things, Ben-Gurion accused Eshkol of sabotaging the agreement with Adenauer and of trying to divert the German loan money from investment in the Negev.[2]

In mid-May 1967, President Nasser ousted the UN force that had patrolled the Gaza Strip for a decade. Ten days later he announced that he was closing the Strait of Tiran, the entrance from the Red Sea to the Gulf of Eilat, and would no longer allow Israeli ships to reach the port of Eilat. The blockade applied also to foreign vessels carrying "strategic cargo" to Israel, including fuel. He then signed a defense agreement with Jordan, to Israel's east; this complemented Egypt's existing cooperation with Syria to the north. Israel was surrounded. The Eshkol government launched a round of diplomatic initiatives. Foreign Minister Abba Eban went from capital to capital to meet with presidents and prime ministers. In the meantime the reserves were called up to active duty. This was the "waiting period"; anxiety spread through the country.

Many citizens came forward to volunteer for the work of the men taken by the army. They delivered mail, drove buses, manned fire stations, worked shifts in the hospitals. Elderly people and schoolchildren prepared bomb shelters, dug trenches, and filled sandbags. The press fostered an atmosphere of "their finest hour," with stories of fearless citizens standing shoulder to shoulder against the enemy, filled with courage and determination. Between the lines, however, a national mood of depression, distress, apprehension and a general sense of helplessness were discernible. People emptied store shelves, and the black-market dollar rate rose by 20 percent. *Maariv*, dutifully optimistic as required by a national emergency, announced that "within two days the stream of people leaving [the country] from the Tel Aviv airport is expected to abate." People listened to the nonstop threats being broadcast on the Arab radio stations. The broadcasts consisted of primitive boasts in bad Hebrew, but they were attended to seriously and were quoted in the press. The Voice of the United Arab Republic reported daily that ships of the U.S. Sixth Fleet were standing ready to evacuate Jews from Israel and predicted that those who remained would be slaughtered. All over the country, one heard and read about the danger that the Arabs were about to "exterminate Israel." The phrase had no precise meaning, but everyone used it: No one said that the Arab armies would "conquer" Israel or that they would "destroy" its cities, not even that they would kill its inhabitants. They said that the Arabs would "exterminate Israel."

Meanwhile, half a dozen bearded men in broad hats and black suits, employees of the Tel Aviv Religious Council, surveyed the city's parks, basketball courts, and vacant lots and sanctified them as cemeteries. They expected tens of thousands of casualties.[3] Only a nation haunted by the memory of mass extermination could plan so meticulously for the next holocaust. Interviewed after the war for the book *The Seventh Day*, one young soldier recalled, "People believed we would be exterminated if we lost the war. We got this idea—or inherited it—from the concentration camps. It's a concrete idea for anyone who has grown up in Israel, even if he personally didn't experience Hitler's persecution. Genocide—it's a real possibility. There are the means to do it. That's the lesson of the gas chambers." He discussed it with the men in his company. "I think it's an idea that everyone in Israel lived with. Everyone thought about it. I myself certainly thought in terms of extermination. Any Israeli feels that all these things are part of his life but also feels—I do, at any rate —the relativity of his existence, not just from the point of view of military danger. The fact of Jewish existence in Israel isn't yet unquestionable.

Historically, it's a very short-term phenomenon. We're also comparatively small numerically, the proportion of Jews who actually live here. *

This was the hour for the Young Turks of Rafi, led by Moshe Dayan and Shimon Peres. Their goal was to sweep Levi Eshkol and his generation out of the national leadership and take their places. Yitzhak Rabin, then chief of staff, wrote:

> They mocked him and chipped away at his image and publicized his weaknesses and made false accusations and claimed that the country did not, in effect, have a defense minister in its most difficult hour. Eshkol was exhausted. The burden of the times and that slander campaign worked together to call his position into question. His authority was damaged in the eyes of a few ministers, and those of senior officers as well. . . . With his wings clipped and his authority curtailed, he lacked the power to impose his will on the government. [5]

According to Rabin, Eshkol understood that there was no escaping war, but the impression created by his rivals was that the protracted waiting period was evidence of weakness, and danger. Eshkol, they contended, was not capable of leading the country to war and victory. Anxiety, increasing from day to day, served his opponents well. They stoked the fires; the papers called for "war now" and demanded a new war cabinet led by a "strong man." At the same time, demonstrations and huge newspaper ads demanded Eshkol's ouster in a well-coordinated public campaign. The army general staff also made its position clear. At the beginning of June, Eshkol handed over the defense ministry to Moshe Dayan. He also brought the opposition into a new national unity government, appointing Menahem Begin to the cabinet. [6]

During those weeks of drumbeating, the newspapers continually identified Nasser with Hitler. The proposals to defuse the crisis by any means other than war were compared with the Munich agreement forced on Czechoslovakia before World War II. A year and a half earlier, Gen.

---

* *The Seventh Day: Soldiers Talk about the Six-Day War*, a book produced entirely from recorded conversations after the war, is an authentic but not unproblematic document. [4] There is no way of knowing when the soldiers revealed their real feelings and when they simply repeated clichés contrived to sustain their image as sensitive fighters—shooting and crying their way through a just war. They may not have known themselves. The Holocaust seems, for some of them, to have been the raw material from which they fashioned their self-image.

Yehoshafat Harkabi, former chief of military intelligence, had published an article in *Maariv* describing what he saw as the classic anti-Semitic elements in the religious and political thinking of the Arab countries, including references to the *Protocols of the Learned Elders of Zion* and racist arguments drawn from Nazi ideology, and his article was distributed to Israeli soldiers by the army's educational corps.[7] During the "waiting period," the motif of anti-Semitic threat appeared in the press more than ever before and served as a central argument for those demanding a more determined leader than Eshkol, one who would immediately launch a war. "It is more than the Strait of Tiran that is at issue now," wrote Eliezer Livneh, a well-known commentator and a former Knesset member for Mapai, in *Haaretz*. "What is at issue is the existence or nonexistence of the Jewish people. We must crush the machinations of the new Hitler at the outset, when it is still possible to crush them and survive. It is irresponsible folly not to believe what Nasser has been writing and saying for the last twelve years. Neither the world nor the Jews believed the sincerity of Hitler's declarations. . . . Nasser's fundamental strategy is the same as Hitler's." *Haaretz* had already printed a catalog of comparable statements by Nasser and Hitler, such as "If Israel wants war—fine: Israel will be destroyed!" (Nasser, 1967); "If the Jews drag the world into war, world Jewry will be destroyed" (Hitler, 1939).[8]

The newspapers also extensively covered Nasser's involvement in the ongoing civil war in Yemen. The Egyptians used chemical weapons there, returning the German scientists to the headlines. All this stirred up old Holocaust anxieties. Fear that Israel was in imminent danger of being obliterated was also widespread among the cabinet ministers, most of whom were European-born. One minister, Moshe Haim Shapira, reached the conclusion that the danger was so great that the country should not go to war; the rest inferred the opposite. Anxiety also plagued Israeli-born Chief of Staff Rabin, who was tormented by a sense of guilt for not having prevented the current threat. Tension, plus an overdose of nicotine, overcame him. He shut himself up at home for two days at the height of the events that preceded the war. "It was a personal malfunction," he explained to Eshkol afterwards, offering his resignation; Eshkol told him to carry on.[9]

War finally erupted on June 5, 1967, and over the next six days the Israeli army conquered the Gaza Strip, the Sinai peninsula, the West Bank together with East Jerusalem, and the Golan Heights. The new territories, three times as large as prewar Israel, contained nearly a million inhabitants. Among the government ministers were some, most notably Menahem Begin, who had long dreamed of winning the West Bank. The war machine that occupied the West Bank was also fueled by the historic frustration of commanders from the War of Independence— among them Moshe Dayan, Yitzhak Rabin, and Yigal Allon—who had failed to take this area in 1948. Before the week was over, everyone knew what many (including some stokers of the prewar anxiety) had known before—the Israeli army was more than a match for all the Arab armies put together.

The threat of "extermination" had not, then, been real. But the fear of it had been real, and fear is what Eshkol's opponents exploited. More than any other factor, fear had prompted the war—the same fear that had contributed to mass immigration in the 1950s and to the Dimona project. Its roots lay in the Holocaust.

The six days of the war were often compared to the six days of creation. The feeling for many was of zero hour, a turning point like the Holocaust and the creation of the Jewish state. It was as if Zionist history had begun all over again. The return to the Western Wall and the other Jewish holy sites in Jerusalem, Hebron, and elsewhere enveloped the victory in a halo of national-spiritual redemption and led to a sudden emotional outpouring of Jewish identification, to the point of ecstasy and messianic mysticism. *Haaretz* wrote, "The majesty of the past is no longer only a distant image; it is now part of the new country. Its splendor will spread its rays on the task of building a Jewish society that is a link in the long chain of the people's history in its country. . . . Jerusalem is entirely ours. Cry out and shout, thou inhabitant of Zion!"[10] *Al Hamishmar*, the newspaper of the left-wing socialist Mapam party, was not to be outdone: "We hear the beating heart of Jewish history and we draw the full measure of strength and faith from the eternal sources of ancient Israel."[11] Yet another columnist wrote: "If they give back Jerusalem, I will die."[12]

The soldiers' fighting spirit and the victory were attributed to, among other things, the Holocaust. "Two days before the war," related Uri Ramon, a young officer, "when we felt that we were at a decisive moment and I was in uniform, armed and grimy from a night patrol, I came to the Ghetto Fighters Museum at Kibbutz Lohamei Hagetaot. I wanted to pay my respects to the memory of the fighters, only some of whom had reached this day when the nation was rising up to defend itself. I felt clearly that our war began there, in the crematoriums, in the camps, in the ghettos, and in the forests." He left the museum "pure and clear and strong for this war."[13] Knesset member Arieh Ben-Eliezer (Herut) said: "We were not as few as people say. At our sides fought the six million, who whispered the eleventh commandment in our ear, 'Thou shalt not be killed'—the commandment that was omitted at Mount Sinai but given to us now, during the recent Sinai battles."[14]

§

The first doubts about the occupation of the captured territories were expressed immediately after the war. In *The Seventh Day* there were those who said that the heritage of the Holocaust made it difficult for them to act as military occupiers.[15] The political debate over the future of the new territories also began immediately after the war, and the Holocaust was also cited here, mostly as a reason why Israel could not return to its previous borders. This position was not held only by the right: Menahem Begin liked to quote Abba Eban, who had described the pre-1967 borders as "Auschwitz lines."[16] Golda Meir also based her hard-line views on the Holocaust.[17]

In the meantime, the war of attrition along the Suez Canal continued. Egypt shelled Israeli outposts. The papers daily printed small photographs of the soldiers killed. The Palestinians launched a terror campaign, hijacking aircraft and blowing them up. In September 1972, terrorists burst into the rooms of the Israeli Olympic team in Munich. Two of the athletes were slain immediately; nine more died in an abortive attempt to save them from the kidnappers. A year later, in September 1973, Palestinian terrorists attacked a passenger train bringing Jews from the Soviet Union to a transit camp in Austria, from which they were supposed to continue on to Israel. Chancellor Bruno Kreisky, capitulating to the terrorists' demands, promised to shut down the transit camp. Both incidents were assaults on symbols central to Israel's very being, on the Zionist dream itself, and both were defeats. They were inevitably linked in the Israeli public mind to the Nazi murder of the Jews.

Then came another war. The surprise was almost complete. On October 5, 1973, the day before the Yom Kippur attack by the Egyptian and Syrian armies, the Israeli estimate was that hostilities were unlikely. The next day, the Day of Atonement, the specter of the Holocaust again stalked the land. In the Sinai campaign, dread came in the wake of the victory and led to withdrawal; in the Six-Day War, it preceded the war and led to victory. In 1973, dread came while the war was still being fought. This "earthquake" shook the very foundations of Israel: it spread fear among the decision makers and undermined the morale of the nation. Moshe Dayan was said to have predicted destruction; Golda Meir was reported to have planned suicide. "This feeling was similar to the sense of helplessness that gripped the Jewish people during the Second World War," wrote Holocaust scholar Leni Yahil.[18] Even if Dayan did not say that the "Third Temple" was about to fall and even if Meir's biographer is correct in saying that she was not in fact ready to take her own life, there can be no doubt that Israel had never been in as much danger as it was during its fifth war.[19] Israel won, but this victory was unlike the previous one. It did no more than preserve the status quo, and at a heavy price—2,500 dead, one out of every thousand Jewish citizens. Only during the War of Independence had more been killed.

The blow to the nation's sense of identity was equally severe: Israel no longer felt invulnerable. "The Yom Kippur War," Col. Ehud Praver, deputy chief education officer in the Israeli army, later recalled, "made us all realize that Israel was not the most secure place in the world." Taught, as most young Israelis were, that Zionism was born as a response to anti-Semitism and that Israel was the guarantee of the Jewish people's security, now and forever, Praver felt that "the whole monolithic system we had brought with us from school—anti-Semitism–Zionism–security —was cracked. There were moments when it seemed to have collapsed entirely."

The myth of invulnerability was based on a heroic interpretation of the Holocaust period: "In school," Praver continued, "we had been mesmerized by the Resistance. We were really spellbound by the idea that 'we' were the Resistance, even though we hadn't been born, and that 'they' were the lambs who went to be slaughtered. Suddenly that was cracked, too—we needed the support of American Jews. I remember someone's writing after Mark Spitz's success in the Olympics that there was an important truth in the fact that the Jewish kid from America swam faster than the Jewish kid from Israel. It wasn't just that we needed financial support; that was normal. We needed political support. Without the Americans, we realized, we would not hold out. We felt totally isolated: the country was about to be destroyed and no one had stepped forward. That was the basis for our identification with those very people whom we had despised, to use Jabotinsky's words, as 'a pit of dust and decay.' " After the realization came reactions. "We rebelled against the Resistance," Praver said. "After all, the Resistance had been a symbol. We saw it as the great lie we had unmasked in the Yom Kippur War.

Until then we believed in the pairing of the words *Holocaust* and *heroism* and identified ourselves with the heroism. The war made us realize the meaning of the Holocaust and the limitations of heroism."[20]

After the Yom Kippur War, Palestinian terrorists struck again and again. Time after time, Israel found itself facing situations that evoked the Holocaust. This was true, for example, in the summer of 1976, when an Air France jet en route from Tel Aviv to Paris was hijacked and forced to fly to Entebbe, Uganda. As concern for the fate of the passengers grew, it was learned that the Israelis had been separated from the rest of the passengers. That action inevitably recalled the "selection" at Auschwitz, where those who were fit were separated from those to be sent to the gas chambers.[21] Prime Minister Yitzhak Rabin and the minister of defense, Shimon Peres, approved an army rescue operation.

Peres, who had been a student in Israel during the Holocaust, belonged to the generation that felt guilt and shame about the extermination of the Jews. The hijacking raised in him the same feelings. Holocaust anxiety was a fixed feature of his psychic makeup. Born in Poland, he had come to Palestine in the early 1930s, at the age of eleven. Despite growing up in Tel Aviv and spending time at a kibbutz, he found it difficult to assimilate the outward signs of Israeliness. In contrast to the stereotypical "new man" of Israel, Peres, formerly Perski, preserved a certain measure of "Polishness," or sentimental Jewishness that may have taken root during his political youth, when he stood in the shadow of Berl Katznelson, Levi Eshkol, and David Ben-Gurion. He was an avid reader and wrote poetry; he never served in the army. When the Perski family had emigrated to Palestine, Peres's grandfather, the head of the local Jewish community, stayed behind in Poland. The Nazis shut him and others up in the synagogue and set it aflame. He was burned alive. During his childhood, Peres had loved no one as much as he did his grandfather. When he asked the government for authorization to send a rescue force to Entebbe, he cited the Holocaust among his arguments.[22]

The triumphant rescue by Mossad commandos reconfirmed the essentially heroic nature of the Israeli "new man," and, at least for the moment, reanimated the myth of the Resistance.

22 | "Hitler Is Already Dead, Mr. Prime Minister"

On November 19, 1977, President Anwar Sadat of Egypt came to Jerusalem and was received by Prime Minister Menahem Begin. A year and a half later Israel and Egypt signed a peace treaty. This was Begin's great historic achievement.

Begin was the first prime minister who didn't belong to the Labor movement led by Mapai, and he was also the first who was a survivor of the Holocaust. A year after World War II broke out he had been arrested by the Soviet secret police, and in 1942 he arrived in Palestine. There were many indications that he had brought with him what was later described as "survivor syndrome"—a sense of guilt for having remained alive. Apparently he also brought, or developed, the notion that he had deserted his people: At the time of his arrest he had been the leader of the Betar youth movement in Poland. Once in Palestine, he was unable to do anything more for the Jews of Europe than the Mapai leaders were doing. In fact, not belonging to the yishuv leadership, he could not do anywhere near as much. Toward the end of the war, however, and even more after it was over, Begin made a great effort to create the impression that he was more loyal to the heritage of the Holocaust than the members of Mapai were. The Holocaust shaped his entire political career—from the great battle against reparations to the anxious period before the Six-Day War. When Levi Eshkol made Begin a minister in his national unity government, Begin received legitimacy for the first time. He was able to claim a share of the victory. To a large extent, his appointment to the cabinet paved the way for his election as prime minister ten years later.

In the 1970s the members of the second generation of the Oriental Jewish community, children of immigrants from the Islamic countries, came of age. They charged that Israeli society was discriminating against them, both denying them equal opportunities and forcing them to give up their own culture. They had trouble accepting the Holocaust as part of their own history—the establishment, led by the Labor movement, did not encourage them to do so—and their protest movements gave voice to that alienation. Early in 1979, Charlie Biton, a young Jerusalem activist of Moroccan descent elected to the Knesset as a Communist, stated: "Anti-Semitism arose in industrial Europe. In Morocco there was no anti-Semitism. The European Jews were an exploitative class, and in Israel they are the same. The Zionist movement came here and turned this country into an offshoot of Europe." Until Biton corrected himself, his statement was interpreted as a defense of the genocide against the Jews.[1]

Members of the ruling coalition sometimes declared the importance of emphasizing that Oriental Jews were also among the victims of the Holocaust; textbooks were eventually revised to this effect.[2] But such efforts came too late to save the Labor movement. Begin understood better than the Labor leaders the sensibilities of the Oriental voters, and he steered them into support for the center-right alignment (Likud) formed in 1973; Begin's Herut party was Likud's largest component. Part of his strategy relied on fostering demagogic populism and nationalistic sentiment. When he promised that he would never give up the West Bank, he was reassuring the Oriental Jews not only with the prospect of national security and the attainment of a national dream but also with the promise of social advancement: The Palestinians in the territories, not the Oriental Jews, were now at the bottom of the social ladder, and as long as the occupation continued, the Orientals would not revert to the lowest rung. Begin knew how to give the Oriental Israelis, especially those who had come from North Africa, the sense that he respected their culture. He restored their most important treasure—their self-respect—stolen from them by the Labor movement. In so doing, he involved them in what had up until then been a solely Ashkenazic privilege—Holocaust consciousness. * The great popularizer of the Holocaust, Begin did more than

* Ultimately, the sharing became essentially complete. A study by Dan Bar-On and Oron Sela of Ben-Gurion University concluded that beginning in the late seventies, the Holocaust became an "event" common to all citizens of Israel, no matter what their origins

anyone else to politicize it. A master of the symbolic historical gesture, he missed no opportunity to exploit the Holocaust in debating his political opponents and in creating his own political image.

The longer he spoke of the Holocaust and used it to justify his policies and to shore up his political position, the more he expropriated Labor's monopoly on it. This had always been one of his goals. He often seemed to believe that, by controlling the memory of the Holocaust, he could control the country. His first action as prime minister was to grant asylum to a group of Vietnamese boat people who had been saved by an Israeli ship. "We all remember the boats of Jewish illegal immigrants in the 1930s who wandered over the seven seas asking for entry to a country, or to many countries, only to be rejected," Begin said.*[5] Begin tended to give the impression that the whole world was tainted with Nazism and that Israel stood alone. Two years before he took office, the UN General Assembly had itself promoted this impression by resolving that Zionism was a form of racism. Israel's ambassador to the UN, Haim Herzog (later elected president), expressed the future prime minister's sentiments particularly well when he told the General Assembly delegates that Hitler would have felt at home among them.[7]

During President Sadat's visit and the ensuing debate over the agreement that required Israel to withdraw from the entire Sinai peninsula, almost everyone referred to the Holocaust; it served both the supporters and the opponents of the treaty. Begin accompanied Sadat on a visit to Yad Vashem, and afterwards—lest anyone accuse him of capitulating to the enemy—gave his guest the standard Israeli version of the Holocaust's lesson: "No one came to save us—neither from the East nor from the West. For this reason, we have sworn a vow, we, the generation of extermination and rebirth: Never again will we put our nation in danger, never again will we put our women and children and those whom we have a duty to defend—if necessary at the cost of our lives—in range of the enemy's deadly fire."[8] The agreement's opponents also used the Ho-

---

and culture.[3] "The patterns of daily behavior of every citizen of the country should be guided by the harsh impact of the events of the Holocaust," affirmed Knesset member Moshe Katsav, a young man of Iranian birth.[4]

* A number of Vietnamese refugees were in fact allowed to settle in Israel, but when, a while later, there was a proposal to allow the entry of several thousand more, Begin reacted like one of the leaders who had avoided giving asylum to Jewish refugees. First there had to be an international agreement, he stated, suggesting that the Knesset approach the world's parliaments to discuss the plight of the refugees.[6]

locaust to justify their position. "For me, it is sufficient to recall the Egyptian president's past during World War II, and his attraction to Berchtesgaden, Hitler's Eagle's Nest, to sense that the destruction of Israel is the factor that motivates his thinking and action," said Dov Shilansky in the Knesset.[9] During World War II Sadat had supported Germany; some time before coming to Jerusalem he had spent a vacation in the Bavarian ski resort of Berchtesgaden. The peace treaty included among its provisions the evacuation of the Israeli settlements in the Sinai. When the residents of the town of Yamit resisted the evacuation, they pinned yellow Stars of David on their clothes, the kind that the Nazis had forced the Jews to wear.

The Holocaust was, especially throughout Begin's term in office, a cornerstone of the basic creed of the State of Israel and the policies of its government. In June 1981, Begin justified the demolition of an Iraqi nuclear facility with the words "We must protect our nation, a million and a half of whose children were murdered by the Nazis in the gas chambers."[10] He often compared Yasir Arafat to Hitler, referring to him as a "two-legged beast"—a phrase he had used, years earlier, to describe Hitler.[11] Begin further compared the PLO's Palestinian National Covenant to *Mein Kampf*. "Never in the history of mankind has there been an armed organization so loathsome and contemptible, with the exception of the Nazis," he liked to say.[12] On the eve of Israel's invasion of Lebanon, in June 1982, Begin told his cabinet: "You know what I have done and what we have all done to prevent war and loss of life. But such is our fate in Israel. There is no way other than to fight selflessly. Believe me, the alternative is Treblinka, and we have decided that there will be no more Treblinkas."[13] A few weeks after the war began, Begin responded to international criticism of Israel by repeating a premise that his predecessors had shared: after the Holocaust, the international community had lost its right to demand that Israel answer for its actions. "No one, anywhere in the world, can preach morality to our people," Begin declared in the Knesset.[14] A similar statement was included in the resolution adopted by the cabinet after the massacres in Sabra and Shatila, the Palestinian refugee camps on the outskirts of Beirut.[15] Referring to the London *Times*, Begin said, as he often had before: "A newspaper that supported the treachery of the Munich agreement [to dismember Czechoslovakia in the 1930s] should be very careful in preaching morality to a small nation fighting for its life. Had we listened to it we would no longer exist."[16] In a letter to President Ronald Reagan, Begin wrote that the destruction of Arafat's headquarters in Beirut had given him the feeling that he had sent the Israeli army into Berlin to destroy Hitler in his bunker.[17]

The war in Lebanon divided the country deeply. The Holocaust was inevitably dragged into the political debate. "Hitler is already dead, Mr. Prime Minister," wrote author Amos Oz, in response to one of Begin's defenses of the bombing of Beirut.

Adolf Hitler destroyed a third of the Jewish people, among them your parents and relatives, among them my family. Often I, like many Jews, find at the bottom of my soul a dull sense of pain because I did not kill Hitler with my own hands. I am sure that in your soul a similar fantasy hovers. There is not and will never be a cure for this open wound in our souls. Tens of thousands of dead Arabs will not heal that wound. But, Mr. Begin, Adolf Hitler died thirty-seven years ago. Unfortunately or not, it is a fact: Hitler is not in hiding in Nabatea, in Sidon, or in Beirut. He is dead and gone.

Again and again, Mr. Begin, you reveal to the public eye a strange urge to resuscitate Hitler in order to kill him every day anew in the guise of terrorists. . . . This urge to revive and obliterate Hitler over and over again is the result of a melancholy that poets must express, but among statesmen it is a hazard that is liable to lead them along a path of mortal danger.[18]

The editor of *Yediot Aharonot*, Herzl Rosenblum, responded to Oz in an article that contained one of the stranger paragraphs ever written in the Hebrew press. Defending Begin's comparison of Yasir Arafat with Adolf Hitler, Rosenblum wrote:

Arafat, were he only to get enough power, would do to us things that even Hitler never imagined. This is not rhetoric on our part. If Hitler killed us with a certain restraint—were Arafat ever to come to power, he would not merely play at such matters. He would cut off our children's heads with a war shriek, rape our women in broad daylight before tearing them to shreds, and throw us off every roof into the street and skin us like hungry tigers in the jungle wherever he came across us, without German "order" and Eichmann's organized transports. . . . This being the case, what did Begin do wrong in mentioning Adolf Hitler? Yes, that despot was a kitten compared to what Arafat will bring. . . . Begin, when he began speaking recently about Hitler, did not exaggerate—in fact, he minimized—the danger lying in wait for us from the mad rise of this mass murderer from Beirut.[19]

A few days earlier the papers reported the most vociferous denunciation ever made by the government's opponents: the scholar Yeshayahu Leibowitz described the war in Lebanon as a "Judeo-Nazi policy."[20] For the first time since Yad Vashem was built, a Holocaust survivor began a hunger strike there: Shlomo Schmelzman, a survivor of the Warsaw ghetto and of Buchenwald, protested both the war and the use of the Holocaust to justify it. His strike prompted more polemics in the press. The Yad Vashem management decided to forbid him to sit on the institution's grounds, and after seven days he gave up.[21]

At the end of that same year, a Jerusalem woman accompanied her soldier son and his comrades from the tank corps on a visit to Yad Vashem, where she attended the lecture given by one of the guides, Yehiam Weitz. The next day she sent a letter to the Israeli army's chief of staff, Maj. Gen. Rafael Eitan, who ordered the immediate cancellation of all visits by soldiers to Yad Vashem. According to the woman, Weitz, the son and grandson of respected Mapai officials, had said that contrary to the usual interpretation, the creation of Israel did not ensure the security of its inhabitants; quite the opposite—it would be much easier to eliminate the Jews in Israel than it would the majority of Jews elsewhere. The woman also wrote that the guide had disparaged the deaths of the victims of the Holocaust and said that it made no difference how one died, whether with honor or in shame.

The guide's words, not surprisingly, had been taken out of context, and army visits to Yad Vashem were soon renewed. Some months before, a military court had begun considering the charges against several soldiers and officers accused of unwarranted violence against residents of the occupied territories. One of the defendants was said to have ordered his soldiers to inscribe numbers on the arms of Palestinians. The board of Yad Vashem was asked to condemn the act. Gideon Hausner, now the board's chairman, squelched the initiative, ruling that it had no relevance to the Holocaust.[22]

Begin's politicization of the Holocaust angered his opponents and inevitably led them to reexamine and redefine some basic, almost sacred, historiographical concepts. In 1980, an article by the well-known columnist Boaz Evron signaled a turning point. Under the provocative headline "THE HOLOCAUST—A DANGER TO THE NATION," the article challenged for the first time the thesis that the extermination of the Jews was unique among the crimes of the Nazis. In fact, Evron noted, they murdered Germans, the retarded, the incurably ill, and Gypsies, and they intended to extend mass extermination to include other nations as well. The thesis that the murder of the Jews was unique was merely a convenience for all concerned, he wrote. It helped the Germans present Nazism as a single outburst of madness, and so paved the way for Germany to return to the family of nations, which fit in with the political and economic interests of the world at large—including Israel. The emphasis on the unique nature of the slaughter of the Jews as the world remained silent advanced the interests of the Zionist movement, and later of the State of Israel. "Every important non-Jewish guest who arrives here is taken, as if it goes without saying, on a mandatory visit to Yad Vashem . . . to make clear the proper mood and sense of guilt expected of him," Evron remarked.

Yet the thesis that the genocide of the Jews was unique had the undesirable effect of removing the Jewish people from the human race, as if they had been created separately. This tendency had deep roots in Jewish tradition, Evron wrote, in the concept of the Jews as a chosen people that "dwells alone." But in addition to being antithetical to the Zionist dream of creating a normal Jewish existence, it could, he maintained, lead to moral blindness. "Since the world is always presented as hating and persecuting us, we see ourselves as released from the need for any moral consideration in our attitudes to it." The paranoid isolation from mankind and its laws, Evron cautioned, was apt to bring certain Jews to the point where, if they had power, they would relate to non-Jews as subhuman and, for all practical purposes, emulate the racist approach of the Nazis. Evron warned also against the growing tendency to identify Arab hostility to Israel with Nazi anti-Semitism. "A leadership cannot be detached from its propaganda; it sees its own propaganda as a reflection of reality," he wrote. "Thus the leadership acts within a world of myths and monsters of its own creation."[23]

This was written two and a half years before Menahem Begin sent the Israeli army to Beirut to destroy Adolf Hitler.

In February 1983 the Knesset held a debate on "Fifty Years since the Nazi Rise to Power—The Day and Its Lessons." Ritual historical debates of this sort had been held before in the Knesset, generally on major anniversaries of various events of the Holocaust. Taken together, they reflect the influence of the changing social and political reality in Israel on the way Israelis perceive the Holocaust. The 1983 debate was initiated by Yair Tsaban (Mapam), a leader of the Israeli peace movement. The most important lesson of the Holocaust, he said, was the universal one: "To be on guard: to be alert to every sign of the erosion of democracy, to every inclination toward dictatorship of any type, in any clothing, even if populist or pseudo-leftist. This lesson is accompanied by another lesson: the terrible peril involved in the conjunction of the destruction of democracy and the rise of dictatorship with the cancerous growth of unrestrained, overpowering nationalist madness." From here, Tsaban launched into a lecture based mostly on the research of American historian George Mosse.[24] The Holocaust's universal lessons had been mentioned in the past, but Tsaban's attempt to bring them to the forefront at the expense of the nationalist lessons was new, an obvious response to Menahem Begin's attempt to present his policies, including the war in Lebanon, as a national moral imperative resulting from the Holocaust.

§

For Begin, however, the lesson never changed. Shortly before Begin became prime minister, German Chancellor Helmut Schmidt had been invited to make a state visit to Israel. Germany was by then a country whose economic, geopolitical, and military importance to Israel was second only to that of the United States, though both Germany and Israel took care not to say that they had "normal" relations. Not long after the Begin government was formed, however, Moshe Dayan, now foreign minister, said that Germany and Israel had "secular" relations.[25] Begin himself promised to do all that his position required, including meeting with German officials, and his government endorsed the earlier invitation to Schmidt.[26]

Schmidt, meanwhile, put off his visit time after time, as if Begin's Israel did not deserve him. In the spring of 1981, Schmidt said upon returning from a visit to Saudi Arabia that Germany's Nazi past imposed on it historical responsibility for a number of European nations, and for the Palestinian people as well. He did not mention the Jewish people or Israel. Begin responded with a fierce personal attack on the chancellor, hinting, among other things, that Schmidt had been an accomplice to Nazi crimes. "Everyone served in the Nazi army, including Mr. Schmidt, who swore personal allegiance to the Führer and lived up to his oath entirely," Begin said.[27] Israel was in the midst of a stormy and violent election campaign. Begin's attack on Schmidt was part of his efforts to stir up emotions, a distant echo of his great anti-German harangues of the 1950s. Begin had already exchanged insults with Austrian Chancellor Bruno Kreisky over Kreisky's ties with Yasir Arafat. "We will overcome the Nazi Arafats and their servants as well, whatever their origins," Begin said, referring to Kreisky's Jewish birth.[28] It is easy to imagine what he might have said had he known that Jewish blood flowed in Helmut Schmidt's veins also. Israel's ambassador to Germany, Yohanan Meroz, who had heard of Schmidt's background from the chancellor himself, decided to keep the information from his superiors. He feared Begin might make use of it and further exacerbate the tension between the two countries.[29] In the end, Schmidt did not visit Israel.

Begin resigned in August 1983. "I can't go on," he explained, and until his death in 1992, he lived a secluded life at home. When he left his office for the last time, German flags waved over the building: Chancellor Helmut Kohl was about to arrive for a visit. It would seem that the tension-racked Begin consciously chose the timing for his resignation. At least he would not have to receive the German.

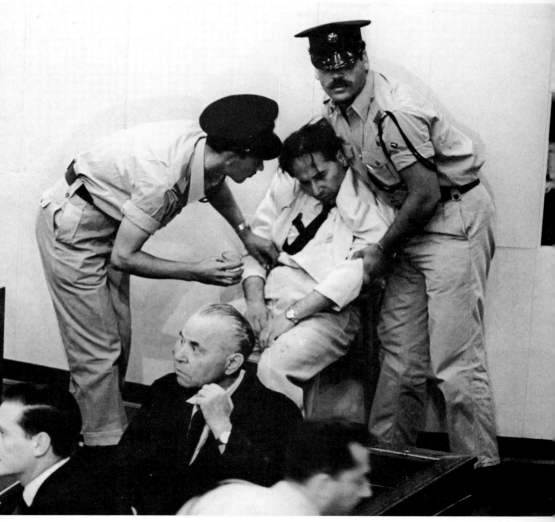

"I see them"
Yehiel De-Nur ("Ka-Tzetnik") seconds after having fainted on the witness stand at the trial of Adolf Eichmann

"Not one of us will leave here as he was before"
Israelis at the Eichmann trial
ISRAELI GOVERNMENT PRESS OFFICE

"I would have shot a bullet into my head"
Adolf Eichmann in court

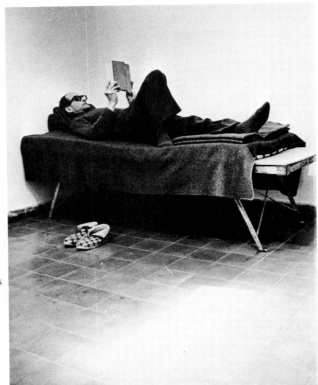

"Defeated before this conundrum"
Adolf Eichmann in his cell

"To point an accusing finger"
Attorney General Gideon Hausner at the Eichmann trial
ISRAELI GOVERNMENT PRESS OFFICE

"From the land of the Holocaust to the land of the living"
Abba Kovner at the Eichmann trial
ISRAELI GOVERNMENT PRESS OFFICE

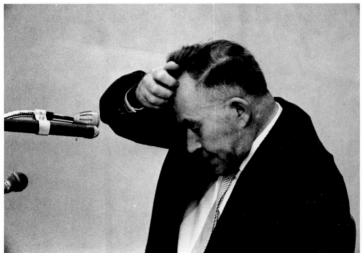

"The shadow of another trial"
Joel Brand at the Eichmann trial
ISRAELI GOVERNMENT PRESS OFFICE

"Self-hatred"
Hannah Arendt at the Eichmann trial
ISRAELI GOVERNMENT PRESS OFFICE

First design for Yad Vashem
by Mordecai Shenhabi
(1943)

"An everlasting name"
The Yad Vashem Pillar of Heroism
in Jerusalem
ISRAELI GOVERNMENT PRESS OFFICE

"Idol worship"
Zyklon B, used to exterminate the
Jews, and bars of soap, supposedly
made of human fat, exhibited on
Mount Zion (Jerusalem, 1972)
ISRAELI GOVERNMENT PRESS OFFICE

"The last desire of my life has been fulfilled"
Mordecai Anielewicz statue at Yad Mordecai
ISRAELI GOVERNMENT PRESS OFFICE

"Every Jew has his own death camp"
Yael Kushnir, Masorti High School
student at Treblinka (1990)

ישראל לקראת מלחמת המפרץ בעיני זאב (הארץ, 3.10.90)

"Never more Jewish"
Waiting for the Persian Gulf War
in Israel as seen by Zeev. Text
reads: "Unification of Germany"
Haaretz (October 3, 1990)

Israeli high school students at Majdanek (1990)

23 | *"Deep in Our Souls"*

In the summer of 1984, some 25,000 Israelis cast their votes for Rabbi
Meir Kahane, electing him to the Knesset. The political establishment
was stunned, for the man had often been compared to Adolf Hitler.
Kahane had come to Israel from the United States. The principles he
proclaimed were, he said, based on the lessons of the Holocaust.[1] At the
start of his public career, as the leader of the militant Jewish Defense
League in the United States, Kahane had won a certain measure of
admiration in Israel. For many, he was the epitome of a proud Jew
unafraid to defend himself.

Kahane liked to say he was a true expression of Zionism. In fact, he
expressed only its dark side. Zionism has a Kahanist element that man-
ifested itself even before Kahane. Kahane's Zionism was racist and pornographic. As he began his activities in Israel, it became clear that he
wished to alter some fundamental values of Israeli life. He demanded
the expulsion of Israel's Arab citizens and the Arab residents of the occupied territories, and he advocated establishing Jewish religious law as
the law of the land. At first, he was dismissed as an eccentric trouble-
maker. From time to time he would organize a demonstration and clash
with the police. At his headquarters in Jerusalem, he ran a kind of little
museum that compared the coming holocaust (in America) with the
previous one in Europe. Kahane's violent anti-Arab, antidemocratic nationalism and religious extremism won most of their support in disad-
vantaged neighborhoods, nourished by a complex of social frustration,

xenophobia (particularly with regard to Arabs), fears for survival, and vague anxieties that Kahane knew how to stir up. He frequently warned that Arabs craved to give vent to their Jew hatred by raping women and children; a series of murders and rapes that enraged the country at that time—some of them perpetrated by terrorists, some by common criminals, and some of which remain unsolved—fed his propaganda machine. But he was ugly and spoke bad Hebrew with a foreign accent. No one thought he had any more influence than lavatory graffiti. Hence the shock of his election to the Knesset.

About a year after his election, Kahane introduced two bills. The first would have restricted Israeli citizenship to Jews. Non-Jews—that is, Arabs—would have the status of "stranger," as defined by Jewish law, and would be subject to "taxes and slavery." The personal rights of every such stranger would be protected, but he or she would have no political rights and so would not be allowed to vote, hold public office, or live in Jerusalem. Non-Jews who refused to accept these restrictions would be expelled from the country, although they would receive compensation. The second bill was called the Law to Prevent Assimilation between Jews and Non-Jews, and for the Holiness of Israel. Its terms included the elimination of all government programs meant to bring about contact between Jews and Arabs. There would be separate beaches for Jews and non-Jews; non-Jews would not be allowed to live in Jewish neighborhoods without the agreement of the majority of the Jewish residents. A Jewish citizen or resident of the country would not be allowed to marry a non-Jew. A Jewish citizen of Israel would be forbidden to have sexual relations with a non-Jew; intermarried couples would be forced to separate immediately.

One member of the Knesset compared the proposed legislation with the Nuremberg laws, section by section, and found many points of similarity. The Knesset's presidium refused to allow Kahane to bring the bills up for debate. Kahane went to the Supreme Court and won, as he had in the past: Justice Aharon Barak ruled that Kahane's bills "awaken horrifying memories" and could harm the democratic character of the State of Israel, but, he wrote, "our strength lies in meticulous preservation of the rule of law and the legality of power, even when this means giving expression to opinions we abhor."[2]

In time it became clear that Kahane himself was less dangerous than Kahanism, which spread through Israel and gained power, especially among young people.[3] As Palestinian terror attacks continued, there were

more and more incidents of mobs of young Israelis attacking Arab passersby and raging through Arab neighborhoods; the cry "Death to the
Arabs" became all too familiar. "The slogan 'Death to the Jews' still
echoes in my ears, and here they change a single word and it comes out
'Death to the Arabs,' " said Knesset member Haike Grossman (Mapam),
a Holocaust survivor. In her darkest dreams, she said, in the nightmares
that pursued her for many long years, she never thought that such a thing
could happen.[4] In July 1985 the Knesset passed an amendment stating
that candidates associated with racist acts or goals could not stand for
election to the Knesset. The Holocaust was frequently invoked in the
debate over the amendment. The Knesset also considered an amendment
to the penal code that would outlaw racist incitement, as well as a law
forbidding a slate of candidates denying Israel's right to exist to run for
the Knesset and another forbidding contacts with the PLO.[5] Kahane was
not allowed to be a candidate in the next elections to the Knesset, but
his place was filled by other Kahanists, who knew how to express their
demand for the deportation of the Arabs in acceptable language, free of
religious fanaticism and pornographic racism, language rooted in Zionist
thinking and the Israeli experience.

Along with the legislative measures aimed at restricting Kahane, the
educational system also sought to protect democracy from racism. The
1986–87 school year was declared the year of "education for democracy";
as a part of the new program, the ministry of education encouraged
meetings between Jewish and Arab students. Radio and television, as well
as the education corps of the army, lent their support to a concentrated
but somewhat pathetic effort to shore up democratic consciousness.

"In the wake of Kahane, we heard more and more about soldiers who,
exposed to the history of the Holocaust, were planning all sorts of ways
to exterminate the Arabs," recalled education-corps officer Ehud Praver.
"It concerned us very much, because we saw that the Holocaust was
legitimizing the appearance of Jewish racism. We learned that it was
necessary to deal not only with the Holocaust but also with the rise of
fascism and to explain what racism is and what dangers it holds for
democracy." According to Praver, "too many soldiers were deducing that
the Holocaust justifies every kind of disgraceful action."[6] In May 1986
the army distributed a set of guidelines for commanding officers, "The
Holocaust and Its Lesson." The two-page document concluded by stating
that the defense of human freedom was the best way of preventing another
outbreak of Nazism.[7] A year later, in April 1987, the education corps

distributed another sheet, called "After the Holocaust," containing the following sentences: "The experience of the Holocaust returns us to man as man. . . . We are commanded to be ready to defend ourselves, but in addition to strength, we are commanded to preserve the moral values that determine our image and the use we make of our power." On the back, a quote from Israeli novelist A. B. Yehoshua presented a dilemma: "Should we endanger ourselves for our moral values? And, in contrast, are we permitted, under serious military circumstances, to deviate from basic moral values?" According to Yehoshua, the very doubts raised by such a dilemma reflect an understanding of the significance of the Holocaust.[8]

A few months later the Intifada broke out, and soon the army decided to suspend visits by soldiers to the Ghetto Fighters Museum at Kibbutz Lohamei Hagetaot. Officially the army contended that the educational programs were not functioning properly and that the guides meant to accompany the soldiers were not properly trained.[9] Unofficially, there were reports that the events in the occupied territories had elicited extreme reactions from the soldiers: some had concluded from what they saw in the museum that brutality like that of the Nazis was the way to deal with rioters. In the summer of 1989 the press revealed that a group of soldiers calling itself the Mengele unit had plotted to kill Arabs. There were also reports of units in which the soldiers termed themselves "Auschwitz platoons" and "Demjanjuks." The army tried at first to prevent publication of these stories and later explained that the idea was no more than black humor on the part of the soldiers.[10]

But violence and black humor were not the only lessons learned at the Ghetto Fighters Museum: some soldiers concluded that they could no longer be accessories to the oppression in the territories. Their refusal to serve in the territories reflected an entire range of existential problems and moral qualms that until then had been ignored or sidestepped. Like the issue of racism, it put democracy to the test; also like the issue of racism, it arose in the shadow of the Holocaust, first appearing during the war in Lebanon. With the war at its height, some soldiers refused to serve on political and moral grounds. Then, as the army suppressed the Palestinian uprising in the territories, sometimes systematically violating human rights, dozens of Israelis refused to participate and were sent to prison. The phenomenon was probably more widespread than was publicly known, because individual cases were dealt with informally and quietly within each unit.[11] Service in the Israeli army had always been seen not only as a necessity but also as a pillar of the personal and collective identities of the Israeli people. Thus the refusal to serve in the territories, much less the army, was tantamount to going into exile. And although this type of protest remained marginal, by the mid-1980s it was already a subject for debate. Like the talk—much more common—of deporting the Arabs, this debate also reflected the polarization of values and culture and the growing extremism of political thinking in Israel. Violent acts against Arabs in the occupied territories—the army described them as "excesses"—were made public in a series of military trials that revived the question of what should be considered a "manifestly illegal order" that a soldier was required to disobey. The Nazi army was cited, usually indirectly, in this context. Those who refused to serve in Lebanon and the territories often cited the Holocaust in defense of their position.

The comparison between Israel and Nazi Germany had been made in the past, as far back as the War of Independence. It had been heard after the Kfar Kassem massacre of 1956 and was occasionally raised in discussions of the question "Can it happen to us, too?" Israeli politics recognized "Hitler" as an insult and as a charge to be leveled in a whole range of debates.[12] Yet its use as a literal comparison was rare and was restricted, generally, to the lunatic fringe. The most extreme ultrareligious sects in the Jerusalem neighborhood of Mea Shearim painted houses with swastikas in condemnation of the government. Ethnic tension led to the coining of such expressions as *Ashken-Nazis*. Not long after Yeshayahu Leibowitz introduced his term *Judeo-Nazis* to protest Israel's actions in Lebanon, Amos Oz exchanged letters with a member of the marginal left, who wrote that the use of successive cold and hot showers to torture Palestinian prisoners "reminds me of something." Oz responded, "That is a demagogic and corrupt comparison."[13] At times various newspapers around the world compared Israel to Nazi Germany. Israel called this anti-Semitism. The authorities in the occupied territories took action against Arab newspapers that made the comparison.[14] But the political extremism that gave birth to Kahanism on the one hand, and to the refusal to perform military service on the other, made Israelis of the 1980s more prone to compare themselves with the Nazis. That shift was the result of, among other things, the extensive rhetorical use to which Begin had put the Holocaust.

In September 1988 *Davar*, a newspaper with ties to the Labor movement, published an article that described the Moledet party—which advocates the expulsion of Arabs from Israel to Arab countries—as "neo-

Nazi"; Moledet lodged a criminal complaint. A few weeks later *Maariv* published a campaign ad against the Labor party's platform of seeking a solution to the Israeli-Palestinian conflict through an international peace conference; the ad contained a large picture of Adolf Hitler at the Munich conference of 1938. *Maariv* apologized.[15] Zeev Sternhell, a Hebrew University expert on the history of fascism, wrote: "The end came to German democracy not on the day the Nazi militias killed their first leftist demonstrator but when a Nazi was sentenced to three months in prison for the same offense for which a Communist was sentenced to three years."[16] A Tel Aviv judge had just sentenced a Jewish citizen to six months of public service for killing an Arab boy. When the mayor of one of the new West Bank settlements tried to require all Arabs entering his town to wear an identification tag, the popular daily tabloid *Hadashot* published an editorial headlined "NO TO THE YELLOW PATCH."[17] "We had better start preparing ourselves and the glass booths in which we will sit when they judge us for what we did to the Palestinian people," declared a well-known songwriter.[18] After Kahane was murdered in the winter of 1990, his followers began to threaten storekeepers and demand that they stop employing Arab workers. Proprietors who complied were given signs certifying that Arabs were not employed on the premises. Yitzhak Arad, current chairman of the Yad Vashem board of directors, told *Hadashot*: "When I heard that, I immediately recalled the German boycott of the Jews." A year later, three judges serving on a special military panel ruled that atrocities committed in the West Bank under orders from Col. Yehuda Meir had wakened in them "unavoidable associations."[19]

The press had previously played up a public scandal that had begun, typically, with statements made in newspaper interviews. In October 1988 A. B. Yehoshua had said in an interview with *Newsweek* that he could understand how Germans who lived through World War II could say they did not know about the Holocaust, "since many Israelis refuse to read the newspapers or watch the news on television. That's how easy it is to disengage oneself from things happening ten kilometers away," he added. Of course there was an uproar. Yehoshua denied having equated the situation in the territories with that in Nazi Germany and tried to explain what he meant:

In our collective and personal subconscious, like it or not, we carry not images of the French in Algeria or the English in Kenya but rather images of the Second World War (and let us not forget that the Holocaust was not just gas chambers but also a horrifying system of humiliation and mistreatment of individuals, old people, women, and children). These are the fundamental images with which we have been raised and which are planted deep in our souls.[20]

For the first time Yehoshua seems to have provided theoretical legitimacy for using the Holocaust as a criterion for comparison. His idea was innovative, perhaps the most consciously daring idea that an Israeli writer had drawn from the Holocaust.

It may be no coincidence that Yehoshua's remarks appeared in a polemic newspaper article and not as part of a literary work: Hebrew fiction has always had a hard time competing with documentary reports of the Holocaust. The best writers—S. Y. Agnon, Amos Oz, and Yehoshua—have seldom touched on the Holocaust itself. One of the two great novels overtly influenced by the Holocaust, *Saul and Joanna* by Naomi Fränkel, concentrates on Jewish life in Germany before the Holocaust and the other, *See Under: Love* by David Grossman, written thirty years after Fränkel's work, focuses on the effects of the Holocaust on survivors in Israel. Neither book directly deals with the horror itself. The same is true of the works of Aharon Appelfeld. As a rule, he does not touch the fire.[21]

In confronting the Holocaust, Israeli writers are up against more than the limitations of language. There is also a tradition of literature, partly echoing the lamentations in the Bible, that is inspired by disaster and repression, by hundreds of years of massacres, persecution, expulsions, and discrimination against Jews. The works of poets like Shaul Tschernikowski and Haim Nahman Bialik, works about the anti-Semitic persecutions of the Middle Ages and the turn-of-the-century pogroms in Russia, always very much present in Hebrew literary consciousness, remained relevant after the Holocaust as well. Uri Zvi Greenberg, whose powerful lamentations have won him recognition as the greatest of the Holocaust poets, belongs, in his own way, to the tradition created by his predecessors.

With the politicization of the Holocaust during the Begin administration, a new, explicit rhetoric marked Israeli prose, poetry, and especially drama. The Lebanon war occasioned numerous comparisons between Israelis and Nazis. Thus the 1982 massacres at the Sabra and Shatila refugee camps near Beirut inspired the following lines by Dalia Rabikowitz.

> Back to camp, *Marsch!* shouted the soldier
> To the screaming women from Sabra and Shatila.
> I had orders to follow.[22]

At the end of 1990 the comparison also found expression in a book of monologues by soldiers who served in the territories.[23]

¶

With each passing year, popularization of the Holocaust increased. From the *Heroism Quiz* on national television, live from Auschwitz, to the publication of a Hebrew edition of *Maus*, an American book that depicts the murder of the Jews in comic-book form, consciousness of the Holocaust became part of everyday life and a staple theme of popular culture: in films and plays, books and television.[24] By the late 1980s there was hardly a day when the Holocaust was not mentioned in one of the newspapers.

These were the same newspapers, in many cases the same editors, that had provided only modest coverage of the Holocaust while it was happening. After the war they seldom dealt with it, either. Except for *Haaretz*, they showed little interest in the Nuremberg trials. Just as they had not considered the murder of Jews a big story, neither did they think the trial of the murderers important. The change came with Adolf Eichmann's capture and trial. In September 1961, *Maariv* printed Yevgeny Yevtushenko's "Babi Yar," devoting its banner headline to the poem.[25] Once the papers had discovered the Holocaust as a story, they did not let it go, giving it ever-increasing attention. They opened their pages to all kinds of historical debates whose main point was a reexamination of accepted truths about the Holocaust and related matters. In the summer of 1988, for example, the press debated whether it was proper or improper to publish Adolf Hitler's *Mein Kampf* in Hebrew. Eventually an abridged version of the book was published.[26] The major media event of the late 1980s took place in Jerusalem: the trial of John Demjanjuk. When he was extradited from the United States at the beginning of 1986, Demjanjuk was sixty-six years old. He had been born in the Ukraine and had emigrated to Cleveland, Ohio, after World War II. He spent most of his life working at a Ford factory. His original name had been Ivan. In the early 1970s, the United States Department of Justice began to investigate his past, suspecting that he had concealed from the American immigration authorities the fact that during the war he had been drafted into the

German forces and had been stationed at the concentration camp at Sobibor, Poland. It seems that the crucial information on his identity reached the American justice department from the Soviet Union, but precisely how has never been properly explained. The American legal proceedings stretched over many years; at a certain stage it became clear that there was not enough material to convict Demjanjuk, but his citizenship was revoked. Israel then requested his extradition—apparently in response to an inquiry by the American authorities, who did not know what to do with the man. For various reasons, the prosecution decided to focus on the crimes Demjanjuk was accused of committing not at Sobibor but at another camp, Treblinka. He was accused of having operated the camp's gas chamber, in which some 870,000 people, the vast majority of them Jews, were murdered. Demjanjuk was also accused of numerous sadistic acts; the charge sheet stated that his unique cruelty had won him the nickname "Ivan the Terrible."

Criminal case 373/86 was based largely on an identity card bearing Demjanjuk's name, picture, and personal details and on the testimony of a long line of Treblinka survivors who claimed to identify him. The identity card was described as one issued to those who attended an SS training camp, Trawniki, in Poland. The document had been brought to Israel from the Soviet Union in the airplane of the Jewish-American millionaire Armand Hammer, in a mission surrounded with mystery and drama. A while later several other such documents were also brought from the USSR. The identification document and the witnesses were necessary because John Demjanjuk claimed that he had never been in Treblinka; the document, in fact, recorded his service in Sobibor, not in Treblinka. Demjanjuk denied having ever been in Sobibor, too. He tried to present the court with an alibi and argued that the documents were forged. All the accusations against him, Demjanjuk maintained, were meant to embarrass the expatriate anti-Soviet Ukrainian community in the United States—a KGB conspiracy. Demjanjuk's counterclaim determined the entire character of the trial. Instead of centering on the tragedy of Treblinka and its lessons, it focused on the riddle of the defendant's identity.

The names of two Ukrainians who had operated the gas chambers at Treblinka had been mentioned at the Eichmann trial: Nikolai and Ivan. Ivan may have been a sadist or a Jew hater. But unlike Adolf Eichmann, he had taken no part in making the decisions that led to the genocide. There is no particular reason for assuming that he identified with Nazi ideology. He was what Israelis called a *rosh katan*—literally, "small head"—a soldier who did as he was told, without thinking, trying his best to evade any responsibility. The Demjanjuk trial could have been made into the trial of the *rosh katan*. It could have declared that people are responsible for their actions, and for the orders they obey. It could have underscored the concept that if they carry out a manifestly illegal order, they will have to answer for their actions, sooner or later, even forty years later. The trial could thus have contributed to the efforts to suppress the active racism that had surfaced in Israel.

The prosecution preferred, however, to recount the horrors of the death camp. One after another the survivors were called to the witness stand to tell in bloodcurdling detail what had befallen them. The courtroom was full. The trial was carried live on radio and television. People everywhere followed the broadcasts. For days and weeks the country watched, hearing testimony of atrocities, including the sexual abuse of children, as if again prostrating itself before horror and death in anger and hatred, as if again digging in and closing itself off from a hostile world. As in the Eichmann trial, it became clear that the trial medium was very limited in its ability to tell history. It had, however, great dramatic power. The atmosphere was charged, the product of the strain between the legalistic correctness that characterized the proceedings and the horrifying reality it revealed. The prosecutor, Michael Shaked, a curly-headed young man, intelligent, diligent, and pleasant, had a sense of mission—historical justice. The impression was that he truly believed John Demjanjuk was Ivan the Terrible. From time to time it seemed that he was the only person who really believed it.

At moments, the defense attorney turned the trial into a farce. Marc J. O'Connor, a garrulous, publicity-minded American lawyer, embroiled himself endlessly in verbal clashes with the judges. He frequently offended the court, sometimes pretentiously throwing in a few words of Hebrew. The court, which gave every impression of being hostile, in turn insulted the defense counsel. At one stage O'Connor demanded that the three judges disqualify themselves; the request was rejected. It began to look as if John Demjanjuk would end up on the gallows mainly because of his odd choice of attorney. Halfway through the trial Demjanjuk and his family dismissed O'Connor, who returned to oblivion in Buffalo, New York, leaving behind a faint odor of aftershave. The public feud between him and his Israeli colleague on the defense team, Yoram Sheftel, was one of the highlights of the trial. Then there was an expert witness who tried to commit suicide after cross-examination revealed that her claim to expertise was spurious. There was another Israeli member of the defense team who killed himself by jumping out a window. At the suicide's funeral, an elderly man threw acid at Sheftel, who only by luck kept his eyesight. One of the three judges had a heart attack.

The trial was held in a hall usually used as a cinema, not in a court-room, and, unlike other trials, was open to photographers and broad-casters. The press, as usual, made no pretense of respecting the principle of sub judice and convicted the defendant before the trial began. The minister of justice did the same; long before the trial opened he was calling Demjanjuk a mass murderer.[27] In that sense, it was a show trial but—strangely enough—a fair show trial. Everything was conducted in keeping with the law and with proper judicial procedure. The defendant was given ample opportunity to defend himself. Every word said in court was simultaneously translated into both Ukrainian and English, for the convenience of the defense team and the foreign press. The defense also received other necessary technical aid, at government expense. Demjan-juk was held in isolation, but in fairly comfortable conditions. His cell had a radio; he studied Hebrew, read newspapers, and was allowed, from time to time, to speak with his family on the telephone. When he felt ill, he received medical care.

Was there ever any chance that Demjanjuk would be acquitted, even on the basis of reasonable doubt? The atmosphere surrounding the trial and the witnesses called to identify him made acquittal almost impossible. Their testimony raised the question of whether it is at all feasible to identify a man after so many years, especially since during the ten years that preceded the trial he had been mentioned in the press and even seen on television. The procedures used to identify him were in many ways irregular, and there was some question as to whether to believe the witnesses' assurances that they had not coordinated their testimony or coached one another. Some of the witnesses had testified about their incarceration at Treblinka at other trials.

One of the trial's hardest moments came during the examination of Eliahu Rosenberg, whose job at Treblinka was to remove bodies from the gas chambers. Prisoners who had tried to escape were punished by being placed in the chambers with an insufficient dose of gas. They died horribly, in agony, over an entire night. Defense attorney O'Connor asked Rosenberg if he had not thought of helping them escape. His question was essentially the same as the one put to witnesses at the Kastner and Eichmann trials. Rosenberg responded with anguish.

ROSENBERG: How could I have done so, your honors? How could I have helped? I had no contact with live people. If I saw people—I saw people who entered the gas chambers. I had no contact with them. They had no time even to raise their heads. What could I have told them?

JUDGE LEVIN: Mr. Rosenberg . . . the question relates to this case. Did you try to help them escape?

PROSECUTOR SHAKED: With all due respect to the court, I think that the witness's response is the best answer to the question that was asked. In my humble opinion this question contains a provocative element. I don't think that the witness should even have to answer such a question.

LEVIN: The question is permissible and germane, and Mr. Rosenberg is requested to answer it.

ROSENBERG: I must answer, your honor?

LEVIN: Yes, yes.

ROSENBERG: That question?

LEVIN: The question as I have explained it to you.

ROSENBERG: I understand, your honor. So I repeat: the people were completely naked. . . . In what way could I have helped them? How? How? By screaming? "Don't enter the gas chamber"? They didn't want to enter the gas chamber. If God forbid one of us had screamed—I don't wish on even you, Mr. O'Connor, to witness what they would have done to him: they would have pushed him alive into a pit full of blood. So don't ask me questions like that, Mr. O'Connor. I beg of you. You were not there. I was. Ask him —Ivan—he'll tell you what he would have done to me . . .

LEVIN: Mr. Rosenberg, Mr. Rosenberg.

ROSENBERG: There were cases . . .

LEVIN: I understand your pain. But as I brought to your attention earlier, we are a court and we must act in accordance with procedures fitting to a court. So there is no need to shout. And there has to be a certain measure of restraint. I ask that you observe this during the rest of the examination.

ROSENBERG: Your honor, I have never been asked such a painful question. Even the worst anti-Semite has never asked me such a thing. Could

I have helped such a miserable creature? Who would have helped
me get out and tell now what happened there?

LEVIN: Fine, Mr. Rosenberg, you have finished your answer to this
question.[28]

Along with the drama and the trivia that surrounded the trial, this
incident brought home the terrible distress of those who had survived
because they had been forced by the Nazis to carry out various tasks
connected to the extermination, such as extracting gold teeth and burning
bodies. They had to live with this truth throughout their years in Israel.
Then the country in which they had made their new lives asked them
to identify a person who was possibly the real murderer, and gave them
a chance to help convict him. It was their last opportunity to do something
for the victims and to redeem themselves. This is one good reason to
treat their testimony with utmost caution.

But it took great courage to look a Holocaust survivor in the eye and
tell him that his testimony was insufficient. The three judges, Dov Levin,
Dalia Dorner, and Zvi Tal, considered themselves part of a historic
mission—to remind mankind of the Holocaust. They apparently feared
that if they acquitted Demjanjuk, even by giving him the benefit of the
doubt, they would be abetting the efforts of anti-Semites and anti-Zionists
to deny that the Holocaust ever occurred. They could not shoulder such
a burden. On April 18, 1988, they convicted the defendant and sentenced
him to death. The sentence was greeted with shouts of vengeance by the
audience.

The verdict fills nearly 450 pages. It is in places written in poetic,
almost biblical language, and at one point it prefers the language of prayer
to that of the law. Among other things it states that the story of the
genocide of the Jews "has been pushed, intentionally or through inattention, into the abyss of oblivion," and the judges are thus charged with
"exposing the truth." The judges wrote that they had composed the verdict
"in holy awe," and ruled that "we must survey the bitter and abrupt fate
of European Jewry during the dark days of the Holocaust. We must walk
the trail of agony and death soaked with their blood and saturated with
the tears of those who were slaughtered, strangled, and martyred by the
German butchers and their collaborators from other nations.[29] The words
"German butchers and their collaborators" were taken from a memorial
prayer, not from the law, which speaks only of "Nazis and Nazi Collaborators." They also wrote that the Jews of Europe were taken "like lambs

to the slaughter."[30] All this places the verdict with the literature of national-religious lamentation and all of it is, actually, superfluous. The court was not asked "to uncover the truth" about the Holocaust. The extermination of the Jews was no longer "consigned to the abyss of oblivion." In fact, it was not even an issue between the prosecution and the defense.

Demjanjuk appealed and was heard, in a dry, undramatic atmosphere, in the Supreme Court. Doubt continued to prevail, and indeed became stronger, when new evidence was discovered in the former Soviet Union. The media covered the hearing only briefly, as if they felt uncomfortable for having placed this man at the center of Holocaust history for so long. After all, he was not Adolf Eichmann.

In July 1993, the Supreme Court in Jerusalem determined, as expected, that Demjanjuk's identity as Ivan the Terrible of Treblinka had not been proven beyond a reasonable doubt and overturned his conviction and death sentence. The court also stated that Demjanjuk had been an SS guard at the Sobibor death camp but could not be convicted on that charge because he had not been given a proper chance to defend himself on it. The judges had to choose between justice and the law; they opted for the law. Israel freed a Nazi war criminal on a legal technicality.

"Legal experts," wrote Elie Wiesel, "will probably maintain that the verdict means a victory for the judicial system. I do not know who the winner is. I know, and I am saying this with deep pain, that the loser is the Jewish memory." Holocaust survivors and a number of Jewish organizations tried to initiate a new trial against Demjanjuk. Once again they appealed to the Supreme Court. Eventually, however, Demjanjuk was allowed to return to the United States. "Let us not share with him the skies that God has put over our heads and over the heads of our children," wrote one of the Supreme Court judges poetically. "Let him not dwell amongst us and our camp shall be holy."

Although there was much talk of its "educational value," the trial of John Demjanjuk seems not to have had any significance at all. Most young Israelis by this time knew more about the Holocaust than did those who had been their age when Eichmann was captured. One hundred thousand Israelis had seen Claude Lanzmann's *Shoah*—it may well be that they learned more from the film than from the trial. In any case, the Holocaust was no longer a dark secret in the survivors' personal biographies; rather it belonged to the country's history, indeed to its collective memory.

PART VIII

MEMORY:

The Struggle to Shape the Past

24 | *"Holocaust and Heroism"*

Up the road in central Jerusalem that bears the name of Theodor Herzl and that leads, at its peak, to his grave, lies the city's central military cemetery. Here are buried the soldiers who have fallen in the wars between Israel and the Arabs. Pine trees shade the graves, enveloping them in timeless tranquillity. One monument honors the 200,000 Jewish soldiers who fell in the ranks of the Red Army during the Second World War. A memorial to them here, among the graves of Israeli soldiers, seems to appropriate them posthumously into the Israeli army and into the Zionist movement. It proclaims, in a way, that they fell not in defense of the Soviet Union in its war against the Nazis but in defense of the Jewish people and for the establishment of the State of Israel. For this reason, they are worthy of being remembered among Israel's heroes, on the memorial mountain, alongside the fathers of Zionism and national leaders.

The victims of the Holocaust have their memorial on the slopes of the same mountain. Those who conceived the site hoped that it would be established on the highest point in the city; they spoke of a "Pantheon" on the peak of Mount Scopus. The minutes of their initial discussions also contain the terms *mausoleum* and *cathedral*. "The first thing clear to all of us is that the proposal [for the site] must be grandiose, fantastic, . . . as immense as the immensity of our catastrophe," one of the organizers said.[1] Their vision was not realized. The place allotted them is unassuming, as if there were reason to hide it. It faces not Jerusalem, Israel's capital, but rather the deserted Judean wilderness. The road leading down to the site branches off from the road to Ein Kerem, the picturesque village in which John the Baptist was born.

The visitor arrives at an unremarkable stone building, four stories high, that houses the offices, the excellent library, with more than 100,000 volumes, and the archives. Next to this are a cafeteria, rest rooms, and public telephones. Across the way is a shop that sells books on the Holocaust, some of them scholarly, some popular, as well as guidebooks to Israel in many languages, including German. There are also postcards and stamps and various knickknacks, key chains, and souvenirs. There are religious items for sale, too—mezuzot and Hanukkah menorahs of copper, silver, and gold. The prices are quoted in dollars, and the buyers receive their purchases in white plastic bags bearing a six-branched black menorah, in memory of the six million dead, and the words "Yad Vashem." The menorah is the institution's seal. The artist who designed it based it on the seven-branched menorah that stood in the Temple in Jerusalem and that is also part of the seal of the State of Israel. Models of the Holocaust menorah, in various sizes, are sold in the shop.

In front of the building is a lawn, on which, during a visit early in May 1990, I saw groups of students and soldiers sitting in circles with their guides, talking about the extermination of the Jews. The head of the institute, Yitzhak Arad, told me that such groups sit there almost daily.[2] No one knows for sure how many people visit; entrance is free and no one counts. Arad estimates that half a million students and soldiers come every year. Before entering his office I lingered a bit in the yard. When the soldiers—paratroopers—entered the lecture room, they left their rifles on the lawn in a neat pile, under the watchful eye of one of their number. The guard sat by the rifles, his legs crossed, and took a paperback Harold Robbins novel, in English, out of his pack. Air-conditioned buses brought visitors from all countries; Arad estimates nearly a million come each year. The tourists wore brightly colored clothes and talked in a babble of languages. They left behind soft-drink cans and crumpled film boxes, as tourists do; Arab workers picked up the trash. Two of the senior officials of the institute crossed the yard. They spoke Polish between them, peppering their conversation with a few words of Hebrew and Yiddish. One had a blue number on his arm. The memorial was established in the spirit of the national vow so sharply expressed by Avraham Shlonsky: "To remember it all / To remember, to forget nothing."[3]

The way to the historical museum takes the visitor past two rows of carob trees; this is the Avenue of the Righteous Gentiles, named for the non-Jews who risked their lives to save Jews from the Nazis. The State of Israel grants them an honorary title and pays some of them a small pension. A special national committee headed by a Supreme Court justice decides who is worthy of the distinction. Over the years the number of the righteous has reached into the thousands. Each of them, or his or her heirs, has the right to plant a tree on the avenue. At the foot of the museum is a copy of a large memorial, the work of sculptor Natan Rappaport, to the Warsaw ghetto uprising; the original stands in Warsaw. The memorial is in the Stalinist heroic style: larger-than-life figures, upright and tense before the leap into battle, muscular bronze arms holding weapons, eyes gazing into the future. Thus it happens that the visitor meets the righteous gentiles and the ghetto rebels, two exceptions in the history of the Holocaust, before learning anything of the extermination of the Jews. This was not the plan. But the second most important national site, after the Western Wall, is a patchwork of improvisations and financial compromises. Yad Vashem has never had enough money.

The museum's chambers are not large; the exhibit is old, and some of the walls are grimy. Most of the exhibits are photographs, some of them revolting: scenes of mass deportation, executions, tortures, "medical experiments," and various other atrocities committed against the inmates of the death camps. The explanations are long, their tone didactic, in Hebrew, English, and Yiddish. The visitor approaches them in chronological order, beginning with the first manifestations of anti-Semitism in Nazi Germany—books, placards, cartoons. The museum does not argue that Nazi anti-Semitism reflected the national character of the German people. It does not portray it as part of German history or as part of the universal phenomenon of racism and xenophobia. It leaves it without explanation, as if it needed none, as if it were natural. Ghetto life is described in a series of photographs that are meant to rouse the viewer to compassion, identification, and revulsion, all at the same time. One shows an old woman selling the yellow armbands with the Star of David that the Nazis forced the Jews to wear.

From here the visitor is channeled into a narrow passageway in the form of a sewer pipe, like those used by the underground ghetto fighters.

The Jewish attempts to resist the Nazis are described in detail, and the visitor gets the impression that the Jews fought a war with the Nazis. In the Israeli culture of memory Holocaust and heroism stand side by side, as if they were equal in force and in historical importance, complementary halves of a single entity.

About halfway through the museum—a bit after the most horrifying of the pictures—there is a placard that tries to raise the visitor up out of the depths of despair and explain that the death of the Jews in the Holocaust was not in vain. They died martyrs, the placard says. Jewish martyrdom, it explains, is not only the death of a Jew who would rather give up his life than betray his religion. According to Maimonides, even a Jew killed not because he refuses to convert but simply because he is a Jew, is also a martyr. The first plans for Yad Vashem spoke, in fact, of the need to memorialize the Jewish martyrology. "A martyr is a person who accepts death or suffering for any noble cause," an early official of Yad Vashem wrote. "To be a Jew, to be different from every other nation, and to suffer for generations for the right to be different is a noble cause."[4]

Apparently not everyone agreed with him. The Hebrew name of the institution refrains from calling the dead "martyrs," as if martyrdom were too "Jewish," too religious a death, not Israeli enough. It was worthy of being included, at most, in the name given in the language of American Jewry. "The Memorial Authority for the Holocaust and Heroism," the direct translation of its Hebrew name, is in English officially called "The Memorial Authority for the Martyrs and Heroes of the Holocaust." Similarly, it is no coincidence that the institution's Hebrew name, unlike the English one, uses the abstract terms "Holocaust" and "heroism" instead of referring to the victims and heroes themselves. Only a small number of Holocaust victims and survivors fit the heroic imagery of the first Israelis. The Hebrew words *Yad Vashem* appear, transliterated, in the English name. The words are taken from the book of Isaiah (56:5): "And to them will I give in my house and within my walls a memorial better than sons and daughters: I will give them an everlasting name [*yad vashem*] that shall not be cut off." It is a problematic verse, since it argues that the "everlasting name" will be "better than sons and daughters"— that is, better than life itself. The verse is carved in the yard of Yad Vashem in huge stone letters, but instead of the words "better than sons and daughters" there is a discreet ellipsis.

Not far from there hangs a little sign that returns the visitor with grotesque suddenness to the routine of terror in Israel: "Watch out for suspicious objects." The adjoining wall is devoted to the connections that the Palestinian leader Haj Amin al-Husseini established with Nazi officials. The visitor is left to conclude that there is much in common between the Nazis' plan to destroy the Jews and the Arabs enmity to Israel. Then comes the story of the illegal immigrant ship, the *Exodus*. The ship stood at the center of a drama that took place some two years after the Second World War ended, but the visitor to the Yad Vashem museum is given the impression that this was a rescue mission during the Holocaust. The visit concludes with the establishment of the State of Israel. One of the last photographs in the museum shows Adolf Eichmann in his glass booth. Thus the museum leads the visitor "from Holocaust to rebirth." The message is "never again."

Before leaving the museum, the visitor can go up one floor, into a half-dark gallery whose design combines a kind of solemnity of mourning with the officious functionalism of a census bureau. This is the "sanctuary of names." Here the names of the victims are recorded on microfilm. Visitors can locate the names of their relatives on the list, and if they do not find them, they are invited to add them to the list by filling out special forms, or "testimonial sheets," available in eight languages. The service is free of charge. It is life's way of fighting death—or, in this case, murder—as is memory itself. The implication is that so long as we do not forget the victim, he or she is in some way among the living. The catalog of names is a way of rescuing each of the millions of victims from anonymity, of restoring each individual's identity as a human being. The forms state: "Since time is running out, and since in less than a generation no one who personally remembers the fallen will remain alive, you should make every effort to question the elders of your family about the fallen, and to register them, while it is still possible." By the fall of 1990 fewer than three million names were on file. Somewhere in the minutes of a board meeting one can find Nahum Goldmann's contention that such a list should not even be started, since it could never contain a full six million names and so would give neo-Nazis cause to argue that six million were not murdered. Such an outcome would cause great embarrassment, the president of the World Jewish Congress warned the Yad Vashem board, since the six million figure served as the basis for the reparations and compensation agreements with Germany.[5] At the exit there are tablets enumerating, by country, the number of Jews killed, including one stating that a million and a half children were murdered. The sum total comes close to 6.5 million.*

Upon exiting the museum the visitor comes into the courtyard where, once a year, an official memorial ceremony is held. At its edge is what is called in English the "Hall of Remembrance," though "Memorial Tabernacle" better catches the connotations of the Hebrew name, *Ohel Yizkor*. It is a blocklike structure made of slabs of basalt, with black cast-iron gates. The interior walls are of concrete, and the ceiling slopes upward to a rectangular hole, a reminder of the holes through which the gas canisters were tossed into the asphyxiation chambers, and of the chimneys of the crematoriums where the bodies were burned. Visitors stand on a raised platform and their gaze is directed downward. The floor is a mosaic with the names of the twenty-two largest death camps. In a corner of the tabernacle, an eternal flame burns in a broken bronze vessel. In a nearby recess in the wall lie ashes collected from the extermination-camp crematoriums. The Hall of Remembrance is used in official ceremonies, including visits by foreign heads of state, somewhat like the graves of the unknown soldiers in other countries. Men who enter are requested to cover their heads, as is the custom in Jewish holy places. As at the Western Wall, a bin of folded black cardboard hats, held together by staples, is available for the unprepared. Those interested can ask the gatekeeper for mimeographed sheets of the kaddish, the memorial prayer, in Hebrew, English, and Yiddish.

The term *tabernacle* is borrowed from the structure Moses built in the desert to house the Ark of the Covenant. Like the word *sanctuary*, the word *tabernacle* forms part of the name of many synagogues in Israel. But the Memorial Tabernacle is not a synagogue; there is no separation of men and women. There is a synagogue in one wing of the museum, but it is not used for prayer services; it is a memorial to the demolished synagogues of Europe. Yad Vashem does not employ a rabbi.

---

* The six million figure received canonical status only gradually. Right after the war one could still hear the phrase "more than five million," and one Knesset member spoke in 1950 of seven million. The Yad Vashem Act (1953), which chartered the institute, cites the six million figure, but draft versions of the law said simply "millions." There was a debate over whether to give legal status to the number of victims, or to leave the subject to the historians. In his opening statement at the Eichmann trial, Attorney General Gideon Hausner said that he was representing "six million accusers," but the charge sheet stated that Eichmann was culpable in the deaths of "millions of Jews," without stating a precise number. The verdict also avoided specific figures and used the phrase "some six million." The *Encyclopedia of the Holocaust*, published by Yad Vashem, gives an "estimate": 5.86 million.[6]

This is no accident: from the very start, Holocaust memorial culture was meant to be an integral part of the secular national symbolism of the Zionist movement and the State of Israel. In September 1946 the burial society of the chief rabbinate asked the members of the Jewish Agency executive to honor with their presence the burial of a box containing the ashes of Jews from the Chelmno death camp. The members of the executive were invited to the ceremony as "the representatives of the Jewish people." The funeral, in Tel Aviv, was well attended, and over time, other such funerals were held.[7] The Jewish Agency executive realized that the rabbinate was gaining control over the memorialization of the Holocaust and had to be prevented from giving this important function a religious cast. In 1949 a Jewish Agency leader warned that the funerals of victims' ashes were liable to compete with the ceremonial reburial of Theodor Herzl, whose remains had been brought to Jerusalem from Vienna.[8]

The issue inspired heated debate, but in the end Yad Vashem was founded as a national-secular institution. The site contains figurative sculptures, in violation of Jewish religious law. The memorial steles and inscriptions make much use of biblical verses, as was the custom in the 1950s, and reflect that period's nostalgia for ancient Hebrew sovereignty in the Land of Israel—skipping over 2,000 years of exile, as well as the religious law that evolved outside Israel.[9] Prayers are said and candles lit at memorial ceremonies, but Yad Vashem generally takes care to invite army rabbis and cantors for this purpose and to keep the religious part of the ceremony to a minimum. The prayers are balanced by readings from secular Israeli poets. Always read is a poem of Haim Guri's that addresses the dead:

> We have avenged your bitter and lonely deaths
> With our fist, heavy and hot.
> We have established a monument here to the burnt ghetto,
> A living monument that will never end.[10]

The monument Guri meant was the State of Israel.

When Mordecai Shenhabi presented the Jewish National Fund with his first proposal for a memorial to the victims of the Nazis, he made his case in a practical tone: "The Jewish National Fund [JNF] needs a new cause that can turn into a pipeline for large sums," he wrote. He supposed that the money would come in the form of contributions from wealthy Jews overseas, but he also projected an income from the memorial activities themselves. People who wished to memorialize their loved ones could plant trees in a special grove, for a price, and could buy memorial certificates and specially designed stone monuments to be erected anywhere in the world where Jews are buried. The expected income would fund immigrant absorption and Zionist settlement, Shenhabi wrote, as early as 1942.[11] The extermination of the Jews had just begun. The memorial plan reflected the tendency to remove the Holocaust from present reality, to treat it as though it were already a chapter in the history of the nation, and to focus public attention on the Zionist future.

Shenhabi, born in Russia, lived at a Hashomer Hatsair kibbutz called Mishmar Haemek. It is hard to say what made him tick. He was one of those creative early Zionists who were constantly coming up with ideas and projects, only some of which could be realized. Quiet, stubborn, and, at times, annoying, Shenhabi was addicted to activism, constantly out to begin something new, and his projects all exhibited a unique blend of fantasy and lust for action. The Yad Vashem proposal included an ideological manifesto, an estimated budget, and an architectural sketch of a tall tower on the top of a hill. Around the tower, Shenhabi imagined a "people's park" that would spread over thousands of acres and contain not only a central Memorial Sanctuary to preserve the names of the victims, a Sanctuary of Battle (Heroism), Holocaust historical museums and archives, but also research institutes devoted to the history of Zionism, a large conference center, hotels, a youth hostel, restaurants, sports facilities, including a stadium, and a cemetery. No tourist would be able to avoid visiting the complex, Shenhabi promised. The minutes record one participant of an early discussion of the plan fantasizing about covering the entire cemetery with glass, so that it could also serve as a greenhouse for tropical plants.[12] At this stage, Shenhabi was not yet thinking of Jerusalem as the site for his project, preferring an agricultural area. The memorial complex was meant to fit in with the JNF's efforts to purchase land for Jewish settlement. "Jerusalem does not represent the Zionist pioneering spirit," ruled Zvi Lurie, another participant in the discussions, also of Hashomer Hatsair.[13]

The establishment of the complex, Shenhabi wrote, was a fundamental precondition for a normal life in Israel. "We are obligated to perpetuate the memory of the century's greatest catastrophe within the framework of our Zionist enterprise," he stated. This was the key. The "monumental" Memorial Sanctuary would point an accusing finger at the non-Jewish world, which offered the Jews "as prey to the enemy's jaws,"

Shenhabi wrote, and it would teach the lesson of "a thousand years of trying to live in countries that are not ours." The purpose of the Sanctuary of Battle, Shenhabi wrote, was to show the value of the war for Jewish and human honor. "In it, our generation will teach and the coming generations will learn that our brothers were not led like 'lambs to the slaughter.' Here we will establish the historical-national fact of how great our part was in the war against the terrible nemesis." By "our part," he apparently meant the Jewish soldiers who fought in the Allied forces. Shenhabi supposed that over the years the number of visitors to the Memorial Sanctuary would go down, since a single visit would suffice, and that the number of visitors to the Sanctuary of Battle would increase. "War must be learned and relearned," he stated in 1944.[14] At one point he went to speak to Ben-Gurion about the plan. Ben-Gurion considered the idea and later indicated that he supported it.[15]

The JNF board discussed the proposal with due gravity but was not, on the whole, enthusiastic. The members feared that the memorial would compete with their own fund-raising efforts and doubted it would earn back the original investment. They also debated the proper way to memorialize the Holocaust, what was permitted and what forbidden. The proposed "Pantheon" would elicit not pride but deep sorrow, judged Eliahu Epstein (who as Eliahu Eilat would later serve as the first Israeli ambassador to Washington); thus it did not fit in with the optimistic attitude of the Zionist movement. Better "to create new life through a living enterprise rather than a stone monument," he said. Neither would people want to spend money commemorating suffering, Epstein added, since "nations are in the habit of erecting monuments not to the memory of failures or sufferings but rather to victories and acts of glory." A colleague dissented on the economics of the program—people would be willing to do something to commemorate their relatives—but he agreed that it was not desirable to emphasize mourning: "The accent should be on building and constructive work," he asserted. Another participant wondered whether it was "permitted to make commercial use of Jewish anguish" but dismissed the question as moot, since after the war the desire to forget the horrors would grow. So it had been after World War I, he realized—people had danced in the streets."[16]

The JNF discussed the plan several more times during the war but displayed no urgency in carrying it out. Instead, beginning in 1942, it put together its own, competing memorial program. The Martyrs' Forest, in the Jerusalem mountains, was a threat to Yad Vashem, since "memorial huts" were to be scattered among the trees, where visitors could commune with the memory of the victims. Shenhabi claimed that the JNF planned the forest secretly and behind his back. "What, after all this, remains of the central memorial project?" he asked angrily when the JNF began to distribute, in Palestine and throughout the world, colorful pamphlets soliciting the purchase of trees for the new forest. Shenhabi saw it as a "cruel curtailment" of his project. Only with great effort did he succeed in persuading the JNF to do without the memorial huts; it would not, however, cancel the plans for the forest itself. The leaders of the JNF did not make any secret of what had motivated them to initiate the project: "It was the very last opportunity to score any kind of financial success," one of the heads of the fund explained. Ben-Gurion gave them a declaration stating that the only fit monument for European Jewry was the State of Israel itself, but he praised them for the initiative in planting a forest "in which the hope that our martyrs sustained in their lives will bloom." *17

Shenhabi kept trying. Chaim Weizmann sent him a letter of encouragement, but he had to nag and badger the nascent state's leaders with letters and memos just to get them to listen to the proposal. At the beginning, Shenhabi still felt he had to justify the importance of memory itself. "With all our might we must fight every sign of forgetting!" he asserted.[19] But the leaders of the yishuv did not see a Holocaust memorial as a high priority: not only were there more urgent tasks, there was no clear precedent—no one really knew how to design collective memory. That question was the subject of many debates, as well as personal, political, and ideological power struggles.

In 1947, Shenhabi convoked, together with the Jewish Studies Institute of the Hebrew University, an international conference whose participants voiced support for Yad Vashem's goals, especially the collection of historical material. In the meantime, Shenhabi rented himself a small office, ordered stationery, and put out a pamphlet—rather a stylish one for those days—in which he proclaimed that the purpose of Yad Vashem was to turn memory into a "great force." The pamphlet was meticulously written, and it preserved, even in its layout, absolute symmetry between Holocaust and heroism. It proposed that people pay two Palestinian

* In the end, the forest project was a disappointment. By 1953 only half a million trees had been purchased. "The Jewish people do not want to remember," the sponsors complained.[18]

pounds (about $8 then) to register the names of family members killed in the Holocaust. The price included a tree; more trees could be planted for an additional charge.[20] At this stage, Shenhabi had refined his memorial plan. Among other things, he now proposed displaying the instruments of torture the Nazis used, as well as replicas of a gas chamber and a crematorium. "We must erect active implements, not passive shells," he wrote, but this part of the plan never left the drawing board.[21]

After the Declaration of Independence in 1948, Shenhabi began to emphasize that a memorial site was necessary to establish clearly for all the world the link between the extermination of the Jews and the establishment of the state and he demanded Yad Vashem be granted a monopoly on the memorialization of the Holocaust. He managed to enlist Prime Minister Ben-Gurion and Foreign Minister Sharett in the effort to scuttle a Holocaust memorial proposed for Paris, the initiative of one Yitzhak Shneurson.

The files that document the fight against this project reveal great indignation: "The entire matter seems very serious from a national and diplomatic point of view," wrote Minister of Education Ben-Zion Dinur to Ben-Gurion. The most appalling part, according to Dinur, was the fact that the Paris project had been the initiative of Jews. Having a memorial site in Paris would weaken Israel's position with other nations; it was a sign of "the Diaspora instinct" to question the centrality of Israel and "give Paris the place of Jerusalem."[22]

The prime minister ordered Israel's ambassadors to "take every step" necessary to terminate the Schneurson plan; the foreign ministry sent out its orders in top-secret cables. Ultimately the government reached an agreement with Schneurson: Yad Vashem was recognized as the central Holocaust memorial project, with the exclusive right to register the names of victims. But the negotiations were not easy; though the Yad Vashem leaders maintained that Israel had won a major victory "in a cultural war of ideas," they chided themselves for having been so late in recognizing "the extent of the danger." The agreement with Schneurson required great "emotional effort" on their part, they wrote. Yad Vashem agreed to recommend to the Claims Conference of the Jewish organizations that the Paris project be given a lump sum of $500,000 to build a monument, for which the Paris project would relinquish the right to conduct any sort of fund-raising campaign in the future. The money would come from German reparations payments. Yad Vashem asked the foreign ministry to tell its diplomats to keep their eyes peeled and to ascertain that Schneurson did not attempt any fund-raising of his own; if he did, Yad Vashem threatened "open war" against him.[23]

Beginning in 1950, Shenhabi also floated another idea aimed at ensuring Israel's monopoly on the Holocaust: a special law should state that every Holocaust victim became, at his death, an Israeli citizen. Shenhabi called his proposal "the Act to Reinstate the Civil Rights of the Victims of the Nazi Extermination Program," as if those victims had sometime in the past been citizens of a future Israel. "The loss of millions is in any case a direct loss to the state of Israel," he asserted. "The extermination of each of those millions, from the point of view of the Israeli state, was like the slaughter of a 'potential citizen.' The State of Israel, as the national expression of the dispersed Jewish people, will bestow its citizenship on the fallen, thus upholding their memory and honor, returning them to the bosom of their homeland, and confuting the Nazi crime for generations to come." His reasoning was, of course, utterly spurious. There is no way of knowing which, or how many, of the Holocaust's victims considered themselves "potential citizens" of Israel. Many of them died precisely because they had preferred not to move to Palestine when that option was open to them. And most of the world's Jews, Holocaust survivors among them, chose not to come to Israel even after the state was founded.

The idea is worthy of note, then, mainly because of the considerable effort the Israeli government put into examining it. Letters and reports and memos and legal opinions piled up. Shenhabi himself took the idea to several world-renowned jurists; some of them were willing to accept it. The JNF's legal counsel asserted that granting citizenship to the Holocaust's victims could help the Israeli government claim the property of those victims who left no heirs. The attorney general disagreed, warning that living heirs of these posthumous citizens would have a strong claim to Israeli citizenship, which should not be granted automatically, because many of these relatives were non-Jews. Both expressed their doubts as to whether other countries could be persuaded to recognize the Israeli citizenship of the victims. The most determined opponent of the idea was the chief counsel of the foreign ministry. From a legal point of view there was no way to grant Israeli citizenship retroactively for a period preceding the establishment of the state, he pointed out. There was no way to grant Israeli citizenship to someone who was not alive when the state was established, and there was no way to grant citizenship to someone who was not in the country and who had not applied for it. Israel's ambassadors reported that the idea was received with discomfort by Jews, both Zionists and non-Zionists. They saw the Israeli initiative as a threat to their status as loyal citizens of their own countries. Some legitimately feared that turning the dead into Israeli citizens would undermine the property rights and even the personal status of the heirs. "The foreign ministry is against it," David Ben-Gurion recorded in his diary.[24]

A proposal for overcoming all these difficulties came from New York. Yaakov Robinson, counsel to the Israeli UN delegation, wrote to President Ben-Zvi that granting citizenship to those who had died before the state was established would be possible if the Declaration of Independence were revoked, creating instead a "doctrine of continuity between the Second Commonwealth [the biblical kingdom of Solomon] and the Third Commonwealth [the new State of Israel]"—that is, an assumption that Israel had not ceased to exist when the nation went into exile in 72 A.D. After all, the nation had never conceded its sovereignty in its own land; all the governments that had risen and fallen during the intervening 2,000 years were nothing but illegal military occupiers. The Declaration of Independence of May 14, 1948, was thus not really a declaration of independence but rather an announcement that the previous barriers to the actualization of this never-conceded sovereignty had been removed. In order to overcome the legal absurdity involved in giving citizenship to the dead, Robinson proposed granting it retroactively to the living, beginning at a given date, such as January 30, 1933, the day Hitler came to power, for German Jewry, and March 10, 1938, the day of the *Anschluss*, for Austrian Jewry. There were still many difficulties, the counsel wrote, but the idea itself was attractive.

Ben-Gurion had already, in February 1951, appointed a special committee to examine the proposal. The committee, chaired by Natan Feinberg, ruled that a declaration of continuity between the "Second Commonwealth" and the current state would cause Israel problems with other countries and that the proposal to grant posthumous citizenship had no precedent in international law and did not conform to accepted definitions of citizenship. On the other hand, the committee asserted that there was no legal reason not to grant the victims of the Holocaust "symbolic and abstract citizenship." The committee used the term *honorary citizenship*. By the time the idea was formed into a legislative proposal, this phrase had been replaced by a new coinage: *memorial citizenship*, with no legal significance.[25] When the Sanctuary of Names was established, it offered certificates of honorary citizenship at a price of $12 each. Yitzhak Arad, head of Yad Vashem, told me that they are not in great demand.

Shenhabi next proposed a bill that would turn Yad Vashem into a national memorial authority. This was not easy. No one raised any objections, but neither did anyone do much to promote the legislation: everyone was busy with more important matters. Shenhabi ran from one Knesset member to another, from journalist to journalist, buttonholing them, warning, demanding, pleading. Everyone told him he was absolutely right, and then quickly crossed the street.

Shenhabi's bill finally came up for consideration in the Knesset in the summer of 1953, and once again the debate reflected the tendency of all the parties to exploit the Holocaust for their own ideological ends. Most of the seats in the chamber were empty, and party leaders assigned junior members to do the floor work, but the battle over the "Holocaust and Heroism Memorial Act—Yad Vashem"—was, in fact, another battle for the country's soul.

Education Minister Dinur, a professor of Jewish history at the Hebrew University, introduced the bill. He started with a definition: *Shoah*, the Hebrew term for the Holocaust, he said, means the destruction of European Jewry and the slaughter of more than six million Jews. "Actually, six and a half million," he noted, giving the breakdown. Later Dinur would say that the term *Shoah* contains a historiographical problem, since it connotes suddenness and surprise.* Yet according to Zionism, the Holocaust was not sudden. It came as a logical development and could have been predicted from the simple fact that Jews were living among other peoples as nationless strangers.[26] The goal of the Nazis, Dinur said, was "to obliterate the name of Israel." Dinur's use of the term *Israel* to indicate the Jewish people was intentional; it not only reflected the common tendency to fall into a traditional, literary style whenever the Holocaust was the subject but reinforced the thesis that the murder of the Jews was a crime against the State of Israel. Dinur also praised the heroism of European Jewry and linked it to the heroism of the yishuv. He recalled the Warsaw ghetto revolt, which "symbolized the entire tragedy." There had been "hundreds of rebellions" in Europe, he said, almost everywhere. He included in his definition of heroism the

---

* The word *Shoah*—literally "catastrophe"—was in common use before the rise of the Nazis. It became the term for the expected murder of the Jews as early as March 1933. In recent years it has again come to refer to events other than the extermination of the Jews: an economic shoah, an ecological shoah, a moral shoah, etc.

people's struggle for their human dignity and for their lives and reached the conclusion that "Holocaust and heroism" were matters of daily life in the ghetto.

Having established the link between the victims of the Holocaust and the State of Israel, and the symmetry between Holocaust and heroism, Dinur turned to the events of 1948, five years after the Warsaw ghetto rebellion. The War of Independence, he said, was "a direct continuation" of the war of the partisans and the underground fighters, as well as that of "more than a million and a half of our soldiers" who fought the Nazis during World War II. The figure was the accepted estimate of the number of Jewish soldiers who had fought in the Allied armies. Jewish heroism is all one, he contended.[27]

Further on, Dinur described memory as a historical imperative imposed on Israel by the victims themselves. In speaking to this point, the minister once more waxed poetic, describing how Jewish communities would be portrayed at Yad Vashem. The communities flowered into idealized images of women "gay and young," "light of foot and life-loving," "modest and simple." The proposed law ordered the new memorial authority to impart "the lesson" of the Holocaust and heroism, as if "Holocaust" and "heroism" were a single entity with a single lesson. The law did not define, however, what the lesson was, other than commanding the authority to foster "a sense of memorial unity." When the debate on the bill began, it became clear that the Knesset was far from unified.

Yaakov Hazan (Mapam) identified the Warsaw ghetto revolt with the youth movements of the left, led by Hashomer Hatsair, Mapam's youth wing. It was the merger of Zionism and socialism that produced the heroism of the ghetto fighters, Hazan argued. Esther Raziel-Naor (Herut) protested—Hazan was making distinctions among the dead, she said, as if they had shown their party cards on the way to the furnaces. In her opinion, the Knesset was not competent to pass the proposed law, since it was the same Knesset that had decided to ratify the reparations agreements with Germany. The Yad Vashem building would undoubtedly be constructed out of German cement and iron; therefore, she announced, her party would not participate in the vote. Beba Idelson (Mapai), a women's activist, demanded that special emphasis be given to the women and children "whose soft flesh was used to make soap." Rabbi Yitzhak Meir Levin (Agudat Yisrael) objected to the secular character of the memorial authority, proposing instead the construction of a "holy place" for the study of Jewish religious texts—in memory of the fallen.

A series of changes in the final version of the law also reflected the political importance everyone attributed to the shape of memory. The committee that put together the final version decided to omit the word *partisan* and replace it with *forest fighters*. The word *partisan* was omitted because its emotional impact served the parties of the left in their effort to glorify the Soviet Union; Mapam predictably wanted to leave the word in. Mapam also demanded the inclusion of the term *fascism* along with *Nazism*—this in keeping with its position that Nazism was nothing but a type of fascism. Another leftist member of the Knesset, Avraham Berman, who raised a similar objection, explained that the intention was to protest the fascist danger of the United States. He referred to Secretary of State John Foster Dulles and Sen. Joseph McCarthy and described the United States as a country of racial discrimination and lynch gangs, a danger to the Jewish people. "Treblinka is likely to be reborn near New York, and Majdanek near Chicago," he declared. Esther Raziel-Naor demanded replacing the term *Nazis* everywhere it appeared with the term *Germans*—all Germans were guilty, she asserted. These amendments were rejected. The members were asked to stand and be counted, and the law was passed without opposition. During the course of the debate, the members of the house had been asked to stand two other times, once in memory of the Holocaust dead and once in memory of the ghetto fighters.[28]

On April 21, 1951, the Knesset decided that the twenty-seventh day of the Jewish month of Nissan would, every year, be Holocaust and Ghetto Rebellion Memorial Day. The date was a compromise. The Warsaw ghetto revolt began on Passover eve. At first it had been commemorated according to its date on the secular calendar, April 19. Each year there were calls to declare a national memorial day. Even though the call was for a nonreligious memorial date, everyone agreed that it should be part of the Hebrew calendar and that it could not coincide with Passover. The twenty-seventh of Nissan was close to the date of the rebellion and, according to Mordecai Nurok (National Religious party), was appropriate also because it recalled the season when European Jews were slaughtered during the Crusades.[29]

The Knesset did not mandate how to commemorate the memorial day. There were memorial ceremonies throughout the country—at Kibbutz Yad Mordecai and Kibbutz Lohamei Hagetaot, on Mount Zion in Jerusalem, and elsewhere. There were organizations of survivors that initiated such ceremonies, as well as municipalities and political parties. "Ghetto Rebellion Memorial Day is turning into a political matter," maintained one Mapai leader during a special discussion held by the party secretariat in March 1953. He said he had looked into the issue and had reached the conclusion that such a day was "an important educational asset." "We should take it out of Mapam's hands," he argued.[30] The ceremonies at Yad Mordecai and Lohamei Hagetaot did, in fact, often serve as platforms for party declarations on current political issues. The government also discussed the issue and decided, partly for the same reason, to legislate the memorial ceremonies. The government did not rush, however; the Holocaust and Ghetto Rebellion Memorial Day bill was submitted to the Knesset only five years later. In the meantime it had become clear that the ceremonies interested largely the survivor activists themselves. For the rest of the country, the twenty-seventh of Nissan was a day like any other. "Places of entertainment are wide open on this day," Rabbi Nurok objected. "The radio plays happy music, dances, and humor, and the display windows glow. Merriment and happiness instead of sorrow and mourning." Nurok proposed enforcing the mourning—closing stores and forbidding lights in display windows, for instance. He also wanted memorial ceremonies in the schools and at synagogues, with workers given time off to participate in them. Films could be screened only by permission of Yad Vashem; radio broadcasts would also accord with the solemnity of the day.[31]

Nurok's bill was not brought to a vote. Instead, the government presented its own law, less draconian than Nurok's and differing from it in one other emotion-charged detail. Instead of the "Holocaust and Ghetto Rebellion Memorial Day Law," it was called the "Holocaust and Heroism Memorial Day Law." This was, of course, more accurate and evenhanded. There had been, after all, other manifestations of heroism, including passive civil resistance. But Mapam took the proposed change as an insult: "They are trying to obliterate the memory of Mordecai Anielewicz," protested one of the party's Knesset members. Anielewicz, a Hashomer Hatsair leader, had been commander of the Warsaw ghetto revolt. Her objection was rejected, but the law itself stated that the memorial day would be devoted to the memory of the Holocaust, acts of heroism, and acts of rebellion. The Knesset enacted the law in April 1959, again without opposition.[32]

Yet the memorial lobby was still not satisfied. Two years later, not long before the Eichmann trial, the Knesset decided to enhance the law and give it a more Jewish character. From then on, observance would begin at sundown the previous day, as for all Jewish holy days, and all places of entertainment, including coffeehouses, would be closed. This amendment was also subject to a lengthy debate. It was agreed that the name would be Holocaust, Rebellion, and Heroism Memorial Day. "It is not easy to fashion an expression of collective grief," sighed one member of the Knesset.[33] Everyone warned against forgetting: "We must breathe each day anew the smoke of the furnaces," declared Aharon Yadlin (Mapai), later minister of education.[34]

The memorial day comes a week after Passover, generally in April. Cinemas and other places of entertainment are closed, in accordance with the law, but many restaurants and coffeehouses are open: the fine they have to pay is less than what they earn by staying open. The atmosphere of mourning is created largely by the national radio and television stations. The form of the programs is fixed, down to the tiniest details. The radio plays testimonies of Holocaust survivors and long symposiums, as well as mournful music—always, it seems, with a solo cello. The news broadcasts come without the musical signal that usually precedes them, and the announcer does not say "Good evening." The television shows films about the Holocaust, though not always documentaries. In 1990, for instance, it presented a movie on the Nuremberg trials starring Spencer Tracy and Marlene Dietrich.

The print media recognize the national and historical importance of the culture of memory, so they print poems, reflections, and pictures for Holocaust Day, with a preference for dark woodcuts. The night editors know how to extract items appropriate for the occasion from the day's news, such as anti-Semitic incidents in Germany and elsewhere.[35] For years it was customary to print articles about the repression of Jews in the Soviet Union. Again and again the papers repeated the Zionist lesson of the Holocaust and underscored the obligation not to forget. This was the day for patriotic declarations. "The most infuriating thing of all about the meeting between President Mitterrand and Yasir Arafat today is that the meeting is being held on Holocaust Day," wrote *Yediot Aharonot*.[36] Over time, the space devoted to Holocaust Day grew. Instead of the brief summary of the events of the day came pages full of news items, opinion articles, and analysis. This expanded coverage was not just a reflection of the general growth in the number of pages each newspaper printed; it revealed also a new concept of journalism—the Holocaust was now a story to be covered.

Since 1959, Holocaust Day has been marked by sirens—a long blast that does not waver as an air-raid warning does. On hearing the siren, people stop whatever they are doing. Drivers stop their cars, pedestrians stop walking, and the entire country freezes in place for a moment of memory, contemplation, and unity. The siren is broadcast on the radio as well, on all stations. It is an impressive moment. The flags on all public buildings, including hotels, are flown at half-mast.

The main ceremony is held on the eve of Holocaust Day, after dark, on the Yad Vashem grounds. Attended by the country's leaders, televised live, it is paramilitary in character. In addition to the customary military bugle call to mark mourning, soldiers bear flags and light torches, and the army's chief rabbi and its head cantor, both in uniform, say the prayers. A week after Holocaust Day, Israel is again in mourning, this time for the soldiers who have fallen in Israel's wars. This memorial day also begins the night before and in accordance with the Hebrew calendar—on the third day of the month of Iyar. But, like Holocaust Day, it too is primarily a national, secular day, with the exception of a few prayers and modes of mourning borrowed from religious rites. The memorial ceremonies are very similar to those held a week earlier, including the siren—except that for the soldiers it is sounded twice, evening and morning. The soldiers' memorial day is actually the model, with Holocaust Day created in its image. The ceremonial similarity between the two has increased each year; the week separating them has turned into almost a single unit of loss, memory, and rehearsal of national values.

From time to time, Yitzhak Arad told me, there have been attempts to use Yad Vashem as a platform for political issues. He tries to keep his institution above such disputes. Speakers may denounce anti-Semitism and the many publications—most of them fairly esoteric—that try to "deny" the Holocaust. They are permitted to declare that the Holocaust proves the need for a strong Israel. They may not, however, go beyond the bounds of the national consensus. The prayers said at the ceremony are carefully worded: the murder of the Jews is described in the passive voice: "those who were tortured, murdered, slaughtered." Generally, the prayers do not identify the murderer. They attribute the horrors to "impure hands," "cruel hands," "the hand of the enemy."[37] Great care is taken not to accuse the German nation; it is customary for the entire diplomatic corps to attend, including the German ambassador. At the 1990 ceremony, a point was made not to condemn the unification of Germany.

§

The religious community has developed its own culture of memory. At some religious schools the Holocaust is memorialized on the fast day of the tenth of Tevet—the day the chief rabbinate has designated for the recitation of the kaddish memorial prayer for those Holocaust victims whose date of death is not known. The fast itself commemorates the beginning of the Babylonian siege of Jerusalem preceding the destruction of the First Temple.* The religious memorialization of the Holocaust replaces some of the fundamental concepts of the secular approach—including the heroic myth of the rebels—with others of its own. Its typical heroes are the ninety-three students of the ultrareligious Beit Yaakov girls' school in Cracow, Poland. The girls are said to have committed suicide rather than let the Nazis turn them into camp prostitutes. A number of yeshivas and Hasidic courts active in Israel consider themselves the direct descendants of Jewish communities destroyed in the Holocaust.

The Holocaust Chamber on Mount Zion was established in 1949, before Yad Vashem was built. The mountain's holiness was emphasized especially after the partition of Jerusalem in the wake of the War of Independence, when worshipers could no longer reach the Western Wall of the Temple's complex. From the top of Mount Zion, one can gaze down on the Temple Mount. The ministry of religion, citing an ancient tradition, proclaimed that Mount Zion was the burial site of King David. Until the Old City was occupied in 1967 and Jewish prayer at the Western

---

* A few months after becoming prime minister, Menahem Begin proposed eliminating Holocaust Day. The proposal was one of several meant to chip away at the Labor movement's version of the national mythology. Begin suggested memorializing the Holocaust on Tisha B'Av, the religious day of mourning for the destruction of the two Temples and other national disasters. The proposal was also meant, perhaps, to give the "rebirth"—the establishment of the state—a holy status as well. Begin suggested a separate celebration of the ghetto rebellions and partisan heroism, on Independence Day. "I have never understood how it was possible to separate blood from blood, heroism from heroism," Begin said. "The ghetto rebels and the partisans fought for our people, and for our people also fought, in Israel, the soldiers of Israel, the Haganah, the Palmach, the Etzel, the Lehi, and Mahal. All are heroes, all are martyrs, all gave their lives for the Jewish people. . . . Let us have a single day for all of Israel's heroes." Begin was expressing the tendency to identify Israel with the Jewish people. He also wished to include the Etzel and the Lehi in the Israeli pantheon of heroism, from which they had been excluded. The Labor movement, which had appropriated the myth of the ghetto rebels for itself, diminished, and often completely ignored, the role that Betar had played in the rebellions. Begin's proposal to create "a single day for all of Israel's heroes" was meant to rob the Labor movement of its monopoly on heroism. The proposal created an uproar and Begin withdrew it.[38] The effort to indoctrinate Israeli youth with the lessons of the Holocaust would not have gained from the proposed change, since Tisha B'Av occurs during summer vacation.

Wall was renewed, Mount Zion was the holiest place in Jerusalem, and many thousands made pilgrimages to it.

One room, with a domed, soot-blackened ceiling, was designated as a memorial to the victims of the Holocaust. On exhibit in glass cases, alongside the memorial candles lit by the worshipers, were various items that had survived the Holocaust—charred Torah scrolls, the striped uniform of a camp inmate, metal canisters that contained the gas used to murder the Jews, a lampshade said to be made of human skin, and bars of soap purportedly manufactured from human fat. Yad Vashem's leaders disliked the Holocaust Chamber on Mount Zion. "In my opinion, what is going on there is idol worship," said a Yad Vashem board member.[39] A few years later people were permitted, for a price, to erect private memorials in the chambers. Knesset member Gideon Hausner protested. The prosecutor at the Eichmann trial, later a government minister, had just been appointed chairman of the Yad Vashem board. The minister of religion responded that this had been the practice on Mount Zion for twenty years, in keeping with the custom at many synagogues. "Yad Vashem is not the only memorial project in the country," the minister said pointedly. "There are other memorial projects, with similar activities."[40]

One such project, Ot Vaed ("Sign and Witness"), defines itself as an educational organization devoted to the Holocaust and its significance for Jewish religious life. Founded in Jerusalem in the early 1980s under the aegis of the National Religious party, Ot Vaed has published a glossy booklet, in Hebrew and English, that reveals that it hopes to develop into a religious Yad Vashem. Alongside its educational activity, it intends "to establish a memorial site that will express the Jewish spirituality of the Holocaust martyrs" and "to gather, assemble, and catalog all written material and living testimonies about the Holocaust, religious life therein, and its place in our Jewish existence." On the booklet, the letters of the name Ot Vaed appear, in gold, in the same typeface used by Yad Vashem, with their associations of flames. The name, like that of Yad Vashem, comes from a verse in the book of Isaiah, only it refers to a prophecy about the spread of Jewish faith to nearby countries, including Egypt.

Like the founders of Yad Vashem almost fifty years earlier, Ot Vaed dreams of a complex on a high spot in the hills of the Etsion Bloc—an area of the West Bank that had been settled by Jews before the War of Independence but lost then. It was regained in the Six-Day War and is now part of the occupied territories, not annexed to Israel. Like Mordecai

Shenhabi, the advocates of the new plan have prepared eye-catching colored drawings. "Around the complex," the booklet promises, "there will be a memorial park. There will be a magical mountain view from its paths."[41]

I asked Yitzhak Arad about competing memorial sites in Israel and elsewhere; the Holocaust memorial in Washington threatens to overshadow Yad Vashem. Arad hesitated. Obviously, he said, he had an interest in seeing that the central Holocaust memorial be the one in Jerusalem, but times have changed. Israel could not fight the Washington Holocaust museum—a project supported by, among others, the president of the United States and by Elie Wiesel, Nobel laureate—as it had fought the Shneurson initiative in Paris. The basic problem remained, however— Jerusalem or Babylonia, Israel or the Diaspora: Which was the center? When Yad Vashem's cornerstone was laid, there was a similar issue: whether to invite only the Israeli president to speak at the ceremony or also to invite Nahum Goldmann, chairman of the World Jewish Congress. "The country's president unites world Jewry," said one participant in the debate. Another disagreed: "The president of Israel is not the leader of all Jews. Diaspora Jewry participates in Yad Vashem. It is therefore proper and fitting that the Diaspora be represented." A third contended, "The president of the country is enough. We must do away, once and for all, with the separation between the State of Israel and the People of Israel!" In the end, the board decided, by a vote of six to five, to invite Goldmann. It was also decided, however, that if President Ben-Zvi objected to there being another speaker, he would be the only one; and this, in fact, is what happened.[42]

Now, though, with no way to fight the American Holocaust centers, Arad said, it was best to cooperate with them. Yad Vashem certainly has an interest in helping any institution that deepens awareness of the Holocaust, he said, cautiously diplomatic. And over the years the political differences with the other centers in Israel have blurred, and there is more common ground. Although they continue to compete, they have learned to share the national memory.

Arad is a short, well-built man from Lithuania. When the Nazis occupied his hometown of Swieciany, the then fifteen-year-old Yitzhak Rodnitzki organized a group of ghetto youths into an underground cell. They managed to steal several rifles from the Germans. Two years later, at the beginning of 1943, he fled into the forests and fought with a band of Soviet partisans until the war ended. In Israel he served in the standing army and, after the Six-Day War, was named chief education officer, with the rank of brigadier general. He has been director of Yad Vashem since 1972 and earned a doctorate with his research on the Holocaust.

In the summer of 1987, Yad Vashem established a memorial to the million and a half children who died in the Holocaust. It is a monument to the magic of light, designed by Moshe Safdie. At the entrance hangs a large sign, on glass, with golden letters stating that this memorial to the 1½ million Jewish children who perished in the Holocaust was erected through the generosity of Abraham and Edita Spiegel of Beverly Hills, California, in memory of their son, Uziel, killed in Auschwitz. The entrance leads into a narrow stone corridor, echoing with faint noises, like a long sigh, or a fluted lament electronically distorted. At the end of the corridor, the visitor is confronted with the face of a child, in stone relief: this is Uziel Spiegel. On the left is a heavy iron door, and beyond it—blackness. A few steps onward is a glass wall containing photographs of children. From here the corridor becomes a narrow ramp, in total darkness. Against the background of the sounds the visitor heard earlier, he now hears names—Moshele Abramowitz, twelve years old, from Lvov; Sarale Zuckerman, three years old, from Vilna; Yaakov Shimonowitz, fourteen years old, from Budapest. The readers, a man and a woman, speak in alternating Hebrew, Yiddish, and English. Then the visitor finds himself in a sea of light. The effect is stunning; one seems to be standing at the center of a black sphere, and as far as the eye can see, to the horizon, there are lights upon lights upon lights—hundreds of thousands, perhaps millions. They are created by a few candles reflected in a clever system of giant mirrors. The pathway leads the visitor, always in darkness, through the lights, always to the sound of the children's names, to the exit. Outside, another large glass sign, identical to the one at the entrance, again notes the names of the donors, a Jewish contractor and his wife. The structure cost nearly $2 million.

Yes, Yitzhak Arad told me, they had many misgivings about whether it was fitting to build such an attraction on a national memorial site. There was also the question of whether Spiegel's millions were enough to justify giving the memory of Uziel precedence over the memories of the other million and half children killed. Arad decided to take the risk. He knew it would be either a total failure or a big hit. It turns out that everyone who visits is impressed, and he, Arad, does not argue with success. Yes, there had been a certain amount of discomfort with the donor's insistence on naming the entire structure after his son. Arad refused absolutely, he told me. After extended negotiations, they compromised on the signs at the doors and the relief sculpture. Otherwise they would have lost the entire contribution, Arad said. The background to our conversation was the sound of bulldozers working in the "Valley of the Destroyed Communities." There, a walkway will lead the visitor between giant, human-dwarfing blocks of stone, each a memorial to a dead community.

What, then, is the lesson of the Holocaust according to Yad Vashem? I asked Arad, currently at work on a wide-ranging project with a $2.5 million budget, meant to document the history of the Holocaust in twenty-five volumes, an official Israeli version. Arad, very cautiously, said that he assumed that over the years a national consensus had developed in Israel, largely independent of party affiliation. Everyone agrees that the Holocaust teaches what awaits a nation in exile that has no state of its own; had Israel been established before the Nazis came to power, the murder of the Jews could not have been possible. Everyone agrees that the Holocaust led to the establishment of the state and that its survivors were at the center of the struggle for its independence.

Here Arad said something that a head of Yad Vashem would not have said in the past: as far as he was concerned, the term *heroism* could be done without; *Holocaust* is sufficient. It says everything. In his lectures, he told me, he cites among the manifestations of heroism not only the underground ghetto armies and the partisans but also the efforts of the ghetto Jews to survive from day to day and their attempt to preserve their dignity, up to the very last. In doing this, he tells his audiences, they frustrated the Nazis' main goal—to banish them from the human race. Young people who hear him now seldom denounce, as they once did, the Holocaust's victims for not having fought back. Now he rarely hears the once-frequent charge that they went "like lambs to the slaughter," Arad said. This change began with the Eichmann trial and took place gradually, somewhere between the Six-Day War and the Yom Kippur War.

Over the years, the character of the day commemorating the six million also has changed. Instead of the generalization that was expressed by the phrase *Holocaust and heroism*, there has been an increasing tendency to identify with the victims of the Holocaust as individuals. On Holocaust Day 1990, stands were set up around the country and equipped with loudspeakers. Passersby were invited to read the names of the fallen out loud. The project, called "Every One Has a Name," attracted large numbers. Among the first participants was Prime Minister Yitzhak Shamir. He read the names of his parents: it was one of the few times that Shamir identified himself publicly as the son of a family murdered in the Holocaust.

25 | *"The Rest of Your Life with Monik and Frieda"*

Kibbutz Yad Mordecai lies about forty miles south of Tel Aviv, near the coastal city of Ashkelon and the valley where David and Goliath fought. The first settlers came there in 1943—a few dozen young members of Hashomer Hatsair who arrived from Poland in the late 1930s. They called their new kibbutz Mitzpe Yam, and they planned to support themselves by fishing. They adopted the name Yad Mordecai about a year after the death of the Warsaw ghetto rebel commander Mordecai Anielewicz. Most of them had not known him personally; they were memorializing a symbol, not a friend. A handbook put out by Hashomer Hatsair in the 1950s stated that "it is important to emphasize the comradeship of fighters of all nations—Poles, Soviets, Jews—all of whom belonged to the revolutionary working class of their people. . . . The national interest in redeeming the honor and lives of the Jewish people is absolutely identical to the international interest in fighting the war against fascism and for the Soviet Union. In this spirit we will uphold the memory of the ghetto rebellion."[1] Yad Mordecai is one of the two Holocaust memorial sites of Hashomer Hatsair. The Holocaust memorial of another, less radical kibbutz movement, Hakibbutz Hameuhad, was established at Lohamei Hagetaot. At the beginning of the 1950s, when the different kibbutz movements were engaged in a heated political war, both Yad Mordecai and Lohamei Hagetaot adopted the Warsaw ghetto uprising as if it were theirs alone.

Not far from the cow sheds at Yad Mordecai, in the sand, there are stone steps with trees planted on both sides. The branches form a roof that forces those ascending to bow their heads. At the top, suddenly, there is a clearing and in it a huge bronze statue of a handsome young man, the work of Natan Rapaport. It is a sort of Israeli version of Michelangelo's *David*, but in battle dress. His open shirt reveals a muscular chest, and his head is tilted slightly back, looking upward. In his right hand is a grenade, ready to be thrown; he is the personification of bravery. This is Mordecai Anielewicz; he gazes out over the houses of the kibbutz that bears his name. Behind him lies a large concrete tank, full of bullet marks, the remains of the kibbutz water tower, destroyed in 1948, during the War of Independence. Engraved next to the statue is a quotation attributed to Anielewicz. It purportedly comes from a letter he wrote to Antek Zuckerman, his deputy, not long before his death: "The last desire of my life has been fulfilled. Jewish self-defense is a fact. I am content, happy that I was among the first Jewish fighters in the ghetto."

The museum is housed in a specially constructed modern concrete building, and there is a charge for admission. Less didactic, more aesthetic, and more emotional than Yad Vashem, the small exhibit was designed under the guidance of Abba Kovner. The visitor descends into a dim basement. A black wall bears the sentence: "In this place try to see what can no longer be seen, to hear what can no longer be heard, to understand what can never be understood." A speaker plays Jewish folk tunes. Hanging on the walls are pictures of children, some wearing *kippot*, the skullcaps signifying their religious background. Here in the basement, Jewish life in Poland before the German occupation is shown. "Most of the people were poor and humble," states the explanation on one wall. "They lived in small towns; their backs were bent and they walked with a stoop." Obviously there were some Jews in Poland who were not "bent"—younger, wealthier residents of large cities. But they do not fit Israel's image of the Exile and are mentioned only in passing. While emphasizing the material poverty of Jewish life in Poland, the text lovingly describes the culture—"their rich milieu and their exalted souls." For more than a thousand years, it says, Polish Jewry "reigned supreme in the history of the people of Israel." In contrast with the Yad Vashem museum, the explanations are written not in Yiddish but only in Hebrew and English.

Then one begins to ascend, and the light becomes brighter as one walks past the history of the Nazi regime, the stages of the attacks on the Jews, and finally their murder—Auschwitz. The second part of the museum, perhaps two-thirds of its space, is devoted to the Jewish resistance to the Nazis and to Yad Mordecai's battle with the Egyptians during the War of Independence. Alongside a model of the bunker that served as the command center of the Warsaw ghetto uprising hangs a large photograph of what is supposedly Anielewicz's last letter, containing the famous quotation engraved next to the monument. The text in the photograph is, however, in Yiddish and is a translated re-creation. The Hebrew original has been lost. Over the years it has been rewritten, from memory, in various versions, some of them probably more heroic than the original.[2] A huge wall, "the wall of rebellion," carries the names of hundreds of "outposts" of the "Jewish resistance movement" in the forests, ghettos, cities, Allied armies, and death camps. The impression is that it was a vast network of popular warfare. Then comes the section describing the briha (flight) and haapala (illegal immigration), as if they were an inseparable part of the Holocaust. The "European exodus" is described as "a drama with no parallel in the history of nations." As at Yad Vashem, there is a photograph of the *Exodus*.

At this point one passes a small window and gazes out at the graves of the members of Yad Mordecai who fell during the War of Independence. Then, turning, one sees a display about the eleven kibbutzim that settled in the Negev on a single night in October 1946. Only the Hebrew date is noted—the night after Yom Kippur. There is a photograph showing how the settlers laid a water pipe in the Negev. The accompanying text expresses a fundamental concept of the Israeli ethos: that the right of the Jews to settle in the country is based, in part, on the fact that they developed it—unlike the Arabs, who neglected it. The style is poetic, almost biblical:

> And they did not wander from well
> To spring, like the sons of the desert,
> But came and laid a pipe
> and brought water from the north
> To the south. And the foothold
> That they gained in one night
> Became a shade-crowned settlement.
> And the water flowed
> Through the pipe like blood
> That grants life to the limbs
> In the body of man.

And blood would flow on the pipe,
On it, the blood of people
Who came out at night
To defend what is more precious
Than anything in the world,
Water.

The museum then guides the visitor to another huge photograph of Mordecai Anielewicz, in his Hashomer Hatsair uniform, brimming with vitality and youth. Alongside are, again, those last words attributed to him: "The last desire of my life has been fulfilled. . . ." Gradually, almost without noticing, but in accordance with precise planning, the visitor leaves the Holocaust museum and enters a museum of War and Victory. Jutting from the chamber's walls are parts of old weapons, including a tank cannon and detailed maps containing a description of the battle for Yad Mordecai and a few other kibbutzim in the area, step by step. There is also a collection of artillery shells. Yad Mordecai was defeated and its defenders retreated; King Farouk of Egypt had his picture taken there, as if it were a conquered city. Later, the Egyptians were defeated and the kibbutz was retaken in a fierce battle.

The man who sold me my entrance ticket also offered me Margaret Larkin's book about the kibbutz, published by the ministry of defense. In English it is called *The Seven Days of Yad Mordecai*; its Hebrew title translates literally as *And the Sun Did Not Stand Still*.[3] The man identified himself as Shika Katsir, one of the founders. He helped the author write this heroic epic; she mentions his name in the preface. He himself presented the book to David Ben-Gurion. If I bought the book, he told me, he would autograph the first page. So he did. Next to his cash register he has postcards and all kinds of souvenirs, among them little ashtrays containing the picture of the Anielewicz statue. Katsir then sent me to visit the battlefield, where the fighters are represented by cutouts.

¶

One evening in April 1989, Tzvika Dror took me for a visit to the Ghetto Fighters Museum at Kibbutz Lohamei Hagetaot, a name that itself means "ghetto fighters." Dror, a teacher and writer, then sixty-three, was at work documenting the history of the kibbutz, which had that week celebrated its fortieth birthday. He opened room after room for me, showing me models of concentration camps, a wooden device on which inmates were tied for beatings, and a metal container that once held poison gas. The museum's central exhibit is the original glass booth in which Adolf Eichmann sat during his trial. The extermination of the Jews is presented at the Ghetto Fighters Museum largely as background to the main subject—the fight against the Nazis. On one wall is a blowup of a letter written by a young man named Ofer Feninger to his girlfriend Yael a few years before he was killed in the Six-Day War:

I have just finished reading [Ka-Tzetnik's] *House of Dolls* and I feel with my entire soul the horrors of that terrible Holocaust. . . . I feel rising in me, out of all the horror and helplessness, a great urge to be strong, strong to the point of tears; sharp as a knife; quiet and terrible; that is what I want to be! I want to know that bottomless eyes will never again gaze from behind electrified fences! They will not gaze that way only if I am strong! If we are all strong! Strong and proud Jews! Never again to be led to the slaughter.

We were alone in the museum, Tzvika Dror and I. In each room he turned on the light as we entered and turned it off as we left; in the corridors we walked in the dark. That same week the kibbutz was to lay the cornerstone for a new structure, a monument to the children killed in the Holocaust. Its cost was estimated at $1.5 million—a donation. There was of course no point in asking why Israel needed a second, and costly, monument for the children after the one at Yad Vashem in Jerusalem. The kibbutz had its own needs. At first it had planned to invest $3 million.*

The museum and the luxurious center next to it cast their shadows on the kibbutz. It is hard to avoid the cliché; it is a geographical fact. The kibbutz's "declaration of settlement," which Tzvika Dror showed me, describes it as a "settlement on the redeemed land of the Western Galilee—a living and productive monument to the ghetto uprising." It was founded by survivors of the Warsaw ghetto, among them Antek

---

* During its first years, Yad Vashem fought against the other memorial sites, including the Ghetto Fighters Museum at Lohamei Hagetaot. The battle was political as much as anything else. "They want to prove that the ghetto rebellion was initiated by members of Hashomer Hatsair," a member of the Yad Vashem board protested. "For this reason there is no way to be sure that their publications will be purely truthful and historical. In my opinion, now, when there is a national institute like Yad Vashem, they should dissolve."

Zuckerman and his wife, Tzivia Lubetkin. They settled on the land of the Arab village of Samariah, which was destroyed during the War of Independence, its inhabitants deported. "A village of terrorists," Tzvika Dror commented as we toured the dark museum. There is no settlement in Israel that better illustrates the link between the Holocaust and the Palestinian tragedy. The history of the kibbutz's name reveals another facet of Israel's complex relation to the Holocaust.

Yitzhak Tabenkin, the group's leader, proposed that they simply call themselves Vilna. Antek Zuckerman was opposed: How could he get on a bus and ask for a ticket to Vilna, he said. The first settlers wanted to preserve the name of the ruined Arab village, so they called the kibbutz Lohamei Hagetaot Samariah. The Jewish National Fund told them that the conjoining of "ghetto fighters" and the memory of Samariah was unthinkable and ruled that the kibbutz should be called Asher, after the Israelite tribe that had inhabited the area in ancient times. The settlers agreed to do without the Arab name but not without the reference to their past as ghetto fighters. The JNF further objected that it was unthinkable to include the term *ghetto* in the name of an Israeli settlement. Tzvika Dror showed me the correspondence, documenting a dispute between the biblical and tribal Hebrew heritage and that of the Jewish ghetto in the Diaspora.

The fierce struggle over the name reflected the tendency of the veterans of the organized Resistance to set themselves apart from the rest of the Holocaust survivors, as if they belonged to some secret noble order. Yet the desire to serve as "a living and productive monument to the ghetto uprisings" was very hard to realize. Poet Haim Guri told me once that when he visited the kibbutz during its first years, at night he could hear tormented cries through the windows of the members' huts. Not all the founders of the kibbutz—not even a majority—had been anti-Nazi fighters. Many of them, I learned, agonized over the fact that they had merely survived the Holocaust but had not rebelled. The myth of heroism was a heavy burden, at odds with their memories and experiences.

Once a year, during Passover, the staff of the kibbutz store prepares a special feast and holds a little party of its own, which I attended. Treating me to chicken in mushroom-wine sauce, the staff members began to reminisce, some in Yiddish. Among those present were elderly people with hard pasts and hard lives. Tzvika Dror pointed to one member, Yehuda Bornstein, who had first been in Auschwitz and then in another camp, Ebensee. Hunger had forced him to eat the bodies of dead prisoners. Many years later, during the Yom Kippur War, Bornstein lost his son, Tzvika Bashan, a pilot. His Israeli-born daughter, Nili, a poet, wrote:

> I yearn for Lodz, and the warm, sweet eyes of my grandparents.
> I yearn for them as for challah on the Sabbath.

Many children of Holocaust survivors in Israel felt this loss and grief. Like their parents, they also suffered from shame, guilt, and sometimes even nightmares about the camps they had never known.[5]

I had come to Lohamei Hagetaot with a stupid question: Had they succeeded in finding happiness at the kibbutz? But I only dared ask whether, in hindsight, they thought they had done the right thing in deciding to grow old together. They said that they did not speak daily of the Holocaust. On the contrary, until Tzvika Dror had forced them to recount the terrors of their pasts in the four volumes of testimonies he prepared, there were those who did not even know the details of their friends' stories. They lived together and were silent together. It had not been easy for him to convince them to tell about their lives. Dror's books are testimony not only of the Holocaust but also of the group therapy that an entire kibbutz participated in through telling its story.[6] Avraham Tsoref said that he could not live among those who had not endured the Holocaust as he had. After the war, while still a prisoner in a maapilim camp in Cyprus, he spent much time thinking about how he would tell people what had happened to him "there," what words he would choose to relate that the Jews of his town were no longer. He felt as if he were the last Jew on earth. When he arrived in the country, no one asked him, and that was horrible, he said. People did not want to know. That whole period was traumatic, he said, finishing his meal, and leaving. He had been in the Stutthof concentration camp.

Afterwards, I went to visit Nina Wangrove. Dror's testimonies contain the story of the horrible tortures she endured in prison.[7] She told me about her life at her kibbutz. Later, she said that she had never told that story before. It was a sad monologue.

> That's a good question, how my life would have been if I hadn't gone to the kibbutz. I've always been very closed off; my husband and I did not talk about what had been during the war. I could have made him talk about it, but I didn't want to. He's also from "there." I don't like to say "Holocaust survivor." The fact is that we did not

survive, we were not saved. To this day we have not been saved.

During the war I wanted only to die. I knew I was doomed to die, but my dream was to live until the end of the war and die a free person, one day after. Like a bird that has flown to every far-off place and in the end spreads its wings and falls.

The war ended. When it ended, something ended inside of me, too. After all the energy I had devoted to living through the war, suddenly there was nothing else worth devoting myself to. It was very, very hard. I so longed for something to give my life meaning. I was eighteen. By chance I met people who told me, maybe go to a kibbutz. That's how I came here.

I was apprehensive. I remember that I told my husband: the kibbutz's ideology is nice. But do you want to live the rest of your life with Monik and Frieda? Monik and Frieda were among the first ones here. That's what I asked my husband: Do you really want to live with them from now on? It turned out that we did: we spent our whole lives with Monik and Frieda.

Other people did not understand us, cannot understand us. That is my feeling today. I don't know what would have happened had they tried to understand us. Perhaps it's best that they didn't try. No one asked us anything. They gave us a work schedule and told us to work. If they had tried to understand us, who knows? Maybe it would not have worked out.

And we didn't try to understand ourselves. So one year went by and then another and another and another. Every year it became harder. Everything. The memories of the Holocaust and the memories from after the Holocaust and the memories from the kibbutz. Every year it is harder.

We were completely confused, in shock, to go from that camp to this—ghetto. Yes, the kibbutz. That's how I feel, like in a camp or in a Jewish ghetto. How can you live this way? In the end I was not happy. Except for my children, there is nothing that ties me here. I can be here and tomorrow I can be there and the day after nowhere. This did not turn out to be a terribly important place to me. Perhaps there really are no terribly important places, or even things. Everything important died.

For many years I still lived in my imagination, in my old house. My homeland was Soviet Russia. My father and mother—I don't know what happened to them. My brother, too. Many years, very many years, I lived in the hope that one day I would see them. More than once I would suddenly leave the kibbutz, go to Haifa, walk down Herzl Street, walk around and around and stand in front of the cinema—who knows, suddenly they might appear among the people. It was horrible. It was horrible for me, it was horrible to explain to my husband where I was going. And then we lived so packed together, everyone on everyone's toes. You couldn't breathe without the whole kibbutz knowing. External things—not what was happening to Nina inside, but where Nina was going, where was she going. And I never found them.

I should have gotten out of that and lived. The kibbutz was never home. Today it is at least tolerable living here. But it was not home, and today, too, it's not home. And I am very dedicated to the place. I worked hard at all sorts of jobs. I did everything that needed doing. I worked with children and in the factory—wherever they needed me. But not like my husband. My husband believed in what he was doing. I did it all out of duty, out of a sense of responsibility. He really believed in the kibbutz. Not me.

The children left. Now I feel strong enough to tell it all. I used to be silent. Simply accepted everything. They gave us this ideology—socialist, full of prohibitions: what to wear and what not to wear, what to think and what not to think, what to say and what not to say. It was all so oppressive. But I accepted it. Accepted it. What would have been had I not gone to the kibbutz? Perhaps I would have been sorry my whole life. Could be.

She was sixty-two when I visited her, tall, sturdy, dark-haired, radiating fortitude and drama. A short while before, she had lost her eyesight. The kibbutz built her a large apartment and gave her a loom, on which she wove pastoral scenes, in wool.

"Father and Mother spoke about nothing else," related the kibbutz secretary, as the elected head of the kibbutz administration is called. "They talked about it all the time. Every conversation, no matter how it began, would get to the Holocaust, sooner or later." She and her brother couldn't stand it, she said. They couldn't stand the annual memorial ceremonies, which were big kibbutz events, because so many important guests always came. Memory weighed on her parents and weighed on their children. Complex relations. Her name is Yael Zuckerman; her parents were the legendary Antek Zuckerman and Tzivia Lubetkin. Every week, on Friday nights, they would meet with friends and admirers. They nurtured the myth throughout their lives. They would talk for a while about current concerns and then begin reminiscing. Yael Zuckerman did not understand a word of it, she told me, and did not want to understand. "Until it was too late. That's the way it always is. By the time a person wants to understand her parents, there's no one left to ask," she said.

Zuckerman, a psychologist, began to take an interest in the Holocaust only after her father's death in June 1981. Then she began to read her parents' books; she traveled twice to Poland. It was a process of maturation, she said, of rethinking her life, of missing her parents. A matter of age, too. She is not obsessed with the Holocaust, she said, but she knows that it is part of her.

The kibbutz has 280 adult members, among them 90 founders. There are 185 children, making for a community of almost 500 people. The parents and founders retired from kibbutz work early, as if their strength were gone, and made way for their children. There was almost no generational struggle, Zuckerman said. The kibbutz is prosperous, well cared for, the lawns vivid green; it owns a factory that makes imitation meat products from soya—a great success, with sales of $21 million a year. Yes, they export to Germany. Members of the kibbutz received compensation from Germany. Like many other kibbutzim, they used the money to build a swimming pool. Some members were still receiving an annual pension from Germany. Not all of them handed the money over to the kibbutz. "It's a problem," Zuckerman said. They have volunteers from other countries, but no Germans. German groups wishing to visit the museum are required to bring a letter of recommendation from Willy Brandt. That is what was decided once, after a long debate.

¶

During the 1980s, anti-Semitism in Germany was discussed again and again in the Knesset, as was the need to bring war criminals to justice, and the problem of how to counter those who claimed the Holocaust never happened. In general, these debates had no practical significance; they reflected the tendency to defend the "holiness" of the heritage. Like the law that protects religious sensibilities, and the honor of the national flag, there was a proposal in 1985 to forbid the use of Nazi symbols for anything but educational purposes and research. Some of these debates were held in a clearly ceremonial atmosphere. The Knesset proceedings frequently note that among those seated in the gallery were prominent Holocaust survivors, and there were also cases when a choir was invited to attend the session, to sing songs about the Holocaust. At times members of the Knesset included poetry, prayer, and personal memories in their speeches. Sometimes the discussions were accompanied by various dramatic symbolic acts. Justice Minister Moshe Nissim announced that the government would award $1 million to whoever could turn Josef Mengele over to Israel. Meir Kahane tore up an Austrian flag on the Knesset podium during a discussion of President Kurt Waldheim's past.[8] There was a certain element of competition involved here: members often tried to show that they were more patriotic or more religious than their opponents; similarly, they competed over faithfulness to the Holocaust. Many were Holocaust survivors, and they tried to induce the Knesset to make all sorts of anti-German gestures, as if they missed those far-off days in the 1950s when such initiatives involved huge outpourings of emotion. One demanded that the Knesset condemn those Israelis who had taken advantage of their legal right to receive German passports, just like tens of thousands of other Israelis with dual citizenship. "Such a step is antipatriotic, anti-Zionist, and immoral," he stated. A colleague protested that Israel had promised to improve Germany's image in school textbooks. A third tried to persuade the Knesset that the president of Israel should not visit Germany.[9] Yet, for all the ceremony, the Holocaust lobby, like the religious lobby, discovered that secular reality is stronger. Many thousands of Israelis requested and received German passports; the Israeli German committee to examine textbooks continued to work undisturbed; President Herzog visited Germany.[10]

Shortly before the Berlin Wall fell in November 1989, the first intensive contacts between East Germany and Israel began. It was a strange, almost necrophilic diplomatic episode. Israel tried to get a dying East Germany to sign a reparations agreement that would obligate a united Germany. Up until then, East Germany had denied its share in the responsibility for the crimes of the Nazis. The contacts were almost a precise reprise of the negotiations that Israel had conducted with West Germany in the 1950s. Now as then, Israel dictated the statement of contrition it demanded. History has seldom seen such continuity and repetition. Almost forty years after the fact the same players played against the same background and represented the same interests. The Israelis wanted money, the Germans a new image. The currency was words.

In April 1990 the East German parliament passed a resolution, one of the last in its history, in which it not only expressed contrition but also, perhaps for the first time, recognized Israel's status as a representative of Jews around the world. From the day Israel was founded it had hoped for such recognition but never won it, partly because of the opposition of Jewish organizations in other countries, especially in the United States. Now it won it, in the form of the last testament of a German state that was about to die. It is hard to imagine anything more ironic.*[11]

The Israeli press reacted to the reunification of Germany with editorials expressing reservation, apprehension, and pain—but written, it would seem, out of a sense that this was how the newspapers of the Jewish state ought to react. Here and there Holocaust survivors raised their voices. Not unexpectedly, Dov Shilansky was their spokesman. "For us it is a day of mourning," the speaker of the Knesset declared.[13] Yet the government was quick to adjust to the new reality. Foreign Minister Moshe Arens flew to Germany to repair the damage done when Yitzhak Shamir initially expressed misgivings. "We have absolute confidence in a united Germany," Arens said in Bonn.[14] *Yediot Aharonot* conducted a survey: 36 percent of those asked said that they saw the unification of Germany as positive. Some 28 percent said that they opposed it. Another 35 percent said that they didn't care, and this is probably the crucial figure: most Israelis no longer considered Germany an enemy.[15]

---

* Just before reunification, the Berlin Philharmonic came to Israel for a series of concerts, its first such tour. It had previously been unable to play in Israel because of the past of its conductor, Herbert von Karajan. On the occasion of the orchestra's visit, just after von Karajan's death, Daniel Barenboim repeated an opinion often heard in the past. The time had come, he said, to be rid of the final taboo and to play Richard Wagner's music in public. The penultimate anti-German taboo had already been broken, with no scandal—orchestras had begun to play the music of Richard Strauss.[12]

26 | *"What Is There to Understand?*
They Died and That's It"

On a small street in Tel Aviv that has known better days stands an auditorium called Ohel Shem. The street, one of the city's oldest, is named after Arthur James Balfour, a British foreign minister who won the honor by writing a crucial letter in 1917. Addressed to Lord Lionel Walter Rothschild, president of the Zionist Federation in England, it stated that His Majesty's government looked with favor on the establishment of a Jewish national home in Palestine. The Balfour Declaration was an important achievement in the Zionist movement's efforts to establish a Jewish state. Ohel Shem ("Shem's Tent") was founded about twelve years later at the instigation of Haim Nahman Bialik, the Zionist movement's national poet. The nearby beach was the home of muscular Judaism; Bialik wanted a hall that would foster cultural Judaism. In his poem "On the Threshold of the House of Prayer," he wrote: "You shall not fall, Shem's tent, I'll build you fast."[1] It was an important cultural center, as secular as Tel Aviv itself, where one could see the city's writers, poets, and scholars; in its prime it drew large crowds. The Israel Philharmonic Orchestra played on its stage, and the Mapai central committee met there, too.

Six decades later, Ohel Shem has lost its greatness. The paint is peeling and faded, and it is used only for marginal events, such as Yiddish theater productions. In September 1990 I went to Ohel Shem to attend the annual reunion of Israelis from Lodz, held in commemoration of the day the Nazis liquidated the ghetto there; I was immediately identified as an outsider. Lodz was the second-largest city in Poland; on the eve of the war about a quarter million Jews lived there, one out of every three inhabitants. Many of them earned their living in the city's textile industry; most were murdered by the Nazis. Those who came to Israel have established their own fellowship organization, as have people from many other European cities and towns. Each of these *Landsmanschafts* holds an annual memorial ceremony; not a month goes by without such a get-together being held somewhere, usually in Tel Aviv.

The majority of people who came to Ohel Shem that night were in their sixties; they had spent most of their adult lives in Israel, speaking Hebrew, but at their annual assembly, part memorial service and part reunion, they fell into Polish and Yiddish. The meeting was held between Rosh Hashanah and Yom Kippur, a time when people tend to think of the changing seasons. The participants asked what had happened since the last time, about health and children. One had had heart surgery, another had opened a new business, one had retired, and another passed away. A daughter had completed officer's training, and the oldest son, the one in Los Angeles, had had another child. This was old, Ashkenazic, well-off Tel Aviv, yet it was as if a collective sigh hovered in the hall the whole time. In coming to Israel these people had lost a world precious to them. They missed it, I thought, or perhaps they missed only their lost youths. Either way, as they grew older, they felt closer to their childhoods. The older ones had experienced the horrors of the Holocaust; some had survived the death camps.

The people still milling about on the sidewalk moved toward the auditorium's entrance; in the lobby, two young people sold the *Holocaust Encyclopedia*, Israel's main contribution to the historiography of the Jewish genocide. In six volumes, it is a semiofficial publication, jointly produced by Yad Vashem, the Mapam-linked publishing house Sifriat Poalim, and *Yediot Aharonot*. Elie Wiesel contributed a preface. At the time it was being marketed with a mass advertising campaign, including radio commercials. Those present at the Lodz convention were offered the set at a discount. A man wandered through the audience selling Shimon Levin cassette tapes from a cardboard box. Levin himself, in black robe and hat, had been invited to lead the audience in the mourners' prayers.

But first the chairman called the meeting to order, addressing the audience as "Dear Lodzers"; then six candles were lit in a memorial menorah set on a box draped in black cloth. Candles and prayers had a place here, but the gathering was clearly secular: though the audience of perhaps three hundred stood for the prayers, the men and women stayed together. Most of the men did not cover their heads, though some covered them with handkerchiefs, the expedient for secular Israel in attending funerals, weddings, and the like. The prayers lasted only a few minutes. Then there were a few words in Yiddish, also an integral part of Israel's memorial culture. The chairman introduced the evening's speaker, Zvi Blumenfrucht, as a writer and a poet. Blumenfrucht warned, in Yiddish, against forgetting. Despite those who would have us forget the Holocaust, he said, we will not forget it; and, as if pledging loyalty to the dead, he repeated, *"Nein, nein, nein!"* Three Israeli flags stood on either side of the stage, for a total of six. Above hung a large color map of the ghetto.

The chairman was an energetic man who seemed to have considerable experience moderating this annual event. He made several announcements about administrative matters. He had hoped, he said, to bring some schoolchildren to tell the group about their trip to Poland, but in the meantime they went into the army. The Lodz immigrants' organization wrote to the army and asked that they be given leave for this evening; he, the chairman, had personally handled the matter. Unfortunately, the army had not agreed. He was nevertheless happy to see several young people in the hall, although not many. It was very important, the chairman said, to pass the story of Lodz on to the younger generation.

Three weeks later the two Germanys were to reunite, but the subject did not come up. Instead, the chairman said something about the "little Hitler" now threatening Israel: Iraqi president Saddam Hussein. In the context of the Gulf crisis, the chairman praised David Ben-Gurion for having had Israel build its own atom bomb. The people in the hall nodded in agreement.

Afterwards, the chairman encouraged the Lodzers to be happy. This was in accordance with a ruling of the chief rabbi of Tel Aviv, he told them. The victims, the martyrs, had willed life to the survivors, and life was happiness, even laughter. They had not lived just to shoulder the grief of the world. Even at memorial services one may laugh, the chairman said, telling them a joke from the Second World War. There was this Japanese boy who asked his father why, really, it had been necessary to bomb Pearl Harbor; wouldn't it have been simpler to buy it? The audience chuckled politely.

And that reminds me, the chairman said, that the organization's bank account is empty. There were many plans—the organization wanted to bring an exhibition of photographs of the Lodz ghetto, now in Frankfurt, to Israel. Among the pictures, believe it or not, was a picture of the chairman of the Judenrat, Haim Rumkovski, in the company of SS commandant Heinrich Himmler. If they could afford it, they would like to hold two memorial ceremonies each year: in the meantime, they were preparing a reunion of the graduates of the Hebrew Gymnasium in Lodz.

The organization's offices, the chairman announced, had recently received, through the generosity of the Polish government, copies of the old Lodz census lists. There was also information on the burial sites of 150,000 Jews who had gone to their reward since the turn of the century. Examination of these documents could save much time for those traveling to visit the graves of their families. There was also a pamphlet advising members of remaining possibilities for demanding compensation from Germany. But all this costs money, and he, the chairman, knew, of course, that his dear Lodzers were warmhearted and generous, and he was sure that now, during the intermission, people would make donations. At the end of the break, though, the chairman announced that he had not received sufficient donations. Apparently some of the members had forgotten to bring their checkbooks, so he expected to receive contributions by mail, he said. The listeners shook their heads skeptically.

The centerpiece of the evening was a pair of historical lectures. Shmuel Cracowski, director of the Yad Vashem historical archive, lectured on the period of the Nazi occupation before the establishment of the ghetto. Dina Porat spoke of the Jewish world's attitude toward the Holocaust, including that of the yishuv. Cracowski is a small, balding man, with an accent that betrays his Polish origins; Porat is an elegant young woman, with the Hebrew of a native-born Israeli. Cracowski spoke with great feeling, and it was not always possible to distinguish between the historian and the public speaker, between the scholar and the eulogizer. He concentrated on describing the atrocities the Nazis committed against the civilian population, acts of barbaric sadism, he called them. When he cited the name of Herbert Fischer, one of the commanders of the Nazi murder bands known as *Einsatzkommandos*, Cracowski commented that "all the commanders of these units were PhDs." The audience again nodded, a brotherhood of "little people," neither doctors nor murderers. When Cracowski spoke of the destruction of synagogues and noted their locations, a wave of murmuring passed through the hall. The names of streets he cited brought people to whisper childhood memories to their neighbors; Cracowski warmed their hearts. Porat, who teaches at Tel Aviv University, was restrained, cold, and academic.

¶

Cracowski and Porat represent two stations on the path of Israeli historiography of the Holocaust. The path leads, step by step, from memorialization to scholarship, passing innumerable ideological, political, and psychological barriers all along the way. The first efforts to commemorate the Jewish communities destroyed in the Holocaust were made during the war, by the communities themselves. Emanuel Ringelblum documented the history of the Warsaw ghetto; his archive, discovered hidden in milk jugs after the war, is a valuable source of information for the study of the Holocaust. Similar archives, as well as diaries, were produced in ghettos, partisan outposts in the forests, and even in the death camps themselves.[2] In Israel there were also efforts at commemoration, and these were made part of the Zionist effort. In July 1947, an international conference in Jerusalem brought together representatives of all the historical institutions involved in gathering material on the Holocaust. Those attending explained that they worked not only with the scholarly aims of studying and understanding the causes and significance of the Jewish genocide but also "out of hope that the lesson of the Holocaust will serve the future of our nation." The conference resolved that Israel, with "Jerusalem in its midst," was the appropriate place to serve as a world center for this study.[3]

The Holocaust and Heroism Memorial Act of 1953 gave Yad Vashem the status of official historian by stating that among the institution's tasks was "to gather, investigate, and publish all evidence of the Holocaust and heroism."[4] The first historical effort made by the institution was, in fact, recording interviews with survivors. These interviews have a certain historical value, but the interviewers did not press their subjects with questions and did not demand proof or confront the survivors with existing information that might contradict their testimony. For witnesses, telling their stories was a holy obligation to the dead, and sometimes also a release for their personal stress, a kind of testimonial therapy. Yad Vashem simply recorded what they had to say.

The *Landsmanschaft* organizations also encouraged their members to record what had happened to them during the war. Over the years, a unique and touching literary genre developed: the memorial, or *Yizkor*, book. Each one memorializes a community destroyed, some of them so small that they can hardly be found on any map. Most of these books came about in the same way: Several survivors from the town got together, exchanged recollections, and wrote down the stories and legends; they gathered photographs, mostly from private family albums that survived and ended up in Israel, who knows how; they searched through old suitcases and opened long-closed drawers and found marriage contracts and death certificates and report cards; here and there they found pages from a young girl's diary, or a love poem, or a drawing, or a child's composition, or a leaflet put out by the partisans in the forest. Every page, every photograph spoke of a lost way of life, from mother's chicken soup to a mass grave in the forest, from the ghetto rebellion to immigration to Israel. A teacher or poet from the town would anthologize the material and add, to the best of his or her abilities, ideals, nostalgia, heroism, and Zionism. Famous persons from the town would be honored with a special place in the book. President Zalman Shazar wrote something about his Stoyvetz, David Ben-Gurion about his Plonsk. The *Landsmanschaft* printed two or three hundred copies in Hebrew and Yiddish, for the survivors who had promised to buy them. The Lodz book came out early, in 1943. In 1990, close to a thousand such books were put on exhibit in the Yad Vashem library.[5] About half of them were printed after the Yom Kippur War.

Hundreds, perhaps thousands, of personal memoirs have also been written. These too, were meant to break the great silence imposed on the Holocaust survivors in Israel and undo the negative stereotypes under which they suffered. The melancholy reflections, cries of pain, calls for revenge, and declarations of loyalty to the Zionist vision that fill these volumes also characterize the work of many of the first Israeli historians who studied the Holocaust. Most of them had also experienced the terrors of the war and survived the death camps. They, too, were concerned for the image of the Holocaust's victims and survivors. They, too, had enlisted in the struggle for the State of Israel and shared the faith in its redemptive power that pervaded the literature and poetry of the time and suffused the Declaration of Independence. "Our death has a dawn," exulted Natan Alterman, as if the single great wish of the victims had been to die for the establishment of the state.[6] In one of his novels, Ka-Tzetnik brings together a man and woman on the Tel Aviv beach. He is a Holocaust survivor, she Israeli-born. It is the night of November 29, 1947, the very night that the UN General Assembly resolved to partition Palestine into two states. "A state! A state! A Hebrew state!" Ka-Tzetnik wrote. "Her legs twined round his loins, the salt water shimmered, intoxicating wine in their kisses. . . . Let me now, my love, and I will kiss this earth at this hour and on this night."[7] The Declaration of Independence reads, "The Holocaust committed against the People of Israel [i.e., the Jewish People] in recent times, during which millions of Jews were slaughtered in Europe, again proved manifestly the necessity of a solution to the problem of the Jewish People, who lack a homeland and independence. The solution is the renewal of the Jewish state in Israel, which will open wide the gates of the homeland to every Jew and which will grant every Jew the status of a people with equal rights among the family of nations."*

The effort to rehabilitate the image of the Holocaust's victims and survivors, to support the ideological struggle of the state, and to shape the memorial culture deterred Israeli historians from trying to understand Nazism. They feared, perhaps, that such an attempt would be interpreted as a justification of it or as a challenge to its abstract, almost mystic status as the symbol of absolute evil. This fear inhibited research and explains why the most important books on Nazism and the extermination of the Jews were not written in Israel. In fact, only a few of these foreign works were translated into Hebrew, generally long after original publication. Translation and publication in 1962 of William Shirer's *The Rise and Fall of the Third Reich* was an almost revolutionary event. Hermann Rauschning's *Conversations with Hitler* and Konrad Heiden's *Der Führer: Hitler's Rise to Power* came out in Hebrew during World War II, but the classic biography of Hitler by Alan Bullock was published in Israel

---

* In similar fashion, any denial of the Holocaust would be seen as an attempt to challenge the right of Israel to exist. "There is a world conspiracy, financed by those who hate Israel, whose goal is to twist the historical truth about the Holocaust," warned one member of the Knesset.[8] In July 1981 the Knesset passed a law that prohibited the denial of the Holocaust: "The publication, in writing or orally, of work that denies the acts committed during the period of the Nazi rule, which are crimes against the Jewish people or crimes against humanity, or that downplays their dimensions with the intention of defending those who committed these crimes or of expressing support for or identification with them is liable to five years' imprisonment."[9] A proposal to impose ten years' imprisonment was not accepted. Thus the extermination of the Jews was no longer a subject for the historians; it was almost as if it had been uprooted from history itself and had become a national doctrine of truth, protected by law, somewhat similar in legal status to religious faith. Indeed, in one way the Holocaust has even a higher status than religion: The maximum punishment for "crass injury" to religious sensibilities or tradition—including, presumably, any denial of God's existence—is one year in prison.[10]

in 1974, almost twenty years after it first appeared in English. Joachim Fest's *Hitler* appeared in Hebrew in 1986, thirteen years after it was first published in German. The Israeli publisher added to the book's original title a subtitle contradicting the book's basic thesis: *Portrait of a Nonperson.* [11]

Hannah Arendt told me once of the pressures that prevented the Israeli publication of her controversial book on the Eichmann trial; she believed that Ben-Gurion himself had demanded that the book be banned. *Eichmann in Jerusalem* is a classic text in the debate over the personality of the Nazi murderer and his motives and in the discussion of human evil in general. Its nonpublication in Hebrew rankled Arendt, but the book itself, she said, was less important than people thought. She had written in anger at what she saw as Israel's attempt to exploit the Eichmann trial for political purposes. She told me that, were she to write it again, she would write it differently. Its subtitle, *A Report on the Banality of Evil,* was blown out of proportion, she argued. Then she added, with the biting irony that characterized her, that *Eichmann in Jerusalem* could at most serve as a guide to reporters on how to cover a historic trial.

Raul Hilberg's basic work on the Holocaust also remains untranslated into Hebrew. Like Arendt, Hilberg placed part of the guilt for the genocide on the Jews themselves, implicating the Judenrats in facilitating the extermination program. The role of the Judenrats has always been one of the most sensitive issues of the Holocaust; it took seven years for Yad Vashem to publish a Hebrew translation of Isaiah Trunk's *Judenrat,* which was first published in New York. Ruth Bondi's *Edelstein against Time*—a humane, balanced account of the moral dilemmas faced by the man whom Eichmann appointed as "Jewish Elder" of the Theresienstadt ghetto—was published only in the early 1980s, when it was seen as shattering a taboo. The same was true of Yehoshua Sobol's play *Ghetto,* produced a few years later.*[12]

---

* Supreme Court Justice Gabriel Bach, who had been a member of the prosecution team at the Eichmann trial, told me that contrary to Arendt's assertion, the prosecution presented "all relevant" evidence with regard to the Judenrats. At one point, Bach recalled, there was a danger of the whole trial's becoming the trial of the Jewish councils instead of Eichmann and the Nazis. One day Eichmann's German defense counsel, Robert Servatius, came and showed Bach fifteen letters he had received from Israeli citizens, all of whom offered to appear as defense witnesses. They were not interested in defending Eichmann; instead, they hoped that while testifying they would have the chance to close old accounts with members of their local Judenrats. These people were boiling cauldrons

Israeli historiography needed almost an entire generation before it produced scholars able to attempt, sometimes successfully, to separate the
Holocaust from their personal biographies, to see it as part of history,
and to investigate it without apologetics and without ideology. This effort
began in the late 1970s. It probably could not have begun earlier; the
Holocaust was too close then, too painful, too oppressive, too political. *[14]

Dina Porat is best known for her book on the yishuv's attitudes toward
the Holocaust. "The yishuv did not alter its way of life and did not change
course because of the Holocaust," she wrote.[16] Her *Trapped Leadership*
is an important book; until its publication in 1986 the failures of the
yishuv's rescue program were a subject that on occasion flared up in
Israeli politics but had never been studied methodically. Only one book
worthy of attention preceded Porat's. Written by a Tel Aviv teacher named
S. B. Beit-Zvi, it was read by few.[17]

Before Porat's talk at the Lodz reunion, the chairman remarked that
the attitude of the yishuv to the extermination of the Jews had troubled
the survivors while they were still "there," in the ghetto. It also troubled
them once they came to Israel, especially since they were despised for
having gone to the death camps "like lambs to the slaughter," instead of
defending themselves, and because in Israel people refused to believe
their stories. The audience murmured in approval. Their first contact
with a country that could respect only dead heroes was a trauma. Many
Holocaust survivors therefore embraced Dina Porat's book, or at least the

---

waiting to explode. Servatius decided not to summon them. He estimated, probably
correctly, that their testimony would only make the court realize how the Nazis wore
down their victims before sending them off to their deaths. "Imagine what would have
happened if all those witnesses, Jews from Israel, had appeared in court and told Judenrat
stories," Bach said. "No one would have remembered Adolf Eichmann." When Servatius
decided to concede this matter, Bach congratulated himself for having advised Eichmann
to take on the German attorney.[13]

* Religious historiography has its own ideological and political problems and taboos, not
the least of which is the difficulty of explaining how God could have permitted the mass
murder of the Jews. Like the secular Zionists, the religious community saw the Jewish
genocide as a link in the long chain of persecutions.

Some believed that the Jews were murdered in punishment for their sins and some
that their fate was meant to speed the arrival of the Messiah; most rabbis chose simply
to say that, while there must be an explanation for the Holocaust, there was no way of
knowing what it was. When Zionists claimed that the rabbinical establishment had
prevented pious Jews from saving their lives by emigrating to Israel, the ultraorthodox
responded by accusing the Zionists of having abandoned them because they were religious:
thus it was the Zionists, not God, who had abandoned them.[15]

many newspaper articles written about it. Porat, however, seemed very cautious, even forgiving. She told the Lodzers that the people in Palestine could not have done a thing for them. They didn't believe the information on the extermination; besides, they could not have understood what it meant because they were, she contended, too decent, and they had other, equally legitimate concerns.

§

More than twenty years earlier, in April 1968, I went with two friends to interview David Ben-Gurion for the Hebrew University student newspaper.[18] Ben-Gurion received us in his small home at Kibbutz Sde Boker. Then eighty-two years old, he was still sharp and radiated power. We came to ask him, in advance of Israel's twentieth Independence Day, to what extent the country was independent. Ben-Gurion liked the question. He was in a mood for historical reflection that morning. He had plenty of time, and we sat with him for almost three hours.

It was the day after the first Holocaust Day following the Six-Day War. The newspaper *Lamerhav* had published a long interview with Saul Friedländer, who was just then beginning to be recognized around the world as one of the important scholars of the Holocaust. "A failure," said Friedländer, himself a Holocaust survivor, when asked about the yishuv's reaction to the extermination of the Jews in Europe. "I do not claim that from a technical-operational point of view they could have done more than they actually did," he explained. "I claim that the yishuv leadership and the public as a whole did not give enough thought to the matter. The rescue of the Jews in Europe was not at the top of the yishuv leaders' list of priorities. For them, the most important thing was the effort to establish the state." Friedländer made it clear that he was speaking of Ben-Gurion's approach. "I believe that Ben-Gurion never understood the nature of the Holocaust," Friedländer added. "True, he visited the refugee camps in Europe after the war, but he did not plumb the depths of the matter. He saw it first as potential for establishing the state." Friedländer linked this approach to Ben-Gurion's general view of Jewish history: "I think that Ben-Gurion and many others are 'ashamed' of the historical heritage of Diaspora Judaism," he said.[19] We asked Ben-Gurion whether this was true. He preferred not to discuss the subject. "I'll read it later," he said about the newspaper interview, and made a note to invite Friedländer to meet with him, as if it were some minor misunderstanding that could be cleared up in a conversation.

Ben-Gurion began talking about his favorite thesis, that "the people of Israel"—that is, the people *in* Israel—must be a "chosen people" and a "light to the nations," a paragon of national morality and spiritual and scientific genius. He told us of his young manhood in Palestine, from the year 1906. He had been a pioneer, he said. This is how the first Zionist settlers saw themselves—a national avant-garde, a nucleus for the creation of a "new man" in a new Hebrew society. For them, Zionism was a rejection of the Diaspora they loathed. This attitude led, after the war, to arrogance and contempt towards the Holocaust's victims and survivors.

Ben-Gurion was twenty when he came, but he said that even as a small child he had known that he would go to live in Israel as a Zionist. His memory might be misleading him on this point, we suggested, but the old man insisted: as early as the age of three he had already known that he would live in Israel as a Zionist. He told us of his efforts to make peace with the Arab countries, and stated, for the first time in public, his position with regard to the territories occupied in the Six-Day War: "If I have to choose between a small Israel, without territories, but with peace, and a greater Israel without peace, I prefer a small Israel."

At moments he was rather intimate and sentimental. Aside from encouraging immigration, there was nothing more important than encouraging a higher birthrate, which he termed "internal immigration." He had wanted another child, a fourth, he told us, but his wife, Paula —who had died a short while before our visit—had not agreed.

We tried again to speak about the Holocaust. "All right," Ben-Gurion said. "The Holocaust. I want you to know that beginning in 1945 I had only one concern: would we survive or would we not survive? It was clear that the British would leave the country and that the Arabs would take their place." For the next twenty minutes he surveyed his efforts to bring about the establishment of the State of Israel, as well as a series of secret operations he ordered to obtain arms for the coming war. He remembered names, dates, places. He briefly reviewed the major stages of the War of Independence; he recounted battles. He wanted to be sure we understood the immensity of the achievement, three young students who could not remember that war. "We were on the brink of extermination," Ben-Gurion said—but of the Holocaust he said not a word.

We returned to the subject for a third time. Friedländer contends that you did not properly understand its significance, we said. Ben-Gurion sank into a long silence: we could hear only the buzzing of a lone desert fly. Suddenly he raised his eyes and said: "What is there to understand?

They died and that's it." He rose from behind his desk and went, without speaking, to a tall ladder leaning against a book-lined wall. He climbed up and up, drew out a dusty volume, leafed through it for a minute or two, and then, still in place at the top of the ladder, a short, stocky old man with a white mane of hair, read to us what he had said to the Histadrut convention in 1934—before the Nazis had been in power for even a year, and five years before World War II began:

> Hitler's regime puts the entire Jewish people in danger, and not just the Jewish people. . . . The Hitler regime cannot last for long without a war of vengeance against France, Poland, Czechoslovakia, and its other neighbors. . . . There can be no doubt that we are now facing a danger of war no less than before 1914, and a war that will be greater in its destruction and its terrors than the last world war. . . . Perhaps only four or five years (if not less) stand between us and that terrible day. During this period we must double our numbers, because the size of the yishuv on that day will, perhaps, determine our future on the day of decision.[20]

Ben-Gurion descended from the ladder and said: "I said exactly what would happen, and I said it five years before the war." Afterwards he told us of the efforts he made, in London, to increase the immigration quota. The greater part of the guilt for holding down immigration, and therefore for preventing the rescue of the Jews, fell on the Palestinian Arabs and the British, Ben-Gurion said. He emphasized the contacts between Haj Amin al-Husseini, the Grand Mufti of Jerusalem, and Adolf Hitler. No, the British could not have saved six million Jews, he said. They could have saved many, but not all. They could, for instance, have bombed Auschwitz and Treblinka, he contended. Here he told us something that coming from him sounded like a historical anecdote. There had been this Jewish man, Ben-Gurion could not remember his name, who arrived with some Nazi proposal to free a million Jews in exchange for ten thousand trucks. "Where could we find ten thousand trucks?" he asked, dumbfounded as if hearing the idea for the first time. There was something almost surreal in the offhand tone in which he spoke of that attempt at rescue.

§

Before leaving Budapest in 1944, Hanzi Brand told me with a shy smile, her husband notified the Jewish Agency representatives in neutral Istanbul that he was coming.[21] They cabled him in response that they would be waiting for him. The cable said that Chaim would be waiting, and she and her husband assumed, of course, that the reference was to Chaim Weizmann. This did not surprise them; Adolf Eichmann's proposal required a decision at the highest level, as well as a great logistic effort, with international cooperation. It meant taking a million Jews out of the Nazi occupation zone, and giving the Nazis ten thousand trucks, all while the war was still raging. Yes, they had believed Eichmann; of course they had believed him. First, because they had no other choice but to believe him. Second, if he didn't mean it, why did he talk to the Jews and send one of them to Istanbul? Yes, they believed him. And it was clear to them that the man who would greet Joel Brand in Istanbul would be Chaim Weizmann. In fact, it was Haim Barlas, one of the Jewish Agency representatives in Istanbul, and Barlas had not even succeeded in getting Brand an entry permit into Turkey.

Somehow Brand reached Istanbul anyway. On his way to Palestine, he was arrested by the British and held for months in a military prison in Cairo. The Hungarians, who knew nothing about the mission the Nazis had entrusted to her husband, arrested Hanzi Brand for interrogation and tortured her in an attempt to make her reveal the nature of the mission. In the meantime the matter had gone from the Jewish Agency executive in Jerusalem to the desks of Churchill, Roosevelt, and Stalin. None of them wanted the deal, each one for his own reason, and for one common reason: they did not know what to do with a million Jews. Eichmann ordered the trains to roll to Auschwitz.

When I visited her, Hanzi Brand was in her eighties. She remembered the mission in detail; she lived it daily. It was hard to know what the Nazis had wanted, she said. Perhaps they had wanted an alibi on the eve of their defeat; perhaps they had wanted a separate peace with the West, without Hitler's knowledge. Either way, Eichmann had called Rezso Kastner in to put together a proposal. Joel and Hanzi Brand had also been there. She gave the impression of having read every word ever written about the episode. Most historians had not understood the events, she ruled, and at least some of them had maliciously distorted it. She had seen Motti Lerner's play *Kastner* three times, in Tel Aviv in 1985; it was part of a wave of Holocaust plays mounted by the Israeli theater.[22] Lerner, she guessed, had meant to write something against Kastner, like everyone else. But what came out was a human Kastner who evoked sympathy, even admiration, a man who had risked his life to save Jews, as he had in fact done.

We spoke of the metamorphosis of Kastner's reputation since the judge ruled in 1955 that he had "sold his soul to the devil." People had many reasons to hate Kastner, Hanzi Brand said. No, not because he was arrogant and ambitious but because Eichmann had allowed him to choose a few hundred Jews to put on a train and send to Switzerland—and he chose. The people he left in Budapest never forgave him for that. Those who were not murdered by the Nazis told all kinds of stories about how he had taken advantage of his position to save his family and the officials of his party and the rich who could pay to be saved. But those who were on the train never forgave him either, because in saving them he put them in his debt—they owed him their lives. No one likes that, she said. And what life could they have afterward? Every morning, when they woke up, they knew that they were living at the expense of those who had not boarded the train.

Kastner, Gerhard Riegner told me, was his own worst enemy. Riegner, an official of the World Jewish Congress, was the man who had given the world the first authoritative information about the Nazi plan to methodically slaughter the Jews of Europe. Eichmann forced Kastner to act in God's place and decide who would live and who would die, Riegner said. It was a horrible position to be in, and Kastner did it. That was his tragedy. After the war he wanted to be an important person. That was his mistake.[23]

In the thirty years since Kastner was murdered in front of his home in Tel Aviv, everything has changed, Hanzi Brand said. At some point people began to understand Kastner's plight. Suddenly they understood what a helpless Jew is. She had a grandchild named after her husband. People sometimes ask him about Joel Brand. Her impression is that there is no hostility in their voices. For them, the name symbolizes the rescue efforts. She is happy for the boy, she said, and told me about the couple's first days in Palestine in 1947. She had not wanted to come. In Palestine they would have to remain silent, she told her husband. No one would let them tell their story. And so it was.

She spent her first period in the country at Kibbutz Givat Haim. Everyone was very nice to her, but they did not want to hear what had happened to her. Instead they spoke of what had happened to them. How the Arabs had attacked the kibbutz. A shell had landed near the chicken coop, they told her over and over again. Even then it seemed to her that they were talking about their war to avoid hearing about hers. They were ashamed of the Holocaust. At one point they suggested that her two sons be sent for psychiatric treatment. She did not send them. One later died, and the second, employed at the Nahal Sorek nuclear plant, was to serve in the Israeli embassy in Bonn. Those people who knew her story always asked her why she and her husband had not done anything against the Nazis early on. And they always, always asked her how she had been saved, until she began to feel that she had to apologize for living. The stories she and her husband told competed with the stories of the Warsaw ghetto uprising, she said, and could not win: They had only fought for their lives, not to be heroes. The country wanted heroes. The Brands could only offer a story of survival. People did not know how hard it had been just to stay alive. They didn't comprehend that; they wanted stories of glory.

It bothered her husband. He felt the need to tell over and over what had happened and how it had happened. That was how he dealt with the horrible feeling that hundreds of thousands of Jews had been murdered because his mission had failed—a feeling that never left him. But no one would listen. He went around Tel Aviv for years with his story and not one journalist showed any interest. He believed all his life that the Jewish Agency leadership bore part of the guilt.

When the British released him from prison, Brand reached Palestine and joined the Lehi. In the past he had identified with Mapai, but the failure of his mission lit the fire of revenge in him, and he wanted to take part in terrorist attacks on the British. After Israel was founded, one of his Lehi commanders proposed that he write a book about the failure of his mission. The story was not known to the public and the man who made the proposal, Yitzhak Jezernitzky (later Prime Minister Yitzhak Shamir), was thinking of the political damage it would cause Mapai. Brand wrote the book but Mapai pressured him not to publish it. Teddy Kollek, the director of the prime minister's office, handled the matter. During the war Kollek had spent some time in Istanbul and after Brand's arrest had used his connections in British intelligence to visit him in prison.

Now Kollek tried to persuade Brand that the publication of the book would cause damage to Israel's political and security interests. Israel's demand that the world support it was based partly on the world's failure to help the Jews during the Holocaust. Any book that revealed that the leaders of the yishuv lost a chance to save Jews would undermine that justification, Kollek explained, and should therefore not be published. Apparently, though, Kollek was even more worried that it would be a blow to Ben-Gurion. Kollek dealt with the matter as only he knew how, with overwhelming charm and an iron fist. He offered money and voiced threats. At one point he persuaded Brand to let the Mapai publishing house issue his book. Brand agreed but of course found it hard to recognize the manuscript when it was returned to him for proofreading. In the end, the original version was published in German. Mapai published the sanitized version, with an afterword by Moshe Sharett. The attempt to suppress the book led to a second book, which Brand wrote with his wife, quoting the letters that Kollek had written to him. Taken together, the two books show Mapai's overwhelming anxiety about its record on the rescue efforts.[24]

A few months after the war, Hanzi Brand met Moshe Sharett and told him that the Jewish Agency still owed her money that she had spent personally, during the war, to finance the agency's activities in Budapest. Sharett did not deny the debt, but asked if she had saved the receipts, because the agency treasurer would have trouble taking care of the matter without receipts. Gerhard Riegner related something similar: When President Roosevelt received the information on the Nazi extermination plan, someone in the White House, or perhaps in the State Department, objected that the information was "unconfirmed." "What could I have done?" Riegner asked bitterly. "I had no bodies to send to Washington."

After almost fifty years, Hanzi Brand is no longer angry. Mayor Kollek even offered to help memorialize her husband, who died in 1964. Looking back, she told me, she can appreciate the efforts David Ben-Gurion and Moshe Sharett made to get the British to agree to the plan. But she still believes that the Jewish Agency leaders did not understand that the mass murder of the Jews required them to step beyond their routine thinking. Instead of dutifully presenting the proposal to the British, they should have established direct contact with the Nazis. They could have sent Eichmann a draft response. They could have pretended that they were willing to negotiate; Eichmann would have believed them. He thought that they were the elders of Zion who ruled the world. They should have played for time. Just time: on the outskirts of Budapest you could already hear the Red Army's artillery. It was a matter of a few months. The agency leaders didn't understand that. They remained obedient to the British. The Zionist movement's main interest was, after the war, to get the Jews a state.

Hanzi Brand did not want to attribute wrong motives to Ben-Gurion. The man had simply erred, she said. The principal blame for the failure of the mission rested on the British. Yet she could not avoid the question.

What had really mattered to David Ben-Gurion during the war? How much time had he devoted to his work in Mapai and how much to rescuing the Jews?

The people in Palestine were deep in their own affairs, Gerhard Riegner said sympathetically. They were facing a Nazi threat in the form of Field Marshal Rommel, who was trying to break through the British line in Egypt and invade Palestine. The persecution of the Jews in Europe was not their main interest, nor was it the main interest of most of the world's countries.

When I visited him, Riegner was a stout man of eighty, a German-born attorney who, like many other yekkes, had never managed to get over his German accent. He had been working for fifty years for the World Jewish Congress, a federation uniting the Jewish communities of different countries. It served its member communities largely through diplomatic contacts. We sat in his office in Geneva; his window looked out over the lake and onto the old League of Nations building. Riegner was then deeply involved in a worldwide struggle, part public and part secret, that the congress was staging to prevent the establishment of a Carmelite convent at the site of the Auschwitz death camp in Poland. The congress had recently failed in its efforts to prevent the election of Kurt Waldheim as president of Austria. I asked him why the issue of the convent was so important. Riegner said that Auschwitz was not only a national memory belonging to the Jewish people that should not be taken by anyone else; it was also an important political asset. Among other things, it served the diplomatic efforts of both the World Jewish Congress and Israel.[25] Then Riegner surrounded himself with a large pile of old, yellowing files, and reminisced.

Like Joel Brand, he had been involved in one of the darkest episodes of the Holocaust. One day, in the summer of 1942, he learned that the Nazis were preparing a plan for the methodical extermination of millions of Jews, apparently with gas. A few weeks later he learned that the plan had become an operational decision. His source was a German industrialist named Eduard Schulte, a man who had contacts as high, apparently, as Adolf Hitler's staff. Riegner did what he had to do—he sent cables to Jewish community leaders in the United States, Britain, and Jerusalem. He related all this to me in the present tense. It is August, people are on vacation, it is hard to reach them. There is a war. It is difficult to send cables. We have to beware of the censor. It is hard to get a telephone connection. There are no airline flights. It is hard to persuade people that the information is accurate; it is convenient for them not to believe it. When they do believe, it is hard to get them to do something.

In his story, bureaucracy was an omnipotent force.

I asked him what the leaders of the free world should have done. Riegner said that they could at least have tried to give Hitler the feeling that they took the matter seriously. They could have made more forceful threats than they did. They could have launched various kinds of retaliatory operations: He had never been able to understand why, when it came down to it, they had not bombed the death camps. He had stayed in Geneva with the World Jewish Congress and tried to enlist the leaders of the Christian churches. Riegner and others also tried to obtain exit permits for Jews and sent them money and packages. One hundred thousand packages. Perhaps they could have done more. They could not have saved six million Jews. They could have saved hundreds of thousands, however, had the gates been open to the United States, Britain, Australia, South America, North Africa, Palestine. Various countries would have taken in Jewish refugees had they been given guarantees that after the war the refugees would leave.

For almost fifty years Gerhard Riegner had refused to reveal the name of the man who told him the terrible secret. Eventually two historians, Walter Laqueur and Richard Breitman, discovered Eduard Schulte's identity for themselves.[26] Riegner was surprised that no one had found out earlier. Why, I asked him, had he not told them? Schulte had every reason to be proud of what he had done. Riegner, correct as always, said that he had promised to keep Schulte's name secret, and he had never been released from that promise, not even after the war. The name made no difference to the study of the Holocaust's history and lessons, Riegner said.

I asked him what lessons he had learned from the episode. He learned, he said, that violent racist organizations should be destroyed while they are still small and should not be allowed to grow to the dimensions of Hitler's Third Reich. He learned that rational means of warfare were of no use when one's enemy acts out of irrational motives, as Hitler did. He had thought more than once of the Palestine partition proposal of 1937: Had Israel been established then, the Holocaust might have been prevented; in any case, the lives of many Jews would have been saved. He learned that in the twentieth century there was almost no possibility of keeping state secrets secret, no matter how confidential, no matter how terrible. He learned that the media's power to change history even after learning, and publishing, the leaked secrets, was extremely limited. The bureaucracy suffered from the same limitation. Everyone knew everything, more or less as it happened, yet no one went beyond the accepted truths of their routine ways of thinking, their routine legalities and strategies. The liquidation of the Jews proceeded according to plan, Riegner said.

Yes, they knew, Ben-Gurion finally told us, but what could they have done? No one could say that he had not taken an interest in the murder of the Jews. He had taken an interest. But there had been other things that had required his attention. No one could say that he was ashamed of the Jews who were murdered—what could they have done? Who helped them? Only a handful of people gave them assistance. He had visited Anne Frank's house in Amsterdam, he told us. He thought of his niece there. She had been burned alive. And he thought of his hometown, Plonsk. No, he was not ashamed of the Diaspora's heritage, as Saul Friedländer claimed. But he had greater appreciation for the spiritual heritage of the Land of Israel. This was true. He thought more of the Bible than of the Talmud. At this point he went off into a long monologue on the nature of God.

§

And that, approximately, is what Dina Porat told the Lodzers at their annual conference at Ohel Shem: The yishuv leadership was preoccupied with local affairs but could not, in any event, have done more to save Jews than it did. She did not condemn the leadership's lack of compassion. The Lodzers were not pleased—in person, Porat sounded more objective, even overly restrained, than she did in her book. Cracowski's lecture had spoken to their hearts. As the whispers and interruptions increased and the stream of notes being sent up to the podium grew, Porat said that the documentation available today enables the historian to determine that the Jews in the Holocaust "endured an impossible trial with great honor." This calmed the audience, somewhat.

The chairman, still speaking of the disgrace that had been imposed on Holocaust survivors, related that one member of the Lodzer organization had checked and discovered that no fewer than seventy-two fighters born in Lodz had fallen in Israel's War of Independence. Before dispersing, the assembly sang "Hatikvah"; the cantor who had previously led them in prayer now led them in the national anthem.

27 | "When You See a Graveyard"

In the three years between the German defeat in World War II and the establishment of Israel, and during the first years of independence, no one really knew how to teach the Holocaust in school. The memorial culture had not yet been created, and Israeli society had not yet decided what was permitted and what forbidden. In 1949, for instance, the papers were flooded with advertisements for "The Seven Dwarfs of Auschwitz," two brothers and five sisters, Hungarian-born Holocaust survivors, all midgets, who traveled from city to city with a song-and-dance show.[1] For many students and teachers, the Holocaust was a personal trauma. The memories were too harsh, too close, and some of the questions were too distressing to discuss. People who were then in school recall their first encounter with the Holocaust as a kind of voyeurism—it was a forbidden secret, as discomfiting and tantalizing as death and sex.[2]

Everyone then was addicted to the present and future. The immediate problems facing the first Israelis—war, immigrant absorption, austerity, and the longing for normalcy—helped them repress the past. If they spoke of the Holocaust at all, they did it on Holocaust Day. Yet one out of every three schools did not even hold a ceremony, and most of the ceremonies that were held were memorial rituals—assemblies with prayers, readings, candle lighting—that did not take advantage of the pedagogical opportunity. In those years, Israeli schools were associated with political parties; this made it even harder to design a common curriculum. The teaching of the Holocaust was already a political problem: Some insisted on a Marxist approach, others on a Zionist perspective.[3]

In October 1953 the Ministry of Education published an eighth-grade history program that, for the first time, had a section on the Holocaust: two whole lessons. It took ten more years for the ministry to issue a comprehensive Holocaust instruction program; and it might have taken longer had the Eichmann trial not intervened.

That trial was the greatest national effort ever made to fit the Holocaust into the Zionist movement's understanding of history. The Jews had been persecuted and murdered in every generation and in every place, and always for the same reason—because they were there, instead of in their own country. Yet in preparing for the trial, assistant state prosecutor Gabriel Bach later recalled, the prosecution set itself the goal of inducing Israeli youth to identify with the Holocaust's victims. This identification, it was hoped, would replace the arrogance that had, up until then, been the main component of the attitudes of young Israelis to the survivors. From this point of view, Bach told me, the trial was a historical and educational turning point.[4]

In the wake of the trial, a program of instruction for the five days leading up to Holocaust Day was introduced; the Ministry of Education recommended devoting six hours to the program, which, in its emphasis on "the Diaspora in its magnificence," reflected the changes that had taken place in Israel's attitude to the Holocaust. Education Minister Zalman Aran announced that his ministry would make an increased effort to deepen the "Jewish consciousness" of the country's schoolchildren.[5] In 1966, and again in 1967, delegations of young people paid visits to the sites of the death camps in Poland. On their return the students were quoted in a Ministry of Education pamphlet as saying, "We left as Israelis and returned as Jews."[6] A few months later the Six-Day War broke out. Poland, like most of the Communist bloc, severed diplomatic relations with Israel, so the visits to the camps ceased.

The anxiety that preceded the Six-Day War and the great victory that followed once again pushed the Holocaust into the forefront of Israeli consciousness. The euphoria—not only in Israel but also in Jewish communities around the world—reinforced the sense that Israel and the Jewish people had a common fate. To instill in Israeli students closer ties to the Diaspora and to deepen their identification with the Holocaust's victims, schools "adopted" certain Diaspora communities and studied their histories from earliest times to their destruction in the Holocaust. Students read books, collected pictures, and heard the stories of those who had come from the "adopted" town, which was usually the birthplace of their teacher. This gave the students an emotional connection with the community and with the Zionist lesson of the Holocaust.[7]

As the 1970s approached, the Ministry of Education put together a sixty-hour unit dealing with the history of the struggle to establish the state. Ten of these hours were devoted to the Holocaust. The teachers were to center their instruction on individuals, such as Anne Frank and Janusz Korczak. Numbers, especially numbers in the millions, were not significant enough and certainly did not elicit a strong emotional reaction, the ministry explained. Emphasizing the tragedy of the individual, instead of the national experience, reflected another change in Israeli life. More and more Israelis were learning to think of themselves in the first person singular. The ordinary "I" began to push aside the heroic "we" that had previously been encouraged.

All this was expressed in textbooks as well. Ruth Firer, a senior teacher and lecturer in the Hebrew University's School of Education, analyzed one hundred textbooks published during the first forty years of the country's existence and before. She discovered a shift in the authors' approach to sensitive subjects, beginning in the 1970s. Up until then, for thirty years, the books hardly revised their views. Noting that the process of composing and publishing textbooks is a long one, Firer pointed out that the changes she identified in books from the 1970s therefore reflected an approach that had been formulated at least five years earlier. During those years the sense was that Israel had entered a new period of its history and that it was time to reexamine old historiographical truths and fossilized myths. In the spirit of the 1960s, the new textbooks expressed rebellion. There was a feeling that the country was ready to exchange the old patriotic clichés for universal humanistic values.[8] Coupled with the debate over the future of the occupied territories and their Palestinian inhabitants, this new sensibility infused the presentation of such key concepts as Holocaust and heroism, genocide and rebellion.

The first textbooks generally treated the plan to exterminate the Jews as an inseparable part of Nazi policy, discernible as early as the 1920s in *Mein Kampf*. In contrast to this "intentionalist" approach, scholarly work on the subject has increasingly adopted a "functionalist" approach, which attributes the extermination of the Jews to historical developments and circumstances over time, with the clear implication that, up until some given point, it would still have been possible to prevent the genocide. The intentionalist view emphasizes the unique character of the Holocaust and thus conforms to the Zionist movement's fundamental assumptions:

that only an independent Israel could guarantee the safety of the Jews. Early Holocaust stories meant for young children therefore usually ended with heroic rescue and regenerative immigration to Israel. This was the story of little Shula: With the help of a magic ring she shattered the ghetto walls, killed the guard, and then went from house to house, street by street, gathering all the Jews. They boarded trains for the seaport and eventually set sail, singing, for the Land of Israel.[9] This tale would seem to fulfill the desires of the education ministry official who wrote, "What should we give these children? We should give them something useful. We should give them the Holocaust in its most beautiful form."[10] The functionalist approach of later textbooks, in contrast, made human choices and actions central at every stage.

Earlier textbooks described the Nazis as "beasts of prey thirsty for human blood"; their deeds were "acts of the devil"; the concentration camps were "the inferno."[11] The demonization of Nazi evil exempted the authors from having to confront the social and political conditions that made Nazism possible, from having to consider the possibility that Nazism was the product of an ordinary human environment. The demonization of Nazism and its mythologizing, in general, were also necessary since the Holocaust served as the main justification for the creation and existence of the State of Israel. Hence the great emphasis on Nazi sadism in the early textbooks, the gruesome descriptions of the "medical experiments" performed on concentration-camp inmates, women in particular, the insistence that the Nazis had made soap out of the bodies of murdered Jews. Later textbooks preferred to describe the horrors through testimony of individual survivors, thus reinforcing the credibility of the information and intensifying the student's identification with the victims.

The first textbooks were careful to describe Jewish resistance in military language, including professional terms used by the Israeli army. Notably, they tended to avoid labeling the rebels as Jews, preferring the terms *Hebrews, Israelites, Defenders of Masada,* or simply *Israelis.* Textbooks published in the 1970s had a different slant: they gave Jewish resistance less space, referred to it as a marginal phenomenon, and no longer depicted it as the height of honor, just as the death of the rest of the victims was no longer depicted as the depth of shame.

In the late 1970s the Ministry of Education proposed a new plan for Holocaust instruction in secondary schools, formulated by a Hebrew University team led by Haim Shatzker. The new thirty-hour study unit was divided into five sections. The Shatzker program no longer put the

Holocaust on the same plane as heroism, and almost completely ignored the link between the Holocaust and the rebirth of Israel. In the spirit of the transformation that the Yom Kippur War brought about, Israel was no longer presented as the alternative to the Holocaust.

Another study unit drafted at about the same time by Arik Karmon of Ben-Gurion University emphasized the Nazis—their ideology, politics, government, mentality. For the first time a Holocaust study unit analyzed Nazism in detail. Critics contended that it taught more about Nazism than it taught about the Holocaust; some protested that it encouraged students to identify with the Nazis instead of with their victims. Teachers argued that high school students were not intellectually advanced enough for either the Shatzker or the Karmon plan; the same could be said for most of the teachers. In the end, both plans were abandoned, not because of their ideological directions but because of pedagogical difficulties.[12] In the meantime, Menahem Begin had become prime minister, and for the first time in the country's history the Ministry of Education was taken from the Labor movement and given to the National Religious party.

In September 1978 Israeli television broadcast the American docudrama *Holocaust*. Its airing had been preceded by an impassioned debate in the Israel Broadcasting Authority's executive committee. On the question of whether to broadcast the program, eleven committee members voted in favor and five opposed. The opponents charged that the miniseries vulgarized the Holocaust; they argued that this American kitsch, as they called it, reflected Begin's penchant for exploiting the Jewish genocide to gain support for his uncompromising, isolationist, and chauvinistic foreign policy. In preparation for the broadcast, the Ministry of Education issued a teacher's handbook that suggested such topics for class discussion as "What may we learn about the Jews who wished to disavow their origins? Is this a common phenomenon in our times? Try to link this with Chancellor Bruno Kreisky's recent remarks." The Jewish Austrian leader had attacked the Israeli government's position on the Middle East conflict, and some attributed his criticism to "self-hatred." Another discussion topic: "The need for a Jewish state is alluded to throughout the program. Do you think that the Holocaust would have been possible had Israel existed then? Does the example of Entebbe illustrate a change in the position of Jews today?"[13] Thus the state used the largest public encounter with the Holocaust since the Eichmann trial to reinforce the contention that Israel protects the Jewish people from a second Holocaust.

In 1979 the Ministry of Education announced that Holocaust studies were to be a standard requirement for senior high school students. Another committee drafted yet another study program emphasizing the student's emotional involvement. "The Holocaust must first of all be felt," declared the committee chairman, "and it must be felt as a fact in and of itself, not as part of the larger historical context and not in the framework of scholarly inquiry."[14] The Israel of Menahem Begin, the Holocaust's great popularizer, was not satisfied: in 1980 the Knesset amended the national education law. This, the most authoritative statement of national values outside the Declaration of Independence, had stated that education should be based on "the cultural values of the people of Israel and their scientific achievements; love of the homeland and loyalty to the state and the Jewish people; training in agricultural work and trades; pioneer training and the aspiration for a society built on freedom, equality, tolerance, mutual assistance, and love for one's fellowman." On March 26, 1980, the Knesset added "awareness of the Holocaust and heroism."[15] Since then, the Holocaust has been taught in both elementary and secondary schools, so an Israeli high school graduate will have studied it twice. Since the early 1980s, questions on the Holocaust have accounted for 20 percent of the overall score in the high school diploma examination in history. The examination frequently asks about the fate of the Jews in the Holocaust, including their life in the ghettos, the resistance, and martyrdom. Questions about the history of Nazi Germany are much less frequent.[16]

But such scholastic efforts have not been particularly effective. In December 1982, sociologist Uri Farago presented a list of four hundred questions to Israeli schoolchildren in an attempt to learn about their attitudes to the Holocaust. The majority of those asked said that most of the information they had about the subject came from television, films, and books. The most commonly cited book was *The Diary of Anne Frank*. They also learned much from the Holocaust Day ceremonies at their schools and from study days at Yad Vashem and other institutions devoted to the Holocaust. Ashkenazic students said that they had learned something from their parents. As a source of information, history classes came in last.

The same survey showed that more than half the country's students thought they should learn more about the Holocaust. The subjects were asked to list three important historical events that affected their lives. Nine percent listed the peace treaty with Egypt, 14 percent the war in

Lebanon, then still in progress. Fifteen percent cited other wars, including the Six-Day and Yom Kippur wars. Twenty percent listed the establishment of Israel and the War of Independence; the largest number, 26 percent, cited the Holocaust (the remaining students mentioned other events). Similar surveys have been conducted periodically since 1965; by the mid-1970s, the Holocaust appeared in third place, after the founding of Israel and the War of Independence and the most recent war at the time of the survey. Close to nine out of every ten students said that they identified with the Holocaust's victims.[17]

§

One day in the fall of 1990 I went to Ashdod, "a small Mediterranean city," as Amos Oz calls it, "that does not pretend to be Paris or Zurich and does not aspire to be Jerusalem."[18] An instructor from the Ot Vaed educational project, a group that specializes in teaching the religious significance of the Holocaust, invited me to attend a class she was giving at one of the city's high schools, a large and depressing concrete structure located on Ghetto Rebels Street. The class consisted of about twenty boys and girls, eleventh- and twelfth-graders. The teacher, an energetic woman in a long skirt, had brought with her a Nazi propaganda film directed by Leni Riefenstahl and a film containing testimony about the medical experiments on twins conducted by Josef Mengele: The survivors describe, in horrifying detail, what Mengele did to them. Between the films the instructor led a discussion on religious faith during the Holocaust and thereafter, based on a mimeographed booklet of short texts that the class read together.[19]

One text tells of a good and pious man whose young sons and daughters had been led to the death pit behind their village. His mind snapped, and on the eve of Yom Kippur, during the Kol Nidre service, he suddenly began to fume and rant against God, denouncing all he had held holy. "To believe in God after Auschwitz is an insult to intelligence, taking God's name in vain, an attack on one's deepest moral sensibilities," the booklet comments. Another selection is written by Elie Wiesel: Several rabbis, inmates of a concentration camp, bring God to trial for the murder of his people; he is found guilty. Another selection is written in the form of a rabbi's memoirs: A prisoner asked the rabbi to rule on a dilemma in accordance with Jewish law. The prisoner had the possibility of saving his young son from being sent to the gas chambers, but he knew that another child would be sent in his child's place. Was he permitted to save his son? The rabbi tried to evade the question: "When the Temple stood, such a question would reach the Sanhedrin," he said, "and here I am in Auschwitz without a single book of Jewish law and without other rabbis to consult and without any ability to concentrate seriously on the question." The man pressed, though the rabbi pleaded that he be left alone; but the man demanded an answer to no avail. Finally, he said, "Rabbi, I have done what the Torah requires of me: I have asked the rabbi a question and there is no other rabbi here. If the rabbi cannot tell me that I am permitted to save my son, it is a sign that he is uneasy about permitting me, since were it permitted beyond any doubt, he would certainly answer that it was permitted. What this means for me is that this thing is forbidden by Jewish law. This is sufficient for me; and since my child will be burned in accordance with Torah and Jewish law, I accept this with love and joy, and I will do nothing to save him because thus the Torah has commanded."

Here, then, were the two alternatives: apostasy and rebellion versus faith and resignation. The teacher asked the teenagers in Ashdod what they thought. The students, only one or two of whom were religious, were silent. Now the teacher presented texts that were more political. One claimed that ultraorthodox, anti-Zionist groups were partly guilty: Had they encouraged Jews to migrate to Palestine instead of preaching that Zionism was heresy, those Jews might have been saved. Countering this was an ultraorthodox text. Trying to be like all other nations, it stated, the Jews had chosen two idols to which to sacrifice—socialism and nationalism. These two idols combined into National Socialism, and here there was a miracle. The National Socialists—the Nazis—became the terrible, wrathful rod that beat the Jews throughout the land: "The very impurity we worship is what strikes at us."

Another text illustrated the belief that the torments inflicted by the Nazis were the tribulations that according to tradition would precede the arrival of the Messiah. A rabbi went to his death joyfully, the text related. His disciples, who accompanied him in the death train, said afterwards that he danced and sang the whole way. One of the passengers turned to him "with a heartbreaking cry and shout" and pleaded that he pray for a miracle, but the rabbi put his hand on the passenger's shoulder, gazed at him with a compassionate smile, and said, "Do not be afraid, we are going to the Messiah." The Jew was not convinced: "Does the Messiah live in Germany?" he asked, and the saintly rabbi said, "Yes, the Messiah is there, bound in irons, suffering and bearing the torments of Israel."

The religious Zionist view was exemplified by the story of a father and son walking on the road. The son grew tired and asked his father, "Where is the country?" The father answered, "Let this be your sign, when you see a graveyard before you, the country is nearby." Rabbi Zvi Yehuda Kook interpreted Ezekiel 20:34, "And I will bring you out from the peoples and I will gather you out of the countries in which you are scattered, with a mighty hand, and with a stretched-out arm, and with anger poured out," as a reference to the Holocaust. The spilled blood of six million, the rabbi said, was indeed horrible, but God's people had become so contaminated with the impurity of other nations that it was necessary to remove it with bloodshed.

Educator Eliezer Berkowitz contributed to the booklet the idea that evil, man's creation, is an inevitable consequence of the freedom of choice God has given him. The final sentence in the booklet is from Yeshayahu Leibowitz: "The Holocaust has no religious significance."

"Well, what do you think?" the teacher asked. The students were silent. "What do you think?" she demanded. "What do you feel? Why can't you accept the simple explanation of sin and retribution? Why?" One student said that he agreed with Berkowitz, another said that he accepted Leibowitz's opinion. There was a short discussion. It was already late, the young people were tired, and they still had to watch the film about the Mengele twins. An oppressive silence pervaded the classroom. Then the teacher said that the question was indeed difficult. The Holocaust is a test for the believer. If it is punishment for sin, why were the ultraorthodox also punished? And do the dimensions of the sin justify the magnitude of the punishment? This was the question that tortured Job. And as for the tribulations that foretell the coming of the Messiah, wasn't the suffering out of proportion? The concept of the Holocaust as an expression of free will is also very difficult, because then where was God? Yes, it is indeed an extremely difficult question. And this, the teacher said, is what she wanted the students to know: There are those who say that it is easier for the believer, because his faith provides him with answers to his dilemmas. In fact, the opposite is true—the believer has a harder time, because he is left with a question mark.

At another school, a religious one, a teacher offered a simple solution: an acrostic proving that it was all written in the Bible. The discovery was made with the aid of a computer at the Technion in Haifa, the teacher told his class. Taking every fiftieth letter, beginning with a certain letter in Genesis, one gets Hitler's name; a similar method reveals, elsewhere in the Bible, the names of several other leaders of the Third Reich. Taking every forty-ninth letter, going backwards, starting at a given point in Deuteronomy, one gets the word *Shoah*, Holocaust.

28 | "What Does It Do to Me?"

One morning in mid-October 1990, 150 high school students arrived at Ben-Gurion airport and, as one might expect, created something of a commotion: Many had never been overseas. The Persian Gulf crisis was threatening to escalate; the Israeli civil-defense corps began distributing gas masks packed in little cardboard boxes that also contained hypodermic needles loaded with an antidote to nerve gas. Inevitably, one of the teenagers waiting for the flight to Warsaw quipped that he had no reason to worry—when Saddam Hussein's missiles hit Tel Aviv, he would be in Auschwitz.

Holocaust jokes abound in Israel, but they are told furtively, like dirty jokes. Tasteless as they are, they provide an outlet for anxiety, like the gallows humor of doctors and soldiers. I noticed that during the trip to the death camps in Poland, the students seldom reverted to such humor. Perhaps it would have been easier for them had they cracked jokes; once or twice they had a very tough time.

They were eleventh- and twelfth-graders from seven schools around Israel; one of the schools designates itself as traditional, two as religious, and the rest as secular. Before joining the students on their journey I took part in their orientation, over the course of two months. They took the preparation seriously, reading books, viewing films, visiting memorial sites, meeting survivors, a total of perhaps thirty hours. Most of the travelers were children of native Israeli Ashkenazic parents. These parents were of the generation that had grown up—like Momik, the hero of

David Grossman's *See Under: Love*—in the great silence that had enveloped the Holocaust during Israel's first years. Nothing better illustrates the change that has occurred in Israel's attitude towards the Holocaust than the journey of these students, members of the third generation, to Treblinka, Majdanek, and Auschwitz. It was a pilgrimage to the Diaspora. Here was a Zionist irony. A single generation after the founding of the state, Israel was sending its children into the Jewish past abandoned by its founding fathers, who hoped to create a "new man," free of the ghetto past. The young people were sent to seek out what secular Israeli society was, apparently, unable to offer them—roots. The trip was a ritual laden with emotion and symbols and a sometimes bizarre obeisance to what Saul Friedländer once described as the union of kitsch and death. Nourished from two sources, one nationalist and the other religious, it had a clear political orientation as well. It exuded isolationism, to the point of xenophobia, rather than openness and love of humanity.

The attempt in the 1970s to include the Holocaust's universalist lessons in the instruction has been almost completely abandoned. A circular sent out by the Ministry of Education containing guidelines for the visits to Poland mentions only in passing the need "to reevaluate" moral values and humanism. A special booklet given by the ministry to the participants in the trip includes no such mention. The booklet does contain, however, a message for the teacher and guide, written by Avraham Oded Cohen, the director of the ministry's youth division.

As we stand beside the death furnaces in the extermination camps, our hearts fill with resentment and tears come to our eyes for the horrible destruction of European Jewry, and Polish Jewry within it. Yet while we weep and suffer pain and sorrow over the destruction, our hearts fill with pride and contentment at the great privilege we have of being citizens of an independent Israel. At the sight of the flag of Israel flying high above the death pits and furnaces, we stand straight and proud and murmur, "The people of Israel live! The eternal one of Israel will not fail us!" We swear before our millions of murdered brothers, "If I forget thee, O Jerusalem, let my right hand lose its cunning!" And it is as if we hear their souls crying out to us, "In our deaths we have commanded you to live. Preserve and defend the State of Israel as your most precious possession." Then we answer, with a full heart, "May the State of Israel live forever!"

Cohen, portly and friendly, his head sporting the knitted *kippah* identifying him as a national-religious Zionist, gave the program its name:
"I Seek My Brothers" (Genesis 37:16). The verse was part of the weekly
Torah reading when Cohen first visited Poland to investigate the possibility of sending groups of students there. The students are called a
"delegation"; the booklet also includes the Prayer for the State of Israel
and the Blessing for the Soldiers of the Israeli Defense Forces. The plan
calls for the students to recite these prayers at Auschwitz. Also included
are rulings by Israel's two chief rabbis, one of them stating that, if certain
restrictions are observed, *cohanim*, hereditary members of the priestly
class who served in the Temple in Jerusalem and who are ritually forbidden to enter cemeteries, may nevertheless visit the former death camps.

At certain sites in Poland the students were also to recite *Yizkor*, the
Jewish memorial prayer, for the victims of the Holocaust. Israel's memorial culture makes use of at least six or seven different versions of this
prayer, differing in length, style, and spirit. One version begins "May
God remember," another "May the Jewish people remember," still another "We remember." One states that the Jews were led "like lambs to
the slaughter," but the others omit this unfortunate expression. Some
versions state that the victims of the Nazis were "martyrs to God," while
others do not. One mentions Jews "who were burned in the holy sanc-
tuaries, on the Torah scrolls," while another speaks of "the hundreds of
fighters who rose to waken a despairing people to heroism." One of the
prayers devotes two lines to the memory of the "righteous gentiles." The
most obvious variation is in the identification of the murderer. Yad
Vashem and the Israeli army make no identification at all. Another
version uses the formulation of law: "Nazis and Nazi collaborators."
Others are more specific—"the German Nazis and their collaborators"
—and some generalize, referring to "the Germans."

The Ministry of Education supplied the student pilgrims with two
versions of the *Yizkor* prayer. Both begin with the words "May God
remember"; both include the expression "like lambs to the slaughter."
One says that the death camps were built by "the diabolical Nazi government of the German nation of murderers." The second version is
more general, referring simply to "the German nation of murderers."
Both versions mention Nazi collaborators "from other nations." Neither
of them takes note of the ghetto rebels. Both contain a paragraph not
used by either Yad Vashem or the army, calling on God "to speedily
avenge before our eyes" the blood of the victims.[2]

A few days before they flew to Poland, the students gathered at a large community center in Jerusalem. There was a sing-along, led by a man with an accordion; the words to the songs were projected on the wall. The selection was made up of patriotic popular songs frequently heard on the radio: "I was born to the nation of two thousand years, a piece of land waits for us, not a piece of heaven"; "Land, our land, land that we love, you are mother and father to us. Land of the people, our land forever, where we were born, where we will live, come what may"; "We won't stop singing. Let the UN tell us to retreat, tell us to give back the land. We won't stop singing."

Shalmi Barmor was late for this event. A forty-five-year-old native of Tel Aviv, Barmor is director of the World Center for the Instruction of the Holocaust at Yad Vashem. He relates to his title, as to himself and life in general, with a measure of ironic skepticism. One of the initiators of the pilgrimages to Poland, Barmor was to lead the students from the Masorti (Traditional) High School in Jerusalem, one of whom was his son, Eyal. In the months of preparation, Barmor did not go easy on the teenagers. He demanded that they grapple with the difficulty of understanding the unique nature and causes of the Holocaust. He hoped to instill open-mindedness in them: From the start he brought the Armenians, the Gypsies, Biafra, and Cambodia into the discussions. Barmor explained on what points the genocide of the Jewish people was different, and on what points it was not. He told the students to consider the mass murder from the Nazi point of view, and to this end he spoke to them about Nazi racism. A colleague of his spoke with them about the personality of the murderer. Hitler was not a madman, Barmor said, just as Saddam Hussein is not a madman. Barmor intentionally entered the firing range on several subjects: the common interests of the Nazis and the Zionist movement, the difficulty of properly understanding the Judenrats established by the Nazis. He told the students that martyrdom required a choice between life and death and that the victims of the Holocaust had no such choice. He spoke with them about the comparison sometimes made between the persecution of the Jews and the repression of the Palestinians and explained why, in his opinion, the comparison did not hold water. The students received a basis for thinking about the Holocaust in historical terms; they would be able to do more than conduct a dialogue with the souls of the dead in the style of the Ministry of Education booklet. Barmor spent many hours, over weeks and months, preparing them. It was impressive.

He also spoke to them about Poland, where his father had been born. When Barmor was nine years old, his father was appointed first secretary of the Israeli delegation in Warsaw. During our visit to Warsaw, he showed me the house where his father's family had lived. It was evening; the picturesque lanes were emptying. Standing by the old cathedral, Barmor told me that, when he first came to Poland, he had a great fear of Christianity. How, I wondered, could a Tel Aviv child be afraid of Christianity? Was it the heritage of a thousand years of troubled relations between Jews and Poles? But Barmor said that the source of his fear was an Israeli children's classic called *Two Friends Set Out* by Yemima Avidar-Tchernowitz and Mira Lube. It is the story of a child, a Holocaust survivor, searching for his lost sister and finding her in a horrifying convent in Italy.[3] The same motif exists in Holocaust poetry: "My sister's eyes search the convent wall / A scarlet cord," Abba Kovner wrote.

> A candle shivers in the hands of the nuns
> Nine holy sisters watch my sister
> As if watching talking dust
> . . . in the yard
> My sister plays with the language of allusions,
> With another God.[4]

I had visited Yaakov Barmor, by then retired, at his home. "Jew hatred is as natural in Poland as blue is to the sky," the former diplomat told me; he had said something similar to his son's students. Shalmi Barmor knew all there was to know about Polish anti-Semitism. He tried to explain its background to his students. He did it the hard way, presenting his students with copies of a recent *Haaretz* article by Shabtai Teveth, Ben-Gurion's biographer, written after he visited Poland. Teveth attacked the Poles for concealing from visitors to Auschwitz the fact that most of those murdered there had been Jews. "The Polish nation," Teveth wrote, "is the victor in the end, and it has despoiled Jewish property and inherited its suffering and its Holocaust; it has made them into a commercial venture."[5] The students read the article and agreed. Many of them clearly identified the Holocaust with Poland. Everywhere they went they searched for—and sometimes found—swastikas on the walls. Shalmi Barmor tried to explain to the students that the Poles were not guilty of the murder of the Jews. Indeed, the Poles felt they had been defeated in the war—they had traded the Nazi conquest for a Soviet occupation.

Anti-Semitism in Poland should not be ignored, Barmor told his students, but he emphasized that the Poles considered the mass murder of the Jews part of their Polish national tragedy. The students argued with him. "Someone, after all, has to be guilty of the Holocaust," one of them said. "We have to hate someone, and we've already made up with the Germans." Standing by the Warsaw ghetto wall, we encountered a garrulous drunk. I suspect that Barmor did not translate everything he said about the Jews.

Shalmi Barmor worked hard to get his students to appreciate the fact that for a long time conditions in Poland were good for Jews; in fact, Poland had been the center of the entire Jewish world. To the writer Yehudit Hendel, the Poland of her childhood seemed to be almost a Jewish country.[6] Eyal Barmor told me afterwards that while he gained an understanding of the Holocaust from visiting the camps, he gained an even greater understanding of the dimensions of the loss from visiting the old Jewish quarter of Cracow. If he told his father that too, he made him proud.

The memorial ceremony next to Natan Rapaport's monument to the Warsaw ghetto uprising came only a few hours after our arrival in Poland, just before nightfall. Maia Morag, one of the students, Shalmi Barmor, and I took advantage of the twilight to sneak away from the group and search for 7 Pawia Street, not far from the monument. This had been the house of Maia's grandfather Eliahu Morag, whose family name had then been Samorog. Grandpa Eliahu had very much wanted his granddaughter to see the street. Two weeks before we came to Poland, I had visited Morag at his home in Givataim, a suburb of Tel Aviv. He is a pleasant sixty-eight-year-old retiree in sandals, a well-known expert on raising poultry. His parents had owned a leather-goods factory in Warsaw; one of the products was walking sticks. Once a year, as May Day approached, the business flourished: the Jewish manufacturer would sell the Communists the sticks they used to beat up their rivals on the right.

A short while before the war, Morag received an immigration certificate to Palestine, on the quota of his Zionist Youth Movement. He had previously been the victim of anti-Semitic attacks. He would never, he said, forget the moment he parted from his mother. It was in the street: "My boy, why are you leaving me?" she wept. He never saw her again. To the best of his knowledge she was murdered at Treblinka, along with his father. He would never be free of his sense of guilt for having left them, he said.

After arriving in Palestine, Morag was among the founders of Kibbutz Nitsanim, some twelve miles north of Yad Mordecai. Nitsanim was also occupied by the Egyptians during the War of Independence, but unlike Yad Mordecai, it did not enter the annals of Israeli heroism; instead it has become a symbol of cowardice and treason, partly because its members did not belong to the right political party. The story is well-known: the members of the kibbutz fought for fifteen hours along with the soldiers sent to defend them, almost to the last bullet. Thirty—nearly a third of them—were killed. When they faced the choice of dying or surrendering to the Egyptians who had already penetrated the kibbutz, they raised their hands and were taken prisoner. "Treacherous behavior," Ben-Gurion ruled in his war diary.[7]

No other story so well illustrates the heavy burden the cult of heroism imposed on Israel. Even before anyone knew what had really happened there, the army put out a "battle sheet"—a kind of brigade newsletter— condemning Nitsanim. "Better to die in the home trenches than to surrender to the murderous invader," it proclaimed. "To surrender so long as the body lives and the last bullet breathes in the magazine is shameful! To be taken prisoner by the invader—shame and death!"[8]

For the next forty years the members of Nitsanim fought to clear their name, but the Israeli ethos refused to forgive them. They were castigated over and over again in books and in army education programs for having been taken prisoner. Like the victims of the Holocaust, the members of Nitsanim, were said to have gone "like lambs to the slaughter." The parallel was no coincidence: The man who imposed ignominy on Nitsanim was none other than Abba Kovner. During the War of Independence, Kovner, a respected member of Hashomer Hatsair, served as education officer in the Israeli army; he was called the political commissar, in emulation of the Red Army. He wrote that "battle sheet." Nitsanim belonged to a rival political movement; some of its members came, as Kovner did, from Vilna. The "battle sheet" was, apparently, a further shot in a dispute that had begun back in Vilna during the Holocaust.

After the War of Independence, Nitsanim was a community of widows, orphans, and defeated fathers returned from Egyptian POW camps. For years they were unable to forgive themselves. They agonized over their past and their image. The fathers were ashamed of themselves, and their sons were ashamed of the fathers. I had gone to Nitsanim one day in an attempt to understand why, actually, they were unable to expunge the stain imposed by the poet-commissar so many years ago. I had, I thought, some sense of the magnitude of the indignity, but I had trouble understanding the meaning of it for them. Why, I asked them over and over again, should they care about that leaflet, so senseless even then? They said that it wasn't rational. I could do nothing but record that, like the Holocaust's survivors, they also secretly believed in their shame; they too were trapped within that same ethos that could glorify only dead heroes and that despised all those who preferred surrender and life to "death with honor." Here was a kibbutz that had died twice.*

Eliahu Morag was among those taken prisoner. The Egyptians held them for nine months, mistreating all, torturing some. Morag has always remembered the first words he heard from his four-year-old son, Giora, upon his return: "Daddy, why are you alive?" His Giora wanted a hero for a father.

Giora Morag, now a banker, clearly remembers the night Nitsanim was evacuated. The children were taken on foot to another settlement: it was a frightening trek; the sky was full of explosions. Twenty-five years later, Giora Morag found himself facing the same enemy, during the Yom Kippur War, as a company commander in the tank corps. In accordance with orders but against his better judgment, Morag attacked. He knew that, like the men of Nitsanim and of the ghettos before him, he had no chance in the battle. The Egyptians wiped out almost the entire company. The preparations his daughter Maia was making for the trip to Poland helped him approach his own father with some questions that he had never dared ask before; the two had become closer, it seemed to me. I thought about all this the night Maia, Barmor, and I went to find 7 Pawia Street, in Warsaw. There is no 7 Pawia Street anymore. Only a vacant lot.

The ceremony at Rapaport's monument had in the meantime reached the singing of "Hatikvah." The students of the Ben-Gurion High School of Petah Tikvah, who were responsible for the ceremony, read poems from a black book with a yellow Star of David on the front cover and a small, plastic Israeli flag on the other. They said almost nothing about

---

* It took forty years before Nitsanim was absolved by history. Previously unpublished documents and testimony revealed, among other things, that the kibbutz had had difficulty obtaining sufficient arms to defend itself because it didn't have the necessary political connections. Had its defenders surrendered earlier, many more of them would have remained alive. They fought too long. The author of the book that cleared them was Tzvika Dror, the historian of Kibbutz Lohamei Hagetaot.[9]

the uprising itself. Other than a tour of the ghetto's ruins, and a short meeting, at the end of the trip, with a man who had known Mordecai Anielewicz, there was little mention of the rebellion. The Ministry of Education's booklet contained half a page on the Jewish theater in the Warsaw ghetto; the rebellion was mentioned only in passing. After five wars, Israelis no longer needed this heroic myth to cancel out the shame of the Holocaust. I would guess that this is also connected to the fact that Mapam, which in the past was a power in Israeli politics, has since become only a marginal group. Shalmi Barmor revealed a little secret to me. Rapaport's monument is not identical in all details to the version standing at the entrance to the Yad Vashem museum in Jerusalem. One of the differences is that the mother image in the Warsaw version has a bared breast; in Jerusalem it is covered.

ℐ

A few weeks before the trip, the students had been given large sheets of poster board and colored markers and told to record their fears. They were afraid of what they would see at the death camps; perhaps they would not be able to withstand the horror and would cry, and others might make fun of them. Some feared that they would make fun of others. There were those who were afraid that they would return from the camps in Poland as "different people." There were those who feared they would have a hard time returning to their studies. Others feared that they would so deeply absorb the experience in Poland that they would be distanced from friends who did not go. Some wrote that, more than anything else, they were afraid that they would feel nothing. They were given preparation for such a possibility: Even if they were to feel nothing, they were told, there was no reason for them to conclude that their emotional makeup was deficient.

As it turned out, that fear was unfounded: each student broke down at one stage or another of the journey, most of them more than once. For most, it happened well before we reached Auschwitz, the last of the death camps on our itinerary. For many it happened at Treblinka. The students from the Masorti school conducted a small memorial ceremony there. Each one lit a memorial candle for his or her relatives. One boy, whose parents had been born in Morocco, lit a candle in memory of the parents of his friends. Teacher Orit Elidar read "An Ode to Those Saved from the Fire," written by her sister: "Every Jew has his own death camp . . . every Jew has his own gas chamber."[10] It was a very personal ceremony; everyone cried. At Treblinka nothing remains, everything is left to the imagination; there are only memorial stones. They are spread over a huge area, as far as the eye can see.

Most of the students broke down at Majdanek. The camp there remains exactly as it was—the shower rooms, barracks, hats, clothes, shoes, furnaces. Nothing is left to the imagination. The level of horror rises as the visit continues from barracks to barracks, to the glass box filled with human bones. Then one comes to a huge basin containing the ashes of the dead, piled high. Dusk was falling; a few German clergymen laid a wreath. A flock of crows passed overhead.

Matan Meridor, an intelligent, amiable boy, told me something he did not think he would tell his friends. While walking through the thousands of shoes left at the Majdanek camp, he looked for the smallest ones, and suddenly he thought of a line in the Betar anthem written by Zeev Jabotinsky: "With blood and sweat a race will rise, proud, generous, and cruel." Then he thought of the testament Samson leaves to his people in a Jabotinsky novel: "Let them gather iron, appoint a king, and learn to laugh."

I told him about the time, thirty years ago, his aunt Hagit Meridor had sparked a lengthy public debate over the meaning of the Holocaust when she told her father, Knesset member Eliahu Meridor, about the visit of a German pastor to her class. The year was 1962, just before Adolf Eichmann's verdict was handed down. The Reverend Bruno Dieckmann was among Israel's good friends in Germany. The foreign ministry had recommended approving his request to visit an Israeli school. After sitting in on an elementary school English lesson, Dieckmann told the students where he was from and asked them if they had anything to pass on to the children of his country. When Hagit Meridor told her father about the visit, Herut swung into action; it enlisted its best people, led by Menahem Begin, to condemn this incident.[11] Matan Meridor— whose father served as Yitzhak Shamir's minister of justice—told me that he has not yet closed his own historical accounting with the Germans. On the visit to Majdanek he carried an Israeli flag. The wind wrapped it around his body like a shroud and, for a moment, he told me, he was not sure he wanted to get out.

On the way to Auschwitz one of the teachers read a few lines from Victor Frankl's *Man in Search of Meaning* into the bus's loudspeaker. Frankl was much quoted during the trip; the Viennese psychiatrist had survived Auschwitz. "It seems that man is able to endure suffering, humiliation, fear, or anger thanks to the image of a loved one that he preserves in his heart," Frankl wrote, "or thanks to religion or a sense of humor, or even thanks to a glance at the people imprisoned with him, or thanks to his belief that in the end all will be well."*[12] The teacher then read a selection from Primo Levi's *Survival in Auschwitz.* Her voice choked; she had trouble going on. It was another three miles to the camp gate. The teacher asked the students to maintain a respectful silence. Everyone was quiet; only the motor of the bus could be heard. At the gate, she spoke into the microphone: "Remember that we have a doctor with us."

The visit to Auschwitz was meant to bring the encounter with the Holocaust to a dramatic and emotional climax, but most of the students could not muster the expected catharsis. Everyone examined themselves, asking, "What does it do to me?" and decided that Majdanek had "done" more, perhaps because it had been the first camp they saw, perhaps because it had not been made into a museum and did not draw as many tourists as Auschwitz. Or maybe it was because they had not assimilated it as a symbol and had not demanded that the visit there "do" something special. By the time they reached Auschwitz, they had no tears left, one of them said.

During the visit the teachers quoted Ka-Tzetnik. One teacher reminded the students that the writer had later retracted what he had said during the seconds before he fainted on the witness stand at the Eichmann trial. Not another planet but part of this world, an expression of human evil. By the gallows on which Rudolf Höss, the camp's commandant, had been hanged, one of the students gave a talk about him. I once met Höss's brother-in-law; during the war, he had visited the camp, peering into every corner, seeing everything. Once he asked Höss how he was able to function in the routine of horror. The commandant answered, so he said, "You would not be able to understand it. We are on another planet here."[13] My impression was that many of the young people preferred to understand Auschwitz as another planet.

During the eight days of the pilgrimage the students endured emotional extremes—sharp swings from outbursts of elation to attacks of weeping, to the point of hysterics. It happened again and again. Each time they

---

* The myth that Frankl discovered the meaning of life at Auschwitz was an invention of his publisher, he once told me; in fact, he had discovered it long before his arrest. Yet, he said, what he had endured at Auschwitz proved that his theory was correct.

conducted a ceremony, a grim mood overcame them; when it was over, it evaporated and was gone. Two or three hours after returning from the visit to Auschwitz, they were dancing at a disco with young Poles. Perhaps that is part of the ideology of the commandment to live. The Ministry of Education songbook contains three sections: "patriotic and Sabbath songs," "songs of the Holocaust and heroism," and "songs for fun."

The students visited the death camps as if they were points isolated from their surroundings: pilgrims to the past, the students learned next to nothing about the revolutionary events then in progress in Poland. It was very much like the way Christian pilgrims visit Jerusalem—they learn nothing about Israel. This comparison came to mind more than once. Where Birkenau once stood, not far from Auschwitz, the teenagers left the bus and walked along the railroad tracks, like Christian pilgrims on the Via Dolorosa. They brought prayers and readings from a special book, a kind of canon, from the psalm "Do not keep silence, O God," to "On Returning to Auschwitz," by Avner Treinin, an Israeli poet. Most of the texts were written in a unique sort of solemn language—several key words were in Yiddish, rather than in Hebrew: Yiddish is to the liturgy of this memorial ritual what Aramaic is to Jewish prayer and Latin to Christian prayer. They also brought special music, on cassette: at the entrance to the Treblinka monument they played a song by Yehuda Poliker, a popular Israeli singer and a son of Holocaust survivors. His lyrics, "Here is the Treblinka station, here is the Treblinka station," sound against a background of percussion and electric guitars, bouzouki, bass guitar, and electric organ. The melody repeats itself endlessly, and the students chanted the litany along with the cassette.

Most of them, most of the time, dressed in a kind of uniform created especially for the purpose: a sweatshirt of bright purple, with a large, stylized white Star of David and the word "Israel" in Roman letters embossed on the back. Some of them frequently walked in formation, waving the Israeli flag. They did this, they explained to me, so that the passersby in the Polish cities would know that there is life after the Holocaust. It was their revenge as Israeli emissaries. Sometimes I noticed gestures whose ritual significance seemed much deeper, mystical. One boy placed a lit memorial candle in the crematorium at Majdanek, then knelt before the candle, his fingers interlaced; others imitated him. It was as if they were relighting the furnace.

Besides their teachers, the students had three spiritual shepherds to guide them along their pilgrimage—Holocaust survivors, referred to as witnesses. On an earlier pilgrimage, one student wrote, "The more I think about it, the more strongly I believe that people who went through the Holocaust have something divine about them, something beyond the human."[14] The witnesses told about their experiences in the camp and shared with the students their views about the lesson to be learned from the Holocaust. Their presence gave the journey a very personal, a very emotional, a very impressive, as well as a very political dimension.

David Sarid, a retired teacher from Tiberias, told the students that the Holocaust he hoped to impart to them would be the fourth pillar of their identities, along with Jewish tradition, the Land of Israel, and the Jewish people, with its liberal and humanistic values. His goal was to inflict a small wound on them, he said, a wound the size of a needle prick, so as to transfuse them with a drop of his own blood. They would pass this blood on from generation to generation, to the end of days, he told them. On his arrival at Auschwitz, Sarid had been younger than the students he was now accompanying. At the site of the train station, he told them how the prisoners were selected: those for immediate death to one side and those for labor to the other. He was chosen to live. The SS men, he told the students, would then herd the prisoners at a run into the camp. Here, like this, said Sarid, now in his sixties, suddenly beginning to run into the empty field where the camp barracks had once stood. He ran, and the students of the Masorti High School ran after him. Run, run, Sarid called, and they ran and ran. It was a grotesque, terrifying moment. Sarid had already run with another group that way; while I was with them he did it over and over again, with different groups of students. That day the temperature at Birkenau reached freezing. When they were cold, Sarid said, the prisoners would huddle together in a single clump, body to body. Come here, he told them, and they huddled together and swayed from side to side, slowly, as if in prayer, and someone began singing a traditional chant. Some of the students said, afterwards, that they had got a little carried away.

On the eve of the Auschwitz visit, at the synagogue in Cracow, Sarid read the students a sort of poem, "My Birkenau," while his wife played the flute. He told them that the Holocaust required them to remember with sorrow and live with joy. During his talks with the students he repeatedly recalled the slaughter of the Gypsies; during the visit to Birkenau he led the students to a small stone plaque, their only monument. He had witnessed their murder while at the camp. The Jewish people, he told the students, must not forget them, just as the rest of the world must not forget the Jews. Teacher Orit Elidar lit a memorial candle under the plaque.

The two other witnesses were Matti Bayski and Miriam Yahav. Bayski, a sturdy man from a town near Lodz, had been at Auschwitz and several other camps. In Israel he worked for the Ministry of Education, where he directed a program to prepare high school students for their army service. This was the second time he had gone with students to Poland. On the way to Majdanek he showed me a letter from a student on his first trip: "I thank you for teaching me to appreciate life and love my country," the boy had written.

Miriam Yahav, a survivor of Auschwitz, Majdanek, and other camps, for many years managed a candy store in Beersheva. She told the students hair-raising horror stories that even Shalmi Barmor found hard to listen to and read poems she had written, some of them in Yiddish. "Suddenly all was gone, nothing was left, only I alone, desolate," she wrote in one poem. "Each day was like a year. Where did I sin? Where? To this day I do not understand how it happened, how I remained, I in particular. How did I emerge from the horror?" At the end of her poems, alongside her name she customarily writes her serial number at the camp—A-15755. The one injunction left them by the victims, Yahav told the students, was revenge, revenge, revenge. Eliezer Lidovski, the Tel Aviv pensioner who told me about his part in the attempts to poison the water supplies of several German cities, always regretted not having done more. "The world would look on Israel differently, had the Jewish people known how to take blood revenge," he said.[15] David Sarid, though, told the students that there is no revenge. Our hearts should not fill with hatred, he reiterated time and again, lest there be no room for love. Miriam Yahav said she found her revenge in, among other things, Poland's poverty. Everything is so gray and sad here, she said when we were in Cracow. "The Polish Jews murdered in the Holocaust took joy with them, and since then there has been no joy in this land": that was her revenge, she said.

Yahav had never spoken about her experience until the Eichmann trial. Since then, she has considered telling her story a mission. She gives talks to students, soldiers, and other groups, including prisoners—her one condition being that there be no Arabs among them. When she described the death apparatus at Treblinka she said: "Everything was so organized with them. They had culture. Not like the Arabs." She was not talking politics, she insisted repeatedly when I asked her about it.

She was saying what she felt. Arabs frightened her. What could she do?—she was from "there." While still working in her candy store, she recounted, she would see how the Arabs came each month to the local social security office to collect their child allowances. It burned her up; they had so many children. They like it, she said as we went down Estherke Street. Estherke had been the Jewish mistress of Casimir the Great, the fourteenth-century Polish king. Miriam Yahav and I were on our way to the synagogue of Rabbi Moshe Isserles, the sixteenth-century codifier of the Ashkenazic legal tradition. It was Saturday morning. She told me how hard it had been for her to become pregnant after the Holocaust; but in the end she had two daughters and a son. One member of her family had been killed in the Six-Day War, another during the Yom Kippur War. Yes, she thought that the best thing would be to expel all the Arabs from the country. On trucks if they want, some other way if they want—so long as they get out, she said. I spent some time on her bus. The students, who came from a religious high school in Petah Tikvah, liked her. They too spoke much about the need to deport the Arabs. No, Yahav swiftly answered in place of the student I had asked, there was no similarity between the deportation of Arabs and the deportation of Jews. The Jews had not sought to do any harm to the gentiles.

Before the trip to Poland, one of the students commented that the planned ceremonies, with the prayers and the flag, were not to her liking. She suspected that someone was trying to indoctrinate them politically. The Holocaust was being presented as if it belonged only to the Jews, and this was not the case, she said. The teachers did what psychologists recommend doing in similar awkward situations: they told the students to talk about it. A fascinating debate ensued. The student who raised the issue said that she would not want to participate in ceremonies that emphasized only Israeli identity. The ceremonies, if there are any, should emphasize Jewish identity, or better yet, human identity. Her friends challenged her. One said that if he was going to Poland to cry, he preferred to do so as an Israeli and as a Jew, not just as a human being. Another said that no distinction should be made between Jewish and Israeli identity. The Nazis, he added, had murdered the Jews because they were Jews, not because they were human beings. Matan Meridor said that the Israeli flag contains Jewish symbols and represents the entire Jewish people. He, personally, could not sing a requiem to the Gypsies while standing before a monument to Jews, he said; he was not going to Poland because of the Cambodian genocide. He had no objection to mentioning, on occasion, that others had also been murdered, but he was going to Poland in the name of the six million.

That discussion continued long into the night; at times it was very emotional, and usually very political. The students could deduce from it that they were not being told the truth when remembrance of the Holocaust was presented to them as a manifestation of national unity. In fact, it was another expression of the divisions in Israeli society between right and left, xenophobia and humanism, divisions confirmed by behavioral scientists Dan Bar-On and Oron Sela in their study of the relation of Israeli youth to the Holocaust. Political polarization made it hard for young people to understand the Holocaust apart from Israeli reality; their conception of that reality inevitably affected their approach to the Holocaust.[16] This overlay of past and present was revealed over and over again during the journey to the death camps in Poland. While walking through the streets of Cracow one Friday evening, returning from a synagogue, several of the teenagers sang Yaakov Rotblit's "Song of Peace," written shortly after the Six-Day War; others sang a song from Bnei Akiva, the national-religious youth movement, improvising a line of their own: "Expel the Arabs, gather in the Jews."

The booklet the Ministry of Education distributed to the students prior to their trip stated that Poland supports self-determination for the Palestinians and Palestinian terrorist organizations, as if these two were one and the same. The students were not told that the right to self-determination is a universal right of every nation. Again and again the students were warned that the Holocaust meant that they must stay in Israel. They were not warned that the Holocaust requires them to strengthen democracy, fight racism, defend minorities and civil rights, and refuse to obey manifestly illegal orders. Meanwhile, surveys revealed the low level of democratic consciousness among Israeli youth; a comparative study conducted by Ben-Gurion University led to the embarrassing conclusion that the level of democratic consciousness among German youth was significantly higher.[17]

Most Israelis, in fact, seem to lack the optimism necessary to accept the humanistic lessons of the Holocaust, and, in recognition of that, some people have gone so far as to advocate forgetting the Holocaust altogether. A few months after the outbreak of the Palestinian uprising in the territories, *Haaretz* launched a public debate by printing a most unusual essay by Yehuda Elkana called "For Forgetting." At the time, Elkana was director of the Institute of the History of Science and Ideas at Tel Aviv University and director of the Van Leer Institute in Jerusalem. A Holocaust survivor, he had been taken to Auschwitz as a ten-year-old child. His experience there led him to the conclusion that "what happened in Germany can happen anywhere, with any people, including my people." Yet he believed it was possible to prevent "such events" through proper education and an appropriate political context.

The article came in the wake of the increasing number of press reports of "excesses" committed by Israeli soldiers in the territories. Elkana had seen all this in the past, he wrote: "I have seen a bulldozer bury people alive, I have seen soldiers who, losing their senses, broke the hands of civilians, including children." He asked himself what the source was of the acts committed by Israeli soldiers in the territories and reached the conclusion that what motivated Israeli society's attitude toward the Palestinians was not personal frustration but rather a deep existential fear nourished by a specific interpretation of the Holocaust and by the willingness to believe that the entire world was against the Jewish people, the eternal victim. "I see in this ancient belief, to which many people subscribe today, Hitler's paradoxical and tragic victory," Elkana wrote. If the Holocaust did not suffuse national consciousness so deeply, the conflict between the Jews and the Palestinians would not have led to so many "aberrant" reactions, and, most likely, the diplomatic efforts would not have led to a dead end, he added.

Like others before him, Elkana laid out the dangers inherent in memory:

An atmosphere in which an entire nation determines its relation to the present and shapes its future by concentrating on the lessons of the past is a danger to the future of any society that wishes to live in relative serenity and relative security, like all other countries. . . . The very existence of democracy is endangered when the memory of the past's victims plays an active role in the political process. All the ideologues of the fascist regimes understood this well. . . . The use of past suffering as a political argument is like making the dead partners in the democratic process of the living.

The professor's conclusion:

I see no greater danger to the future of Israel than the fact that the Holocaust has been instilled methodically into the consciousness of the Israeli public, including that very large part that did not endure the Holocaust, as well as the generation of children that has been born and grown up here. For the first time I understand the seriousness of what we have done, when for decades we have sent every child in Israel to visit Yad Vashem over and over again. What did we expect tender children to do with this experience? Our minds, even hearts, closed, without interpretation, we have proclaimed "Remember!" What for? What is a child supposed to do with these memories? For a great many of them, the horror pictures were likely to be interpreted as a call for hatred. "Remember" could be interpreted as a call for long-standing, blind hatred. It may well be that the world at large will remember. I am not sure of that, but in any case that is not our concern. Each nation, including the Germans, will decide for itself, in the context of its own considerations, whether it wishes to remember. We, on the other hand, must forget. I do not see any more important political or educational stance for the country's leaders than to stand up for life, to give oneself over to the construction of our future—and not to deal, morning and evening, with symbols, ceremonies, and lessons of the Holocaust. The rule of historical remembrance must be uprooted from our lives.[18]

The responses to Elkana's article were strong, bearing titles such as "For Memory," "For Learning," and "Holocaust of Forgetting." Yisrael Eldad, former Lehi leader and right-wing polemicist, branded it "a moral, educational, and psychological atrocity."[19]

The value of memory was also debated in the teachers' lounge of the Masorti school when the trip to Poland was first proposed. Someone there charged that the students were being exposed to undesirable emotional and nationalistic manipulation. When I mentioned the trip to Hanzi Brand, the woman who had negotiated with Adolf Eichmann, she asked me why they had to go to those monuments, in Poland. "We have enough monuments to dead people here. This country is full of them," she said. But Yehudit Hendel's reaction was different: "I think that, just as one is required to serve in the army," she wrote, "one should be required to go to Auschwitz."[20]

On the plane back from Poland, flight attendants handed out newspapers reporting the bloody incident in the Jerusalem neighborhood of Bakaa in which a Palestinian from the West Bank stabbed three Israelis to death on the street. Bakaa was once inhabited by wealthy Arabs, who fled in 1948 and were replaced by Jewish immigrants, some of whom were refugees from Arab countries and others of whom were Holocaust survivors. In the 1980s the neighborhood began to be gentrified by white-collar workers and professionals, many of them supporters of the Israeli peace movement.

In addition to the three murders, the terrorist also wounded a boy—the grandson of Abba Kovner. One of the victims, a soldier, had previously been Orit Elidar's student at the Masorti school. By the time the teacher had recovered from the shock of seeing the young woman's picture in the newspaper, the plane was ready to land. On the plane's telescreen a video clip appeared, accompanied by the song "Our land forever, where we will live, come what may." So the students brought back from Poland nothing more than what Moshe Dayan had said in 1956 over the grave of a soldier killed in a clash with Arabs near the Gaza Strip: "Millions of Jews who were killed because they had no country now gaze at us from the dust of Israeli history and command us to settle and raise up, once again, a land for our people."[21]

§

A few months later the students endured their third war. Since they were born around the time of the Yom Kippur War, the first war they could actually remember was the one in Lebanon. They would soon be going into the army; there was every reason to believe that their war would be the Intifada. Then the Persian Gulf War broke out.

Like all previous wars, this one too brought the Holocaust to the forefront of public consciousness. It was also used to revive animosity toward Germany, now reunited Germany. That response was almost inevitable. Saddam Hussein was compared to Hitler; everyone assumed that he had chemical weapons manufactured with the help of German firms. The anxiety that swept the country was a rerun of the feeling before the Six-Day War, when the Egyptian army in Yemen used poison assumed to have been developed with assistance Egypt had received from German scientists. Now the Israeli press spouted articles and letters linking united Germany with the Third Reich. There was even a demonstration outside the German embassy in Tel Aviv. Some of the speakers identified themselves as Holocaust survivors. The reports of German involvement with chemical weaponry in Iraq reopened old wounds and reawakened dormant fears. The organization that had organized the "Life March" of Israeli and American youth at the extermination camp sites in Poland published a large notice addressed to the German government: "Just let us live in this country," it entreated.[22]

When Iraq began to attack Israel with missiles, therefore, the German foreign minister was quick to bring Israel a check, a contribution toward repairing the war's damages. This did not leave a good impression, so the Germans then sent a few batteries of antimissile missiles to reinforce those the United States had previously stationed in Israel. An anti-German tone continued to ring in the press. When the civil-defense authorities began to distribute gas masks to the civilian population, *Yediot Aharonot* published an article by Noah Klieger explaining why he had refused to accept a gas mask. "I did not survive the Auschwitz death camp and the gas chambers of Birkenau in order, more than forty-five years later, to walk around an independent Jewish state with antigas equipment, against gas developed and manufactured by Germans. Thanks, not me."[23]

It is difficult to know to what extent these things came out of the depths of the soul and to what extent they expressed the repetition of a rhetorical ritual. In any case, the war with Iraq made it clear that the legacy of the Holocaust has passed out of the hands of the anti-German lobby of Holocaust survivors and their children. Awareness of the Holocaust no longer demands animosity toward Germany. Its power lies within it, and it has become part of the existential experience of all Israelis.

The anxiety that pervaded Israel at the outbreak of the war was real, and for the first time since the country was founded, it was an anxiety provoked by a sense of threat not to collective existence but to individual citizens, their families, and their property. Israel as a country was not in danger; tens and hundreds of thousands of Jewish immigrants from the Soviet Union were pouring in, the largest and most promising wave of immigration in the country's history. Israelis did not endure a war at the front or in public shelters. They experienced it within their own homes. It was the common experience of everyone; radio and television broadcasts reinforced the sense of national togetherness. Israeli television also broadcast a melodramatic American series about the Holocaust based on Herman Wouk's *War and Remembrance*, starring Robert Mitchum, John Gielgud, and Topol. The series was sponsored by Tivol, Kibbutz Lohamei Hagetaot's soya-product enterprise. Yet, even though everyone was facing the same external danger and was gripped by the same fear at the very same moments, those air-raid sirens, rising and falling in a blood-freezing wail, split society into its components, each person for himself and his family, in his sealed room, isolated within his gas mask. Thousands of Tel Avivers abandoned their homes, seeking refuge in more secure areas of the country; the Israeli myth had suffered no greater blow since the surrender of Nitsanim. Those who remained at home huddled together, helplessly expecting the worst. Never before had so many Israelis shared so Jewish an experience.

Epilogue

In the summer of 1990 I went to visit General Yossi Peled, who was then serving as commander of Israel's northern region, bordering on Lebanon and Syria.[1] His parents had once lived in Warsaw. Peled said he has no idea what his father did for a living, though once he had heard that he was involved in the diamond business—which might explain how he succeeded, shortly before the war, in fleeing with his wife and two daughters to the diamond-trading center of Antwerp. Their family name was Mendelevitch; when their son was born in 1941, they called him Jefke, a Polish nickname for Joseph. Belgium was by then already under Nazi occupation, and the condition of the Jews steadily declined. Fearing the worst, the Mendelevitches decided to hand their three children over to a Belgian–Catholic foster family; not long afterwards, the elder Mendelevitches were sent to Auschwitz.

The foster-parents were not young; one of their sons served in the Belgian army. Though the Mendelevitches paid them, the couple apparently sheltered the Jewish children out of humanitarian motives as well, since there was real danger involved. Peled said he remembers them fondly, like a father and mother. They brought up the three children as Catholics. He learned to pray, in Flemish, before meals and before going to sleep. On Sundays he went to church. Thus passed the war years.

His father was killed at Auschwitz, but his mother managed to survive and returned to Antwerp to claim him. He did not want to go with her; he did not remember her. It soon became clear that she was unable to care for him, and then she once again gave him up, this time to a Jewish orphanage. The six-year-old was told that he was Jewish and should stop saying the prayers he had grown up with. He adjusted only with difficulty; for a while he continued to pray secretly, in his bed, after the lights were turned off. In 1949, the children were taken, via France, to Israel. Their mother did not come with them. A stranger, their uncle, awaited them at the Haifa port and took them with him to his kibbutz, Negba. A few months previously the State of Israel had been established and the War of Independence had come to an end. Yosef, as he was now called, was almost eight.

Kibbutz Negba lies twelve kilometers east of the city of Ashkelon. It was founded in 1939 by immigrants from Poland, members of Hashomer Hatsair. When it was founded, it was the southernmost Jewish settlement in Palestine. When Yosef Mendelevitch and his sisters arrived, Negba was still recovering from the battles of the War of Independence and had already become one of the symbols of Israeli heroism. Time and again, the Egyptians had threatened the kibbutz, shelling it from the air, and each time the kibbutz managed to repel them. The battles, states a pamphlet the kibbutz has printed, taught them that "the way to life is war and steadfastness under all conditions."[2] The kibbutz would soon commission a huge monument from Natan Rapaport: two muscular youths and a woman with a kerchief on her head, in bronze.

The kibbutz children tormented Yosef: he was a refugee, without parents, a boy who knew only a few words of Hebrew and spoke with a foreign accent that he has never completely overcome. Yoskia, as they called him maliciously, did not admit to his tormentors that his father had been killed at Auschwitz. His father died in the Warsaw ghetto uprising, he lied to them, and tried hard to be accepted. It was a very difficult time: Yosef lived in constant fear that he would again be uprooted. He was full of resentment and suspicion. His past oppressed him; for many years he repressed it, an embarrassing secret.

In December 1985, Peled saw one of the three films on the Holocaust made by poet Haim Guri together with Jako Erlich, and wrote Guri a letter, on the stationery of his office in the Israeli army general staff. He felt "a deep and strong need" to share his childhood memories with Guri, the general wrote in a sudden outburst of emotion: It is an unusual document.

> Yesterday I sat and watched *The Face of Revolt*, and the tempest of my childhood in that difficult time was again brought to life by a

surge of emotion. I, born into the inferno; I, the Jewish baby of six months old given over to a Christian family for some years; I, the Jewish child of six returned to Judaism by the Jewish Brigade—I find myself as an officer in the Jewish army, gazing years back, feeling and understanding the source where we have suckled, aware or unawares, the heroism of this nation.

I want you to know, Haim Guri: sometimes, when I am by myself, I go back decades in my thoughts, remembering only snatches of things. Pictures like the entry of the Nazis into the house of a Christian family, looking for Jewish children . . . a section of railroad track . . . the Christian church . . . the coming of the Allies . . . the strange woman (I am already six) presented to me as my mother . . . my resistance against entering a restaurant with a Star of David on it, and this I say to my mother who has just returned from Auschwitz. . . . All these memories sometimes make me suddenly feel tears streaming from my eyes, and when I gaze at these tears, despite my being an adult experienced in life, a veteran of several wars, I see that these are the tears of a four-year-old, five-year-old Jewish child.

As I grow older the link with my past becomes stronger, and my past, which is the past of our nation, becomes stronger and more important. . . . Many of the things I have done for years have their source in that horrible period. To be honest, the effort to make sure that what happened to my family and to the six million will not happen to my two sons, born in Israel, that is the real drive that motivates me.[3]

He could guess, Peled told me, what would emerge were he to lie on the psychoanalyst's couch, but as far as he knows it was not the Holocaust that motivated him to become an officer. It was his brigade commander, Mordecai Tsipori, who later became a member of Begin's cabinet. Peled had not previously intended to stay in the army after his basic duty. When his term was up, Tsipori called him and told him about the shortage of officers and asked him to stay on for six more months. Thirty years went by. "I envy the lucky officers who at the age of twenty had Theodor Herzl appear to them in their dreams and order them to remain in the army in order to fortify the Zionist movement," Peled said sarcastically. "Herzl never appeared in my dreams." Quite the opposite, he added—it took years before military service became natural to him, he said. Either way, the Israeli army had supplied him with a challenge, friends, and a home.

In the army they began to call him Yossi, and later he changed his last name to Peled, Hebrew for "steel." He was close to Yitzhak Rabin, the chief of staff during the Six-Day War, and now prime minister, and married a member of his staff. They had two sons. The oldest never asked anything; the younger has shown great interest in the Holocaust, and Peled would like him to go to Poland.

As defense minister in 1987, Rabin asked Peled to go with him on an official visit to West Germany; they visited Dachau, where Rabin made a speech. "I wish to tell you here that we won," Rabin said.[4] As he spoke, General Peled turned his head and cried. Two years later, in a clash with Palestinian guerrillas in the north, two Israeli paratroopers under Peled's command were killed. Some of their comrades wept. Reporters heard Peled tell them that there was nothing wrong with tears. Chief of Staff Dan Shomron, though, said the next day that real fighters don't cry. "It was a foolish statement," Peled told me. "Why not cry, if you want to? The question is whether you do the work right. The night after they cried over their fallen friends, the paratroopers had to fight again, and they were fine. Whoever needs to cry, should cry." Peled saw the expression of emotion as a sign of maturity. He spoke out of experience, he said: as he grew, he found himself losing the tough exterior he had assumed when he enlisted in the army, thirty years before.

Yet it was only unwillingly that Peled revealed to me that he had one recurring dream: he is running through a large forest, fleeing for his life, the Nazis chasing him. In reality it never happened. Other than this, the Holocaust does not trouble him, he said. But sometimes, when he stands before students, he remembers himself at their age, and he relives the series of separations that have marked his life from the day his parents gave him to that family in Antwerp. Once he flew over the city in a helicopter as a guest of the Belgian army chief of staff. He was able to direct him to the neighborhood in which he grew up, locating from the sky the Catholic church he had prayed in. No, he told me, he did not live the Holocaust every hour of the day. As far as he remembered, he had never thought of it during a battle, and he has fought in every war and on every front since the Six-Day War.

When we talked, in the summer of 1990, Peled said he assumed that there were those in the army who thought he was trying to use his story to promote his personal ambitions, so he was careful not to make himself into a symbol. Nevertheless, his story is dramatic; it can't help but symbolize Jewish vitality, and Peled knew it.

Once he learned that he had no reason to be ashamed of his past, he allowed Israeli television to produce a film on his life. Ever since then, he has been overwhelmed with invitations to lecture. He accepts the ones from schools. He tells the students that it is hard to be sure whether Israel would have been established had the Holocaust not happened. But he has no doubt that the Holocaust accelerated the process that brought about the country's creation. "In fact," he said, "this country was founded on a silver platter made of six million bodies." Peled was using the expression attributed to Chaim Weizmann: "A people does not get a country on a silver platter." Natan Alterman was inspired by these words to write a poem that over the years gained the status of a hymn, frequently quoted at official memorial services for fallen soldiers. For Alterman, the "silver platter" on which the country was given to the nation was a boy and girl, "flowing with the dew of Hebrew youth"—members of the generation that fought the War of Independence.[5] Forty years later, the general in "the Jewish army," as he called it, so oppressed by the Sabra ethos in his boyhood, passed the silver platter back from the first Israelis to the last Jews. In the meantime, the Israelis had learned to live with their Jewish past.

¶

Israelis are obsessed with history. They are the offspring of a nation, a religion, and a culture that has dismissed the present and left the future in the hands of faith and fate. The past thus becomes an object of worship. Since the beginning of the 1980s, they have been worshiping *moreshet hashoah*—a somewhat peculiar term, meaning "the heritage of the Holocaust." The story of Yossi Peled, like that of Yehiel De-Nur (Ka-Tzetnik) is a concrete example of this dramatic development in the Israelis' attitude to the Holocaust. The contempt that many members of the yishuv felt toward the Diaspora did not disappear during the Holocaust. Rather, it deepened. And after the war the yishuv's condescending attitude to the survivors, a posture born of regret and shame, gave rise to the great silence that surrounded the Holocaust through the 1950s. These were the years when Israelis refused to speak or even think about the Holocaust, almost to the point of denial. Over the last decades, in contrast, the Holocaust has increasingly become a major factor in shaping Israeli identity and a constant and intense preoccupation. Viewed dispassionately, though, the recent eagerness to embrace the past is often no less problematic and charged with contradiction than the earlier tendency to deny it.

There are a number of explanations, both political and cultural, for the current intensity of involvement with the Holocaust. Israel differs from other countries in its need to justify—to the rest of the world, and to itself—its very right to exist. Most countries need no such ideological justifications. But Israel does—because most of its Arab neighbors have not recognized it and because most of the Jews of the world prefer to live in other countries. So long as these factors remain true, Zionism will be on the defensive. As a justification for the State of Israel, the Holocaust is comparable only to the divine promise contained in the Bible: It seems to be definitive proof of the Zionist argument that Jews can live in security and with full equal rights only in their own country and that they therefore must have an autonomous and sovereign state, strong enough to defend its existence. Yet, from war to war, it has become clear that there are many places in the world where Jews are safer than in Israel. Moreover, the extermination of the Jews during the Holocaust was an obvious defeat for the Zionist movement: The Zionists were unable to convince the majority of the world's Jews to come to Palestine before the war, while that was still an option. And though the yishuv leaders certainly could have displayed greater compassion for and identification with the Jews of Europe, they could not have done more to save them; the yishuv was helpless when faced with the Nazi extermination program.

In order to resolve these contradictions, the State of Israel put forth the thesis that, had it existed during the Holocaust, it could have prevented the slaughter of European Jewry. "We, the soldiers of the Israeli Defense Forces, have come to this place fifty years later, perhaps fifty years too late," said Chief of Staff Ehud Barak during a visit to Auschwitz.[6] And Prime Minister Yitzhak Shamir said, "The State of Israel's highest obligation is to stand ready to defend the Jewish people anywhere in the world where evil has come upon them."[7] The first spontaneous reaction in Israel to the rescue of several thousand Ethiopian Jews in 1991 was: Had we only had a country during the Second World War, we could have saved European Jewry as well. This is, of course, an ideological, not a historical, statement; it illustrates the great difficulty of separating rhetoric from reality.

But if the Holocaust could be used politically as a justification for statehood, it could also be used culturally to substitute for certain aspects of the Zionist program. The yishuv leadership desired to build a new nation, detached from the oppressive two-thousand-year history of Jewish existence in the Exile. The "new man" that Zionism wished to create would be the opposite of the persecuted and submissive "old Jew" who had earned his living through various kinds of commerce. The new Zionist society would represent creative, socialist, secular progress, imbue its children with sovereign pride and with the ability to defend themselves and their honor. But this Zionist ideal, too, was complicated by reality: the "new man" lacked a dimension of depth; he had no past, no link with Jewish history, and no connection to the experience of most Israelis.

Israel's founders revived the use of the Hebrew language in its biblical Sephardic pronunciation, but that fulfilled only part of their dream. Most of the immigrants—those who survived the Holocaust as well as those who arrived from the Islamic world—did not come to Israel because they wished to escape the Exile; they came because there was no other country that would take them. They were refugees, not Zionist idealists. Many of them, therefore, exhibited little enthusiasm for trading their existing culture and identities as Jews for the hypothetical identity of the "new man." It soon became clear that two thousand years of history could not be obliterated.

On the contrary. As the years went by, the similarity between life in the sovereign Israeli state and the traditional life of Jewish communities around the world increased. The country was isolated, set apart from its surroundings. Its religion, culture, values, and mentality were different. It lived in insecurity. Time and again, Israelis were forced to recognize that, for its very existence, Israel is largely dependent on outside assistance, including the support of wealthy and influential Jews abroad. Israeli legislation increasingly draws on traditional Jewish law.[8] Like members of Jewish communities elsewhere, members of the Jewish community of Israel have a dual identity. They are both Israeli and Jewish. They represent no "new man."

All this explains why so many Israelis held fast to their Jewish roots— why, indeed, they have sought them anew. There were those who found their way into non-Zionist ultraorthodox circles. There were those whose particular integration of religion and Zionism inspired them to settle the territories occupied in the Six-Day War. There were those who left the country, choosing, for the most part, to join the world's largest Jewish community—in America. Many Israelis reverted to using the original Jewish names that they had Hebraicized upon moving to Israel. These moves, however, were radical, demanding, and difficult. Emotional and historical awareness of the Holocaust provides a much easier way back into the mainstream of Jewish history, without necessarily imposing any real personal moral obligation.

The "heritage of the Holocaust" is thus largely a way for secular Israelis to express their connection to Jewish heritage. And its importance in daily life has increased year by year as Israel has become more "Jewish" and less "Israeli." Beginning in the 1980s, not a day has gone by without the Holocaust being mentioned in some context or other in one of the daily newspapers; it is a central subject of literature and poetry, of theater, cinema, and television. From time to time, new institutes for the study of the Holocaust spring up, devoted to a variety of subjects, including the real and imagined distress of the children of Holocaust survivors. In the 1950s and 1960s, Masada, the symbol of Hebrew rebellion and pride, was the object of pilgrimage for Israeli youngsters; soldiers scaled its sharp cliffs to swear fealty to the army and to receive their first rifles. Now many receive their weapons at the Western Wall in Jerusalem; tens of thousands of Israeli high-school students have already made the pilgrimage to the death-camp sites in Poland, and more are doing so each year. Nine out of ten of these young people have said on their return that the Jewish experience they underwent strengthened their Israeli identity.[9] All research has shown that the consciousness of the Holocaust is increasing accordingly. A 1992 study of Israeli identity among teachers' college students found that close to 80 percent of those asked identified with the statement, "We are all Holocaust survivors."[10] Oded Peled, an Israeli-born poet (no relation to the general), wrote: "Mother, I am with you in Bergen-Belsen . . . I am there with you always—after all, it is you and I, Mother: you and I and the terrible snow that will remain with us always."[11]

The Holocaust now occupies the same place in the Israeli self-image for those of European ancestry and those whose origins lie in the Arab world. Indeed, it has come to be so dominant a component of Israeli identity that a Druse member of the Knesset, Zeidan Atshi, once claimed the right to share it. Atshi intervened in a debate between Prime Minister Begin and another member of the Knesset. The argument led, as so often before, to the Holocaust. Begin demanded that Atshi not interfere. "This is a dispute between two Jews," he shouted at him. Atshi was deeply hurt. "Then what am I doing here?" he protested, as if inclusion in the heritage of the Holocaust were a matter of equal civil rights.[12]

As the consciousness of the Holocaust increased and became, along with religion and Zionist ideology, a crucial source from which Israelis draw the elements of their identity, it played an ever more pivotal role in the ongoing debate over what fundamental values ought to guide Israeli society. It is in the framework of this debate that some have suggested that Israelis would do best to forget the Holocaust entirely, because they were not learning the proper lessons from it. Indeed, the "heritage of the Holocaust," as it is taught in schools and fostered in national memorial ceremonies, often encourages insular chauvinism and a sense that the Nazi extermination of the Jews justifies any act that seems to contribute to Israel's security, including the oppression of the population in the territories occupied by Israel in the Six-Day War. The assumption is that the Holocaust requires the existence of a strong Israel and that the failure of the world to save the Jewish people during the Second World War disqualifies it from reminding Israel of moral imperatives, including respect for human rights. The sense that the Holocaust was inevitable, in accordance with Zionist ideology, and the identification with the Jew as a victim are liable to lead Israelis to conclude that their existence depends solely on military power, and so to limit their willingness to take the risks involved in a compromise peace settlement. Paradoxically, the fatalistic lessons of this Holocaust heritage sabotage the realization of the Zionist dream—the Zionists, after all, dreamed that the Jewish people would become a nation like all other nations, a country like all other countries.

Yet it does not follow from the risks inherent in Israeli memorial culture that Israelis would do best to forget the Holocaust. Indeed, they cannot and should not forget it. They need, rather, to draw different conclusions. The Holocaust summons all to preserve democracy, to fight racism, and to defend human rights. It gives added force to the Israeli law that requires every soldier to refuse to obey a manifestly illegal order. Instilling the humanist lessons of the Holocaust will be difficult as long as the country is fighting to defend itself and justify its very existence; but it is essential. This is the task of the seventh million.

Notes

꙳

ABBREVIATIONS

BGA: Ben-Gurion Archives, Sde Boker.
BGD: Ben-Gurion Diary, at the BGA.
CC: Central Committee.
CZA: Central Zionist Archives, Jerusalem.
DFPSI: *Documents on the Foreign Policy of the State of Israel* (Jerusalem: National Archives).
DCO: *District Court Opinions* (Jerusalem: Ministry of Justice).
DOD: Division of Oral Documentation.
EC: Executive Committee.
FM: Foreign Ministry.
GPO: Government Printing Office, Jerusalem.
JAE: Jewish Agency executive, of the CZA.
KP: *Knesset Proceedings* (from Tenth Knesset on, the number of the Knesset is sometimes included: *KP10*, etc.).
LA: Labor Archives, Tel Aviv.
LPA: Labor Party Archives, Bet Berl, Tsofit.
NA: National Archives, Jerusalem.
NGA: Nahum Goldmann Archives, at the CZA.
PC: Political Committee.
PF: Personal file, not open to research.
PMO: Prime Minister's Office.
SCO: *Supreme Court Opinions* (Jerusalem: Ministry of Justice).
YHOG: *Yediot Hitahdut Oley Germanya/Mitteilungsblatt der Hitachdut Olej Germania*, the bilingual newsletter of the German Immigrants' Association.

The name changed several times, sometimes including Austrian immigrants as well. Articles were published in both Hebrew (translated here) and German.

YVA: Yad Vashem Archives.

Articles and books published in Israel are in Hebrew unless otherwise indicated; their Hebrew titles, though, are given in English translation.

PROLOGUE: KA-TZETNIK'S TRIP

1. The following pages are based largely on two extended interviews with Yehiel De-Nur, his wife, his daughter, and his doctor. See Tom Segev, "Ka-Tzetnik's Trip," *Koteret Rashit* 234 (27 May 1987), pp. 16 ff.; Ka-Tzetnik 135633, *Shivitti: A Vision* (San Francisco: Harper and Row, 1989; Tel Aviv: Hakibbutz Hameuhad, 1987). See also Yehiel De-Nur's testimony at the Eichmann trial, session no. 68 (7 June 1961), records, YVA; Haim Guri, *Facing the Glass Booth* (Tel Aviv: Hakibbutz Hameuhad, 1962), pp. 124 ff.; Tzvika Dror, *They Were There* (Tel Aviv: Hakibbutz Hameuhad, 1992).

PART I: HITLER: *The Yekkes Are Coming*

1   "THE STREETS ARE PAVED WITH MONEY"

1. "The Red Flag Was Lowered from Atop the German Consulate in Jerusalem," *Hazit Haam*, 2 June 1933, p. 1.
2. "Hitler Is Chancellor of Germany," *Haaretz*, 31 Jan. 1933, p. 1.
3. *Haaretz*, 8 Feb. 1933, p. 1.
4. B.K.: "What Time Will Do," *Haaretz*, 8 March 1933, p. 2; *Haaretz*, 9 April 1933, p. 1; Yoav Gelber, "Zionist Policy and the Haavara Agreement 1933–1935," *Yalkut Moreshet* 17 (Feb. 1974), pp. 99 ff.
5. Editorial, *Doar Hayom*, 1 Feb. 1933, p. 2.
6. Editorial, *Davar*, 1 Feb. 1933, p. 1; editorial, *Davar*, 6 Feb. 1933, p. 1.
7. Yitzhak Laufban, "In the Shadow of the Swastika," *Hapoel Hatsair*, 21 March 1933, p. 1; S. Savorai, "The Leaders of Millions and Their Times," *Hapoel Hatsair*, 10 March 1933, p. 3.
8. Yitzhak Laufban, "Satan's Ally," *Hapoel Hatsair*, 26 May 1933, p. 1.
9. H. Ben-Yeruham (Merhavia), *The Betar Book* (Tel Aviv: Havaad Lehotsaat Sefer Betar, 1973), II:1:173.
10. Avraham Harabi, "Criticism of Our Relations with Germany," *Haaretz*, 17 March 1933, p. 8.
11. Laufban, "Shadow of the Swastika."

12. "The Masses of Hebrew Jerusalem Identify with Jabotinsky's Position against Germany," *Hazit Haam*, 2 June 1933, p. 2.

13. Zeev Jabotinsky, "The Lofty Zionism," *Speeches, 1927–1940*, p. 187, quoted by Rafaela Bilski-Ben-Hur, *Every Individual a King: The Social and Political Thought of Zeev Jabotinsky* (Tel Aviv: Dvir, 1988), p. 221.

14. Shabtai Teveth, *The Burning Ground*, vol. III of *The Lamentations of David* (Tel Aviv: Schocken, 1987), p. 437.

15. Laufban, "Shadow of the Swastika."

16. Teveth, *Kinat David*, p. 284.

17. Moshe Beilinson to Berl Katznelson, 8 May 1933, quoted by Anita Shapira, *Berl* (Tel Aviv: Am Oved, 1980), p. 403.

18. Arthur Ruppin, *Chapters of My Life*, vol. III, *Building the Land and the People, 1920–1942* (Tel Aviv: Am Oved, 1968), p. 222.

19. Ibid., p. 223; see also Ruppin, *Sociology of the Jews* (Hebrew) (Warsaw: Stibel, 1931), pp. 33 ff.

20. Ruppin, *Chapters of My Life*, III:322.

21. "Wieviel Kostet ein Haushalt in Palästina?" (unsigned), *Jüdische Rundschau* (Berlin), 28 April 1933, p. 169; Moshe Beilinson, "Haushaltskosten in Palästina," *Jüdische Rundschau*, 30 May 1933, p. 7.

22. Shaul Esh, *Essays on the Research of the Holocaust and Contemporary Judaism* (Jerusalem: Hebrew University Press, 1973), pp. 33 ff.; David Yisraeli, *The German Reich and Israel* (Tel Aviv: Bar-Ilan University Press, 1974); Gelber, "Zionist Policy," p. 100; Yoav Gelber, *A New Homeland* (Jerusalem: Yad Ben Zvi, Leo Beck Institute, 1990), pp. 32 ff.; Werner Feilchenfeld, Dolf Michaelis, and Ludwig Pinner, *Haavara-Transfer nach Palästina* (Tübingen: J. C. B. Mohr, Paul Siebeck, 1972), p. 31; Edwin Black, *The Transfer Agreement* (New York: Macmillan, 1984).

23. Theodor Herzl, *The Jewish State*, intro. Menahem Begin (Tel Aviv: Yediot Aharonot, 1978), pp. 30 ff.

24. Ben-Gurion and Shertok: Black, *Transfer Agreement*, p. 294; Meyerson: ibid., p. 366; Begin: Aviezer Golan and Shlomo Nakdimon, *Begin* (Tel Aviv: Idanim, 1978), p. 39.

25. Black, *Transfer Agreement*, p. 248.

26. Ibid., p. 379.

27. Feilchenfeld et al., *Haavara*, p. 76.

28. "The Debate on Haavara at the Vaad Haleumi Meeting" (unsigned), *Davar*, 17 Nov. 1935.

29. Y. Soker, "Upon Hitler's Rise," *Hapoel Hatsair*, 3 Feb. 1933, p. 1.

30. Abba Ahimeir, "Questions of the Moment," *Doar Hayom*, 10 Oct. 1928.

31. "A Fair Ending to the Peace Preaching of Magnes-Bentwitch," *Hazit Haam*, 6 May 1932, p. 4.

32. Abba Sikra, "The Third Zionist Organization," *Hazit Haam*, 28 March 1933, p. 2.

33. Editorial, *Hazit Haam*, 31 March 1933, p. 1.
34. Yosef B. Schechtman, *Zeev Jabotinsky* (Tel Aviv: Karni, 1956), II:283 (this also includes the response of the editor of *Hazit Haam*); Zeev Jabotinsky, speech on Polish radio, reprinted in *Hauma*, issue 1 (5) (June 1963), p. 56; "Jerusalem Masses," *Hazit Haam*, p. 2.
35. Quoted in Gelber, "Zionist Policy," p. 129.
36. "The Unknown Transfer," *Hayarden*, 10 Nov. 1935, p. 1; "The Shame of the Haavara," *Hayarden*, 13 Nov. 1935, p. 2.
37. David Ben-Gurion to Heschel Frumkin, 16 Sept. 1930, in Yehuda Erez, ed., *Ben-Gurion's Letters* (Tel Aviv: Am Oved, 1974), III:145.
38. Chaim Weizmann to Felix M. Warburg, 11 Dec. 1939, in Barnet Litvinof, ed., *The Letters and Papers of Chaim Weizmann* (New Brunswick, N.J.: Transaction Books, Rutgers University, 1978), XV:65; Weizmann to Morris Rotenberg, 31 Jan. 1931, ibid., XV:98.
39. Yitzhak Laufban, "Issues of the Day," *Hapoel Hatsair*, 23 Sept. 1932, p. 1.
40. Zeev Jabotinsky, "The Red Swastika," *Hazit Haam*, 4 Nov. 1932, p. 2.
41. David Ben-Gurion at Beit Haam in Tel Aviv, 18 Feb. 1933. The full version of the speech appears under the title "Against Strike-Breakers at Frumkin and in Petah Tikvah," *Davar*, 21 March 1933.
42. Ben-Gurion to Haim Guri, 15 May 1963, BGA, quoted in Michael Bar-Zohar, *David Ben-Gurion* (Tel Aviv: Am Oved, 1978), III:15–16. See also Ben-Gurion to Eliahu Dobkin (comparing Jabotinsky to Hitler), 11 April 1933, Erez, *Ben-Gurion's Letters*, III:572; Teveth, *Burning Ground*, p. 163; Uri Zvi Greenberg, "Arlosoroff's Hitlerada," *Die Welt* 7 (Yiddish; Warsaw), 9 June 1933; Yohanan Pogravinski, "The Stalin–Ben-Gurion–Hitler Pact," *Hazit Haam*, 16 June 1933, p. 2.
43. Anita Shapira, *Berl*, p. 403.
44. Laufban, "Satan's Ally," p. 1; Shechtman, *Zeev Jabotinsky*, I:422.
45. David Ben-Gurion at the Mapai PC, 19 Nov. 1933, LPA, 23/33.
46. Pogravinski, "Pact," p. 2.
47. Shabtai Teveth, *The Arlosoroff Murder* (Tel Aviv: Schocken, 1982); State of Israel, *The Report of the Commission of Investigation into the Murder of Dr. Haim Arlosoroff*, 1985.
48. Yoav Gelber, "Zionist Policy"; Yisraeli, *German Reich and Israel*; David Yisraeli, "The Third Reich and the Transfer Agreement," *Journal of Contemporary History* 6 (1971), pp. 129–48; Eliahu Ben-Elisar, *The Extermination Conspiracy: The Foreign Policy of the Third Reich and the Jews, 1933–1939* (Tel Aviv: Idanim, 1978).
49. "The Debate on Haavara," p. 4.
50. Ibid.
51. Ibid.
52. Rabbi Benyamin, "Quiet and Considered," *Doar Hayom*, 13 Dec. 1935, p. 2.

53. "The Debate on Haavara," p. 4.
54. David Ben-Gurion at the JAE, 23 Nov. 1935, CZA.
55. B.D.: "Issues of the Day," *Doar Hayom*, 13 Dec. 1935, p. 2.
56. "On David Ben-Gurion's Speech at the Vaad Haleumi," unsigned, *Haboker*, 17 Dec. 1935, p. 1.
57. Yitzhak Gruenbaum at the JAE, 13 Nov. 1938, CZA.
58. Gruenbaum at the JAE, 11 May 1937, CZA.
59. David Ben-Gurion at the Mapai CC, 7 Dec. 1938, LPA, 23/38.
60. Shabtai Teveth, "Ben-Gurion and the Holocaust Blunder," *Haaretz*, 10 April 1987, p. B5.
61. Arthur Ruppin, "The Settlement of German Jewry in Israel," *Davar*, 1 Sept. 1933, p. 6; Georg Landauer to Dr. Hartenstein, 17 Aug. 1933, CZA, S/7 84.
62. Quoted in Gelber, *New Homeland*, p. 131.
63. "On David Ben-Gurion's Speech," p. 1.
64. Black, *Transfer Agreement*, p. 329.
65. Esh, *Essays*, pp. 47 ff.; Black, *Transfer Agreement*, pp. 348 ff.
66. Esh, *Essays*, pp. 54–55; Menahem Begin, 15 May 1963, *KP*, XXXVII:1859.
67. John and David Kimche, *Secret Ways: The Migration of a Nation "in Violation of the Law"* 1938–1948 (Jerusalem: Jerusalem Post, 1955), pp. 21 ff.
68. David Ben-Gurion and Arthur Ruppin to whom it may concern, 21 Jan. 1935, CZA, S/7 219.
69. Tuchler Report: *Erlebnisse und Beobachtungen in den ersten vier Hitlerjahren*, undated document, YVA, 01/24.
70. Von Lim (Leopold Itz von Mildenstein), "Ein Nazi fährt nach Palästina," *Der Angriff*, 26 Sept.–9 Oct. 1934; Jacob Boas, "A Nazi Travels to Palestine," *History Today* 30 (Jan. 1980), p. 33; Yehuda Koren, "Zioninazi," *Monitin* 112 (Jan. 1988), pp. 26 ff.
71. Tuchler Report.
72. Police interrogation of Eichmann, Israel Police, national headquarters, Bureau 06, *Adolf Eichmann*, I:91 ff.; report of the visit (prosecution exhibit 37 at the Eichmann trial), YVA; the Eichmann trial records, session 18, 24 April 1961, pp. 48 ff., YVA; testimony of Dieter Wisliceny, YVA (6) TR 3; Folkes file, Haganah Archive, 119 private archive; Alex Doron, "Folkes, Mystery Man," *Maariv* (weekend supplement), 5 Aug. 1988, pp. 26 ff.
73. Teddy Kollek, *For Jerusalem* (London: Weidenfeld and Nicolson, 1978), p. 31; for another meeting between a Jewish Agency representative and Eichmann, see Ehud Avriel, *Open Gates* (Tel Aviv: Sifriat Maariv, 1976), pp. 76 ff.; see also Dov Goldstein, "Five Meetings with Eichmann," *Maariv*, 27 June 1960, p. 6; and "Minister Shapira Saw Him in 1938," *Maariv*, 24 May 1960, p. 2.

74. Kimche and Kimche, *Secret Ways*, p. 46.
75. Testimony of Dr. Walter Shen, Hans Friedenthal, and Leo David (the Bal-Kaduri collection), YVA, 01/229; 01/130; 01/277.
76. Black, *Transfer Agreement*, p. 131.
77. Mimeographed notice, 29 June 1932, Jabotinsky Institute, B-21 (circulars).
78. Collection of Betar pamphlets from Germany, Jabotinsky Institute, B-21; Ben-Yeruham, *Betar Book*, I:528.
79. Ben-Yeruham, *Betar Book*, II:1:350.
80. "Participation of Jews in the Berlin Olympics: Optional or Mandatory?" *Haaretz*, 1 July 1936, p. 2; see also editorials in the sports section of *Haaretz* on 3 and 14 July 1936, pp. 7 and 14, respectively.
81. Ben-Yeruham, *Betar Book*, II:1:799.
82. Shlomo Lev-Ami (Levi), *Struggle and Revolution: The Haganah, Etzel, and Lehi (1918–1948)* (Tel Aviv: Ministry of Defense), p. 148; Natan Yellin-Mor, *Freedom Fighters of Israel: People, Ideas, Adventures* (Haifa: Shikmona, 1975), pp. 71–84; Yosef Heller, *Lehi 1940–1949* (Jerusalem: Keter, 1989), pp. 125 ff.
83. Yellin-Mor, *Freedom Fighters*, p. 73.
84. For the draft version of the notice, see CZA, S/7 321, and *Davar*, 6 Dec. 1935.
85. David Ben-Gurion in Kfar Yedidya, 6 Nov. 1948, LPA, 15/43.

2 "A SON OF EUROPE"

1. All these figures are based on varying estimates. The differences are the result of, among other things, different computational methods—whether according to origin or citizenship, and depending on which borders of the Reich were used. A thorough statistical discussion of the emigration of German Jewry may be found in Herbert A. Strauss, "Jewish Emigration from Germany: Nazi Policies and Jewish Responses," published in two parts in the 1980 and 1981 *Leo Beck Institute Yearbooks* (London: Secker and Warburg), pp. 313 ff. and 343 ff. respectively; Eva Belling, *Die Gesellschaftliche Eingliederung der Deutschen Einwanderer in Israel* (Frankfurt: Europäische Verlagsanstalt, 1967); Yoav Gelber, *A New Homeland* (Jerusalem: Yad Ben Zvi, Leo Beck Institute, 1990), pp. 51 ff.; Shlomo Erel, *The Yekkes: 50 Years of Immigration* (Jerusalem: Reuven Mass, 1985), pp. 33 ff.; Miriam Getter, "Immigration from Germany in the Years 1933–1939: Socio-Economic Absorption Versus Socio-Cultural Absorption," *Kathedra* 12 (July 1979), pp. 125 ff.; see also Moshe Sikron, *Immigration to Israel 1948–1953* (Jerusalem: Falk Center, 1957), pp. 14 ff., "Immigration in the Mandatory Period," and 105 ff., bibliography.
2. Erel, *Yekkes*, p. 12.
3. Ibid., p. 445; see also Richard Willstädter, *From My Life* (New York:

W. A. Benjamin, 1965); Ronald W. Clark, *Einstein: The Life and Times* (New York: World, 1965), pp. 474 ff.

4. Zweig to Freud, 21 Jan. 1934, in Ernst L. Freud, ed., *The Letters of Sigmund Freud and Arnold Zweig* (London: Hogarth, 1970), p. 57.

5. Ibid.

6. Zweig to Freud, 12 Aug. 1934, ibid., p. 87.

7. Zweig to Freud, 1 Sept. 1935, ibid., p. 109.

8. Ibid., p. 113.

9. Zweig to Freud, 15 Feb. 1936, ibid., p. 120.

10. Zweig to Freud, 22 Nov. 1935, ibid., p. 114.

11. Zweig to Freud, 15 Feb. 1936, ibid., p. 121.

12. Zweig to Freud, 1 Feb. 1937, ibid., p. 136; and Zweig to Freud, 21 March 1937, ibid., p. 137; and others.

13. Freud to Zweig, 21 Feb. 1936, ibid., p. 122.

14. Zweig to Freud, 23 March 1939, ibid., p. 179.

15. Zweig to Freud, 16 July 1938, ibid., p. 165.

16. Ibid.

17. Zweig to Freud, 8 Aug. 1939, ibid., p. 183.

18. Freud to Zweig, 28 June 1938, ibid., p. 163; and Freud to Zweig, 5 March 1939, ibid., p. 178.

19. Arnold Zweig, "Verwurzelung," *Orient*, 3 July 1942, p. 2.

20. Zeev Tsahor, "Ben-Gurion and the Haapala, 1934–1948," in Benyamin Pinkas, ed., *Eastern European Policy Between Holocaust and Rehabilitation* (Beersheva: Ben-Gurion University Press, 1987), pp. 422 ff.

21. Dan Michman, "Zeev Jabotinsky: The Evacuation Program and the Problem of Anticipation of the Holocaust," *Kivunim*, issue 7, May 1980, pp. 119 ff.

22. Yohanan Bader, 26 Dec. 1949, *KP*, III:319.

23. Shmuel Dotan, *The Partition Debate in the Mandatory Period* (Jerusalem: Yad Ben-Zvi, 1980).

24. H. Ben-Yeruham (Merhavia), *The Betar Book* (Tel Aviv: Havaad Lehotsaat Sefer Betar, 1973), II:2:799 ff.

25. Chaim Weizmann to Blanche Dagdale, 1 Dec. 1935, in Barnet Litvinof, ed., *The Letters and Papers of Chaim Weizmann* (New Brunswick, N.J.: Transaction Books, Rutgers University, 1978).

26. German Immigrants' Association to the Immigration Department, 29 Dec. 1933, CZA, S/26, 2564.

27. Immigration Department to the Palestine office, 28 Nov. 1934, CZA, S/7 149.

28. Henrietta Szold to Georg Landauer, 19 Aug. 1934, CZA, S/7 70, and others. See also German Immigrants' Association to Henrietta Szold, 11 Jan. 1934, CZA, S/7 563 S/7 78.

29. Georg Landauer to the Immigration Department, 12 March 1934, CZA, S/7 70.

30. Martin Rosenblüt to Georg Landauer, 27 Oct. 1937, CZA, S/7 581; Walter Ettinghausen to Leo Cohen, 20 Sept. 1938, CZA, S/25 2482.
31. Werner Senator to the Palestine office in Berlin, 30 Jan. 1935, CZA, S/7 142.
32. Summary of meeting, 6 Jan. 1935, CZA, S/25 2576.
33. Yitzhak Gruenbaum to Nahum Goldmann, 16 Oct. 1935, CZA, S/7 3637.
34. Quoted by Gelber, *New Homeland*, p. 136.
35. Eliahu Dobkin to Martin Rosenblüt, 15 Jan. 1936, CZA, S/6 3637.
36. Arthur Handke to Martin Rosenblüt, 24 April 1933, CZA, L/13 138. See also memo by Ernst Levi, 19 Oct. 1934, CZA, S/7 26.
37. Yehoshua Heschel Farbstein at the JAE, 14 July 1933, CZA.
38. Arthur Ruppin and Yehuda Leib Fischman at the JAE, 29 Nov. 1936, CZA.
39. Werner Senator and Yitzhak Gruenbaum at the JAE, 29 Nov. 1936.
40. Yitzhak Gruenbaum at the JAE, 22 March 1936, CZA.
41. Immigration Department to the Palestine offices, 1 Nov. 1938, CZA, S/7 790.
42. Immigration Department to the Palestine offices, 28 Nov. 1934, CZA, S/7 149.
43. "Wieviel Kostet ein Haushalt in Palästina?" (unsigned), *Jüdische Rundschau* (Berlin), 28 April 1933, p. 169; Moshe Beilinson, "Haushaltskosten in Palästina," *Jüdische Rundschau*, 30 May 1933, p. 7. Erel, *Yekkes*, pp. 149 ff.; Margarete Turnowsky-Pinner, *Die zweite Generation mitteleuropäischer Siedler in Israel* (Tübingen: J. C. B. Mohr, Paul Siebeck, 1962), pp. 48 ff.; Getter, "Immigration from Germany," p. 126; Aharon Kedar, "The German Immigration as an Apolitical Opposition in the Kibbutz Movement During the Fifth Aliya," *Kathedra* 16 (July 1980), pp. 137 ff.; Gelber, *New Homeland*, pp. 317 ff.
44. "Wieviel Kostet?"; Beilinson, "Haushaltskosten," p. 7.
45. "This Country's Diseases," *YHOG*, special issue, June 1936.
46. Survey by Dr. P. Lander, 30 Nov. 1933; P. Karmeli to Kibbutz Givat Hashlosha, 13 Sept. 1934, CZA, S/7 83, and others.
47. Belling, *Deutschen Einwanderer*, p. 87.
48. Doron Niderland, "The Influence of Immigrant Doctors from Germany on the Development of Israeli Medicine, 1948–1933," diss., Hebrew University, 1982, p. 24.
49. Hermann Zondek, *Auf Festem Fusse, Errinerungen eines Jüdischen Klinikers* (Stuttgart: Deutsche Verlagsanstalt 1973), pp. 163 ff.
50. Niderland, pp. 77 ff.
51. Ruth Bondi, *Shiba* (Tel Aviv: Zmora Bitan Modan, 1981), p. 91.
52. Max Kreutzberger (Central European Immigrants' Association), memo, Nov. 1941, CZA, S/7 2105.
53. Kedar, "German Immigration," p. 140; German Immigrants' Association, Report of a Visit to Petah Tikvah, 9 May 1934; Moshe Brechman to

A. Levi, 27 Sept. 1934, CZA, S/7 83, and others; lecture by Moshe Brechman at a meeting of the German Immigrants' Association, 24 Jan. 1935, CZA, S/7 118.

54. Zionist Organization Executive, *The 19th Zionist Congress: Stenographic Report* (Tel Aviv: Dvir, 1937), p. 333.

55. Menahem Ussishkin at Central Council for the Supremacy of Hebrew, Sept. 1941, CZA S/7 2081.

56. A. Beilin, "Our Yekkes," *Davar*, 12 Sept. 1941, p. 2.

57. M. Y. Ben-Gavriel, "Ein Wort an die Einwanderer aus Deutschland," *Jüdische Rundschau*, 12 Sept. 1933, p. 511; David Ben-Gurion at a study day for western European immigrant activists, Kfar Yedidya, 6 Nov. 1943 (response to the debaters, p. 6), LPA, 15/43.

58. "German Jewry and the Yishuv" (unsigned), *YHOG*, 10 March 1939, p. 1.

59. Remarks by Y. Sandbank at the Hebrew Conference of German Immigrants, Tel Aviv, March 1935. German Immigrants' Association, "On the Question of Cultural Activity," pamphlet 3, 1935; Martin Buber, "Das Ende der deutsch-jüdischen Symbiose," *YHOG*, 10 March 1934, pp. 5 ff.

60. Ozer Ben-David, "German Jews in Palestine," *Davar*, 20 Aug. 1933, p. 3; Nagi Margalit-Auerbach, "Your Duty to the Immigrants," *Davar*, 9 Oct. 1933, p. 3.

61. Azriel Karlebach, "Winds That Blew," *Journalists' Yearbook* (Tel Aviv: Agudat Haitonaim, 1943), p. 89.

62. S. Bach, "German Jews in Palestine," *Davar*, 1 Sept. 1933, p. 7.

63. Avivi, "Zionism of the Heart and Zionism as a Career," *Haboker*, 20 Feb. 1941, p. 2.

64. Beilin, "Our Yekkes," p. 2.

65. Memos and correspondence on this subject in the CZA, S/7 464, and in S/7 614.

66. Various correspondence in the Tel Aviv Municipal Historical Archives, division 4, files 5/A (89) and 5/A (91).

67. Meir Dizengoff to Haim Bograshov, 20 Feb. 1934, Tel Aviv Municipal Historical Archives, division 4, file A/5 (89).

68. B. Krugliakov to Moshe Kaspi, 19 June 1944, Tel Aviv Municipal Historical Archives, division 4, file 5/A (91).

69. Minutes of the Central Council for the Supremacy of Hebrew, survey of the committee's activities, Heshvan-Av 5701 (1941), CZA, S/7 2081.

70. "An Unthinkable Act" (unsigned), *Haaretz*, 13 March 1939, p. 4; Robert Weltsch, "In the Matter of the *Jüdische Rundschau*," *Haaretz*, 14 March 1939, p. 3; "Declaration of the German Immigrants' Association and Austrian Immigrants' Association," *Haaretz*, 24 March 1939, p. 3.

71. Max Jacobson (Megged), "On the Question of the Foreign-Language Press," *Haaretz*, 9 March 1941, p. 2.

72. Minutes taken at a meeting between representatives of the Central Council

for the Supremacy of Hebrew and representatives of the German and Austrian Immigrants' Association, 20 March 1941, and accompanying documents; minutes from a meeting of the presidium of the Central Council for the Supremacy of Hebrew, 22 April 1941, CZA, S/7 2081.

73. Menahem Ussishkin at a meeting of the presidium of the Central Council for the Supremacy of Hebrew, 22 April 1941, CZA, S/7 2081.

74. Walter Preuss at study day for western European-born immigrant activists, Kfar Yedidya, 6 Nov. 1943, debate on the Ben-Gurion speech, p. 3 , LPA 15/43.

75. "They Are Killing Themselves" (unsigned), *YHOG*, Aug. 1939, I:16.

76. Beilin, "Our Yekkes."

77. Yeshayahu Wolfsberg, "The German Immigration and the Cultural Question," *YHOG*, 10 March 1939, p. 1.

78. "The Virtue of Tact in Public" (unsigned), *YHOG*, Oct. 1939, p. 12.

79. The German and Austrian Immigrants' Association, in cooperation with the Czechoslovakian Immigrants' Association and the religious association Emet Veemunah in Jerusalem, course offerings of the *beit midrash amami* for the summer of 1942; see also *YHOG*, special Hebrew-language issue, April 1935, I:6; "The Position of the German and Austrian Immigrants' Association," *Haaretz*, 9 March 1941, p. 3.

80. "The German Jews Are Guilty" (unsigned), *YHOG*, Oct. 1939, p. 12.

81. Gustav Krojanker, "J'accuse," *Haaretz*, 16 March 1941, p. 2; Gustav Krojanker, "Tolerance or Extremism?" *Haaretz*, 23 March 1941, p. 2.

82. Franz Eisenberg, "Zur methodik des Hebräischen," *YHOG*, 24 Jan. 1941, p. 2.

83. Alexander Zak, "Kampf um Hebräisch," *YHOG*, 24 Jan. 1941; Sonja Gottgetreu, "Zum Thema Jaecke," *YHOG*, 10 Oct. 1941, p. 4.

84. Remarks by Y. Sandbank at the Hebrew assembly of German immigrants, Tel Aviv, March 1935. German Immigrants' Association, "On the Question of Cultural Activity," pamphlet, no. 3, 1935.

85. Ernst Simon, "Deutsche Juden in Eretz Israel," *Jüdische Rundschau*, 10 March 1933, p. 97.

86. Joseph Marcus, "Tozereth Haaretz," *YHOG*, Feb. 1938, I:5; "You Will Eat Your Bread in Clamor" (unsigned), *YHOG*, Aug. 1939, II; G. Stulz, "The Hebrew Book and the German Immigrant," *YHOG*, Sept. 1936, I:16.

87. Wolfsberg, "German Immigration."

88. Georg Landauer to Moshe Shertok, 15 April 1934, CZA, S/7 83.

89. Krojanker, "J'accuse."

90. C. Z. Klötzel, "Das Antijeckentum," *YHOG*, 3 Oct. 1941, p. 6.

91. David Ben-Gurion at Kfar Yedidya, 6 Nov. 1943, response, p. 7, LPA, 15/43.

92. Gustav Krojanker, "Haavara: A Litmus Test for the Zionist Movement,"

German Immigrants' Association, pamphlet no. 4, 1936, pp. 4 ff.; "For the Haavara," *YHOG*, Nov. 1935, II:24.

93. "Aufruf!" (unsigned), *YHOG*, Dec. 1935, I:3.

94. Dan Horowitz and Moshe Lisak, *From Yishuv to State: The Jews of Palestine During the British Mandate as a Political Community* (Tel Aviv: Am Oved, 1977), p. 335.

95. David Ben-Gurion at Kfar Yedidya, 6 Nov. 1943 (esp. p. 8), and his response to the debaters (esp. p. 3), LPA, 15/43; S. Goralik, "Because of Zionism or Because of the Tribulation?" *Haaretz*, 29 Dec. 1939, p. 2; "Sünden gegen den Einwanderer" (unsigned), *YHOG*, 28 Feb. 1941, p. 2.

96. "Jüdische Vornamen-Wichtig für deutsche Staatsangehörige im Ausland," *YHOG*, No. 5, 1938, pp. 10 ff.; Fritz Stein to the German consulate in Jerusalem, 6 Nov. 1938, NA, P/1080/500.

97. "The Authority and the Individual" (unsigned), *YHOG*, Aug. 1939, II:12.

98. David Ben-Gurion at Kfar Yedidya, 3 Nov. 1943, opening remarks, pp. 3 ff., LPA, 15/43.

99. Susan Lee Hattis, *The Bi-National Idea During Mandatory Times* (English) (Haifa: Shikmona, 1970).

100. *Mitteilungsblatt*, 8 Dec. 1944, p. 1.

101. Erich Goldstein to Felix Rosenblüth, 26 June 1947, CZA, J/18 44.

102. Felix Rosenblüth at a meeting of the Aliya Hadasha executive, 1 Jan. 1948, CZA, J/18 38.

103. Gustav Krojanker, "Segregation or a Living Bridge?" *Haaretz*, 20 July 1942, p. 2; "Wer ist der glehrige Hitler-Schüler?" (unsigned), *YHOG*, 14 Aug. 1942, p. 4.

104. Ruth Bondi, *Felix* (Tel Aviv: Zmora Bitan, 1990).

105. Georg Landauer to Felix Rosenblüth, 31 Jan. 1948, CZA, J/18 45; Pinhas F. Rosen, "Aus Erinnerungen an die Jahre 1939–1948," in Hans Trammer, ed., *In Zwei Welten* (Tel Aviv: Bitaon, n.d.), pp. 271 ff.

106. Shimon Kanowitz, "At the Change of the Generations," *Deot* (Hebrew edition of *YHOG*), May 1960, p. 5.

107. Georg Landauer to Martin Rosenblüt, 17 Nov. 1938; see also Erich Rot, memo on collection for ransoming Austrian and German prisoners, 25 Jan. 1939, CZA, S/7 756; Landauer to Kurt Blumenfeld, 26 Aug. 1941, CZA, S/7 913.

108. Landauer to Blumenfeld, 18 March 1943, CZA, S/7 2016.

PART II: HOLOCAUST: *It Was in the Papers*

3 "ROMMEL, ROMMEL, HOW ARE YOU?"

1. S. Goralik, "The Good Soldier and the Enlistment Poster," *Haaretz*, 13 Sept. 1939, p. 2.
2. Haviv Canaan, *Two Hundred Days of Fear* (Tel Aviv: Mol Art, 1974), p. 137.
3. Georg Landauer to Kurt Blumenfeld, 18 March 1943, CZA, S/7 2016.
4. David Horowitz, *The Development of the Israeli Economy* (Jerusalem: Bialik Institute, Dvir, 1948); Nadav Halevy, "The Economic Development of the Jewish Yishuv, 1917–1947," talking paper no. 7914 (Jerusalem: Falk Center, 1979).
5. Moshe Sharett at the JAE, 27 April 1941, CZA; Uri Brenner, ed., *Facing the Threat of a German Invasion of Palestine in the Years 1940–1942: Sources and Testimony* (Tel Aviv: Yad Tabenkin, 1984), p. 61 (Levi Eshkol).
6. Canaan, *Two Hundred Days*, p. 137.
7. Ibid., pp. 137, 139, 168, 209.
8. Moshe Sharett at the JAE, 8 June 1941, CZA.
9. Canaan, *Two Hundred Days*, p. 210 (India); Brenner, *Facing the Threat*, p. 25 (U.S.), pp. 47 ff. (plans for evacuating settlements); decisions of the JAE, 30 June 1942, CZA (evacuation).
10. Brenner, *Facing the Threat*, p. 38 (Aran), p. 40 (Yaari).
11. "Outlines for Peace Proposals" (unsigned, undated document), CZA, S/25 4752.
12. Werner Senator at the JAE, 30 June 1942, CZA; Dina Porat, *Trapped Leadership* (Tel Aviv: Am Oved, 1986), p. 57.
13. Yehuda Bauer, *Diplomacy and the Underground* (Tel Aviv: Sifriat Poalim, 1963), pp. 144 ff.; Brenner, *Facing the Threat*, pp. 58 ff., 138 ff.
14. Undated handwritten copy with note signed YBZ (Yitzhak Ben-Zvi?), CZA S25/4752; Moshe Sharett at the JAE, 5 July 1942, CZA; "Jewish-Arab Cooperation against the Germans," in Brenner, *Facing the Threat*, p. 178.
15. Moshe Shapira and Werner Senator at the JAE, 30 June 1942, CZA.
16. Brenner, *Facing the Threat*, pp. 29, 43, 36, 185; Natan Alterman, "The Night of the Siege" (in "The Joy of the Poor"), *Poems from Then* (Tel Aviv: Hakibbutz Hameuhad, 1972), p. 217.
17. Moshe Shapira and Werner Senator at the JAE, 30 June 1942, CZA.
18. Yitzhak Gruenbaum at the JAE, 30 June 1942, CZA.
19. Brenner, *Facing the Threat*, pp. 63, 176 ff.; Yoav Gelber (ed.), *"Masada": Defending Israel During the Second World War* (Tel Aviv: Bar-Ilan University, 1990).
20. "Outlines for Peace Proposals." It looks as if Moshe Sharett initialed this

document, to indicate that he had seen it. Another unsigned document, attached to this one, is dated 23 May 1941.

21. "Upon the Ringing of the Bells" (unsigned), *Hapoel Hatsair*, 10 May 1943, p. 1.
22. "Terror," *Davar*, 30 June 1942, p. 1.
23. "Martyrs," *Hatsofeh*, 18 March 1942, p. 3.
24. "A Horrible Report of Nazi Cruelty: Massive Numbers of Polish Jews Put to Death with Poison Gas," *Davar*, 8 Oct. 1942, p. 2.
25. "700,000 Jews Murdered So Far in Poland by the Nazis and the Fifth Column," *Davar*, 28 June 1942, p. 1.
26. "The Nazi Atrocity in Kharkov," "Great Football Victory for Maccabee Damascus," *Haaretz*, 13 Jan. 1942, p. 2.
27. Moshe Prager, "Six Million Jews and a Million Children in Danger," *Davar*, 30 Nov. 1942, p. 2; see also Shmuel Schnitzer on Israel Army Radio, in Yitzhak Goren and Tirtza Yuval, *The Past Reexamined*, transcript of a broadcast in the Yad Vashem Library.
28. "Half a Million Jews Exterminated in Romania?" *Davar*, 10 Aug. 1942, p. 1.
29. Elisheva Ayalon, "Palcor: The Story of the Jewish Agency's News Agency," *Kesher* (Tel Aviv) no. 4 (Nov. 1988), pp. 71 ff.
30. Jewish Agency announcement, *Haaretz*, 23 Nov. 1942, p. 1.
31. "The State of the Jews in Europe," JAE, 22 Nov. 1942.
32. Zeev Laqueur and Richard Breitman, *The Terrible Secret* (Tel Aviv: Schocken, 1981) and *Breaking the Silence* (Tel Aviv: Schocken, 1988).
33. Moshe Shapira, Eliezer Kaplan, and Dov Yosef at the JAE, 22 Nov. 1942, CZA.
34. Yoav Gelber, "The Hebrew Press in Palestine on the Extermination of European Jewry," Research Papers on the Holocaust and the Resistance, Second Series A (Tel Aviv: Hakibbutz Hameuhad, 1969), pp. 30 ff.; S. B. Beit-Zvi, *Post-Ugandan Zionism in the Crisis of the Holocaust* (Tel Aviv: Bronfman, 1977), pp. 37 ff.; Porat, *Trapped Leadership*, pp. 64 ff.; Yehiam Weitz, "Positions and Approaches in Mapai Regarding the Holocaust of European Jewry, 1939–1945," diss., Hebrew University of Jerusalem, 1988, pp. 81 ff.
35. "Deathblow to the Enemy at Stalingrad," *Haaretz*, 23 Nov. 1942, p. 1; "Big Victory for Russians at Stalingrad," *Davar*, 23 Nov. 1942, p. 1.
36. Berl Katznelson at the Histadrut convention, 19 April 1942, *Davar*, 22 April 1942, p. 1; see also *Katznelson's Works* (Tel Aviv: Mapai, 1950), V:53.
37. Yitzhak Gruenbaum, *In the Days of Destruction and Holocaust* (Tel Aviv: Haverim, 1946), p. 27 (first published in *Haolam*, 30 May 1940).
38. Lecture at a seminar for the Mapai Young Guard, 6 June 1944, in *Katznelson's Works*, XII:218.

39. Moshe Sikron, *Immigration to Israel 1948–1953* (Jerusalem: Falk Center, 1957), p. 19; A *Survey of Palestine* (Jerusalem: Government of Palestine, 1946), I:141.
40. Uri Zvi Greenberg, *The River Roads* (Tel Aviv: Schocken, 1968), p. 53.
41. "They Murdered Children," *Haaretz*, 21 Dec. 1942, p. 1, "The Clowns," ibid., p. 3; "The Voice of the Dying" (editorial), *Haaretz*, 21 March 1943, p. 2; Yehuda Bergman, "Crumbs for Purim," ibid.; "Purim in Mourning," *Haaretz*, 22 March 1943, p. 2; notice for student party, *Davar*, 10 March 1944, p. 4; "Pinocchio," *Davar* (afternoon edition), 4 Feb. 1942, p. 2.
42. Advertisement for "Kiwi," *Haaretz*, 17 Oct. 1943, p. 4; "The Way to Victory" advertisement, *Haaretz*, 21 Dec. 1942, p. 4; "Rommel, Rommel" advertisement, *Haaretz*, 31 Dec. 1942, p. 3.
43. Lecture, 6 June 1944, *Katznelson's Works*, XII:218.
44. Golda Meir at the Histadrut EC, 26 May 1943, LA.
45. B. Hacohen, "After the Declaration," *Hamashkif*, 25 Dec. 1942, p. 2.
46. B. Hacohen, "The Way They Look," *Hamashkif*, 11 Dec. 1942, p. 2; "After the Declaration"; "The Yishuv and Rescue Activities," *Hamashkif*, 24 March 1944, p. 2.
47. Gruenbaum, *Days of Destruction*, pp. 63, 67, 69, 131 ff.; "A Sensational Announcement from Y. Gruenbaum," *Haboker*, 7 Dec. 1942, p. 2; Eliahu Dobkin at the Mapai CC, 20 May 1942 ("Forbidden to publish"), LPA; Eliahu Dobkin at the Histadrut Council, 26 May 1942 ("We are required to keep silent"), p. 61, LA; Yosef Sprinzak at the secretariat of the Histadrut EC, 11 Feb. 1943 (no publication of news of the Jewish police, for fear of embarrassment and "political repercussions"), LA; diary of Dov Yosef, 26 Nov. 1942, CZA, S/25 1510.
48. David Ben-Gurion at a gathering of Mapai activists, 8 Dec. 1942, LPA, 3/6.
49. Eliahu Dobkin at the Mapai CC, 30 Nov. 1942, LPA.
50. Georg Landauer to Kurt Blumenfeld, 18 March 1943, CZA, S/7 2016.
51. Association of Cinema Owners to the Jewish Agency, 11 Nov. 1942, CZA, S/26 1513.
52. "To the People of Israel in Time of their Mourning and Anger," *Haaretz*, 17 Dec. 1942, p. 1.
53. George Bernard Shaw to the Writers' Association, 30 Sept. 1944, the Aviezer Yellin Archive on Jewish Education in Israel, Tel Aviv University, 5.153 (1932).
54. Dina Porat, " 'Al Domi': Israeli Intellectuals Facing the Holocaust, 1943–1945," *Hatsionut* 8 (Tel Aviv University and Hakibbutz Hameuhad, 1983), pp. 245 ff. The Al Domi files: Aviezer Yellin Archive on Jewish Education in Israel, Tel Aviv University, 5.153 (1932). Rabbi Benyamin episode: editorial, *Haaretz*, 6 June 1944, p. 2; "Why I Lost My Temper," 9 June 1944; editorial, 11 June 1944, p. 2; letters to the editor, 20 and 27 June 1944.

4 "HAPPY IS THE MATCH"

1. Dina Porat, *Trapped Leadership* (Tel Aviv: Am Oved, 1986), p. 308.
2. David Ben-Gurion at the Mapai CC, 12 Sept. 1939, LPA. 23/39.
3. Ben-Gurion at the Mapai CC, 24 Aug. 1943, LPA, 23/43.
4. Ben-Gurion at the Mapai CC, 12 Sept. 1939, LPA, 23/39; "Outlines of Zionist Policy," 15 Oct. 1941, CZA, Z/4 14632.
5. Moshe Sharett at the JAE, 30 June 1942, CZA.
6. Yoav Gelber, *The History of Volunteerism*, vol. III: *The Flagbearers* (Jerusalem: Yad Ben-Zvi, 1983).
7. Dalia Ofer, *Treading the Sea: Illegal Immigration During the Holocaust* (Jerusalem: Yad Ben-Zvi, 1988), pp. 470 ff.
8. Moshe Sharett, 4 Feb. 1940, *Political Diary* (Tel Aviv: Am Oved, 1979), V:19.
9. Yehiam Weitz, "Positions and Approaches in Mapai Regarding the Holocaust of European Jewry, 1939–1945," diss., Hebrew University of Jerusalem, 1988, pp. 105 ff.
10. Eliahu Golomb at the Mapai PC, 26 Jan. 1944, LPA, 26/44.
11. David Ben-Gurion at the JAE, 12 Sept. 1943, CZA.
12. Mania Shochat at the Mapai CC, 28 Jan. 1942, LPA, 23/42; Ben-Gurion at the JAE, 29 Nov. 1942, CZA.
13. Porat, *Trapped Leadership*, pp. 413 ff.; Yoel Palgi, *A Great Wind Comes* (Tel Aviv: Am Oved, 1978), p. 17.
14. Porat, *Trapped Leadership*, p. 416; Weitz, "Positions and Approaches," pp. 125 ff.
15. *Hannah Senesh: Her Life, Mission, and Death* (Tel Aviv: Hakibbutz Hameuhad, 1959), p. 224.
16. Haike Grossman, "Forty Years Later," *Yalkut Moreshet* 39 (May 1985), p. 90.
17. Haim Hermesh, *The Amsterdam Operation* (Tel Aviv: Maarahot, 1971), pp. 155 ff.
18. Palgi, *Great Wind*, pp. 25, 243.
19. Berl Katznelson at the Histadrut EC, 29 Nov. 1939, LA.
20. Teddy Kollek, *One Jerusalem* (Tel Aviv: Maariv, 1979), pp. 56, 59.
21. Porat, *Trapped Leadership*, p. 263. See also Zeev Venya Hadari, *Against All Odds: Istanbul 1942–1945* (Tel Aviv: Ministry of Defense, 1992).
22. Report of the Rescue Committee, submitted to the 22nd Zionist Congress, Dec. 1946, pub. by the Jewish Agency, 1946; Arieh Morgenstern, "The United Rescue Committee of the Jewish Agency and Its Activity in the Years 1943–1945," *Yalkut Moreshet* 13, June 1971, pp. 60 ff.; Benyamin Mintz to Yitzhak Gruenbaum, 23 Sept. 1943, CZA S/46 280.
23. Report of conversation in the Gruenbaum house with Consul Lowell Pinkerton, 7 June 1944, CZA, S/26 1232; Porat, *Trapped Leadership*, pp. 392 ff.

24. Yitzhak Gruenbaum to Leib Yafeh, 22 May 1944, CZA S/26 1232; Gruenbaum at the Zionist EC, 18 Jan. 1943, CZA, S/25 1851; Gruenbaum, *Days of Destruction*, p. 68.

25. Ofer, *Treading the Sea*, pp. 212, 255; Porat, *Trapped Leadership*, pp. 302, 258.

26. Porat, *Trapped Leadership*, pp. 309 ff.; Efraim Ofir, "Was It Possible to Rescue 70,000 Jews from Transnistria?" *Yalkut Moreshet* 33 (June 1982), pp. 103 ff.; Hava Wagman-Eshkoly, "The Transnistria Opportunity for Rescue or Deception?" *Yalkut Moreshet* 27 (April 1979), pp. 155 ff.

27. Ben-Gurion at the Mapai secretariat, 10 Feb. 1943, LPA, 24/43; see also Hannah Turuk-Yablonka, "The Europa Plan," diss., Hebrew University of Jerusalem, 1984.

28. Porat, *Trapped Leadership*, pp. 328 ff. Avraham Fuchs, *I Called and There Was No Answer* (Jerusalem: Hamehaber, 1985).

29. Moshe Sharett at the JAE, 20 Oct. 1944, CZA. The description of the episode is based primarily on Porat, *Trapped Leadership*, pp. 347 ff.; Yehuda Bauer, "Joel Brand's Mission," *Yalkut Moreshet* 26 (Nov. 1978), pp. 23 ff.; Amos Elon, *Zero Hour* (Idanim, 1980).

30. Yitzhak Gruenbaum, David Ben-Gurion, and Eliahu Dobkin at the JAE, 25 May 1944, CZA.

31. Eliezer Kaplan at the JAE, 23 July 1944, CZA.

32. Eliahu Dobkin at the secretariat of the Histadrut EC, 11 Oct. 1944, LA; Yehuda Bauer, "The Negotiations between Sally Meyer and SS Representatives, 1944–1945," from *Rescue Attempts and Activities during the Holocaust* (Jerusalem: Yad Vashem, 1976), pp. 11 ff.

33. *Attorney General vs. Adolf Eichmann, Verdict and Sentence* (Jerusalem: Merkaz Hahasbara, 1972), 1962, p. 133.

34. Heinrich Himmler, Vermerk 10, Dec. 1942, Bundesarchiv Koblenz Bestand, Schumacher 240/I (copy in the Moreshet Archive, D. I 5753).

5 ''A WARM JEWISH HEART''

1. Shabtai Teveth, *The Burning Ground*, vol. III of *The Lamentations of David* (Tel Aviv: Schocken, 1987), p. 444.

2. David Ben-Gurion at the JAE, 6 Dec. 1942.

3. Theodor Herzl, *The Jewish State* (Tel Aviv: Yediot Aharonot, 1978), p. 22.

4. Moshe Sharett at the Zionist EC, 18 April 1943, CZA, S/25 1851.

5. Yitzhak Damiel-Shweiger, "And Return," *Davar*, 27 Nov. 1942, p. 3.

6. David Ben-Gurion at a gathering of Mapai workers, 8 Dec. 1942, LPA, 3/6.

7. Teveth, *Burning Ground*, p. 444; S. B. Beit-Zvi, *Post-Ugandan Zionism in the Crisis of the Holocaust* (Tel Aviv: Bronfman, 1977), p. 130; Reuven

Dafni, ed., *David Ben-Gurion and the Holocaust of European Jewry* (Jerusalem: Yad Vashem and Merkaz Hahasbara, 1987); see also Avihu Ronen, "Halinka's Mission," *Yalkut Moreshet* 42 (Dec. 1986), pp. 55 ff.; Tuvia Friling, "The Emotional Components of David Ben-Gurion's Attitude toward the Jews of the Diaspora during the Holocaust," reprint from the collection *Jewish National Solidarity in the New Era* (Beersheva: Ben-Gurion University, 1988).

 8. David Ben-Gurion at a gathering of Mapai activists, 8 Dec. 1942, LPA; Ben-Gurion to Arthur Lurie, 8 Dec. 1942, quoted in Yoav Gelber, "Zionist Policy and the Fate of European Jewry, 1939–1942," Yad Vashem, *Collected Research* 13 (1980), p. 147.

 9. Ben-Gurion to Yehoshua Kastner, 2 Feb. 1958, NA, PMO, 5432/16.

10. Diary of Dov Yosef, 26 Nov. 1942, CZA, S/25 1510.

11. Anita Shapira, *Berl* (Tel Aviv: Am Oved, 1980), p. 672.

12. Yitzhak Gruenbaum to the Rescue Committee, 29 June 1944, CZA, S/26 1238/a.

13. Apolinari Hartglass, "Comments on Aid and Rescue," undated memorandum, CZA, S/26 1232 (quoted with stylistic corrections).

14. David Ben-Gurion at the JAE, 23 July 1944.

15. B. Hacohen, "The Way They Look," *Hamashkif*, 11 Dec. 1942, p. 2.

16. Dina Porat, *Trapped Leadership* (Tel Aviv: Am Oved, 1986), pp. 450 ff.; Tuvia Friling, "Ben-Gurion's Positions in the Children's Rescue Episode, Nov. 1942–May 1945," *Yalkut Moreshet* 38, Dec. 1984, pp. 32 ff.

17. Y. Bahar to David Ben-Gurion, 23 July 1944, CZA, S/25 85.

18. Golda Meir at the secretariat of the Histadrut EC, 24 Jan. 1943, LA.

19. Yitzhak Gruenbaum and others at the Zionist EC, 18 Jan. 1943, CZA, S/25 1851; Gruenbaum, *Days of Destruction*, p. 68.

20. Gruenbaum and Eliezer Kaplan at the JAE, 25 Oct. 1942, CZA.

21. Porat, *Trapped Leadership*, pp. 169 ff.

22. Shmuel Dayan at the PC, 2 Nov. 1939, LPA, 23/39.

23. "A Terrible Report on the Cruelty of the Nazis," *Davar*, 8 Oct. 1942, p. 2.

24. P. Heilprin, "We Are Guilty," *Davar*, 24 Dec. 1941, p. 2; see also Y. Gan-Zvi, "The Yishuv's Position in the Troubles of the Big Brothers," 18 April 1940, p. 2; H. Rosenblum, "Whence the Apathy?" *Haboker*, 2 July 1941, p. 2.

25. "We did not notice": Yosef Sprinzak at the JAE, 6 Dec. 1942, CZA. "We have done nothing": Melech Neustadt at the Histadrut Council, 26 May 1942, LA, and Histadrut EC, 13 Dec. 1942, LA; "Did We Do Enough?" *Haaretz*, editorial, 29 Nov. 1942, p. 2. "*Davar* didn't publish": Eliahu Dobkin at the Histadrut EC, 31 Dec. 1942, LA. "No one has any doubt": David Remez, ibid. "Full of sin": Aharon Tzisling at the secretariat of the Histadrut EC, 11 Feb. 1943, LA; Beba Idelson at the Histadrut EC,

18 Nov. 1943, LA. "Shame": Golda Meir at the secretariat of the Histadrut EC, 29 April 1943, LA.

26. "Cooperation with the British during the War," report by Reuven Shiloah (Zaslani), CZA, S/25 7902.

27. Nana Sagi, *German Reparations* (English) (Jerusalem: Magnes Press, 1980), pp. 14 ff.; Anita Shapira, *Berl*, p. 604.

28. "Justicia" to the Jewish Agency, 7 Dec. 1942, CZA, S/26 1325. See also memoranda on reparations (1941 onward): CZA, S/26 1325; S/25 5188; S/90 526; S/90 527; Eliahu Dobkin at the JAE, 6 Dec. 1942, CZA; Gershom Bendam, "What Will Be the Future of the Jews of Europe?" *Haaretz*, 30 Jan. 1942, p. 2; "Is Anyone Giving Thought to the Stolen Property of European Jewry?" (unsigned), *Haaretz*, 20 Jan. 1943, p. 2; M. Rubenstein, "What about Property Stolen from Jews?" *Haaretz*, 14 March 1943, p. 2; Siegfried Moses, "The Jews' Reparation Claim," *Haaretz*, 21 June 1943, 19 Oct. 1943, p. 2, and 10 Feb. 1944, p. 2; Natan Feinberg, "The Reparations Claim of the German Jews," *Haaretz*, 7 Sept. 1943, p. 2, 4 Jan. 1944, p. 2; Ben-Gurion in Weitz, "Positions and Approaches," p. 317.

29. Shenhabi's proposal (10 Sept. 1942) in the Hashomer Hatsair-Kibbutz Haartsi Archives (Shenhabi personal archive), VI 1 (4); Shenhabi Plan (2 May 1945) in CZA, S/26 1326, as well as the YVA ("The Old Yad Vashem"), YV/9–YV/10.

30. *Haaretz*, 2 Dec. 1942, p. 1 (Lamentations); *Davar*, 6 Nov. 1943, p. 1 ("Cry, Jerusalem"); *Davar*, 17 Dec. 1942, p. 1 ("The Vale of Murder"); *Davar*, 14 Jan. 1943, p. 1 ("The Vale of Sorrow"); *Haaretz*, 2 Dec. 1942, p. 2 ("The Valley of Weeping"); *Davar*, 31 Dec. 1942, p. 1 ("How has she been left exiled and penniless"); *Davar*, 22 Dec. 1942, p. 1 ("Satan's plot").

31. Moshe Sharett and David Ben-Gurion at the Mapai CC, 7 Dec. 1938, LPA.

32. Ben-Gurion at the JAE, 26 Oct. 1943, CZA.

33. Chaim Weizmann at the JAE, 22 Oct. 1942, in Michael J. Cohen, ed., *The Letters and Papers of Chaim Weizmann*, vol. XX, series A (Jerusalem: Israel Universities Press, 1979), pp. 67 ff.

34. Advertisement, *Davar*, 7 May 1944, p. 4.

35. "How the Revisionists Behaved in the Enlistment Collection Drive" (unsigned), *Davar*, 13 March 1944, p. 1; B. Hacohen, "The Yishuv and the Rescue Operations," *Hamashkif*, 24 March 1944, p. 2.

36. "Yes, Rescue Is Possible" (unsigned), *Herut*, 1 Feb. 1943, p. 2.

37. Eliezer Don-Yehia, "Cooperation and Conflict between Political Camps: The Religious Camp and the Labor Movement and the Crisis of Education in Israel," diss., Hebrew University of Jerusalem, 1977, pp. 499 ff.; Ernst Simon, "The Theory of Zionist Education in Light of the Question of the

Tehran Children," *Haaretz*, 5 July 1943, p. 2, and 6 July 1943, p. 2; M. Shenfeld, "The Tehran Children Accuse" (Jerusalem: Agudat Yisrael EC, 1943); *Tsror Mihtavim*, 135 (200), 30 April 1943, pp. 248 ff., 136 (201), 14 May 1943, pp. 266 ff., 137 (202), 4 June 1943, pp. 292 ff.; Ben-Zion Tomer, *Red and White and the Smell of the Oranges* (Jerusalem: Hasifria Hatsionit, 1971).

38. "Ugly Repercussions of the Immigration of the Tehran Children," *Haaretz*, 14 March 1943, p. 6.

39. "What the Tehran Children Can Teach Us," *Haaretz*, 22 March 1943, p. 2.

40. Eliahu Dobkin, David Remez, and Golda Meir at the Mapai CC, 20 May 1942, LPA, 23/42.

41. Secretariat of the Histadrut EC, 29 April 1943, LA.

42. Benyamin Mintz to Yitzhak Gruenbaum, 23 Sept. 1943, CZA, S/26 280.

43. Ibid.

44. Report on the Package Operation, 2 March 1944, CZA, S/25 5649. See also Arieh Morgenstern, "The United Rescue Committee of the Jewish Agency and Its Activity in the Years 1943–1945," *Yalkut Moreshet* 13, June 1971, pp. 60 ff.; Hava Wagman-Eshkoly, "The Dispute over the Collection of Funds for Rescue Activities," 1943, Leni Yehiel et al., eds., *Papers for the Study of the Holocaust Period*, Collection 3 (Tel Aviv: Hakibbutz Hameuhad, 1984), pp. 123 ff.

45. Avraham Woronowski, "Our Children's Reaction to the Holocaust in the Diaspora," *Hed Hahinuch* 258 (1945), p. 34; response from Gustav Krojanker, "Our Children's Reaction to the Holocaust in the Diaspora," *Amudim*, 16 Feb. 1945, p. 1.

46. Berl Katznelson, "After a Conversation on the Diaspora," 6 June 1944, *Works of Katznelson* (Tel Aviv: Mapai, 1950), XII:218; Yehiam Weitz, "The Yishuv's Self-Image and the Reality of the Holocaust" (English), *Jerusalem Quarterly*, Fall 1988, pp. 1 ff.

47. Yitzhak Gruenbaum at the Zionist EC, 18 Jan. 1943, CZA, S/25 1851.

48. "Why Don't the Jews of Hungary Defend Themselves?" *Davar*, 22 June 1944, p. 1.

49. Y. Gan-Zvi, "On Slaughter and Silence," *Hatsofeh*, 18 Jan. 1942, p. 2.

50. Haim Nahman Bialik, "In the City of Slaughter," *Collected Works* (Tel Aviv: Dvir, 1941), p. 83.

51. Abba Kovner, Declaration read at a pioneering youth rally in Vilna, 1 Jan. 1942, in Yitzhak Arad, ed., *The Holocaust Documented* (Jerusalem: Yad Vashem, 1978), pp. 544 ff.; Gustav Krojanker, "And the Crooked Was Set Straight," *Haaretz*, 1 Jan. 1942, p. 2.

52. "To the People of Israel," *Davar*, 17 Dec. 1942, p. 1; announcement of the Vaad Leumi, "The Cry of Israel from Zion," 30 Nov. 1942, CZA, S/25 5183.

53. Haim Barlas, "Report on the Activities in Turkey Concerning Immigration and Rescue, Oct. 1943–Sept. 1944," CZA, S/25 5206; Zeev Schind at the Histadrut EC, 6 Sept. 1944, LA.
54. Uri Keisari, "We Have Mourned and Now We May Go On," *Yediot Aharonot*, 16 March 1945, p. 2.

PART III: ISRAEL: *The Last Jews*

6 "AT FIRST I THOUGHT THEY WERE ANIMALS"

1. David Ben-Gurion at the JAE, 28 Sept. 1944, CZA.
2. David Ben-Gurion, "Eternal Israel," *Government Yearbook 1954* (Jerusalem: GPO, 1954), p. 37.
3. Ben-Gurion at the JAE, 11 Feb. 1945, CZA.
4. Ben-Gurion at the JAE, 20 June 1944, CZA.
5. Ben-Gurion, Y. L. Fishman, Yitzhak Gruenbaum, and Moshe Shapira at the JAE, 20 June 1944, CZA.
6. Ben-Gurion at the JAE, 20 June 1944, CZA.
7. BGD, 4 Dec. 1944.
8. BGD, 8 May 1945.
9. BGD, 30 July 1945.
10. BGD, 19 Oct. 1945, 23 Oct. 1945, 26 Oct. 1945, 27 Oct. 1945.
11. Testimony of Ruth Aliav, BGA, DOD, p. 53.
12. Ben-Zion Yisraeli at the Mapai secretariat, 24 July 1945, LPA, 24/45.
13. Yehezkel Sakharov, 3 Oct. 1945, CZA, S/25 5243; Sakharov to Dov Yosef, 9 Oct. 1945, CZA, S/25 5238; Yehiel Duvdevani to Eliahu Dobkin, 5 Sept. 1945, CZA, S/26 1198.
14. Yoav Gelber, *History of Volunteerism* (Jerusalem: Yad Ben-Zvi, 1988), III:376; Yehuda Bauer, *The Briha* (Tel Aviv: Moreshet and Sifriat Poalim, 1974), pp. 80 ff.
15. Hoter-Yishai report (July 1945), LA, VII 126 69.
16. Aliav testimony, p. 61.
17. N. Silberblatt, "The Camp Residents Are Losing Patience," *Haaretz*, 6 Aug. 1947, p. 2.
18. Yosef Bankover at the Histadrut EC, 5 Sept. 1945, LA.
19. Eliahu Dobkin at the Mapai CC, 29 April 1946, LPA, 23/46; at the Histadrut EC, 5 Sept. 1945, LA, JAE, 30 April 1946, CZA.
20. Yitzhak Laufban, "In the Shadow of the Swastika," *Hapoel Hatsair*, 21 March 1933, p. 1; Chaim Weizmann at the 20th Zionist Congress, stenographic report, Zionist Organization and Jewish Agency, 1937, p. 33; see also Dalia Ofer, "From Survivors to Immigrants: The Remnant Facing Immigration," in Yisrael Gutman and Adira Drechsler, eds.,

Sheerit Hapletah, 1947–48 (Jerusalem: Yad Vashem, 1990), pp. 375 ff.; Hannah Turuk Yablonka, "The Absorption and Integration Problems of the Remnants in Israeli Society in Formation: 29 Nov. 1947 to the end of 1949," diss., Hebrew University, 1990, p. 1.

21. Soldier's letter, quoted by Gelber, *History of Volunteerism*, III:434, 449; Eliahu Dobkin at the Mapai CC, 29 April 1946, LPA, 23/46; Haim Yahil, "The Actions of the Mission to the Survivors, 1945–1949," *Yalkut Moreshet* 30 and 31 (Nov. 1980 and April 1981), pp. 135, 172.

22. Yahil, "Actions of the Mission," p. 31; Yablonka, "Absorption and Integration," p. 21.

23. Yael Danieli, "The Heterogeneity of Postwar Adaptation in Families of Holocaust Survivors," in Randolph L. Braham, ed., *The Psychological Perspectives of the Holocaust and of Its Aftermath* (Boulder: East European Quarterly, 1988), pp. 109 ff.

24. Testimony of Sammy Levi, Hebrew University, Institute of Contemporary Judaism, DOD, 14(4), p. 25.

25. Eliahu Dobkin at the Mapai CC, 29 April 1946, LPA, 23/46.

26. Yahil, "Actions of the Mission," pp. 7–40, 135, 140, 174.

27. David Shaltiel at the Mapai CC, 11 Sept. 1945, LPA, 24/45.

28. Zeev Iserson at the Mapai CC, 11 Sept. 1945, LPA, 24/45.

29. David Ben-Gurion at the Mapai CC, 22–23 July 1949, LPA, 24/49; on "the natural selection" during the Holocaust, see also Eliahu Dobkin, *Immigration and Rescue during the Holocaust Years* (Reuven Mass, 1946), p. 114.

30. Arieh Gelblum, "Fundamental Problems of Immigrant Absorption," *Haaretz*, 28 Sept. 1945, p. 3.

31. Yahil, "Actions of the Mission," p. 11.

32. Aliav testimony, p. 55.

33. BGD, 20 Oct. 1945; 26 Oct. 1945; David Ben-Gurion at the JAE, 21 Nov. 1945, CZA.

34. Ben-Gurion at the JAE, 24 Feb. 1946, CZA.

35. Eliahu Dobkin at the JAE, 21 Sept. 1944, CZA; Shaul Meirov Avigur at the Mapai secretariat, 24 Dec. 1944, LPA, 24/44.

36. Aharon Hoter-Yishai in Bauer, *Briha*, p. 102.

37. Yehiam Weitz, "Positions and Approaches in Mapai Regarding the Holocaust of European Jewry, 1939–1945," diss., Hebrew University of Jerusalem, 1988, p. 58.

38. Eliahu Golomb at the Mapai PC, 26 Jan. 1944, LPA, 24/44; Pinhas Lubianiker at the Histadrut EC, 5 Sept. 1945, LA; on a "great holocaust," see also Yonah Kosoi at the Mapai CC, 14 Aug. 1945, LPA, 23/45.

39. David Ben-Gurion at the JAE, 24 Feb. 1946, CZA.

40. Shaul Meirov Avigur at the Mapai secretariat, 3 May 1943, LPA, 24/43; also Weitz, "Positions and Approaches," pp. 56 ff.

41. Dobkin, *Immigration and Rescue*, pp. 61 ff.
42. David Ben-Gurion at the JAE, 11 Feb. 1945, CZA; Weitz, "Positions and Approaches," pp. 139 ff.
43. Eliahu Dobkin at the Mapai secretariat, 24 Nov. 1942, LPA, 24/42.
44. David Ben-Gurion at the Mapai CC, 24 Feb. 1943, LPA, 23/43.
45. Moshe Shapira at the JAE, 20 June 1944; Yaakov Zerubavel at the JAE, 2 Nov. 1948, CZA.
46. Eliezer Kaplan at the JAE, 19 Aug. 1949, CZA.
47. Yitzhak Refael at the JAE, 19 Aug. 1949, CZA.

7   "A CERTAIN DISTANCE"

1. Yoav Gelber, *History of Volunteerism* (Jerusalem: Yad Ben-Zvi, 1988), III:357.
2. "The Jewish Diaspora in 1946," lecture by Leib Levite to the council of the Ahdut Haavoda-Poalei Zion party, *Davar*, 4 Feb. 1947, p. 2.
3. Eliahu Dobkin at the JAE, 30 April 1946, CZA.
4. Yehuda Bauer, *The Briha* (Tel Aviv: Moreshet and Sifriat Poalim, 1974), pp. 82 ff.; Irit Keinan, "The Remnants: Olim or Immigrants?" *Iyunim* 1 (1991), p. 343 ff.; Tad Szulc, *The Secret Alliance: The Extraordinary Story of the Rescue of the Jews Since World War II* (New York: Farrar, Straus and Giroux, 1991).
5. Arieh Pialkov, ed., *Seminar on Yehuda Bauer's "The Briha"* (Tel Aviv: Yad Tabenkin, 1975), p. 61.
6. Bauer, *Briha*, p. 122.
7. Haim Yahil, "The Actions of the Mission to the Survivors, 1945–1949," *Yalkut Moreshet* 30 and 31 (Nov. 1980 and April 1981), p. 36.
8. Gelber, *History of Volunteerism*, III:534.
9. Testimony of Eliezer Lidowski, Hebrew University, Institute of Contemporary Judaism, DOD, 62 (4).
10. Testimony of Dov Gur (Robert Grossman), Haganah Archives, 2302.
11. Karmi Ptael, ed., *The Doubles* (Jerusalem: Mossad Bialik, 1990); Gelber, *History of Volunteerism*, III:666.
12. Aliav testimony, p. 34.
13. Yahil, "Actions of the Mission," p. 169.
14. Ibid.
15. Eliahu Dobkin at the JAE, 21 Sept. 1944; David Ben-Gurion at the JAE, 17 Dec. 1944; Ben-Gurion and Nahum Goldmann at the JAE, 27 Oct. 1944, CZA; BGD, 1 Nov. 1945.
16. Aviva Halamish, *Exodus: The Real Story* (Tel Aviv: Am Oved, 1990), pp. 69 ff.
17. David Ben-Gurion at the JAE, 21 Nov. 1945, CZA.

18. Natan Alterman, "The Nation and Its Agent," *The Seventh Column* (Tel Aviv: Hakibbutz Hameuhad, 1977), I:85.

19. Golda Meir, *My Life* (Tel Aviv: Maariv, 1975), p. 152; Halamish, *Exodus*.

20. Aviva Halamish, "Haapala: Values, Myth, and Reality," in Nurit Gretz, ed., *Vantage Point* (Tel Aviv: Open University, 1988), p. 93; see also Anita Shapira, ed., *Haapala: A Collection on the History of Rescue, the Briha, the Haapala, and the Remnants* (Tel Aviv: Am Oved, 1990).

21. Idit Zertal, "Lost Souls: The Maapilim and the Mossad Lealiya Bet in the Struggle to Establish the State and Thereafter," *Hatsionut* 14 (Aug. 1989), pp. 107 ff.

22. Shaul Avigur, Yeshayahu Trachtenberg (Shaike Dan), and David Ben-Gurion at the Mapai secretariat, 9 Dec. 1947, LPA, 24/47; Gedalia Yogev, ed., *State and Diplomatic Documents, Dec. 1947-May 1948* (Jerusalem: National Archive, 1980), p. 19; Zeev Venya Hadari, *Refugees, Defeat, and Empire* (Tel Aviv, Hakibbutz Hameuhad), pp. 195 ff.

23. Eliahu Dobkin at the Mapai CC, 29 April 1946, LPA, 23/46.

24. Weitz, "Positions and Approaches," pp. 177 ff.

25. Yehiel Duvdevani at the Mapai secretariat, 15 Jan. 1946, LPA, 24/46.

26. Pinhas Lubianiker (quoting a telegram from Mordecai Oren) at the Histadrut EC, 5 Sept. 1945, LA; David Ben-Gurion to his wife (attached to the diary), 9 Feb. 1946.

27. Lubianiker at the Mapai secretariat, 27 Aug. 1946, LPA, 24/46.

28. Golda Meir at the JAE, 28 July 1947, CZA.

29. Yahil, "Actions of the Mission," pp. 156 ff.; Levi testimony, pp. 27 ff.; "Why Did They Kill Eitan Avidov?" *Koteret Rashit* 164 (21 Jan. 1986), p. 9.

30. Zeev Mankowitz, "Ideology and Politics Among the Remnants in the American Occupation Zone in Germany 1945–1946," diss., Hebrew University, 1987; David Shaari, *The Cyprus Deportation, 1946–1949* (Jerusalem: Hasifria Hatsionit, 1981), pp. 274 ff.; Nahum Bogner, *The Deportation Island* (Tel Aviv: Am Oved, 1991).

31. Yahil, "Actions of the Mission," pp. 21, 40.

32. Shaari, pp. 274 ff.

33. Yahil, "Actions of the Mission," p. 175.

8 "SIX MILLION GERMANS"

1. Yehuda Bauer, *The Briha* (Tel Aviv: Moreshet and Sifriat Poalim, 1974), p. 16.

2. Testimony of Abba Kovner, Hebrew University, Institute of Contemporary Judaism, DOD 2 (4) A; See also Levi Arieh Sarid, "Revenge: History, Image, and Activity," *Yalkut Moreshet* 32 (April 1992), pp. 35 ff.

3. Eliahu Dobkin at the Histadrut secretariat, 11 Oct. 1944, p. 8, LA,

24/44; see also Dobkin, *Immigration and Rescue during the Holocaust Years* (Reuven Mass, 1946), p. 114.

4. Unpublished study of Aliyat Hanoar graduates. I wish to thank Professor Reuven Feurstein, Dr. Yaakov Rand, and Ms. Ada Oz of the Hadassah-WIZO Canada Research Institute (founded by Aliyat Hanoar) for having kindly agreed to make the results of the study available to me.

5. Tzivia Lubetkin, *The Last on the Walls* (remarks to the 15th convention of Hakibbutz Hameuhad at Kibbutz Yagur, 8 June 1946) (Tel Aviv: Hakibbutz Hameuhad, 1947), p. 46.

6. Testimony of Yitzhak Avidov (formerly Pasha Reichman), Hebrew University, the Institute for Contemporary Judaism, DOD, 160 (4).

7. Testimony of Abba Kovner, Moreshet Archive, 1062 A, p. 46; Avidov testimony.

8. Avidov testimony.

9. Kovner testimony, Hebrew University.

10. Abba Kovner at the Histadrut CC, 19 Aug. 1945, LA.

11. Meir Yaari to Yehuda Tubin, 24 July 1945; letter from London, 21 Aug. 1945, Yaari Archive, Hashomer Hatsair Archives, B-2 (5a); Yaari to Tubin, 15 Jan. 1946; Yaari to Moshe Zertal, 12 Feb. 1946, Yaari Archives, B-2 (5); Anita Shapira, "The Yishuv's Encounter with the Remnant," *Walking on the Horizon* (Tel Aviv: Am Oved, 1989), pp. 325 ff.; Anita Shapira, "The Yishuv's Encounter with the Remnant," in Gutman and Drechsler, *Sheerit Hapletah*, pp. 71 ff.; see also Meir Yaari's reaction ("Nonsense and Lies"), *Koteret Rashit* 151 (23 Oct. 1985), p. 24; Kovner testimony, Moreshet Archive.

12. Kovner testimony, Hebrew University, Moreshet Archive, and Haapala project of Tel Aviv University. Internal cables on his arrest: to "Artzi" from "Sidney," 18 Dec. 1945; to "Kasuto" from "Artzi," 25 Dec. 1945; to "Ben-Yehuda" from "Kasuto," 25 Dec. 1945, all in the Haganah Archive, 14/175; "Yaakobi" to "Haverim," 8 Jan. 1946, Haganah Archive, 100/14. Also see Yoav Gelber, *History of Volunteerism* (Jerusalem: Yad Ben-Zvi, 1988), III:639; Zeev Mankowitz, "Ideology and Politics Among the Remnants in the American Occupation Zone in Germany 1945–1946," diss., Hebrew University, 1987, p. 331; Mordecai Naor, *Laskov* (Tel Aviv: Misrad Habitahon and Keter, 1988), p. 148; Michael Bar-Zohar, *The Avengers* (Tel Aviv: Levin Epstein, 1969), pp. 47 ff.; Michael Elkins, *Forged in Fury* (New York: Ballantine, 1971), pp. 235 ff.; Chronologies 1945, Weizmann Archive.

13. Avidov testimony.

14. Tzvika Dror, "Pain and Shouting," *Davar*, 15 June 1990, p. 19; compare also with Yitzhak (Antek) Zuckerman, *Those Seven Years* (Tel Aviv: Hakibbutz Hameuhad and Beit Lohamei Hagetaot, 1990), pp. 530 ff.

15. "Poison Bread Fells 1900 German Captives in U.S. Prison Camp Near

Nuremberg," *New York Times*, 20 April 1946, p. 6; "Prison Plot Toll of Nazis at 2283," *New York Times*, 23 April 1946, p. 9.

16. Kovner testimony, Hebrew University.
17. Ibid.; see also Levi Arieh Sarid, "Kovner's Answer to His Provokers," *Yalkut Moreshet* 47 (Nov. 1989), pp. 7 ff.
18. Avidov testimony.
19. Testimony of Michael Ben-Gal, Hebrew University, Institute of Contemporary Judaism, DOD, 95 (4); Gelber, *History of Volunteerism*, III:432.
20. Hanoch Bartov, *Pimples* (Tel Aviv: Am Oved, 1965), p. 47.
21. Ms. on the brigade's future, undated, CZA, S/25 6064.
22. Gelber, *History of Volunteerism*, III:306 ff.
23. Testimony of Dov Gur (formerly Robert Grossman), Haganah Archive, 2302.
24. Yisrael Karmi, *Fighters' Way* (Tel Aviv: Sifriat Tarmil, 1966), p. 116.
25. Ibid.
26. Testimony of Shalom Giladi, Haganah Archive, 3947 (as published in *Haolam Hazeh*, 29 March 1961).
27. Kovner testimony, Hebrew University.
28. Ben-Gal testimony.
29. Testimony of Haim Laskov, Haganah Archive, 4357.
30. Quoted by Arieh Preiss, "The Reactions of the Underground Movements in Palestine to the Extermination of European Jewry," *Masua* 8 (April 1980), p. 56.
31. Unsigned poem, *Haaretz*, 30 Nov. 1942, p. 1; Natan Gurdus, "Let the World Cry Out!" *Haaretz*, 26 Nov. 1942, p. 2; "Revenging the Blood of Thy Servants," *Haaretz*, 2 Dec. 1942, p. 1; similarly in *Haboker*, 2 Dec. 1942, p. 1; Shlomo Z. Shragai, "The Demand for Revenge," *Hatsofeh*, 9 June 1942, p. 2.
32. Call of the CC of the Writers' Association, *Davar*, 26 Nov. 1942, p. 1.
33. Quoted by Preiss, "Reactions," p. 71.
34. Apolinari Hartglass, "Ways of Response and Rescue," *Haolam*, 27 Dec. 1942, p. 1; Moshe Kleinman, "The Problem of Revenge," *Haolam*, 31 Dec. 1942, p. 1; letter from M. A. Bodley, ibid., p. 3.
35. P. Heilprin, "There Will Be No Revenge," *Davar*, 18 June 1942, p. 2.
36. Unsigned editorial, "Destruction," *Haaretz*, 24 Nov. 1942, p. 2.
37. Unsigned item, *Mishmar*, 24 Oct. 1943, p. 4; see also Shlomo Ginzberg, "Peace without Revenge," *Moznaim* 16 (1943), pp. 273 ff. Response: "On Forgiving" (unsigned), *Haboker*, 1 Sept. 1943, p. 2; Azriel Karlebach, "To Me Belongs Vengeance and Recompense When Their Foot Stumbles," *Hatsofeh*, 16 Jan. 1942, p. 2.
38. Quoted in Sarid, "Revenge," p. 79.
39. Meir Argov, 30 June 1959, *KP*, XXVII:2395.

40. Rozka Korczak at the Kibbutz Haartsi EC, 3 Jan. 1945, Moreshet Archive, A 990.
41. Menahem Begin, 16 March 1965, *KP*, XLII:1544.

9 "A BARRIER OF BLOOD AND SILENCE"

1. Moshe Sikron, *Immigration to Israel from 1948 to 1953* (Jerusalem: Falk Center, 1957), p. 16.
2. Hannah Turuk Yablonka, "The Absorption and Integration Problems of the Remnants in Israeli Society in Formation: 29 Nov. 1947 to the end of 1949," diss., Hebrew University, 1990, p. 13.
3. Smadar Golan, "The Story of Michael Gilad," *Koteret Rashit* 204 (29 Oct. 1986), pp. 24 ff.; Tom Segev, "The 82nd Blow," *Haaretz*, 20 Nov. 1987, p. B5.
4. Yaakov Kurtz, *Book of Testimony* (Tel Aviv: Am Oved, 1943), p. 6.
5. Testimony of Miriam Akavia, videotaped (raw footage for the film *Return to Life*), preserved in the Diaspora Museum and quoted with the kind permission of the museum and the subject. This testimony contains most of the elements included in countless other testimonies preserved in various archives, at Yad Vashem, Moreshet, and elsewhere. See also Tzvika Dror, ed., *Pages of Testimony: Ninety-six Members of Kibbutz Lohamei Hagetaot Tell Their Stories* (Kibbutz Lohamei Hagetaot: Katznelson Ghetto Fighters' Museum, Hakibbutz Hameuhad, 1984).
6. Rozka Korczak at the Kibbutz Haartsi EC, 3 Jan. 1945, Moreshet Archive, A. 990.
7. Yablonka, "Absorption and Integration," p. 29.
8. "Dramatic Meeting between a Mother and Her Soldier Son," *Maariv*, 9 Feb. 1949, p. 4.
9. Ada Fishman at the Mapai immigration and absorption committee, April 1948, pp. 26 ff., LPA, 7/24/48; Haim Yahil, "The Actions of the Mission to the Survivors, 1945–1949," *Yalkut Moreshet* 30 and 31 (Nov. 1980 and April 1981), p. 31; Yehiel Duvdevani at the Mapai secretariat, 15 Jan. 1946, LPA, 24/46.
10. Elie Wiesel, "Questions That Remain Unanswered," papers for research on the Holocaust, collection 7, p. 4, Haifa University, 1989.
11. Eliahu Dobkin at the Mapai CC, 29 April 1946, LAP, 23/46.
12. Testimony of Hanche Sheich, Moreshet Archive, A 964.
13. S. Davidson, "Holocaust Survivors and Their Families: A Psychotherapeutic Clinical Experiment," *Rofeh Hamishpaha* 10 (Aug. 1981), pp. 313 ff.; Yael Danieli, "The Heterogeneity of Postwar Adaptation in Families of Holocaust Survivors," in Randolph L. Braham, ed., *The Psychological Perspectives of the Holocaust and of Its Aftermath* (Boulder: East European Quarterly, 1988), pp. 109 ff.

14. Tzivia Lubetkin, *The Last on the Walls* (remarks to the 15th convention of Hakibbutz Hameuhad at Kibbutz Yagur, 8 June 1946) (Tel Aviv: Hakibbutz Hameuhad, 1947), p. 5.
15. State prosecutor to minister of justice, 28 Aug. 1949, NA, PMO, 5437/9; undated memo, NA, PMO, 5437/19.
16. Yablonka, "Absorption and Integration," p. 284.
17. The Division for Immigrant Care (Histadrut) to the Immigration Department (Mapai), 25 Jan. 1945, LA, IV 2351–2061; Ada Fishman at the Mapai bureau, 8 April 1947, LPA, 25/47; David Remez, Shaul Avigur, and David Ben-Gurion at the Mapai bureau, 12 Feb. 1945, LPA, 25/45; Giora Yoseftal at the Mapai CC, 14 Dec. 1948, LPA, 23/48.
18. Heshel Frumkin at the Mapai CC, 9 Aug. 1948, LPA, 23/48.
19. Shaul Avigur at the Mapai secretariat, 22 April 1949, LPA, 24/49; Giora Yoseftal at the Mapai secretariat, 22 April 1949, LPA, 24/49; Yablonka, "Absorption and Integration," p. 36.
20. Tom Segev, *1949: The First Israelis* (New York: Free Press, 1986), pp. 68 ff.
21. Giora Yoseftal at the Mapai CC, 14 Dec. 1948, LPA, 23/48.
22. Eliahu Dobkin and Zalman Aharonowitz at the Mapai CC, 22 April 1949, LPA, 24/49; Shaul Avigur and David Ben-Gurion at the Mapai bureau, 12 Feb. 1945, LPA, 23/45; Ben-Gurion at the Mapai secretariat, 22 April 1949, LPA, 24/49; Ben-Gurion to Dr. Sofer, 5 Feb. 1948, BGA, correspondence; see also Ben-Gurion at the Zionist EC, 22 Aug. 1948, CZA, S/5 323.
23. Arieh Gelblum, "Fundamental Problems of Immigrant Absorption," *Haaretz*, 28 Sept. 1945, p. 3.
24. Golda Meir at the Histadrut EC, 29 April 1946, LA.
25. Regina Fertig Hitter file, CZA, S/6 242 I/4.
26. Yitzhak Salant to Haim Rokah (undated), LPA, 10-1-5.
27. Mapai Haifa to Rokah, 26 Sept. 1948; Absorption Department to Avramowitz, 21 Dec. 1948, LPA, 10-1-2.
28. B.A. to Karmi, 21 May 1946, LA, 208 IV 4298.
29. Absorption Department to activists committee, 5 Jan. 1950; Absorption Department to senior members committee, 8 March 1950, LPA, 10-1-3.
30. Emanuel Gutman, *Election Results for the First, Second, and Third Knessets and Local Bodies in 1950 and 1955* (Jerusalem: Hebrew University, 1957); Asher Tsidon, *The House of Representatives* (Jerusalem: Ahiasaf, 1965), pp. 382 ff.
31. Recha Freier, *Rooted: The Foundation of Aliyat Hanoar and Its Early Years* (Jerusalem: Tamar, n.d.), p. 16; Tom Segev, "A Woman of Love and Hate," *Haaretz* (weekend supplement), 19 Dec. 1980, pp. 12 ff.
32. Yablonka, "Absorption and Integration," p. 190.
33. Freier, *Rooted*, p. 10.

34. Aliyat Hanoar PF 14424. The personal files of the Aliyat Hanoar charges have been preserved, but are not open for research. The following section is based on several hundred of these files that were opened to me through the generosity of the Hadassah-WIZO Canada Research Institute.

35. Aliyat Hanoar PF 15209.

36. Aliyat Hanoar PF 11698.

37. Quoted by Haim Shatzkar, "Aliyat Hanoar and Its Part in the Rescue, Absorption, and Rehabilitation of Holocaust Refugee Children," in Yisrael Gutman and Adira Drechsler, eds., *Sheerit Hapletah, 1947–48* (Jerusalem: Yad Vashem, 1990), pp. 331 ff.

38. Ben-Zion Tomer, *Red and White and the Smell of Oranges* (Jerusalem: Hasifria Hatsionit, 1971), p. 287.

39. Ibid.

40. Letters on questions about joint education, Ein Harod, July 1943, CZA, S/75 1866.

41. Reuven Feurstein, Yaakov Rand, Ada Oz, unpublished Hadassah-WIZO Canada Research Institute study on Aliyat Hanoar.

42. Aliyat Hanoar PF 25965; 8918; 11299; 7336.

43. Aliyat Hanoar PF 18105.

44. Aliyat Hanoar PF 4004; 1958; 14315; 19634.

45. Michael Tel Tsur, *Alim*, Aug.–Oct. 1947, p. 30, quoted in Shatzkar, "Aliyat Hanoar."

46. Ibid.

47. Zeev Hever, "Children Tell Their Stories," *Davar*, 22 Oct. 1943, p. 2.

48. Aliyat Hanoar PF 8797.

49. Yitzhak Pessach to Dr. A. Simonzon, 15 Dec. 1949, Aliyat Hanoar PF 19634.

50. Feurstein et al.

51. Aliyat Hanoar PF 11719; 1950; 3957.

52. Givat Brenner to the Histadrut, 20 April 1945, LA, IV 221-2-517.

53. Zeev Iserson et al. at the Mapai bureau, 16 March 1948, LPA, 25/48.

54. Avraham Harzfeld and Shmuel Dayan at the Mapai CC, 30 Nov. 1948, LPA, 23/48; Immigration Department of the Histadrut in Haifa to the department management in Tel Aviv, 18 Nov. 1946, LA, 208 IV 4298.

55. Conclusions of a committee to examine the possibility of organizing immigrants in work brigades and groups, NA, PMO, 1/160; State of Israel, Public Opinion Research Institute, "Public Opinion on the Extent of Immigration," Oct. 1949, p. 12.

56. "4,000 Immigrants Opened Absorption Episode of the 100,000," *Haaretz*, 18 June 1946, p. 2.

57. Eliahu Dobkin at the Mapai CC, 23 Oct. 1945, LPA, 23/45; Shaar Haamakim to Histadrut immigration center, 24 June 1944, LA, IV 211-2-531; Kvutsat Usha to the immigration center, 25 July 1944; Kibbutz Elon to Jewish Agency, 25 Sept. 1944, etc., LA, IV 211-2-525.

58. Ayelet Hashahar to the Jewish Agency Immigration Department, 24 Oct. 1945; Usha to the immigration center, 16 Nov. 1943, 26 July 1944; Elon to the Jewish Agency, 25 Sept. 1944, LA, IV 211-2-515.

59. Kvutsat Schiller to the Histadrut immigration center, 12 Sept. 1944, LA, IV 211-2-531; Afikim to the Jewish Agency, 27 Sept. 1945; Haim Rokah to Usha, 27 Oct. 1943, Usha to Rokach, 16 Nov. 1943, LA, IV, 211-2-515.

60. Malka Schlein to Rokach, 22 Feb. 1951, LPA, 10-1-4.

61. Levi Eshkol to JAE, 19 June 1949, CZA.

62. Yablonka, "Absorption and Integration," p. 180.

63. Eliahu Dobkin to the Mapai CC, 23 Oct. 1945, LPA, 23/45.

64. Testimony of Yoel Peles (Florsheim), Moreshet Archive, A 972.

65. Hillel Klein, "Families of Holocaust Survivors in the Kibbutz: Psychological Studies," *International Psychiatry Clinics* 8 (1971), pp. 67 ff.

66. Yablonka, "Absorption and Integration," pp. 141, 161, 169, 183.

67. Ibid., p. 141.

68. Ibid., p. 67.

69. David Ben-Gurion to Zeev Schind, 18 March 1948, in Gershon Rivlin and Elhanan Oren, eds., *War Diary* (Tel Aviv: Ministry of Defense, 1982), I:302; Dov Yosef at the JAE, 11 Jan. 1948, CZA; the Mossad in Israel to the Mossad overseas, 30 March 1948, CZA, S/6 5067.

70. Yablonka, "Absorption and Integration," p. 74.

71. Ibid., p. 83.

72. Ibid., p. 64. See also Emanuel Sivan, *The Generation of '48: Myth, Profile, and Memory* (Tel Aviv: Maarahot, 1991), pp. 73 ff.

73. Yablonka, "Absorption and Integration," p. 74; BGD, 14 June 1948.

74. Haim Guri, *Until Dawn Comes* (Tel Aviv: Hakibbutz Hameuhad, 1950), p. 85.

75. Gabi Daniel (Benjamin Haroshowsky-Harshav), "Peter the Great," *Igra* 2 (1986), p. 199; Sivan, *Generation of '48*, pp. 73 ff.

76. Yablonka, "Absorption and Integration," p. 104.

77. Ibid., p. 113.

78. Eliahu Dobkin at the Mapai CC, 2 May 1942, LPA, 23/42; David Ben-Gurion at the Mapai CC, 22 April 1949, LPA, 24/49.

79. According to the film *Cloudburst*, produced by Orna Ben-Dor-Niv and Dafna Kaplanski, first broadcast on Israeli television in June 1989.

80. *Writers at a Meeting Summoned by the Prime Minister, 27 March 1949* (Jerusalem: GPO, 1949); see Anita Shapira, *Land for Power* (Tel Aviv: Am Oved, 1992).

81. Gelblum, "Fundamental Problems."

82. Aharon Appelfeld, *Struck by Light* (Tel Aviv: Hakibbutz Hameuhad, 1980), p. 61; *Tsror Mihtavim* 7, no. 6 (169) 131, 22 Jan. 1943, p. 143.

83. *The Sixth Histadrut Convention* (Tel Aviv: Histadrut, 1945), p. 302; see also Yehuda Tubin et al., eds., *Rozka* (Tel Aviv: Sifriat Poalim, 1988),

p. 213; Dina Porat, "Rozka Korczak and the Yishuv," *Yalkut Moreshet*, April 1992, pp. 9 ff.

84. Moshe Smilansky, "Lesson," *Haaretz*, 10 May 1945, p. 2.

85. Avraham Shlonsky, "Omens," *Poems* (Tel Aviv: Sifriat Poalim 1971), IV:72.

86. Yahil, "Actions of the Mission," p. 174.

87. Haim Baltzan, "The Jews Among the War Criminals," *Haaretz*, 3 June 1945, p. 2.

88. Aliav testimony, BGA, p. 57.

89. Testimony of Dov Shilansky, Jabotinsky Institute, 6/29/18.

90. Shapira, *Walking on the Horizon*, pp. 328 ff.; also Yosef Bankover at the Histadrut EC, 5 Sept. 1945, LA.

91. Tom Segev, "Had You Only Sent a Messenger," *Koteret Rashit* 63 (15 Feb. 1984), pp. 14 ff.

92. Yoel Palgi, "A Great Wind Comes" (Tel Aviv: Am Oved, 1978), p. 243.

93. Yad Vashem secretariat, 26; Tom Segev, "The Soap Myth," *Koteret Rashit* 205 (5 Nov. 1986), p. 11; "The Jewish Soap Atrocity Is Confirmed," *Haaretz*, 26 Dec. 1945, p. 2; Uzi Benziman, "The Good, the Bad, and the Ugly," *Haaretz*, 23 June 1989, p. B3; Uri Zvi Greenberg, 23 Jan. 1950; *KP*, IV:593; Moshe Sharett, 13 March 1951, *KP*, VIII:1322; Menahem Begin, 2 April 1951, *KP*, VIII:1548; Arieh Ben-Eliezer, 10 Aug. 1951, *KP*, X:242; Yoram Kanuik, *Man Son of Dog* (Tel Aviv: Amikam, 1969), p. 112; Ruth Firer, *Agents of the Lesson* (Tel Aviv: Hakibbutz Hameuhad, 1989), pp. 27 ff., p. 53.

94. Moshe Sharett at the Histadrut EC secretariat, 29 April 1943, LA. See also Anita Shapira, *Land and Power* (Tel Aviv: Am Oved, 1992) pp. 451 ff.

95. Yablonka, "Absorption and Integration," p. 187.

96. Aviva Halamish, "Haapala: Values, Myth, and Reality," in Nurit Gretz, ed., *Vantage Point* (Tel Aviv: Open University, 1988), p. 88; Idit Zertal, "Lost Souls: The Maapilim and the Mossad Lealiya Bet in the Struggle to Establish the State and Thereafter," *Hatsionut* 14 (Aug. 1989), pp. 107 ff.

97. "Toward the Future," speech to a gathering of writers, June 1943, Yitzhak Gruenbaum, *In the Days of Destruction and Holocaust* (Tel Aviv: Haverim, 1946), p. 127.

98. Haim Baltzan, "Like Foam on the Water," *Haaretz*, 31 Jan. 1947, p. 2.

99. David Remez at the Histadrut EC, 26 May 1943, LA.

100. Eliezer Kaplan at the JAE, 20 June 1944, CZA.

101. Ada Fishman at the Histadrut EC, 23 Jan. 1946, LA.

102. S. Eisenberg at the JAE, 9 Oct. 1949, CZA.

PART IV: RESTITUTION: *How Much Will We Get for Grandma and Grandpa?*

10 "ADD A FEW MORAL ARGUMENTS"

1. Menahem Bader and David Ben-Gurion, 28 Nov. 1951, *KP*, X:942.
2. Mordecai Nurok, 29 June 1949, *KP*, I:867.
3. Yermiah Yafeh to Ben-Gurion, undated, NA, FM, 2418/15.
4. Ora Shem-Or, "Let No German Foot Tread in Tel Aviv!" *Yediot Aharonot*, 4 Sept. 1949, p. 1.
5. Gershom Schocken, "We and the Germans," *Haaretz*, 2 Sept. 1949, p. 2.
6. Walter Eitan to Moshe Shapira, undated (based on a consultation of 15 Dec. 1949), NA, FM, 2539/1; press release from the Government Press Office, 28 Dec. 1949, NA, FM, 2413/2.
7. Director of the legal division to the director-general, 10 Jan. 1950, NA, FM, 2413/2.
8. Gershon Avner to Daniel Levin, 27 Nov. 1949, in Yemima Rosental, ed., *Documents on the Foreign Policy of Israel May–December 1949* (Jerusalem: National Archive, 1986), IV:650.
9. The Foreign Trade Commission to the Minister of Finance and the Foreign Minister, 14 Sept. 1949, NA, FM, 2413/2.
10. Michael Bar-Zohar, *Ben-Gurion* (Tel Aviv: Am Oved, 1978), II:912; III:1320.
11. Walter Eitan to the Israeli overseas delegations, 31 Aug. 1950, NA, FM, 2413/2.
12. Moshe Sharett to the Mapai CC, 21 April 1952, LPA, 23/52.
13. Summary of meeting, 22 Dec. 1949, NA, FM, 2413/2; see also Yeshayahu A. Jelinek, "Like an Oasis in the Desert: The Israeli Consulate in Munich," *Studies in Zionism* (Tel Aviv, English) (1988), pp. 81 ff.
14. Eliahu Livneh to the consular department, 20 Sept. 1950, and Gershon Avner to Livneh, 28 Sept. 1950, NA, FM, 2539/1.
15. Yeshayahu Förder and Moshe Shapira, 1 Jan. 1951, *KP*, VII:617.
16. Yehoshua Freundlich, ed., *Documents on the Foreign Policy of Israel*, vol. V, 1950 (Jerusalem: National Archive, 1988), p. 609.
17. Shlomo Ginossar to Gershon Avner, 2 Nov. 1950, ibid., V:617.
18. Mordecai Kidron to Walter Eitan, 9 Jan. 1950, NA, FM, 2413/2.
19. Gideon Rafael to Abba Eban, 19 Feb. 1951, NA, FM, 2413/2.
20. Elyashiv Ben-Horin to Gershon Avner, 6 Nov. 1950, in Freundlich, *Documents*, V:629; and Ben-Horin to Avner, 6 Nov. 1950, NA, FM, 2539/1 (I).
21. Michael Amir to the Western European division, 13 Nov. 1950, in Freundlich, *Documents*, V:650; Shlomo Ginossar to Avner, 2 Nov. 1950, ibid.,

V:617; see also the opinion of the Israeli consul in Munich, ibid., V:666.

22. Walter Eitan to Amir, 22 Nov. 1950, NA, FM, 2413/2.

23. Michael Brecher, *Decisions in Israel's Foreign Policy* (London: Oxford University Press, 1974); Yehudit Auerbach, "Foreign-Policy Decisions and Changes of Position: Israel-Germany 1950–1965," diss., Hebrew University, 1980; Yitzhak Gilad, "Israeli Public Opinion on Israel–West German Relations, 1949–1965," diss., Tel Aviv University, 1984; Ludolf Herbst and Constantin Goschler, eds., *Wiedergutmachung in der Bundesrepublik Deutschland* (Munich: R. Oldenburg, 1989).

24. Nana Sagi, *German Reparations: A History of the Negotiations* (English) (Jerusalem: Magnes Press, Hebrew University, 1980), pp. 7 ff.; Yeshayahu A. Jelinek, "Israel und die Anfänge der Shilumim," in Herbst and Goschler, *Wiedergutmachung*, pp. 119 ff.

25. Memo by Paul März, 17 March 1943, CZA, S/25 5188; for other memos on the matter of reparations (1941 and onward), see S/26 1325; S/25 5188; S/90 526; S/90 527.

26. Israel Ministry of Foreign Affairs, *Documents Relating to the Agreement between the Government of Israel and the Government of the Federal Republic of Germany* (English) (Jerusalem: GPO, 1953), pp. 9–11.

27. Sagi, *German Reparations*, p. 36; Haim Yahil at the Mapai CC, 13 Dec. 1951, LPA, 23/51.

28. "Martin Buber Explains His Reasons for Accepting the Goethe Prize from the University of Hamburg," *Haaretz*, 31 Dec. 1951; Mordecai Nurok, 19 Dec. 1951, *KP*, X:717; Haim Boger, 9 Jan. 1952, *KP*, X:934, etc.; for other reactions see Gershom Scholem, *There Is a Reason* (Tel Aviv: Am Oved, 1982), p. 121, and letter to the editor, *Haaretz*, 20 Dec. 1951; Martin Buber, *Briefwechsel aus sieben Jahrzehnten* (Heidelberg: Lambert Schneider, 1975), III:308 ff.

29. Pinhas Rosen, 5 Dec. 1949, *KP*, III:228 ff.; Avraham Sheftel and Yonah Kosoi, *KP*, III:235.

30. Walter Eitan to Zeev Sherf, 22 Dec. 1949, NA, FM, 2539/1.

31. Eliezer Kaplan to Moshe Sharett, 21 March 1950, NA, FM, 2417/1.

32. Gershon Avner to Daniel Levin, 27 Nov. 1949, in Rosental, *Documents*, p. 650.

33. CZA, S/35 70; the Mendelsohn report is also in the NA, FA, 2417/1; see there also comments by Arieh Yehuda David of the Ministry of Commerce and Industry, during a joint meeting of the JAE and the cabinet, 2 May 1950.

34. Shmuel Tulkowsky to Ernst Ostermann, 27 Oct. 1950; Ostermann to Tulkowsky, 10 Jan. 1951; Moshe Sharett to Gershon Meiron, 8 March 1951; Meiron to Sharett, 12 March 1951; all in NA, FM, 2417/1.

35. Sharett to Eliezer Kaplan, 2 July 1950, NA, FM, 2417/1.

36. Karl Marx, "Bekenntnis zur Verpflichtung: Interview der *Allgemeinen* mit

Bundeskanzler Dr. Adenauer," *Allgemeinen Wochenzeitung der Juden in Deutschland,* 25 Nov. 1949, pp. 1 ff.

37. Shlomo Kadar to Moshe Sharett, 29 Dec. 1950, NA, FM, 2417/1.

38. Ministry of Foreign Affairs, *Documents Relating to the Agreement,* pp. 13–24, 28–39.

39. Gershon Avner to Maurice Fischer, 6 April 1951; Fischer to Avner, 3 May 1951, etc., NA, FM, 2543/4; David Horowitz, *Life at the Focus* (Tel Aviv: Masada, 1975), p. 89.

40. "Sharett: There Have Been No Contacts with the Germans in Paris on the Matter of Compensation," *Haaretz,* 25 Dec. 1951, p. 1.

41. Horowitz, *Life,* pp. 86 ff.; Fischer to Avner, 3 May 1951, etc., NA, FM 2543/4.

42. Deutscher Bundestag, 27 Sept. 1951, copy of the minutes, NA, FM, 2543/6; see also Ministry of Foreign Affairs, *Documents Relating to the Agreement,* pp. 41 ff.; Eliezer Shinar, *Under the Burden of Duty and Emotion* (Tel Aviv: Schocken, 1967), p. 20.

43. Gershon Avner to Ester Herlitz, 11 Nov. 1951, NA, FM, 2543/6.

44. Avner to Walter Eitan, 21 Aug. 1951, NA, FM, 2417/3.

45. Two drafts of Adenauer's declaration, NA, FM, 2543/6; another draft on the stationery of a restaurant in Wiesbaden, Germany, NA, FM, 532/8; see also Kai von Jena, "Versönung mit Israel? Die deutsch-israelischen Verhandlungen bis zum Wiedergutmachungsabkommen von 1952," *Vierteljahreshefte für Zeitgeschichte* 34 (1986), pp. 457 ff.; Rudolf Huhn, "Die Wiedergutmachungsverhandlungen in Wassenaar," in Herbst and Goschler, *Wiedergutmachung,* pp. 141 ff.

46. Nahum Goldmann to Moshe Sharett, 14 Sept. 1951, CZA (Nahum Goldmann), Z-6 2345.

47. Gershon Avner to Walter Eitan, 21 Aug. 1951, NA, FM, 2417/3.

48. BGD, 25 Sept. 1951.

49. Walter Eitan to Eliahu Livneh, 24 Sept. 1951, NA, FM, 532/8; see also Gershon Avner to Rafael, 25 Sept. 1951, NA, FM, 2417/3.

50. Draft of reaction with comment by Walter Eitan, NA, FM, 2417/3.

51. Ministry of Foreign Affairs, *Documents Relating to the Agreement,* pp. 44 ff., 56 ff.

52. "Dr. Adenauer's Declaration," *Haaretz,* 3 Oct. 1951, p. 2.

53. Ministry of Foreign Affairs, *Documents Relating to the Agreement,* pp. 56 ff.; see also Moshe Sharett to Walter Eitan, 20 Nov. 1951, in Rosental, *Documents,* p. 821.

54. Nahum Goldmann, *Memoirs* (Jerusalem: Weidenfeld and Nicolson, 1972), p. 236.

55. Moshe Sharett to the Mapai PC, 5 May 1952, LPA, 26/52.

56. Yosef Sprinzak at the Mapai CC, 13 Dec. 1951, LPA, 23/51.

57. Azriel Karlebach, "Amalek," *Maariv,* 5 Oct. 1951, p. 3.

58. Avraham Sheftel at the Mapai CC, 13 Dec. 1951, LPA, 23/51.
59. Meir Dworzecki at the Mapai CC, 13 Dec. 1951, LPA, 23/51.
60. David Ben-Gurion at the Mapai CC, 13 Dec. 1951, LPA, 23/51.
61. Ibid.

11   "GAS AGAINST JEWS"

1. BGD, 30 Oct. 1951; David Ben-Gurion at the Mapai CC, 13 Dec. 1951, LPA, 23/51.
2. Natan Alterman, "Three Things about the Claim from Germany," *The Seventh Column* (Tel Aviv: Hakibbutz Hameuhad, 1978), III:386; Arieh Gelblum, "Buber on the Question of Contacts with Germany," *Haaretz*, 7 Jan. 1952, p. 1.
3. "Public Opinion Survey on Compensation Concluded," *Maariv*, 9 Jan. 1952, p. 4; on the operation of the survey, see *Maariv*, 3 Jan. 1952, p. 1, and thereafter.
4. "Menahem Begin Calls for Enlistment and Action," *Herut*, 1 Jan. 1952, p. 1.
5. "Begin at Mass Demonstration at Zion Square in Jerusalem," *Herut*, 8 Jan. 1952, p. 1.
6. Eric Silver, *Begin* (London: Weidenfeld and Nicolson, 1984), p. 7.
7. "The Blood of the Slaughtered Will Not Be Silent," *Herut*, 2 Jan. 1952, p. 1.
8. "Nothing in the World Would Justify Negotiations with the German Nation of Murderers," *Herut*, 6 Jan. 1952, p. 1.
9. Placards on reparations, Jabotinsky Archives, 9/8/3 1 H.
10. "Nothing in the World."
11. *Herut*, 4 Jan. 1952, p. 1.
12. "We Will Not Be in One Camp with Hitler's Heirs," *Al Hamishmar*, 8 Jan. 1952, p. 1; see also Karlebach, "Amalek."
13. *Herut*, 7 Jan. 1952, p. 1.
14. Menahem Begin, 7 Jan. 1952, *KP*, III:891.
15. David Ben-Gurion, ibid., III:897.
16. Elimelech Rimalt, ibid., III:899.
17. "Begin at Mass Demonstration."
18. "Bloody Rioting of Fascist Mob in Jerusalem," *Davar*, 8 Jan. 1952, p. 1; "Herut Rally and Clashes," *Haaretz*, 8 Jan. 1952, p. 1.
19. "Begin at Mass Demonstration."
20. Menahem Begin, 7 Jan. 1952, *KP*, X:906.
21. "Police in 2-Hour Street Battle" (English), *The Jerusalem Post*, 8 Jan. 1952, p. 1.
22. Yaakov Hazan, 10 March 1949, *KP*, I:55.
23. David Ben-Gurion at the Mapai CC, 13 Dec. 1951, LPA, 23/51; see also Zalman Aran, 8 Jan. 1952, *KP*, X:922.

24. David Ben-Gurion, *Vision and Way* (Tel Aviv: Mapai, 1953), III:278.
25. Yosef Sprinzak et al., 7 Jan. 1952, *KP*, X:901 ff.
26. Shalom Rosenfeld, "Day of Eruption and a Storm of Hatred in Jerusalem," *Maariv*, 8 Jan. 1952, p. 2.
27. Yohanan Bader, *The Knesset and I* (Tel Aviv: Ianim, 1979), p. 62.
28. Menahem Begin, 7 Jan. 1952, *KP*, X:905.
29. BGD, 6 Jan. 1952.
30. Rosenfeld, "Day of Eruption"; *KP*, X:905.
31. Menahem Begin, 7 Jan. 1952, *KP*, X:906 ff.
32. S. Svislovsky, "The Knesset Wept," *Yediot Aharonot*, 8 Jan. 1952, p. 2.
33. BGD, 11 Jan. 1952.
34. Ben-Gurion, *Vision and Way*, III:278.
35. "Ben-Gurion Was About to Outlaw Herut," *Yediot Aharonot*, 9 Jan. 1952, p. 1.
36. Telegrams of support and letters from citizens, 7–13 Jan. 1952, BGA.
37. Isser Harel, *Security and Democracy* (Tel Aviv: Ianim, 1989), p. 190.
38. Michael Bar-Zohar, *Ben-Gurion* (Tel Aviv: Am Oved, 1978), II:925 ff.
39. "The Street Will Not Rule," *Haaretz*, 8 Jan. 1952, p. 2; Azriel Karlebach, "This Is the Limit," *Maariv*, 8 Jan. 1952, p. 4.
40. 9 Jan. 1952, *KP*, X:962 ff.
41. Haim Landau, 21 Jan. 1952, *KP*, X:1036; Meir Argov, 9 Jan. 1952, *KP*, X:944.
42. Yohanan Bader, 17 March 1952, *KP*, XI:1588.
43. Arieh Ben-Eliezer, 8 Oct. 1951, *KP*, X:242.
44. Haim Landau, 21 Feb. 1955, *KP*, XVII:880.
45. Landau, 5 Dec. 1949, *KP*, III:234; Yohanan Bader, III:232.
46. Moshe Sharett, 15 March 1950, *KP*, VIII:1320 ff.; see also Ministry of Foreign Affairs, *Documents Relating to the Agreement*, pp. 20 ff.
47. Menahem Begin, 2 April 1951, *KP*, VIII:1548.
48. Emanuel Gutman, *Election Results for the First, Second, and Third Knessets and Local Bodies in 1950 and 1955* (Jerusalem: Hebrew University, 1957), p. 5.
49. Bader, *Knesset and I*, p. 49.
50. Ibid., p. 50.
51. Gutman, *Election Results*, p. 4.
52. Bader, *Knesset and I*, pp. 54 ff.
53. Ben-Gurion at the Mapai CC, 13 Dec. 1951, LPA, 23/51.
54. Bader, *Knesset and I*, pp. 58, 62.
55. Menahem Begin, 7 Jan. 1952, *KP*, X:905.

1 2   "THE BABY WENT FOR FREE"

1. All of Israel's diplomatic documentation of the negotiations with Germany is open for research in the National Archives in Jerusalem. The Nahum Goldmann Archive is kept in the Central Zionist Archives. Konrad Adenauer and Nahum Goldmann recounted the negotiations in their memoirs. Several officials, both Israeli and German, have also published their memoirs. A chronology of the negotiations, based mainly on the published autobiographical material, can be found in Gilad, "Israeli Public Opinion"; a description of the negotiations, particularly from the point of view of the Jewish organizations, can be found in Nana Sagi, *German Reparations*, and in Yehudit Auerbach, *Ben-Gurion and Reparations from Germany* (Jerusalem: Yad Ben-Zvi, forthcoming). The German side is described in Ludolf Herbst and Constantin Goschler, eds., *Wiedergutmachung in der Bundesrepublik Deutschland* (Munich: R. Oldenburg, 1989).
2. Konrad Adenauer, *Erinnerungen* 1953–1955 (Stuttgart: Deutsche Verlags-anstalt, 1966), p. 144.
3. Shinar, *Under the Burden*, p. 28.
4. Huhn, "Wiedergutmachungsverhandlungen," p. 143.
5. Yeshayahu Ben-Porat, *Conversations* (Tel Aviv: Idanim, 1981), pp. 44 ff.
6. Ibid., pp. 9 ff.
7. Adenauer, *Erinnerungen*, p. 137.
8. Ibid., p. 141.
9. NGA, Z-6 1998.
10. Eliahu Tabin in tape-recorded interview with the author, 9 May 1990; Maurice Fischer to the Foreign Minister, 6 April 1952, NA; memorandum by Eliezer Dorot, 9 April 1952, NA, FM, 2544/1.
11. Eliezer Shinar to Walter Eitan, 23 Dec. 1951, NA, FA, 2417/3; on contacts with East Germany, both direct and indirect (through the Soviet Union), see there 2418/3–15, 2544/1, etc.
12. Memorandum of the Investigation Division, 5 Aug. 1952, NA, FM, 2543/9.
13. Moshe Tsuriel to Nahum Goldmann, 22 July 1954, NGA, Z-6 2016.
14. Abba Eban to Dean Acheson, 3 April 1952, NGA, Z-6 1985; also Acheson to Moshe Sharett, 3 June 1952, ibid.
15. Jacob Blaustein, *A Dramatic Era in the History of New York* (New York: American Jewish Committee, 1966), pp. 7 ff.
16. Drafts of letters from John McCloy and Harry S. Truman to Konrad Adenauer, written apparently by Nahum Goldmann, NGA, Z-6 2010; see also Goldmann, *Memoirs*, pp. 240 ff.
17. Maurice Fischer to the reparations delegation, 4 June 1952, NA, FM, 2417/6; on Klein's mission see also Huhn, op. cit., p. 143.
18. Shinar, *Under the Burden*, pp. 31 ff.

19. Nahum Goldmann to Konrad Adenauer, 19 May 1952, NGA, Z-6 1998; Goldmann, *Memoirs*, pp. 241 ff.; Adenauer, *Erinnerungen*, pp. 146 ff.
20. Reparations delegation to the prime minister, 13 June 1952, NA, FM, 2417/6.
21. Ministry of Foreign Affairs, *Documents Relating to the Agreement*, pp. 125 ff.
22. Michael Michaeli, *Foreign Trade and Import Capital in Israel* (Tel Aviv: Am Oved, 1963), pp. 32, 431.
23. Shinar, *Under the Burden*, pp. 44 ff.; Moshe Sharett at the Mapai PC, 5 Sept. 1952, LPA, 26/52; also on 26 March 1953.
24. Shinar, *Under the Burden*, pp. 52 ff.; Zalman Aran at the Mapai CC, 14 April 1953, LPA, 23/53; Haim Landau and David Ben-Gurion, 3 April 1953, *KP*, XIII:862 ff.
25. Dov Shilansky, *In a Hebrew Jail: From the Diary of a Political Prisoner* (Tel Aviv: Armoni, 1980), pp. 21, 26.
26. Tom Segev, "The Goal Sanctifies," *Haaretz* (supplement), 26 Feb. 1982, pp. 7 ff.
27. Shilansky, *Hebrew Jail*, pp. 10 ff.
28. BGD, 17 April 1953.
29. Conversation with the author.
30. "Head of Betar Movement Arrested," *Maariv*, 7 Sept. 1953, p. 1.
31. Goldmann, *Memoirs*, p. 250.
32. David Ben-Gurion to Nahum Goldmann, 2 July 1952, 17 Sept. 1953, BGA.
33. Ibid., 2 July 1952.
34. Bank of Israel, *Reparations and Their Effect on the Israeli Economy* (Jerusalem: Bank of Israel, 1965), pp. 65 ff.
35. Shinar, *Under the Burden*, p. 63.
36. Hillel Dan, *On an Unpaved Road: The Story of Solel Boneh* (Tel Aviv: Schocken, 1963), p. 342.
37. Bank of Israel, *Reparations and Their Effect*, pp. 171 ff.
38. Michaeli, *Foreign Trade*, pp. 38 ff.
39. Bank of Israel, *Reparations and Their Effect*, p. 111.
40. Hans Günter Hockerts, "Anwälte der Verfolgten: Die United Restitution Organization," in Herbst and Goschler, *Wiedergutmachung*, pp. 249 ff.; Norman Bentwich, *The United Restitution Organization, 1948–1968* (London: Vallentine, Mitchell, n.d.).
41. The quotations that follow are taken from the material contained in tens of thousands of claims files preserved in the offices of the United Restitution Organization (URO), Tel Aviv. I wish to express my gratitude to the late Avner Rom, the organization's director, for allowing me to examine the files, on condition that they not be identified, so as not to constitute an invasion of privacy. Several thousand such files are also preserved in the Central Archive for the History of the Jewish People in Jerusalem, and are

still sealed. See also Christian Pross, *Wiedergutmachung: Der Kleinkrieg gegen die Opfer* (Frankfurt: Athenaeum, 1988).

42. Yosef Falk to Walter Eitan, 9 Jan. 1956; Benyamin Ilsar to Falk, 20 Jan. 1956, NA, FM, 2545/1.

43. Michael Landsberger, *The Effect of Personal Compensation from Germany on Consumption and Savings in Israel* (Jerusalem: Bank of Israel, 1969), p. 6.

44. Israel Weinberg, atty., vs. the Attorney General, SCO, 1973, XXVII(2): 314 ff.

45. The attorney general to the prime minister, foreign minister, and finance minister, 10 April 1956, NA, FM, 2545/1; Levi Eshkol, 31 Dec. 1956, KP, XXI:600; Benyamin Mintz, 31 Dec. 1956, KP, XXI:601; for further debates on this subject see KP for 28 Jan. 1957, XXI:873 ff.; 9 Apr. 1957, XXII:1767 ff.; 26 March 1957, XXII:1520 ff.; 10 April 1957, XXII:1772 ff.; 29 May 1957, XXII:2033 ff.; 3 Feb. 1960, XXVIII:543 ff.; 18 July 1960, XXIX:1893 ff.; 19 June 1963, XXXVII:2131 ff.

46. Landsberger, *Effect of Personal Compensation*, p. 21.

47. Quoted by Dan Giladi, "The Effect of Personal Compensation from Germany in the Kibbutz Movement," submitted to the Institute for Labor and Social Research of the Histadrut and to Tel Aviv University, 1976, p. 18.

48. Moshe Sharett, 13 March 1951, KP, VIII:1230.

49. Shinar, *Under the Burden*, p. 75.

50. Deutscher Bundestag, 10 Wahlperiode, *Bericht der Bundesregelung über Wiedergutmachung und Entschädigung für nationalsozialistisches Unrecht sowie über die Lage der Sinti, Roma, und verwandter Gruppen*, Drucksache 10/6287, Bonn, 31 Oct. 1986, p. 30.

51. Eliahu Livneh to Walter Eitan, 27 Nov. 1952, NA, FM, 2413/2.

52. David Ben-Gurion, *The Renewed State of Israel* (Tel Aviv: Am Oved, 1969), I:423.

53. Quoted in Giladi, "Effect . . . in Kibbutz Movement," p. 17.

54. Eri Jabotinsky and Golda Meir, 27 March 1950, KP, IV:1153 ff.

PART V: POLITICS: *The Kastner Affair*

13 "IT IS HARD FOR US, THE JUDGES OF ISRAEL"

1. "The Man Who Set Off the Kastner Explosion," *Haolam Hazeh*, 23 June 1955, p. 4.

2. "Israel: On Trial," *Time*, 11 July 1955, pp. 19 ff.

3. Shalom Rosenfeld, *Criminal Case 124* (Tel Aviv: Karni, 1955), p. 18; see also the verdict of the Jerusalem District Court (original), p. 2, and verdict of the Supreme Court (original), p. 128, both at the Yad Vashem Library, Jersualem, also SCO, 1958, XII:2017 ff.

4. BGD, 29 Dec. 1947; 10 Jan. 1948; 22 June 1951.

5. Rosenfeld, *Criminal Case*, pp. 100, 182.
6. Israel Rudolf Kastner, *Der Kastner Bericht über Eichmanns Menschen-handel in Ungarn* (Munich: Kindler, 1961).
7. Mordecai Nurok, 29 June 1949, *KP*, I:868.
8. "Attack on Jew Suspected of Collaboration with the Gestapo," *Haaretz*, 6 Jan. 1946, p. 3.
9. Dov Shilansky, *In a Hebrew Jail: From the Diary of a Political Prisoner* (Tel Aviv: Armoni, 1980), p. 18.
10. David Ben-Gurion at the JAE, 24 Feb. 1946, CZA.
11. Testimony of Ruth Aliav, BGA.
12. Roman Friester, *Without Compromise* (Tel Aviv: Zemora Beitan, 1987), pp. 290 ff.
13. Shin, "Collaborators," *Hatsofeh*, 9 Jan. 1946, p. 2.
14. Eliahu Dobkin at the Histadrut EC, 5 Sept. 1945, LA, XVII:34.
15. "Proposed Law Against Jewish War Criminals," *Haaretz*, 10 Nov. 1949, p. 4.
16. Mordecai Nurok, 29 Nov. 1949, *KP*, III:187 ff.
17. "Proposed Law."
18. *DCO*, 1951–1952, V:146 ff.
19. Ibid.; see also *SCO*, 1964, XVIII:2:85 ff.
20. *DCO*, 1951–1952, V:152 ff.
21. *SCO*, 1959, XIII:1056.
22. Quoted by Roni Stauber, "The Political Debate over the Kastner Trial in the Party Press," *Hatsionut* 13 (1988), p. 226.
23. Dov Yosef, *The Dove and the Sword* (Tel Aviv: Masada, 1975), pp. 321 ff.
24. Dan Ofri, "My Husband Spoke Only the Truth," *Yediot Aharonot (Shiva Yamim* supplement), 17 March 1967, pp. 5 ff.
25. Yehiel Gutmann, *The Attorney General versus the Government* (Tel Aviv: Idanim, 1981), p. 89.
26. Tom Segev, "The Conscience and Justice of Haim Cohen," *Haaretz* (supplement), 13 March 1981, p. 7. See also Michael Shashar, *Haim Cohen, Supreme Court Judge* (Jerusalem: Keter, 1989), p. 98; Gutmann, *Attorney General*, p. 89.
27. Moshe Sharett, 23 May 1954, *Personal Diary* (Tel Aviv: Sifriat Maariv, 1978), II:510.
28. "Dr. Kastner Testifies," *Haaretz*, 19 Feb. 1954, p. 8; "Kastner: Counter-intelligence Knew of the Paratroopers' Arrival in Hungary," *Haaretz*, 1 March 1954, p. 1; "Eichmann Told Me: I Am Prepared to Sell You a Million Jews," *Haaretz*, 2 April 1954, p. 8.
29. Uri Avneri, "Man of the Year: Shmuel Tamir," *Haolam Hazeh*, 14 Sept. 1955, p. 3.
30. Quoted in Isser Harel, *The Truth about the Kastner Murder* (Tel Aviv: Idanim, 1985), pp. 152 ff.

31. BGD, 6 July 1953.
32. Harel, *Truth*, pp. 55 ff.; *DCO*, 1958, XV:233 ff.; *SCO*, 1958, XII:1541 ff.
33. Rosenfeld, *Criminal Case*, pp. 242 ff.
34. Ibid., p. 248.
35. "The Man Who Set Off."
36. R. Ben-Shushan, "How Not to Buy," *Haaretz*, 3 Dec. 1953, p. 3; "More on the Wheat Deal," *Haaretz*, 25 March 1954, p. 2.
37. Rosenfeld, *Criminal Case*, p. 194.
38. Benyamin Halevy to David Ben-Gurion, 22 Dec. 1953, BGA; see also Eliakim Rubinstein, *Judges of the Land* (Tel Aviv: Schocken, 1980), p. 135.
39. Verdict of the Supreme Court (original), p. 167; also: *SCO*, 1958, XII:2017 ff.
40. Rosenfeld, *Criminal Case*, p. 36.
41. Ibid., p. 51.
42. "The Verdict in the Gruenwald-Kastner Trial," *Haaretz*, 27 June 1955, p. 4.

14   "HIS SOUL TO THE DEVIL"

1. Quoted by Roni Stauber, "The Political Debate over the Kastner Trial in the Party Press," *Hatsionut* 13 (1988), pp. 226 ff.; see also p. 225.
2. Tom Segev, "Dear Reader," *Koteret Rashit*, 13 May 1987, pp. 20 ff.
3. "The Avneri-Tamir Affair," *Yediot Aharonot*, 26 Oct. 1980, p. 11.
4. Harel, *Truth*, p. 331.
5. Uri Avneri, "Man of the Year: Yisrael Kastner," *Haolam Hazeh*, 26 Sept. 1954, pp. 3 ff.
6. Ibid.
7. Ibid.
8. Harel, *Truth*.
9. Teddy Kollek, *For Jerusalem* (London: Weidenfeld and Nicolson, 1978), p. 53.
10. Sharett, *Personal Diary*, II:376, 392, 414, 425, 430, 443, 463, 479, 483, 508, 425, 543, 562.
11. Ibid., 9 June 1954, II:543; "Sharett Recounts Brand's Rescue Mission," *Maariv*, 6 June 1954, pp. 3, 6.
12. Sharett, 29 July 1954, *Personal Diary*, II:562.
13. The verdict of the Jerusalem District Court is quoted here from the original, at the Yad Vashem Library, p. 179; see also *SCO*, 1958, XII:2017 ff.
14. The verdict of the Jerusalem District Court, quoted here according to the original copy, pp. 20 ff.
15. Ibid., pp. 38, 51, 53.

16. Ibid., pp. 117, 125 ff.
17. Ibid., pp. 157 ff.
18. Sharett, 22 June 1955, *Personal Diary*, IV:1073.

15 "THE WALLS ARE BEGINNING TO CRACK"

1. Quoted by Roni Stauber, "The Political Debate over the Kastner Trial in the Party Press," *Hatsionut* 13 (1988), pp. 230 ff.
2. Uri Avneri, "The Sharett Trial," *Haolam Hazeh*, 30 June 1955, pp. 3 ff.
3. "About the Verdict," *Hapoel Hatsair*, 28 June 1955, p. 3.
4. Sharett, 24 June 1955, *Personal Diary*, IV:1073.
5. "On Reading the Verdict," *Haaretz*, 24 June 1955, p. 2.
6. Moshe Keren, *Passing and Permanent Problems*, 1977 (Jerusalem: Keren, 1978), p. 210.
7. Ibid., p. 188.
8. Menahem Begin and others at the Herut CC, 26 June 1955, Jabotinsky Archives, H/1-6/o/9.
9. 28 June 1955, *KP*, XVIII:2107 ff.
10. Sharett, 28 June 1955, *Personal Diary*, IV:1074.
11. Mapai Knesset caucus, 28 June 1955, LPA, 11–2–6.
12. 29 June 1955, *KP*, XVIII:2146 ff.
13. Sharett, 4 July 1955, *Personal Diary*, IV:1081.
14. Ibid., 5 and 6 July 1955, IV:1081 ff.
15. Kollek, *For Jerusalem*, p. 47; Arthur D. Morse, *While Six Million Died* (New York: Ace, 1967); Ben Hecht, *Denial* (Tel Aviv: Israel Press, 1970).
16. Yonah Kesse and others, Mapai secretariat, 12 July 1955, LPA, 24/55.
17. Natan Alterman, "More on Two Ways," *The Seventh Cross* (Tel Aviv: Hakibbutz Hameuhad, 1981), II:426.
18. Natan Alterman, *On Two Ways*, ed. Dan Laor (Tel Aviv: Hakibbutz Hameuhad, 1989).
19. Quoted in Stauber, pp. 234 ff.
20. David Ben-Gurion to A. S. Stein, 17 Aug. 1955, BGA.
21. Yehoshua Kastner to Ben-Gurion, 19 Jan. 1958; Ben-Gurion to Kastner, 2 Feb. 1958, NA, PMO, 5432/16.
22. Ben-Gurion to A. S. Stein, 18 Aug. 1955, BGA.
23. "Ben-Gurion Refused to Refute the False Alibi of War Criminal Krumey," *Herut*, 7 Feb. 1965, p. 1.

16 "JEREMIAH THE PROPHET, FOR EXAMPLE"

1. David Ben-Gurion and Menahem Begin, 17 Oct. 1956, *KP*, XXI:110 ff; Begin, 7 Nov. 1956, *KP*, XXI:197.
2. Irving Sider and Harold Greenberg, "Otto Skorzeny: The Nazi behind

Nasser," *Maariv*, 19 Oct. 1956, p. 4; picture of *Mein Kampf*: *Maariv*, 5 Nov. 1956, p. 2; "Without Intermediaries" (editorial), *Maariv*, 5 Nov. 1956, p. 4; Eliezer Wiesel: "The SS Officer Who Planned the Egyptian Deportation," *Yediot Aharonot*, 23 Dec. 1956, p. 2; Uri Zvi Greenberg, "The Right Time for Words and the Right Time for Rain," *Maariv*, 27 July 1956, p. 3.

3. Yitzhak Meir Levin, 7 Nov. 1956, *KP*, XXI:209; see there also Baruch Azanya (Mapai), XXI:212.

4. David Ben-Gurion, *The Renewed State of Israel* (Tel Aviv: Am Oved, 1969), p. 546; Mordecai Bar-On, *Challenge and Strife* (Beersheva: Ben-Gurion University, 1991), p. 85. Also Bar-On, *The Gates of Gaza: Israel's Defense and Foreign Policy, 1955–1957* (Tel Aviv: Am Oved, 1992).

5. BGD, 8 Nov. 1956.

6. Michael Bar-Zohar, *Ben-Gurion* (Tel Aviv: Am Oved, 1978), III:1281, 1294.

7. David Ben-Gurion, "Address to IDF Officers" (4 April 1957), *Uniqueness and Purpose* (Tel Aviv: Maarahot, 1972), p. 294.

8. SCO, 1960, XLIV:410; Moshe Kordov, *Eleven Green Berets on Trial* (Tel Aviv: A. Narkis, 1959); Tom Segev, "Kfar Kassem: The Black Flag," *Haaretz* (supplement), 22 Oct. 1981, pp. 5 ff.

9. Sharett, 21 June 1957, *Personal Diary*, VIII:2219.

10. Avner (Walter) Bar-On, *The Stories Not Told* (Tel Aviv: Idanim, 1981), pp. 81 ff.; Esther Vilenska, 13 Nov. 1956, *KP*, XXI:248; David Ben-Gurion, 12 Dec. 1956, *KP*, XXI:462.

11. Poles, "How Could It Have Happened?" *Haaretz*, 28 Dec. 1956, p. 2; Natan Alterman, "The Triangular Area," *Davar*, 7 Dec. 1956, p. 3; Uri Avneri, "The Seed of Destruction," *Haolam Hazeh*, 19 Dec. 1956, p. 3; Rabbi Benyamin, "Kfar Kassem at the Gates of the Knesset," *Ner*, Nov.–Dec. 1956, p. 19; Yehoshua Bar-Yosef, "On the Kfar Kassem Incident," *Davar*, 18 Dec. 1956, p. 2; Yeshayahu Leibowitz, letter, *Haaretz*, 28 Oct. 1958; letters to the editor, *Haaretz*, 2 Nov. 1958; "The Terrible Incident of Kfar Kassem," *Davar*, 17 Oct. 1958, p. 1; see also Dan Horowitz, "A Severe but Necessary Judgment," *Davar*, 31 Oct. 1958, p. 2; Ron Linenberg, "The Kfar Kassem Episode as Reflected in the Israeli Press," *Medina Vemimshal* 6 (Winter 1972), pp. 48 ff.

12. Editorial, *Yediot Aharonot*, 13 Dec. 1956, p. 2; S. Svislotzki, "This Was a Horrible and Terrifying Event," *Yediot Aharonot*, 13 Feb. 1956, p. 2; Yair Amikam, "Lynch in the Name of 'Thou Shalt Not Kill,'" *Yediot Aharonot*, 21 Dec. 1956, p. 2; Shmuel Segev, "Kfar Kassem to Receive a Quarter of a Million Liras," *Maariv*, 12 Dec. 1956, p. 2.

13. SCO, 1960, XLIV:410.

14. Aharon Zisling at cabinet meeting, 27 June 1948, Hakibbutz Hameuhad Archive (Zisling), section 9, container 9, file 3.

15. Shimon Peres, *David's Sling* (Jerusalem: Weidenfeld and Nicolson, 1970), p. 56.

16. BGD, 29 Dec. 1957.

17. BGD, 4 Sept. 1956.

18. Yehudit Auerbach, "Foreign-Policy Decisions and Changes of Position: Israel-Germany 1950–1965," diss., Hebrew University, 1980, pp. 162 ff.; David Ben-Gurion, 24 Dec. 1957, *KP*, XXIII:484; Menahem Begin, 7 Jan. 1958, *KP*, XXIII:564.

19. Ben-Gurion, 7 Jan. 1958, *KP*, XXIII:589.

20. Ben-Gurion to Yitzhak Ben-Aharon, 14 Feb. 1958, BGA.

21. Ben-Gurion, 24 Dec. 1958, *KP*, XXIII:483.

22. Ben-Gurion to Yariv Ben-Aharon, 3 July 1963, 14 July 1973; Ben-Aharon to Ben-Gurion, 9 July 1963, BGA.

23. Uri Avneri, "The Verdict," *Haolam Hazeh*, 15 Jan. 1958, pp. 3 ff.

24. The Supreme Court verdict is quoted here according to the original, pp. 156, 23, 175, 131, 47, 56, 93, 103, 195; SCO, 1958, XXII:2017 ff.

25. Harel, *Truth*, p. 200.

26. Ibid., p. 203.

27. Ofer, "My Husband."

28. Aharon Megged, "Milestone," *Masa*, 22 March 1957, p. 1.

29. Pinhas Rosen to Haim Cohen, 17 Jan. 1958, NA, PMO, 5432/16.

30. Shmuel Tamir, Uri Avneri, and others, 6 Jan. 1971, *KP*, LIX:861 ff.; see also Harel, *Truth*, pp. 287 ff.; and Gutmann, *Attorney General*, p. 351.

17   "THERE IS NO CERTAINTY THAT OUR CHILDREN WILL REMAIN ALIVE"

1. "Granaten aus Haifa," *Der Spiegel*, 26 June 1959, p. 18.

2. David Ben-Gurion at the Mapai CC, 28 June 1959, LPA, 23/59; see also Yehudit Auerbach, "Foreign-Policy Decisions and Changes of Position: Israel-Germany 1950–1965," diss., Hebrew University, 1980, pp. 170 ff; Yitzhak Gilad, "Israeli Public Opinion on Israel–West German Relations, 1949–1965," diss., Tel Aviv University, 1984, pp. 175 ff.

3. Ben-Gurion at the Mapai CC, 28 June 1959, LPA, 23/59.

4. "Arms Sales to Germany: A Question of Conscience," *Haaretz*, 26 June 1962, p. 2.

5. 15 Nov. 1954, *KP*, XVII:85 ff.

6. David Ben-Gurion at the Mapai CC, 28 June 1959, LPA, 23/59.

7. Ibid.

8. Moshe Sneh and Levi Eshkol, 24 June 1959, *KP*, XXVII:2360.

9. 29 June–1 July 1959, *KP*, XXVII:2371 ff.

10. Shimon Peres, *David's Sling* (Jerusalem: Weidenfeld and Nicolson, 1970), p. 58.

11. Gilad, "Israeli Public Opinion," pp. 201 ff.
12. 16 March 1960, *KP*, XXVIII:918 ff; David Ben-Gurion, 20 Jan. 1960, *KP*, XXVIII:420 ff.; Isser Harel, *Security and Democracy* (Tel Aviv: Idanim, 1989), p. 328.
13. Ben-Gurion, *Renewed State*, p. 563; Bar-Zohar, *Ben-Gurion*, III:1371 ff.; Inge Deutschkron, *Bonn and Jerusalem: The Strange Coalition* (New York: Chilton, 1970), pp. 117 ff.
14. Gilad, "Israeli Public Opinion," pp. 220 ff.; 5 Jan. 1960, *KP*, XXVIII:247 ff.; 16 March 1960, *KP*, XXVIII:918 ff.

PART VI: TRIAL: *Eichmann in Jerusalem*

18 "LET THEM HATE, AND LET THEM GO TO HELL"

1. Isser Harel, *The House on Garibaldi Street* (Tel Aviv: Maariv, 1975), pp. 161 ff., 22 ff.
2. *Attorney General vs. Adolf Eichmann, Verdict and Sentence* (Jerusalem: Merkaz Hahasbara, 1972), pp. 72 ff.
3. Simon Wiesenthal, *Ich Jagte Eichmann* (Stuttgart: Gütersloh Mohn, 1961); Tuvia Friedman, *Nazi Hunter* (English) (Haifa: Institute for the Documentation of Nazi War Crimes, 1961).
4. Isser Harel, *Security and Democracy* (Tel Aviv: Idanim, 1989), pp. 319 ff.; Isser Harel, *The German Scientists Crisis, 1962–1963* (Tel Aviv: Maariv, 1982), pp. 146 ff. See also Tom Bower, *The Pledge Betrayed* (Garden City, N.Y.: Doubleday, 1982), p. 396.
5. BGD, 6 Dec. 1959, quoted in Michael Bar-Zohar, *Ben-Gurion* (Tel Aviv: Am Oved, 1978), III:1374.
6. BGD, 15 May 1960, ibid., III:1,375; Harel, *House on Garibaldi*, pp. 161 ff., 253 ff.
7. David Ben-Gurion, 23 May 1960, *KP*, XXIX:1291.
8. Natan Alterman, "The Scales of Justice," in *The Seventh Column* (Tel Aviv: Hakibbutz Hameuhad, 1981), II:497.
9. "The Prosecution against Eichmann Must Be Prepared Meticulously," *Haaretz*, 27 May 1960, p. 2.
10. Harel, *House on Garibaldi*, pp. 161 ff., 22 ff.
11. David Ben-Gurion to Frieda Sason, 24 May 1960, BGA.
12. "The Beast in Chains," *Time*, 6 June 1960, pp. 24 ff.
13. Alterman, "Scales of Justice," II:400.
14. David Ben-Gurion to Yitzhak Y. Cohen, 10 April 1961, BGA; Ben-Gurion to Nahum Goldmann, 2 June 1960, BGA.
15. "The Eichmann Case as Seen by Ben-Gurion," *New York Times Magazine*, 18 Dec. 1960.

16. David Ben-Gurion, 12 June 1962, *KP*, XXXIV:2294.

17. Gershon Hall, "Eichmann to an International Court in Jerusalem," *Haboker*, 31 May 1960, p. 1; Rafael Bashan, "Weekly Interview," *Maariv*, 27 Jan. 1961, p. 10.

18. David Ben-Gurion to Nahum Goldmann, Goldmann to Ben-Gurion, 2 June 1960, BGA.

19. Ben-Gurion at the Mapai CC, 2 June 1960, LPA, 23/60; Moshe Meisels, "The Ben-Gurion–Goldmann Duel," *Maariv*, 3 June 1960, p. 2.

20. Ben-Gurion to Goldmann, 2 June 1960, BGA.

21. Ibid.; Ben-Gurion to Yitzhak Y. Cohen, 10 April 1961, BGA.

22. Herbert B. Ehrman to Ben-Gurion, 28 Feb. 1961; Ben-Gurion to Ehrman, 13 March 1961, BGA.

23. Joseph M. Proskauer to Ben-Gurion, 31 May 1960; Ben-Gurion to Proskauer, 18 July 1960, BGA.

24. "Eichmann Case Seen by Ben-Gurion."

25. David Ben-Gurion to Joseph M. Proskauer, 18 July 1960, BGA.

26. Ben-Gurion to Yitzhak Y. Cohen, 10 April 1961, BGA.

27. Ibid.

28. Ben-Gurion to Proskauer, 18 July 1960, BGA.

29. "Eichmann Case Seen by Ben-Gurion."

30. "The Day of the Great Shock," *Maariv*, 24 May 1960, p. 1; "Eichmann Is Not a Man," *Maariv*, 3 June 1960, p. 4; Herzl Rosenblum, " 'Sheheheyanu!' " *Yediot Aharonot*, 24 May 1960, p. 2; Moshe Sneh, 8 June 1960, *KP*, XXIX:1471; Shmuel Tamir, "The Trial of the Devil," *Yediot Aharonot*, 27 May 1960, p. 2; Verdict of the Supreme Court (original copy), pp. 15, 103, 4, reprinted in *SCO*, 1958, XII:297 ff.

31. Moshe Sneh, 8 Aug. 1960, *KP*, XXIX:2106.

32. Yitzhak Olshan, *Deliberations* (Tel Aviv: Schocken, 1978), pp. 315 ff.

33. Lead article, *Davar*, 28 May 1960, p. 1; Moshe Sneh, 8 Aug. 1960, *KP*, XXIX:2106.

34. Haim Ben-Asher and Rachel Cohen, 26 Dec. 1949, *KP*, III:313 ff.; see also 21 March 1950, IV:1103 ff.

35. Yosef Lamm and Menahem Begin, ibid.

36. Pinhas Rosen, 27 March 1950, *KP*, IV:1147, 1161.

37. Zorach Warhaftig, 27 March 1950, *KP*, IV:1152; Nahum Nir Rafalkes, 1 Aug. 1950, *KP*, VI:2393.

38. *DCO*, 1951–1952, V:172.

39. Pinhas Rosen, 27 March 1950, *KP*, IV:1147; Nahum Nir Rafalkes, 1 Aug. 1950, *KP*, VI:2393.

40. Moshe Erem, 27 March 1950, *KP*, IV:1151.

41. Zorach Warhaftig, 27 March 1950, *KP*, IV:1147.

42. Avraham Zeliger, "Bureau 06," *Rivon Mishteret Yisrael* 4, no. 13 (Feb. 1962), pp. 8 ff.

43. Rachel Auerbach, "Witnesses and Testimony at the Eichmann Trial," *Yediot Yad Vashem* 28 (Dec. 1961), pp. 35 ff.

44. Yitzhak Gilad, "Israeli Public Opinion on Israel–West German Relations, 1949–1965," diss., Tel Aviv University, 1984, pp. 241 ff., 370.

45. Gideon Hausner, *The Jerusalem Trial* (Tel Aviv: Beit Lohamei Hagetaot and Hakibbutz Hameuhad, 1980), pp. 294–305.

46. Olshan, *Deliberations*, pp. 315 ff.

47. Rafael Bashan, "Weekly Interview," *Maariv*, 3 Oct. 1969, p. 16.

48. 18 Jan. 1961, *KP*, XXX:754 ff.; 31 Jan. 1961, *KP*, XXX:855 ff.; see also Eliakim Rubenstein, *Judges of the Land* (Tel Aviv: Schocken, 1980), pp. 162 ff.

49. 8 Aug. 1960, *KP*, XXIX:2106.

50. Hannah Arendt, *Eichmann in Jerusalem: A Report on the Banality of Evil* (New York: Viking, 1965), p. 4.

19   "SIX MILLION TIMES NO!"

1. Gideon Hausner, *The Jerusalem Trial* (Tel Aviv: Beit Lohamei Hagetaot and Hakibbutz Hameuhad, 1980), pp. 312 ff.

2. *Attorney General vs. Adolf Eichmann, Verdict and Sentence* (Jerusalem: Merkaz Hahasbara, 1972), pp. 137 ff.

3. Gideon Hausner to David Ben-Gurion, 24 March 1961; Ben-Gurion to Hausner, 28 March 1961, BGA.

4. Hausner, *Jerusalem Trial*, pp. 324 ff.

5. *Attorney General vs. Adolf Eichmann, Opening Statement* (Jerusalem: Merkaz Hahasbara, 1972), p. 7.

6. "Six Million Souls Stand and Shout Before You," *Haaretz*, 21 May 1947; Dov Shilansky, *In a Hebrew Jail: From the Diary of a Political Prisoner* (Tel Aviv: Armoni, 1980), p. 20; SCO, 1959, XIII:1056.

7. David Ben-Gurion, "Eternal Israel," *Government Yearbook 1954* (Jerusalem: GPO, 1954), pp. 18, 9, 14.

8. *Attorney General vs. Eichmann, Opening*, p. 127.

9. Hausner, *Jerusalem Trial*, pp. 324 ff.

10. Haim Guri, *Facing the Glass Booth: The Jerusalem Trial* (Tel Aviv: Hakibbutz Hameuhad, 1962), p. 13.

11. Natan Alterman, "The First Day," in *The Seventh Column* (Tel Aviv: Hakibbutz Hameuhad, 1981), II:501.

12. *Attorney General vs. Eichmann, Opening*, p. 124.

13. Hausner, *Jerusalem Trial*, pp. 327, 245.

14. Guri, *Facing*, p. 73.

15. Rivka Joselewska at the Eichmann trial, session 30, records, Yad Vashem Library.

16. Gabriel Strassman, "What Did the Eichmann Trial Give Us?" *Maariv*, 11 Dec. 1981, p. 27.
17. Moritz Fleischman, session 16, records, Yad Vashem Library; Guri, *Facing*, pp. 33, 245, 268.
18. Hausner, *Jerusalem Trial*, pp. 341, 344; Pinhas Freudiger at the Eichmann trial, session 51; Joel Brand at the Eichmann trial, session 56, records, Yad Vashem Library.
19. Tamir's request and accompanying newspaper articles are preserved in the Beit Jabotinsky Archives and in the Yad Vashem Library.
20. Hausner, *Jerusalem Trial*, p. 344.
21. *Attorney General vs. Eichmann, Verdict*, p. 183.
22. Tzivia Lubetkin and Yitzhak (Antek) Zuckerman at the Eichmann trial, session 25; Abba Kovner at the Eichmann trial, session 27, records, Yad Vashem Library.
23. Hausner, *Jerusalem Trial*, p. 334.
24. Ibid., p. 349.
25. Ibid., p. 351.
26. Eichmann testimony, sessions 75 ff., records, Yad Vashem Library.
27. *Attorney General vs. Eichmann, Verdict*, p. 280.
28. Guri, *Facing*, pp. 146, 154, 176, 183, 187.
29. Hausner, *Jerusalem Trial*, p. 390.
30. *Attorney General vs. Eichmann, Verdict*, p. 42; Hausner, *Jerusalem Trial*, p. 351.
31. Guri, *Facing*, p. 187.
32. *Attorney General vs. Eichmann, Verdict*, pp. 279 ff.
33. Ibid., pp. 285 ff.
34. "Do It!" *Maariv*, 15 Dec. 1961, p. 1.
35. Elisabeth Young-Bruehl, *Hannah Arendt: For Love of the World* (New Haven: Yale University Press, 1982), p. 332.
36. Yerahmiel Cohen, "On the Question of the Responsibility of the Jews for Their Extermination by the Nazis as Expressed in the Writings of Bruno Bettelheim, Raul Hilberg, and Hannah Arendt, and the Debate Surrounding Them," M.A. diss., Hebrew University of Jerusalem, 1972, pp. 45 ff.
37. F. A. Krummacher, ed., *Die Kontroverse Hannah Arendt, Eichmann, und die Juden* (Munich: Nymphenburger Verlagshandlung, 1964); Jacob Robinson, *And the Crooked Shall Be Made Straight* (New York: Macmillan, 1965); Arieh Leon Koboby, "A Criminal Country versus a Moral Society," M. Mushkat, "Eichmann in New York," and Natan Eck, "Hannah Arendt's Hateful Articles," all in *Yediot Yad Vashem* 31 (Dec. 1963), pp. 1 ff.; exchange of letters between Gershom Sholem and Hannah Arendt, *Yediot Irgun Olei Merkaz Eropa* 33 (16 Aug. 1964); see also Gershom Scholem, *Significant Acts* (Tel Aviv: Am Oved, 1982), p. 91; A. E. Simon, "A Portrait of Hannah Arendt," *Molad* 21, pamphlet 179–180, pp. 239

ff.; Ruth Firer, *Agents of the Lesson* (Tel Aviv: Hakibbutz Hameuhad, 1989), pp. 138 ff.

38. Hausner, *Jerusalem Trial*, pp. 409 ff.
39. David Ben-Gurion, 12 June 1962, *KP*, XXXIV:2293.
40. Guri, *Facing*, pp. 245 ff.
41. Schmuel Hugo Bergmann to Geula Cohen et al., 27 July 1961, Bergmann Archives, National and University Library, Arc. 40 1502/1558.
42. Schmuel Hugo Bergmann, *Tagebücher, Briefe, 1948–1975* (Königstein: Jüdischer Verlag bei Athenaeum, 1985), II:415 (1 June 1962); p. 395 (21 Dec. 1961).
43. Martin Buber Archives, National and University Library, unit 630.
44. Pinhas Rosen to Martin Buber, 29 April and 7 May 1962, ibid.; Hausner, *Jerusalem Trial*, p. 428.
45. Buber et al. to Yitzhak Ben-Zvi, 30 May 1962, Buber Archives.
46. Yehuda Bacon, 7 June 1961, Eichmann trial, session 68, records, Yad Vashem Library; see also "Paintings from Hell," *Haolam Hazeh*, 17 May 1961, pp. 12 ff.
47. Bacon to Martin Buber, 4 Nov. 1958, Buber Archives.
48. Bergmann, *Tagebücher*, II:415 (1 June 1962).
49. Rafael Bashan, "Weekly Interview," *Maariv*, 27 Jan. 1961, p. 10; "Philosopher's Plea," *Time*, 23 March 1962, p. 23; Hausner, *Jerusalem Trial*, p. 445.
50. Arendt, *Eichmann*, p. 252.
51. Michael Shashar, *Yeshayahu Leibowitz on the World* (Jerusalem: Keter, 1987), XXXII:79 ff.

20   "GLOOM SHALL NOT PREVAIL"

1. "The Atom," *Time*, 26 Dec. 1960, p. 11; David Ben-Gurion, 21 Dec. 1960, *KP*, XXX:545; Levi Eshkol, 18 May 1966, *KP*, XLV:1469.
2. Ben-Gurion at the opening of the Institute for Nuclear Physics at the Weizmann Institute, 20 May 1958, BGA, file on "Ben-Gurion, Scientists, and Humanists."
3. Yisrael Dostrovsky, "The Establishment of the Atomic Energy Commission," *David Ben-Gurion and the Development of Science in Israel* (Jerusalem: Israel National Academy of Sciences, 1989), pp. 44 ff.
4. Yaakov Hazan and Tawfik Tubi, 6 Aug. 1962, *KP*, XXXIV:3059 ff.
5. Yehuda Ben-Moshe, "Twenty-Five Years before Vanounou," *Koteret Rashit*, 26 Nov. 1986, p. 16.
6. Shimon Peres, 23 May 1966, *KP*, XLV:1480 ff.
7. David Ben-Gurion at the Mapai CC, 13 Dec. 1951, LPA, 23/51.
8. Moshe Dayan at the Mapai CC, 28 June 1959, LPA, 23/59.

9. Dostrovsky, "Establishment of the Atomic Energy Commission," pp. 44 ff.

10. E. D. Bergmann to Meir Yaari, 25 July 1966, Hashomer Hatsair–Kibbutz Haartsi Archives (Yaari personal archive), B-11 (3).

11. 3 Nov. 1964, *KP*, XLI:223 ff.; Esther Raziel-Naor, 27 Jan. 1960, *KP*, XXVIII:486.

12. Isser Harel, *The German Scientists Crisis, 1962–1963* (Tel Aviv: Maariv, 1982), p. 65.

13. 20 March 1963, *KP*, XXXVI:1568 ff.

14. Harel, *German Scientists Crisis*, pp. 74 ff.

15. David Ben-Gurion, 7 April 1963, *KP*, XXXVI:1748.

16. Teddy Kollek, *For Jerusalem* (London: Weidenfeld and Nicolson, 1978), p. 154.

17. David Ben-Gurion, 13 May 1963, *KP*, XXXVII:1821; Abba Sikra, "The Third Zionist Organization," *Hazit Haam*, 28 March 1933, p. 2. See also Michael Bar-Zohar, *Ben-Gurion* (Tel Aviv: Am Oved, 1978), III:1546; Abba Ahimeir, "From a Fascist's Notebook," *Herut*, 15 Aug. 1955, p. 2; "Ben-Gurion-Ahimeir Debate," *Maariv*, 26 Nov. 1964, p. 6.

18. Yitzhak Gilad, "Israeli Public Opinion on Israel–West German Relations, 1949–1965," diss., Tel Aviv University, 1984, pp. 270 ff.

19. David Ben-Gurion to Haim Guri, 15 May 1963, BGA, quoted by Bar-Zohar, *Ben-Gurion*, III:1547.

20. Kollek, *For Jerusalem*, p. 155.

21. David Ben-Gurion, 13 May 1963, *KP*, XXXVII:1823; Menahem Begin, 17 March 1964, *KP*, XXXIX:1427; Gilad, "Israeli Public Opinion," pp. 270 ff.

22. Gilad, "Israeli Public Opinion," pp. 369 ff.; Rachel Auerbach, "Witnesses and Testimony at the Eichmann Trial," *Yediot Yad Vashem* 28 (Dec. 1961), pp. 193 ff.; Haim Yehil to Moshe Sharett, 22 March 1953, CZA (NGA) Z6 2016.

23. 28 July 1954, *KP*, XXVII:2229; Moshe Sharett, 24 April 1955, *Personal Diary* (Tel Aviv: Maariv, 1978), IV:958; 15–17 July 1957, *KP* XXII:2389 ff.; 24 Dec. 1957, *KP*, XXIII:481 ff.

24. "Israel and Germany," *Haaretz*, 19 July 1954, p. 2; Gershom Schocken to Moshe Sharett, 19 July 1954, NA, FM, 2413/3.

25. 2 July 1956, *KP*, XX:2154 ff.; Yaakov Tsur, *Paris Diary* (Tel Aviv: Am Oved, 1968), p. 272.

26. Elimelech Rimalt, 12 Oct. 1964, *KP*, XLI:11.

27. Eliezer Shinar, *Under the Burden of Duty and Emotion* (Tel Aviv: Schocken, 1967), pp. 93 ff.; Moshe Sneh, 10 Dec. 1963, *KP*, XXXVIII:473.

28. 20 May 1964, *KP*, XL:1860 ff.; 19 Oct. 1964, *KP*, XLI:57 ff.; 18 Nov. 1964, *KP*, XLI:384 ff.; Gilad, "Israeli Public Opinion," pp. 349 ff.

29. 16 March 1965, *KP* XLII:1540 ff.
30. Gilad, "Israeli Public Opinion," pp. 434.
31. Yeshayahu Ben-Porat, *Conversations* (Tel Aviv: Idanim, 1981), p. 25; see also Amos Elon, "No One Is Too Old to Learn Something New," *Haaretz*, 5 May 1966, p. 1; Elon, *In a Land Haunted by the Past* (Tel Aviv: Schocken: 1967).
32. Levi Eshkol, 23 May 1966, *KP*, XLV:1518; "Adenauer Left After a Discussion of State Affairs with Eshkol," *Maariv*, 10 May 1966, p. 1.
33. Esther Raziel-Naor, 17 May 1966, *KP*, XLV:1443; Yaakov Solomon, *My Way* (Tel Aviv: Idanim, 1980), pp. 274 ff.; "An Apparently Superfluous Clash," *Haaretz*, 6 May 1966, p. 2.
34. Rolf Pauls, tape-recorded interview with author, 23 Nov. 1989.
35. 15 July 1953, *KP*, XIV:1946; 23 May 1955, *KP*, XVII:1241; 10 Dec. 1956, *KP*, XXI:429.
36. Levi Eshkol, 12 July 1966, *KP*, XLVI:2100.
37. 18 Oct. 1961, *KP*, XXXII:134 ff.; 2–3 Jan. 1962, *KP*, XXXII:580 ff.; 9 Jan. 1962, *KP*, XXXII:902 ff.
38. Haim Bar-Lev, 13 Feb. 1985, *KP*, I:1620.

PART VII: GROWING UP: *From War to War*

2 1   "EVERYONE THOUGHT ABOUT IT"

1. *Nitsots* 15 (undated, apparently February–March 1967); Natan Shacham, "We Need More Daring," *Maariv*, 7 July 1967, p. 13.
2. David Ben-Gurion, 23 May 1966, *KP*, LV:1508 ff.
3. Shimon Samet, "Tel Aviv at a Time of Crisis," *Haaretz*, 2 June 1967, p. 2; R. Ben-Shoshan, "The Economy Withstood the Test," *Haaretz*, 9 June 1967, p. 3; "With Courage and Decisiveness," *Haaretz*, 1 June 1967, p. 2; "Within Two Days the Stream of Those Leaving from Lod Will Slow Down," *Maariv*, 29 May 1967, p. 8; Attallah Mansour, "Shukeiry's Voice of Palestine Calls on Israeli Arabs to Rebel," *Haaretz*, 1 June 1967, p. 2; Michael Bar-Zohar, *The Longest Month* (Tel Aviv: Levin-Epstein, 1968), p. 153.
4. *The Seventh Day*, recorded and edited by a group of young kibbutz members (London: André Deutsch, 1970), pp. 160 ff.
5. Yitzhak Rabin, *Service Book* (Tel Aviv: Maariv, 1979) p. 148.
6. Shlomo Nakdimon, *Toward the Zero Hour* (Tel Aviv: Ramdor, 1968); Eitan Haber, *Tomorrow Will Be War: The Memoirs of Brig. Gen. Yisrael Lior, Military Secretary to Prime Ministers Levi Eshkol and Golda Meir* (Tel Aviv: Idanim, 1987), pp. 157 ff.

7. Yehoshafat Harkabi, *Between Israel and the Arab World* (Tel Aviv: Maar-ahot, 1968), pp. 39 ff.
8. Eliezer Livneh, "The Danger of Hitler Returns," *Haaretz*, 31 May 1967, p. 2; "Between Hitler and Nasser," *Haaretz*, 5 June 1967, p. 2; see also "Return to Munich," letters to the editor, *Haaretz*, 31 May 1967, p. 2; Yohanan Lahav, "Diary of the Crisis," *Yediot Aharonot*, 2 June 1967, p. 17.
9. Rabin, *Service Book*, p. 161; Michael Brecher, *Decisions in Israel's Foreign Policy* (New Haven: Yale University Press, 1975), pp. 333 ff.
10. "Cry Out and Shout, Thou Inhabitant of Zion!" (editorial), *Haaretz*, 8 June 1967, p. 2.
11. "Great Events" (editorial), *Al Hamishmar*, 8 June 1967, p. 1.
12. Silvi Keshet, "My Dear Uzi," *Haaretz*, 8 June 1967, p. 2.
13. Uri Ramon, "The Consciousness of the Holocaust during the Six-Day War," *Dapim Leheker Hashoah Vehamered*, collection A, 1969, pp. 59 ff.
14. Arieh Ben-Eliezer, 22 July 1968, *KP*, LII:2729.
15. *Seventh Day*, pp. 160, 173.
16. Menahem Begin, 20 June 1977, *KP*, LXXX: 67.
17. Meiron Medzini, *The Proud Jewess* (Tel Aviv: Idanim–Yediot Aharonot, 1990), p. 406.
18. Leni Yahil, "How Can We Discuss the Holocaust?" *Gesher* 1 and 2 (1979), pp. 144 ff.
19. Medzini, *Proud Jewess*, p. 434.
20. Ehud Praver, tape-recorded interview with the author, 15 June 1990.
21. See also Amnon Lin, 26 June 1985, *KP*, CI:3147.
22. Matti Golan, *The Road to Peace: A Biography of Shimon Peres* (New York: Warner Books, 1989), p. 152; Peres in tape-recorded interview with the author, 27 Aug. 1990; Shimon Peres, *Entebbe Diary* (Tel Aviv: Idanim, 1991), pp. 68, 92.

22 ''HITLER IS ALREADY DEAD, MR. PRIME MINISTER''

1. Omri Mishor, "Panel Discussion in Musrara," *Al Hamishmar*, 27 Feb. 1979, p. 4; Gabriel Stern, "The Lesson of the Holocaust for Sephardim and Ashkenazim," *Al Hamishmar*, 27 April 1979, p. 4.
2. Yitzhak Navon, 14 March 1978, *KP*, LXXXII:2047.
3. Dan Bar-On and Oron Sela, "The Vicious Circle between Relating to Reality and Relating to the Holocaust among Young Israelis," research report, Ben-Gurion University, Department of Behavioral Sciences, 1990, p. 39.
4. Moshe Katsav, 14 March 1978, *KP*, LXXXII:2058.
5. Menahem Begin, 20 June 1977, *KP*, LXXX:65.

6. Begin, 20 June 1979, *KP*, LXXXIV–LXXXVI:3115, 3126.

7. Gershon Jakobson, "Before All at the UN, Herzog Tore the Condemnation of Zionism to Shreds," *Yediot Aharonot*, 11 Nov. 1977, p. 1.

8. Menaham Begin, 20 Nov. 1977, *KP*, LXXXI:463.

9. Dov Shilansky, 27 Sept. 1979, *KP*, LXXXIII:403; see also *KP*, LXXXIII:3800 (parliamentary question no. 2059).

10. Gideon Alon, "Begin: If Iraq Tries Again to Build a Nuclear Reactor, We Will Act against It," *Haaretz*, 10 June 1981, p. 1.

11. Menaham Begin, 2 April 1951, *KP*, VIII:1548.

12. Begin, 1 Sept. 1977, *KP*, LXXX:752; also 15 Aug. 1977, *KP*, LXXX:674.

13. Arieh Naor, *Government at War: How the Israeli Government Functioned during the Lebanon War*, 1982 (Tel Aviv: Yediot Aharonot, 1986) pp. 47 ff.

14. Menaham Begin, 29 June 1982, *KP*10, II:2973.

15. *Report of the Investigatory Commission on the Events in the Beirut Refugee Camps*, 1983, p. 55.

16. Menaham Begin, 18 June 1982, *KP*10, II:2747.

17. Arieh Zimuki, "Begin to Reagan: I Feel Like I Have Sent the Army into Berlin to Destroy Hitler in His Bunker," *Yediot Aharonot*, 3 Aug. 1982, p. 1.

18. Amos Oz, "Hitler Is Already Dead, Mr. Prime Minister," *Yediot Aharonot*, 21 June 1982, p. 6.

19. Herzl Rosenbloom, "Childish Blabber," *Yediot Aharonot*, 2 July 1982, p. 2.

20. "Prof. Leibowitz Calls Israel's Policy in Lebanon Judeo-Nazi," *Yediot Aharonot*, 21 June 1982, p. 7.

21. Lili Galili, "The Yad Vashem Directorate Forbade Hunger Strike on Its Grounds," *Haaretz*, 13 Aug. 1982, p. 3.

22. Hanoh Bartov, "Out of Bounds," *Maariv*, 11 Jan. 1983, p. 5. See also Yehiam Weitz, "Tempest in a Teacup," *Davar*, 10 Jan. 1983, p. 5.

23. Boaz Evron, "The Holocaust: A Danger to the Nation," *Iton* 77 21 May–June 1980), pp. 12 ff.; see also Yehuda Bauer, "An Attempt at Clarification," *Iton* 77 22–23 (Sept.–Oct. 1980), pp. 18 ff.; Boaz Evron, "Clarification of Clarification," *Iton* 77 24 (Nov.–Dec. 1980), pp. 36 ff.

24. Yair Tsaban, 21 Feb. 1983, *KP*, C:1423 ff.

25. Moshe Dayan, 5 July 1978, *KP*, LXXXIII:3391.

26. Yoram Aridor, 23 Nov. 1977, *KP*, LXXXI:499.

27. Menaham Begin, 3 June 1981, *KP*, XCI:2896 ff.; see also Amnon Rubinstein, 3 June 1981, *KP*, XCI:2894.

28. Begin, 9 July 1979, *KP*, LXXXIV-LXXXVI:3391.

29. Yohanan Meroz, *Was It for Nothing?* (Tel Aviv: Sifriat Poalim, 1988), p. 67.

23 "DEEP IN OUR SOULS"

1. Meir Kahane, *Thorns in Your Eyes* (Jerusalem: Institute for the Jewish Idea, 1980).
2. Yair Kotler, *Heil Kahane* (Tel Aviv: Modan, 1985), pp. 292 ff.; SCO, 742/84, verdict, 31 Oct. 1985; see also Tel Aviv-Jaffa Magistrate's Court, civil case 45860/90, Meir Kahane vs. Yitzhak Lior et al. (in author's possession); SCO, vol. 39(2), p. 302 and vol 42(4), p. 197.
3. Displays of racism among schoolchildren and the educational system's inattention: *KP*, 2 Jan. 1985, C:1,023 ff.; Van Leer Institute report on the danger of extremism among youth: 26 June 1985, *KP*, CII:3132; "In the wake of surveys of youth: not democratic hysteria but sober Zionist and political-military history": 2 Dec. 1985, *KP*, CVI, pp. 688 ff. See also Dahaf Research Institute and Van Leer Institute, *Political and Social Positions among Youth*, 1987.
4. Haike Grossman, 25 Nov. 1986, *KP*, CVI:397.
5. 29 July 1985, *KP*, CII:3751; 31 July 1985, *KP*, CII:3865, 3898.
6. Tape-recorded interview with Col. Ehud Praver, 15 June 1990.
7. Israeli Defense Forces, Education Corps, Guidelines for the Commander, 5 May 1986, quoted by permission of the IDF spokesman.
8. Israeli Defense Forces, Education Corps, "On the Agenda," 26 April 1987, quoted by permission of the IDF spokesman.
9. Praver interview.
10. Dan Sagir, "In the Battalion They Knew That We Were a Killer Company," *Haaretz*, 31 July 1989, p. 11.
11. Uzi Baram and Yitzhak Rabin, 2 Aug. 1989, *KP*12, I:3616.
12. See, for example, Gershom Schocken, 2 Jan. 1956, *KP*, XIX (2):685.
13. Tom Segev, "The Case of Mohammed Abu Wardi," *Koteret Rashit* 203 (22 Oct. 1986), p. 11.
14. Ori Nir, "The Civil Administration Has Forbidden Distribution of *Al-Fajr* for Publishing an Anti-Semitic Cartoon," *Haaretz*, 18 Sept. 1988, p. 2.
15. Zvi Harel, "Moledet Has Filed a Criminal Complaint for Libel against *Davar*," *Haaretz*, 26 July 1989, p. 5; "International Conference" (adv.), *Maariv*, 30 Oct. 1988, p. 2; "Apology," *Maariv*, 31 Oct. 1988, p. 18.
16. Zeev Sternhell, "Banai, Struzman, Farago," *Hadashot*, 2 June 1986, p. 11.
17. "No to the Yellow Patch," *Hadashot*, 2 June 1989, p. 2.
18. Dan Almagor, "I Regret," *Yerushalaim (Yediot Aharonot)*, 16 Dec. 1988, p. 23.
19. Doron Meiri, "I Thought of the Boycott the Germans Staged against the Jews," *Hadashot*, 27 Nov. 1990, p. 8; special military court M/1/90, Chief Military Prosecutor vs. Col. Yehuda Meir, verdict, p. 13 (in author's possession).

20. "Israel Has Room for All," *Newsweek*, 17 Oct. 1988, p. 64; Yerah Tal, "We Are Beginning to Grow Accustomed to It: A Dangerous Repression," *Haaretz*, 11 Oct. 1988, p. 2; Aharon Megged, "Things of No Truth," *Haaretz*, 14 Oct. 1988, p. C3; David Avidan, "Tell It Not in Gath," *Hadashot Shel Shabbot*, 14 Oct. 1988, p. 23.

21. Sidra DeKoven Ezrahi, "Aharon Appelfeld: The Search for a Language," in Jonathan Frankel, ed., *Studies in Contemporary Jewry*, 1984, I:366.

22. Dalia Rabikovitz, "You Don't Kill a Baby Twice," *True Love* (Tel Aviv: Hakibbutz Hameuhad, 1987), p. 64.

23. Roli Rosen and Ilana Hammerman, *Poets Will Not Write Poetry* (Tel Aviv: Am Oved, 1990); see also Hannah Yaoz, "Hebrew Holocaust Literature as Historical and Transhistorical Literature," *Eked* 1980; Avraham Hagorny-Green, "On the Holocaust in Our Poetry," *Eked* 1970.

24. Art Spiegelman, *Maus* (Hebrew edition) (Zemora Beitan, 1990).

25. Stan Johnson, "Unprecedented Debate on Anti-Semitism and the Holocaust in the Soviet Union," *Maariv*, 27 Sept. 1961, p. 1.

26. Noah Klieger, "Not 'Another Book,' " *Yediot Aharonot*, 18 Aug. 1988; Yoram Harpaz, "Don't Shoot the Translator," *Kol Hair*, 28 April 1989, p. 31; Moshe Zimmerman and Oded Heilbrunner, eds., *Chapter from Hitler's "Mein Kampf"* (Jerusalem: Akademon, 1992).

27. Moshe Nissim, 25 June 1985, *KP*, CI:3061.

28. *State of Israel vs. Ivan John Demjanjuk, Trial Record*, 2 March 1987, pp. 1065 ff. (in author's possession).

29. *State of Israel vs. Ivan John Demjanjuk, Verdict*, 18 April 1988, pp. 1 ff. (in author's possession). See also Tom Teichholz, *The Trial of Ivan the Terrible* (New York: St. Martin's Press, 1990); Wilhelm L. Wagenaar, *Identifying Ivan* (Cambridge: Harvard University Press, 1989).

30. *Israel vs. Demjanjuk, Verdict*, p. 9.

PART VIII: MEMORY: *The Struggle to Shape the Past*

24 "HOLOCAUST AND HEROISM"

1. Avraham Levinson, consultation on the question of the proposed Diaspora Memorial, 4 June 1945, YVA, container YV/1-YV/9 (file 14); see also the symposium organized by Yad Vashem, 10 June 1956, NA, FM, 2388/16.

2. Yitzhak Arad in tape-recorded interview with author, 12 May 1990.

3. Avraham Shlonsky, "Vow," in *Poems* (Tel Aviv: Sifriat Poalim, 1971), IV:84.

4. Arieh Leon Kokobi, "The Criminal Country versus the Moral Society," *Yediot Yad Vashem* 31 (Dec. 1963), pp. 1 ff.

5. Nahum Goldmann to the Yad Vashem executive, 1 Feb. 1956, minutes, NA, FM, 2388/16.

6. Haim Ben-Asher, 27 March 1950, *KP*, IV:1158; Attorney General vs. Adolf Eichmann, verdict (Jerusalem: Merkaz Hahasbara, 1962) pp. 189 ff.; "Holocaust and Heroism Memorial Act" (undated draft), NA, FM, 2388/15/A; *KP*, XIV:2455; see also Yaakov Rosenthal, "Yad Vashem, Memorialization of Martyrs and Legislative Attempts," *Haaretz*, 13 April 1953, p. 2; Yisrael Gutman, ed., *The Encyclopedia of the Holocaust* (Jerusalem: Yad Vashem, Sifriat Poalim, 1990), V:1282.

7. D. Z. Pinkas to JAE, 4 Sept. 1946, CZA, S 26 1326; "Ashes of Polish Martyrs to Burial in Tel Aviv," *Haaretz*, 12 Sept. 1946, p. 4.

8. Yaakov Zerubavel and Berl Loker at the JAE, 26 June 1949, CZA.

9. Yosef Gorny, *The Quest for Collective Identity* (Tel Aviv: Am Oved, 1986), p. 106.

10. Haim Guri, "From That Fire," in *Readings for Holocaust and Heroism Memorial Day* (Jerusalem: Merkaz Hahasbara and Yad Vashem, 1975), p. 60.

11. Mordecai Shenhabi, proposal to the main office of the Jewish National Fund, 10 Sept. 1942, and related material (1942–1945), Hashomer Hatsair archives (Shenhabi archive), 4-1-F; see also YVA, YV/1–YV/9 and YV/10–YV/19; Yehuda Koren, "To Weep for the Fire," *Davar Hashavua*, 29 Aug. 1986, pp. 8 ff.; ibid., 5 Sept. 1986, pp. 6 ff.

12. Shenhabi proposal.

13. Memorandum of meeting with the Hashomer Hatsair CC, 18 June 1946, YVA, YV/1–YV/9 (file A).

14. Basic Assumptions for the Planning of the Memorial Mountain, 8–9 April 1956, NA, FM, 2388/16.

15. Mordecai Shenhabi, notes, 14 Aug. 1944, 21 Aug. 1944, YVA, YV/1–YV/9 (file A).

16. Shenhabi proposal.

17. David Ben-Gurion to Avraham Granot, 21 April 1952, BGA, correspondence.

18. Mordecai Shenhabi to Granot, 6 Nov. 1951; Yosef Weitz and others to main office of Jewish National Fund, 3 Feb. 1953, YVA, YV/1–YV/9 (file X); see also Shenhabi to Abba Houshi, 21 Oct. 1954, NA, FM, 2388/15/A.

19. "Yad Vashem, Memorial Project for the Destroyed Diaspora," 2 May 1945, YVA, YV/10–YV/19 (file II).

20. "Yad Vashem," publicity leaflet, 1 March 1948, NA, FA, 2388/15/A; Vaad Haleumi discussions, YVA, YV/1–YV/9 (file 14); Yad Vashem conference (13 July 1947), container YV/10–YV/19 (file I); see also decisions of the CZA convention, 1326 S/26.

21. "Yad Vashem": elements of the plan (undated), YVA, container YV/10–YV/19 (file II).

22. Ben-Zion Dinur to David Ben-Gurion, 3 April 1953, NA, PMO, 5564/2.

23. Yad Vashem to Foreign Ministry public-relations department, 6 Jan 1954, NA, FM, 2388/15/A; see also 2520/13/A; public-relations department to Israeli delegations overseas, 24 March 1953, NA, FM, 2388/15/A.

24. BGD, 26 June 1951.

25. Correspondence with experts on international law, correspondence with David Ben-Gurion and Moshe Sharett, opinions of attorneys, and report of the Feinberg commission, YVA, management archive, vol. 1950–1952; proposed legislation, Robinson opinion, and further correspondence, NA, FM, 2388/15/A; see also 2388/16.

26. Ben-Zion Dinur at Yad Vashem executive, 1 Feb. 1956, NA, FM, 2388/16. See also Hannah Zeifeld, "The Beginnings of the Term 'Shoah,' " *Masua* 15 (1987), pp. 101 ff.

27. Dinur, 12 May 1953, *KP*, XIV:1310 ff. See also Holocaust and Heroism Memorial Act, Yad Vashem, 1953, undated draft, NA, FM, 2388/15/A.

28. 12 May 1953, *KP*, XIV:1310 ff.; 18 May 1953, XIV:1331 ff.; 19. Aug. 1953, XIV:2402 ff.

29. 12 April 1951, *KP*, IX:1655 ff.

30. Mapai secretariat, 20 March 1953, LA 24/53.

31. Mordecai Nurok et al., 18 June 1958, *KP*, XXIV:2118 ff.

32. Holocaust and Heroism Memorial Day Law, 10 March 1959, *KP*, XXVI:1385.

33. Baruch Azania et al., 8 March 1961, *KP*, XXXI:1264 ff., 1300 ff., 1504 ff., 1590.

34. Aharon Yadlin, 13 March 1961, *KP*, XXXI:1313.

35. Shlomo Shamgar, "Neo-Nazi Gangs Riot in Berlin," *Yediot Aharonot*, 22 April 1990, p. 2.

36. Aviezer Golan, "The Meeting in Paris," *Yediot Aharonot*, 2 May 1989, p. 2.

37. *Readings for Holocaust and Heroism Memorial Day* (Jerusalem: Merkaz Hahasbara and Yad Vashem, 1975), pp. 12 ff.

38. Motions, 2 Aug. 1977, *KP*, LXXX:564 ff.

39. Moshe Kol at Yad Vashem administration, 1 Feb. 1956, NA, FM, 2388/16.

40. Gideon Hausner, Zorach Warhaftig, 16 Dec. 1968, *KP*, LIII:698; see also S. Z. Kahane to Zeev Sharef, 7 June 1956, NA, PMO, 5564/2; Judith T. Baumel, *A Voice of Lament: The Holocaust and Prayer* (Ramat Gan: Bar-Ilan University, 1992); Menahem Friedman; "The Haredim and the Holocaust," *The Jerusalem Quarterly*, no. 53 (Winter 1990), pp. 115 ff.

41. *Ot Vaed*, unattributed and undated publicity pamphlet (in the author's possession).

42. Meir Dvorzetzki, Avraham Granot, and Yitzhak Gruenbaum at Yad Vashem executive, 16 July 1954, NA, FM, 2388/15/A.

2 5   "THE REST OF YOUR LIFE WITH MONIK AND FRIEDA"

1. Quoted in Nili Keren, "The Influence of Opinion Leaders and of Holocaust Research on the Development of the Educational Discussion and Curriculum on the Holocaust in Secondary Schools and in Informal Education in Israel, 1948–1981," diss., Hebrew University, 1985, p. 29.
2. Yitzhak ("Antek") Zuckerman, *Those Seven Years* (Tel Aviv: Hakibbutz Hameuhad, Beit Lohamei Hagetaot, 1990), pp. 304 ff.
3. Margaret Larkin, *The Sun Did Not Stand Still* (Tel Aviv: Maarahot, 1984).
4. Meir Dvorzetzki at Yad Vashem administration 13 Dec. 1954, YVA, Administration archive vol. 1953–1955.
5. Nili Bornstein, *I Ask to Wait* (Tel Aviv: Hakibbutz Hameuhad, 1973), p. 27; Dina Vardi, *Bearers of the Sign: Dialogues with Members of the Holocaust Second Generation* (Jerusalem: Keter, 1990); Aaron Hass, *In the Shadow of the Holocaust* (Ithaca: Cornell University Press, 1990); Amnon Neustadt, *Israels Zweite Generation* (Berlin, Bonn: Verlag J.H.W. Dietz, 1987); Dan Bar-On and Oron Sela, *Psycho-Social Effects of the Holocaust on the Second and Third Generations* (Beersheva: Ben-Gurion University, Division of Behavioral Sciences, 1991).
6. Tzvika Dror, ed., *Testimonies of 96 Members of Kibbutz Lohamei Hagetaot* (Tel Aviv: Hakibbutz Hameuhad, 1984).
7. Ibid., I:13 ff.
8. Proposed legislation to forbid the use of Nazi symbols and terms, 19 Feb. 1986, *KP11*, II:798 ff.; Holocaust and Heroism Memorial Law, Yad Vashem (amendment re honorary citizenship for righteous gentiles), 14 Jan. 1985, *KP11*, I:1152; 25 March 1985, p. 2156; announcement of minister of justice of prize of $1 million to whoever would bring Mengele to justice in Israel, 7 May 1985, *KP11*, I:2374; Meir Kahane, 11 June 1986, *KP*, CVII:3067.
9. Debate on 40th anniversary of the defeat of Nazi Germany and its puppets, 6 May 1985, *KP11*, I:2367 ff.; Holocaust and Heroism Memorial Law, Yad Vashem (amendment), proposal, 19 Feb. 1985, *KP11*, I:1712; extradition of Archbishop Tarifa to Israel, 21 Jan. 1985, *KP11*, I:1276 ff.
10. Israeli requests to receive German citizenship, 13 Feb. 1985, *KP*, CI:1655 ff.; parliamentary question 1000, 1002, 5 June 1985, *KP*, CII:2767 ff.; cabinet approval of president's visit to Germany, 3 Dec. 1986, *KP*, CVI:570.
11. Hans Mordow to Yitzhak Shamir, 2 March 1990; declaration of the East German parliament, 23 April 1990 (complete version in possession of the author, quoted by permission of the Ministry of Foreign Affairs).
12. Michael Handelsaltz, "Only the Israeli Philharmonic Can and Should Break the Wagner Boycott," *Haaretz*, 12 April 1990, p. A5.
13. "Revolution and Its Dangers," *Maariv*, 12 Nov. 1989, p. 14; Yeshayahu

Ben-Porat, "Against the Unification of Germany," *Yediot Aharonot*, 12 Nov. 1989, p. 2; Yeshayahu Ben-Porat, "No to One Germany," *Yediot Aharonot*, 29 Nov. 1989, p. 2; "Israel and the Unification of Germany," *Haaretz*, 20 Feb. 1990, p. B1; "A New Power," *Maariv*, 2 Oct. 1990, p. 12; Dov Genihovski, "The Unification of Germany," *Yediot Aharonot*, 2 Oct. 1990, p. 2; "Knesset Speaker: The Jewish People Should Wear Sackcloth and Ashes," *Maariv*, 3 Oct. 1990, p. 1; "Knesset Speaker: For Us It Is a Day of Mourning," *Yediot Aharonot*, 3 Oct. 1990, p. 1; Bronia Klebansky, "We Should Be Apprehensive about the Unification of Germany" (letter), *Haaretz*, 23 March 1990, p. B9; "Knesset Speaker: Broadcast of the Rock Concert from Germany: Insensitivity and Boorishness," *Yediot Aharonot*, 20 July 1990, p. 8.

14. Shaul Ben-Haim, "Foreign Minister Arens in Bonn: We Have Absolute Confidence in United Germany," *Maariv*, 16 Feb. 1990, p. 3; see also "Ministers: Arens's Acquiescence in the Unification of Germany Is a Sin Against History and Contempt for the Holocaust," *Maariv*, 16 Feb. 1990, p. 1; Akiva Eldar, "Arens Denies," *Haaretz*, 18 Feb. 1990, p. A3.

15. "The Public's Position on the Unification of Germany," *Yediot Aharonot*, 6 July 1990, p. 1. See also *Der Speigel Special* no. 2 (1992), pp. 61 ff.

26   "WHAT IS THERE TO UNDERSTAND? THEY DIED AND THAT'S IT"

1. Haim Nahman Bialik, "On the Threshold of the House of Prayer," *Complete Works of H. N. Bialik* (Tel Aviv: Dvir, 1941), p. 7.

2. Shmuel Cracowski, "Memorial Projects and Memorial Institutions Initiated by Survivors," in Yisrael Gutman, Adina Drechsler, eds., *The Remnant, 1944–1948* (Jerusalem: Yad Vashem, 1991), pp. 351 ff.

3. Decisions of the Commission on the Study of the Holocaust and Heroism, 13–14 July 1947, CZA, 1326 S 26.

4. Holocaust and Heroism Memorial Law, Yad Vashem, 1953, *KP*, XIV:2455.

5. Avraham Wine, "Memorial Books as a Source for the Study of the History of Jewish Communities in Europe," *Yad Vashem*, Collection of Studies on the Holocaust and Heroism, vol. IX (1973), pp. 209 ff.; Jack Kugelmass and Jonathan Boyarin, *From a Ruined Garden: The Memorial Books of Polish Jewry* (New York: Schocken Books, 1984).

6. Natan Alterman, "The City Falls," in *Poems That Were* (Tel Aviv: Hakibbutz Hameuhad, 1972), p. 220.

7. Ka-Tzetnik, *The Conflict* (Tel Aviv: Levin Epstein-Modan, 1975), p. 114.

8. Pinhas Sheinman, 14 March 1978, *KP*, LXXXII:2050.

9. Proposed Law Forbidding the Denial of the Holocaust, 15 July 1985, *KP*, C:3452 ff.; CVIII:3533, 3479.

10. Criminal Code (Attacks on Religious and Traditional Sensibilities), paragraph 173, in Eliahu Winograd, ed., *Dinim*, XXI:9336.

11. William L. Shirer, *The Rise and Fall of the Third Reich* (New York: Simon and Schuster, 1960); Hermann Rauschning, *Conversations with Hitler* (Tel Aviv: Sifriat Rimon, 1940); Konrad Heiden, *A Man Provoking Europe* (Tel Aviv: Linman, 1940); Alan Bullock, *Hitler: Anatomy of a Dictatorship* (Tel Aviv: Hakibbutz Hameuhad, 1974); Joachim Fest, *Hitler: Portrait of a Nonperson* (Jerusalem: Keter, 1986). See also Uri Avneri, *The Swastika* (Tel Aviv: Sifrei Mada Veinformatsia, n.d.).

12. Hannah Arendt, *Eichmann in Jerusalem: A Report on the Banality of Evil* (New York: Viking, 1965); Raul Hilberg, *The Destruction of European Jewry* (Chicago: Quadrangle, 1961); Isaiah Trunk, *Judenrat* (Jerusalem: Yad Vashem, 1979); Ruth Bondi, *Edelstein against Time* (Tel Aviv: Zemora Bitan Modan, 1981); Yehoshua Sobol, *Ghetto* (Tel Aviv: Or Am, 1984).

13. Gabriel Bach in tape-recorded interview with the author, 17 May 1990.

14. Yisrael Gutman and Gideon Greif, eds., *The Holocaust in Historiography: Lectures and Discussions at the Fifth International Conference of Holocaust Researchers* (Jerusalem: Yad Vashem, 1978).

15. S. Salomon, *The Zionist Crimes in the Destruction of the Diaspora*, published by the author, 1988.

16. Dina Porat, *Trapped Leadership* (Tel Aviv: Am Oved, 1986), p. 493.

17. S. B. Beit-Zvi, *Post-Ugandan Zionism in the Crisis of the Holocaust* (Tel Aviv: Bronfman, 1977).

18. Yosef Avner, Avraham Kushner, and Tom Segev, "Nitsots's Conversation with David Ben-Gurion," *Nitsots*, 28 April 1968, p. 2.

19. Uriel Reingold, "I Chose? I Cannot Escape It," *Lamerhav*, 25 April 1968, p. 3.

20. David Ben-Gurion, *The Renewed State of Israel* (Tel Aviv: Am Oved, 1969), p. 57.

21. Hanzi Brand in an interview with the author, 30 Aug. 1990.

22. Motti Lerner, *Kastner* (Tel Aviv: Or Am, 1988); Ben-Ami Feingold, *The Holocaust in Hebrew Drama* (Tel Aviv: Hakibbutz Hameuhad, 1989).

23. Gerhard Riegner in a tape-recorded interview with the author, 23 June 1989.

24. Joel and Hanzi Brand, *The Devil and the Soul* (Tel Aviv: Ledori, 1960); see also "Joel Brand Sent by Those Sentenced to Die," Tel Aviv: *Ayanot*, 1957; Amos Elon, *Zero Hour* (Tel Aviv: Idanim, 1980).

25. See also the Polish government's intention of establishing a Catholic convent at Auschwitz, parliamentary question no. 1970, 8 April 1986, *KP*, CVII:2589; motions, 28 May 1986, *KP*, CVII:2842 ff.

26. Walter Laqueur and Richard Breitman, *Breaking the Silence* (Tel Aviv: Schocken, 1988); Walter Laqueur, *The Horrible Secret* (Tel Aviv: Schocken, 1980).

27 "WHEN YOU SEE A GRAVEYARD"

1. "The Seven Dwarfs from Auschwitz," *Haaretz* 19 July 1949, p. 1.
2. Bilha Noy, *The Holocaust in Israeli Elementary Schools in the 1940s and 1950s as Reflected in the Memories of Graduates*, unpublished, quoted with permission of the author.
3. Nili Keren, "The Influence of Opinion Leaders and of Holocaust Research on the Development of the Educational Discussion and Curriculum on the Holocaust in Secondary Schools and in Informal Education in Israel, 1948–1981," diss., Hebrew University, 1985, pp. 31 ff. See also Anita Shapira, *Land and Power* (Tel Aviv: Am Oved, 1992), p. 485.
4. Gabriel Bach in tape-recorded interview with the author, 17 May 1990.
5. Keren, "Influence," pp. 71 ff.; see also debate on the teaching of Jewish consciousness in the schools, 4 March 1958, *KP*, XXIII:504.
6. Quoted in Keren, "Influence," p. 143.
7. Quoted in ibid., p. 180.
8. Ruth Firer, *Agents of the Lesson* (Tel Aviv: Hakibbutz Hameuhad, 1989).
9. Quoted in ibid., p. 31.
10. Ibid., p. 35.
11. Ibid., pp. 97 ff.
12. Keren, "Influence," pp. 224 ff.
13. Ibid., pp. 196 ff.
14. Tom Segev, "Dealing with the Holocaust," *Haaretz* supplement, 14 Sept. 1979, p. 9.
15. 26 March 1980, *KP*, LXXXVIII.
16. Diploma examinations, in possession of the author, quoted with permission of the Ministry of Education and Culture.
17. Uri Farago, "Consciousness of the Holocaust Among Youth Studying in Israel: 1983," *Dapim Leheker Tekufat Hashoah*, collection C (Tel Aviv: Hakibbutz Hameuhad, 1984), pp. 159 ff.
18. Amoz Oz, *Here and There in Israel, Fall 1982* (Tel Aviv: Am Oved, 1983), p. 178.
19. *Sources for Discussion on the Subject of the Believing Jew during the Holocaust and Thereafter*, mimeographed booklet printed by Ot Vaed; see also *Faith in the Holocaust: An Examination of the Jewish-Religious Significance of the Holocaust* (Jerusalem: Ministry of Education and Culture, 1980).

28 "WHAT DOES IT DO TO ME?"

1. *I Seek My Brothers: Youth Trip to Poland* (Jerusalem: Ministry of Education and Culture, 1990).

2. Ibid., pp. 61 ff.; *Friday-Night Prayers in Cracow* (Jerusalem: Ministry of Education and Culture), p. 38.

3. Yemima Avidar-Tchernowitz and Mira Lube, *Two Friends Set Out* (Tel Aviv: Bronfman, 1972).

4. Abba Kovner, "My Little Sister," quoted in Natan Gross, Itamar Yaoz-Kaset, and Rina Klinov, eds., *The Holocaust in Hebrew Poetry: A Selection* (Jerusalem: Yad Vashem and Hakibbutz Hameuhad, 1984), p. 184.

5. Shabtai Teveth, "Snapshots: Russia, Poland," *Haaretz*, 31 Aug. 1990, p. B4; see also his "To Whom Does Auschwitz Belong?" *Haaretz*, 7 Sept. 1990, p. B2; Yoram Brunovski, "From Anti-Semitism to Anti-Polism," *Haaretz*, 7 Sept. 1990, p. 135.

6. Yehudit Hendel, *By Silent Villages* (Tel Aviv: Hakibbutz Hameuhad, 1987), p. 31.

7. BGD, 18 June 1948.

8. Tzvika Dror, *Nitsanim: The Twice-Built Kibbutz* (Tel Aviv: Hakibbutz Hameuhad and Ministry of Defense Publications, 1990), p. 17.

9. Ibid.

10. Mira Kedar, "Song Saved from Fire," *Fig Tree Branches* (Tel Aviv: Sifriat Poalim, 1990), p. 8.

11. Zeev Jabotinsky, "The Betar Song," in *Poems* (Jerusalem: Eri Jabotinsky, 1947), p. 25; Zeev Jabotinsky, *Samson* (Tel Aviv: Maariv, 1976), p. 271; 18 Oct. 1961, *KP*, XXXII:134 ff.; 2–3 Jan. 1962, pp. 580 ff.; 9 Jan. 1962, pp. 902 ff.

12. Tom Segev, "Is It Worth Living?" *Haaretz* (supplement), 11 June 1981, pp. 12 ff.

13. Tom Segev, *Soldiers of Evil* (New York: McGraw-Hill, 1987), pp. 211.

14. Memorial booklet summing up the trip to Poland of students from Ben-Gurion High School, Petah Tikvah (October 1989), in the author's possession.

15. Eliezer Lidowski in interview with the author, 13 July 1989; see also Lidowski testimony, HU, ICJ, DOD, 62 (4); Eliezer Lidowski, *And the Spark Did Not Go Out* (Tel Aviv: Organization of Partisans, Ghetto Fighters, and Ghetto Rebels, 1986).

16. Dan Bar-On and Oron Sela, "The Vicious Circle between Relating to Reality and Relating to the Holocaust among Young Israelis," discussion paper, Ben-Gurion University, Department of Behavioral Sciences, 1990, p. 58.

17. Ibid.

18. Yehuda Elkana, "For Forgetting," *Haaretz*, 16 March 1988, p. 18.

19. Nili Keren, "For Learning," *Haaretz*, 16 March 1988, p. 18; Nira Feldman, "For Remembering," *Haaretz*, 23 March 1988, p. 13; Yisrael Eldad, "The Apparent Holocaust of Forgetting," *Haaretz*, 14 April 1988, p. 9; see also *Politika*, no. 8, June–July 1986.

20. Yehudit Hendel, *Silent Villages*, p. 60.
21. Moshe Dayan, *Milestones* (Tel Aviv: Idanim, 1976), p. 191.
22. Notice of the Center for the Heritage of Jewish Heroism, *Haaretz*, 29 Jan. 1991; see also "Without a Red Carpet" (editorial), *Haaretz*, 25 Jan. 1991; Yehiam Weitz, "Yes, It Happened to Us, Too," *Davar*, 25 Jan. 1991, p. 18; Gideon Alon, "Daily Interview with Miriam Zeiger," *Haaretz*, 27 Jan. 1991, p. A2; Lili Galili, "Survey: 50 Percent of Tel Aviv and Haifa Residents Suffer Anxiety," *Haaretz*, 28 Jan. 1991, p. A3; Anat Meidan, "Holocaust Survivors and the Gas Mask," *Hadashot*, 5 Feb. 1991, p. 20; Jurgen Keil, "How Do You Feel as a German?" *Haaretz*, 21 Feb. 1991, p. B2.
23. Noah Klieger, "Why Not?" *Yediot Aharonot*, 7 Oct. 1990, p. 20.

EPILOGUE

1. Yossi Peled in recorded interview with the author, 2 July 1990.
2. Quoted in *The History of the War of Independence*, foreword by David Ben-Gurion (Tel Aviv: Maarahot, 1959), p. 272.
3. Yossi Peled to Haim Guri, 18 December 1985 (copy in author's possession), quoted with the kind permission of Yossi Peled and Haim Guri.
4. Yitzhak Rabin at Dachau, 8 Sept. 1987 (complete text in author's possession), quoted with the kind permission of the Office of the Minister of Defense.
5. Natan Alterman, "The Silver Platter," *The Seventh Column* (Tel Aviv: Hakibbutz Hameuhad, 1977) I:154.
6. Ehud Barak at Auschwitz, 7 April 1992 (complete text in author's possession). Quoted with the kind permission of the Office of the Chief of Staff.
7. Yitzhak Shamir in Jerusalem, 6 July 1972 (complete text in author's possession), quoted with the kind permission of the Office of the Prime Minister.
8. Nahum Rackover, *Jewish Law in Knesset Legislation* (Jerusalem: Hebrew Law Library, 1988).
9. Uri Farago, "Holocaust Consciousness Among High School Students in Israel—1983," *Dapim Leheker Tekufat Hashoah*, collection (Tel Aviv: Hakibbutz Hameuhad, 1984), pp. 159 ff.
10. Yair Oron, *Jewish-Israeli Identity* (Tel Aviv: Kibbutz College School of Education, 1992), p. 58.
11. Oded Peled, *Letters to Bergen-Belsen* (Tel Aviv: Hakibbutz Hameuhad, 1978), p. 7.
12. Zeidan Atshi and Menahem Begin, 3 June 1981, *KP* XCI:2897.

Index

Abramowitz, Moshele, 443
Abs, Hermann, 232, 315n, 318
Acheson, Dean, 231
Act against Jewish War Criminals, 260
Adenauer, Konrad, 190, 305n, 330; anti-Semitic incidents during administration of, 318; Begin denounces, 216; development loan from, 319–20, 388; and Egyptian missiles, 371; and Eichmann trial, 340–41, 365; and establishment of diplomatic relations, 377; in Israel, 380–82; and military relations, 303, 313, 375; negotiates treaty with Israel, 227–35; and reparations, 199–205, 208, 214, 225, 332, 340; retirement of, 376; during Sinai campaign, 240
Af Al Pi Chen (ship), 133
Agami, Moshe, 326
Agnon, Shmuel Yosef, 80, 411
Agranat, Shimon, 306–7
Agudat Yisrael, 39, 102, 263, 297, 347n, 435
Ahdut Haavodah, 136, 285–86, 290, 293, 303, 304, 313, 316, 317
Ahimeir, Abba, 23, 374
Akavia, Miriam (formerly Weinfeld), 153–57, 159
Al Domi, 80–81
Aleichem, Sholem, 349
Al Hamishmar (newspaper), 293, 299, 392
Aliav, Ruth Klieger, 115n, 116, 128, 259
Aliya Hadasha, 58, 61–63
Aliyat Hanoar, 46, 166–71
Allon, Yigal, 316, 392

Alterman, Natan, 70, 131, 184, 211, 292, 299, 308, 320, 326, 327, 350, 463
Altmeier, Jacob, 203
American Jewish Committee (AJC), 330, 331
American Jewish Congress, 26, 83, 92
Amikam, Eliahu, 301
Amir, Michael, 195–96
Amit, Meir, 371, 374
Angriff (newspaper), 30
Anielewicz, Mordecai, 182, 293, 437, 446–49, 495
Anschluss, 31, 33, 433
Appelfeld, Aharon, 168, 180, 411
Arab High Committee, 70n
Arabs, 68, 90, 192, 325n, 387, 448, 471; British and, 469; compromise with, 277, 368, 468; and establishment of Jewish state, 62, 134; expulsion of, 113–14, 161–62, 405, 409, 451, 504–5; Germans and, 71, 319, 326, 378, 403, 425; Kahane and, 405–7, 410; in Knesset, 219, 222; massacre of, 398–402; nuclear capability of, 370; wars against, 133, 297, 389–95, 421
Arad, Yitzhak, 410, 422, 435, 442–44
Arafat, Yasir, 399–401, 404, 438
Aran, Zalman, 69, 235, 298, 383, 478
Arendt, Hannah, 36, 344, 357–60, 365, 465
Arens, Moshe, 457
Argov, Meir (formerly Grabovski), 147–48, 151–52, 209–10, 222, 288
Ariav, Haim, 289
Arlosoroff, Haim, 20–21, 25, 32, 264, 308